MW00846499

GET THE MOST FROM YOUR BOOK

SPRINGER PUBLISHING
CONNECT™

VOUCHER CODE:

LEYTEL6H

Online Access

Your print purchase of *Lifespan Development* includes **online access via Springer Publishing Connect**™ to increase accessibility, portability, and searchability.

Insert the code at http://connect.springerpub.com/content/book/978-0-8261-8279-1 today!

Having trouble? Contact our customer service department at cs@springerpub.com

Instructor Resource Access for Adopters

Let us do some of the heavy lifting to create an engaging classroom experience with a variety of instructor resources included in most textbooks SUCH AS:

INSTRUCTOR'S MANUAL

POWERPOINTS

TEST BANK

Visit **https://connect.springerpub.com/** and look for the **"Show Supplementary"** button on your **book homepage** to see what is available to instructors! First time using Springer Publishing Connect?

Email **textbook@springerpub.com** to create an account and start unlocking valuable resources.

Lifespan Development

Cultural and Contextual Applications for the Helping Professions

J. Kelly Coker, PhD, LCMHC, NCC, BC-TMH
Kristi B. Cannon, PhD, LPC, NCC
Savitri V. Dixon-Saxon, PhD, LCMHC
Karen M. Roller, PhD, MFT

 SPRINGER PUBLISHING

Copyright © 2023 Springer Publishing Company, LLC

Springer Publishing Company, LLC
11 West 42nd Street, New York, NY 10036
www.springerpub.com
connect.springerpub.com/

Acquisitions Editor: Rhonda Dearborn
Compositor: Exeter Premedia Services Private Ltd.

ISBN: 978-0-8261-8278-4
ebook ISBN: 978-0-8261-8279-1
DOI: 10.1891/9780826182791

SUPPLEMENTS:
Instructor Materials:

 SPRINGER PUBLISHING CONNECT™ | A robust set of instructor resources designed to supplement this text is located at **http://connect.springerpub.com/content/book/978-0-8261-8279-1.** Qualifying instructors may request access by emailing **textbook@springerpub.com.**

Instructor's Manual ISBN: 978-0-8261-8287-6
Instructor's Test Bank ISBN: 978-0-8261-8288-3
Instructor's PowerPoints ISBN: 978-0-8261-8289-0

Chapter Podcasts ISBN: 978-0-8261-8281-4
Chapter podcasts may be accessed at http://connect.springerpub.com/content/book/978-0-8261-8279-1

22 23 24 25/ 5 4 3 2 1

Library of Congress Cataloging-in-Publication Data

Names: Coker, J. Kelly, author.
Title: Lifespan development : cultural and contextual applications for the
  helping professions / edited by J. Kelly Coker, PhD, MBA, LCMHC, NCC,
  BC-TMH, Kristi B. Cannon, PhD, LPC, NCC, Savitri Dixon-Saxon, PhD, LPC,
  NCC, Karen Roller, PhD, MFT.
Description: New York, NY : Springer Publishing Company, [2023] | Includes
  bibliographical references and index.
Identifiers: LCCN 2022002501 (print) | LCCN 2022002502 (ebook) | ISBN
  9780826182784 (paperback) | ISBN 9780826182791 (ebook)
Subjects: LCSH: Developmental psychology. | Life cycle, Human
Classification: LCC BF713 .C645 2023 (print) | LCC BF713 (ebook) | DDC
  155--dc23/eng/20220208
LC record available at https://lccn.loc.gov/2022002501
LC ebook record available at https://lccn.loc.gov/2022002502

Contact sales@springerpub.com to receive discount rates on bulk purchases.

Publisher's Note: **New and used products purchased from third-party sellers are not guaranteed for quality, authenticity, or access to any included digital components.**

Printed in the United States of America by Gasch Printing.

The authors wish to dedicate this book to the caregivers of the world, those in the holy and thankless work of doing everything possible to meet the needs of those they can while trying not to need too much themselves.

Contents

Podcast Contributors   xi
Preface   xiii
Acknowledgments   xvii
Podcast List   xix
How to Use This Book   xxi
Instructor Resources   xxv

PART I: WHAT IS LIFESPAN DEVELOPMENT?

1. Lifespan in Context   3
   History of Developmental Theories in Context to Helping Professions   3
   Rationale for Learning and Applying Developmental Theories   4
   Fundamental Issues in Lifespan Development   5
   Socio-Political Impact on Development   7
   The Interactive Nature of This Book   9
   Let the Story Begin: An Exploration of the Gestational Period   10
   Summary   14

2. The Roots of Lifespan Developmental Theories   21
   Introduction to Developmental Theory   21
   Theories of Ego Development   22
   Theories of Cognitive Development   32
   Theories of Moral Development   39
   Theory of Attachment   46
   Theories of Adult Development   48
   Perspectives From the Field: Podcast   53
   Summary   54

3. Cultural and Contextual Development Models   61
   Introduction to Cultural and Contextual Models of Development   61
   Human Development and Social Justice: Allyship, Advocacy, and Activism   62
   Models of Identity Development   63
   Systemic and Contextual Models of Development   76
   Theories in Context: Recent and Relevant Research   81
   Summary   84

PART II: AGES AND STAGES

4. Cultural and Contextual Factors of Infancy Through Early Childhood   95
   Case Study 4.1: The Case of Xquenda   95
   Infancy Through Early Childhood   96
   Cultural Factors: Infancy Through Early Childhood   99
   Toddlerhood   103
   Contextual Factors: Infancy Through Early Childhood   106
   Bullying and Peer Abuse   107
   Custody   109
   Unaccompanied Minors and DACA   109
   Runaways, Abductions, and Trafficking   110
   Foster Care and Adoption   110
   Neurodevelopmental Differences and Difficulties   111
   COVID-19   113
   Perspectives From the Field: Podcast   117
   Summary   118

5. Developmental Theories of Infancy Through Early Childhood   133
   Introduction   133
   Case Study 5.1: The Case of Xquenda   133
   Infancy Through Early Childhood   134
   Perspectives From the Field: Podcast   157
   Summary   157

6. Cultural and Contextual Factors of Middle Childhood Through
   Adolescence   171
   Case Study 6.1: The Case of Dev   171
   Middle Childhood Through Adolescence   172
   Cultural Factors: Middle Childhood Through Adolescence   173
   Contextual Factors: Middle Childhood Through Adolescence   186
   Clients in Middle Childhood and Adolescence: Clinical Considerations   193
   Perspectives From the Field: Podcast   194
   Summary   195

7. Developmental Theories of Middle Childhood Through Adolescence   199
   Case Study 7.1: The Case of Dev   199
   Middle Childhood Through Adolescence   200
   Piaget's Cognitive Development Theory   201
   Erikson's Psychosocial Development   208
   Perspectives From the Field: Podcast   217
   Summary   217

8. Cultural and Contextual Factors of Emerging Adulthood Through
   Early Adulthood   221
   Case Study 8.1: The Case of Bi'lal   221
   Emerging Adulthood   222
   Emerging Adulthood and Early Adulthood   223

Cultural Factors: Emerging Adulthood 224
Contextual Factors: Emerging Adulthood 229
Cultural Factors: Early Adulthood 236
Contextual Factors: Early Adulthood 240
Clients in Emerging and Early Adulthood: Clinical Considerations 245
Perspectives From the Field: Podcast 248
Summary 248

9. Developmental Theories of Emerging Adulthood Through Early
    Adulthood 253
    Case Study 9.1: The Case of Mystic 253
    Introduction to Adult Development Theory 254
    Carl Jung and Personality Theory 258
    Psychosocial Identity Development Theory 261
    Clients in Emerging and Early Adulthood: Clinical Considerations 275
    Perspectives From the Field: Podcast 278
    Summary 278

10. Cultural and Contextual Factors of Middle Adulthood 281
     Case Study 10.1: The Case of Ellen 281
     Middle Adulthood 282
     Cultural Factors: Middle Adulthood 282
     Contextual Factors: Middle Adulthood 287
     Clients in Midlife: Clinical Considerations 296
     Perspectives From the Field: Podcast 299
     Summary 299

11. Developmental Theories of Middle Adulthood 303
     Case Study 11.1: The Case of Ellen and Clark 303
     Middle Adulthood 304
     Personality Development in Middle Adulthood 304
     Psychosocial Development 305
     Ego Development 312
     Moral Development 316
     Other Factors Impacting Development in Middle Adulthood 324
     Perspectives From the Field: Podcast 325
     Summary 325

12. Cultural and Contextual Factors of Late Adulthood Through End
     of Life 329
     Case Study 12.1: The Case of Rose 329
     Late Adulthood 330
     Cultural Factors: Late Adulthood 331
     Model of Disability Identity Development 338
     Contextual Factors: Late Adulthood 341
     Clients in Late Adulthood: Clinical Considerations 352
     Perspectives From the Field: Podcast 353
     Summary 354

13. Developmental Theories of Late Adulthood Through End of Life   359
   Case Study 13.1: The Case of Rose   359
   Late Adulthood   359
   Lifespan Development in Late Adulthood   361
   Theories of Late Adult Development   361
   Cultural Factors and Aging   380
   Contextual Factors and Aging   383
   Clinical Considerations   388
   Perspectives From the Field: Podcast   389
   Summary   390

Index   395

Podcast Contributors

William Barkley, PhD, Dean Emeritus, School of Counseling, Walden University, Minneapolis, Minnesota

Ramone Ford, PhD, Psychologist, Psychology of the Western Reserve, Northfield, Ohio

Stephanie J. W. Ford, PhD, Professor, Liberty University, Lynchburg, Virginia

Nina Nabors, PhD, ABPP, Dean, Walden University, Minneapolis, Minnesota

Brian L. Ragsdale, PhD, Director of Student Success, Walden University, Minneapolis, Minnesota

Stacee Reicherzer, PhD, LPC-S, Associate Professor, Adler University, Chicago, Illinois

Emmett R. Roberts, Jr., PhD, LCSW, Core Faculty, Walden University, Minneapolis, Minnesota

Donna S. Sheperis, PhD, Professor and Associate Chair, Palo Alto University, Palo Alto, California

Judyth Weaver, PhD, Founder and Past Chair, Somatic Psychology Program, Santa Barbara Graduate Institute, Santa Barbara, California

Chenobia Webster-Hill, DSW, LCSW, Core Faculty, The Barbara Solomon School of Social Work, Walden University, Minneapolis, Minnesota

Preface

When the authors of this textbook got together to brainstorm what to include in this book, we collectively and immediately agreed we wanted to offer a different framework for understanding human development. As a mental health professional in training, you are most likely required to take a course or two in lifespan or human development. You may have even taken a class in human development in your undergraduate psychology or sociology or human services or social work programs, so you might be thinking, "Ugh, not *another* class learning about tired old developmental theories!"

OVERALL GOAL OF THE BOOK

As the authors of this textbook represent women of different ages, cultural backgrounds, professional identities, and experiences as clinicians and professional educators, we felt that we could work together to try to bring to life, in new ways, the theories and models of lifespan development to benefit you, the future mental health professional, in applying them to your real-world work with future clients. Whether you are training to become a professional counselor, psychologist, social worker, marriage and family therapist, or other mental health professional, you will engage with clients/patients across the lifespan. As humans navigate the different ages of life, they pass through different stages of development. Mental health professionals rely on various theories, treatment modalities, and ongoing research to inform their best practice; we hope this text will support you to do so in a culturally responsive, humble, self-reflective way, in order that your clients will be ethically and effectively served across the lifespan.

DISTINGUISHING FEATURES AND LEARNING TOOLS

This textbook is organized in a way that we believe makes it interesting, entertaining, and relevant. In Chapters 1, 2, and 3, we introduce important concepts related to lifespan and human development, discuss foundational models and theories of development that serve as the roots of the field, and discuss how theories and models of development should be viewed through contextual and cultural frameworks, and updated, empirically based research.

In Chapters 4 through 13, we talk about different ages and stages of development, but we do this a bit differently than what you might normally see in a textbook of lifespan development. We first introduce you to a case study that will be a client or client family representing a particular age and stage. In the first chapter for each age and stage, we start with cultural and contextual considerations, and then in the subsequent chapter, we focus on two to three developmental theories that help us to conceptualize this age/stage of development. By having you *first* consider how cultural frameworks and models of development and understanding of people from different backgrounds and experiences move through their lifespan, and how this movement is facilitated or hindered by other relevant contextual factors, we can begin to understand the developmental process in a richer, more dynamic way. You will be challenged to critically analyze the theories that are presented, and to seek and understand new information and research that help to consider how theories of lifespan development are either limited in their abilities to describe development, enhanced by more current research that considers a broader cultural and contextual framework, or sometimes even both.

Take Erik Erikson, for example. Erikson, a German-born American psychologist, is considered by many to be one of the key framers of one of the best-known theories, Psychosocial Development. Erikson developed a stage model of development, initially based on a very narrow set of personal experiences in his own practice. In addition, he developed his eight-stage model of development, where children, adolescents, and adults resolve key conflicts at each stage, based on normative experiences of White males in Western, industrialized society. Does this mean that we should disregard Erikson's contributions to our understanding of development? The short answer is no, because we also can learn from subsequent research and writing from other theorists (and in this case, from Erikson himself, who continued to refine his theory, with the help of his wife, Joan, well into his 90s). The answer should also be, "It depends." Just because Erikson gets a lot of play in lifespan development textbooks, like this one, for example, does not mean we just indiscriminately embrace his theoretical tenets and what they mean for clients. So, we encourage you to take a "both/and" approach to this material. Learn what you can about the theorist and theories themselves—the roots, if you will—and then evaluate them against cultural and contextual factors, recent and relevant research, and your own critical thinking skills to make informed choices about their utility in your future clinical practice.

INTENDED AUDIENCE

This text aims to (a) prepare emerging mental health professionals for licensure exams with an understanding of foundational developmental theories by introducing you to some of the White, Western, industrialized, male-centered developmental theories that have dominated medical model mental health practice for the last century, and to (b) take a critical look at limitations of those theories, introducing you to updated research and more inclusive, diverse, culturally responsive, relational, collectivistic, trauma-informed approaches to lifespan development and its place in clinical care. We hope to inspire you to be lifelong learners as scientists–practitioners, with ongoing openness to revising what you "know," even as you become more clear about what appears to be self-evident.

The Latin etymology of *psychology* is the study of the *psyche* (the soul, mind, or spirit). Psychology has come to be interpreted as the study of the mind and/or behavior; however, Greek philosophers were only beginning to categorize and differentiate the mind from the body from the soul or spirit. It was René Descartes's reductionistic split of mind as superior over matter that underlies much of White, Western, industrialized, male philosophy and psychological theory today, leaving the spirit or soul out altogether. This schism seeks to be remedied in the West now through integrative, holistic, sometimes feminist practices of medicine, therapy, and counseling, as well as allied healing arts that belong to unbroken lineages rooted in collectivistic cultures around the world. Insurance-funded government agencies are beginning to employ acupuncture to reduce juvenile recidivism, and mindfulness-based stress reduction for a panoply of medical and psychological diagnoses; insurance money generally goes where there is expected to be a return on the investment, and integrated approaches are showing measurable improvement when proper methods are employed. It is our hope that clinicians of all stripes will behold their clients' inherent wholeness, and support their clients' ability to pick up pieces they may have lost along the way, using methods that honor their sense of belonging just as they are, rather than compared to expectations within the dominant cultures in which they must find a way to survive and thrive.

Instead of filling up the reader with information to memorize, which will not really serve you or your clients, the authors wish to engage in the Latin etymology of *education*, "educare" or "educere"; "e" is the prefix for *out* as in *e-gress* or *e-xit*, while *du-ca-re* means *to mold/train* and *du-ce-re* means *lead*. We want to balance these efforts of training and leading out; we wish for these words to reach inside and connect with your own lived experiences, help pull them out to be considered, appreciated, nurtured, honored, mourned, challenged, questioned, and held in their complex context as much as possible. We intend to help you explore your own cultural conditionings, to see where your experiences with subjugation, power and privilege, gaining and losing, being centered or marginalized, and being connected or estranged come together to make meaning throughout your development. Because we aim to write from a trauma-informed perspective, we invite you to let go of judgments about "what is wrong" with people to act the way they do, and to instead be curious about "what happened" to them, in the spirit of collective healing and liberation.

To breathe a little life into these developmental theories, we provide case studies which are amalgamations of clients we have served over the years. Many details that one would eventually hold as a time-tested and trusted clinician have been left out of these vignettes in service of showing you how hungry the brain will be to know more, to have certainty, to complete the puzzle and be done not knowing. As people's stories are complex and mysterious and cannot be fully known, and good trauma-informed care means one must prioritize secure relationship-building over obtaining data bits, we have left many questions unanswered; we think that it is in the best interest of your future clients for you to come to peace with the time and patience it takes to earn client trust enough that they choose to volunteer more details in the timing that is right for them and their healing.

We enrich our case studies through podcasts with cross-disciplinary pioneers and leaders in their specializations who share their experience and insights into how they might work with the client systems presented; we hope these voices give you a taste of how various clinicians apply developmental theory in a culturally responsive manner, and inspire you to work as a supportive member of interdisciplinary teams. We further hope that no matter the license you pursue, no matter the systems you report to in exchange for secure employment and the opportunity to be of meaningful service, that you foster your own compassion satisfaction by developing rich, nourishing relationships with clients, colleagues, supervisors, and beloveds in your personal life all across your lifespan. Human beings know themselves through relationships, and are sustained across the lifespan through healthy relationships. The podcasts may be accessed at http://connect.springerpub.com/content/book/978-0-8261-8279-1.

INSTRUCTOR'S RESOURCES

For instructors considering adopting this textbook, we want to provide you with dynamic and supportive teaching tools to facilitate engagement with your students and to promote deeper experiences of your students. Each chapter is accompanied by PowerPoints that can be used to frame interactive discussions with students on the material presented including suggested activities to bring the reflections in each chapter to life as classroom-based interactions. We also provide a test bank for each chapter consisting of a combination of multiple-choice, true-false, and essay questions. This test bank will be able to be easily integrated into learning management systems (LMSs) for use in online learning spaces.

CONTENTS

This book is organized into two parts. Part I covers the topic, What Is Lifespan Development? Part I of the textbook uses three chapters to provide an overview of lifespan development (Chapter 1), theories of human and lifespan development (Chapter 2), and theories of intersectionality and identity development (Chapter 3). These chapters provide the foundation from which to explore relevant developmental concepts as they apply to people at various ages and stages of development.

Part II covers different ages and stages of development. Each age and stage is presented in a two-chapter sequence. The first chapter in each sequence introduces a case study of a client belonging to a particular age group. Once the case is introduced, relevant contextual and cultural factors are identified as students consider the lens through which to examine each stage. A podcast is included as a resource from an expert in the field who will discuss the case study from their discipline and perspective applying at least one theory of development to their conceptualization of the case. Students have opportunities for reflection on the case through sidebars and additional instructor resources and activities. The second chapter in each age and stage anchors specific theories, models, and clinical interventions to working with the identified case presented in the previous chapter. New and relevant research is included to further contextualize the application of the theory.

It is our hope that by anchoring our discussion of different theories of development to a specific case after having noted relevant cultural and contextual factors, you will be able to conceptualize these cases in a rich and robust manner. Reflections, podcasts, and suggestions for additional resources and information will round out the content of this book. Happy reading, and we hope to break the stereotype of lifespan development being just one of those topics you "have to" learn about, and instead that it becomes for you one of the favorite topics you "get to" learn about!

A robust set of instructor resources designed to supplement this text is located at http://connect.springerpub.com/content/book/978-0-8261-8279-1. Qualifying instructors may request access by emailing textbook@springerpub.com.

Acknowledgments

The authors thank three groups of critically important beloveds—those teachers to whom we owe our careers and whom we emulate in our more skillful moments: Señora Crane, Joyce Garvey, Kate Kaufman, Rae Johnson, Jill Kern, Aline LaPierre, Herbert Exum, Tracy Robinson-Wood, DiAnne Borders, Pam Paisley, Randy Lyle, Ray Wooten, Audrey Temple, Lois Connally; our own caregivers and partners, who made sure we were clean, fed, attended to, loved, nurtured, safe enough to learn, free enough to grow, valued enough to share what was hard, and rooted in our sense of belonging: Martha Peterson-Saffer and Chuck Saffer, Jim and Susana Coan, Bill Coker, Brenda and Richard Dixon, Wilma and Mike Roller, Dale and Jim Bordovsky, Jon Cannon; and our precious children, to whom we aim to pass on these legacies: Liam Coker, Saniyya Saxon, Sage Roller, Finley Cannon, Rowan Cannon, Fallon Cannon.

Podcast List

Organized below by chapter, the *Lifespan Development* podcasts are available as support and provide explanatory information. The majority of chapters include a podcast. The first presented podcast, the author discussion in Chapter 2, helps contextualize the framework for the textbook. In Chapters 4 through 13, Perspectives From the Field podcasts are short conversations between the textbook authors and experts who share their perspectives of the presented case studies, the relevant cultural and contextual factors of the age and stage of development, and developmental theories attributed to the presented age and stage. Access the podcasts at http://connect.springerpub.com/content/book/978-0-8261-8279-1.

Chapter 2
Podcast Chapter 2: Why Did We Write This Book?
Author discussion among Drs. Kelly Coker, Kristi Cannon, Savitri Dixon-Saxon, and Karen Roller: Perspectives From the Field

Chapter 4
Podcast Chapter 4: Cultural and Contextual Considerations of Early Childhood: The Case of Xquenda
Dr. Karen Roller's conversation with Dr. Judyth Weaver: Perspectives From the Field

Chapter 5
Podcast Chapter 5: Developmental Perspectives of Early Childhood: The Case of Xquenda
Dr. Karen Roller's conversation with Dr. Judyth Weaver: Perspectives From the Field

Chapter 6
Podcast Chapter 6: Cultural and Contextual Factors of Middle Childhood Through Adolescence: The Case of Dev
Dr. Kristi Cannon's conversation with Dr. Stacee Reicherzer: Perspectives From the Field

Chapter 7
Podcast Chapter 7: Developmental Theories of Middle Childhood and Adolescence: The Case of Dev
Dr. Kristi Cannon's conversation with Dr. Stacee Reicherzer: Perspectives From the Field

Chapter 8
Podcast Chapter 8: Cultural and Contextual Factors of Emerging Adulthood Through Early Adulthood: The Case of Bi'lal
Dr. Savitri Dixon-Saxon's conversation with Dr. Brian Ragsdale and Dr. Emmett Roberts: Perspectives From the Field

Chapter 9

Podcast Chapter 9: Developmental Theories of Emerging Adulthood Through Early Adulthood: The Case of Bi'lal and Mystic
Dr. Savitri Dixon-Saxon's conversation with Dr. Stephanie J. W. Ford and Dr. Chenobia Webster-Hill: Perspectives From the Field

Chapter 10

Podcast Chapter 10: Cultural and Contextual Factors of Middle Adulthood: The Case of Ellen
Dr. Kelly Coker's conversation with Dr. Donna Sheperis: Perspectives From the Field

Chapter 11

Podcast Chapter 11: Developmental Theories of Middle Adulthood: The Case of Ellen and Clark
Dr. Kelly Coker's conversation with Dr. Donna Sheperis: Perspectives From the Field

Chapter 12

Podcast Chapter 12: Cultural and Contextual Factors of Late Adulthood: The Case of Rose
Dr. Savitri Dixon-Saxon's and Dr. Kelly Coker's conversation with Dr. Stephanie J. W. Ford and Dr. Ramone Ford: Perspectives From the Field

Chapter 13

Podcast Chapter 13: Developmental Theories of Late Adulthood: The Case of Rose
Dr. Savitri Dixon-Saxon's and Dr. Kelly Coker's conversation with Dr. Nina Nabors and Dr. William Barkley: Perspectives From the Field

HOW TO USE THIS BOOK

Lifespan Development is a course that many in the helping professions need to take but can be intimidating or even boring. The features of this book were developed by the authors to bring to life, in new ways, the theories and models of lifespan development to benefit you, the future mental health professional, in applying them to your real-world work with future clients! The following features, recognizable by their easy-to-find design elements, appear consistently in the chapters that will help you navigate a different framework for understanding human development.

LEARNING OBJECTIVES

Upon completion of this chapter, students will be able to:

1. Describe the perinatal and early childhood periods of human development.

2. Identify risk and resiliency factors for infancy and early childhood.

3. Recognize contextual factors that may merit therapeutic attention for early individual and relational healing.

4. Describe how cultural humility and trauma-informed care may be applied for early developmental needs in families, as well as longitudinal effects from this foundational period.

Learning Objectives: Help you focus on learning outcomes for each chapter.

CASE STUDY 4.1: THE CASE OF XQUENDA

Meet Xquenda (aka "Miguel" at school), a 5-year-old child assigned male at birth, currently presumed to be cisgender based on self-referential pronouns and gender presentation such as, "Yo soy el único que juega con la camioneta" (I am the only one (male) who plays with the truck). Xquenda is referred to you, a mental health practitioner at a public elementary school, in a migrant rural residential suburb surrounded by strawberry fields. The teacher's chief complaint is that Xquenda regularly disrupts the kindergarten classroom with tantrums and potty accidents, and has difficulty with transitions.

Case Studies: Chapters are organized by lifespan development phases. Two chapters cover each phase. The first chapter discusses cultural and contextual features of the age and stage presented through a unique case study client the student can follow as they explore the age and stage.

While his sister's zero-to-five years experience was all contained within the community embrace of multigenerational family members looking after her when her parents needed to work, with on-demand breastfeeding because her mom was able to work in the fields nearby and either wear her or take breaks when she needed her, Xquenda had to tolerate long hours away from his mom while she worked away from the home during his infancy. In fact, because mom had delivery complications with Xquenda, she ultimately had an unplanned C-section, and was hooked up to a bag of antibiotics in the hospital for 3 days after Xquenda's birth, which interrupted their bonding processes (Pilch, 2015; Sakala et al., 2020; van Reenen & van Rensburg, 2013). Xquenda had difficulty latching and the parents could not afford a lactation consultant, so he was given formula in the hospital and the parents were not encouraged to keep trying breastfeeding (Jenco, 2020). Xquenda was also given broad spectrum antibiotics in the hospital, which upset the fragile development of the intestinal microbiome environment necessary to begin digesting comfortably, resulting in chronic colic (Azad et al., 2013; Leung & Hon, 2019), and though he was able to room-in with his mom, she was not allowed to have visitors for more than 1 hour at a time.

Student Reflection Boxes: Invite you to think critically about, apply assessments to, or reflect on your own developmental histories and futures in context to case studies or examples represented in the book.

SESSION EXCERPT 4.1

Mental health professional: Can you tell me what it was like for you to be pregnant?

Inda Jani: Well (exhales audibly, and pauses, looking at Surem with a small smile), we weren't really planning for Xquenda the way we were with Nayeli. With Nayeli, we had been together a few years, and we were ready to start our family, and things were pretty easy with all our family around. And she was such a happy baby, ate so well, always affectionate and ready to play. But then as the big farm started encroaching on our lands, and we were finding their trash in our river, the whole community was trying to figure out what to do. We tried talking to the bosses, but nothing. Then the woods started getting clear cut, and we knew we couldn't stay much longer. And that's when I missed my moon (period) again, with Xquenda. We knew it would be harder to find a new living situation with a baby, we knew finding work in the city would be harder ... we knew no one. We just didn't know how far we would have to go to find a place we could be. And the money to live (tears well up in her eyes).

Session Excerpts: These are narratives between a mental health professional and case study family members. The narratives further illuminate concepts relevant to the chapter's age and stage, including cultural and contextual considerations.

PERSPECTIVE FROM THE FIELD: PODCAST

Access this podcast at http://connect.springerpub.com/content/book/978-0-8261-8279-1/part/part02/chapter/ch04

The goal of this chapter was to provide you with an initial understanding of how infancy and early childhood are shaped by the experiences, contexts, and cultures in which they are embedded. As we prepare to move into the next chapter and dig more deeply into additional theories and models specific to this age of development, I invite you to listen to Dr. Judyth Weaver speak more directly to the developmental considerations we should bear in mind when working with a client like Xquenda. Dr. Weaver is a Reichiean psychologist, practicing clinician certified in multiple somatic modalities, educator, and the founder of Somatic Reclaiming. She is also a leader in the field of pre- and perinatal psychology, facilitating therapeutic processes for groups, families, and individuals to complete unfinished business from gestational and birth imprints.

Perspective from the Field: Podcasts – Focus on cultural and contextual dimensions of development and on particular theories with interviews of experts in the field who are applying this theory to their work with clients.

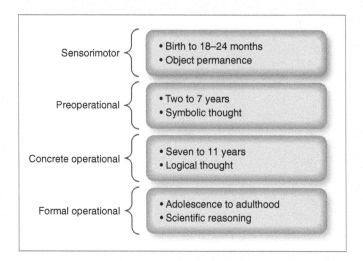

Figure 2.1 Piaget's four stages of cognitive development.

Source: Adapted from Isaacs, N. (2015). *A brief introduction to Piaget: The growth of understanding in the young child and new light on children's ideas of number*. Algora Publishing.

Many visual illustrations, tables, and figures help to make the book more readable, engaging, and dynamic.

The authors would like to hear your thoughts and feedback on the first edition. If you would like to share your thoughts on corrections, updates, or anything else, please contact us at SpringerLifespanbook@gmail.com

Instructor Resources

A robust set of resources designed to supplement this text is located at http://connect
.springerpub.com/content/book/978-0-8261-8279-1. Qualifying instructors may
request access by emailing textbook@springerpub.com

Available resources include:

- Instructor's Manual:
  - Accreditation Mapping
  - Learning Objectives
  - Key Words
  - Multiple Choice Questions
  - Activities/Homework Assignments
  - Additional Resources
- Test Bank
- Chapter-Based PowerPoint Presentations
- Podcasts: Organized by chapter, the supporting podcasts present perspectives
  from experts in mental health disciplines to expand on chapter content.

PART I

WHAT IS LIFESPAN DEVELOPMENT?

CHAPTER 1

Lifespan in Context

LEARNING OBJECTIVES

Upon completion of this chapter, students will be able to:

1. Identify key features of lifespan development models.
2. Recognize cultural and contextual factors of lifespan development theories.
3. Discuss limitations of lifespan development theories.
4. Discuss how lifespan development theories inform your understanding of the mental health professions.

HISTORY OF DEVELOPMENTAL THEORIES IN CONTEXT TO HELPING PROFESSIONS

Developmental theories present systematic ways of evaluating how human beings grow from birth to death, and the various changes they undergo along the way. The origins of lifespan development theory are centered in the field of developmental psychology in late 19th-century Europe, where the scientific study of children and adolescents first began. This was followed by a significant period of exploration in the early 20th century, where more pronounced research and theory development occurred—all with the goal of understanding human behavior and, at that time, childhood development. Early influencers on this process were the scholars John Lock, Jean-Jacques Rousseau, and Charles Darwin, who each developed theories on human behavior (Developmental Psychology, 2020; Koops, 2015). Their emphasis on nature versus nurture, genetics, and environment gave rise to subsequent developmental theories related to the lifecycle including intellectual development, moral development, personality development, and psychosocial development.

Lifespan development theories arose in the nascent Western mental health profession as an attempt to organize and make sense of human capacities and limitations across the lifespan, and originally, to create some normed expectations which would guide where and how therapeutic intervention was to be directed for clients' optimal well-being and ongoing development. As the mental health profession has become more diversified and decentralized, a growing body of researchers around the world have performed cross-cultural studies highlighting how worldview informs what is considered normative. As a result, developmental theory has started to become more nuanced and self-reflective—though there is still much room for growth in honoring the wide variety of human experience. As the mental health profession becomes more interdisciplinary and holistic, developmental theories are now incorporating more trauma-informed research from sociology, anthropology, history, medicine, interpersonal neurobiology, physiology, and adjacent fields, while still creating culture-syntonic norms for medical model treatment. Mental health professionals need to be aware of how their work sites use developmental theories to justify medical necessity of clinical treatment, while being sensitive to their clients' worldviews and expectations for treatment, in order that skillful, trauma-informed care can be delivered and received.

And that is where this text comes in. Throughout the remainder of this book you explore a variety of developmental theories, some born out of traditional Western thought and considered foundational to development theory. Others are more contemporary and reflect advances in the mental health field that support the more interdisciplinary and holistic approaches so fundamental and necessary for work in the allied helping professions. As a future mental health professional you will be tasked with considering a multitude of factors to support those you work with, one of which is their development. As you read forward in this chapter and text, we hope you will begin to understand not only the value of developmental theory, but the ways in which it is, by nature, evolving. We encourage you to appreciate the roots of developmental theory as well as the ways in which it has branched out across time. We simultaneously hope you will grow stronger in your understanding of human nature and the individual experience, all while developing a critical eye for reviewing and applying developmental theory.

RATIONALE FOR LEARNING AND APPLYING DEVELOPMENTAL THEORIES

As you begin to engage with developmental theories you may be asking yourself why these theories are important to your future work and how you would ultimately apply them. At the core, developmental theories provide us with important frameworks to understand those around us. They help contextualize experiences, give us a point of reference to understand growth and barriers to progress, and, particularly important to the mental health professions, they help us to understand where traumas, life circumstances, and areas of concern may have manifested or are creating limitations for the clients we will serve.

We spend a good portion of this text emphasizing the uniqueness of development and the ways in which our individual contexts and cultures shape the developmental process. However, it is also important to note that research in the area of human development has found considerable overlap in experiences from person to person. For example, the vast majority of us are born and continue to physically grow and mature (Bogin, 2020). As we move into adolescence, most of us experience puberty and the associated hormonal and body changes accompanying that experience, even when there are deviations in when and how this occurs (De Silva & Tschirhart, 2016). Similarly, our brains develop, and cognitive capacity shifts and expands across time (Stiles & Jernigan, 2010). From a social–emotional development perspective, we have some shared experiences as well. As relational beings, we largely move in and through the world engaging with others and evolving in our intra- and interpersonal experiences accordingly (Melé & Cantón, 2014).

The theorists discussed in this text have spent considerable time researching and evaluating the human experience and have sought ways to help us understand some of the universal experiences we may share as people. They offer us a point of comparison and a framework to understand general expectations for such things as cognitive, identity, and personality development. In this way, developmental theories can be viewed as a ruler—they help us gauge where a person is on particular developmental trajectories, relative to what the theorist deemed to be a "normative" experience. This can be a very helpful way for us to understand what our clients are experiencing and where issues may be coming from in their lives. Developmental theories offer us a lens to help clarify what we are seeing and hearing with those we serve, and a jumping off point to start or continue that work.

Developmental theories, as you will see, also come with limitations. They are born out of the experiences of specific theorists, often over-generalized to individuals and populations on whom and for whom they were not developed, and can fail to consider the contextual and cultural implications tied into the development process. To that end, it is also helpful to remember that developmental theories serve as an imperfect tool for understanding. The proverbial lens we are viewing through may be foggy, or the ruler incorrectly marked. As a future mental health professional, it is important to consider the value of developmental theories in helping you understand a broad view of human development, while also recognizing that each individual experience is unique.

FUNDAMENTAL ISSUES IN LIFESPAN DEVELOPMENT

Lifespan development is a composite of all the elements of our growth and experience across time, from conception to death. In the social sciences these often get broken down into the areas of physiological, cognitive, and social–emotional development. Although each area offers some distinct insights into human development, the interplay between and among these areas is significant. As mental health professionals we use the information from these areas of development to help us understand where our clients are, where they have come from, and where we may need to focus in our work.

Physiological Development

Physiological development encompasses the physical and genetic portions of our developmental experiences. This includes our genetic make up, body growth, hormonal changes, the impact of physical deformities and disabilities, diseases, and illnesses. As you might imagine, physiological development begins long before our birth, as genetics and the impact of our ancestral development first dictate which traits are inherited from our biological parents. In the years to follow, our bodies move through various stages of physical growth and maturity, including hormonal, neurological, and musculoskeletal. Our physiological development results from the combination of genetics, lifestyle, and environment—some of which we can control, and much of which we cannot. Understanding the physiological changes associated with various stages or ages of life can be an important way to contextualize what is occurring for individuals in those years. This is especially true when we consider the ways in which physiological development ties into cognitive and social–emotional development.

Cognitive Development

Cognitive development includes the neurological changes of the brain and the resulting impact on the areas of language, memory, and intelligence. When we consider cognitive development, we are often concerned with how individuals learn to think, explore the world around them, and use knowledge to problem-solve. As you might expect, the most significant period of neurological and cognitive growth is from conception to late childhood, when the brain grows to 90% of its adult volume (Stiles & Jernigan, 2010). However, the brain continues to mature in size through adolescence, and the prefrontal cortex and other regions of the brain are not fully developed until the mid-20s (Arain et al., 2013). As individuals age, cognition varies but begins to deteriorate across multiple domains in late adulthood (Tucker-Drob et al., 2019). Just like physiological development, cognitive changes across the lifespan have direct implications for other areas of development and the more holistic human experience.

Social–Emotional Development

Social–emotional development includes our growth in and through relationships with others in our lives. It involves learning to form and value relationships with others, feelings about self, and social adjustment to a variety of interactions over time. Just like physiological and cognitive growth, we begin our life with certain social experiences and we continue to evolve, grow, and be influenced by different relationships across the span of our lives. These relationships impact not only how we see others, but how we view ourselves and respond emotionally as well. Our initial social interactions are primarily with family, which are distinctly influenced by culture and context. As we grow, social influence expands to include friends, partner relationships, and communities. The extent to which we engage with certain people, and the emotional outcomes of those interactions, can vary across individuals and be specific to developmental ages across time.

Manifesting Lifespan Development Issues

Rarely do our clients present with issues stemming from only one area of development. Instead, we often see this playing out in a variety of developmental arenas across their lives. As you consider this information, it may be helpful to think about what this might look like when presented in real life, and why understanding the implications of these developmental arenas is so important to us in the helping professions. Let's take, for example, Ariana. Ariana was born into poverty and a home with eight additional children. As a result, she was neglected as a child and suffered malnutrition. As she moved into her early school years, she demonstrated delayed cognitive development, resulting from the neglect. While in school Ariana was teased for her lack of intelligence and the clothes she wore, which led to behavioral problems and a struggle to form positive peer relationships. As she continued to develop, she struggled to trust others in her life. Now, as an adult, Ariana has few peer supports, cannot maintain a healthy partner relationship, and struggles to hold down a job. As a future mental health professional, are you able to see the various developmental issues Ariana faced, and how those have intersected to get her to this point?

SOCIO-POLITICAL IMPACT ON DEVELOPMENT

Development, as noted, is a highly intersectional experience. It is also an experience that occurs against the backdrop of a combination of social and political factors, which are equally impactful on the development process. One of the key considerations we have for you in this text is to understand how the context of each individual shapes their experience, and socio-political factors are integral to this understanding. All too often you will find development framed as a global experience. That is to say that *everyone* develops in much the same way or that everyone *should* achieve specific milestones across their lifespan. When we talk of *socio-political* considerations, we are considering such things as economic influence, political factors, and sociological trends that have a direct impact on the life of each individual. These are factors that create opportunities for privilege and marginalization, and can also significantly shift the experience of developmental milestones depending on where someone is on the continuum of each.

Let's begin with economic influence. As in the case with Ariana, access to financial means or the lack thereof can significantly impact the developmental process. Not having financial security or access to basic needs can directly influence physical, cognitive, and social–emotional development. Had Ariana, for example, been born in a home with more financial means, she likely would have had the food resources necessary to foster her physical and cognitive growth, and her developmental experience, even into adulthood, may have been vastly different. And, while economic considerations are important when evaluating each family system, it is also important to think about the economic influence, or lack thereof, at the societal level. For example, the number of resources and economic support put into public education for lower income or minority children has a direct impact on the developmental experience (Heuer & Stullich, 2011). This means that even if Ariana came from a financially stable home, if she attended a high-poverty school, her development could also be impacted. Understanding how financial resources and the economic environment impact persons individually and collectively is an important part of understanding the developmental experience.

Political factors are another important consideration to the development process and can often overlap with economic issues. These include the formal laws and policies that impact individuals within their environments, but also include things like the political forces and influences that may impact access to or the experience of different elements in society. Consider, for example, the COVID-19 pandemic and the associated vaccine. While largely tied to economics, the question of access to vaccines is also a political one that has direct ties to development. Once vaccine development was ready and approved, countries, states, regions, and communities had to determine who would be first in line to receive vaccines and who would follow. This meant consideration for who was most at risk, but also whose job was determined to be "essential" or "front line." There was also consideration around global supply and who would gain access based on location of vaccine development, wealth, or connection as geopolitical allies (Haass, 2020, July 14). Other political considerations tied to the pandemic included who had direct access to healthcare and which legal and regulatory bodies could require mandates for vaccines and masks. The long-term impact of the pandemic and the associated political association are yet to be determined; however, we know there will be considerable health and educational implications to development for decades to come. As you move forward through this textbook, keep these types of political considerations in mind as you factor in how policies and practices shape the development of those you will serve.

Sociological trends is an additional area to consider when we think about human development and the life cycle. The influence of society—shifts in demographics, the ways in which people live, work, and think—has a significant impact on how people experience their growth and developmental process. Consider, for example, the movement within the United States on the topic of gay marriage. From 1997 to 2021, support of legalized marriage for same-sex couples increased from 27% to 70% (McCarthy, 2021). This was a significant societal shift in acceptance that took place across the span of 25 years. As you might imagine, for gay persons born in the United States and raised prior to the 21st century, the developmental experience was likely very different than those who were born thereafter. What is also important to consider is that not all countries or regions have demonstrated this same level of social change and acceptance when it comes to views on homosexuality (Poushter & Kent, 2020). Individuals you may work with in the future will come from all walks of life and many different cultures. As such it will be important for you to bear in mind the sociological beliefs of each person's family and cultural origins, as well as how those translate in current society.

Exploring Developmental Theories With a Contextual Lens and Contemporary Perspectives

There is a reason that lifespan development theories came to be. Just like you, the theorists associated with each developmental model or theory were looking to understand the people around them, and maybe even themselves. They wanted to know how we came to learn, engage with others, develop our personalities, overcome obstacles, and age within the contexts of our lives. We actually owe a great debt to the theorists who spent much of their lives investigating and publishing these developmental theories. These theories were, and in many ways still are, ways of creating meaning and understanding for those of us in the helping professions who are charged with working with clients across the developmental continuum. Their work contributed to the field of psychology and the various mental health and human service sectors, and their theories have been researched, expanded, and enhanced to get us where we are today. This does not, of course, mean they are always accurate to each person, context, culture, or time.

In the upcoming chapters you will have the opportunity to engage with some of the most significant and influential developmental theories to date. Our goal for this text was to provide you with the necessary exposure to traditional developmental theories, allowing you to appreciate them in the context of their development and for what they continue to contribute to the field. At the same time, research on human development has continued since many of these theories were first established—challenging some of their assumptions or otherwise addressing gaps that were identified across time. As a result, we also use the chapters ahead to provide you updated information and critiques grounded in more recent research of these traditional theories.

Within this text we explore, *first*, what it means to consider culture and context through the lens of development. You will see our emphasis on these areas as we begin each new developmental stage with a case study client. In starting with the person first, we switch the lens in which we explore developmental theory. Rather than applying a theory to a client, where the focus is on the theory and how much the client "fits" or "does not fit," we seek to have you apply the client to the theory—taking the whole person of the client and considering how they fit into the theoretical perspective, or not. In doing so, we explore traditional and seminal theories of development. We spend time outlining what those theories assert and how this is applied at various stages across development. We also explore critiques of these theories, emphasizing the ways in which additional research and consideration of socio-political factors have altered understanding for each theory since their inception. Finally, we spend time exploring areas of new research or theoretical perspectives that give more expansive or alternative perspectives.

THE INTERACTIVE NATURE OF THIS BOOK

As we, the authors, sat down to plan and write this book, we had some fairly strong ideas of what we wanted to include, what we wanted to avoid, and what we felt was most salient for readers like you, who are becoming mental health professionals. Our end goal was to provide you with a resource that was engaging and built on a foundation of applied learning that would be meaningful to your understanding of the lifespan development process. We know this content is important—it will help lay the foundation for how you view, support, and respond to the needs of those you work with in the future. It may also be necessary as a form of preparation for future licensure or certification exams for your profession. At the same time, we wanted to avoid the mistakes we have seen in many theory-focused texts—making it overly dense, boring, or hard to understand, or otherwise minimizing the influence of culture and context in the conversation of the development process.

We also recognized that sometimes the best way to learn about others is to continue to reflect on ourselves. This is a critical part of your professional development and you will be challenged to do so many times in your graduate program and professional careers. To that end, we have prepared a text that is story focused, highly reflective, application based, and emphasizes context and culture at the core. We present multiple case studies throughout this text that will anchor you in a client experience. We not only share the client's story with you, but provide you direct session excerpts to illustrate how developmental theory is used in interactions between the case study client and the mental health professional. Similarly, we have built in reflections, field work perspectives, and context-driven sidebars that are designed to have you think further and more critically about the content you are learning. Finally, you will find podcasts available with this text. These are designed to give you yet another perspective, from clinical professionals in the field, on how to understand and apply developmental theory with a focus on context and culture.

We want you, as mental health professionals-in-training, to engage in self-reflection about your own complex contextual conditioning as a person growing up, developing, and making sense of yourself in relationship to those on whom you have depended for survival and fulfillment. We also want to help you begin making the shift from receptive student to professional teammate, by working with these fictional clients along with your classmates. As you will soon be in experiential training, responsible for making sense out of the context of your clients' struggles and capacities, we want you to begin practicing this clinical judgment with compassion and a willingness to take in supervisory guidance, aware that you will be embedded in a professional hierarchy and need to work effectively with colleagues. Toward that end, the case studies, student reflections, and podcasts are intended to help you stay open-minded to others' experiences while noticing what arises for you, the assumptions you make based on life experience, and the emotional labor to navigate all of this with professional boundaries and client-centered advocacy. We also hope to inspire you to be lifelong learners, as we can never know everything.

LET THE STORY BEGIN: AN EXPLORATION OF THE GESTATIONAL PERIOD

As we launch into the initial chapters of this text, we thought it might be valuable to set the stage with an understanding of pre-birth experiences and their potential impact on development. Recognizing that we are the culmination of experiences, cultures, contexts, and family systems that contributed to our existence, it felt important to factor in these gestational considerations as we move further into the developmental theories that come after. As you consider the information that follows, we encourage you to begin the process of story-first, and think through your own gestational experiences. We also ask you to carry this information forward as you look at the case studies and developmental theories that come later, considering their potential impact.

Historical Context

Your lifespan, and that of everyone you meet, is the result of innumerable conditions that had to come together in a mathematically improbable way in order that embodied life take form exactly as and where it has by the *accident of birth*. Whether you ascribe to the Big Bang theory, the Great Spirit or Mystery, the Creation of Genesis, the pre-existence of Muhammad, the ultimate immutability of Brahman, the doctrine of Dependent Origination, another cosmology, or none at all, to experience your own life out of context with everything necessary to make it possible runs the risk of reducing your wonder about how you came to be and still exist as you do, with your exact body, brain, identities, beliefs, relationships, challenges, gifts, and possibilities. Such reductionism also runs the risk of objectifying others, which is contrary to ethical guidelines in clinical practice. Let us, therefore, aim to explore the fuller context of human development in a way that supports our connection and service to each other across our lifespans.

Hominids, the primate family to which *Homo sapiens* belongs, appear to have evolved about 1.8 million years ago on the African continent (Gibbons, 2010). Following current archeological and genetic data, it appears we evolved as a species for most of our time as nomadic hunter–gatherers on the African continent (Ember, 2020), and then in waves that have proceeded and receded, pushed out into new lands and climates, with our DNA and behavior mutating to survive and conserve the species along the way (*National Geographic*, n.d.). Agrarian societies arose about 11,000 years ago in the Fertile Crescent of the Middle East (Ghose, 2013), mostly shifting the nomadic lifestyle into one of territorial cultivation and food storage that, in combination with climate changes, allowed for the human population to explode by 1000-fold (Zahid et al., 2016). However, some hunter–gatherer societies do survive today, and give a window into our shared developmental history as a species (Hawkes et al., 2018). Agrarian society gave rise to country boundaries and resulting politics (Midlarsky, 1992); prior to this, nomadic groups moved on as food and safety requirements dictated.

Homo sapiens colonized the entire habitable planet over hundreds of thousands of years, and people mostly stayed in genetically related and allied family bands within walking distance of each other, until crowding, plagues, war, and torture in the European Middle Ages spurred a surge of re-colonization (Menakem, 2017). Europeans with more powerful weapons and technologies then crossed oceans in search of yet more land and resources, committing genocide against approximately 1 million members of the First Nations of the Americas, enslaving and committing further crimes against humanity on approximately 12.5 to 30 million Africans and their descendants (Menakem, 2017, *Trans-Atlantic Slave Trade - Downloads*, 2019); then the Industrial Revolution began around 1750 CE (Buchanan, 2020). These traumatic disruptions systematically broke family bands and communities apart. From this long-view historical context, your biological parental lineage somehow survived long enough to bring you into being. As we will touch on in this text, the transgenerational transmission of that experience informs your body–mind and its development across the lifespan, as well as the biobehavioral socialization processes your body has gone through to make it this far.

Pre- and Perinatal Development

Pre- and Perinatal Psychology (i.e., PPN or PPP) focuses on human development from pre-conception through the first year after birth. Coalescing the fields of anthropology, sociology, embryology, evolutionary biology and psychology, medicine, and mental health, PPN systematically explores the lived experience of implicit memory as it relates to beliefs and behaviors, as well as the risk and potential associated with variations in conception, gestation, and the early bonding experience, considered to be the foundation of one's life cycle to follow (Castellino, 2000; Chasnoff, 1989; Chasnoff et al., 1990, 1998, 2005, 2015, 2018; Evertz et al., 2021; Gilliland et al., 1999; Heller & LaPierre, 2012; Verny, 1984, 1996, 2014; White & Rhodes, 2014).

Because the genetic material that is transforming into embodied human consciousness during gestation is subject to the physical, relational, emotional, neurochemical, political, and spiritual experience of the gestating parent, a trauma-informed, relational, experiential, holistic interview and intervention process is the hallmark of PPN psychoeducation, advocacy, and therapeutic treatment in industrialized societies (Evertz et al., 2021; Monk et al., 2012; Seng & Taylor, 2015). Expanding this frame is *neuroanthropology*, which investigates how the brain develops within culture, and how culture is in turn shaped by the brain (Domínguez et al., 2009). From a clinical perspective, these interplays are often addressed referencing Bronfrenbrenner's Ecological Model of Development, and Relational-Cultural Theory, both of which we'll explore throughout this text.

PERSONAL APPLICATION 1.1: SELF-CARE MOMENT

Before reading on, bring your attention to where your skin makes contact with gravity, holding you to the Earth. Feel the strength and stability of your bones, providing structure and support for your flexible muscles and mobilizing joints. Sense how the nerve endings in the skin tell you where you end and the outside world begins. Stay curious about how the intelligence of your cells knows exactly how to become the organs that filter and sustain your individualized awareness. Can you bring your full attention to this very inhale? And this very exhale?

Conception

The egg that would become you was probably floating around in your biological mother when she was 5 months along gestating inside your maternal grandmother, a process called *oogenesis* (Irving, 1999). Assigned females appear to be born with their ova intact, and thus are developing the ova that will become any future conceptions while still in utero (unless future research can demonstrate that ovarian stem cells are producing new eggs after birth). This means that, most likely, the eggs are exposed to the circumstances unfolding while your biological mother was gestating in your maternal grandmother, and possibly reacting with epigenetic silencing or expression based on how life was requiring those elders to respond (Cooney, 2006; Jiang et al., 2004; Serpeloni et al., 2017; Sloane et al., 2015). Longitudinal studies on cohorts with shared histories of famine versus abundance show that there are also statistically significant increases in specific diseases (such as cancer, diabetes, and cardiovascular disease) when future fathers were impacted just before puberty, and that cultural trauma appears to carry forward on both parents (Jawaid, et al., 2018; Lehrner & Yehuda, 2018; Vågerö et al., 2018). Thus, with Western science, epigenetic effects on both maternal and paternal lines are beginning to be traced back at least two generations in humans, though many wisdom traditions suggest it is closer to seven generations that inform how our genes are impacted by our ancestors' experiences; animal studies are beginning to gather affirmative data on those concerns (Guerrero-Bosagna et al., 2013; Interlandi, 2013; Manikkam et al., 2012).

To be born requires that each of us inherits genetic material (i.e., Nature) from both a maternal and paternal line, and then gestates within a bio-psycho-social-spiritual being who is subject to their own lived experience (i.e., Nurture, aka epigenetics, or "over/on top of" genetics); therefore, cultural beliefs, expectations, and practices have informed our development even before we were born.

PPN purports that the emotional tenor and resulting neurochemical environment present through the process of conception do not have a null effect (Evertz et al., 2021). Whether both genetic donors were desiring to conceive at that time, the degree of safety and love versus fear, the sense of free choice versus force, tend to arise among the emotional and behavioral patterns present when a baby is conceived. If one genetic donor is trading sexual favors in exchange for food or housing security, drugs or protection, or has no say at all in the intercourse, presumably that is a less desirable situation to conceive in than if one is safe, securely attached, financially stable, free of substances, experiencing naturally generated neurochemical cascades of serotonin, dopamine, and oxytocin, emotionally open to conceiving, and supported by one's community to do so. If previous miscarriages, abortions, or a vanishing twin have occurred and not been fully resolved emotionally and therefore neurochemically, PPN suggests that the *haunted womb* might result in disenfranchised grief for birth parent and/or subsequent babies, as well as increased risks of mental health diagnoses (Boklage, 1990; Courtney, 2020; Evertz et al., 2021; Markin, 2018; Song et al., 2021).

Gestation

Pleasure and survival neurochemistry, nutrition, medicine, recreational and unintentional substance exposure can cross the placental barrier into the developing fetus; thus, babies are born with both ancient and situation-specific programming of what to expect from their environment upon birth, and are vulnerable to environmental and stress toxins that can impact brain and nervous system development, sometimes for life (Chasnoff, 1989; Chasnoff et al., 1990, 1998, 2005, 2015, 2018; Perry, 1997; Ross et al.,

2015; Verny, 2021). Traits and practices that are long-conserved have been maintained by Nature as they are advantageous for the species; departing too far from that which has been long-conserved tends to be disadvantageous, and sometimes disastrous for the individual or group, even if the species will keep going on (Lewis et al., 2000). For example, *teratogenic* ("malformation-causing") substances such as alcohol, drugs, agricultural fertilizers, petrochemicals, plastics, and pesticides are very recent inventions compared to the ancient evolution of the human body, and our developing bodies do not process them without damage (Carlos-Wallace et al., 2016; Fisher et al., 2012; Latini et al., 2006; Ragusa et al., 2021; Roberts & Karr, 2012). Sex and gender identity also appear to begin being formed in utero, as hormonal signaling between birth parent and fetus, and possibly epigenetic exposures, inform the developing baby's body and brain as sex and gender are being determined (Foreman et al., 2019; Leinung & Wu, 2017; Ristori et al., 2020). Furthermore, prenatal adversity is implicated in the subsequent development of personality, neurological, and behavioral disorders (Krzeczkowski & Van Lieshout, 2019; Monk et al., 2012; O'Connor et al., 2013; Schwarze et al., 2013).

Modern medicine, psychiatry, and psychology are increasingly finding that there are lifelong implications for well-being associated with this most impactful stage of our development (Barker et al., 2018; Fleming et al., 2018; Goldstein et al., 2021; Stephenson et al. 2018; Verny, 2021), and in fact, that the transgenerational transmission of trauma can be traced to epigenetic stressors having genetic effects in family lines (Jawaid et al., 2018; Perroud et al., 2014), in addition to the now widespread understanding that substance exposure in utero results in acquired brain and nervous system injury resulting in lifelong self-regulation and learning difficulties (Chasnoff, 1989; Chasnoff et al., 1990, 1998, 2005, 2015, 2018; Ross et al., 2015).

PERSONAL APPLICATION 1.2

Religious and political beliefs about conception, pregnancy, and women's and fetus's rights are deeply held and emotionally charged. How will you use supervision to work through any differences you have with your clients' beliefs to avoid values imposition around pregnancy decisions, while still offering psychoeducation as your clients are sufficiently receptive?

When gestating people are well supported and have Maslow's hierarchy of needs met consistently, they are more able to stay neurophysiologically regulated and within optimal limits while growing their babies, which when done with intentional attention such as touch, soothing voice, and healthy boundaries, is considered *early parenting* in PPN (Mckee et al., 2018) (Figure 1.1). When gestating people are not well supported or are otherwise not getting their hierarchy of needs met regularly, the ensuing stress necessarily impacts the neurochemical signals the baby is receiving during this most critical phase of development, which can interrupt both size and organization of the baby's various biological systems upon which their subsequent development must scaffold (Evertz et al., 2021). Compounding these interruptions is any substance ingestion that is not caught by the first-pass metabolism of the liver, thus crossing the placental barrier and impacting the neurophysiological development of the fetus (Ross et al., 2015). Birth weight, Apgar score, ability to latch and soothe can all show signs

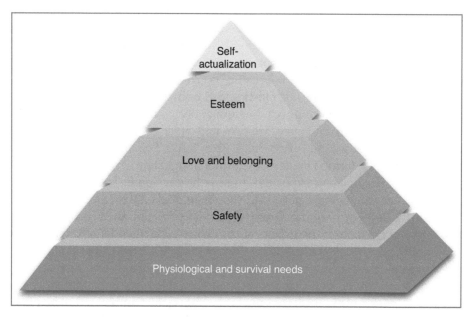

Figure 1.1 Maslow's hierarchy of needs.

of perinatal stress and trauma, as well as health and well-being (Hasanjanzadeh & Faramarzi, 2017). Clinically, helping gestating people get their hierarchy of needs met in good time allows them to increase their intentional focus on prenatal bonding with their baby, while preparing logistically and emotionally for the major changes to come.

SUMMARY

Developmental theories serve as a framework to understanding our clients and their respective development across time. As the theoretical landscape has expanded and shifted from its origins in the late 19th century, we have seen an increased need to focus on the influence of cultural and contextual factors and their impact on development. Similarly, we are seeing a greater expansion in the helping professions to include interdisciplinary approaches and a more holistic view of the developmental process. Understanding human development and the associated developmental theories that make meaning of that process is not only a requirement of your training program, but will provide you one of the most necessary tools in your future work as a mental health professional. The goal of this chapter was to start you on that journey.

Within this chapter we began our exploration of developmental theory by evaluating where developmental theory first evolved. We followed this with a discussion of the rationale for using developmental theory in the mental health professions and how the material from this text can be directly applied to the work you will do in the helping professions. We also evaluated the primary areas of physiological, cognitive, and social–emotional development that are the foundation of development, paying particular attention to how they work together to influence the developmental process. Finally, we spoke to the socio-political influences that must be considered as part of human development. These include economic influences, political factors, and sociological trends.

In preparation for reading the remainder of this book, we spent some time orienting you to how we conceptualized the theories for this text, including the use of traditional theory, critical analysis, and updated research. We laid out how this text is different and emphasized our particular focus on context and culture as key considerations in the evaluation of lifespan development. We also spoke to the interactive nature of our book and the ways in which we have emphasized a story-first approach that includes significant use of case studies, session excerpts, personal reflections, field work boxes, and supplementary podcasts featuring interviews with experts in the helping professions. To wrap up this chapter we explored the gestational development process as an origin to development. You were presented with key considerations for genetic influence and pre- and perinatal psychology using a trauma-informed perspective.

Our hope is that this material collectively set the stage for the chapters to come and has helped you to understand both the significance and value of developmental theory, context, and culture. In the following chapter you will begin evaluating the foundational developmental theories used in the mental health professions. These will be clustered into the primary developmental areas associated with psychological development and give a high-level overview of the most significant concepts associated with these traditional theories. As you move into Chapter 3 you will begin to explore the concept of intersectionality and identity development models and will provide additional theories and models that highlight contextual and cultural considerations tied to development. The combination of theories and content from these first few chapters will be carried forward to the remaining chapters of the text where you will evaluate and engage with developmental ages and stages and begin to apply your learning to client case studies. We hope you find this material engaging and informative to your growing understanding of lifespan development and your future work as a mental health professional.

REFERENCES

Arain, M., Haque, M., Johal, L., Mathur, P., Nel, W., Rais, A., Sandhu, R., & Sharma, S. (2013). Maturation of the adolescent brain. *Neuropsychiatric Disease and Treatment*, 9, 449–461. https://doi.org/10.2147/NDT.S39776

Barker, M., Dombrowski, S. U., Colbourn, T., Fall, C. H. D., Kriznik, N. M., Lawrence, W. T., Norris, S. A., Ngaiza, G., Patel, D., Skordis-Worrall, J., Sniehotta, F. F., Steegers-Theunissen, R., Vogel, C., Woods-Townsend, K., & Stephenson, J. (2018). Intervention strategies to improve nutrition and health behaviours before conception. *The Lancet*, 391(10132), 1853–1864. https://doi.org/10.1016/S0140-6736(18)30313-1

Bogin, B. (2020). *Patterns of human growth (Cambridge studies in biological and evolutionary anthropology)* (3rd ed). Cambridge University Press.

Boklage, C. E. (1990). Survival probability of human conceptions from fertilization to term. *International Journal of Fertility*, 35(2), 75, 79–80, 81–94.

Buchanan, R. A. (2020, November 18). *History of technology*. Encyclopedia Britannica. https://www.britannica.com/technology/history-of-technology

Carlos-Wallace, F. M., Zhang, L., Smith, M. T., Rader, G., & Steinmaus, C. (2016). Parental, in utero, and early-life exposure to benzene and the risk of childhood leukemia: A meta-analysis. *American Journal of Epidemiology*, 183(1), 1–14. https://doi.org/10.1093/aje/kwv120

Castellino, R. (2000). The stress matrix: Implications for prenatal and birth therapy. *Journal of Prenatal & Perinatal Psychology & Health*, 15(1), 31–62. https://login.paloaltou.idm.oclc.org/login?url=https://www.proquest.com/scholarly-journals/stress-matrix-implications-prenatal-birth-therapy/docview/198685748/se-2?accountid=25325

Chasnoff, I. J. (1989). Drug use and women: Establishing a standard of care. *Annals of the New York Academy of Sciences, 562*(1), 208–210. https://doi.org/10.1111/j.1749-6632.1989.tb21019.x

Chasnoff, I. J., Anson, A., Hatcher, R., Stenson, H., Iaukea, K., & Randolph, L. A. (1998). Prenatal exposure to cocaine and other drugs. Outcome at four to six years. *Annals of the New York Academy of Sciences, 846,* 314–328. https://doi.org/10.1111/j.1749-6632.1998.tb09748.x

Chasnoff, I. J., Barber, G., Brook, J., & Akin, B. A. (2018). The child abuse prevention and treatment act: Knowledge of health care and legal professionals. *Child Welfare, 96*(3), 41–58.

Chasnoff, I. J., Landress, H. J., & Barrett, M. E. (1990). The prevalence of illicit-drug or alcohol use during pregnancy and discrepancies in mandatory reporting in Pinellas County, Florida. *The New England Journal of Medicine, 322*(17), 1202–1206. https://doi.org/10.1056/NEJM199004263221706

Chasnoff, I. J., McGourty, R. F., Bailey, G. W., Hutchins, E., Lightfoot, S. O., Pawson, L. L., Fahey, C., May, B., Brodie, P., McCulley, L., & Campbell, J. (2005). The 4P's plus screen for substance use in pregnancy: Clinical application and outcomes. *Journal of Perinatology, 25*(6), 368–374. https://doi.org/10.1038/sj.jp.7211266

Chasnoff, I. J., Wells, A. M., & King, L. (2015). Misdiagnosis and missed diagnoses in foster and adopted children with prenatal alcohol exposure. *Pediatrics, 135*(2), 264–270. https://doi.org/10.1542/peds.2014-2171

Cooney, C. A. (2006). Germ cells carry the epigenetic benefits of grandmother's diet. *Proceedings of the National Academy of Sciences of the United States of America, 103*(46), 17071–17072. https://doi.org/10.1073/pnas.0608653103

Courtney, J. A. (2020). *Infant play therapy: Foundations, models, programs and practice.* Routledge. https://doi.org/10.4324/9780429453083

De Silva, N. K., & Tschirhart, J. (2016). Puberty-defining normal and understanding abnormal. *Current Treatment Options in Pediatrics, 2*(3), 121–130. https://doi.org/10.1007/s40746-016-0061-9

Developmental Psychology. (2020, August 25). *New World Encyclopedia.* https://www.newworldencyclopedia.org/p/index.php?title=Developmental_psychology&oldid=1041275

Domínguez, J. F., Lewis, E. D., Turner, R., & Egan, G. F. (2009). The brain in culture and culture in the brain: A review of core issues in neuroanthropology. *Progress in Brain Research, 178,* 43–64. https://doi.org/10.1016/S0079-6123(09)17804-4

Ember, C. R. (2020). Hunter-gatherers. In *Explaining human culture.* Human Relations Area Files. http://hraf.yale.edu/ehc/summaries/hunter-gatherers

Evertz, K., Janus, L., & Linder, R. (Eds.). (2021). *Handbook of prenatal and perinatal psychology.* Springer International Publishing. https://doi.org/10.1007/978-3-030-41716-1

Fisher, P. A., Kim, H. K., Bruce, J., & Pears, K. C. (2012). Cumulative effects of prenatal substance exposure and early adversity on foster children's HPA-axis reactivity during a psychosocial stressor. *International Journal of Behavioral Development, 36*(1), 29–35. https://doi.org/10.1177/0165025411406863

Fleming, T. P., Watkins, A. J., Velazquez, M. A., Mathers, J. C., Prentice, A. M., Stephenson, J., Barker, M., Saffery, R., Yajnik, C. S., Eckert, J. J., Hanson, M. A., Forrester, T., Gluckman, P. D., & Godfrey, K. M. (2018). Origins of lifetime health around the time of conception: Causes and consequences. *The Lancet, 391*(10132), 1842–1852. https://doi.org/10.1016/S0140-6736(18)30312-X

Foreman, M., Hare, L., York, K., Balakrishnan, K., Sánchez, F. J., Harte, F., Erasmus, J., Vilain, E., & Harley, V. R. (2019). Genetic link between gender dysphoria and sex hormone signaling. *The Journal of Clinical Endocrinology and Metabolism, 104*(2), 390–396. https://doi.org/10.1210/jc.2018-01105

Ghose, T. (2013). Evidence of ancient farming in Iran discovered. *Live Science.* https://www.livescience.com/37963-agriculture-arose-eastern-fertile-crescent.html

Gibbons, A. (2010). The human family's earliest ancestors: Studies of hominid fossils, like 4.4-million-year-old "Ardi," are changing ideas about human origins. *Smithsonian.* https://www.smithsonianmag.com/science-nature/the-human-familys-earliest-ancestors-7372974

Gilliland, A. L., Verny, T. R., & Psych, D. (1999). The effects of domestic abuse on the unborn child. *Journal of Prenatal & Perinatal Psychology & Health, 13*(3/4), 235.

Goldstein, J., Cohen, J. E., Mareckova, K. M., Holsen, L., Whitfield-Gabrieli, S., Gilmann, S., Buka, S. L., & Hornig, M. (2021). How we handle stress at 45 linked to prenatal exposure. *The Harvard Gazette*. https://news.harvard.edu/gazette/story/2021/04/how-we-handle -stress-at-45-linked-to-prenatal-exposure

Guerrero-Bosagna, C., Savenkova, M., Haque, M. M., Nilsson, E., & Skinner, M. K. (2013). Environmentally induced epigenetic transgenerational inheritance of altered Sertoli cell transcriptome and epigenome: Mmolecular etiology of male infertility. *Public Library of Science*. https://doi.org/10.1371/journal.pone.0059922

Haass, R. N. (2020, July 14). *The politics of a COVID-19 vaccine*. Council on Foreign Relations. https://www.cfr.org/article/politics-covid-19-vaccine

Hasanjanzadeh, P., & Faramarzi, M. (2017). Relationship between maternal general and specific-pregnancy stress, anxiety, and depression symptoms and pregnancy outcome. *Journal of Clinical and Diagnostic Research, 11*(4), VC04–VC07. https://doi.org/10.7860/JCDR/2017/24352.9616

Hawkes, K., O'Connell, J., & Blurton Jones, N. (2018). Hunter-gatherer studies and human evolution: A very selective review. *American Journal of Physical Anthropology, 165*(4), 777–800. https://doi.org/10.1002/ajpa.23403

Heller, L., & LaPierre, A. (2012). *Healing developmental trauma*. North Atlantic Books.

Heuer, R., & Stullich, S. (2011). *Comparability of state and local expenditures among schools within Districts: A report from the study of school-level expenditures*. Office of Planning, Evaluation and Policy Development, US Department of Education.

Interlandi, J. (2013). The toxins that affected your great-grandparents could be in your genes: Biologist Michael Skinner has enraged the chemical community and shocked his peers with his breakthrough research. *Smithsonian*. https://www.smithsonianmag.com/innovation/ the-toxins-that-affected-your-great-grandparents-could-be-in-your-genes-180947644/?c= y&story=fullstory#Skinner-ingenuity-birds-main-473.jpg

Irving, D. N. (1999). When do human beings begin? Scientific myths and scientific facts. *International Journal of Sociology and Social Policy, 19*(3/4), 22–46. https://doi.org/10.1108/ 01443339910788730

Jawaid, A., Roszkowski, M., & Mansuy, I. M. (2018). Transgenerational epigenetics of traumatic stress. *Progress in Molecular Biology and Translational Science, 158*, 273–298. https://doi.org/ 10.1016/bs.pmbts.2018.03.003

Jiang, Y.-H., Bressler, J., & Beaudet, A. L. (2004). Epigenetics and human disease. *Annual Review of Genomics and Human Genetics, 5*, 479–510. https://doi.org/10.1146/annurev.genom.5 .061903.180014

Koops, W. (2015). No developmental psychology without recapitulation theory. *European Journal of Developmental Psychology, 12*(6), 630–639. https://doi.org/10.1080/17405629.2015.1078234

Krzeczkowski, J. E., & Van Lieshout, R. J. (2019). Prenatal influences on the development and stability of personality. *New Ideas in Psychology, 53*, 22–31. https://doi.org/10.1016/j.newide-apsych.2018.01.003

Latini, G., Del Vecchio, A., Massaro, M., Verrotti, A., & De Felice, C. (2006). In utero exposure to phthalates and fetal development. *Current Medicinal Chemistry, 13*(21), 2527–2534. https:// doi.org/10.2174/092986706778201666

Lehrner, A., & Yehuda, R. (2018). Cultural trauma and epigenetic inheritance. *Development and Psychopathology, 30*(5), 1763–1777. https://doi.org/10.1017/S0954579418001153

Leinung, M., & Wu, C. (2017). The biologic basis of transgender identity: 2D: 4D finger length ratios implicate a role for prenatal androgen activity. *Endocrine Practice, 23*(6), 669–671. https://doi.org/10.4158/EP161528.OR

Lewis, T., Amini, F., & Lannon, R. (2000). *A general theory of love*. Vintage Books.

Manikkam, M., Guerrero-Bosagna, C., Tracey, R., Haque, M., Skinner, M. K., & Shioda, T. (2012). Transgenerational actions of environmental compounds on reproductive disease and identification of epigenetic biomarkers of ancestral exposures. *Public Library of Science*. https:// doi.org/10.1371/journal.pone.0031901

Markin, R. D. (2018). "Ghosts" in the womb: A mentalizing approach to understanding and treating prenatal attachment disturbances during pregnancies after loss. *Psychotherapy, 55*(3), 275–288. https://doi.org/10.1037/pst0000186

McCarthy, J. (2021, June 8). *Record high 70% in U.S. support same-sex marriage*. Gallup. https://news.gallup.com/poll/350486/record-high-support-same-sex-marriage.aspx

Mckee, C., Stapleton, P., & Pigeon, A. (2018). History of pre and perinatal (PPN) parenting education: A literature review. *Journal of Prenatal & Perinatal Psychology & Health, 32*(3).

Melé, D., & Cantón, C. G. (2014). Relational dimensions of the human being. In *Human foundations of management*. IESE Business Collection. Palgrave Macmillan. https://doi.org/10.1057/9781137462619

Menakem, R. (2017). *My grandmother's hands: Racialized trauma and the pathway to mending our hearts and bodies*. Central Recovery Press.

Midlarsky, M. I. (1992). The origins of democracy in agrarian society. *Journal of Conflict Resolution, 36*(3), 454–477. https://doi.org/10.1177/0022002792036003003

Monk, C., Spicer, J., & Champagne, F. A. (2012). Linking prenatal maternal adversity to developmental outcomes in infants: the role of epigenetic pathways. *Development and Psychopathology, 24*(4), 1361–1376. https://doi.org/10.1017/S0954579412000764

National Geographic. (n.d.). *Natural selection*. https://www.nationalgeographic.org/encyclopedia/natural-selection

O'Connor, T. G., Monk, C., & Fitelson, E. M. (2013). Practitioner review: Maternal mood in pregnancy and child development--implications for child psychology and psychiatry. *Journal of Child Psychology and Psychiatry, and Allied Disciplines, 55*(2), 99–111. https://doi.org/10.1111/jcpp.12153

Perroud, N., Rutembesa, E., Paoloni-Giacobino, A., Mutabaruka, J., Mutesa, L., Stenz, L., Malafosse, A., & Karege, F. (2014). The Tutsi genocide and transgenerational transmission of maternal stress: Epigenetics and biology of the HPA axis. *The World Journal of Biological Psychiatry, 15*(4), 334–345. https://doi.org/10.3109/15622975.2013.866693

Perry, B. D. (1997). Incubated in terror: Neurodevelopmental factors in the 'cycle of violence.' In J. Osofsky (Ed.), *Children, youth and violence: The search for solutions* (pp. 124–148). Guilford Press.

Poushter, J., & Kent, N. (2020, June 25). *The global divide on homosexuality exists: But increasing acceptance in many countries over past two decades*. Pew Research Center. https://www.pewresearch.org/global/2020/06/25/global-divide-on-homosexuality-persist

Ragusa, A., Svelato, A., Santacroce, C., Catalano, P., Notarstefano, V., Carnevali, O., Papa, F., Rongioletti, M. C. A., Baiocco, F., Draghi, S., D'Amore, E., Rinaldo, D., Matta, M., & Giorgini, E. (2021). Plasticenta: First evidence of microplastics in human placenta. *Environment International, 146*, 106274. https://doi.org/10.1016/j.envint.2020.106274

Ristori, J., Cocchetti, C., Romani, A., Mazzoli, F., Vignozzi, L., Maggi, M., & Fisher, A. D. (2020). Brain sex differences related to gender identity development: Genes or hormones? *International Journal of Molecular Sciences, 21*(6), E2123. https://doi.org/10.3390/ijms21062123

Roberts, J. R., Karr, C. J., & Council On Environmental Health. (2012). Pesticide exposure in children. *Pediatrics, 130*(6), e1765–e1788. https://doi.org/10.1542/peds.2012-2758

Ross, E. J., Graham, D. L., Money, K. M., & Stanwood, G. D. (2015). Developmental consequences of fetal exposure to drugs: Wwhat we know and what we still must learn. *Neuropsychopharmacology: Official Publication of the American College of Neuropsychopharmacology, 40*(1), 61–87. https://doi.org/10.1038/npp.2014.147

Schwarze, C. E., Mobascher, A., Pallasch, B., Hoppe, G., Kurz, M., Hellhammer, D. H., & Lieb, K. (2013). Prenatal adversity: A risk factor in borderline personality disorder? *Psychological Medicine, 43*(6), 1279–1291. https://doi.org/10.1017/S0033291712002140

Seng, J., & Taylor, J. (2015). *Trauma-informed care in the perinatal period*. Dunedin Academic Press.

Serpeloni, F., Radtke, K., de Assis, S. G., Henning, F., Nätt, D., & Elbert, T. (2017). Grandmaternal stress during pregnancy and DNA methylation of the third generation: An epigenome-wide association study. *Translational Psychiatry, 7*(8), e1202. https://doi.org/10.1038/tp.2017.153

Sloane, M. A., Nunez, A. C., Packham, D., Kwok, C. T., Suthers, G., Hesson, L. B., & Ward, R. L. (2015). Mosaic epigenetic inheritance as a cause of early-onset colorectal cancer. *JAMA Oncology, 1*(7), 953–957. https://doi.org/10.1001/jamaoncol.2015.1484

Song, H., Fang, F., Larsson, H., Pedersen, N. L., Magnusson, P. K., Almqvist, C., & Valdimarsdóttir, U. A. (2021). Loss of a co-twin at birth and subsequent risk of psychiatric disorders. *ELife, 10*, e63514. https://doi.org/10.7554/eLife.63514

Stephenson, J., Heslehurst, N., Hall, J., Schoenaker, D. A. J. M., Hutchinson, J., Cade, J. E., Poston, L., Barrett, G., Crozier, S. R., Barker, M., Kumaran, K., Yajnik, C. S., Baird, J., & Mishra, G. D. (2018). Before the beginning: Nutrition and lifestyle in the preconception period and its importance for future health. *The Lancet, 391*(10132), 1830–1841. https://doi.org/10.1016/S0140-6736(18)30311-8

Stiles, J., & Jernigan, T. L. (2010). The basics of brain development. *Neuropsychology Review, 20*(4), 327–348. https://doi.org/10.1007/s11065-010-9148-4

Trans-Atlantic Slave Trade - Downloads. (2019). https://Www.Slavevoyages.Org/Voyage/Downloads#full-Versions-of-the-Trans-Atlantic-Slave-Trade-Database/0/En

Tucker-Drob, E. M., Brandmaier, A. M., & Lindenberger, U. (2019). Coupled cognitive changes in adulthood: A meta-analysis. *Psychological Bulletin, 145*(3), 273–301. https://doi.org/10.1037/bul0000179

Vågerö, D., Pinger, P. R., Aronsson, V., & van den Berg, G. J. (2018). Paternal grandfather's access to food predicts all-cause and cancer mortality in grandsons. *Nature Communications, 9*(1), 5124. https://doi.org/10.1038/s41467-018-07617-9

Verny, T. R. (1984). Prenatal psychology: Implications for the practice of medicine. *Canadian Family Physician Medecin de Famille Canadien, 30*, 2115–2118.

Verny, T. R. (1996). Isolation, rejection and communion in the womb. *International Journal of Prenatal and Perinatal Psychology and Medicine, 8*, 287–294.

Verny, T. R. (2014). What cells remember: Toward a unified field theory of memory. *Journal of Zahid Prenatal & Perinatal Psychology & Health, 29*(1), 16.

Verny, T. R. (2021). The pre- and perinatal origins of childhood and adult diseases and personality disorders. In K. Evertz, L. Janus, & R. Linder (Eds.), *Handbook of prenatal and perinatal psychology*. Springer. https://doi.org/10.1007/978-3-030-41716-1_5

White, K., & Rhodes, J. (2014). Trends and influences in pre- and perinatal psychology a summary. *Journal of Prenatal & Perinatal Psychology & Health, 28*(3), 198–211.

Zahid, H. J., Robinson, E., & Kelly, R. L. (2016). Agriculture and population growth. *Proceedings of the National Academy of Sciences, 113*(4), 931–935. https://doi.org/10.1073/pnas.1517650112

CHAPTER 2

The Roots of Lifespan Developmental Theories

LEARNING OBJECTIVES

Upon completion of this chapter, students will be able to:

1. Identify theories of human development.
2. Describe key tenets of theories of human development.
3. Recognize terminology associated with specific theories of human development.
4. Identify how human development needs may be addressed with the seminal theory.

INTRODUCTION TO DEVELOPMENTAL THEORY

So where do we begin? One challenge with determining which seminal theories to introduce in a lifespan development textbook is to try to establish a workable foundation from which to expand and explore. What you will likely find as you move through the ages and stages of development is that each theorist focused on development from a different perspective of the human experience. That is to say, there is not one all-encompassing theory of human development. Instead, theories were developed, researched, and can be categorized across domains of development, such as cognitive and personality development. What is also true is that theories are often categorized based on the age of development and the associated milestones with particular points in the life cycle. The earliest developmental theories, for example, focused solely on child and adolescent development, whereas adult developmental theories came later and reflect different experiences. In addition, some theories are broader than others, encompassing a full lifespan, while others are highly specific to a time period, an experience, or a cultural identity. In truth, there are a multitude of developmental theories and many ways in which these can be presented.

In order to best equip you with an understanding of development theory, we felt it was important to spend some time exploring the most seminal theories of lifespan development and anchoring those into specific domain areas. The goal is to help you begin conceptualizing development and the multilayered and multidimensional ways in which humans come to be who they are, and we must first do this by laying the foundation. Within this chapter you will explore the key areas of ego development, cognitive development, moral development, attachment theory, and adult development, as well as some of the most prominent theorists and theories associated with them. Each theory in this chapter is laid out with the intent of being a foundational reference point for you. While we hope to effectively cover the most salient elements of each theory in the sections that follow, the goal is not to allow this material to stand alone. Instead, you will find it referenced in more specific and applied detail as you move into the age and stage chapters that follow. When necessary, we invite you to refer back to this chapter, as your foundation, for additional clarification and understanding of the applied content you will read later.

THEORIES OF EGO DEVELOPMENT

Sigmund and Anna Freud, as well as Erik Erikson, examined development through the lens of personality and biologically based drives. These are commonly referred to as psychoanalytic and psychodynamic theories of ego development and are tied to personality. In other words, how do we understand who we are? How do our unconscious drives and impulses interact with our environments to shape our sense of self? How do we grow, mature, and evolve into beings who have a sense of self and a sense of place in our worlds? These theories are the roots of developmental theory and the place where we will start our theories discussion.

Freud's Psychosexual Theory

Sigmund Freud is the first White Western medical professional credited with formal exploration of how the physical, neurological, and relational experience of the embodied human gives rise to psychological experience from developmental imprints. Freud was a Monrovian (now Czech) Austrian neurologist who valued understanding the patient's inner world in order to help resolve their suffering, thus inventing "the talking cure," fathering psychoanalytic theory, inadvertently founding traumatology, and laying the groundwork for all mental health study and practice to follow. He was also a cisgender man in a heterosexual marriage with five children in Victorian Vienna, with upper middle–class status and a significant sphere of influence, the context of which we will explore a bit (Gay, 2006).

Freud conceptualized the inborn lifeforce as a fundamentally sexual drive, or *libido*, a primary human impulse that organizes *libidinal phases of development* to make initial contact with the world and society. This included the psychological effects known as *oral, anal, phallic, latent,* and *genital libido* phases, which culminated in the "altruistic" act of procreation (Brill, 1938). Freud's emphasis on lifeforce energy as fundamentally sexual highlights how central to identity sex and gender are from his frame of reference. Though it is important to consider that these also reflect a cisnormative, heteronormative, misogynistic bias.

FREUD'S STAGES OF PSYCHOSEXUAL DEVELOPMENT

Here we will focus primarily on development within a psychoanalytic framework, specifically the psychosexual phases. We will maintain awareness of Freud's *social location* (Anthias, 2013) as we explore the brave attempt he made from his particular privileged and limited position, to make sense of the human condition (Table 2.1).

Table 2.1 Freud's Psychosexual Stages of Development

STAGE	AGE	EROGENOUS ZONE	CONSEQUENCE OF FIXATION
Oral	Birth to 1 year old	Mouth	Latent aggressive or passive tendencies
Anal	1 to 3 years old	Anus and bladder	Anal retentiveness (orderly, rigid, obsessive) or anal expulsiveness (messy, wasteful, destructive)
Phallic	3 to 6 years old	Genitals	Roots of fixation with the opposite-sex parent (Oedipus or Electra complex)
Latent	7 to 12 years old	Dormant sexual feelings	Inability to form healthy relationships as an adult
Genital	13 years old and above	Mature sexual feelings	Unable to develop meaningful healthy relationships

Source: Adapted from Brill, A. A. (Ed.). (1938). *The basic writings of Sigmund Freud*. Random House.

The Oral Phase.   The *oral* phase, from birth through the first year, is centered on sensory and emotional gratification that results in some measure of age-appropriate biobehavioral co-regulation through nursing, suckling, and exploring objects by placing them in the mouth. Teething and apoptosis of the gums happen during the second half of this phase, which are soothed by chewing and rubbing the gums, but the rooting and ingestion necessary for a neonate to grow into a toddler is thought to create patterns of expectation based on this repeated survival and formative soothing experience. If sufficient caregiver contact, holding, acceptance, availability, and supportive nourishment are provided through breastfeeding and oral exploration during this first year of life, the baby tends to learn to relax, be at ease in their body, trust that their needs will be met, and thus be in secure, pleasurable contact with the world around them (e.g., caregivers are perceived as *good objects*; Westen, 1991). This pleasurable contact protects the baby from getting caught up in frustrated fixation on oral gratification, allowing them to move on to the next phase with the right timing as their body matures (Fisher & Greenberg, 1996); the loss of this reliable connection may be implicated in a characterological tendency toward depression (Desmet, 2013).

If, however, there is not sufficient satisfaction of regulation through timely oral gratification, there can be tendencies toward ongoing bodily tension, angry aggression, mistrust, and a subconscious longing to return to this phase of being cared for in order to finally gratify it, rather than carry the grief forward; such patterns may be coupled with anxious ingestion later in life (e.g., substance use, eating disorders, nervous chewing of nails and writing implements; Fisher & Greenberg, 1996), as well as depression (Desmet, 2013; Oppenheim et al., 1997). These stored experiences of not enough or too much are thought to result in a residue of *neuroses*, anxious compensation that can cause lifelong difficulties in subsequent relationships where the caregiving patterns get reactivated (Brill, 1938). Modern analysts might suggest that the unconscious desire to merge with a lover and lose personal boundaries in becoming a "we" is anchored in this phase of relatively undifferentiated connection, and the tendency to idealize authority figures and romantic partners who are sufficiently responsive as indicative of an oral character structure, anchored to this phase of needs fulfillment.

The Anal Phase.   From about the first birthday to age three, Freud posited that developmental and libidinal energy moved from being centralized around the mouth to the bladder and anus (Brill, 1938). This *anal* phase is when pressure to become toilet trained increases as the child ages, and the medically capable child gains sphincter control to be aware of the need to defecate and urinate. If attuned parenting via strength-based praise and encouragement during the oral phase has set the toddler up to be relatively relaxed and trusting, the caregiving patterns are likely to hold, and the transition to the anal phase is presumed to occur without undue emotional charge from shame or fear of dismissive or over-bearing parenting; the toddler will increasingly show interest in being able to self-direct to toileting independently, with resulting pride of accomplishment, productivity, and ease of letting go. If, on the other hand, the caregiving environment has been withholding, punitive, disorganized, or otherwise overwhelming, or becomes so in the new demands of attuning to an increasingly complex and differentiating baby, or by some invasive trauma, the patterns that carry through the toilet training phase may lead to a child who is fixated on the anal phase, resulting in an *anally retentive or expulsive* character (Brill, 1938).

Unresolved tension from this phase is theorized to result in neurotic (unproductive, unhealthy) power struggles and control dynamics, such as uptight anxiety, perfectionism, and obsessive tendencies if the child is unable to meet overly high expectations or is punished for asserting their budding independence. Power struggles can also take the form of demanding parental attention and structure by intentionally making a mess and spreading one's waste around physically and emotionally (Brill, 1938). Modern analysts might suggest that patterns giving rise to irritable bowel syndrome, encopresis or enuresis, obsessive compulsive disorder, conspicuous consumerism, and process addictions may be linked to unresolved stressors and traumas of this phase (U.S. Association for Body Psychotherapy Board meeting, personal communication, November 2020).

The Phallic Stage.   Age three to six encapsulates Freud's *phallic* stage, when preliminary sexual and gender identity processes become more central to a child's developing sense of self and their place in the family (Brill, 1938). Freud's Oedipus and Electra complexes arise here, where a preschooler's innocent infatuation with their parents' affection and approval can purportedly give rise to fantasies of dominion over their competing parent's love and attention, usually theorized as a jealousy toward the same-sex parent and attraction toward the opposite sex parent, resulting in desires to replace the same-sex parent, and guilt over such feelings. This is obviously situated in a cis- and heteronormative frame of reference, and further reified in the misogyny and violence of the era by *fears of castration* and *penis envy* (Brill, 1938). Most modern clinicians look askance at the literal interpretation of these complexes; however, updated traumatology research would largely agree that long-standing relational, intimacy, and self-esteem issues can persist if this developmental phase creates problematic emotional charges regarding how fundamentally safe, accepted, and loved one is by any valued caregiver (Barnum & Perrone-McGovern, 2017; Levine, 2003; Levine & Kline, 2008).

If the innocent emotional and attentional desires of the preschooler are honored with healthy boundaries and a securing parental subsystem that is not unduly challenged by these competing needs for affection, the preschooler will emerge from this phase feeling inherently lovable and worthy, including in their inborn sexual attraction across the lifespan (Brill, 1938), though the oppression informing Freud's cis-heteronormativity would not have allowed that pride and security for LGBTQ+ children. If sexual boundary violations, parental shame or jealousy toward the child occur during this phase, lifelong anxiety about emotional and sexual intimacy could be the result (Barnum & Perrone-McGovern, 2017). Modern analysts might suggest that an integrated sense of one's sexuality and gender identity and expression are owed to this phase being navigated without undue interruption, and that tension of disapproval or other emotional shocks occurring during this phase of ego development might have long-term implications in felt security of romantic relationships and self-expression, including as Type II, "relational/developmental" (Kira, 2001) or Type III, "complex" trauma (Solomon & Heide, 1999). The updated case study of one of Freud's most famous *phallic* client examples, "Little Hans, exemplifies how the Type II traumas of child abuse and erratic parental behavior within the home can graft onto a young child's developing awareness of genitalia, a part of their wholeness and safety, and result in phobias and fears (Ross, 2007), informed by cultural context and expectations.

STUDENT REFLECTION 2.1

"Little Hans" (Herbert Graf) was a 5-year-old boy who exhibited a phobia of horses and castration anxiety. His mom had been a patient of Freud's, so the family had some acculturation to Freud's theories and methods. Hans was brought to Freud's attention for psychoanalysis by his father, though Freud was minimally involved. Freud altered his famous couch work and exchanged suggestions through letters with the father sharing Hans's art and reports; Freud gifted Hans a wooden rocking horse at age 3 as gentle exposure therapy to help uncouple his fear for horses in a way that would likely not lead to scary experiences (Midgley, 2006). As time went on, it became clear that Hans's mom was threatening to cut off his penis if he wouldn't stop touching it (Blum, 2007). Hans also witnessed close-up a horse-drawn carriage topple over and harm many people while walking on the street with his babysitter (Blum, 2007). Hans was able to work through his traumatic reactions to horses while moving through the phallic stage that was tinged with danger and threat. Later interviews reveal that Hans's mother was emotionally and physically abusive toward her husband and the children; Hans's sister died by suicide as an adult, possibly as a result of unresolved developmental trauma (Ross, 2007).

The Latency Phase.   The *latency* period is from six to puberty. During latency, the lifeforce Freud conceptualized as *libido* is sublimated, or channeled, into intellectual and social pursuits of entering larger society through the demands of school and other people's expectations outside of the home (Brill, 1938). In industrialized societies, this period is so all-consuming socially that the lifeforce is usually seamlessly absorbed in keeping up with those extra-familial relationships and academic pursuits. Children who have emotional charges left over from earlier phases may be required to repress (subconsciously hold down) or suppress (consciously hold down) the work remaining to fit in socially, and/or might find themselves fixated on an earlier developmental phase when they enter this one, which could then be theorized to result in an immature ability to form age-typical friendships upon school entry and fulfilling adult relationships later on in life (Brill, 1938). Modern analysts might point to difficulties integrating this phase as being the source of commitment-phobic tendencies in adulthood (Knight, 2014).

The Genital Phase.   The *genital* phase is from puberty to death. During the genital phase, the libido is reactivated and expressed not just in pursuit of personal satisfaction, as it was during early childhood, but in ever-maturing mutuality toward love interests. If previous stages were resolved effectively, there will be low conflict over getting needs met and contributing to loving relationship; if unresolved emotional charges remain from previous psychosexual phases, the fixation and neuroses will result in difficulty with warmth, caring, and empathy for others (Brill, 1938; Lantz & Ray, 2021).

FINAL THOUGHTS ON FREUD

Sigmund Freud founded psychoanalysis—the bedrock of human development— psychology, and counseling as medicine-adjacent fields. What Freud proposed as normative or ideal for developmental tasks was focused on the individual, even though the core conflicts he identified are all rooted in unrepaired traumatic ruptures in significant attachment relationships. Considering the timeframe, context, and identity of Freud, we see how his White, Western, cisgendered, heterosexual, financially privileged identity infused his definition of what was "normal"; he pathologized females and gay males directly and has been interpreted as having engaged in victim-blaming of incest survivors, though Bettelheim (1983) asserts that is due to mistranslation of his Viennese German into English. His publications and lectures created an uproar as they began to air out dirty laundry of Viennese elite society, which he was expected to protect. Imperfect in its tightly culture-bound limitations, his initial conceptualization of early needs and experiences having long-term implications for ego development broke open the medical sciences and paved the way for subsequent developmental theorists to fine tune the rough sketch he had drawn.

Erikson's Psychosocial Development Theory

Erik Erikson offers us another perspective on ego development; however, his is centered on the influence of social dynamics and evaluates the developmental process into adulthood. Erikson was the first developmental theorist to emphasize the complete lifespan in a development theory, resulting in his significant influence in the mental health fields across time. While stage-focused, like Freud, Erikson was interested in how biological, psychological, and societal factors influenced development from birth through death.

Initially trained by Anna Freud (Target, 2018), daughter of Sigmund, and later inducted as a member of the American Psychoanalytic Society, Erikson had no formal degrees in psychology or graduate education. He was born in Frankfurt, Germany, in 1902, raised for many years by a single mother, and was trained as a Montessori teacher. In spite of this he later moved to the United States where he was a practicing psychoanalyst; a university lecturer at Harvard, Yale, and the University of Berkeley; received a Pulitzer Prize for his work *Gandhi's Truth*; and authored one of the most prominent theories of personality development (Maree, 2020). Unlike his predecessor Freud, Erikson believed personality development spanned the full life cycle and ultimately reflected a series of eight developmental stages tied to psychosocial experiences, crises, and strengths.

THE STAGES OF PSYCHOSOCIAL DEVELOPMENT

Much like many other theorists, Erikson developed a stage theory that was founded on the belief in *epigenetics*, or the idea that people's personalities are developed across time through a particular sequence of prescribed developmental milestones (Maree, 2020). The milestones in focus in this theory tie specifically to personality development and how this is shaped through our interactions with others and with specific tasks tied to our agency at that time. Depending on how we are able to navigate those—positively, negatively, or not at all—we ultimately develop strengths or face a developmental identity crisis that can plague us in future stages.

Unlike other stage theories that require particular success in a stage before progressing forward, the expectation is that individuals progress based roughly on age and expected adherence to the milestones associated with that age and stage. Failure to effectively deal with the developmental tasks of a particular stage will not prevent progression but will likely result in those "problems" resurfacing in later stages (Maree, 2020). Alternatively, if we are able to successfully navigate the developmental task at each stage, we foster personality strengths that will aid in our identity development and carry over into our future interactions and stages. In this way, Erikson's stages should be viewed as a broader continuum of development where optimal psychological health is achieved through successfully addressing the crises of each stage (Dunkel & Harbke, 2017) (Table 2.2).

Stage 1: Basic Trust Versus Basic Mistrust.   In infancy through approximately a baby's first birthday, or even a little beyond, infants face the developmental task of establishing a sense of trust for their caregivers. Changing a baby's diaper, feeding them when they are hungry, keeping them warm and dry, giving them snuggles and smiles, all reinforce feelings of basic trust. Through the establishment of this trust, babies gain the psychosocial strength and virtue of *hope*. Hope allows a young child, when moving into the next stage of development, to carry with them a sense of security, safety, and trust in their caregivers and their ability to be cared for (Capuzzi et al., 2016). If the developmental task of this first stage is not successfully reconciled, such as in cases where infants' basic needs are not adequately met, then the infant can experience the crisis of distrust. From a clinical perspective, then, the client who has difficulty trusting others may look at the world with anxiety, fear, and mistrust (Chung, 2018).

Stage 2: Autonomy Versus Shame and Doubt.   After the first year and into toddler years, children typically become mobile and inquisitive and start exploring the world around them. In addition, toddlers start to use their words, bodies, and emotional expression to make their needs and wants known. If you have ever raised a child, you probably remember well the stage of "No!" "Mine!" and the middle-of-the-grocery-store-temper-tantrum because your little darling couldn't have the sugary cereal. This flexing of independence is, however, important in Erikson's view. When caregivers can provide realistic opportunities for children at this stage to exert their will, to make some choices, and to celebrate the emerging individual who is separate from the caregiver, they are setting the stage for the successful resolution of the task of

Table 2.2 Erikson's Psychosocial Stages of Development

AGE	STAGE	DEVELOPMENTAL TASK	CRISIS	PSYCHOSOCIAL STRENGTH
1 to 2 years: Infancy	Basic trust vs. Mistrust	Infants interact with caregivers and begin to visualize and develop trust related to attaining needs	Infants create a feeling of distrust due to a disruption in the care-giving pattern	Hope
2 to 4 Years: Early Childhood	Autonomy vs. Shame and Doubt	Children start exploring their environment and begin distinguishing themselves from others	An identity crisis occurs when parents punish their children for not accomplishing expected tasks (e.g., toilet training)	Will
4 to 5 Years: Preschool Age	Initiative vs. Guilt	Children begin interacting with peers, distinguish between right and wrong, and complete certain tasks successfully on their own	Children who try to exert too much power experience disapproval, resulting in a sense of guilt	Purpose
5 to 12 Years: School Age	Industry vs. Inferiority	Children start to build their own social networks and become more competent and adept at carrying out increasingly complex tasks	Children develop a sense of inferiority if their performance is not appreciated	Competence
13 to 19 Years: Adolescence	Identity vs. Role Confusion	Individuals start developing their belief system, values, sense of self, and goals as they grow more independent and self-confident.	Individuals who fail to accommodate both external recognition and self-satisfaction ultimately struggle with developing their sense of self	Fidelity
20 to 40 Years: Emerging Adulthood	Intimacy vs. Isolation	Young adults decide whether they will establish, maintain, and promote intimate relationships with people they trust	Individuals refrain from creating friendships and resort to emotional stress and isolation	Love

40 to 65 Years: Adulthood	Generativity vs. Stagnation	Individuals begin giving back to their social system, focus on their professional life, and are concerned about raising children	Stagnation will prevail leading to disengagement in productive life activities	Care
65+: Maturity	Ego Integrity vs. Despair	Individuals re-evaluate their lives and reflect on their achievements as they confront the idea of dying and their mortality	Individuals who feel they have failed to cease opportunities in their lives enter a state of despair and surrender to frustration	Wisdom

Source: Adapted from Dunkel, C. S., & Harbke, C. (2017). A review of measures of Erikson's stages of psychosocial development: Evidence for a general factor. *Journal of Adult Development, 24*(1), 58–76. https://doi.org/10.1007/s10804-016-9247-4; Karkouti, I. M. (2014). Examining psychosocial identity development theories: A guideline for professional practice. *Education, 135*(2), 257–263; Maree, J. G. (2020). The psychosocial development theory of Erik Erikson: Critical overview. *Early Child Development and Care.* https://doi-org.ezproxy.snhu.edu/10.1080/03004430.2020.1845163

distinguishing oneself from others and developing the psychosocial strength and virtue of *will*. If toddlers are not afforded the opportunity to exert themselves, to develop self-control when something happens they do not like, and to develop the foundation of self-esteem, then the resulting crisis of development can be to feel stuck in feelings of shame, inadequacy, and doubt (Capuzzi et al., 2016).

Stage 3: Initiative Versus Guilt.   The preschool years, about ages 3 to 5, are when children have the developmental task of learning to interact with others outside of the caregiver and immediate family unit, often including peers, teachers, and other adults. This is also the period of development where Erikson suggested that moral development begins to occur. Understanding the difference between right and wrong and starting to connect with a sense of direction can lead to the psychosocial strength and virtue of *purpose* (Chung, 2018). Preschoolers have broadened their vocabulary and also their thirst for knowledge. Asking endless questions, including the often used "why?," is typical at this stage. Because children at this age may find themselves, at times, away from their primary caregiver, either in learning environments or social environments, they naturally will be learning to initiate. Their ability to take initiative in these situations and to successfully engage with the world around them will minimize frustration and therefore guilt. The crisis that can occur at this stage is when children are scolded, admonished, or receive disapproval for trying to exert too much power and control, causing a feeling of guilt (Chung, 2018).

Stage 4: Industry Versus Inferiority.   The school-aged years, about ages 6 through 12, represent opportunities for children to develop meaningful friendships and to engage in increasingly difficult tasks. Through schoolwork, household chores, and social and familial expectations and interactions, children learn about how their contributions impact others and potentially benefit the world around them. Mastery, competence, and ability are regularly measured and evaluated, and if children feel that their efforts are recognized and rewarded, they achieve the psychosocial strength and virtue of *competence* (Capuzzi et al., 2016). Children who do not gain this sense of industry can instead develop the crisis of inferiority, where now and in the future their ability to make decisions, problem-solve, and have faith in their own abilities is reduced.

Stage 5: Identity Versus Role Confusion.   The teenage years, ages 13 through 19, is a time marked by asking the question, "who am I?" and "who do I want to be?" This search for identity can lead adolescents to enter young adulthood with the psychosocial strength and virtue of *fidelity*, which Erikson and Erikson (1997) describe as both as the capacity to trust others and to be trustworthy to others. If adolescents can examine their own beliefs, values, sense of who they are to themselves and others, they will emerge from this tumultuous stage confident and more independent. A crisis at this stage could be marked by an inability to establish a sense of identity, potentially leading to confusion about oneself and one's place in the world (Chung, 2018).

Stage 6: Intimacy Versus Isolation.   During early adulthood into full adulthood, ages 20 to about 40, young adults are working to establish meaningful relationships. There is a tricky balance to strike, from Erikson's point of view, between achieving autonomy and independence (please note a very Western idea of development) and connection, interdependence, and intimacy with others (Chung, 2018). Also notice the wide age range represented in this stage: 20 to 40. Much happens in the lives of emerging adults and young adults during this time period. Individuals in their early 20s are still physically maturing; the brain does not reach full maturity until at least the mid-20s (Chung, 2018). So, while young adults are continuing to build social networks and relationships, and completing increasingly complex tasks including going to college, starting to make a living, or living on their own, they often are still at least partially dependent on their parents or other caregivers. A crisis at this stage of development could result in experiences of isolation, loneliness, and difficulty making meaningful connections with others. The psychosocial strength and virtue developed when this stage is successfully resolved is *love* (Capuzzi et al., 2016). According to Erikson and Erikson (1997), the psychosocial strength of *love* represents a "...mutuality of mature devotion" (p. 82) which prepared young adults to enter into the stage of middle age.

Stage 7: Generativity Versus Stagnation.

The Psychosocial Stages of Development Model suggests this stage of life occurs between about 40 and 65 years of age. The developmental task of this stage involves looking beyond oneself and beginning to consider how to give back, either to future generations, to younger coworkers, to the community. In short, how to work in service to others. This represents generative work, where one's action may be focused around raising a family, pursuing a career, and supporting older parents (Chung, 2018). Erikson and Erikson (1997) identified this stage as the time where even as we age, we strive for relevance. How do we generate new products, new ideas, and new opportunities for ourselves and others? If we are able to tap into our generative spirit during this stage of life, the psychosocial strength of *care* is cultivated. If, however, the adult in middle age is not able to engage in meaningful and generative actions, then the crisis of stagnation can occur, leading to a sense of disengagement from a productive life and activities (Capuzzi et al., 2016).

Stage 8: Ego Integrity Versus Despair.

What does it mean to be "old"? Our definition of old age continues to shift as in most developed countries, individuals are living longer and longer. Some developmental theorists talk about the "old," between ages of about 65 to 80, and then the "old old," from about age 80 until end of life (Cronin & King, 2010). When Erikson first developed his theory, he created only eight stages, believing that this final stage represented the key developmental tasks of the old. Once he himself was among the "old old," however, Erikson, along with his wife Joan, developed a ninth stage for consideration, which we will briefly highlight here. For those between about 65 and 80, the developmental task to resolve is how to successfully re-evaluate one's life, to reflect on achievements and contributions, and develop a strong sense of self based on a life well lived (Erikson & Erikson, 1997). The psychosocial strength and virtue developed from this work is *wisdom*; that in fact, because of the wisdom gained through the lessons and experiences of life, one takes on a mentoring role for those who come behind. If, however, the individual in later life does not feel a sense of accomplishment upon reflection, the crisis experienced is one of despair (Capuzzi et al., 2016).

In his later years, Erikson and his wife Joan wrote a final book called *The Life Cycle Completed* where they introduced a ninth stage for the very old, where the conflict of Ego Integrity versus Despair is magnified and where individuals reflect on all previous stages as they contemplate and reflect on their lives (Erikson & Erikson, 1997).

FINAL THOUGHTS ON ERIKSON

Erik Erikson's contributions to the field of psychology and human development cannot be overstated. In fact, you will see his theory come up several times in this textbook as we look at different ages and stages of development. A word of caution, however, as you examine this and other theories. Notice that much of what Erikson proposed as resolutions for developmental tasks and corresponding virtues were focused on the individual. Consider the timeframe, context, and identity of Erikson himself as you examine his theory of development. In the 1950s and 1960s, Erik Erikson was a White, Western male whose conceptualizations of the developmental process were largely based on reflections of the White, Western male experience (Wurgaft, 1995).

STUDENT REFLECTION

In 1995, Lewis Wurgaft wrote a paper describing a postmodern view of identity development. In that writing, he critiqued Erikson and other identity theorists by stating:

"Both from a clinical and a broadly cultural perspective, concepts like identity have been linked to a discursive strategy in Western thought that has sought to impose a sense of order and coherence on a subjective experience riddled by the contradictions and displacements inherent in language and desire" (p. 70).

What do you think of this statement? What does it say to you about how to examine ego identity theories of development? How does it inform your thinking about your own developmental milestones so far?

THEORIES OF COGNITIVE DEVELOPMENT

While theorists like Freud and Erikson considered development through the lens of a developing ego and personality, other theorists focused on how individuals, children in particular, develop cognitively. In other words: How do children learn to understand the world around them through their ability to think, reason, understand, and know? Jean Piaget and Albert Bandura are two theorists who focused on the developing cognition of children to help inform our understanding of human development.

Piaget's Cognitive Development Theory

Piaget is one of the most well-known developmental theorists in the mental health professions. His work during the 20th century laid the foundation for many cognitive developmental theories and models that have come since, and his focus on constructivist learning has been incorporated into many pre-school and primary education programs (Lutz & Huitt, 2004). Born in Switzerland, Piaget was trained in biology and philosophy and grew interested in how children think while working in Alfred Binet's IQ lab in Paris (Lutz & Huitt, 2004). Through his research, Piaget sought to understand "how we come to know" what we know, ultimately believing what separated human beings from animals was our ability to think abstractly.

Using his own children as his primary source for research and experimentation, Piaget wrote and published prolifically on his observations of cognitive development, including several books: *The Language and Thought of the Child, Judgment and Reasoning in the Child, The Child's Conception of the World, The Child's Conception of Physical Causality,* and *The Moral Judgment of the Child*. Piaget believed cognitive growth was the result of three specific experiences: (a) social interactions with others whereby children see, adapt, and respond to other perspectives outside of their own; (b) physical interaction and exploration of properties and objects; and (c) logico-mathematical experiences in which knowledge is gained from actions carried out on objects, versus from the objects themselves (Mallon, 1976).

THE FOUR STAGES OF COGNITIVE DEVELOPMENT

Piaget's cognitive development theory is a stage theory that assumes learning is predicated on prior experiences and capabilities that occur over time in a step-like fashion (Flavell, 1996; Mallon, 1976). Movement through one stage offered a specific set of skills and learning that represented both a neurological ability, paired with opportunities to engage and manipulate elements in the environment, resulting in learning and cognitive development. In this way, Piaget believed the child was the active agent in their own learning (Isaacs, 2015). Piaget also recognized the influence of biological processes tied to learning and development. His stage theory reinforced that neurological development and specific biological capabilities, known as *cognitive structures*, must first be in place before specific learning could occur (Flavell, 1992). Once present, increased intelligence and more complex understanding would follow (Mallon, 1976). That is to say, Piaget did not believe children simply accumulated more knowledge over time, but that there was a fundamental shift in how they thought, relative to time, age, and development that laid the foundation for his four stages (Figure 2.1).

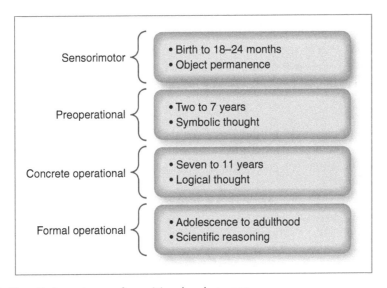

Figure 2.1 Piaget's four stages of cognitive development.

Source: Adapted from Isaacs, N. (2015). *A brief introduction to Piaget: The growth of understanding in the young child and new light on children's ideas of number*. Algora Publishing.

The Sensorimotor Stage. The sensorimotor stage of development occurs from birth to the age of 2 years and is a significant period of cognitive development. According to Piaget, during this stage infants and young children gain knowledge through sensory experiences associated with engaging directly with objects in their environment (Isaacs, 2015). Toddlers and infants in this stage of development use their senses of touch, sound, smell, vision, and taste to take in the world around them and begin to conceptualize objects and people as different from them. This stage is also the foundational stage for language development, as children begin to understand and name objects that are separate from them. Additionally, babies in this stage begin to develop *object permanence*, which is the ability to understand that objects continue to exist even when they can no longer be seen or heard (Jackson, 2008).

The Preoperational Stage. The preoperational stage of cognitive development occurs between the years of 2 and 7. This stage of development centers on an expansion of language and the ability to think symbolically such as in imaginative play (Mallon, 1976). Children in this stage show significant gains in their understanding of and ability to articulate thoughts and now have the ability to use words and pictures to represent objects in the world. This phase of development is often associated with *egocentrism* or the inability to see someone else's perspective or point of view (Heo et al., 2011). So, according to Piaget, while children in this developmental period engage more in social and pretend play, they can struggle to perspective-take or perceive experiences outside of their own.

The Concrete Operational Stage. The concrete operational stage of cognitive development occurs between the ages of 7 and 11. This stage is characterized by an increase in logical and organized thought. While children in this stage are generally considered to persist in concrete thinking, they are better able to perspective-take and begin to understand that their experiences, thoughts, and feelings may be unique to them and not necessarily shared by others in the same situation. This is also the stage in which children begin to develop an understanding of *conservation*, the idea that a mass, distance, number, and so forth, remains constant regardless of how it is subdivided (Isaacs, 2015). That is to say, they can now understand that a cup of water poured into a tall and skinny glass is the same amount of water if poured into a wide and short cup. This form of logical thinking is a key milestone for the concrete operational stage.

The Formal Operational Stage. The formal operational stage of cognitive development occurs at approximately age 12. This final stage of cognitive growth is marked by the development of abstract thought. According to Piaget, it is in this stage that children are capable of deductive reasoning and demonstrate increased logical thinking. In addition, they are able to see multiple solutions to problems and reason out hypothetical situations (Mallon, 1976). This is also a stage where Piaget believed children could engage and reason through moral, social, and ethical situations for the first time because they now have the necessary theoretical and abstract thinking ability required for this depth of thought.

CENTRAL CONCEPTS

Cognitive development theory and the associated stages are built from some key conceptual elements. First, Piaget believed in the concept of schemes as the foundational building block for all learning. According to Piaget, *schemes* or *schemas* are the categories of knowledge we use to understand and interpret our world and ultimately develop out of our interaction with it (Jesinoski, 2010; Young, 1998). The more experience we have with a scheme, the more it gets internalized and generalized into our thinking. Take, for example, the idea of food. According to Piaget's cognitive development theory, even young children begin to learn and categorize the experience of food based on interactions with receiving it, playing with it, and eating it on a daily basis. In that way, they develop a schema for food. They make sense of something mushy and colorful being set in front of them and learn that it represents something they can then touch, interact with, and ultimately eat.

Schemes are modified, expanded, and changed through the processes of assimilation and accommodation. From Piaget's perspective assimilation is the most foundational element of the learning and development process (Isaacs, 2015). *Assimilation* occurs when we take in information and organize it based on our existing schemes (Flavell, 1963). That is to say, our existing schemes help us identify something new when we apply existing knowledge and understanding to it. In the earlier example, once the scheme for food was established, a new type or color of mushy food set in front of a child would be assimilated into the scheme and identified as food.

The modification of a scheme results from the complementary process of accommodation. In *accommodation*, new information is received that does not fit clearly or cleanly into an existing scheme and therefore changes it (Isaacs, 2015). The response is an adaptive change in behavior (Mallon, 1976). Consider, for example, when a baby goes from drinking a bottle or nursing to the point they are eating solids for the first time. Initially, the scheme around food reflected a very specific experience tied to bottle feeding or nursing. Once the baby engaged with grabbing food, holding a spoon, and being fed a new mushy substance, the scheme of food had to accommodate the new information and experience of interacting with solid food.

Piaget ultimately believed it was through the process of assimilation and accommodation that children made intellectual progress and that cognitive structures, required for future stages, were created, developed, and modified into new structures (Mallon, 1976). This continuous movement and balance of engaging with the environment, taking in new information and assimilating or accommodating it is referred to as *equilibration* (Mallon, 1976). That is to say, Piaget believed new structural and cognitive development was established from the balance and equilibrium that developed between the interplay of assimilation and accommodation. Further, once that balance was effectively met around the milestones of a particular stage, the child was able to progress into a future cognitive developmental stage and the equilibration process would start again (Young, 1998).

FINAL THOUGHTS ON PIAGET

Piaget was a pioneer in the field of cognitive development and his work continues to influence learning environments of children and adolescents to this day. This is largely due to the fact that he disagreed with the idea that intelligence in children was fixed and instead emphasized the interplay between biological maturation and children's interaction with the surrounding environment. While significant to our continued understanding of children's cognitive growth, Piaget, not unlike other White male theorists of the 20th century, produced a theory of cognitive development that reflected his own Western middle-class cultural background (Babakr et al., 2019; Matusov & Hayes, 2000). He devised his theory using children, including his own, from his own cultural background and for whom he had direct access. So, while he developed a universal theory of cognitive development he believed was applicable to all humanity, his research was culturally biased and does not always effectively represent the cultural implications tied to how and what certain cultures learn.

Bandura's Social Cognitive Learning Theory

If Piaget was interested in how children learn to interpret their world, Albert Bandura wanted to understand how children, and even adolescents and adults, learn from the models in their environment. Albert Bandura was a Canadian-born psychologist who spent his career developing and testing theories of development. Bandura attended the University of British Columbia where he majored in psychology, and then completed his PhD in clinical psychology from the University of Iowa in 1952. He was hired at Stanford University where he remained until he retired in 2010 (Nabavi, 2012). Albert Bandura died in 2021 after years of dedicated service to the field of educational and developmental psychology, even receiving the National Medal of Science from President Barack Obama in 2016 (MacCormick, 2021).

Bandura is sometimes categorized as a behavioral theorist, sometimes as a cognitive theorist, but where he arguably fits best is straddling the two camps as a social learning theorist. Social Learning Theory (SLT) posits that we learn from our interactions with others in a social context, and that it is this social element, specifically, that allows us to learn and integrate new information. It is through this cycle of observation, imitation, and modeling that people learn and continue to inform who they are (Nabavi, 2012). Throughout his professional career, Bandura studied and refined his theory so that over the last 30 years or so, SLT has become increasingly cognitive in its focus on learning and development. By the mid 1980s, SLT had morphed into Social Cognitive Learning Theory (SCLT; Nabavi, 2012). The increased focus on cognition grew out of studies that demonstrated learning can occur without corresponding behavior change, meaning that it can represent a cognitive or internal process. Bandura explained this internal developmental process as the interplay between environment and social factors, personal factors including cognitive, affective, and biological events, and behavior. In other words, human beings have the capacity to learn behavioral and cognitive strategies by observing models in their environment, and that this learning process may or may not include a resulting behavior change (Bandura, 1999).

Unlike other developmental theorists, Bandura did not conceptualize his theory as a stage model, with children, adolescents, and adults moving through and mastering development at specific stages. Instead, he presented a theory that showed how at any stage of life, people use the interplay of personal factors (i.e., cognitive, affective, biological), environment factors, and behavior that creates conditions for learning and therefore an impact on internal beliefs such as self-efficacy, self-regulation, and motivation (Figure 2.2; Bandura, 1999). In addition, Bandura believed that our internal processes and ways of making sense of our world can also then impact our behavior, environment, and further enhance our sense of self. This *interactive agency*, the ability to have a sense of control over how one interacts with their environment and the people

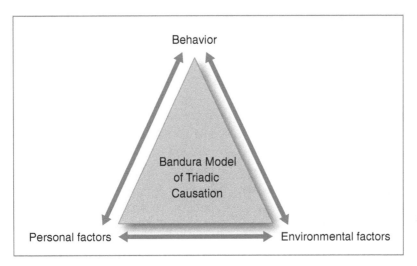

Figure 2.2 Bandura model of triadic causation.

Source: Adapted from Bandura, A. (1999). A social cognitive theory of personality. In L. Pervin & O. John (Eds.), *Handbook of personality* (pp. 154–196). Guildford Press.

in it, is a key construct that differentiates Bandura from behaviorists like Watson and Skinner, who might instead suggest that individuals only respond and react to stimuli in the environment (Bandura, 1999).

In many ways, Bandura was revolutionary in challenging more traditional views of human development with his own more integrative and interactive model of social cognitive learning. According to Bandura (1999), other theories of development were built on foundations of *Unidirectional Causality* or *Bidirectional Causality*. In *Unidirectional Causality*, the idea is that human beings' development is shaped largely by forces outside of their control, like Freud's biological drives and impulses or behaviorists such as Skinner's and Watson's stimulus-response model. At the time of one of his writings in 1999, Bandura suggested that more modern theories of the day were moving away from this idea that we as human beings do not have agency, or some control, over our own developmental process. Certainly, some theories that developed on the heels of Ego Development theories were at least *Bidirectional* or identifying that two things can interact to have a causal effect on one another. Bandura (1999) felt that these models, such as those identified by Erikson and Piaget, only partially tell the story of development, because they suggest that during a particular stage of development, there is a specific set of tasks or conflicts to master or overcome to move one into the next stage of development. For Bandura a *Triadic Causation* more effectively describes the developmental process as it suggests an ongoing and dynamic interplay between the individual and their thoughts, feelings, and biology; their environment including the people and models within it; and their behavior (Bandura, 1999).

A WORD ABOUT SCLT AND GENDER IDENTITY DEVELOPMENT

Like many theorists, Albert Bandura continued to study and therefore refine his theory throughout his life. One area that he looked at along with a colleague, Kay Bussey,

STUDENT REFLECTION

Let us consider an example of how SCLT might explain the development of new learning given the Triadic Causation interaction. Imagine you are a school counselor in a high school. You are working with a teenager, Carla, who regularly gets in trouble for fighting at school. Now you know that Carla lives in a home with a single mother who left an abusive relationship with Carla's father when Carla was just a small child. For many years, it has just been Carla and her mother, but Carla harbors resentment toward her mother for removing her from her father's life, a man she felt was "strong" and fought for what he wanted in life. In contrast, Carla thinks of her own mother as "weak" and someone she has to take care of. Around school, Carla is seen as tough, aggressive, and someone to "stay away" from if you know what's good for you.

So, what has Carla learned about her environment and the models in it that impact her development and how she makes meaning of her world? Carla may have internalized the thinking that in order to survive, you have to develop a thick skin and stand up for yourself. By witnessing the conflict between her parents, she learned that being aggressive was a way to get what you want and being submissive was a sign of weakness. The interplay between Carla's personal factors (stay tough, don't be weak, develop a thick skin) was impacted by her environmental factors of witnessing her parents' fights, and then impacts her own behavior of picking fights with others. We can also look at this cycle in a different, interactive way. Carla's beliefs about being strong and weak are reinforced by picking fights with others and continues to negatively impact her relationship with her mother. Or another way: Carla's fighting with others and lack of stability in her family relationships reinforces her feelings of needing to be "strong" and not show any sign of weakness or vulnerability. Bandura (1999) emphasizes that this complex interplay is best understood in terms of how the interactions continue to reinforce, shape, and change how people think about events, people, and behaviors. Carla's experiences, therefore, with her home life, her relationship with her mother and father, her aggressive behaviors, and the reactions to those behaviors, all reinforce how she thinks about herself and herself in relation to the world around her. So, from a clinical perspective using a SCLT framework, Carla's school counselor might look at how to offer different models of behavior and interactions and different ways to engage and interact with Carla's environment to shift both Carla's behavior and ultimately her thoughts and feelings. Carla's school counselor can serve as a new model in Carla's life, as could positively influencing peers. For an intervention strategy, Carla's school counselor might invite Carla to join a Social Skills group where she can learn from others and in turn internalize new learning that can impact future behavior.

What about you? How else do you think Triadic Causation could explain and inform a school counselor's work with a student like Carla? Can you think of how models in your own life may have shaped who you are now?

---

was how SCLT could be used to explain how one's gender identity is formed. In the next chapter, you will learn more about theories of different identity developments (i.e., gender, race, sexual orientation), so this will simply provide a sneak peek into how we also want to think about theories of development in context to other factors, such as gender.

In an interesting article addressing distinguishing SCLT from other theories that seek to explain gender development, Bussey and Bandura (1999) offered an argument for how SCLT, specifically, provides a good framework from which to understand how we develop gender identities. At the time of their writing, most literature focused on the dichotomous roles of gender identity, "female" or "male." Today, we increasingly strive to understand a broader range of gender identity and gender expression, and in fact SCLT does hold up as a possible developmental foundation for all forms of gender identity development. According to Bussey and Bandura (1999), the modeling aspect of SCLT plays a key and pivotal role in the development of a gender identity. Modeling is present from birth, and the earliest models in babies and young children's lives are usually their primary caregivers. As young children begin to develop a sense of agency, or ability to interact with and even sometimes control the environments around them, they can increasingly seek out models to emulate.

In Western society, and many other cultures, the differences between what is considered masculine and what is considered feminine are key constructs that we as developing human beings strive to make sense of and integrate into our own sense of who we are. As we grow and go to school, meet friends, and extended family, our circle of potential models expands, and we have access to new sources of information. It is through this powerful process of modeling that Bussey and Bandura (1999) postulate that children learn and internalize gendered norms, behaviors, and stereotypes from observing those around them. Once we have access to models, we also engage in cognitively reorganizing our understanding of who we are, including our own gender identity. Younger children, when faced with the choice to emulate same-sex gendered models or other-sex gendered models tend to learn to focus on and attend to the behaviors of same-sex models (Bussey & Bandura, 1999).

There is no shortage of gender stereotypes demonstrating traditional gender roles from which to draw. Increasingly, however, young children are learning that women can be doctors and welders and lawyers and accountants and pilots as well as nurses, teachers, and mothers. Men can similarly occupy roles that are less gender-stereotyped, so the models in children's environments today expand their thinking about their own gender roles and how they can be represented. How these roles are internalized and help shape a sense of self can be, in part, understood through SCLT.

THEORIES OF MORAL DEVELOPMENT

Tied to the concept of cognitive development is the parallel construct of moral development. That is to say, how do we develop morality across our lifespans and how much of this is predicated on cognitive capacity, social influence, and theoretical versus applied moral dilemmas? Influenced by and building on the work of Piaget's two-stage process of moral development, Lawrence Kohlberg developed a six-stage model of moral development that is anchored in seeking and maintaining fairness and justice and remains one of the most influential theories of moral development to date. Offering an alternative perspective and one that emphasizes a heightened awareness of relational implications in the understanding of morality, Carol Gilligan, a then-colleague of Kohlberg at the Harvard Graduate School of Education, developed a three-stage theory of moral development centered on the concept of connection and care.

Kohlberg's Theory of Moral Development

Lawrence Kohlberg was a developmental psychologist who was born in 1927 to a wealthy family in Bronxville, New York. His parents separated when he was 4 years old and he spent the subsequent years rotating every 6 months between his Christian Protestant mother and Jewish father until at age 14 he ultimately chose to live with his father and stepmother (Goldschmidt et al., 2021). Kohlberg was known for his significant intellect, which ultimately allowed him to complete his bachelor's degree from the University of Chicago in only 1 year (Walsh, 2000). Kohlberg also had a strong belief in justice and morality, often finding himself at odds with social rules and principles he found arbitrary. This culminated in his experience as a U.S. Merchant Marine where he smuggled Jewish refugees to the then-British controlled Palestine and laid the groundwork for his interest and future research in moral development (Goldschmidt et al., 2021; Walsh, 2000).

From his preliminary work, Kohlberg came to believe in "the child as a moral philosopher" (Walsh, 2000, p. 37). That is, Kohlberg was one of the first to view moral development as something children generate on their own through social relationships and emotions as opposed to something imposed on them by adults (Walsh, 2000). Heavily influenced by Piaget's work with children, Kohlberg developed a fascination with how children and adolescents develop a sense of morality. In his 1958 doctoral dissertation Kohlberg proposed a six-stage theory of moral development based on interviews with 72 White boys in Chicago. Within the interviews, participants were provided the moral dilemma of Heinz—a fictional man who struggled financially and who ultimately stole medication from a druggist (the inventor of the drug) to help his dying wife. Based on this scenario and the participant responses, Kohlberg created his six-stage theory of moral development and the subsequent *moral judgment interview* (MJI). The MJI consists of three forms and three hypothetical moral dilemmas and was used by Kohlberg to assess where individuals fell within the six stages of his moral development model (Woods, 1996).

KOHLBERG'S STAGES OF MORAL DEVELOPMENT

Significant to Kohlberg's theory were the assumptions that (a) moral development progressed in hierarchical stages over time and experience and was irreversible, (b) there were three possible approaches to resolving moral dilemmas, (c) justice was the most fundamental moral principle, and (d) moral development was a universal experience (Linn, 2001; Woods, 1996). That is to say, Kohlberg believed that all humans developed morality in the same linear way, with some reaching higher or lower levels of overall moral development based on a justice-oriented perspective.

Kohlberg's stages of moral development consist of three primary levels (Preconventional, Conventional, and Postconventional) with two progressive stages within each level (Table 2.3). In reference to his theory, the term *conventional* is used to indicate the level to which one understands and conforms to the conventions of society (Kohlberg, 1981). Therefore, each of the levels and stages of moral development reflect the extent to which decision-making is tied to societal conventions, from Preconventional Stage 1 (Punishment and Obedience Orientation) to Postconventional Stage 6 (Universal–Ethical Principles Orientation). It was not until the late 1970s and early 1980s, and in response to criticisms that his sixth and highest stage of moral development was too aspirational, that Kohlberg made slight modifications to his theory to

Table 2.3 Kohlberg's Stages of Moral Development

LEVEL AND AGE	STAGE	WHAT DETERMINES RIGHT FROM WRONG?
Pre-Conventional Morality (Up to about age 9)	Stage 1: Punishment and Obedience Orientation	Child is "good" to avoid being punished. Punishment equals being "wrong."
	Stage 2: Instrumental-Relativist Orientation	Child begins to understand elements of fairness and reciprocity but this is based on a physical, pragamatic understanding ("You scratch my back and I'll scratch yours").
Conventional Morality (Most adolescents and adults)	Stage 3: Interpersonal Concordance (Good Boy/Nice Girl Orientation)	Individual seeks approval of others and wants to be viewed as "good"; behavior is often judged by intention ("She means well").
	Stage 4: Law and Order Orientation	Individual is aware of wider rules of society so moral judgments include obeying rules of law.
Post-Conventional Morality (20s and beyond)	Stage 5: Social Contract and Legalistic Orientation	Individual is aware that there are times when rules and laws work against the interests of particular individuals, and sometimes the moral action is to work to change unjust laws and rules.
	Stage 6: Universal–Ethical Principle Orientation	Individuals develop their own set of moral guidelines that they feel apply to everyone including justice, equality, and the rights of individuals.

Source: Adapted from Kohlberg, L., & Hersh, R. H. (1977). *Moral development: A review of the theory.* American Psychological Association.

remove the sixth stage from his model of moral development. Moving forward Stage 5 became the highest practical stage (Goldschmidt et al., 2021; Linn, 2001); however, all six stages are still frequently referenced and cited in the mental health fields.

Preconventional Morality. The level of *Preconventional Morality* accounts for the earliest stages of moral development where there is little understanding of the nuances and complexities of societal conventions or their impact on morality (Kohlberg, 1981, Kohlberg, 1982). This period of moral development is associated with childhood and is considered to persist until age 9. Within this level, children base their decision-making on an understanding of rules and consequences and are largely shaped by the expectations of adults. In a preconventional moral world, there are not great considerations beyond the immediate family, school, or social sphere, nor is there a personal moral code. Instead, children often view "good" and "bad" in response to rewards and consequences.

Stage 1 of the Preconventional Level is known as *Obedience and Punishment Orientation* and is focused largely on the avoidance of punishment (McLeod, 2013). If, for example, someone is punished, a child in this stage of moral development would assume that person must have been doing something wrong. Stage 2 reflects a slightly higher level of moral development known as *Instrumental–Relativist Orientation* (McLeod, 2013). Within this stage children have learned that there is not a singular perspective or authority that determines right or wrong. Instead, they understand that people have different perspectives and needs that can drive responses to situations. They have also learned the concept of reciprocity (Cherry, 2021). That is to say, they view morality in terms of what is good for them and others through exchange. If it is mutually agreeable between parties or deemed "fair," it is a morally good action.

Conventional Morality.   The level of *Conventional Morality* is achieved next and occurs when individuals begin to accept and internalize the social rules and moral standards established by society and those of valued adult role models (Kohlberg, 1981, Kohlberg, 1982). Kohlberg believed that most adolescents and adults fell within this level (McLeod, 2013). Here, the focus is on conforming to authority and the norms of the larger societal system to which the person belongs. An awareness of social order and the responsibilities of relationships ultimately influences views of what is right or wrong at this level.

Stage 3 is known as the *Interpersonal Concordance (Good Boy/Nice Girl) Orientation*. Individuals within this stage seek to be viewed as "good" by others and therefore make decisions based on the approval of others (Kohlberg, 1981, Kohlberg, 1982). That is to say, if others in a social group view something as either good or bad, a person in this stage will abide by that belief system. In Stage 4, known as the *Law and Order Orientation*, the concern with broader society begins to impact decision-making (McLeod, 2013). Within this stage the individual is aware of the rules, customs, and laws of society and seeks to uphold them as a form of moral good.

Postconventional Morality.   *Postconventional Morality* is the highest level of moral development and occurs when individuals develop and abide by abstract principles of morality that exceed rules of law or socially agreed upon norms (McLeod, 2013). Examples include a belief in the preservation of life at all costs and the importance of human dignity, even if it meant breaking a law or going against the beliefs of society. At the postconventional level judgment is founded on self-chosen principles and beliefs related to individual rights and justice. According to Kohlberg (1982), only 10% to 15% of people would ever reach the postconventional stages of development.

In the highest practical stage of moral development, Stage 5: *Social Contract and Legalist Orientation*, individuals are aware that while rules and laws exist for the good of the greater society, there are times when they are at odds with the interest of particular individuals (McLeod, 2013). As a result, they make choices consistent with what they believe is the just and right thing to do for the individual, in spite of the social rules or expectations. Using the Heinz example, an individual in Stage 5 would agree with Heinz's action to steal the drug in an effort to save the wife's life, even though stealing is against the law. While generally adhering to the belief in law and order, and the understanding that the collective determined those laws and put them in place, a person in this stage recognizes the nuance and individual situations that may warrant a different approach. In Stage 6, the *Universal–Ethical Principles Orientation*, the movement toward an individualized view of moral belief is even greater. Here, individuals develop their own moral guidelines and "good" action is based on those personally held principles (McLeod, 2013). This is true even if they are at odds with what is customary or legal. The person in this stage will be prepared to defend their principles even if it means violating the rules of society and dealing with legal consequences or disapproval.

Gilligan's Theory of Moral Development

Carol Gilligan is a psychologist who was born into a privileged Jewish family in New York in 1936. She studied at Swathmore and Radcliffe Colleges before getting her PhD from Harvard in 1964, where she later took a teaching position alongside Erik Erikson and Lawrence Kohlberg (Vinney, 2021). Gilligan was heavily influenced by the work of Lawrence Kohlberg, for whom she originally worked as a research assistant and initially developed an interest in moral reasoning. However, Gilligan struggled with Kohlberg's universal theory of moral development noting two significant critiques: (a) It utilized male-only research participants and (b) it relied on hypothetical ethical dilemmas (Cam et al., 2012; Gilligan, 2018; Linn, 2001).

Reflecting on her own experiences and those of women around her, Gilligan realized that the field of psychology and the associated theories had largely been developed through research on privileged, White men and then overgeneralized to all people. Further, when this was done, women and other marginalized populations were not only left out of the conversation but misrepresented along the way. She responded by noting "Wait a minute, what the field of psychology presents as the truth *is a voice*. And how do you show that? By introducing *a different voice*" (Gilligan, 2018, p. 25). As a result, she began researching and publishing on women's psychological development, first in her article "In a Different Voice: Women's Conceptions of the Self and Morality" (Gilligan, 1977) and later in her book *In a Different Voice* (Gilligan, 1982).

Using preliminary research on women, Gilligan found that women's moral development, as well as the moral development of people of color (Walsh, 2000) and different societies (Cam et al., 2012) were not effectively captured in Kohlberg's theory or were otherwise noted to fall short of male moral development by virtue of the emphasis on justice as the determinant of moral development (Linn, 2001; Woods, 1996). The challenge Gilligan noted with the justice and individual rights orientation was that it emphasized growth and moral development through separation, which was considered to reflect a male-oriented perspective (Gilligan, 2018; Linn, 2001; Vreeke, 1991). What this left out was the emphasis on relationships and the ways in which women and other cultures viewed moral dilemmas in terms of connection and care versus independence and separation. For Gilligan, the premise that the goal of development was centered on the separation of reason from emotion or that we could fully understand moral responses based on hypothetical situations rather than real-life situations we were facing was inaccurate, at least for many (Gilligan, 2018). Born out of a response to this, Gilligan proposed her own theory of moral development that encompassed care as part of the moral decision-making process.

GILLIGAN'S STAGES OF THE ETHICS OF CARE

Using Kohlberg's same preconventional, conventional, and postconventional levels to frame her theory, Gilligan proposed that girls and women were not inferior to men, but developed based on the alternative frame of moral judgment known as the ethic of

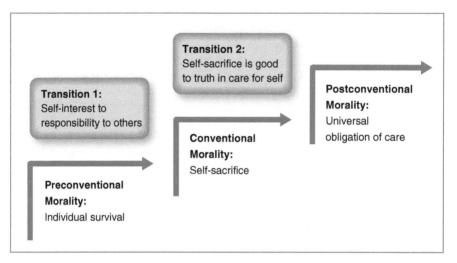

Figure 2.3 Gilligan's stages of the ethic of care.

Source: Adapted from Vinney, C. (2021, August). *The Carol Gilligan theory and a woman's sense of self*. Verywell Mind. https://www.verywellmind.com/the-carol-gilligan-theory-and-a-woman-s-sense-of-self-5198408

care (Gilligan, 1982) (Figure 2.3). Through her research on girls and women, Gilligan found that from a care-based perspective, moral dilemmas are viewed from the lens of tensions or disconnections in relationships and were deeply context dependent (Vreeke, 1991). That is to say, women considered the relational and real-world implications of the dilemma in making their decisions and moral development progressed on a continuum from those decisions. However, rather than view the shifts between levels as a result of age or cognitive development as Kohlberg had, movement through Gilligan's levels of moral development were based on *transitions* tied to changes in the sense of self (Carol Gilligan's Theory of Moral Development, 2012; Vinney, 2021). Gilligan did not assign ages to her stages but generally saw them as progressive and acknowledged that not every woman would reach the highest level (Vinney, 2021).

Preconventional Morality.   In the initial level of the ethics of care the primary focus is on the self and the need to survive (Gilligan, 1982). Individuals at this level are solely focused on making decisions centered on their own self-interest and survival, even when others are involved. The transition from preconventional morality to conventional morality occurs when the individual recognizes and internalizes a responsibility to others (Carol Gilligan's Theory of Moral Development, 2012; Gilligan, 1982; Vinney, 2021).

Conventional Morality.   At the conventional level there is a focus on caring for others which ultimately supersedes self-interest and results in decisions based on self-sacrifice (Gilligan, 1982). This is the stage often associated with normed concepts of "feminine goodness" or "maternal morality," where the understanding of what is good is tied to caring for others (Carol Gilligan's Theory of Moral Development, 2012; Gilligan, 1982; Vinney, 2021). The transition from conventional morality to postconventional morality is marked by an awareness of the need to balance self-interest with the needs of others. In this transition there is a movement away from that sense of "goodness" to one of honest assessment and "truth" in the sense that one must be cared for as well (Carol Gilligan's Theory of Moral Development, 2012; Gilligan, 1982; Vinney, 2021).

Postconventional Morality.   At the highest level of Gilligan's theory of moral development, the focus is on a universal obligation of care—to oneself and to others (Gilligan, 1982). At this level the individual has learned to balance the care they offer to others with the care they provide to self and ultimately sees these as interconnected. That is, a person who cares for others is caring for self and vice versa. However, there is an expectation that while maintaining that ethic of care, the individual avoids harm or exploitation of self or others (Carol Gilligan's Theory of Moral Development, 2012; Gilligan, 1982; Vinney, 2021).

FINAL THOUGHTS ON KOHLBERG AND GILLIGAN

There is clear influence and overlap between Kohlberg's and Gilligan's theories of moral development, with the key differentiator tied to foundational differences in how males and females view moral dilemmas and respond to them. Using the Heinz example described previously, Gilligan demonstrated clear distinctions between two 11-year-old children's responses on whether or not Heinz should steal the drug. Jake, the male example, expressed that Heinz should steal the drug, noting the emphasis on human life over money and that his reasoning was tied to solving "a math problem with humans" (Gilligan, 1982, p. 26). Amy, the female example, had an alternative perspective that emphasized the need for Heinz and the druggist to talk through the issue and find an alternative solution so that Heinz would not ultimately end up in jail and leave his wife to get sicker without him (Gilligan, 1982, p. 28). Both responses indicated a dilemma and the need to address it, but they provided very different approaches to thinking through the dilemma: rules and justice versus care and relationship.

Gilligan's efforts to research and highlight female development have been critical to the field of mental health and to subsequent developmental theory. They have illustrated, at minimum, that there is more than one way to view morality and moral development and much of this is tied to our societal norms and the ways in which we are raised. However, like Kohlberg, Gilligan's theory has faced criticisms of rigor and sex bias. Further, research post-Kohlberg and post-Gilligan has demonstrated that both men and women use justice and care orientations in moral decision-making and that there are no significant differences between the sexes on justice or care orientations (Woods, 1996). What does seem to make the most significant difference is whether or not the moral dilemmas were real life or hypothetical. In situations where real-life dilemmas were used responses reflected a care orientation, whereas hypothetical dilemmas resulted in justice-type orientations (Woods, 1996).

In addition to theseconsiderations, it is important to note that both Gilligan and Kohlberg were born into White families of privilege and their theories largely reflect Western populations. When it comes to what is moral, it is critical to consider that these theories are culture bound and therefore may not reflect the moral values or beliefs of all people in all societies. In that same vein, it is important to consider who maintains power within cultures when it comes to determining "right" and "wrong" and ultimately defining moral development (Woods, 1996).

THEORY OF ATTACHMENT

When we look at the development of children across time, we must consider the familial context of that development, and, in particular, the way in which children bond with caregivers during their early years of life. These early bonds not only shape the way a child interacts with those in their childhood and youth, but also influence the ways in which they develop relationships later in life. Attachment is therefore considered a critical part in understanding safety and security for individuals and is both adaptive as well as necessary as part of survival. For that reason, it is a highly important piece to factor into the developmental process. In the next section we explore the significant influence of John Bowlby and Mary Ainsworth on the origins of attachment theory in the mental health fields.

Bowlby and Ainsworth's Attachment Theory

John Bowlby, a child psychiatrist, was born to an affluent family in London in 1907 and is considered the first attachment theorist (Bretherton, 1992). Bowlby's interest in attachment resulted from a combination of factors including his own childhood experience of being raised and emotionally nurtured by nannies and nursemaids rather than his parents, along with his experiences working with maladaptive and delinquent children later in life (Van Dijken, 1998). Having experienced the loss of his beloved nursemaid, Winnie, at age 4 and then being sent to boarding school at age 7, Bowlby's personal experiences with bonding and loss had a significant impact on him. His later experiences working with and researching children at the Tavistock Clinic provided further observation of caregiver–child relationships and became the basis for his attachment theory. In particular, Bowlby noted observations of protest, despair, or detachment in children when separated from primary caregivers (Ainsworth, 1992; Bowlby, 1969). These observations and his work with Mary Ainsworth would ultimately lead to the development of attachment theory and the multitude of research that has come after.

Mary Ainsworth, a child psychologist who, herself, had been researching infant–mother dyads, later came to work with Bowlby to conduct research on attachment. While Bowlby is attributed with developing the basic tenets of attachment theory, Ainsworth is noted for having developed the methodology used to test the theory and is largely responsible for the way it expanded across time (Bretherton, 1992). Ainsworth was born in the United States in 1913 and then moved to Canada with her White, middle-class family. Ainsworth was the oldest of three daughters and closest, emotionally, to her father, which ultimately created tension between her and her mother (Gale, 2017). She later married Leonard Ainsworth and moved to Uganda where she completed naturalistic observation of infant–mother dyads and further enhanced her understanding of attachment (Ainsworth, 1967). It was back in the United States and in her work at Johns Hopkins that Ainsworth conducted her famous *Strange Situation* study of 12- to 18-month-old babies that she identified three types of attachment: (a) secure attachment, (b) ambivalent–insecure attachment, and (c) avoidant–insecure attachment. Ainsworth's methodology was later used at the Tavistock Clinic, in order to test whether these categories appeared to hold across cultures and relational configurations (Bretherton, 1992).

ATTACHMENT TYPES

The prominent underpinning of attachment theory is the biological perspective and belief that attachment is grounded in behavioral and motivational patterns (Cherry, 2019). That is to say that while children are dependent on their caregivers for food and nourishment, it is in the safety and security of the nurturing response that children foster attachment bonds and develop a secure base for future attachment. According to Bowlby, children have an innate drive to form attachments and do so in an evolutionary capacity (Cherry, 2019). When caregivers are available and attentive to the needs of a child, it allows the child to develop a sense of security and feel safe to explore. When those opportunities for nurturance and response are not tended to or are provided on an inconsistent basis, children can develop insecure attachment styles that ultimately impact behaviors and relationships in the future (Cherry, 2019).

Bowlby and Ainsworth used the Strange Situation methodology to research and categorize children's attachment. This consisted of the caregiver and child starting in a room alone together where the child was allowed to freely explore. Shortly thereafter a stranger would come in and speak briefly to the caregiver before moving toward the child as the caregiver quietly left the room. After a brief period of time the caregiver was brought back in to reunite with the child (Bretherton, 1992). Depending on the level of safety and security the child experienced with the caregiver, they were deemed as either having a secure attachment or one of two insecure attachment styles. Ainsworth's protege, Mary Main, and fellow attachment researcher, Jude Solomon, later added a fourth insecure attachment style based on subsequent research (Main & Solomon, 1986).

Secure Attachment.   Children in the secure attachment category are noted to have a safe and dependable bond with their caregiver. In the experimental situation they are upset when their caregiver leaves and joyful upon their return. While the child feels distress when their caregiver is away, they have confidence in knowing the caregiver will ultimately return. Children in this category feel comfortable seeking care and reassurance when scared (Cherry, 2019).

Ambivalent–Insecure Attachment.   Children in this category become highly upset when their primary caregiver leaves but do not find reassurance or comfort when their caregiver returns. Resulting from poor or limited parental presence, these children have learned that they cannot depend on their primary caregiver to be there when they need them and may passively reject them or demonstrate aggression toward them (Cherry, 2019, 2020). This attachment style is the least common, affecting roughly 7% to 15% of U.S. children (Cassidy & Berlin, 1994).

Avoidant–Insecure Attachment.   Children in this category tend to avoid their caregivers, indicating no preference for the caregiver over the stranger. This response can be particularly pronounced after the absence of the caregiver. While these children may not reject attention from their caregivers, they have also learned they cannot depend on it, so they do not seek it out. This attachment style may result from abuse or neglect where children have learned to avoid seeking help (Cherry, 2019, 2020).

Disorganized–Insecure Attachment.   Children in this category demonstrate a combination of behaviors including appearing dazed, apprehensive, or confused when left alone. Upon the caregiver's return these children may avoid or resist the caregiver. This response reflects the lack of a clear attachment pattern that is often associated with inconsistent caregiver behavior. When this occurs, caregivers may provide both a place of comfort and fear for the child, resulting in disorganized behavior (Cherry, 2019, 2020).

Evolutionary and Security Theories

Taking the long view of human evolution, let's start where all our roots began, in the motherland of Africa some 1.8 million years ago. Attachment theory posits that it would have been advantageous for small, dependent, fragile offspring to be very aware of their primary protector should any danger (such as a large predator) come about, and thus evolution selected for those of us who skillfully kept our caregivers close and allowed appropriately protective parents to succeed in procreating and raising those children to sexual maturity (Belsky et al., 2010; Crittenden & Marlowe, 2013; McLeod, 2009; Simpson, 1999). Because of the demands of doing so successfully, parents who can keep reliable co-parents and alloparents nearby and involved in an *attachment network* (Dagan & Sagi-Schwartz, 2018; Gillath et al., 2019; Riggs & Riggs, 2011) will also be able to share the burden of protection while securing provisions for the tribe, and still keep the children alive, thus nurturance of others' children and a certain willingness for children to seek out, receive care from, and respond to reliable back-up adults is also long-conserved in our species (Crittenden & Marlowe, 2013).

In light of that historically shared responsibility, humans as a whole are still wired to prefer a primary and consistent caregiver above all others—the central figure, or *monotropy*, in what Bowlby called the *hierarchy of attachment* (1969). Even in cultures where primary caregivers significantly or even primarily apportion caregiving across several trusted members of the community, the *internal working model of relationships* held by the child (or eventual adult) still seeks the primary caregiver, or *secure base* (Bowlby, 1988), when truly distressed (Bretherton, 1999; Fivush, 2006). When the *fear system* is not activated, and the secure base is not presently needed for safety and comfort, attention may move out into exploration, where more varied social and environmental engagement is a natural byproduct (Cassidy & Shaver, 1999).

There are obvious advantages for children and primary caregivers in having several reliable caregivers at one's disposal, as is often the case in collectivistic cultures. What has also become clear through numerous studies over time is that it is not necessarily the number of caregivers, but the quality of attuned caregiving, particularly from the primary caregiver (if there is one) that defines the child's attachment security outcome. When the primary caregiver is not appropriately reliable and responsive to the child's attachment needs, or the caregiving is too diffusely spread across a broad swath of caregivers, the result is likely some version of insecure attachment (Cassidy & Shaver, 1999; Karen, 1998). Because attachment theory has been and continues to be researched from a sociological standpoint, not just a Western psychological one, it has solid and ever-growing empirical support for Relational–Cultural considerations (Jordan, 2018).

THEORIES OF ADULT DEVELOPMENT

Many of the theories we have discussed in this chapter focus primarily on development in childhood. Some theories, like those of Erikson and Bandura, consider developmental milestones or new learning opportunities for adults, but there are two theorists we want to mention whose work focused specifically on the development of adults. "Adulthood" represents a wide expanse of time without clear markers of when it begins. After all, Freud marked his Genital Stage of development from puberty to death! Jeffrey Arnett is a modern theorist who gave us the first theory of its kind with a focus on what he termed *Emerging Adulthood* (Arnett, 2000). Daniel Levinson was one of the first theorists to focus specifically on adult development, starting with his book, *The Seasons of a Man's Life* published in the 1970s that followed 40 adult men between the ages of 35 and 45 (Levinson, 1978). Both of these theorists paved the way for a real consideration of the developmental experiences and milestones of adults.

Jeffrey Arnett and Emerging Adulthood

When our parents and grandparents were in their late teens and early twenties, what was considered normal and typical development? My (Coker's) mother and father got married at ages 20 and 23, respectively. My mother's mother and father were married at age 17 and 19, respectively. My mother was a parent at age 20 and her mother was a parent at age 18. I (Coker) also have a son who at the time of this writing is 21, and I cannot imagine (nor can he), being a spouse or parent at this time in his life. Why not? What is different between then and now? One key difference is the delaying of marriage and parenthood in most industrialized societies, sometimes well into the late 20s and even 30s, if at all. So, if young adults are not entering typical and traditional roles of "adulthood," what are they doing? Many are engaged in a prolonged period of exploration, continued learning, and emerging world views (Arnett, 2000). According to Arnett (2000), for those between the ages of about 18 and 25, the stage of emerging adulthood is pivotal and therefore deserving of its own developmental focus. Arnett did not, like some of his predecessors, develop a stage or transition model of emerging adulthood. Rather, he focused his attention on what emerging adults uniquely face during this stage of life. Following are the key concepts of emerging adult development as outlined by Arnett.

EMERGING ADULTHOOD IS DEMOGRAPHICALLY DISTINCT

More than 95% of adolescents in industrial societies live at home (Arnett, 2000). Emerging adults, however, do not follow any typical demographic patterns in terms of residency, and in fact their demographic status is quite variable. Some emerging adults go to college, about one third of those in the United States. Roughly 40% leave home for independent living and full-time work, but for emerging adults, about 40% of them also end up back in their parents' home, at least once (Arnett, 2000). Increasingly, emerging adults are attending college, and about one third of those who graduate seek higher degrees beyond their bachelors. This extension of education is another way in which movement into more typical adult roles is delayed.

EMERGING ADULTHOOD IS SUBJECTIVELY DISTINCT

Even emerging adults, themselves have difficulty naming this period of time in their lives. Mostly they do not identify with being an adolescent, but many also have a hard time considering themselves an adult. It is only when individuals reach their late 20s and early 30s do they identify clearly with being an adult (Arnett, 2000). As we consider the development of emerging adults, it is important to remember that this ambiguity about one's own sense of what it means to be an adult is typical and represents the subjective nature of this identity.

EMERGING ADULTHOOD IS A TIME FOR IDENTITY EXPLORATION

Emerging adulthood represents a time for practice, experimentation, and exploration. Therefore, seeking opportunities for testing out and trying on work roles, love relationships, and changing worldviews and ideas allows for identity exploration (Arnett, 2000). There is a shift from ideas of love and work, for example, from adolescence into emerging adulthood. Teenagers may date and have part-time jobs, both opportunities allowing for practicing of these more adult roles and experiences, but it is emerging adults whose choices around love, work, and training are geared toward really exploring future adult responsibilities (Arnett, 2000).

FINAL THOUGHTS ON ARNETT

This time of life is particularly important, from Arnett's perspective, because it highlights that emerging adulthood is not adolescence, nor is it young adulthood. Arnett also reminds us that there is a diversity of experience among emerging adults that is impacted by many factors, including access and opportunity. For example, there are numerous studies on the experiences of college students because this is an accessible group to study. We know less about those who do not attend college after high school, however, because they are less accessible (Arnett, 2000). Similarly, what Arnett proposes to represent the experiences and development of emerging adults is firmly rooted in a Western, industrialized mindset. Therefore, emerging adulthood is not a universal stage of development but instead one experienced by those between adolescence and adulthood in environments where movement into adulthood is delayed. This delay occurs in industrialized societies where higher education is expected, marriage and parenthood are increasingly delayed, and families have the means to allow their emerging adult children to engage in this period of exploration and interdependence.

In a subsequent writing, Arnett (2007) focused on myths and realities of emerging adults. He reminded us that we tend to think of emerging adults as selfish, as brooding and suffering, and refusing to grow up. Arnett challenged Erikson's idea of an identity crisis to overcome during this time period, and instead pointed to studies that showed that, by and large, emerging adults can move into identity exploration with ".... some anxiety but without trauma" (Arnett, 2007, p. 24). In fact, evidence suggests that emerging adults, overall, are content with their lives as they are and are optimistic about the future. To address the myth of selfishness among this age group, Arnett pointed to evidence showing that emerging adults are more likely than ever before to engage in volunteer work and to have a more global mindset (Arnett, 2007). Finally, to the question of whether emerging adults are inherently "slack" and just don't want to grow up, Arnett contrasted concepts of *failure to launch* with the fact that more young Americans are now, more than ever, obtaining post-secondary training. This points to emerging adults' ability to both use this time in life to explore possibilities while also retaining a grasp on the realities of adulthood (Arnett, 2007).

Daniel Levinson's Theory of Adult Development

When developing his theory of emerging adulthood, Arnett credited Daniel Levinson as making a key contribution to our understanding of adult development (Arnett,

2000). Levinson, in turn, credited Erikson for starting the important conversation about adult development through his psychosocial stage model (Levinson, 1986). Daniel Levinson was born in New York City in 1920. After completing his doctoral work at the University of Berkley, Levinson had the opportunity to study with other psychologists including Erik Erikson at Harvard University. Erikson's influence helped to shape Levinson's research focus and theory generation on looking specifically at adult development, which he pursued once moving to Yale University in 1966 (Daniel Levinson: Biography & Theory, 2015). Levinson's groundbreaking research included following a cohort of 40 men between the ages of 35 and 45 and examining common patterns in their lives. He followed up this research with conducting the same inquiry with a cohort of women, ages 35 to 45, to further refine his theory. His book *Seasons of a Man's Life* was published in 1978, and his research on women was published posthumously by his wife in 1996 in *Seasons of a Woman's Life*.

The metaphor of seasons was important to Levinson, as he articulated in his discussion of the *life course* and the *life cycle* (Levinson, 1986). For Levinson, the process of development did not stop in childhood or adolescence. He postulated that the life course represented opportunities for studying life as it unfolds over time, not just focused on a single moment or point in time. The cycle of life extends beyond our understanding of the life course and suggests that there is an underlying order in the human life course, even as we have individual and unique experiences. This order is represented by different phases or seasons. Levinson felt that the metaphor of the *season* best captures a way to explore adult development, specifically. Just as there are seasons in a year, and seasons within a single day, there are seasons within a life representing change, renewal, transition, and time (Levinson, 1986). Levinson (1986) focused his life's work on the study of adult development, because he determined that most theorists focused on children (e.g., Freud and Piaget) and then skipped into the field of gerontology and old age without really examining, in depth, the years in between.

ERAS AND STRUCTURE OF ADULT DEVELOPMENT

Levinson (1986) conceptualized his theory of adult development in terms of *eras* and *structures* (Figure 2.4*). Eras* represent the macrostructure of the life cycle, or the major changes that adults transition through during adulthood. A *cross-era transition* overlaps one era into the next and lasts about 5 years. The three eras defined by Levinson are *Preadulthood, Early Adulthood, and Late Adulthood*. The transitions in between are marked by the *Early Adult Transition* and the *Midlife Transition*.

Within the broader *eras* are *structures*, similar to stages, that mark the specific developmental periods. According to Levinson (1986), the life structure is the fundamental design of a person's life at a given time. In other words, it is a way of conceptualizing the question, "What is my life like right now?" For each period, adults go through structure building and structure changing. In many ways, Levinson's theory of development is more cyclical than linear, in that he proposes that at each transition, we enter a phase as a novice, and then as we successfully navigate the current life structure, we enter a culminating phase, which prepares us for the next era (Levinson, 1986). Our life structures consist of an interplay between our own identities and the world around us. They are shaped by relationships, cultures, institutions, objects, or

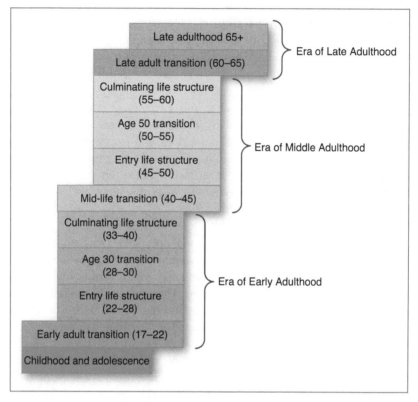

Figure 2.4 Levinson's structures and eras of adult development.

Source: Adapted from Levinson, D. J. (1986). A conception of adult development. *American Psychologist*, *41*(1), 3–13. https://doi.org/10.1037/0003-066X.41.1.3

places—in other words, the external environment. Life structures are made up of patterns, and it is these patterns of relationships that give "... shape and substance to our lives" (Levinson, 1986, p. 6).

The Life Structures developmental model is built upon research conducted by Levinson first on middle-aged men, then replicated with a cohort of middle-aged women, and suggests that while a given life structure may have many diverse components, there are central components that have primary significance. These tend to be marriage and/or family and occupation (Levinson, 1986). Within the *Early Adult Era*, the individual is moving beyond adolescence and is starting to create their first adult life structure. Though flawed, this entry-level life structure represents the novice's attempts to figure out their life structure, to question and modify it, and to finally settle on the life structure in the culminating phase of the era. Then, with entry into the *Middle Adulthood Era* through the midlife transition, there is a period of both an ending and a new beginning. As we leave behind our young adult years, we once again become a novice in navigating our new-found maturity, figuring out what these life structures hold, and continuing to refine and modify our roles and relationships. We culminate our experiences as we ready ourselves to transition into late adulthood, where we once again will become a novice navigating a new life structure (Levinson, 1986).

FINAL THOUGHTS ON LEVINSON

Levinson focused his work on the span of early adulthood through middle adulthood and did not spend time on what might happen once someone enters late adulthood. While Erikson gave us a bit more in terms of stages and structures of this phase of life, Levinson felt that his model, in particular, told us as much about the transitions we go through as we exit one and enter the subsequent era as it does those actual stages or structures within each era. Levinson (1986) pointed to relevant research on transitions themselves: When we experience key periods of change—whether through major life events such as marriage/coupling, childbirth, divorce, new careers, retirement, or loss of a loved one—we experience opportunities for growth, change, and new learning.

PERSPECTIVES FROM THE FIELD: PODCAST

Access this podcast at http://connect.springerpub.com/content/book/978-0-8261-8279-1/part/part01/chapter/ch02

You will notice opportunities throughout this textbook to hear different perspectives, viewpoints, opinions, and expertise of mental health professionals through short podcasts. These podcasts will be linked to chapters throughout the book that introduce a particular age and stage of development by presenting a clinical case study and then examining that case, age, and stage through cultural and contextual lenses. Podcast interviewees were selected for their expertise and ability to speak to the case study presented. We hope you will find this a rich addition to the information presented in this book and a way to have the material presented come to life.

In this chapter on some of the seminal lifespan development theories, we wanted to give you an opportunity to hear from us, the authors of this textbook. We are four women representing different fields of mental health; of different areas of clinical and mental health expertise; of different ages; different races; and certainly other notable differences in family structure, spiritual faith, hobbies, talents, and points of view. What we share, though, is a passion for training mental health professionals and, in this period of MeToo, the Black Lives Matter movement, and COVID-19, that we can bring a new lens through which to understand lifespan development and the central and pivotal role it can play in our work with clients. We invite you to listen to us, Dr. Kelly Coker, Dr. Kristi Cannon, Dr. Savitri Dixon-Saxon, and

Dr. Karen Roller, talk about our reasons for writing this book, what we hope it will provide to you, the emerging mental health professional, and how we hope you will be able to view the marvel of human development through cultural and contextual lenses.

SUMMARY

There are many theories of lifespan development, and this chapter was designed to introduce you to some of the recognized and seminal theories from which we have understood different aspects of development at different points in the lifespan. The theories presented here were grouped into types of theory, theoretical perspectives, and ages and stages of development.

We started with two theories of ego development, Freud's Theory of Psychosexual Development and Erikson's Theory of Psychosocial Development. Both of these stage model theories postulated the stages of development from the perspective of the developing ego, or self. For ego psychologists, development is viewed as largely a process driven by drives and impulses. As children (and then adolescents and adults from Erikson's framework) move through different developmental stages, their ability to resolve the conflicts of the stage will determine whether they are engaged in healthy ego development or maladaptive ego development, which could have a lasting impact.

Cognitive theorists, such as Piaget and Bandura, moved beyond the notion that innate drives and impulses are responsible for development, and focused on the process of learning. Piaget's cognitive model illuminates how children, at different ages and stages of development, use cues in the world around them along with their own physiological development, to make sense of their world and who they are within it. Bandura expanded our thinking about cognitive development through emphasizing the very important role of models in children's lives and how observation of others in the social environment impacts development of behaviors, cognition, a sense of self, and our own subsequent impact on the environment.

Kohlberg and Gilligan examined moral development, and identified stages that people move through to develop a sense of morality and right and wrong. These two theories provided us with a gendered lens through which to view their work, with Kohlberg suggesting that for boys and men, the development of the moral construct, *justice,* was the primary moral edict while for Gilligan focusing her research on girls and women, the development of *care* as representing morality was more often identified. The examination of these theories, in particular, give us an important glimpse into how to consider the limitations of focusing on a more homogeneous group from which to make inferences. Both Kohlberg and Gilligan have been criticized for having potential bias in their theories given their exclusion of one gender for the other.

Bowlby and Ainsworth zeroed in on the earliest stages of development with their focus on how early attachments with primary caregivers shape our ability to engage in secure attachments and healthy relationships throughout life. A primary caregiver who provides this secure attachment to their infants and young children creates a condition from which the child can venture forth and explore their world, knowing they can always come back to a safe base. Attachment theory also encourages us to think beyond our own existence and experiences, and to also consider the role that evolution plays in our innate need as young children to feel secure, and how this security is necessary for survival.

Arnett and Levinson encourage us to zoom out from a focus on how development in childhood shapes our experiences, and to consider that even as adults, we are still learning, growing, and forming an identity and sense of place in the world. Arnett introduced us to a newer stage of development not previously identified, that of emerging adulthood, a time of life that straddles adolescence and adulthood and has its own developmental tasks, features, and opportunities. Levinson pioneered work on understanding the development process of adults and explored how men and women transition through different eras where they experience the structure of young adulthood, middle adulthood, and late adulthood as they develop a sense of identity, refine that identity, and then start again to explore new identities.

As you move into an exploration of different ages and stages of development throughout this book, you will see these and other developmental theorists again. In these subsequent chapters, we will zoom in on the particular components of a theory that is relevant to that age and stage. Know that you can always come back to Chapter 2 if you feel you need more information about the foundations of the theory as you apply it to a particular age and stage. You will also be introduced along the way to other theories of development that we did not cover in this chapter; in those cases, you will get a more comprehensive description of the theory.

The next chapter in this book includes developmental and identity theories and models that will help you connect to the contextual and cultural factors that inform human development and our understanding of different ages and stages. As we state in the podcast that accompanies this chapter, we encourage you to examine theories and theorists with a critical eye; to question the applicability of theories across different groups of people; and to read and understand both critiques of these theories as well as recent and relevant research that may inform new ways to understand and apply developmental theories.

REFERENCES

Ainsworth, M. S. (1967). *Infancy in Uganda: Infant care and the growth of love.* Johns Hopkins Press.

Ainsworth, M. S. (1992). John Bowlby (1907–1990): Obituary. *American Psychologist, 47*(5), 668–668. https://doi.org/10.1037/0003-066X.47.5.668

Anthias, F. (2013). Hierarchies of social location, class and intersectionality: Towards a trans-locational frame. *International Sociology, 28*(1), 121–138. https://doi.org/10.1177/0268580912463155

Arnett, J. J. (2000). A theory of development from the late teens through the twenties. *The American Psychologist, 55*(5), 469–480. https://doi.org/10.1037/0003-066X.55.5.469

Arnett, J. J. (2007). Suffering, selfish, slackers? Myths and reality about emerging adults. *Journal of Youth and Adolescence, 36*(1), 23–29. https://doi.org/10.1007/s10964-006-9157-z

Babakr, Z. H., Mohamedamin, P., Kakamad, K., & Soran University. (2019). Piaget's cognitive developmental theory: Critical review. *Education Quarterly Reviews, 2*(3), 517–524. https://doi.org/10.31014/aior.1993.02.03.84

Bandura, A. (1999). A social cognitive theory of personality. In L. Pervin & O. John (Eds.), *Handbook of personality* (pp. 154–196). Guildford Press.

Barnum, E. L., & Perrone-McGovern, K. M. (2017). Attachment, self-esteem and subjective well-being among survivors of childhood sexual trauma. *Journal of Mental Health Counseling, 39*(1), 39–55. https://doi.org/10.17744/mehc.39.1.04

Belsky, J., Houts, R. M., & Fearon, R. M. P. (2010). Infant attachment security and the timing of puberty: Testing an evolutionary hypothesis. *Psychological Science, 21*(9), 1195–1201. https://doi.org/10.1177/0956797610379867

Bettelheim, B. (1983). *Freud and man's soul.* Vintage.

Blum, H. P. (2007). Little Hans: A centennial review and reconsideration. *Journal of the American Psychoanalytic Association, 55*(3), 749–765. https://doi.org/10.1177/00030651070550030201

Bowlby, J. (1969). *Attachment: Attachment and loss.* Basic Books.

Bowlby, J. (1988). *A secure base: Parent-child attachment and healthy human development.* Routledge.

Bretherton, I. (1992). The origins of attachment theory: John Bowlby and Mary Ainsworth. *Developmental Psychology, 28*(5), 759–775. https://doi.org/10.1037/0012-1649.28.5.759

Bretherton, I. (1999). Updating the "internal working model" construct: Some reflections. *Attachment & Human Development, 1*(3), 343–357. https://doi.org/10.1080/14616739900134191

Brill, A. A. (Ed.). (1938). *The basic writings of Sigmund Freud.* Random House.

Bussey, K., & Bandura, A. (1999). Social cognitive theory of gender development and differentiation. *Psychological Review, 106*(4), 676–713. https://doi.org/10.1037/0033-295x.106.4.676

Cam, Z., Seydoogullari, S., Cavdar, D., & Cok, F. (2012). Classical and contemporary approaches for moral development. *Educational Sciences: Theory and Practice, 12*(2), 1222–1225.

Capuzzi, D., Stauffer, M. D., & O'Neil, T. (2016). Theories of human development. In M. D. Stauffer & D. Capuzzi (Eds.), *Human growth and development across the lifespan: Implications for counselors.* John Wiley & Sons.

Carol Gilligan's Theory of Moral Development. (2012, October 30). *Study.com.* https://study.com/academy/lesson/carol-gilligans-theory-of-moral-development.html

Cassidy, J., & Berlin, L. J. (1994). The insecure/ambivalent pattern of attachment: Theory and research. *Child Development, 65*(4), 971–991. https://doi.org/10.2307/1131298

Cassidy, J., & Shaver, P. (Eds.). (1999). *Handbook of attachment: Theory, research, and clinical applications.* The Guilford Press.

Cherry, K. (2019, July). *What is attachment theory? The importance of early emotional bonds.* Verywell Mind. https://www.verywellmind.com/what-is-attachment-theory-2795337

Cherry, K. (2020, June). *The different types of attachment styles.* Verywell Mind. https://www.verywellmind.com/attachment-styles-2795344#citation-8

Cherry, K. (2021, April). *Kohlberg's theory of moral development.* Verywell Mind. https://www.verywellmind.com/kohlbergs-theory-of-moral-development-2795071

Chung, D. (2018). The eight stages of psychosocial protective development: Developmental psychology. *Journal of Behavioral and Brain Science, 8*(6), 1–35. https://doi.org/10.4236/jbbs.2018.86024

Crittenden, A. N., & Marlowe, F. W. (2013). Cooperative child care among the Hadza: Situating multiple attachment in evolutionary context. In N. Quinn & J. M. Mageo (Eds.), *Attachment reconsidered: Cultural perspectives on a Western theory.* Palgrave.

Cronin, A., & King, A. (2010). Power, inequality and identification: Exploring diversity and intersectionality amongst older LGB adults. *Sociology, 44*(5), 876–892. https://doi.org/10.1177/0038038510375738

Dagan, O., & Sagi-Schwartz, A. (2018). Early attachment network with mother and father: An unsettled issue. *Child Development Perspectives, 12*(2), 115–121. https://doi.org/10.1111/cdep.12272

Daniel Levinson: Biography & Theory. (2015, August 25). *Study.com.* https://study.com/academy/lesson/daniel-levinson-biography-theory.html

Desmet, M. (2013). Some Preliminary Notes on an Empirical Test of Freud's Theory on Depression. *Frontiers in Psychology, 4*(158). https://doi.org/ doi:10.3389/fpsyg.2013.00158.

Dunkel, C. S., & Harbke, C. (2017). A Review of Measures of Erikson's Stages of Psychosocial Development: Evidence for a General Factor. *Journal of Adult Development, 24*(1), 58–76. https://doi.org/ doi:10.1007/s10804-016-9247-4.

Erikson, E., & Erikson, J. M. (1997). *The life cycle completed: Extended version with new chapters on the ninth stage of development.* W. W. Norton & Company.

Fisher, S., & Greenberg, R. P. (1996). *Freud scientifically reappraised: Testing the theories and therapy.* John Wiley & Sons.

Fivush, R. (2006). Scripting attachment: Ggeneralized event representations and internal working models. *Attachment & Human Development, 8*(3), 283–289. https://doi.org/ doi:10.1080/08912960600858935.

Flavell, J. H. (1963). Piaget's contributions to the study of cognitive development. *Merrill-Palmer Quarterly of Behavior and Development, 9*(4), 245–252. https://doi.org/ doi:10.1111/j.1467-9280.1996.tb00359.x.

Flavell, J. H. (1992). Cognitive development: Past, present, and future. *Developmental Psychology, 28*(6), 998–1005. https://doi.org/ doi:10.1037/0012-1649.28.6.998.

Flavell, J. H. (1996). Piaget's legacy. *Psychological Science, 7*(4), 200–203. https://doi.org/ doi:10.1111/j.1467-9280.1996.tb00359.x.

Gale, G. (2017). *A study guide for psychologists and their theories for students: Mary Salter Ainsworth.* Cengage Learning.

Gay, P. (2006). *Freud: A life for our time.* W. W. Norton & Company.

Gillath, O., C Karantzas, G., & Lee, J. (2019). Attachment and social networks. *Current Opinion in Psychology, 25,* 21–25. https://doi.org/ doi:10.1016/j.copsyc.2018.02.010.

Gilligan, C. (1977). In a different voice: Women's conceptions of self and of morality. *Harvard Educational Review, 47*(4), 481–517. https://doi.org/ doi:10.17763/haer.47.4.g6167429416hg5l0.

Gilligan, C. (1982). *In a different voice: Psychological theory and women's development.* Harvard University Press.

Gilligan, C. (2018). Revisiting "in a different voice." *LEARNing Landscapes, 11*(2), 25–30. https://doi.org/ doi:10.36510/learnland.v11i2.942.

Goldschmidt, L., Langa, M., Alexander, D., & Canham, H. (2021). A review of Kohlberg's theory and its applicability in the South African context through the lens of early childhood development and violence. *Early Child Development and Care, 191*(7–8), 1066–1078. https://doi.org/ doi:10.1080/03004430.2021.1897583.

Heo, J., Han, S., Koch, C., & Aydin, H. (2011). Piaget's egocentrism and language learning: Language egocentrism (LE) and language differentiation (LD). *Journal of Language Teaching and Research, 2*(4), 733–739. https://doi.org/ doi:10.4304/jltr.2.4.733-739.

Isaacs, N. (2015). *A brief introduction to Piaget: The growth of understanding in the young child and new light on children's ideas of number.* Algora Publishing.

Jackson, L. (2008). Object permanence. In N. J. Salkind & K. Rasmussen (Eds.), *Encyclopedia of educational psychology* (Vol. 2, pp. 742–743). SAGE Publications. https://link.gale.com/apps/doc/CX2660600209/GVRL?u=nhc_main&sid=GVRL&xid=27c09d57

Jesinoski, M. S. (2010). *Young's schema theory: Exploring the direct and indirect links between negative childhood experiences and temperament to negative affectivity in adulthood.* Utah State University All Graduate Theses and Dissertations. https://digitalcommons.usu.edu/etd/845

Jordan, J. V. (2018). *Relational–cultural therapy* (2nd ed.). American Psychological Association. https://doi.org/ doi:10.1037/0000063-000.

Karen, R. (1998). *Becoming attached: First relationships and how they shape our capacity for love.* Oxford University Press.

Kira, I. A. (2001). Taxonomy of trauma and trauma assessment. *Traumatology, 7*(2), 73–86. https://doi.org/ doi:10.1177/153476560100700202.

Knight, R. (2014). A hundred years of latency: Ffrom Freudian psychosexual theory to dynamic systems nonlinear development in middle childhood. *Journal of the American Psychoanalytic Association, 62*(2), 203–235. https://doi.org/ doi:10.1177/0003065114531044.

Kohlberg, L. A. (1981). *The philosophy of moral development: Moral stages and the idea of justice.* Harper & Row.

Kohlberg, L. A. (1982). *The psychology of moral development: The nature and validity of moral stages.* Harper & Row.

Lantz, S. E., & Ray, S. (2021). Freud developmental theory. In *StatPearls.* StatPearls Publishing. https://www.ncbi.nlm.nih.gov/books/NBK557526

Levine, P. (2003). *Sexual healing: Transforming the sacred wound.* Sounds True.

Levine, P., & Kline, M. (2008). *Trauma-proofing your kids.* North Atlantic Books.

Levinson, D. J. (1978). *The seasons of a man's life.* Ballantine Books.

Levinson, D. J. (1986). A conception of adult development. *American Psychologist, 41*(1), 3–13. https://doi.org/ doi:10.1037/0003-066X.41.1.3.

Linn, R. (2001). The insights of Kohlberg and Gilligan into moral development and counseling. *Social Behavior & Personality: An International Journal, 29*(6), 593–600. https://doi.org/doi:10.2224/sbp.2001.29.6.593.

Lutz, S. T., & Huitt, W. G. (2004). Connecting cognitive development and constructivism: Implications from theory for instruction and assessment. *Constructivism in the Human Sciences, 9*(1), 67–90.

MacCormick, H. A. (2021, July 30). *Stanford psychology professor Albert Bandura has died*. Stanford News: Stanford University Communications. https://news.stanford.edu/2021/07/30/psychology-professor-albert-bandura-dead-95

Main, M., & Solomon, J. (1986). Discovery of a new, insecure-disorganized/disoriented attachment pattern. In T. B. Brazelton & M. Yogman (Eds.), *Affective development in infancy* (pp. 95–124). Ablex.

Mallon, E. J. (1976). Cognitive development and processes: Review of the philosophy of Jean Piaget. *The American Biology Teacher, 38*(1), 28–47. https://doi.org/doi:10.2307/4445437.

Maree, J. G. (2020). The psychosocial development theory of Erik Erikson: Critical overview. *Early Child Development and Care*. https://doi.org/doi:https://doi-org.ezproxy.snhu.edu/10.1080/03004430.2020.1845163.

Matusov, E., & Hayes, R. (2000). Sociocultural critique of Piaget and Vygotsky. *New Ideas in Psychology, 18*(2–3), 215–239. https://doi.org/doi:10.1016/S0732-118X(00)00009-X.

McLeod, S. (2009). *Attachment theory*. Consultado en. www.simplypsychology.org/attachment.html

McLeod, S. (2013). *Kohlberg's theory of moral development*. SimplyPsychology. https://www.simplypsychology.org/kohlberg.html

Midgley, N. (2006). Re-reading "Little Hans": Freud's case study and the question of competing paradigms in psychoanalysis. *Journal of the American Psychoanalytic Association, 54*(2), 537–559. https://doi.org/doi:10.1177/00030651060540021601.

Nabavi, R. T. (2012). *Bandura's social learning theory & social cognitive learning theory*. https://www.researchgate.net/publication/267750204

Oppenheim, D., Emde, R. N., & Warren, S. (1997). Children's narrative representations of mothers: Ttheir development and associations with child and mother adaptation. *Child Development, 68*(1), 127–138.

Riggs, S. A., & Riggs, D. S. (2011). Risk and resilience in military families experiencing deployment: The role of the family attachment network. *Journal of Family Psychology, 25*(5), 675–687. https://doi.org/doi:10.1037/a0025286.

Ross, J. M. (2007). Trauma and abuse in the case of Little Hans: Aa contemporary perspective. *Journal of the American Psychoanalytic Association, 55*(3), 779–797. https://doi.org/doi:10.1177/00030651070550031601.

Simpson, J. A. (1999). Attachment theory in modern evolutionary perspective. In J. Cassidy & P. R. Shaver (Eds.), *Handbook of attachment: Theory, research, and clinical applications* (pp. 115–140). The Guilford Press.

Solomon, E. P., & Heide, K. M. (1999). Type III trauma: Toward a more effective conceptualization of psychological trauma. *International Journal of Offender Therapy and Comparative Criminology, 43*(2), 202–210. https://doi.org/doi:10.1177/0306624X99432007.

Target, M. (2018). 20/20 Hindsight: A 25-year programme at the Anna Freud Centre of efficacy and effectiveness research on child psychoanalytic psychotherapy. *Psychotherapy Research, 28*(1), 30–46. https://doi.org/doi:10.1080/10503307.2017.1349351.

Van Dijken, S. (1998). *John Bowlby: His early life: A biographical journey into the roots of attachment theory*. Free Association Books.

Vinney, C. (2021, August). *The Carol Gilligan theory and a woman's sense of self*. Verywell Mind. https://www.verywellmind.com/the-carol-gilligan-theory-and-a-woman-s-sense-of-self-5198408

Vreeke, G. J. (1991). Gilligan on justice and care: Ttwo interpretations. *Journal of Moral Education, 20*(1), 33–46. https://doi.org/doi:10.1080/0305724910200103.

Walsh, C. (2000). The life and legacy of Lawrence Kohlberg. *Society, 37*(2), 36–41. https://doi.org/doi:10.1007/BF02686189.

Westen, D. (1991). Social cognition and object relations. *Psychological Bulletin, 109*(3), 429–455. https://doi.org/ doi:10.1037/0033-2909.109.3.429.

Woods, C. J. P. (1996). Gender differences in moral development and acquisition: A review of Kohlberg's and Gilligan's models of justice and care. *Social Behavior and Personality, 24*(4), 375–383. https://doi.org/ doi:10.2224/sbp.1996.24.4.375.

Wurgaft, L. D. (1995). Identity in world history: A postmodern perspective. *History and Theory, 34*(2), 67. https://doi.org/ doi:10.2307/2505435.

Young, J. E. (1998). *The young schema questionnaire: Short form* (1st ed.). New York Cognitive Therapy Centre.

CHAPTER 3

Cultural and Contextual Development Models

LEARNING OBJECTIVES

Upon completion of this chapter, students will be able to:

1. Identify key tenets of racial and ethnic identity development.
2. Identify key tenets of sexual and gender identity development.
3. Discuss the roots of privilege and oppression.
4. Recognize personal experiences of privilege and oppression in relation to others.
5. Identify theories of development rooted in systemic, contextual, and social ecology models.

INTRODUCTION TO CULTURAL AND CONTEXTUAL MODELS OF DEVELOPMENT

While critical to understanding the developmental process, culture and context are widely expansive concepts which include far more than any one chapter or text can cover. And yet, our charge is to help expose you, a burgeoning mental health professional, to what these concepts mean and how they tie back to developmental theory. As such, this chapter is intended to be an initial touchstone for your understanding of culture and contextual models of development. In an effort to orient you to the remainder of the book and to the developmental theories that come later, we have selected specific models and interventions within this chapter that highlight frames of reference not previously explored or that were overlooked in traditional theories of development. This includes theories on social, systems, and ecological development. We have also chosen to explore facets of identity development that result from marginalization, privilege, oppression, and the intersection of those identities—information that is important for your work with future clients as well as for you, the future mental health professional and social justice advocate.

What you will find in this chapter is the beginning, not the end, of a cultural and contextual understanding of development. The theories and models explored in this chapter are not intended to be exhaustive. They are, instead, intended to provide you with new and updated perspectives of development that apply to specific cultures or contexts and to encourage your thoughtful exploration of developmental theory as an evolving and expansive part of understanding those you will work with in your future career. Born out of research and alternative experiences, these theories add additional layers and provide alternative frameworks for understanding the clients you will soon serve. However, just as with traditional theories, these models and interventions were developed at specific points in time, under unique contexts, and with a particular cultural lens. Recognizing their strengths and their limitations is just as important as it is for you to consider any other theory of development you will find in this text. Before we move into a discussion of these models and theories, let's first begin with a look at your role as a social justice advocate.

HUMAN DEVELOPMENT AND SOCIAL JUSTICE: ALLYSHIP, ADVOCACY, AND ACTIVISM

Dignity is a human birthright. When dignity is stripped from people in any way, that is an oppressive act. Ethical guidelines for all mental health professionals uphold the responsibility to act from beneficence and work toward a more just society and world by protecting human rights, including dignity. In the stilted, shocking, heartbreaking, cyclical, and slow movement toward a more just world, mental health professionals may start as passive *allies*, develop into more engaged *advocates*, and finally evolve into *activists*, whose commitment to human rights is evidenced in constantly leveraging their power and access in proactive service to the marginalized (El-Mekki, 2018; Melton, 2018).

Because of the ongoing implications of colonization and power-over on this planet, there is great variance in the opportunities, resources, and rights people may enjoy. By the accident of one's birth, one may or may not have access to a nurturing family, clean water, sufficient nutrition, safe shelter, attainable healthcare, unpolluted agricultural land, natural wildlands, affordable and meaningful education, welcoming and accommodating communities in which to explore, appreciated work, role models with the free time to invest in mentorship, enriching social support, and healthy creative outlets. The more access one has to these environmental and relational blessings, the more likely one will be able to achieve optimal development of one's specific abilities, capacities, and dreams. The less access one has to these environmental and relational blessings, the more stress will be required to work toward optimal development, and the less likely "optimal" will be comparable to one with greater access (Murry et al., 2018; Sheidow et al., 2014; Wadsworth & Rienks, 2012). That lack of access in an unjust world should in no way diminish one's right to dignity, but is the cause of much grief and suffering for people the world over.

Allies enjoy membership to one or more privileged in-groups (e.g., White, able-bodied, cis-gendered); feel compassion for the suffering of those in one or more marginalized out-groups; and aim to soothe suffering by standing with marginalized members, offering empathy and support (Mizock & Page, 2016) rather than intentionally acting against marginalized members. Allies have a burgeoning awareness of their social rights and freedoms, a component of their majority group *privileges*, and may often feel unsure how to help or whether to speak up, and may seek appreciation for the discomfort they feel taking risks on behalf of those with less privilege.

Mental health professionals are charged with proactive advocacy responsibilities to reduce barriers to access for those we serve, utilizing the privileges we *do* have in service of those who do not. This means learning the tangible resources available where we work geographically, as well as the informational and digital ones relevant to our clients. Advocacy also means facilitating our clients' access to those resources through networking, referrals, introductions, psychoeducation, translation and interpretation, and completion of applications as necessary. *Advocates* feel compassion for the suffering *and* take concrete action to reduce it by seeking out education, training, and supervision/guidance to learn effective helping strategies and facilitate access to fulfill needs as they present. Advocates do this while maintaining awareness of power and privilege, staying away from self-indulgent hero–victim narratives or seeking recognition (Mizock & Page, 2016).

Mental health professionals who evolve into *activists* do the observable actions of allyship and advocacy, and *also* create necessary change by collaborating with interdisciplinary colleagues locally, nationally, and internationally to work toward a more just society and world through direct service, education, and policy development, elevating the voices of those who have historically been dismissed. *Activists* do not just react to a momentary need as it presents itself, but live in a state of awareness about the constant need and inequities, and devote their careers and significant personal time to try to bring justice where there is injustice, to feed where there is hunger, to bring solace where there is pain, and to interrupt the feedback loops that protect the privileged while harming the oppressed (Mizock & Page, 2016).

To do social justice and advocacy work effectively, we must stay in a constant process of dissolving the internal barriers that were installed through socialization processes beyond our control throughout our own development. As we liberate ourselves from internalized colonization, we are more able to be an effective activist for those we serve, which necessarily envelops skillful advocacy, maintaining the dignity of all (Lewis et al., 2018; Lucero, 2011; Morrow & Malcoe, 2017). The following models were forwarded by mental health professionals who achieved activist-level engagement with their considerable wisdom and access, serving diverse clients at various points across the lifespan, helping move the needle toward a more just world through their clinical and academic offerings.

MODELS OF IDENTITY DEVELOPMENT

Here we explore identity development models that honor the multiple sources of culture, group membership, relativity, access, and barriers that inform the complexity of human development. Each of these models takes a different lens on power imbalances that lead to chronic and toxic stress, but they are mutually reinforcing and operationalize each other in different ways. As you read this material we encourage interactive dialogue with classmates and colleagues about the ways your own socialization processes have, and continue to include these themes.

Intersectionality

Hays (1996, 2008) coalesced the ADDRESSING model as an acronym to structure intake, assessment, rapport-building, and ongoing treatment centered around clients' multiple identities, all of which *intersect* to create a unique individual who belongs to various groups with shared experiences as a multicultural being (Table 3.1). The ADDRESSING model reminds mental health professionals to maintain cultural humility and consideration while gently inviting clients to share over time what they will regarding **a**ge, developmental **d**isabilities, acquired **d**isabilities, **r**eligion, **e**thnicity,

Table 3.1 Hays's ADDRESSING Model of Intersectionality

CULTURAL CHARACTERISTIC	POWER	LESS POWER
Age and Generational Influences	Adults	Children, adolescents, elders
Developmental Disability	Temporarily able-bodied	*Individuals* with disabilities
Disability Acquired Later in Life	Temporarily able-bodied	*Individuals* with disabilities (e.g., multiple sclerosis; dementia caused by stroke)
Religion and Spiritual Orientation	Christians	*Non-Christian*
Ethnicity/Race Identity	White or Caucasian	*Person of color*
Socioeconomic Status	Owning and Middle Class (access to higher education)	People of lower status because of occupation, education, income, or rural habitat
Sexual Orientation	Heterosexuals	Gay, lesbians, and bisexual people
Indigenous Heritage	Non-native	Native
National Origin	U.S born	Immigrants, refugees, and international students
Gender	Male	Women, transgender, and intersex people

Source: Adapted from Hays, P. A. (2016). *Addressing Cultural Complexities in Practice: A Framework for Clinicians and Counselors* (3rd ed.). American Psychological Association.

sexual orientation, socioeconomic status, indigenous group membership, nationality, and gender (2008). Because dominant/privileged groups have ascribed relative values to each of these domains, there may be anxiety, fear, and even trauma when making emotional contact with marginalized identities; feeling vulnerable and protective when assessing the trustworthiness of the mental health professional is a normal experience when clients do not regularly occupy privileged positions.

Mental health professionals are, of course, complex, multicultural beings, with varying membership among these different dimensions of identity development. Our own group membership and social shaping create a complex lens through which we must work to connect effectively with our diverse client populations. The more we self-reflect on our own experiences of privilege and oppression in the ADDRESSING domains, the more we can be sensitized to our clients' experiences of relative privilege and oppression, and effectively care for the ways our clients have been traumatized, marginalized, and "othered," while also working with ways they have been buffered and protected—sometimes problematically—from consequence. Hays is an activist for multicultural competency and inclusion; her published works focus on underserved populations and increasing mental health professionals' sensitivity to specific cultural needs and preferences.

Privilege and Oppression

Ken Hardy specializes in training mental health professionals on the liberatory work of privilege and oppression in family therapy. His publications focus on multicultural competency (Hardy & Laszloffy, 2017) and confront the ongoing centering of Whiteness

Which domains from the ADDRESSING model feel fun and interesting for you to share about yourself? Which domains feel perhaps more stressful or risky? Which domains make you feel proud? Are there any that bring up pain or a sense of not wanting to share them in a mixed group to which you've been assigned? How would it be for you to have a clinician give you a handout with these domains and invite you to share what you would like about them? What would increase your willingness and desire to share? What would make you wary or fully shut down?

(Hardy, 2022). Hardy has created the privileged and subjugated task (PAST) model (2016), acknowledging that we often have a mix of relative privilege and subjugation, or oppression, in each circumstance. Hardy also emphasizes that when we act from our subjugated self when the situation requires we enact the tasks of our privilege, we are likely to cause harm; this is usually the case when we are the more privileged person in the encounter. For example, one measure of privilege is not having to think or feel anything about a particular topic, because it does not affect you or those you care about; having the freedom to be indifferent about a topic because it does not impact your life or sense of safety can result in callousness toward those impacted by it. On the other hand, not having the option to even think about what it would mean to have access to certain rights and opportunities is a measure of oppression; the oppressors put the oppressed "in their place," and have the power and protection to determine where that is.

Hardy notes that shame interferes with connection and healing for the privileged (Hardy, 2016). This author (Roller) asserts that shame and guilt are insufficient in those with narcissistic and antisocial tendencies (American Psychiatric Association, 2013), thus a therapeutic dose of each may be necessary to keep the more privileged, powerful, and protected from causing harm, while too much shame is what freezes people biobehaviorally and requires tremendous emotional resources to up-regulate back into functional social interaction (Porges & Dana, 2018; Terrizzi & Shook, 2020). Shame in larger doses does make people withdraw into a self-protective stance (Terrizzi & Shook, 2020); this is the basis of White fragility (D'Angelo, 2018), and the province of White privilege (Allen, 2018), not evidenced sufficiently in overt acts of White supremacy (Pulido, 2015). However, an appropriate amount of shame, guilt, and remorse is necessary to act as a yield sign for oppressing socialization and aggressive impulses (Terrizzi & Shook, 2020). In Spanish, the derogatory term *sin vergüenza* means *shameless*, and it is used to describe one who does not care about the impact of their actions, often mentioned with a downcast shaking head and clucking tongue after harm has been caused. Many of us have probably sent or received an "smh" text in response to shameless behavior (Table 3.2).

Hardy encourages the subjugated to focus on their health and well-being right now, to liberate themselves from the toxic effects of oppression that will continue throughout their lives. This liberatory work does not have an end in sight, and it is therefore even more important that the subjugated prioritize their own care and joy. Hardy asserts that the more privileged person holds more responsibility for how the interaction unfolds; this has complex implications for clinicians with marginalized identities who are serving those with more social privilege, as more privileged clients may demand, belittle, or otherwise dismiss their mental health professional's interventions.

Table 3.2 Hardy's Tasks of the Privileged and Subjugated

TASKS OF THE SUBJUGATED	GENERIC TASKS	TASKS OF THE PRIVILEGED
1. Unlearn voicelessness; free yourself from the belief that speaking up is a waste of time.	1. You are the expert in your own experience, no one else's.	1. Do not rank suffering, or compare yours to others'.
2. Release internalized messages of subjugation.	2. Tell your own story.	2. Even when intentions are good, consequences may be bad. When consequences are hurtful, take ownership and make repair.
3. Free yourself from trying to change the privileged.	3. Honor thoughts and feelings.	3. Accept that history still impacts current events and experiences.
4. Channel righteous rage for your own protection.		4. Repair over and over; develop stamina for being called out on your insensitivity.
		5. Do not frame others' experiences

Source: Adapted from Dr. Kenneth V. Hardy's Tasks of the Privileged and the Subjugated. Retrieved from https://artsmidwest.org/sites/default/files/KenHardyTasks_Handout.pdf.

It also means that where the mental health professional has more privilege, they must take great care to not oppress clients and colleagues with it. Hardy is an activist for racial equity and decolonization in family systems, the mental health profession, and society at large.

STUDENT REFLECTION 3.2

Which of Hardy's tasks are the most validating for you? Which are the most challenging? As you imagine yourself in different settings, with different groups of people, which tasks become the most salient? How do you think these tasks will show up for you as a mental health professional advocating for your clients? How do you think these tasks will show up for you interfacing with authority figures and colleagues at your work sites? What support will you need to navigate these challenges? How can you connect with that support?

RACIALIZED TRAUMA AND SOMATIC EXPERIENCING

Further operationalizing liberatory clinical practice is the sensory awareness offerings of Menakem (2017), who is both a licensed clinical social worker and somatic experiencing practitioner specializing in racialized trauma. Menakem explains how racial oppression was incubated in the Dark Ages of Europe, and then "blown out" through traumatized and oppressed Europeans. As those Europeans who were oppressed tried to escape oppression, they took their more powerful technologies and weapons (and traumatized bodyminds) to colonize lands across the world, and thus became the traumatizing oppressors of the bodyminds of Brown and Black people the world over. This transgenerational transmission of trauma obviously continues to this day, resulting in ongoing externalized and internalized oppression (Ginther, 2020; Scrine, 2021; Trinh,

2020). Further research is needed to determine best practices for engaging healthy fight for resistance while resolving embodied overwhelm, but it is clear oppression lands on the body and is a primary social determinant of health (Bates et al., 2009; Knibb-Lamouche, 2012; Nowotny & Kuptsevych-Timmer, 2018). Menakem is an activist for racial equity and decolonization; he has stopped referring to "bodies of color" and has replaced that phrase with "bodies of culture" to reclaim wholeness in spite of the ongoing embodied effects of colonization, initiating the field of cultural somatics (Tippett, 2021, April 15).

Ta-Nehisi Coates mourns that oppression existed in many areas of Africa before the slave ships arrived, for to have people to sell, those with more power rounded up those with less and traded them away for generations, though not knowing these people would be treated so much worse than livestock (Coates, 2015). Coates, like Ignatiev and Garvey (1996), notes that the fallacy of Whiteness did not exist until it served as a means for colonists to obtain and retain power over those they had enslaved

> .... the elevation of being White (was achieved) ... through pillaging of life, liberty, labor and land; through the flaying of backs; the chaining of limbs; the strangling of dissidents; the destruction of families; the rape of mothers; the sale of children...(p. 8).

Such caste systems have also co-existed with any imperial reign throughout Asia and the Americas, thus a ranking of the relative value of human life has a long and storied history that shows up in our bodies, our minds, our beliefs, our laws, our policing policies, our social politics, and our personal and professional relationships. Effectively dismantling the external structures of oppression can only follow the dismantling of internal barriers to empathy, respect, caring, connection, and mutuality that allow for dignity, and we each have our tasks in protecting that dignity for each other.

STUDENT REFLECTION 3.3

What do you know about your inherited lineage's experience with colonization? What messages may have been internalized that could benefit from attending and releasing? What practices might be helpful for you to release activation from interactions rooted in power-over?

NON-VIOLENT COMMUNICATION

Clinical psychologist Marshall Rosenberg (1934–2015) developed non-violent communication (NVC) in response to the violence that was erupting during the Civil Rights Movements of the 1960s. Decades of research are now showing that, with diligent practice, NVC can increase "emotional empathy, perspective-taking, (and) empathic concern" (Juncadella, 2013, p. 46), all of which are central to embodying multicultural competencies and protecting dignity. From a concrete practice standpoint, seeking training in NVC can operationalize the steps one takes to honor (in spoken word and behavior) the needs and feelings of our colleagues and clients, even when confronted with strategies that might put us in conflict (Rosenberg, 2003). NVC offers a process and structure by which one may stay curious and open about the needs that are going unmet when another uses a strategy that causes conflict, to grieve when it is clear we will not get our needs met with certain people and situations, and to develop the flexibility to seek out and get our needs met where that is possible.

NVC emphasizes that when our needs are getting met, we experience positive affect, and when they are not getting met, we experience negative affect; it is our strategies for getting our needs met (not our needs or our feelings) that vary and can cause conflict (Rosenberg, 2003). A primary practice of NVC is that when we cannot feel empathy for another, it means we need to give it to ourselves first; in this self-soothing, we may down-regulate our negative affect to then practice curiosity about what needs the other person is trying to meet with their strategies that hurt. For a relationship to be functional long-term, the need for mutuality must be met by all parties involved being able to oscillate smoothly (conceptualized by movement along the infinity symbol) between *honesty* and *empathy*; when people get stuck on honesty, they are likely to say or do things in a hurtful way without concern for how that effects the other(s) involved. Conversely, when people get stuck on empathy, they are likely to not be asserting their needs sufficiently, resulting in an imbalanced relationship that can lead to resentment.

Using Maslow's hierarchy (or NVC materials available online and through structured training) as a guide, mental health professionals may listen closely and assess the unmet needs driving their clients' emotional pain. If there is pain, there are unmet needs. In being curious about and naming the universal needs and taking a full inventory of them, mental health professionals can prioritize the foundational survival and security needs first, advocating to get those immediate safety needs met so that clients' nervous systems can settle from fight-or-flight mode. As safety and security needs are met, mental health professionals can then move up the needs hierarchy to relational and personal fulfillment needs with their clients. Rosenberg was an activist for peace and non-violence focusing mostly on marginalized groups through education and facilitating reconciliation processes. His students further diversified his work and began applying it in training programs, drop-in role-plays, and as an adjunct to couples and family counseling. Depending on the client constellations you serve, you may do most of this work individually, with couples and family systems, with groups, or interfacing between your client systems and the larger systems they inhabit.

Racial and Ethnic Identity Development

The following models serve as the foundation for ongoing research into the experience of integrating racial, ethnic, and cultural identity across the lifespan (Quintana, 2007). Due to the effects of ongoing oppression, those with marginalized racial, ethnic, and/or cultural identities will likely be confronted with painful experiences of subjugation that require life force, time, and attention to process and make sense of. These models articulate that process, and may help the mental health professional normalize and validate their own and their clients' experiences of identity development with regard to acculturative, assimilative, and phenotype-related stress in a White supremacist society (Ward & Geeraert, 2016).

ABOUT ETHNIC IDENTITY DEVELOPMENT

Ethnic identity refers to the degree to which one develops a sense of affiliation and identification with one's ethnic group. Ethnic identity development is marked by moving from a stage of being less mature to being more mature with regard to ethnic identity (Phinney & Ong, 2007). Ethnic belonging and ethnic exploration are the two dimensions of ethnic identity development. According to Phinney (1989) there are four identity statuses based on exploration and commitment. The exploration in ethnic identity involves learning about one's group and how that group membership will impact that person's life. Commitment refers to the process of making a decision about the meaning of one's ethnicity and the way one will live as a group member (Phinney & Ong, 2007).

The four identity statuses are diffuse, foreclosed, moratorium, and achieved, each describing a different combination of exploration and commitment to the identity. The person who is in the identity diffuse status has neither engaged in exploration, nor does that person demonstrate any commitment. This person has not made a decision about identity that is based on their own study or comparison of other ideas and demonstrates no belonging to the ethnic group.

The person in the foreclosed status of ethnic identity development is committed to an ethnic identity, but this commitment is not based on that individual's exploration. Instead, this person has adopted the ethnic identity of the community or family of origin without question and the person has not explored the meaning of that identity.

The person in moratorium has engaged in exploration but has not committed to the ethnic identity. This is the person who is still searching to understand whether or not they can really accommodate the most obvious ethnic group membership. Often the person in moratorium struggles to understand how the ethnic group identity will co-exist with parts of the identity that are not aligned with the ethnic group. The identity-achieved person has engaged in both exploration and commitment, and really understands what it means to be a part of the ethnic group.

Ethnic identity is always a part of a person's development because it starts with family socialization, when children start to learn how a family loves, worships, does family, eats, exercises, recreates, speaks, and celebrates. For the young child, this is a way of life; however, as the young person starts to understand that there are differences between what he, she, or they think is normal and what other people think is a normal way of being, and that what they think is normal is a way of being that is shared by others, is when the young person starts the process of developing an ethnic identity (Phinney, 2006).

As Phinney (2006) explains, these shared group differences may be thought of as negative or positive in certain contexts, and the process of developing an ethnic identity involves resolving positive and negative attitudes about your group and other groups, and understanding who you are in relationship to either. Because of the pervasive hierarchy of power and privilege in American society, those people who belong to nondominant ethnic groups are much more aware of their ethnic identity than those who belong to dominant ethnic groups. As children, the understanding of differences is based on observing characteristics like skin color and clothing and later language and food preferences. Later, children start to understand behaviors and interactions that suggest or are prejudiced (Phinney, 2006). It is not uncommon for elementary school-aged children to report in-school experiences with teachers and administrators that feel discriminatory. By adolescence, young people can start to understand that their membership in an ethnic group means that they belong to a larger community of people who have shared experiences, both positive and negative, that have significant implications for how they live and function in the world (Phinney, 2006).

ABOUT RACIAL IDENTITY DEVELOPMENT

In 1971, William Cross presented his Nigrescence theory to the world, a theory that has been a mainstay of racial identity development since that time. Several other theorists have since used Cross's model as the foundation for their own work conceptualizing racial identity development. Cross's original conceptualization of racial identity included five identity stages: Pre-Encounter, Encounter, Immersion–Emersion, Internalization, and Internalization Commitment. These stages were the labels given to racial identity that at its most undeveloped was White referent, White affirming, and anti-Black, to being anti-White and pro-Black, to becoming humanity affirming. Movement from one stage to the next involves experiences and knowledge that create cognitive dissonance, resulting in the attitudes and beliefs of the current status being too absolute and no longer useful. There were subsequent revisions in 1991 and 2000 (Worrell et al., 2001).

Initially, Cross conceptualized the Pre-Encounter stage of development as Pro-White and Anti-Black, to the degree that the person at the Pre-Encounter phase demonstrated Black-Hatred. However, later iterations were reflective of the diversity and complexity of Black racial identity and Cross and Vandiver (2001) conceptualized Pre-Encounter with two identity clusters: Assimilation and Anti-Black. The person with an assimilated attitude is very dominant-group or White referent. However, the person with the Anti-Black attitude has negative feelings about Blackness and Black people. These attitudes are usually a result of being in environments where Blackness and Black people are only presented in a negative and stereotypical light. As a result, the person internalizes these negative attitudes and it is reflected in self-hatred (Vandiver et al., 2001).

The next stage is the Immersion–Emersion stage, called that because it represents the individual's experience of being completely immersed in the positive aspects of Blackness to the point that the person believes that only that which is Black or Afrocentric is right, and that which is White is bad and wrong. The Immersion identities are therefore referred to as Intense Black Involvement and Anti-White (Vandiver et al., 2001). The person in the Intense Black Involvement cluster is immersed in Black culture—music, literature, art—and is extreme in embracing everything Black. It is as if this person is devouring everything that has been previously denied them with regard to Black culture. However, this stage is often accompanied by anger when the individual realizes that there has been limited or no access to information that would have been the foundation for more positive feelings about the historical contributions, talent, and intelligence of Black people. There is anger directed to those who have created and perpetuated systems that denied them this information. For example, it is quite common that an individual in the Immersion stage targets public school education and educators who did not provide them with a more affirming picture of Black people, and they often feel guilt for not being more insightful about experiences of systematic racism and for their own negative attitudes about Black people and Black culture (Worrell et al., 2001).

As a result of the anger felt in the initial part of Immersion, the second part of Immersion is marked by Anti-White attitudes. This new insight about the systematic oppression of Black people and the deliberate activities to subordinate Black people results in hostility, distrust, and anger toward White people. Interestingly, there has been an evolution with regard to how individuals in this Anti-White period are likely to respond. For example, in the post–Civil Rights Movement, Cross asserted that this anger could result in some outwardly hostile acts, but in the 1990s, the hostility and anger were more likely to be reflected in the thought life of an individual, manifested in fantasies and daydreams about doing harm to White people (Worrell et al., 2001). For this reason, the helping professional needs to be very attuned to the context of the individual. One could assume that the more pronounced racism and the subjugation of Black people and Black culture are in the individual's context, the more pronounced the Anti-White sentiments. It is important to note that not all people emerge from this stage of development given the pervasiveness of racist subjugation.

Emersion is used to describe the time of emerging from the absolutism and romanticized ideas of Blackness typical of the Immersion state and marks the transition to Internalization (Worrell et al., 2001). In his first iteration of the Nigrescence model, the stage that followed Immersion–Emersion was Internalization, and Cross (1971) offered that this stage resulted in self-actualization, indicating greater self-acceptance and better psychological functioning (Worrell et al., 2001). However, in his first revision of the model, there were two notable changes in the conceptualization of Internalization. The first was the rejection of the idea that Internalization was synonymous with the ideals of universal or humanist views. Second, he decoupled greater self-acceptance from better psychological functioning, because there was a recognition that depression and other forms of suffering and mental illness could still exist in an individual who accepts and feels pride about their Blackness. The most significant change in the person's attitude at the stage of Internalization is that the person is no longer only dominant-group referent. The revision describes three identities in the Internalization stage: Black Nationalism, Biculturalism, and Multiculturalism.

While Black Nationalism is often equated with extreme attitudes and movements, Cross maintained that there were two kinds of attitudes that a person demonstrating Black Nationalism exhibits: separatist views or views of inclusion. The separatist ideology is one that emerged from the Pan-Africanist ideology that directed Black people to return to Africa or build separate communities for Black people in the United States. A contemporary example of separatist behavior is families in Georgia pooling their resources to buy 92 acres of land to create a safe space for themselves and their families. The new buyers of this Georgia town Toomsboro say they were prompted to create a cooperative where Black people provide for their own needs as a community and a space that is safer for African American people in light of the killings of George Floyd and Breona Taylor (Kirkland, 2020).

In the Internalization stage of development, Black Nationalism is vital to the internalized identity, particularly because it does represent the attitude of Black empowerment. However, Cross maintained that Black nationalist attitudes have the potential to make it hard for the individual to work with people from other groups and cultures. Therefore, it is important for mental health professionals to make a distinction between the Black Nationalism that may be evident in someone in the Immersion–Emersion stage of identity development and the Black Nationalism of the Internalization stage. The difference between the two is the person who expresses attitudes of Black

Nationalism in the Internalization stage is not likely to romanticize everything Black (Worrell et al., 2001).

Initially, Cross described individuals in the Internalization stage as bicultural, humanist, and cross-cultural. However, feeling that the emphasis on race is too narrow to really describe the identity of the people at the Internalization stage, Cross (1991) revised the Internalization stage to expand the identities beyond race. The internalized Bi-Cultural identity in this stage is marked by non-romanticized acceptance of being both Black and American. The internalized Multicultural identity represents self-acceptance around the racial identity and at least two other identities like being female, being gay, being a person with a disability. The person with a Multicultural identity is able to unite with others from other racial and cultural groups and accepts people from other backgrounds (Worrell et al., 2001).

In 2001, Cross used the Cross Racial Identity Scale to expand the Nigrescence model. As a result, Anti-Black was dropped from the Pre-Encounter Subscales and it was changed to Pre-Encounter Assimilation (Worrell, 2008), Pre-Encounter Miseducation, and Pre-Encounter Self (Vandiver et al., 2001) because his results indicated that a person could have negative attitudes about Black people because they have not been educated in a way that supports different perceptions about Black people and not demonstrate self-hatred. In addition, a new subscale emerged from this research, and the Internalization identity was expanded to include Internalization Multicultural Racial to indicate acceptance of all racial minority groups, and the Multiculturalist subscale was renamed to reflect the acceptance of all people and was renamed Multiculturalism–Inclusive (Worrell et al., 2001).

The Nigrescence model is not considered by some to be a developmental theory, because there is the belief that it is a racial identity attitudinal framework and that there is no stepwise progression through stages. In the 2001 expanded version of the Nigrescence model, Vandiver et al. (2001) moved from referring to the statuses as stages to frames of reference and identity clusters (Worrell, 2008). The Nigrescence theory is more aptly described as an attitudinal theory that allows for the multidimensionality and complexity of racial identity. However, Cross and Fhagne-Smith (2001), in their study of racial identity development from infancy to adulthood, emphasized the contextual and cultural nature of identity development and that racial identity attitudes were primarily the result of the kinds of racial and cultural messages a child was exposed to at home and in community. They argue that the racial identity a person has during adolescence is similar to their racial identity across adulthood.

Female Identity Development

Gilligan (1979) articulated that developmental models had been based on historically Western White male ideals of achievement and autonomy, foregoing attachment and relatedness as worthy activities. Her *ethic of care*, first explored in chapter 2, is a theory of female moral development that centers relationality as a key priority and counterpoint to individualistic and justice-oriented involvement in moral decision-making. Beyond asserting a formal theory of female moral development, Gilligan was concerned that the voice of women was lost in all of the models of development and in the research being conducted to develop them. This culminated in her landmark 1982 book, *In a Different Voice*, which included three studies on women and outlined psychological theory and women's development (Gilligan, 1982). In this text, Gilligan argued that psychological theory mischaracterized women for failing to individuate, separate reason from emotion, and seek independence. Rather, Gilligan's work emphasized that women sought out relationships and interdependence and that this was not a failure to achieve a particular milestone or developmental threshold, but a reflection of their different way of viewing and constructing problems around them (Gilligan, 2018). The fact that women's voices were lost in both the research aspect of theory development as well as in the ways optimal developmental stages were deemed to be achieved was seated within a patriarchal framework (Gilligan, 2011).

Following her publication of *In a Different Voice* Gilligan continued her research with girls. This included a research partnership with Lyn Mikel Brown in which they conducted a longitudinal study on nearly 100 girls between the ages of 6 and 18 to evaluate how they made connections through their relationships (Brown & Gilligan, 1992). The findings of this study were captured in Brown and Gilligan's work, titled *Meeting at the Crossroads: Women's Psychology and Girls's Development* (1992) which highlighted how girls lose their voice as they move from middle childhood into adolescence. This resulted from learning social expectations—the preferences of adults and society for girls to respond in particular ways—and modifying their responses and behaviors accordingly. According to Gilligan, this separation of the self from relationships and movement from relational thinking to separate thinking occur for girls in adolescence but also for boys at the much earlier ages of 4 to 7 (2018). For boys this can manifest in psychological distress in school—learning problems, depression, and acting out behaviors, and for girls, where this occurs later, in depression, eating disorders, cutting, and other self-destructive behaviors (Gilligan, 2018). For Gilligan, understanding these developmental experiences of being "initiated" into codes of manhood and womanhood are critical to understanding development and the broader patriarchal society in which they are seated (Gilligan, 2011).

While Gilligan is known for her work on female development, she is hardly the only feminst scholar or theorist who has contributed to this area. Downing and Rousch (1985) also formulated a feminist identity development model based on Cross's Nigrescence model; they assert "women who live in contemporary society must first acknowledge, then struggle with, and repeatedly work through their feelings about the prejudice and discrimination they experience as women in order to achieve authentic and positive feminist identity" (p. 1). Downing and Rousch assert that for women to reach a stage of consolidated positive identity around their gender, they go through "passive acceptance, revelation, embeddedness-emanation, synthesis, and active commitment" (p. 1).

In an updated review of how this theory and related research has evolved, Hansen (2002) notes that similar to Cross' Nigrescense model, the Feminist Identity Scale has moved away from a stage model, or linear, sequential process. Rather, 16 years of research reveal that Revelation, Embeddedness–Emanation, and Active Commitment are more "dynamic ... women are doing things ... seeing the world differently finding their place ... and initiating social change" (p. 89), while Passive Acceptance and Synthesis are more "static" ends of a spectrum, either "denying gender-based oppression and discrimination ... or living with a positive self-concept despite experiences of sexism" (p. 89).

Sexual Orientation Identity Development

In 1979, Vivienne Cass published a model of sexual orientation identity formation that has had a lasting impact on our understanding of identity development for gay men and women and the associated research that continues in this area today. While not the first or only developmental model to explore the experiences of identity development in gay and lesbian people, Cass's remains one of the most well known and referenced in the research literature (Adams & Phillips, 2009; Marszalek III et al., 2004). Particularly noteworthy was Cass's rejection of a singular path to a gay sexual identity development and the assumed belief that the integration of gay identity would always be perceived negatively (Cass, 1984). Instead, she believed there were multiple dimensions associated with this process that could shift and shape the level of identity integration or identity foreclosure one ultimately had. Driven by a desire to understand (a) how individuals come to see themselves as lesbian or gay; (b) how this self-image shifted to a more formal transition in identity through interaction with others; (c) the various affective, cognitive, and behavioral ways this identity was managed in daily interactions; and (d) how the new identity ultimately integrates in the overall sense of self, Cass developed a six-stage model of identity development designed to reflect the experiences of gay women and men (Cass, 1984).

The initial stage of Cass's model is known as *Identity Confusion* (Cass, 1979). Within this stage individuals are first beginning to question whether or not they are gay. They evaluate their behavior, actions, thoughts, and feelings in an effort to understand how they fit or do not fit in with an assumed heterosexual normative experience (Cass, 1984). This stage is often associated with curiosity, confusion, anxiety, and considerable questioning and culminates in how positively or negatively the individual views the possibility of being gay (Degges-White et al., 2000). Those who engage positively in the questioning process may begin exploring information to further flesh out the potential of a gay identity and are likely to move to the next stage of development. However, others in this stage may respond negatively to the initial questioning and maintain an approach of denial or cisgender identity (Cass, 1979).

The second stage of Cass's model is known as *Identity Comparison* (Cass, 1979). As its name implies, this stage is a period of reflection and comparison to their heterosexual identity and community. Individuals in this stage are moving toward greater acceptance of a gay or lesbian orientation, having accepted the potentiality of this identity for themselves (Cass, 1984). However, they are now facing the consequences of what this means. In particular, they are considering how this translates to differences between themselves and others who are cisgender. Moreover, they are now considering how they will be received or rejected by others in their lives and feeling increasingly alienated from their heterosexual identity. Depending on how the individual perceives these experiences and the emotions that go with them, they may experience greater acceptance of their gay identity and progress to the next stage, or fear being ostracized and therefore continue denying their gay identity (Cass, 1984).

Cass's third stage of sexual orientation identity formation is known as *Identity Tolerance* (1979). Within this stage individuals are more likely to acknowledge "I probably am gay" (Degges-White et al., 2000). As they begin to recognize and internalize this identity, they may begin to actively seek out connection with others in the gay community to serve social, emotional, and sexual needs. However, rather than this reflecting a full and positive acceptance of their identity, these efforts are often associated with meeting basic needs and something to be "tolerated" (Cass, 1984). Additionally, individuals in this stage often keep their gay identity limited to friends and acquaintences in the gay community while maintaining a heterosexual presentation in public or with family. Depending on how positive or negative the experiences are with others in the gay community, individuals in this stage may continue in their path toward even greater acceptance in the next stage or continue to struggle with their gay sexual identity (Cass, 1984).

The fourth stage of Cass's model is known as *Identity Acceptance* (Cass, 1979). Individuals in this stage have increasingly accepted their gay sexual idenity and are engaging more with the LGBTQ+ community through the development of friendships and a peer support network. This stage represents a significant change in identity acceptance because the questions of "Who am I?" and "Where do I belong?" are largely resolved (Cass, 1984). However, while there is an increased level of self-acceptance and participation in the LGBTQ+ community, individuals in this stage may continue to identify as cisgender in public or in specific areas of their lives. To the extent that individuals accept their gay identity in both public and private and view their lesbian or gay identity as positive, they are more likely to move to the next stage of sexual identity development. Individuals who view their gay identity negatively or do not believe they can openly display or acknowledge this in public may continue in this stage of development (Cass, 1984).

Cass's fifth stage of sexual identity development is known as *Identity Pride* (Cass, 1979). As the name implies, the hallmark of this stage is the pride individuals have with being gay and the signifcant loyalty they hold for the LGBTQ+ community. Individuals in this stage have moved from a place of questioning to acceptance and now to a place of strong self-identity (Degges-White et al., 2000). Those in this stage will choose identification with and support of the LGBTQ+ community over the heterosexual community, often seeing this as an effort to revalue the experience and needs of those who have been marginalized by heterosexual society. Individuals in this stage often serve as advocates and may actively confront heterosexual societal rules or institutional values that they view as rejecting of their identity. While associated with a strong self-acceptance of gay identity, individuals in this stage may feel significant frustration, anger, and alienation from the larger cisgender community, including friends and family who belong to it (Cass, 1984). If individuals in this stage receive positive responses from heterosexual friends and family, they are likely to continue to the final stage of Cass's model. Alternatively, if they are faced with negative reactions they are likely to avoid interactions with heterosexuals and maintain at this stage (Cass, 1984).

The final stage of Cass's sexual identity model is called *Identity Synthesis* (Cass, 1994). This stage occurs when individuals have integrated their sexual identity as a part of their overall identity. Moving away from stage five and the sense of dichotomy between the heterosexual community and the LGBTQ+ community, individuals in this stage continue to feel pride but no longer view their gay identity as the singular part of who they are (Cass, 1984; Degges-White et al., 2000). Instead, the individual has integrated their gay sexual identity as part of a collective understanding of who they are. There is a sense of peace and stability that comes with this stage, as the individual is able to integrate their public and private selves (Cass, 1984).

APPLICATIONS OF CASS'S THEORY TO LESBIANS AND ETHNIC LGBTQ+ POPULATIONS

Sexual identity development is complex and highly individualized, just as many other facets of our developmental process are. And while Cass's model of sexual identity development has demonstrated validity for gay men, on whom she developed the model (Cass, 1984; Marszalek III et al., 2004), it, too, is culture-bound. Research on lesbians and various ethnic groups has demonstrated that her model cannot be universally applied to all LGBTQ+ populations or ethnic cultures (Adams & Phillips, 2009; Degges-White et al., 2000; Ferdoush, 2016). In particular, qualitative research with lesbian women found that while stages one (Identity Confusion) and four (Identity Acceptance) were universal for all participants in the study, movement between those stages was more complex and less direct than Cass's model proposed. Further, it was found that stage five (Identity Pride) was not experienced by any of the participants in the study, reflecting what may be a shift in societal acceptance of lesbian women and therefore making that stage obsolete for lesbian women (Degges-White et al., 2000).

Research on gay Native Americans (Adams & Phillips, 2009) and Bangladeshi Kotis (transgender Muslim females; Ferdoush, 2016) also demonstrates distinctions from Cass's original model. Both studies emphasize the importance and influence of social acceptance and stigma on the identity development process. Adams and Phillips (2009) used in-depth interviews with six self-identified two-spirit, lesbian, or gay (TsLG) Native Americans. Findings from their study show that while Cass's model did align for some of the participants, there was also a secondary pathway where some participants never experienced discomfort or questioning of their TsLG identity. This contradicts Cass's assumption that all gay people first self-identify as heterosexual and that all cultures are homophobic. Instead, the authors argue that social location and the degree of acceptance within one's ethnic community can play a significant role in acceptance and integration of identity (Adams & Phillips, 2009).

Ferdoush (2016) also found a strong societal tie associated with the stages of identity that were achieved on Cass's sexual orientation identity model, but on the other end of the spectrum. Using interviews of 18 self-identified kotis, Ferdoush found that their participants developed identities in keeping with Cass's first four stages of development; however, none made it to stages five or six. According to Ferdoush (2016), the societal stigma associated with feeling pride for, being visible as, or living as a koti would never be tolerated in Bangladeshi society, so these individuals are forced to hide and never fully integrate in accordance with Cass's model.

SYSTEMIC AND CONTEXTUAL MODELS OF DEVELOPMENT

Systemic and contextual models of development highlight a more comprehensive, inclusive, and holistic awareness of how historical injustice impinges on opportunities for the oppressed, while affording unearned access to the more privileged, creating *multiple stressors* for marginalized families. Bearing these socio-political inequities in mind, systemic and contextual models of development seek to assess, address, and intervene on the multiple stresses negatively impacting clients' systems, while leveraging access to needed resources around the client systems to increase opportunities for ongoing development. These models also focus attention on the interactions within and between the client system and all the other systems upon which they depend in their movement toward optimal development, advocating for change not just within the individual or the limited relationships around them, but as broadly as possible to reduce impingements and increase ease, access, and opportunity wherever possible.

Vygotsky's Sociocultural Theory

A developmental perspective that specifically accounts for the impact of context on development is that of Sociocultural theory. Developed through the work of Russian theorist, Lev Vygotsky, Sociocultural theory is a cognitive development theory that emphasizes social and cultural influences on individual development (Vygotsky, 1962, 1978; Vygotsky et al., 1997). Central to Sociocultural theory is the recognition that individual development cannot be understood without acknowledging the broader social system within which it is encased (McLeod, 2020). As a counterpoint to more behavioral developmental models of the time, which largely emphasized individualism, Vygotsky began researching cognitive development with a specific focus on the influence of society, culture, and context (Jovanović, 2020). While his initial research, writing, and death occurred in the first half of the 20th century, it was not until the 1960s and 1970s that much of his work was translated or began to significantly impact Western views of the social sciences (Wertsch, 1988).

THE MORE KNOWLEDGEABLE OTHER

There are several components of Vygotsky's work that coalesce and reflect the intersection of learning, language, culture, and social influence. According to Vygotsky (1978), early childhood learning is shaped through social interactions with a tutor or *more knowledgeable other*. As the name implies, a more knowledgeable other is anyone in the child's life that has more knowledge or understanding of a task, concept, or process (McLeod, 2020). When the child witnesses or engages with a more knowledgeable other, they are able to internalize what they have seen and use it to shape their own understanding and future performance. To this end, the social experience of engaging with and witnessing another precedes the internal or individualized learning of the child (Vygotsky et al., 1997). To understand this, consider, for example, a child's process of learning to tie their shoes. It is through the process of observing someone else tie a bow and through the communication that comes from that interaction that the child then has the understanding of how to tie their shoes. They can then internalize that information and begin to practice tying bows on their own, with the ultimate goal of tying their own shoes.

ZONE OF PROXIMAL DEVELOPMENT

Vygotsky (1978) took this concept a step further and emphasized that learning occurs best in the *zone of proximal development*. The zone of proximal development is a theoretical construct built on the idea of scaffolded learning. Within the scaffold, there are things we can do on our own, things we can do with help, and things that are beyond our ability to do even with the assistance of others. The zone of proximal development is the middle space—the place where we can grow beyond our own learning, with the help of others. It is not too far beyond our developmental capabilities and existing knowledge but requires the assistance of a more knowledgeable other to help guide us. Simultaneously, the zone of proximal development requires a basic developmental readiness so that whatever learning is intended is not beyond the capacity of the person learning. If we use the preceding example and consider a 2-year-old child, we know that they are not going to be able to tie their shoe, regardless of how capable their more knowledgeable other is. By virtue of not yet having the physical dexterity or sensory–motor development to tie a bow, tying one's shoes is simply beyond the reach of the zone of proximal development. Instead, learning what a shoelace is or that we tie our shoes to keep them on our feet would be a more appropriate lesson for this age. Regardless of what is being learned, Vygotsky (1978) believed that it was through interaction with more skillful or knowledgeable peers that skills and strategies are best developed and can be applied to future challenges or tasks.

LANGUAGE

Vygotsky (1962) also saw language as critically important to the developmental process and intimately tied to social and cultural interactions. For Vygotsky, language was both the primary tool for transmitting information as well as fostering internal cognitive adaptation and learning. According to Vygotsky (1987), there are three types of language: social speech, private speech, and inner speech. *Social speech* is the speech we use to communicate to others and is developed around the age of 2 years (McLeod, 2020). This is the type of speech we use when speaking with each other—our goal is to transfer our thoughts and ideas to someone else. *Private speech* is self-directed speech that we develop around age 3 and use to process or guide our own learning, overcome obstacles, enhance imagination, and foster conscious awareness (McLeod, 2020). Five-year-olds who talk themselves through the process of tying their shoes are demonstrating a form of private speech. While it may be audible, it is meant to drive their own internal problem-solving and reflects verbal thinking. As children continue to grow to around age 7, the audible forms of private speech often become internal and reflect a higher order of verbal thought known as *inner speech* (McLeod, 2020). Inner speech also has a self-regulatory purpose in that it allows us to think through situations, process responses, and problem-solve but without the audible elements of private speech.

Bronfenbrenner's Bioecological Model

Urie Bronfenbrenner (1917–2005) was a Russian-born, cisgendered male who moved to the United States at age 6, and went on to become a child psychologist. He is widely credited with situating individual child (and later, adult) development within the nested systems the individual inhabits, ultimately developing the bioecological model of human development (1979, 1994). In 1965 Bronfenbrenner co-founded Head Start, a concrete outgrowth of his hundreds of publications in child development pulling together sociology, psychology, economy, medicine, and biology to highlight how epigenetic forces act on genetic inheritance, creating synergistic effects he called *proximal processes* (Ashiabi & O'Neal, 2015; Merçon-Vargas et al., 2020; Tudge et al., 2009). Bronfenbrenner proposed that, by enhancing proximal processes and environments, it is possible to "increase the extent of actualized genetic potentials for developmental competence" (1994, p. 1). Bronfenbrenner's extensive body of work encourages mental health professionals to pay close attention to the environmental systems acting on the individual's development and to work to improve the feedback loops impinging on the individual's development, leveraging resources available in each layer around the individual, and mediating processes between the layers.

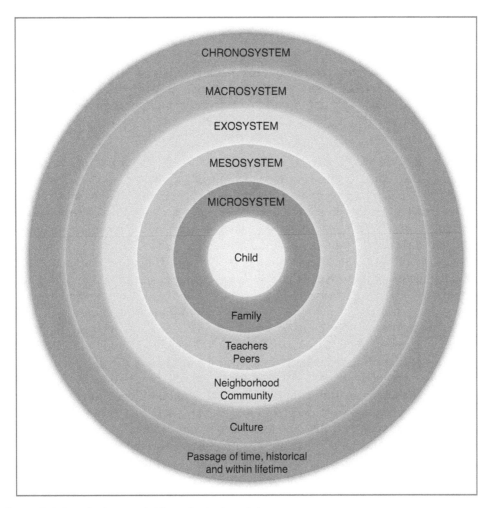

Figure 3.1 Bronfenbrenner's bioecological model.

Bronfenbrenner's nested layers around the individual are the micro- (family, friends), meso- (school), exo- (neighborhood), macro- (culture), and chrono- (changes over time) systems (Figure 3.1). The various clinical training tracks prioritize differently between the nested systems; individual counseling tends to focus on how the individual is fairing in the micro system within all these systems (Lau & Ng, 2014; Yakushko & Chronister, 2005), while couples and family therapy intentionally incorporates the micro- and macrosystems (Eppler, 2019), school-based treatment partners with the mesosystem (Gutkin, 2012; Seginer, 2006), and social work tends to focus on optimizing access to the exosystem (Eriksson et al., 2018; Fearnley, 2020; Houston, 2017). Depending on the clinician's scope, role, training, and duration of treatment, there may be the opportunity to integrate these approaches and advocate among them while significantly considering changes from the chronosystem (Shelton, 2018).

In his later years, Bronfenbrenner increasingly emphasized how central the role of the family is to the well-being of their children, and how fast-paced society was breaking down families, which was breaking down children, which in turn negatively impacts adults and society. He expressed concern for the rise in violence among children and toward them, and begged for a course correction of priorities to protect children's development. His work is seen as having three mutually reinforcing themes:

> developing theory and corresponding research designs at the frontiers of developmental science; laying out the implications and applications of developmental ... research for policy and practice; and communicating the findings .... to undergraduate students, the general public, and decision-makers. (Lang, 2005, para. 13).

Bronfenbrenner's co-creation of the federally funded program Head Start was the pinnacle of his success as an activist for marginalized families and children, reducing barriers to educational access for the underprivileged, and creating a template for others seeking to create more equitable access and opportunity on a national scale. His *proximal processes* framework for educational access and related success may be considered a corollary to the field of medicine's conceptualization of *social determinants of health* (United States Department of Health and Human Services, n.d.). As the unbroken history of oppression's impact lands on marginalized communities, families, and individuals' well-being, it shows up in elevated blood pressure and heart rate, increased diabetes, lower birth rates, higher infant mortality rates, shorter lifespans, and elevated rates of other non-communicable disease-related chronic illness and death (Bambra et al., 2010; Braveman & Gottlieb, 2014; Stringhini et al., 2017; Taylor et al., 2016). Just reacting to the individual symptoms in each patient, student, or family is not going to interrupt the feedback loops that hold these national inequalities in place over generations, requiring that each new generation suffers through them anew. Bronfenbrenner created a pathway toward greater educational access and opportunity for all children in the United States, which has been shown to enhance multiple quality-of-life domains for children and their families, while the evidence shows there is still much more work to do to create equity for poor and underserved communities (Bierman et al., 2014; Burchinal et al., 2011; Shager et al., 2013).

McGoldrick's Family Life Cycle

Monica McGoldrick is a fourth-generation, cisgendered Irish-American woman born in Brooklyn, New York. Director of the Multicultural Family Institute in Highland Park, New Jersey and prolific author of family systems therapy books and training videos, she is also adjunct faculty at the Robert Wood Johnson Medical School (Catanzariti & Datchi, 2018). Dr. McGoldrick's (h.c.) work anchors and expands Murray Bowen's family genograms as a powerful method of drawing out family cultures, history, trauma, and other patterns that inform how family systems cope, and hopefully thrive (McGoldrick et al., 2016). Raised primarily by her White mother and African American caregiver, Margaret Bush, Dr. McGoldrick acknowledges that culture and power were not explicitly addressed during her White, privileged upbringing, but rather a slow dawning which became a more centered treatment focus after a family trip to Ireland. Her own childhood experience of being raised by powerful women (Kehram, 2019, Nov. 21), followed by being mentored by many significant female leaders such as Virginia Satir, probably catalyzed her into a feminist multicultural lens on family therapy (Siegel, 2016).

McGoldrick and her colleagues' approach to family development is to see each member, and the system as a whole, interacting in feedback loops across time; this includes the necessary changing of roles as members are born, age, and die (McGoldrick et al., 2016). When expected transitions are anticipated and prepared for skillfully, there tends not to be much dysfunction in response, but if expected transitions are not prepared for skillfully, or unexpected transitions bring up historical pain and problematic coping, dysfunction can hobble the system as a whole (McGoldrick & Carter, 2011). McGoldrick, therefore, encourages the use of genograms to map out patterns in family systems, so that treatment planning can mindfully address likely trigger points for a crisis, as well as resolve historical pain that leads to emotionally charged reactions.

McGoldrick has spent her career increasingly centering racial, ethnic, and cultural identity formation in family systems work (McGoldrick et al., 2005). Like other feminist clinicians and scholars, she ascribes value to relational- and community-focused behaviors that support and enhance development among and between the generations, as opposed to prioritizing individualistic achievement. Her textbooks and teaching highlight the importance of understanding each family system's worldview with regard to cultural values, rituals, beliefs, and practices, and how to honor each family system's way of cohering across time through these beliefs and practices. McGoldrick is an activist for multicultural inclusivity and systemic clinical competency.

THEORIES IN CONTEXT: RECENT AND RELEVANT RESEARCH

Ethnic and Racial Identity Development

Critical race theory holds that race is socially constructed, as there are no biological differences among racial groups (Goodman, 2000; Roithmayr, 2019; Shih et al., 2007; Smedley & Smedley, 2005). Due to the power of social construction in a colonized world, phenotypic variation still drives oppressive practices the world over, and thus our one species continues to wrestle with social stratification and unjust meaning-making ascribed by those with more power over those with less. The lifelong implications of these oppressive practices are now being identified in how parents and grandparents must prepare their children to cope with the social world, in addition to increased risks with social determinants of health.

In 2018, the Lifespan Model of the ERI Study Group convened to formulate a lifespan model of ethnic–racial identity (ERI; Rogers et al., 2020). This group built their methodology and questions on the critiques and strengths of Phinney, Cross, and others, noting that the last decades have seen exponential growth in ethnic–racial identity research, but that Erikson's norming of development on White populations needs to be further deconstructed in order to articulate relevant outcomes for specific groups across the lifespan. The study group sees ERI development, not as a separate process anchored to a crisis point, but rather as integrated with overall identity development from infancy, incorporating explicit and implicit proximal and distal processes occurring across the lifespan, moderated by supportive relationships (Williams et al., 2020).

The ERI Study Group posits that ethnic–racial *priming* is an "important foundation for implicit ERI perceptions and explicit ERI cognitions in later developmental periods" (Williams et al., 2020, p. 8). For example, infants recognize and show a preference for same-race faces (Beiers, 2013; Timeo et al., 2017; Xiao et al., 2013), not born of animus, but rather a *perceptual narrowing* between 3 and 9 months onto familiar social, cultural, and ethnic–racial stimuli (Williams et al., 2020), which accords with attachment timing and processes. They also note that elementary-aged children's behavior is moderated by positive ERI (e.g., pride in one's ethnic–racial group/s; Marcelo & Yates, 2019; Serrano-Villar & Calzada, 2016): Children can recognize incidents of bias (Brown et al., 2011) and have meaningful conversations about being a member of their respective ethnic–racial group/s (Rogers & Meltzoff, 2017; Turner & Brown, 2007). Furthermore, rather than cognitive development informing children's capacity to self-reflect on their ERI development, it appears that identity-relevant experiences from socialization, discrimination, and other race "encounters" (Cross, 1991; Neville & Cross, 2017) influence when and how ERI develops, and that "two topics warrant greater attention and specificity in empirical and theoretical ERI scholarship: *implicit socialization* and *sociopolitical and historical moments*" (Rogers et al., 2020, para.18). For instance, the murder of Michael Brown, an unarmed Black teenager in Ferguson, Missouri, by a White police officer, shifted the narratives of how children described their racial identity over time (Rogers et al., 2020).

A further concern of the ERI study group was the tendency of developmental models to forward an assumption of what *healthy adjustment* is, often proxied by academic attainment and a lack of externalizing behavior. However, when accounting for the toxic stress of colonizing practices in educational settings in a racially and ethnically stratified society, defining healthy adjustment is not neutral (Philip et al., 2018). For instance, Black youth who attained college scored higher on psychosocial well-being indicators, while significantly worse on physical health measures (Brody et al., 2013). Similarly, with the *model minority myth*, Asian Americans are characterized as successful at the expense of mental well-being (Suárez-Orozco et al., 2006), while Asian American, Pacific Islander, and Muslim students experience increased rates of depression and anxiety due to perceived discrimination (Chen et al., 2014; Tineo et al., 2021). Latinx students who attain college report similar chronic stressors impacting various domains of health and well-being (Cheng et al., 2020; Deckard et al., 2021; Maiya et al., 2021), and Native American college students experience disproportionate rates of victimization, which negatively impact retention (Fish et al., 2017). Developing a sense of belonging moderates these chronic stressors, and thus is central to clinical support for minoritized students (Vaccaro & Newman, 2016).

The research on multiracial populations lags far behind monoracial groups, especially given this is the fastest growing demographic in the United States, slated to be the largest group by 2050. The research that does exist highlights that biracial children tend to show more flexibility in social and learning preferences than monoracial children, including *styleswitching* language to match their interaction partners (Gaither et al., 2014). From a stressor standpoint, multiracial microaggressions elicit multiple chronic stressors, potentially compounded by various targeted group membership experiences (Harris, 2017). It is clear these social determinants of health are absorbed at great cost, possibly leading to chronic inflammation, the foundation of all illness along inherited stress pathways (Cunliffe, 2016; Liu et al., 2017). Rooted in this concern is the ongoing centering of Whiteness as the norm, equated with being "American," and fostering an assumption among White people that they do not have a racial identity, thus can revert to ethnic identity exploration alone, and do not bear responsibility to reflect on how their own racial identity development and processes impact relationships and society (Williams et al., 2020).

The ERI Study Group calls for future research to build on current explorations of ERI bi-directional development among parents, children, and grandparents; to increasingly integrate intersectionality with ERI development; to further deconstruct oppression among intersecting domains of identity (e.g., ERI with gender and sexuality, religion, ability status, age); and to enhance understanding of ERI development for relationships and society (Williams et al., 2020).

Bronfenbrenner

Bronfenbrenner's updated Process–Person–Context–Time model (PPCT) has been described as the most appropriate research design of his theory; this model has been applied in support of public health promotion across the globe, with the World Health Organization using Bronfenbrenner's holistic framework to emphasize mental health as a primary component of quality of life for almost five decades (Eriksson et al., 2018).

Given that Bronfenbrenner's theory evolved through three distinct phases over his lifetime (Bronfenbrenner & Ceci, 1994; Bronfenbrenner, 1979, 1986), scholars sometimes struggle to identify which components of his theory are being utilized in research that references his model (Tudge et al., 2009), which necessarily complicates policy development. The complexity of operationalizing measurable impacts from environmental pressures in various proximities to any given individual means that the bioecological research program is still generating and constructing theory, and is not yet at saturation phase. However, as research in general becomes more interdisciplinary and co-constructive, application of Bronfenbrenner's model highlights that mental health professionals need to be sensitized to many environmental pressures that impinge on our clients, in addition to how our clients' influence the systems they inhabit, and bear in mind how important is the passage of time through developmental phases and multiple contexts, rather than assume the current moment stands outside of ongoing context (Hayes, 2021).

What is abundantly clear is that *cumulative stress* increases the risk for mental health and behavioral problems across the lifespan, though intervention needs to be tailored across the identity spectrums, and in varying distal and proximal processes that impede the individual (Allen et al., 2014; Atzaba-Poria et al., 2004). Parsing whence originates the stressors, and how the stressors interact between the nested systems around the individual requires skillful supervision and ongoing training to intervene effectively.

One recent meta-analytical application of the PPCT approach outlines the multiple impingements on refugees, a growing population now reaching 80 million worldwide that is clearly exposed to multiple chronic and acute risk factors, while still accessing protective factors for resilience. The PPCT model highlights that some children are spending their entire childhood in refugee camps (Hayes, 2021). Because mental health professionals' reach to intervene on distal and even proximal pressures is limited in many ways, we are cautioned against over-emphasizing personal agency in clinical work with any such child, and encouraged to instead,

> place greater emphasis on promoting positive proximal processes operating between an active, evolving refugee child and "significant others" (parents, peers, adults, teachers and support staff), symbols (belief system, language,

culture) and objects (policies and institutions) in their daily environment. (Arakelyan & Ager, 2021, p. 22)

Such an awareness of the many factors beyond any individual's control, even in less chronically stressful circumstances, can render the mental health professional frustrated and overwhelmed with where to start and how to proceed with clients suffering from multiple impingements. While allies may provide empathy for the individual or client system experiencing the stressors, advocates seek out necessary resources to reduce burdens and increase access, and activists continually confront the systemic barriers embedded in oppressive practices, creating opportunities wherever possible for the less privileged by working in interdisciplinary teams to effect lasting and meaningful change to the exo- and macrosystems impinging on microsystems across the chronosystem. Because of the ongoing emotional labor involved to be civically engaged as an activist long term, this author team encourages you to find like-minded practitioners as supports and mentors, and create a self-care plan and team around yourself, to prevent compassion fatigue.

SUMMARY

Context and culture shape every part of the developmental process. In this chapter we began exploring this concept with a focused attention on developmental models, theories, and updated research that recognize facets of culture and context in human development. Though not exhaustive, the theories and models in this chapter were intended to provide a framework for understanding the ways in which who we are, where we live, when we live, and all of the intersecting elements of our privilege and marginalization impact our lifespan trajectories.

We began the chapter with a discussion of human development and social justice with a particular focus on your role as a mental health professional ally, advocate, and activist. This was followed by an introduction to some key models of identity development. We first began with an exploration of Pamela Hays's ADDRESSING model of intersectionality. This was followed by a discussion of privilege and oppression and an emphasis on Ken Hardy's Privileged and Subjugated Task model. We also presented initial information on racial and ethnic identity development through the works of Jean Phinney and William Cross. Next, we explored female identity development and the contributions Carol Gilligan, Nancy Downing, and Kristin Roush made to this area. Finally, we wrapped up this section of the chapter with a look at sexual orientation identity development and the work of Vivenne Cass.

The chapter continued with a look at systemic and contextual models of development. While considered more "traditional," these models factor in an understanding of social impact, ecology, and family systems as part of the developmental process. Within this section we explored Lev Vygotsky's Sociocultural theory, Urie Bronfenbrenner's Bioecological model, and Monica McGoldrick's Family Lifecycle. Recognizing that culture and context also shape theories developed with these particular lenses in mind, in the final section of this chapter we looked at some of the important updates and relevant research that is tied to the cultural and contextual models of this chapter. In particular, we explored developments in Critical Race theory, ethnic–racial identity, and Bronfenbrenner's updated Process–Person–Context–Time model.

Some of the models and theories you were exposed to in this chapter will be expounded upon in future chapters, whereas others may not. Alternatively, you will find that there are additional culture- and context-driven theories in future chapters that were not covered here. Though we have attempted to highlight some of the most significant models of development that factor in culture and context, we recognize we could not do justice to them all in a single text. Instead, our goal is that you use the information from this chapter as a conceptual frame to foster critical analysis and understanding of culture and context as you explore additional theories and models moving forward.

REFERENCES

Adams, H. L., & Phillips, L. (2009). Ethnic related variations from the cass model of homosexual identity formation: the experiences of two-spirit, lesbian and gay Native Americans. *Journal of Homosexuality*, 56(7), 959–976. https://doi.org/10.1080/00918360903187895

Allen, J., Balfour, R., Bell, R., & Marmot, M. (2014). Social determinants of mental health. *International Review of Psychiatry*, 26(4), 392–407. https://doi.org/10.3109/09540261.2014.928270

Allen, W. (2018). *The somatic experience of white privilege: A dance/movement therapy approach to racialized interactions*.[Expressive Therapies Dissertations]. https://digitalcommons.lesley.edu/expressive_dissertations/59

American Psychiatric Association. (2013). *Diagnostic and Statistical Manual of Mental Disorders* (5th ed.). https://doi.org/10.1176/appi.books.9780890425596

Ashiabi, G. S., & O'Neal, K. K. (2015). Child social development in context: An examination of some propositions in Bronfenbrenner's bioecological theory. *SAGE Open*, 5(2).

Atzaba-Poria, N., Pike, A., & Deater-Deckard, K. (2004). Do risk factors for problem behaviour act in a cumulative manner? An examination of ethnic minority and majority children through an ecological perspective. *Journal of Child Psychology and Psychiatry*, 45(4), 707–718. https://doi.org/10.1111/j.1469-7610.2004.00265.x

Bambra, C., Gibson, M., Sowden, A., Wright, K., Whitehead, M., & Petticrew, M. (2010). Tackling the wider social determinants of health and health inequalities: evidence from systematic reviews. *Journal of Epidemiology and Community Health*, 64(4), 284–291. https://doi.org/10.1136/jech.2008.082743

Bates, L. M., Hankivsky, O., & Springer, K. W. (2009). Gender and health inequities: a comment on the Final Report of the WHO Commission on the Social Determinants of Health. *Social Science & Medicine*, 69(7), 1002–1004. https://doi.org/10.1016/j.socscimed.2009.07.021

Beiers, S. (2013). *Infant perceptions of mixed-race faces: An exploration of the hypodescent rule in 8.5 month-old infants*. Pitzer Senior. Theses Paper 46. http://scholarship.claremont.edu/pitzer_theses/46

Bierman, K. L., Nix, R. L., Heinrichs, B. S., Domitrovich, C. E., Gest, S. D., Welsh, J. A., & Gill, S. (2014). Effects of Head Start REDI on children's outcomes 1 year later in different kindergarten contexts. *Child Development*, 85, 140–159. https://doi.org/10.1111/cdev.12117

Braveman, P., & Gottlieb, L. (2014). The social determinants of health: it's time to consider the causes of the causes. *Public Health Reports*, 129(1_suppl2), 19–31. https://doi.org/10.1177/00333549141291S206

Brody, G. H., Yu, T., Chen, E., Miller, G. E., Kogan, S. M., & Beach, S. R. H. (2013). Is resilience only skin deep?: rural African Americans' socioeconomic status-related risk and competence in preadolescence and psychological adjustment and allostatic load at age 19. *Psychological Science*, 24(7), 1285–1293. https://doi.org/10.1177/0956797612471954

Bronfenbrenner, U. (1979). *The ecology of human development: Experiments by nature and design.* Harvard University Press.

Bronfenbrenner, U. (1986). Ecology of the family as a context for human development: Research perspectives. *Developmental Psychology, 22*(6), 723–742. https://doi.org/10.1037/0012-1649 .22.6.723

Bronfenbrenner, U., & Ceci, S. J. (1994). Nature-nurture reconceptualized in developmental perspective: a bioecological model. *Psychological Review, 101*(4), 568–586. https://doi.org/10 .1037/0033-295x.101.4.568

Brown, C. S., Alabi, B. O., Huynh, V. W., & Masten, C. L. (2011). Ethnicity and gender in late childhood and early adolescence: group identity and awareness of bias. *Developmental Psychology, 47*(2), 463–471. https://doi.org/10.1037/a0021819

Brown, L. M., & Gilligan, C. (1992). *Meeting at the crossroads: Women's psychology and girls' development.* Harvard University Press. https://doi.org/10.4159/harvard.9780674731837

Burchinal, M., Kainz, K., & Cai, Y. (2011). How well do our measures of quality predict child outcomes? A meta-analysis and coordinated analysis of data from large-scale studies of early childhood settings. In M. Zaslow, I. Martinez-Beck, K. Tout, & T. Halle (Eds.), *Quality measurement in early childhood settings* (pp. 11–31). Paul H. Brookes Publishing Co.

Cass, V. C. (1979). Homosexual identity formation: a theoretical model. *Journal of Homosexuality, 4,* 219–235. https://doi.org/10.1300/J082v04n03_01

Cass, V. C. (1984). Homosexual identity formation: Testing a theoretical model. *The Journal of Sex Research, 20*(2), 143–167. https://doi.org/10.1080/00224498409551214

Catanzariti, D., & Datchi, C. (2018). McGoldrick, Monica. In J. Lebow, A. Chambers, & D. Breunlin (Eds.), *Encyclopedia of Couple and Family Therapy.* Springer, Cham. https://doi .org/10.1007/978-3-319-15877-%208_682-1

Chen, A. C.-C., Szalacha, L. A., & Menon, U. (2014). Perceived discrimination and its associations with mental health and substance use among Asian American and Pacific Islander undergraduate and graduate students. *Journal of American College Health, 62*(6), 390–398. https://doi.org/10.1080/07448481.2014.917648

Cheng, H. L., McDermott, R. C., Wong, Y. J., & McCullough, K. M. (2020). Perceived discrimination and academic distress among Latinx college students: A cross-lagged longitudinal investigation. *Journal of Counseling Psychology, 67*(3), 401–408. https://doi.org/10.1037/ cou0000397

Coates, T.-N. (2015). *Between the world and me.* Spiegel & Grau.

Cross, W. E. (1971). *The Negro-to-Black conversion experience* (pp. 13–27). Black World.

Cross, W. E. (1991). *Shades of black: Diversity in African-American identity.* Temple University Press.

Cross, W. E., & Fhagen-Smith, P. (2001). Patterns of African American identity development: A life span perspective. In B. Jackson & C. Wijeyesinghe (Eds.), *New perspectives on racial identity development: A theoretical and practical anthology* (pp. 243–270). New York University Press.

Cross, W. E., & Vandiver, B. J. (2001). Nigrescence theory and measurement: Introducing the Cross Racial Identity Scale (CRIS). In J. G. Ponlerott, J. M. Casas, L. M. Suzuki, & C. M. Alexander (Eds.), *Handbook of Multicultural Counseling* (2nd Ed). Sage.

Cunliffe, V. T. (2016). The epigenetic impacts of social stress: how does social adversity become biologically embedded? *Epigenomics, 8*(12), 1653–1669. https://doi.org/10.2217/epi-2016-0075

Deckard, F. M., Goosby, B. J., & Cheadle, J. E. (2021). Debt stress, college stress: Implications for black and latinx students' mental health. *Race and Social Problems,* 1–16. https://doi.org/10 .1007/s12552-021-09346-z

Degges-White, S., Rice, B., & Myers, J. E. (2000). Revisiting Cass' theory of sexual identity formation: A study of lesbian development. *Journal of Mental Health Counseling, 22*(4), 318.

Downing, N. E., & Roush, K. L. (1985). From passive acceptance to active commitment: A model of feminist identity development for women. *The Counseling Psychologist, 13*(4), 695–709. https://doi.org/10.1177/0011000085134013

El-Mekki, S. (2018). Educational justice: Which are you — an advocate, ally, or activist? *The Education Trust.* https://edtrust.org/the-equity-line/educational-justice-which-are-you-an-advocate-ally-or-activist

Eppler, C. (2019). Ecosystem in family systems theory. In J. L. Lebow, A. L. Chambers, & D. C. Breunlin(Eds.), *Encyclopedia of Couple and Family Therapy.* Springer, Cham. https://doi.org/10.1007/978-3-319-49425-8_260

Eriksson, M., Ghazinour, M., & Hammarström, A. (2018). Different uses of Bronfenbrenner's ecological theory in public mental health research: what is their value for guiding public mental health policy and practice? *Social Theory & Health, 16*(4), 414–433. https://doi.org/10.1057/s41285-018-0065-6

Fearnley, B. (2020). Becoming a reflexive and reflective practice educator: considering theoretical constructs of Bronfenbrenner and Bourdieu for social work student field placements. *Social Work Education,* 1–13. https://doi.org/10.1080/02615479.2020.1796954

Ferdoush, M. A. (2016). Revisiting cass's model of homosexual identity development in context of bangladesh society. *SAGE Open, 6*(2). https://doi.org/10.1177/2158244016651913

Fish, J., Livingston, J. A., VanZile-Tamsen, C., & Wolf, D. A. P. S. (2017). Victimization and substance use among native american college students. *Journal of College Student Development, 58*(3), 413–431. https://doi.org/10.1353/csd.2017.0031

Gaither, S. E., Chen, E. E., Corriveau, K. H., Harris, P. L., Ambady, N., & Sommers, S. R. (2014). Monoracial and biracial children: effects of racial identity saliency on social learning and social preferences. *Child Development, 85*(6), 2299–2316. https://doi.org/10.1111/cdev.12266

Gilligan, C. (1979). Woman's place in man's life cycle. *Harvard Educational Review, 49*(4), 431–446. https://doi.org/10.17763/haer.49.4.h1365735413g463

Gilligan, C. (1982). *In a different voice: Psychological theory and women's development.* Harvard University Press.

Gilligan, C. (2011). *Looking back to look forward: Revisiting in a different voice.* Center for Hellenic Studies. http://nrs.harvard.edu/urn3:hlnc.essay:Gilligan.Looking_Back_to_Look_Forward.2011

Gilligan, C. (2018). Revisiting "in a different voice." *LEARNing Landscapes, 11*(2), 25–30. https://doi.org/10.36510/learnland.v11i2.942

Ginther, A. M. (2020). My body is a map, my voice is the path:(trans) racialized somaticities and Roy Hart voice work. In *In Somatic Voices in Performance Research and Beyond* (pp. 98–111). Routledge.

Goodman, A. H. (2000). Why genes don't count (for racial differences in health). *American Journal of Public Health, 90*(11), 1699–1702. https://doi.org/10.2105/ajph.90.11.1699

Gutkin, T. B. (2012). Ecological psychology: Replacing the medical model paradigm for school-based psychological and psychoeducational services. *Journal of Educational and Psychological Consultation, 22*(1–2), 1–20. https://doi.org/10.1080/10474412.2011.649652

Hansen, N. D. (2002). Reflections on feminist identity development: Implications for theory,measurement, and research. *The Counseling Psychologist, 30*(1), 87–95. https://doi.org/10.1177/0011000002301005

Hardy, K. V. (2016). Anti-racist approaches for shaping theoretical and practice paradigms. In M. PenderGreene & A. Siskin (Eds.), *Anti-racist strategies for the health and human services.* Oxford University Press.

Hardy, K. V. (2022). *The enduring, invisible, and ubiquitous centrality of whiteness: Implications for clinical practice and beyond.* W. W. Norton, Incorporated.

Hardy, K. V., & Laszloffy, T. A. (2017). The cultural genogram key to training culturally competent family therapists. In K. V. Hardy & T. Bobes (Eds.), *Promoting cultural sensitivity in supervision: A manual for practitioners.*

Harris, J. C. (2017). Multiracial college students' experiences with multiracial microaggressions. *Race Ethnicity and Education, 20*(4), 429–445. https://doi.org/10.1080/13613324.2016.1248836

Hayes, S. W. (2021). Commentary: Deepening understanding of refugee children and adolescents using Bronfenbrenner's bioecological and PPCT models - A Commentary on Arakelyan and Ager (2020). *Journal of Child Psychology and Psychiatry, and Allied Disciplines, 62*(5), 510–513. https://doi.org/10.1111/jcpp.13403

Hays, P. A. (1996). Addressing the complexities of culture and gender in counseling. *Journal of Counseling & Development, 74*(4), 332–338. https://doi.org/10.1002/j.1556-6676.1996.tb01876.x

Hays, P. A. (2008). *Addressing cultural complexities in practice, second edition: Assessment, diagnosis,and therapy.* American Psychological Association. https://doi.org/10.1037/11650-000

Ignatiev, N., & Garvey, J. (1996). *Race traitor.* Routledge.

Jovanović, G. (2020). How lost and accomplished revolutions shaped psychology: Early Critical Theory (Frankfurt School), Wilhelm Reich, and Vygotsky. *Theory & Psychology, 30*(2), 202–222. https://doi.org/10.1177/0959354320917216

Juncadella, C. M. (2013). *What is the impact of the application of the Nonviolent communication model on the development of empathy? Overview of research and outcomes* [Thesis for MSc in Psychotherapy Studies]. University of Sheffield.

Kehram, E. (2019, November 21). *Marriage and family therapy.* https://multiculturalfamily.org/tag/podcast

Kirkland, P. (2020, September 12). *19 families by nearly 97 acres of land in Georgia to create a city safe for Black people.* Video file. https://www.cnn.com/2020/09/12/us/freedom-black-cooperative-toomsboro/index.html

Knibb-Lamouche, J. (2012). Culture as a social determinant of health. In *Commissioned paper prepared for the Institute on Medicine, Roundtable on the Promotion of Health Equity and the Elimination of Health Disparities, Seattle, WA.*

Lang, S. (2005, September 26). Urie Bronfenbrenner, father of Head Start program and preeminent "human ecologist," dies at age 88. *Cornell Chronicle.* https://news.cornell.edu/stories/2005/09/head-startfounder-urie-bronfenbrenner-dies-88

Lau, J., & Ng, K. M. (2014). Conceptualizing the counseling training environment using bronfenbrenner's ecological theory. *International Journal for the Advancement of Counselling, 36*(4), 423–439. https://doi.org/10.1007/s10447-014-9220-5

Lewis, M. E., Hartwell, E. E., & Myhra, L. L. (2018). Decolonizing mental health services for indigenous clients: A training program for mental health professionals. *American Journal of Community Psychology, 62*(3–4), 330–339. https://doi.org/10.1002/ajcp.12288

Liu, Y. Z., Wang, Y. X., & Jiang, C. L. (2017). Inflammation: The common pathway of stress-related diseases. *Frontiers in Human Neuroscience, 11,* 316. https://doi.org/10.3389/fnhum.2017.00316

Lucero, E. (2011). From tradition to evidence: decolonization of the evidence-based practice system. *Journal of Psychoactive Drugs, 43*(4), 319–324. https://doi.org/10.1080/02791072.2011.628925

Maiya, S., Carlo, G., Davis, A. N., & Streit, C. (2021). Relations among acculturative stress, internalizing symptoms, and prosocial behaviors in Latinx college students. *Journal of Latinx Psychology, 9*(2), 77–91. https://doi.org/10.1037/lat0000177

Marcelo, A. K., & Yates, T. M. (2019). Young children's ethnic-racial identity moderates the impact of early discrimination experiences on child behavior problems. *Cultural Diversity & Ethnic Minority Psychology, 25*(2), 253–265. https://doi.org/10.1037/cdp0000220

Marszalek III, J. F., Cashwell, C. S., Dunn, M. S., & Jones, K. H. (2004). Comparing gay identity development theory to cognitive development: An empirical study. *Journal of Homosexuality, 48*(1), 103–123. https://doi.org/10.1300/J082v48n01_05

McGoldrick, M., & Carter, B. (2011). Families transformed by the divorce cycle: Reconstituted,multinuclear, recoupled and remarried families. In M. McGoldrick, B. Carter, & N. Garcia-Preto (Eds.), *The expanding family life cycle* (pp. 317–335). Pearson.

McGoldrick, M., Garcia Preto, N. A., & Carter, B. A. (2016). *The expanding family life cycle: Individual, family, and social perspectives* (5th ed). Pearson.

McGoldrick, M., Giordano, J., & Garcia-Preto, N. (Eds.). (2005). *Ethnicity and family therapy.* Guilford Press.

McLeod, S. (2020). Lev Vygotsky's sociocultural theory. Simply Psychology. https://www.sim-plypsychology.org/vygotsky.html

Melton, M. L. (2018). Ally, activist, advocate: Addressing role complexities for the multiculturally competent psychologist. *Professional Psychology: Research and Practice, 49*(1), 83–89. https://doi.org/10.1037/pro0000175

Menakem, R. (2017). *My grandmother's hands.* Central Recovery Press.

Merçon-Vargas, E. A., Lima, R. F. F., Rosa, E. M., & Tudge, J. (2020). Processing proximal processes: What bronfenbrenner meant, what he didn't mean, and what he should have meant. *Journal of Family Theory & Review, 12*(3), 321–334. https://doi.org/10.1111/jftr.12373

Mizock, L., & Page, K. V. (2016). Evaluating the ally role: Contributions, limitations, and the activist position in counseling and psychology. *Journal for Social Action in Counseling & Psychology, 8*(1), 17–33. https://doi.org/10.33043/JSACP.8.1.17-33

Morrow, M., & Malcoe, L. H. (Eds.). (2017). *Critical inquiries for social justice in mental health.* University of Toronto Press.

Murry, V. M., Butler-Barnes, S. T., Mayo-Gamble, T. L., & Inniss-Thompson, M. N. (2018). Excavating new constructs for family stress theories in the context of everyday life experiences of black american families. *Journal of Family Theory & Review, 10*(2), 384–405. https://doi.org/10.1111/jftr.12256

Neville, H. A., & Cross, W. E. (2017). Racial awakening: Epiphanies and encounters in black racial identity. *Cultural Diversity & Ethnic Minority Psychology, 23*(1), 102–108. https://doi.org/10.1037/cdp0000105

Nowotny, K. M., & Kuptsevych-Timmer, A. (2018). Health and justice: Framing incarceration as a social determinant of health for black men in the united states. *Sociology Compass, 12*(3), e12566. https://doi.org/10.1111/soc4.12566

Philip, T. M., Bang, M., & Jackson, K. (2018). Articulating the "how," the "for what," the "for whom," and the "with whom" in concert: A call to broaden the benchmarks of our scholarship. *Cognition and Instruction, 36*(2), 83–88. https://doi.org/10.1080/07370008.2018.1413530

Phinney, J. S. (1989). Stages of ethnic identity development in minority group adolescents. *The Journal of Early Adolescence, 9*(1–2), 34–49. https://doi.org/10.1177/0272431689091004

Phinney, J. S. (2006). Ethnic Identity Exploration in Emerging Adulthood. In J. J. Arnett & J. L. Tanner (Eds.), *Emerging adults in America: Coming of age in the 21st century* (pp. 117–134). American Psychological Association. https://doi.org/10.1037/11381-000

Phinney, J. S., & Ong, A. D. (2007). Conceptualization and measurement of ethnic identity: Current status and future directions. *Journal of Counseling Psychology, 54*(3), 271–281. https://doi.org/10.1037/0022-0167.54.3.271

Porges, S. W., & Dana, D. (2018). *Clinical applications of the polyvagal theory: The emergence of polyvagal-informed therapies* (Norton series on interpersonal neurobiology). WW Norton Company.

Pulido, L. (2015). Geographies of race and ethnicity 1: White supremacy vs white privilege in environmental racism research. *Progress in Human Geography, 39*(6), 809–817.

Quintana, S. M. (2007). Racial and ethnic identity: Developmental perspectives and research. *Journal of Counseling Psychology, 54*(3), 259–270. https://doi.org/10.1037/0022-0167.54.3.259

Rogers, L. O., Kiang, L., White, L., Calzada, E. J., Umaña-Taylor, A. J., Byrd, C., Williams, C. D., Marks, A., & Whitesell, N. (2020). Persistent concerns: Questions for research on ethnic-racial identity development. *Research in Human Development, 17*(2–3), 130–153. https://doi.org/10.1080/15427609.2020.1831881

Rogers, L. O., & Meltzoff, A. N. (2017). Is gender more important and meaningful than race? An analysis of racial and gender identity among Black, White, and mixed-race children. *Cultural Diversity & Ethnic Minority Psychology, 23*(3), 323–334. https://doi.org/10.1037/cdp0000125

Roithmayr, D. (2019). Introduction to critical race theory in educational research and praxis. In *In Race is… race isn't* (pp. 1–6). Routledge.

Rosenberg, M. B. (2003). *Nonviolent communication: A language of life*. PuddleDancer Press.

Scrine, E. (2021). The limits of resilience and the need for resistance: Articulating the role of music therapy with young people within a shifting trauma paradigm. *Frontiers in Psychology, 12*, 26. https://doi.org/10.3389/fpsyg.2021.600245

Seginer, R. (2006). Parents' educational involvement: A developmental ecology perspective. *Parenting:Science and Practice, 6*(1), 1–48. https://doi.org/10.1207/s15327922par0601_1

Serrano-Villar, M., & Calzada, E. J. (2016). Ethnic identity: Evidence of protective effects for young, Latino children. *Journal of Applied Developmental Psychology, 42*, 21–30. https://doi.org/10.1016/j.appdev.2015.11.002

Shager, H. M., Schindler, H. S., Magnuson, K. A., Duncan, G. J., Yoshikawa, H., & Hart, C. M. D. (2013). Can research design explain variation in head start research results? A meta-analysis of cognitive and achievement outcomes. *Educational Evaluation and Policy Analysis, 35*(1), 76–95. https://doi.org/10.3102/0162373712462453

Sheidow, A. J., Henry, D. B., Tolan, P. H., & Strachan, M. K. (2014). The role of stress exposure and family functioning in internalizing outcomes of urban families. *Journal of Child and Family Studies, 23*(8), 1351–1365. https://doi.org/10.1007/s10826-013-9793-3

Shelton, L. G. (2018). *The Bronfenbrenner primer: A guide to develecology*. Routledge. https://doi.org/10.4324/9781315136066

Shih, M., Bonam, C., Sanchez, D., & Peck, C. (2007). The social construction of race: biracial identity and vulnerability to stereotypes. *Cultural Diversity & Ethnic Minority Psychology, 13*(2), 125–133. https://doi.org/10.1037/1099-9809.13.2.125

Siegel, J. (2016). A journal of family social work conversation with Monica McGoldrick, LCSW. *Journal of Family Social Work, 19*(1), 56–64. https://doi.org/10.1080/10522158.2015.1133954

Smedley, A., & Smedley, B. D. (2005). Race as biology is fiction, racism as a social problem is real: Anthropological and historical perspectives on the social construction of race. *The American Psychologist, 60*(1), 16–26. https://doi.org/10.1037/0003-066X.60.1.16

Stringhini, S., Carmeli, C., Jokela, M., Avendaño, M., Muennig, P., Guida, F., Ricceri, F., d'Errico, A., Barros, H., Bochud, M., Chadeau-Hyam, M., Clavel-Chapelon, F., Costa, G., Delpierre, C., Fraga, S., Goldberg, M., Giles, G. G., Krogh, V., Kelly-Irving, M., & LIFEPATH consortium. (2017). Socioeconomic status and the 25 × 25 risk factors as determinants of premature mortality: a multicohort study and meta-analysis of 1·7 million men and women. *Lancet, 389*(10075), 1229–1237. https://doi.org/10.1016/S0140-6736(16)32380-7

Suárez-Orozco, C., Todorova, I., & Qin, D. B. (2006). The well-being of immigrant adolescents: A longitudinal perspective on risk and protective factors. In F. A. Villarruel & T. Luster (Eds.), *Child psychology and mental health. The crisis in youth mental health: Critical issues and effective programs. Disorders in adolescence* (Vol. 2, pp. 53–83). Praeger Publishers/Greenwood Publishing Group.

Taylor, L. A., Tan, A. X., Coyle, C. E., Ndumele, C., Rogan, E., Canavan, M., Curry, L. A., & Bradley, E. H. (2016). Leveraging the social determinants of health: What works? *PloS One, 11*(8), e0160217. https://doi.org/10.1371/journal.pone.0160217

Terrizzi, J. A., & Shook, N. J. (2020). On the origin of shame: Does shame emerge from an evolved disease-avoidance architecture? *Frontiers in Behavioral Neuroscience, 14*, 19. https://doi.org/10.3389/fnbeh.2020.00019

Timeo, S., Farroni, T., & Maass, A. (2017). Race and color: Two sides of one story? Development of biases in categorical perception. *Child Development, 88*(1), 83–102. https://doi.org/10.1111/cdev.12564

Tineo, P., Lowe, S. R., Reyes-Portillo, J. A., & Fuentes, M. A. (2021). Impact of perceived discrimination on depression and anxiety among Muslim college students: The role of acculturative stress, religious support, and Muslim identity. *The American Journal of Orthopsychiatry, 91*(4), 454–463. https://doi.org/10.1037/ort0000545

Tippett, K. (2021, April 15). Resmaa Menakem: Notice the rage, notice the silence. *On Being*. https://onbeing.org/programs/resmaa-menakem-notice-the-rage-notice-the-silence

Trinh, T. C. (2020). *The somatic experience of Asian Americans in dominant culture spaces: The effects of internalized racism* [Doctoral dissertation]. Pacifica Graduate Institute.

Tudge, J. R. H., Mokrova, I., Hatfield, B. E., & Karnik, R. B. (2009). Uses and misuses of bronfenbrenner's bioecological theory of human development. *Journal of Family Theory & Review*, *1*(4), 198–210. https://doi.org/10.1111/j.1756-2589.2009.00026.x

Turner, K. L., & Brown, C. S. (2007). The centrality of gender and ethnic identities across individuals and contexts. *Social Development*, *16*(4), 700–719. https://doi.org/10.1111/j.1467-9507.2007.00403.x

United States Department of Health and Human Services. (n.d.). Retrieved September 21, 2021, from https://health.gov/healthypeople/objectives-and-data/social-determinants-health/literature- summaries/early-childhood-development-and-education

Vaccaro, A., & Newman, B. M. (2016). Development of a sense of belonging for privileged and minoritized students: An emergent model. *Journal of College Student Development*, *57*(8), 925–942. https://doi.org/10.1353/csd.2016.0091

Vandiver, B. J., Fhagen-Smith, P. E., Cokley, K. O., Cross, W. E., & Worrell, F. C. (2001). Cross's nigrescence model: From theory to scale to theory. *Journal of Multicultural Counseling and Development*, *29*(3), 174–200. https://doi.org/10.1002/j.2161-1912.2001.tb00516.x

Vygotsky, L. S. (1962). *Thought and language*. MIT Press. https://doi.org/10.1037/11193-000

Vygotsky, L. S. (1978). *Mind in society: The development of higher psychological processes*. Harvard University Press.

Vygotsky, L. S. (1987). Problems of general psychology. In R. W. Rieber & A. S. Carton (Eds.), *The collected works of L. S. Vygotsky* (Vol. 1). Plenum Press.

Vygotsky, L. S., Rieber, R. W., & Wollock, J. (Eds.). (1997). Problems of the Theory and History of Psychology. (R. van Der Veer, Trans.). In *The collected works of LS. Vygotsky* (Vol. 3). Plenum Press.

Wadsworth, M. E., & Rienks, S. L. (2012, July). *CYF News*. http://www.apa.org/pi/families/resources/newsletter/2012/07/stress-mechanism

Ward, C., & Geeraert, N. (2016). Advancing acculturation theory and research: the acculturation process in its ecological context. *Current Opinion in Psychology*, *8*, 98–104. https://doi.org/10.1016/j.copsyc.2015.09.021

Wertsch, J. V. (1988). Psychology: L. S. Vygotsky's "new" theory of mind. *The American Scholar*, *57*(1), 81–89. http://www.jstor.org/stable/41211493

Williams, C. D., Byrd, C. M., Quintana, S. M., Anicama, C., Kiang, L., Umaña-Taylor, A. J., Calzada, E. J., Pabón Gautier, M., Ejesi, K., Tuitt, N. R., Martinez-Fuentes, S., White, L., Marks, A., Rogers, L. O., & Whitesell, N. (2020). A Lifespan Model of Ethnic-Racial Identity. *Research in Human Development*, *17*(2–3), 99–129. https://doi.org/10.1080/15427609.2020.1831882

Worrell, F. C. (2008). Nigrescence attitudes in adolescence, emerging adulthood, and adulthood. *Journal of Black Psychology*, *34*(2), 156–178. https://doi.org/10.1177/0095798408315118

Worrell, F. C., Cross, W. E., & Vandiver, B. J. (2001). Nigrescence theory: Current status and challenges for the future. *Journal of Multicultural Counseling and Development*, *29*(3), 201–213. https://doi.org/10.1002/j.2161-1912.2001.tb00517.x

Xiao, W. S., Xiao, N. G., Quinn, P. C., Anzures, G., & Lee, K. (2013). Development of face scanning for own- and other-race faces in infancy. *International Journal of Behavioral Development*, *37*(2), 100–105. https://doi.org/10.1177/0165025412467584

Yakushko, O., & Chronister, K. M. (2005). Immigrant women and counseling: The invisible others. *Journal of Counseling & Development*, *83*(3), 292–298. https://doi.org/10.1002/j.1556-6678.2005.tb00346.x

PART II
AGES AND STAGES

CHAPTER 4

Cultural and Contextual Factors of Infancy Through Early Childhood

LEARNING OBJECTIVES

Upon completion of this chapter, students will be able to:

1. Describe the perinatal and early childhood periods of human development.
2. Identify risk and resiliency factors for infancy and early childhood.
3. Recognize contextual factors that may merit therapeutic attention for early individual and relational healing.
4. Describe how cultural humility and trauma-informed care may be applied for early developmental needs in families, as well as longitudinal effects from this foundational period.

CASE STUDY 4.1: THE CASE OF XQUENDA

Meet Xquenda (aka "Miguel" at school), a 5-year-old child assigned male at birth, currently presumed to be cisgender based on self-referential pronouns and gender presentation such as, "Yo soy el único que juega con la camioneta" (I am the only one (male) who plays with the truck). Xquenda is referred to you, a mental health practitioner at a public elementary school, in a migrant rural residential suburb surrounded by strawberry fields. The teacher's chief complaint is that Xquenda regularly disrupts the kindergarten classroom with tantrums and potty accidents, and has difficulty with transitions. Recently, Xquenda
hit a classmate in the head with a toy truck, and then did not show any apparent remorse for the hurt caused, which greatly concerned the teacher.

Xquenda's parents, Inda Jani and Surem, speak enough Spanish to negotiate for commercial goods and interface independently with local professionals, but their mother tongues are Zapotec and Yaqui in origin. Their children have become fluently Spanish speaking in the shared home, and their daughter Nayeli is now also fluent in English due to bilingual immersion in school.

Through the interpreter, you learn from the parents that after 6 years of slowly losing their family lands due to corporatization of agriculture in their sending country (Oxfam, 2016), the parents discovered they were pregnant again and decided to liquidate their meager holdings in search of more potential security for their growing family. They migrated from their land to a local town, where there was no consistent work, then to the nearest city, where there was no real opportunity to find affordable housing in a safe area (Garcini et al., 2019). They eventually realized they would have to keep moving to find steady work and be able to send some money to their parents and grandparents, who were all struggling to pay rent in the local town.

As trust develops with the parents over the next several months, they share further about the stress of traveling north for many weeks while pregnant, caring for their young daughter while on foot and hitchhiking, and carefully alluding to some mysterious event they suffered at the hands of the *coyote*, or smuggler who carried them across the border (Cleaveland & Kirsch, 2020; de Arellano et al., 2018). They were so grateful to finally arrive at the busy home of their neighbors' cousins in this farm laborers' community, where they have both found seasonal work in the fields and canneries in order to rent one room, provide for their children, and send a little money home to help sustain their now uprooted elders (Pew Trust, 2016).

Since you have consistently demonstrated that you are not an authority figure focused on their documentation status, the parents reveal to you that 3 months after they crossed the border, Xquenda was born with a difficult temperament (Thiel et al., 2020). He was not as easy to soothe as his older sister, did not latch well or nurse to satiation. He was colicky and had a more reactive startle response, and his long hours of frustrated crying caused tension in the household providing hospitality for the family. The parents admit that they had a hard time enjoying Xquenda's infancy, and that taking turns caring for him took a toll on their marriage even more than folding their firstborn into their lives. They also acknowledge that they had a hard time managing the pressure of this while trying not to upset their new housemates, and that they feared they would need to find an apartment, which was beyond their means.

The family has been to the doctor for regular check-ups, but they could not afford preschool, did not know about Head Start, and are all now suffering chronic upper respiratory ailments that seem never to abate (Mamane et al., 2015; Tarmure et al., 2020). They are concerned for Xquenda's behavior and well-being, and very much want to know how to help him.

INFANCY THROUGH EARLY CHILDHOOD

This stage of life is focused on pre-conception through about ages 5 through 8, depending on the theory to which one most ascribes. Most Western child development theories start development at birth; however, as developmental science is becoming more diversified and inclusive, early childhood and ongoing lifespan development is now acknowledging that pre-birth experiences must be included for clinical assessment and intervention (Evertz et al., 2021; Mckee et al., 2018; Seng & Taylor, 2015; Stephenson et al., 2018; Verny, 1984, 1989, 1996, 2014). Of particular concern are the neurological, emotional, behavioral impacts of in utero *teratogen* ("malformation-causing") exposure (Chasnoff, 1989; Chasnoff et al., 1990, 1998, 2005, 2015, 2018; Latini et al., 2006; Ragusa et al., 2021; Ross et al., 2015) and innumerable other forms of trauma and toxic stress that impact medical and mental health (Danese & Lewis, 2017; Fleming et al., 2018; Gilliland et al., 1999;

Goldstein et al., 2021; Schwarze et al., 2013; Herzog & Schmahl, 2018), even trans-generationally (Jawaid et al., 2018; Lehrner & Yehuda, 2018; Perroud et al., 2014; Serpeloni et al., 2017). This chapter introduces the reader to theory and research related to early childhood development, including the bi-directional developmental impact children and parents/caregivers have on each other (Crouter & Booth, 2003; Gouze et al., 2017; Schrock & Woodruff-Borden, 2010; Simmons et al., 2021).

STUDENT REFLECTION 4.1

Looking at Xquenda's experience of conception and gestation compared to his older sister's, his parents were in a much less stable lived experience when he was growing in utero. They were probably grieving the inevitable loss of ancestral land as corporate agriculture moved in around them (Garcini et al., 2019). Depending on their water source, they may have been exposed to fertilizer and/or pesticide runoff, made to have toxic effects on living organisms (Asghar et al., 2016; Beyond Pesticides, n.d.; Roberts & Karr, 2012). The painful decision to leave the home they'd known and loved for generations likely led to waves of grief and fear as they looked for viable solutions nearby, only to be forced to accept that they would need to keep moving further away from home and family. Losing access to critical buffering relationships of beloved elders and peers to help provide emotional regulation and practical support, the parents would have to increasingly rely on each other for empathy, encouragement, and role tasks (Garcini et al., 2019); this can increase the pressure on a couple to contain stress and attune effectively under growing duress, which can often result in conflict or withdrawal when one is overwhelmed in adult attachment relationships (Johnson, 2019). It is also likely that food security and necessary rest to break down stress neurochemistry was intermittent, and sometimes insufficient, to mitigate their impact on the developing fetus (Barker et al., 2018; Monk et al., 2012; Evertz et al., 2021; Hasanjanzadeh & Faramarzi, 2017; McGowan & Matthews, 2018; Nelson, 2020; Thiel et al., 2020).

While his sister gestated in a mother who was surrounded by loved ones, on land they knew and loved, with cohering rituals and relative emotional ease due to consistent support, enjoying food and housing security, Xquenda's mom would have been more inflamed with stress neurochemistry (Talge et al., 2007; Liu et al., 2017) from being sad and scared for much of her pregnancy with him, and letting go of much that regulated her in search of future stability in a time of upheaval and loss. The sense of focus on Xquenda's well-being would have been shifted to survival needs of the family, sending neurochemical signals of distress to the developing fetus (Lobmaier et al., 2020). While this struggle and suffering could not be avoided, and is clearly not mom or the family's "fault," her elevated heart rate and inflammation of stress pathways may have set Xquenda's baseline in a more activated state, and grown his reptilian brain to be more reactive, even taking up more real estate in the finite container of the fetal skull (McGowan & Matthews, 2018; Thayer et al., 2018); this would likely be the case for anyone in this family's shoes.

While we cannot know for sure the quantity or impact of these variables, clinically, the family may need focused time and clinical support to process, digest, and release the stored survival neurochemistry generated before, during, and after Xquenda's gestation, to slowly let go of past overwhelm that still colors their reactions to stress, which will be ongoing in the acculturation and assimilation experience in a White supremacist culture. Additionally, in utero substance exposure, whether accidental, recreational, or due to addiction, can interrupt the optimal development of the reptilian and lower mammalian layers of the triune brain, both of which regulate sympathetic neurophysiological responses such as fight-flight-freeze-fawn, and parasympathetic responses of rest-and-digest (Fisher et al., 2012). Xquenda may therefore need deeply attuned support to complete the stress and potential toxic exposure of this critical developmental phase, where he was literally fused with his mother, experiencing the stress and toxins she was experiencing, but he will need ongoing trauma-informed care to build the trust necessary to do that more vulnerable work.

Clinically, initial trauma-informed, open-ended prompts to learn from the parents (first away from the kids) about how they perceived stress and support during pregnancy can help unpack unresolved overwhelm and begin pointing to themes that need completion for the well-being of the family, which can then be done together, being mindful not to activate too much stress at one time (Andrighetti et al., 2017). Working through an interpreter who does not specialize in this phase of life or the circumstances the family has lived through will require slower pacing and thoughtful timing so as not to rush the parents through their emotional processing; therefore, lots of space around the questions would likely be indicated.

What components of intake and assessment with this family would you need supervision and consultation to perform skillfully?

SESSION EXCERPT 4.1

Mental health professional: Can you tell me what it was like for you to be pregnant?

Inda Jani: Well (exhales audibly, and pauses, looking at Surem with a small smile), we weren't really planning for Xquenda the way we were with Nayeli. With Nayeli, we had been together a few years, and we were ready to start our family, and things were pretty easy with all our family around. And she was such a happy baby, ate so well, always affectionate and ready to play. But then as the big farm started encroaching on our lands, and we were finding their trash in our river, the whole community was trying to figure out what to do. We tried talking to the bosses, but nothing. Then the woods started getting clear cut, and we knew we couldn't stay much longer. And that's when I missed my moon (period) again, with Xquenda. We knew it would be harder to find a new living situation with a baby, we knew finding work in the city would be harder ... we knew no one. We just didn't know how far we would have to go to find a place we could be. And the money to live (tears well up in her eyes).

Surem: (Swallows audibly, looks at Inda Jani with warmth.) My wife has worked so hard for our family. We did not think it would be this way. (Places his head in his hands, looking at the floor.) I am so tired and wish there was more I could do to help. My son needed to be on our land. If only we could have stayed there, he would be learning to help my father and his cousins, and I know he would be happier. My wife, the things that she's been through to get here, none of that should have happened.

Mental health professional: You've both lost so much help, and support ... and maybe even hope? I want to know more about what you've been through, so we can help some of that stress finish for you. And when you feel ready, we can do that with Nayeli and Xquenda, too.

STUDENT REFLECTION 4.2

Validated assessment of perinatal stress and resilience can follow a variety of qualitative and quantitative methods (Banti et al., 2011; Evertz et al., 2021). A basic semi-structured interview could begin with some of the following:

What were you hoping for during the pregnancy?

How did you experience support throughout your pregnancy?

What helped you feel better when you were worried or stressed?

Who did you turn to with your needs?

What did you need that you didn't get during the pregnancy?

Which of those unmet needs are still present today?

How have you grieved those unmet needs?

How would you describe your child's temperament while the child was growing inside you?

CULTURAL FACTORS: INFANCY THROUGH EARLY CHILDHOOD

Humans are sexually reproductive mammals, born into family systems, whether or not they will stay and be raised within those family systems, given to another family system, and/or be surrendered to some form of institution. Family systems and those who procreate in them, and/or raise others' offspring, are shaped and formed by multicultural identities, experiences, and expectations. Conception, pregnancy, birth, bonding, child rearing, parenting, and caregiving are therefore relationally and culturally embedded experiences. Research shows that one way culture is sustained is through parenting practices; therefore, let's explore some relational and cultural considerations of infancy through early childhood.

Infancy

Development in the first year of life outside the womb—infancy—continues to be marked by a high degree of physical dependency to have all of the baby's needs provided for by caregivers (Evertz et al., 2021). At birth, a neonate's only available defenses are to close its eyes, turn its head, and shut out overwhelming sensation by falling asleep (Brazelton & Nugent, 1995); from a pre- and perinatal perspective, this is also when dissociation starts as a short-term coping mechanism to shut off overwhelming, disorganizing sensations (Lyons-Ruth et al., 2006).

As social mammals, human babies are born equipped with physical and behavioral traits that have evolved to hijack healthy caregiver attention, elicit caregiving, and increase chances the baby's needs are tended to (Kringelbach et al., 2016). Smelling a baby generally reduces testosterone, lowering aggression and the need to roam; it also increases estrogen, oxytocin, prolactin, and leads to dopaminergic surges associated with reward-based learning—even more so in experienced gestational parents (Lundström et al., 2013). When this does not happen for biological and/or social–emotional reasons, there is increased risk of postpartum depression, and aggression, for parents (University of Southern California, 2017).

Newborn babies need the womb re-created for the *fourth trimester* outside (Karp, 2002). They stay regulated with skin-to-skin contact, being held with their ear against the heart so they can hear it beating, on-demand breastfeeding, shooshing white noise and swaying movement like they experienced all throughout gestation (Cleveland et al., 2017); this is especially critical for pre-term babies, though is widely beneficial for all babies (Campbell-Yeo et al., 2015; Heidarzadeh et al., 2013; Sharma et al., 2018). *Babywearing*, or carrying the baby against the caregiver's body in a sling, papoose, or other material wrap, is common in Africa, Asia, and among the First Nations of the Americas to facilitate co-regulation of these needs while caregivers simultaneously tend to other responsibilities, and Western researchers have found babies do stay regulated for higher portions of time when tended to with sensitive care in this proximity (Hunziker & Barr, 1986; Reynolds-Miller, 2016). A longitudinal study has found 20-year benefits for babies who were worn compared to those who were not (Charpak et al., 2017). There are safe and unsafe ways to wear a baby, or multiples, so consulting with experienced babywearers is recommended to make sure the baby's head is properly supported while allowing for ease of breathing and access to the caregiver's face (Marcin, 2019).

According to Dunstan, babies around the world have about five distinct recognizable sounds of discomfort that will escalate into cries that issue from related areas in the abdomen or chest cavity to signal their various reasons for being distressed (Iftikhar, 2020). When caregivers can accurately assess these sounds to deliver the needed comforting and care (e.g., change diaper, help pass gas or poop, feed, burp, wrap and soothe for sleep or otherwise address temperature regulation), the baby will down-regulate and be settled again (Iftikhar, 2020). Preliminary research shows caregivers experience less stress compared to controls if they know how to recognize and respond to these early sounds of distress (Pineda et al., 2016), and parental caregiving aptitude is correlated with conferring secure attachment in children (Hong & Park, 2012; Lewis et al., 2001).

Babies who are born pre-term, or with other medical or physical difficulties, may have a lot of invasive intervention occuring at this fragile developmental stage. Where the evolutionary mandate would be for a long *lying in* to rest and allow the baby to stick to the caregiver so both can gather strength physically and emotionally (Dennis et al., 2007; Murfin, 2012), advances in medical technology in industrialized societies can now lead to life-saving interventions for babies that would otherwise die, but that are likely overwhelming for baby and parents (Porges et al., 2019). There are also myriad decisions to make, balancing personal, familial, and cultural beliefs and expectations with professional opinion regarding immunization, sleep training and arrangements, feeding and elimination habits, visitation, shared caregiving, exposure to the outer world, and so on.

Infants spend much of their time sleeping (decreasingly so across the first year), but when they are awake, they want caregiver proximity, attuned interaction, physical and emotional comfort, facial mirroring, reliable empathy, cooperation, support, mutuality, and regulated emotional and attentional stimulation (Porges et al., 2019). These elements together operationalize *contingent responsivity* of the caregivers to baby (Dunst & Kassow, 2008). The more of that they have, the more regulated they will stay, and the more they will trust that their caregivers will provide what is needed in good timing (Beebe & Steele, 2013). Cultural preferences for functional interdependence in collectivistic societies will support ongoing proximity and relatedness as the infant develops toward toddlerhood (Behrens, 2010; Crittenden & Marlowe, 2013; Dawson, 2018; Jin et al., 2012; Lai & Carr, 2018; Rothbaum & Kakinuma, 2004; Sagi, 1990); cultural preferences for independence in individualistic societies result in a push toward increasing infant attention on objects and projects, with an emphasis on infants to explore the world around them independently with growing physical capacity and mental curiosity (Alcock, 2013; Bowlby & King, 2004; Fox, 1977; Keller et al., 2005; Kratzer, 2019; Main, 1990; Mesman et al., 2016; Strand et al., 2019; van Ijzendoorn & Sagi-Schwartz, 2008).

As their strength grows, if they have no medical difficulties that interrupt or delay the next phases, babies evolve from needing to always be on their backs in order to breathe safely, to being able to hold their heads up for several moments during *tummy time*, which allows them to strengthen their backs in preparation for eventually crawling (Hewitt et al., 2020). As they get ready for crawling, they start strengthening the muscles to roll over from their back to their tummy, and begin little pushups, which then allow them to get up on knees and hands, rocking back and forth.

Crawling is a midline movement that connects the left and right hemispheres of the brain across the corpus callosum for better neurological organization; forsaking crawling to begin walking early has been linked with learning difficulties, and thus extending crawling through daily interactive floor games can be protective and preventive for neurological organization (Stiles & Jernigan, 2010). As physically able babies gain strength through crawling, they begin to pull up on available supports, developing the muscles of the legs to hold up their disproportionately big heads (Adolph et al., 2011). Bouncing while holding on leads to side-stepping with hands on supports, known as *cruising,* to lifting hands up to stand freely, to taking first unstable steps somewhere close to the first birthday. These wobbly, top-heavy first launches into the world are the beginning of *toddling,* and result in lots of falls in the learning process; real injury can occur if the surroundings are not appropriately protective for these first walks (e.g., steps, stairs, concrete, bodies of water, startled pets, cars all can be life-threatening; Peden et al., 2008), and caregiver response to the bumps and bruises can be experienced on a spectrum from neglectful to dismissive to minimizing to regulated and soothing (Koralek, 1992). The baby's brain continues to throw on grey matter at a rapid pace here; receptive language is being encoded as an infant also verbalizes with coo's, discernable cries, intentional sounds, and often their first caregiver titles and favorite object neologisms by the end of the first year (Mayo Clinic, 2021, March 25).

In the diminishing hunter–gatherer tribes around the world today, the way all of our ancestors lived until agrarian and then industrial societies arose (very recently in human history), babies co-sleep with parents and nurse until at least 3 years—but often up to 6—when the *milk teeth* fall out (Diamond, 2012; University of Notre Dame, 2010), and toddlers are known to handle knives and fire-related tools to meaningfully assist in food preparation for the greater good (Apicella & Crittenden, 2015). Safely co-sleeping regulates the baby's heart rate variability and breathing patterns, and also eases breastfeeding transitions to enhance bonding and co-regulation of the parent–baby dyad while reducing exhaustion for the breastfeeding parent (Burbidge, 2017; Weissinger et al., 2014). Though there are innumerable physical similarities and developmental milestones that inform what is normative for early human development within any given culture, there are perhaps as many variants on how those evolutionary potentials are prioritized across societies, which continue to shape how individuals within those cultures develop.

STUDENT REFLECTION 4.3

While his sister's zero-to-five years experience was all contained within the community embrace of multigenerational family members looking after her when her parents needed to work, with on-demand breastfeeding because her mom was able to work in the fields nearby and either wear her or take breaks when she needed her, Xquenda had to tolerate long hours away from his mom while she worked away from the home during his infancy. In fact, because mom had delivery complications with Xquenda, she ultimately had an unplanned C-section, and was hooked up to a bag of antibiotics in the hospital for 3 days after Xquenda's birth, which interrupted their bonding processes (Pilch, 2015; Sakala et al., 2020; van Reenen & van Rensburg, 2013). Xquenda had difficulty latching and the parents could not afford a lactation consultant, so he was given formula in the hospital and the parents were not encouraged to keep trying breastfeeding (Jenco, 2020). Xquenda was also given broad spectrum antibiotics in the hospital, which upset the fragile development of the intestinal microbiome environment necessary to begin digesting comfortably, resulting in chronic colic (Azad et al., 2013; Leung & Hon, 2019), and though he was able to room-in with his mom, she was not allowed to have visitors for more than 1 hour at a time.

Xquenda's mom recalls this period with tears in her eyes, saying how lonely and overwhelmed she felt while her husband and daughter could not be with her and the new baby, and that she could not soothe him with breastfeeding as she had been able to do with her daughter (Mlynek, 2019; Mueller et al., 2015; Murray, 2020; Putignani et al., 2014; Walker, 2010; World Health Organization, 2011; Yang et al., 2016). Though she doesn't "know" it, the oxytocin she generated while naturally birthing and breastfeeding her first child helped bond them emotionally to block out much of the pain and exhaustion of this massive undertaking; she did not generate as much of this bonding neurochemistry with her son due to the interrupted birth and breastfeeding experience (Feldman et al., 2013; Kim & Strathearn,

2017; Kim et al., 2017; Mah et al., 2015; Scatliffe et al., 2019). Where the difficult time she had during the pregnancy and birth could have been partially mitigated by support to successfully breastfeed, as well as rest more deeply when the baby slept, the built-in support she had with her community and family was not available to her with her second child. This increased the risk of postpartum depression, potentially resulting in diminished patience, enjoyment, and contingent responsivity with the baby (Office of the Surgeon General, n.d.; World Health Organization, 2021).

What do you know about your own birth and bonding experience? Are there any patterns that run in your family that might be worth exploring and resolving through personal counseling?

TODDLERHOOD

Subsequent development of the toddler to young child is also relationally and culture bound. Indeed, even if a young child spends time away from primary caregivers and *allo-parents* (kin or non-blood-related, chosen and trusted members of the family), to attend a formally structured day care or preschool environment will inform what developmental milestones (such as toilet-training and tolerating shoes) must have been achieved to be considered "normal" by pre-determined ages. Whether or not a child is born in a state society will inform what caregiving and disciplinary practices are permitted, sanctioned, required, or litigated (Jonson-Reid et al., 2017); this has implications when mental health professionals are serving migrant families who may not have been informed of all the local rules and consequences of the dominant culture, and merits supervisory support to ensure ethical informed consent and clinical care.

Toddlerhood is generally considered to start at 1 year of age, and last until about 4, though there is no official upper limit that is widely recognized (Barker, 2001). Toddlers suddenly go from being relatively easy to contain, because the adults are faster than they are, to quite capable of getting themselves and others into physical danger quickly. Coupled with the fact they have very little appreciation of the risks they can run with their newfound freedom to walk, run, and wield increasingly heavy objects, toddlers create a whole new demand for caregiving supervision (Barker, 2001). To compensate for this risk, Nature imbued us with shame, which acts as a psychic leash with just a look and a shout; when a caregiver notices we are about to hurt ourselves or someone else, they can yank that leash and stop us in our tracks, even at a physical distance (Terrizzi & Shook, 2020). This yank gets us to drop our chin and roll our shoulders forward, turning our attention inward and shortening the breath, in addition to emotional rumination on this ostracized state (Schore, 1991). While effectively stopping us from what we were doing, this state can be difficult for toddlers to self-regulate for too long, and requires that we be soothed and brought back into the tribe with forgiveness and encouragement, along with the lesson delivered (Barrett et al., 1993; Herman, 2018).

Toddlerhood's explosive neurological development can lead to a lot of busy projects, many of them imitating bigger people and their skills, even if the skills don't make sense (Tellis, 2010). Receptive language acquisition is increasingly evident in the daily expressive language that begins to pour forth, often in delightful ways (Mayo Clinic, 2021, March 25). Gross motor skills such as climbing, tumbling, and dancing, as well as interest in manipulating adult tools for daily living, all come online in varying rates among toddlers and preschoolers (Kid Sense, n.d.). Biological males have the highest ratio of testosterone-to-body weight at age 3 (Vesper et al., 2015), which shows itself in sheer energy level, as well as quickness to anger. Fine motor skills are slower to graft on at this stage, but greater dexterity begins to unfold, and handedness becomes clarified (Occupational Therapy for Children, n.d.). Toddlers' emotions continue to be felt very strongly, with frustration tolerance typically low and resistance to boundaries being enforced too often (Schore, 1991). However, toddlers who have a history with responsive caregivers tend to be amenable to soothing and redirection toward what they are allowed to touch and do, and generally want to please loving caregivers (Dennis, 2006). In cultures where young children are incorporated into the whole group activities, imitation leads to procedural learning of adult behaviors, with ongoing desire for proximity, physical contact, and shared attention to the task at hand (Krassner et al., 2017; Rubin et al., 2006).

Socially, young toddlers in same-age cohort groups or drop-in public settings such as parks commonly engage in co-ed *parallel play*, next to each other, where they are often doing their own solitary play in proximity to peers (Brigano, 2011). Through a combination of natural and socialization processes, they may slowly develop reciprocal and increasingly gender-based play as they age through toddlerhood, and increasingly show interest and skill at collaborating in cooperative play, while also showing strong preferences for types of materials and activities that define with whom they play (Änggård, 2011). Younger toddlers tend to have more fluid gender-based play, and increasingly show more consolidated gender identity by the time they reach school age (though social pressure can thwart this for gender non-conforming children) (Kung et al., 2018; Rafferty, 2018, September 18). Strong peer loyalties and alliances can be formed at this age, as can bullying, and imaginal play can alternate between practicing adult roles, and engaging in fantastical, larger-than-life abilities (Holmes et al., 2015). Delays in movement toward collaborative and cooperative play, age-typical language capacity, or emotional regulation tend to garner concerned attention, and may become a focus of early clinical and educational assessment based on this author's experience.

STUDENT REFLECTION 4.4

While Xquenda's sister's toddlerhood would have been focused on life skills specific to survival and contribution within her local community (with likely more than one regulated adult available for line-of-sight supervision at all times), spending lots of free time outdoors and developing gross and fine motor skills based on her interests, Xquenda's toddlerhood in the shared home of his parents' acquaintances was not as free and self-directed, as the family was trying not to impose or annoy the hosting family. Xquenda heard "No" a lot more than his older sister at this same age, and his impulse to run and climb was often interrupted because there was no fence around the suburban house making it safe for him to discharge his wild young energy outside. Xquenda was often told to be quiet and not touch other people's belongings, and the host family's kids would sometimes tease Xquenda by playing with their toys near him, but then taking them away when he tried to play with them.

What aspects of Xquenda's early experience are similar to yours? What aspects are different, and how? If you were to take one key question to your supervisor about how to best proceed serving Xquenda's family thus far, what would it be? Clinically, what repairs do you think would be helpful to better bond parents and son?

Early Childhood

For our purposes here, we will define early childhood from about 4 or 5 years old until kids go on to become fully *school-aged* at 8 (Committee on the Science of Children Birth to Age 8, et al. 2015). Early childhood, as opposed to toddlerhood, is commonly marked by medically capable neurotypical children being reliably potty-trained unless a rare accident occurs, because they finally have sphincter control (Clifford & Gorodzinsky, 2000); increasing ability to verbally self-report needs such as hunger; having the ability to follow simple multi-step directions, and understand many consequences for not doing so; and increasing interest in connecting socially with others outside the family-of-origin (Committee on the Science of Children Birth to Age 8: Deepening and Broadening the Foundation for Success; Board on Children, Youth, and Families; Institute of Medicine; National Research Council, 2015). If the entrance to an aged-cohort day care or school setting has not yet occurred, preparations to do so often begin at this age in industrialized societies. Cultural preferences for ongoing relational closeness in collectivistic societies often result in high regard for teachers as significant and respected authority figures worthy of reverence and the right to influence one's offspring, with high expectations of children to treat teachers with deferential respect, like a family elder (Klassen et al., 2010). Repetition of experience begins to show itself in relative mastery compared to peers in social settings; thus in patriarchal societies, a general acceptance and tolerance between most young preschool-aged peers begins to give way to competitiveness and power-over dynamics, as cohort members vie for authority and attention (Andersen et al., 2013).

The physical, emotional, and cognitive leaps made by young children year-over-year are remarkable to caregivers as they look back during this young stage. What a neurotypical 5-year-old of relative privilege can try to do is vastly different than what a neurotypical 8-year-old of the same relative privilege can reliably do. If given the opportunity to engage in hours per day of free off-screen play, movement, and quiet time, the integration of gross and fine motor skills for medically capable children typically begin to translate into stronger and more graceful movement, while expressive language expands into colorful story-telling, and the ability to imagine into others' experiences increases exponentially (Beaudoin et al., 2020; Madigan et al., 2019). Preferences for school subject matter may begin to result in exploratory imitative play, and as children begin to read in addition to drawing and creative expression, their excitement about fictional storylines and non-fiction subject matter can turn into dramatic performances and science experiments (McNaughton, 1997; Rhodes et al., 2020). Tolerance and stamina for non-preferred academic and life-skill activities typically begin to increase for neurotypical children, with fewer tantrums and more willingness rooted in growing understanding about the need for good hygiene, safety, and some semblance of justice and responsibility (Crosby et al., 2019; Li et al., 2016). Many traits on a spectrum start to consolidate here, such that relative extraversion–introversion, easy going–slow to warm–difficult temperament, and cognitive processing speed become less likely to change much with each passing year (Roberts et al., 2000).

CONTEXTUAL FACTORS: INFANCY THROUGH EARLY CHILDHOOD

In industrialized societies, in utero substance exposure, chronic medical needs, other Type II relational/developmental trauma (Terr, 2003), and neurological or chromosomal learning differences or delays will become a focus of parental involvement with child development professionals as children this age become more involved in public and private educational settings, and those professionals (who have often spent decades in direct service to this age and stage) make recommendations and referrals based on variations from typical age cohort patterns (Crawley et al., 2020; Shonkoff & Phillips, 2000). If caregivers have been suffering in silence; are rooted in cultural groups that are more marginalized, private or even insular; are avoiding authority figures out of fear of reprisal or legal implications; or for other contextual reasons have more rigid boundaries around the family system, the young child with special needs' growing ability to assert and express themselves may result in families being forced to interface with mental health and allied professionals, even if they would rather not (Berger & Font, 2015; Ellis, 2019; Sudland, 2020). Our sensitive empathy and care for the disenfranchised grief and rational fear often held here can help families begin to engage in services while their children's neuroplasticity and identity development are more receptive to beneficial change (Kolb & Gibb, 2011; Novak, 2019). The following topics are primary reasons socially just mental health services are needed for young children and their caregivers, with prevalence rates when they are known.

Discrimination

Being systematically targeted or overlooked due to any identity feature that is marginalized causes toxic stress and is among the causes of Types II and III trauma, which have the highest incidence of becoming complex PTSD (Solomon & Heide, 1999, 2005). Racism, misogyny, ableism, homo and transmisia all fall on young bodies, severing them from a sense of safety and inherent goodness as they find themselves stuck in belittling or life-threatening interactions in their families or out in the widening world. Suicide rates for young children have only recently begun being studied, but patterns show that suicide for young Black boys is increasing, and suicide rates for LGBTQIAA + kids is 7 to 9 times higher than heterosexual and cisgender youth (Sheftall et al., 2016; Youth.gov, n.d.b).

Systemic White supremacy, ableism, cis- and heteronormativity play themselves out in which services and opportunities are available to whom, where, and how, as well as what attributions are made regarding why a child is behaving the way they are, including among highly educated healthcare workers (Ellis, 2019; Trent et al., 2019). In this way, adults in positions of authority often wield access and make split-second decisions about who gets supportive versus punitive intervention when a child is acting out or just happens to be in the wrong place at the wrong time.

Fear of police brutality and murder can result in Black, Indigenous, and other People of Color (BIPOC) parents using corporal punishment to try to teach their children how seriously they must not bring attention to themselves in certain places due to the deadly risk, and requires that BIPOC parents have *the talk* with their kids about protecting themselves from the police, usually while still in elementary school (DeGruy, 2017). The number of police murders has led to the civilian development of 10 survival tips for children of Color (Atlanta City Review Board, n.d.). Black children are six times more likely and Latinx children are three times more likely to be killed by police than White children overall (Badolato et al., 2020). About one in 1000 Black boys will be killed by police, while American Indian/Alaska Native boys are about 1.5 times more likely, and Asian/Pacific Islander boys are only slightly less likely to be killed by police than White boys. Black and American Indian/Native Alaskan girls' rate of being shot by police is about twice that of White and Latina girls, while Asian and Pacific Islander girls' rate is currently the lowest (Edwards et al., 2019). That parents even need to consider the risk of their children being killed by police as a component of their effective child-rearing is a predominantly American phenomenon, though it is also a significant factor in many migrant-sending countries (McCarthy, 2017, January 18). Further considerations regarding the risk of children dying by gun violence follows below.

BULLYING AND PEER ABUSE

Bullying starts in preschool (Saracho, 2017). It can often begin as kids just grabbing toys from each other and not showing remorse for sadness caused when they are small, which is normal for young toddlers, given the limits to their neurological development and therefore ability to sublimate personal desires in preference for respectful peer relationships. However, if left consistently unaddressed as neurological development unfolds and *Theory of Mind* increasingly allows for empathy regarding how others feel (Beaudoin et al., 2020), that can escalate to hitting and name-calling, and kids outnumbering targeted individuals to threaten and torture them emotionally and physically. Cross-cultural research is beginning to show that access to sufficient shared materials and emotional support appears to be implicated in preschooler aggression, and that cultural variations for how to interact with same-age peers has demonstrable difference by preschool age (Metin Aslan, 2018). The risk for discrimination being played out with bullying and peer abuse increases with more marginalized identities and capacities, particularly when the kids targeted are more introverted and less likely to stick up for themselves or have peers who help them find safety (Repo & Sajaniemi, 2015). Kids can also become quickly savvy about finding places away from adult view to enact their abuse on peers, including low-visibility areas such as behind sheds on school playgrounds, bathrooms, buses, and behind closed doors at home (Levine & Kline, 2008; Levine & Tamburrino, 2014).

Sexual abuse between young peers can and does happen in buses and schools, as well as in homes (Levine & Kline, 2008; Tremblay-Perreault & Hébert, 2020). All children involved in either side of this peer abuse may potentially be referred for clinical care if the abuse or resulting trauma behaviors are identified, and it is also possible they go untreated for a long time. Erin's Law is a prevention-oriented child sexual abuse program that is on its way to being enacted in every state (Erin's Law, n.d.), but much sexual abuse happens before children reach the elementary school age at which this program is being delivered (Singh et al., 2014).

Bullying and peer abuse, which tend to escalate as children move through elementary school, are known to increase the risk of suicidal and homicidal behavior in children once they hit 10 years old (Centers for Disease Control and Prevention, 2019). Though schools often publicize they have a zero-tolerance policy for bullying, there can be a lack of operationalization for how intervention will be implemented; this merits supervisory support and meaningful advocacy for school-based mental health professionals, particularly to uphold social justice ethics re: how the children are treated by various authorities. I (Roller) have seen mental health professionals place aggressor and victim in dyad counseling without reporting back to caregivers any updates, while bullying continued unimpeded by school administration.

Gang recruitment and affiliation (2%–5%), begins in elementary school (Youth.gov, n.d.a). When children are born into situations where their role model options are limited, the appearance of protection and belonging a gang initially provides can be quite compelling (Sharkey et al., 2011). Affiliating begins with simply wearing colors, flashing numbers, *mad-dogging* and talking trash to opposing members, but once kids go through the rite of passage of getting *jumped in*, they must begin to avoid certain territories and people in fear for their life, as well as perform prescribed acts to prove their loyalty and worth (Dmitrieva et al., 2014).

Kids who cannot avoid gang affiliation due to family involvement will find it nearly impossible to extricate themselves once they've been jumped in (Dmitrieva et al., 2014). Officially leaving the gang requires another rite of passage of accepting another gang beating, but this time there are truly hard feelings, rather than just one having to prove their courage and loyalty (Dong & Krohn, 2016). Training in diversion and restorative justice approaches is necessary for mental health professionals attempting to penetrate this chain of command to build up the "pulls" away from gang involvement (Young & Gonzalez, 2013), in addition to highly nuanced joining and family therapy with the influential adults to help support the children's differentiation and safety from these subcultural pressures. Success rates for leaving a gang are highest when the family and/or other prosocial enticements help cut ties, which can sometimes require relocation (an option not often available for the working poor; Young & Gonzalez, 2013).

Civilian Gun Violence

Gun violence in the United States has consistently been on the rise over the last several decades with increased gun ownership; there are now 120 guns for every 100 people in the United States. According to the Center for Violence Prevention at Children's Hospital of Philadelphia:

> gun injuries are the second-leading cause of death among U.S. children and teens and the leading cause of death among high school students.... Among younger children (ages 0–12 years) ... 85% are killed in their own home (Children's Hospital of Philadelphia, 2020, December).

There have been 237 school shootings and 403 related deaths or injuries since the Columbine shooting in 1999 (Rowhani-Rahbar & Moe, 2019). Drive-by shootings do not have reliably accurate reporting, but best estimates suggest they result in hundreds of U.S. shootings every year, with 18% of those being children, and 46% being at home (Children's Defense Fund, n.d.).

CUSTODY

About 50% of children in the United States will find themselves in a shared custody situation before age 18, and up to age 13, will not be included in the court's decision-making about their living arrangements unless there are liability-causing determinants the court gives merit (e.g., substantiated child protective services [CPS], DUI, or DV reports on file; Chen et al., 2021). Parents in prison often retain legal custody, even though they cannot provide physical custody, and thus can block children from accessing mental health services unless a judge overturns and mandates that service, which requires the custodial parent have legal representation to get that instituted, which is a privilege (Tuthill, 2021). Mental health agencies sometimes have intake paperwork requirements to reduce legal risks related to split custody, but those who have not yet had to manage an aggressive or threatening parent may not be prepared for this eventuality.

Children caught in high conflict separations, or who are experiencing significant chaos due to changing custody arrangements, may have great fear about voicing their needs and feelings related to a situation where their core safety and security are at risk. The emotional turmoil of this disenfranchised grief and loss requires great sensitivity to navigate successfully, and children can find themselves bouncing between two very different worlds, with multiple challenges and demands placed upon them, while holding their attachment needs for when they can get met (O'Hara et al., 2019). Developmental disruptions are predictable with this ongoing interruption, and require both child-centered and family therapy to resolve as well as possible (Chen et al., 2021; Gil, 2006).

UNACCOMPANIED MINORS AND DACA

According to the Migration Data Portal, "the U.S. Border Patrol (USBP) apprehended nearly 69,000 unaccompanied children in 2014, 40,000 in 2015 and 60,000 in 2016. In 2016, 61 percent of apprehended unaccompanied minors in that year were from El Salvador and Guatemala" (USBP, 2016), and "in recent years, the number of children migrating unaccompanied by guardians has increased. In 2015–2016, there were five times as many children estimated to be migrating alone than in 2010–2011" (UNICEF, 2017b). The number of unaccompanied and separated children applying for asylum in countries other than the European Union increased from 4,000 in 2010 to 19,000 in 2015 (Migration Data Portal, n.d.). These trends make it clear that mental health professionals need to be prepared to effectively serve children whose families may not be traced or available, and try to appreciate the incomprehensible loss such a survival move represents, while helping children navigate the labyrinth of local requirements for them to obtain their education and have a pathway toward self-sustainability.

Deferred Action for Childhood Arrivals (DACA) is a legal policy currently protecting about 800,000 children (Boundless, n.d.) who may or may not have families with them. Recent policy changes aim to uphold these protections and provide support to the 1.8 million children currently eligible for DACA. While the supports are intended for high school graduates or GED-holders, steps need to be taken when children are young to maintain their eligibility. Supervision and advocacy are necessary to protect this opportunity for childhood arrivals.

RUNAWAYS, ABDUCTIONS, AND TRAFFICKING

The incidence of small children running away in the United States is extremely low and not accurately known, but when a small child truly runs away (as opposed to just wandering off for a brief moment) the historical literature attributes this to serious maltreatment, which is linked with multiple increased risks as children become teens (Pergamit, 2010). According to the National Estimate of Missing Children, the incidence of abducted children over the last decade is estimated to be 18.8 out of 1000, with 11.4 reported as being missing (Office of Juvenile Justice and Delinquency Prevention, 2017). Furthermore, "9% are kidnapped by a family member in a custody dispute; 3% are abducted by non-family members, usually during the commission of a crime such as robbery or sexual assault. The kidnapper is often someone the child knows; only about 100 children (a fraction of 1%) are kidnapped each year in the stereotypical stranger abductions you hear about in the news, and about half of these 100 children come home."

According to the Office of Child Labor, Forced Labor, and Human Trafficking (OCFT), approximately 4 million children are currently trapped in forced labor, including about 27% of them in forced sexual labor. As awareness of this widespread systemic abuse continues to grow, and children are rescued from these circumstances, it is likely that mental health professionals will increasingly need specialized training to effectively treat the complex trauma that results from such prolonged, egregious abuse (Department of Labor Bureau of International Labor Affairs, n.d.). I (Roller) served children involved in these circumstances who had to grow up in foster care; their charts revealed STIs sometimes as early as 1 year old, and the global effects on their social, emotional, and cognitive functioning were truly heartbreaking.

FOSTER CARE AND ADOPTION

In the United States, there are currently approximately 419,000 children who have been removed from their families of origin due to egregious or unremitting child abuse and neglect, or who were thrown away, who arrived as unaccompanied minors, or whose caregivers have been deported, incarcerated, or died in a calamitous event. They will often face ongoing loss and developmental disruption as the foster care system attempts to find stable placement for them when suitable kinship care is not available (The Imprint, 2020). It cannot be overstated how devastating the lifelong impact of such disruptions can be if a child does not find their forever family, if they are also separated from their siblings, if they are not supported to grieve all that they have lost, and if they are not given every possible stabilizing resource that helps them to experience themselves as whole, loveable, worthy, capable, resilient, connected, and belonging. Unfortunately, the compassion fatigue that plagues Child Protective Services and the foster care system means that children in it are often left to fend for themselves emotionally and behaviorally (Kapoulitsas & Corcoran, 2015; Scott, 2021). Because there are insufficient qualified foster parents to hold all the children who need a forever home, children in care often have their wounds re-traumatized by the system to which they are handed as they get passed from temporary placement to placement.

Fost-Adopt is a bridge program, usually reserved for younger children, whose families of origin have failed *reunification,* so the children have been relinquished or placed in *permanency planning,* where hope for living with their families again must now be grieved (Barth et al., 2017). As children age through permanency planning, their chances of being adopted out of foster care reduce with each passing year. It is nothing short of miraculous when a child in foster care finds a *sweetheart placement* with a healthy and loving adoptive family that takes them in as their own, commits to keeping them for life, and takes over the reliable, enriched therapeutic and educational care that they need to recover and thrive. In lieu of that, a patchwork of paid professionals and occasionally volunteers will find themselves trying to provide some semblance of continuity without fomenting unrealistic hopes about the child's need for security, positive predictability, trustworthy and reliable adults, and a chance to finally exhale deeply and stop packing their life into one bag to be shuttled to the next temporary place.

Mental health professionals serving children in foster care will often find themselves helpless to influence many circumstances beyond the child's control, and yet must strive to provide evidence that some adults are reliable. Neurosequential organization through predictable session length, time, placement, and activities is crucial for many children in foster care; empowering children with as much choice about activities, topics, and timing of transitions also restores a little bit of safety and worth for kids who otherwise have almost no say in what is happening to them (Perry, 2006).

NEURODEVELOPMENTAL DIFFERENCES AND DIFFICULTIES

Autism Spectrum Disorders (ASD; incidence rate 3%) are neurologically based differences with likely genetic roots exacerbated by inflammatory epigenetic events during the second trimester (Christensen et al., 2019; Madore et al., 2016). Experienced birth parents often notice immediately if their neonate appears overwhelmed by tactile stimulation and gazing when awake. Leaky gut syndrome, stereotypical movement patterns, self-stimulatory humming and neologisms, flat affect, restricted diets and fixated play interests, phobias, lining up objects, and blunted social reciprocity may occur in young children *on the spectrum* (Sivberg, 2003). The evidence-based practice for treatment of ASD is called Applied Behavioral Analysis (ABA), which is a specific paraprofessional intervention performed at home, in the community and school, not billable to mental health services (Odom et al., 2020). Mental health providers may perform auxiliary support for social anxiety in kids with ASD, as well as family therapy to help with the stress on family dynamics. Holistic interventions for building the microbiota and healing the digestive tract may also be employed by appropriate allied professionals (Ding et al., 2017; Fowlie et al., 2018; Srikantha & Mohajeri, 2019).

Fetal Alcohol Spectrum Disorder (FASD; approximately 5%–10% incidence), one of the most under- and mis-diagnosed of all neurodevelopmental difficulties, encapsulates all forms of substance exposure (not just alcohol), and applies to more children than the ones showing the recognizable facial dysmorphology typical of this clinical presentation (Centers for Disease Control and Prevention, 2021, February 4; Chasnoff et al., 2015). FASD increases comorbid risk of: sensory integration disorders (SID); reactive attachment disorders (RAD); encopresis and enuresis; receptive/expressive language development delays; learning disabilities (LD); Attention Deficit Hyperactivity Disorder (ADHD) and Attention Deficit Disorder (ADD); mood disorders; conduct disorders (CD); and antisocial tendencies (Chasnoff et al., 2015). Occupational therapy (OT) is often incorporated in the child's Individualized Education Plan (IEP) as part of their educational accommodations, with ongoing wraparound services to help with social–emotional development.

ADHD and ADD can also stand alone (9.4%) and appear to have genetic roots (Centers for Disease Control and Prevention, 2020, November 16). These diagnoses are common complaints of elementary school teachers, though teachers are not formally trained to accurately diagnose. There are ongoing discussions among mental health professionals regarding epigenetic patterns in industrialized societies that may be contributing to higher rates of ADHD and ADD; quality of involved parental caregiving, quantity of neurologically integrating body-based activities, and screen use are often implicated in these conversations (Weissenberger et al., 2017). Both tend to be treated with a combination of pharmacotherapy and behavioral interventions, with some parents conflicted about ever using medicine, while others cannot imagine trying to raise their child without it.

Psychotic process rarely blossoms fully by early childhood, even though symptoms are as common as 17% in small children (attributed to cognitive processing differences in young children) but when traced back retrospectively, eventual diagnosis of true psychotic process in adolescence or young adulthood is highly correlated with receptive–expressive language delay as early as age 2 (Klosterkotter et al., 2011; Ruhrmann et al., 2010) and a stilted, if any, transition from parallel to cooperative play. Parents of children who went on to be diagnosed with a psychotic process have stated to this author (Roller) that their child has always had a flatter affect and less interest in social interaction than their other children, somewhat like kids on the spectrum may present. Because psychotic process advances as the myelin sheath of the brain further deteriorates, early detection and treatment are paramount (Raballo et al., 2020). For young children exhibiting early *negative* symptoms (e.g., poverty of thought, delayed speech and language, flat affect, low social reciprocity), this is done with a combination of specialized assessment, family therapy, and behavioral interventions to develop skills of daily living; as children age and demonstrate more *positive* symptoms (e.g., sensory hallucinations, paranoia, delusions, word salad), pharmacotherapy and further wraparound mental health service are added to protect access to education and developmentally appropriate skills of daily living (Polanczyk et al., 2010).

Pediatric Autoimmune Neuropsychiatric Disorders Associated with Streptococcal Infections (PANDAS, possible incidence of 1 in 200) can result in tics and other behaviors associated with Obsessive–Compulsive Disorder (OCD) and Tourette's syndrome; ongoing research is pointing to up to 25% of OCD cases being caused by PANDAS (PANDAS, 2018). Pediatric OCD (2%–3% prevalence) can also stand alone, not caused by strep, and has genetic roots, exacerbated by epigenetic stress (Adams et al., 2018). If caught early, PANDAS can remit with antibiotics, but both PANDAS and OCD can become all-consuming if not treated effectively, and both often go undetected or misdiagnosed (Lewin, 2019). Early signs tend to be hand, head, and/or vocal tics; distraction due to cognitive rumination; avoidance of stressful stimuli associated with phobias; compulsions such as handwashing or repetitive yet not fruitful habits (e.g., checking doorknobs, lining up objects, washing until skin bleeds; Adams et al., 2018).

Mental health professionals serving families with young children exhibiting any symptoms of these clinical presentations need to seek supervision quickly; insist on medical, psychiatric, and neuropsychological referrals to perform adequate rule-outs; utilize indicated validated measures to assist with differential diagnoses; do thorough genograms to help assess for genetic risk factors; and optimize early neuroplasticity for therapeutic benefit (Lewin & Piacentini, 2010, April). A combination of occupational therapy, pharmacotherapy, family play therapy, parental and teacher psychoeducation, and skillful collaboration with collateral professionals is often necessary to effectively support families whose children have neurodevelopmental difficulties.

COVID-19

During the COVID-19 pandemic, families who were living in industrialized societies found themselves overseeing their children's online schooling in some format. Young students were regularly required to sit at a computer for 4 to 6 hours per day, often while parents blessed with professional jobs were simultaneously working from home and not able to provide the quantity or quality of social support, play, or pedagogical skill as their children would have normally received at school (Fontenelle-Tereshchuk, 2021). Further complicating this was how children whose parents did not have the luxury of working from home, or who did not have reliable access to the internet, were required to adjust and compensate without the stable structure of a school community to normalize the stress and developmental needs that continued to unfold for over a year. Low-resource families were devastated by the demands placed upon them (Montenovo et al., 2020). Accessing medical and clinical care was largely facilitated by telehealth, if at all, and the vast majority of developmentally appropriate embodied enrichment in the community was intermittent at best, or fully evaporated.

While the long-term effects of these widespread adjustments will not be known for some time, it is clear both parents and children experienced a tremendous sense of stress during the ongoing losses and demands of this global crisis; hundreds of thousands of families lost members without being able to hold them and say goodbye, which complicates the grief even further. Substance abuse was reportedly on the rise, and loss of jobs led to loss of medical insurance, housing, food security, and relational cohesion (Russell et al., 2020; Van Lancker & Parolin, 2020). The circumstances giving rise to child abuse and neglect only increase under times of great duress, and yet children's access to mandated reporters and respite care was nearly completely cut off. At the time of this writing, posts on listservs for mental health professionals were predicting a tidal wave of counseling referrals and CPS interventions once children began returning to in-person school (Torjesen, 2020).

Clients in Infancy and Early Childhood and Their Families: Clinical Considerations

While Xquenda's sister grew up within a consistent group of diverse-aged caregivers and playmates in an attachment network who had known her since conception up until her family moved away, giving her more fluid access up and down the developmental spectrum depending on her needs at the time, Xquenda made an earlier transition to outside society. Xquenda's launch to kindergarten was marked by being handed off to non-relative professionals who have not been part of his family or community while he was a baby, where he also has to become part of a large group of same-age peers overseen by one or two regulated adults, who don't necessarily "love" him or speak his preferred languages, and being directed to spend a bulk of time learning fine motor and reading skills, with only short breaks for child-centered gross motor discharge and development. Furthermore, the pressures felt by Western public school teachers to uphold externally determined standards for achievement and behavior in their outnumbering charges tends to result in stress-based feedback when children are non-compliant or falling short of expectations, without the luxury of time to repeatedly demonstrate and scaffold toward the preferred behavior in a patient way (Klassen et al., 2013).

As a kindergartener, adjusting to the emotional demands of being one among 24 in a group of 5-year-olds expected to sit still and attend academically, and transition willingly, an early assessment and intervention conversation with a mental health professional might look something like this:

SESSION EXCERPT 4.2

Mental health professional (who also meets with family regularly): Hola, Xquenda.... I'm so glad to see you today … (Calm and welcoming tone, soothing prosody, gentle smile, watching Xquenda's facial expression and body posture to quietly ease into his awareness without overstepping his personal space, letting him determine proximity so long as mental health professional and child are both safe.)

Xquenda/Miguel: Ruben took my truck and teacher won't give it back to me! (Anger in voice.)

Mental health professional: Oh, you must be so frustrated … (Validating, gently modeling 6-count exhales to soothe the nervous system.)

Xquenda/Miguel: Rah! It's MINE!! He can't take it from me!! (Signs of sympathetic arousal in flushed face, tight jaw, wide open eyes.)

Mental health professional: So frustrating … you feel mad right now …(Intentionally soothing tone, maintaining 6-count exhales to down-regulate child's nervous system, not rushing to shut down safe expression of activation.)

Xquenda/Miguel: It's MINE!!!! Ruben always takes mine!

Mental health professional: That mad is all in your chest and fists ... I can see how mad you are feeling right now … (Intentional soothing tone, staying focused and present, not trying to shift child out of activated feeling state with words, as he is not able currently.)

Xquenda/Miguel: I never get the truck! He always takes it from me! And teacher lets him!!!

Mental health professional: I would be so sad, to want something so much and have it taken away (Normalizing and modeling being with sadness, softening ground for addressing grief and processing/differentiating from past grief and traumatic loss in upcoming family sessions.)

Xquenda/Miguel: (Showing anger through stomping, banging fist, giving way to downturned mouth and fleeting signs of sadness in downcast eyes and breath catching in throat.)

Mental health professional: Sometimes what helps me is to go outside and throw clay ... would you like to go let your mads out with me? (Gentle redirection to channel discharge of anger and make space for vulnerable sadness underneath protective anger.)

Xquenda/Miguel: (Moves toward door so mental health professional gets up and leads the way to trees outside, brings plywood rectangle, ground sheet for front of target, and block of clay kept for this purpose.)

Mental health professional: Here, let's break off a chunk of clay for you, and you roll it up into a strong ball, while I go put the target up for you. (Empowering with healthy outlet for directing reactive energy, supporting age-appropriate impulse control through successive approximation with engaging alternative for aggressive discharge.)

Xquenda/Miguel: (Throws clay before mental health professional is out of way of target.)

Mental health professional: Oops, we both have to be safe, remember? (Calm, neutral tone, not giving too much attention to the unpreferred act having predicted the mild testing would occur). Ok, now I'm far enough away for your strong arm ...

Xquenda/Miguel: (breaks off more clay chunks and throws at target silently for several minutes while mental health professional calmly encourages, assists only when client bids for attention).

Mental health professional: Look at you, so in charge of yourself! You're focusing... (Ten minutes of client-centered outdoor play, much time non-verbal, being an empathic presence, providing strength-based feedback for what is expected of him in school setting, while giving his body and brain necessary time to break down adrenaline and cortisol generated when he lost something he deeply wanted, again.) Ten more minutes, and then we'll go back to class ... (Gentle preparation for transitions is crucial for young children, and most clients processing overwhelm.)

Xquenda/Miguel: Can I play with your trucks? (Finding ways to fill up where he has more choice and less competition.)

Mental health professional: Of course. Do you want to throw a few more times? Or use all that time to play with trucks? (Giving a sense of agency wherever possible, as children in school are often not given choice about what happens next, and this can mount as frustration).

Being Differently Abled. Xquenda has some special needs that are beginning to be identified by educational and clinical professionals, as even with his colic and difficulty being soothed and latching, the general medical professionals did not see anything they needed to offer the family. With skillful wraparound prevention and intervention, including environmental accommodations at home and school, he will be able to realize his fullest potential emotionally and academically. How might this developmental stage look if a baby's special physical or other developmental needs are identified at birth by medical professionals, for instance, with Down's syndrome, cerebral palsy, or blindness? How might this developmental stage materialize if a baby's special physical or other developmental needs are not immediately apparent at birth, but come to be realized over time, as is often the case with *failure to thrive*, deafness, Autism Spectrum Disorder, celiac disease, hemophilia, and learning differences and disabilities? What special developmental needs do you feel pretty confident you could help with? How will you use supervision, consultation, and referral to ensure families with children of differing abilities and special needs get access to appropriate support and opportunity, especially if you don't have previous training to effectively support these families?

Fetuses, infants, toddlers, and young children are minimally differentiated from the systems they inhabit. They depend physically and emotionally on the systems they inhabit to protect and provide for them, and to alter as necessary for their survival and well-being, as well as their emotional integration of a complicated and often dangerous world. Clinically, it is necessary to bear in mind and support the systems (relationships) our youngest members inhabit, in order that those systems can best provide for them. Toward that end, critically examining the interactions among Xquenda's micro-, meso-, and exosystems can support the mental health professional to perform effective client-centered advocacy and identify linkage needs, while also normalizing stressors the parents and teachers are feeling as the family is pressured to assimilate to the dominant culture. Clinically buffering where possible, using one's privilege and access to help navigate systems with more power, can help reduce the burden of stress on a marginalized family. Facilitating access to necessary resources and community support can help the family create a new network of care and continue to build resilience against the ongoing toxic stress they will likely experience. Supporting this clinical intervention is Relational–Cultural Theory, which aims to facilitate the Five Good Things: (a) a desire to move into more good-feeling relationships; (b) a sense of zest; (c) increased knowledge of oneself and the other person; (d) taking action in and outside of the growth-fostering relationship; and (e) an overall increased sense of worth (Robb, 2006).

Helping Xquenda and his family have these mutually growth-fostering relationships through our own clinical attunement and responsiveness can inspire reasonable hope that another network of support might be formed in this new place, and reduce pressure on the nuclear family to provide everything necessary for Xquenda to thrive, which in turn could help them to recover from some of what they have lost and continue their own *post-traumatic growth,* integrating their strengths and capacities to take on demands as they evolve, even while grieving (Perreira & Ornelas, 2013; Umer & Elliot, 2021). Examples include empowering the family to maintain connection to their cultural identities and practices (e.g., asking the parents what name they would like each family member to be addressed by, rather than assuming the names used at school are preferred; Baima & Sude, 2020); inquiring about how they may connect with their spiritual practices in this new place (Koerner et al., 2013); and using time in session to connect with the family's lineage in ways that feel sustaining, to support their inherent wholeness within dominant systems (Cervantes, 2010; Comas-Díaz, 2006; Nader et al., 2013).

Children born with congenital or acquired disabilities or illnesses will need more alteration, accomodation, and consideration from their micro-, meso-, and exosystems in order to have relatively fair access to developmental opportunities within their communities. The more marginalized and subjugated identities and experiences a child absorbs, the more toxic stress they are likely to face as they develop, and the more their optimal development will likely be impinged upon due to this toxic stress. Mental health and allied professionals serving infants, toddlers, young children, and their families often need further education, training, supervision, and experience to be sensitized and effective in anticipating and providing support services needed for children with special needs and/or marginalized identities, as well as navigating oppressive systems on behalf of underserved clients. Thus mental health professionals are encouraged to maintain holistic awareness of fairness not being "same" between clients, but rather, what is needed for each client to meet their optimal potential.

STUDENT REFLECTION 4.6

How would you support Xquenda and his family if you were to work with them at this developmental phase? What interventions would you use to try to bring balance among the limitations they are facing? How would you use supervision to process any expectations you have about how families behave at this developmental stage? How would you collaborate with preschool teachers if you were asked to provide assessment at this phase?

PERSPECTIVE FROM THE FIELD: PODCAST

Access this podcast at http://connect.springerpub.com/content/book/978-0-8261-8279-1/part/part02/chapter/ch04

The goal of this chapter was to provide you with an initial understanding of how infancy and early childhood are shaped by the experiences, contexts, and cultures in which they are embedded. As we prepare to move into the next chapter and dig more deeply into additional theories and models specific to this age of development, I invite you to listen to Dr. Judyth Weaver speak more directly to the developmental considerations we should bear in mind when working with a client like Xquenda. Dr. Weaver is a Reichiean psychologist, practicing clinician certified in multiple somatic modalities, educator, and the founder of Somatic Reclaiming. She is also a leader in the field of pre- andperinatal psychology, facilitating therapeutic processes for groups, families, and individuals to complete unfinished business from gestational and birth imprints.

SUMMARY

Key cultural considerations for families experiencing pregnancy, birth, early bonding of infancy, and the transition to toddlerhood and early childhood include joining with the entire family in support of what regulates and sustains them as a system during these most critical developmental foundations, while grieving losses with the family system. The physical, emotional, and financial demands of early parenthood have historically been shared and absorbed by a greater number of regulated and devoted adults than most contemporary parents in industrialized societies can access regularly, therefore linkage, and facilitating proactive use of internal and external resources, helps shore up families who do not have sufficient support systems for the demands, and is a primary clinical objective. Contextual factors include being sensitive to the pressures placed on families due to conflicting beliefs and behaviors between their own backgrounds and any dominant system (e.g., medical care, education, law enforcement) with which they must interface, to help honor and empower family strengths in their caregiving, which ultimately serves their offspring. Using our professional access to relationships and resources to reduce toxic stress on the family can help reduce risk of prenatal adversity and Adverse Childhood Experiences (ACEs), which in turn optimizes the child's and family's development (Felitti & Anda, 2010).

Every client we serve survived their gestational, birth, early bonding, infancy, and subsequent stages; the work to do so on their part, and their caregivers', can be extraordinary, and may have left emotional residue with behavioral implications. Many clients we will serve were subject to chronic and even toxic and traumatic stressors during these critical periods, wiring their brains, nervous systems, and therefore implicit beliefs with reasons to be fearful and reactive to subsequent stressors, including the emotional complexity of another human being. The more accumulated and unresolved overwhelm a little one has to hold, the more internal pressure is there, ready to tip into emotional distress and resulting behaviors that may appear regressive. In utero substance exposure, malnutrition, violence, and loneliness are disadvantageous for the developing fetus, babies, and young children; a sense of being safe, wanted and lovable, supported, provided for, attended to, and prized all lead to a more secure base moving forward and out into the wider world. Using our trauma-informed mental health training while accessing all necessary allied services to provide socially just and regulating support to all members of a child's family optimizes that child's chances of navigating each developmental stage to the best of their ability.

REFERENCES

Adams, T. G., Kelmendi, B., Brake, C. A., Gruner, P., Badour, C. L., & Pittenger, C. (2018). The role of stress in the pathogenesis and maintenance of obsessive-compulsive disorder. *Chronic Stress, 2*, 247054701875804. 10.1177/2470547018758043

Adolph, K. E., Berger, S. E., & Leo, A. J. (2011). Developmental continuity? Crawling, cruising, and walking. *Developmental Science, 14*(2), 306–318. 10.1111/j.1467-7687.2010.00981.x

Alcock, S. (2013). Toddlers' complex communication: Playfulness from a secure base. *Contemporary Issues in Early Childhood, 14*(2), 179–190. 10.2304/ciec.2013.14.2.179

Andersen, S., Ertac, S., Gneezy, U., List, J. A., & Maximiano, S. (2013). Gender, competitiveness, and socialization at a young age: Evidence from a Matrilineal and a patriarchal society. *The Review of Economics and Statistics, 95*(4), 1438–1443. 10.1162/REST_a_00312

Andrighetti, H. J., Semaka, A., & Austin, J. C. (2017). Women's experiences of participating in a prospective, longitudinal postpartum depression study: Insights for perinatal mental health researchers. *Archives of Women's Mental Health, 20*(4), 547–559. 10.1007/s00737-017-0744-7

Änggård, E. (2011). Children's gendered and non-gendered play in natural spaces. *Children, Youth and Environments, 21*(2), 5. Retrieved May 6, 2021, from http://www.jstor.org/stable/10.7721/chilyoutenvi.21.2.0005

Apicella, C. L., & Crittenden, A. N. (2015). Hunter-gatherer families and parenting. In D. M. Buss (Ed.), *Handbook of evolutionary psychology*. John Wiley & Sons.

Asghar, U., Malik, M. F., & Javed, A. (2016). Pesticide exposure and human health: A review. *Journal of Ecosystem and Ecography, S5*, 005. https://doi.org/10.4172/2157-7625

Atlanta City Review Board. (n.d.). *Get home safely: 10 rules of survival*. Retrieved August 30, 2021, from https://acrbgov.org/education/get-home-safely-10-rules-of-survival

Azad, M. B., Konya, T., Maughan, H., Guttman, D. S., Field, C. J., Chari, R. S., Sears, M. R., Becker, A. B., Scott, J. A., & Kozyrskyj, A. L. (2013). Gut microbiota of healthy Canadian infants: Profiles by mode of delivery and infant diet at 4 months. *Canadian Medical Association Journal, 185*(5), 385–394. 10.1503/cmaj.121189

Badolato, G. M., Boyle, M. D., McCarter, R., Zeoli, A. M., Terrill, W., & Goyal, M. K. (2020). Racial and ethnic disparities in firearm-related pediatric deaths related to legal intervention. *Pediatrics, 146*(6), e2020015917. 10.1542/peds.2020-015917

Baima, T., & Sude, M. E. (2020). The whole name exercise: A self of the therapist activity to support culturally attuned and inclusive communities in MFT training. *International Journal of Systemic Therapy, 32*(1), 1–22. 10.1080/08975353.2020.1761225

Banti, S., Mauri, M., Oppo, A., Borri, C., Rambelli, C., Ramacciotti, D., Montagnani, M. S., Camilleri, V., Cortopassi, S., Rucci, P., & Cassano, G. B. (2011). From the third month of pregnancy to 1 year postpartum: Prevalence, incidence, recurrence, and new onset of depression. Results from the Perinatal Depression–Research & Screening Unit study. *Comprehensive Psychiatry, 52*(4), 343–351.

Barker, M., Dombrowski, S. U., Colbourn, T., Fall, C. H. D., Kriznik, N. M., Lawrence, W. T., Norris, S. A., Ngaiza, G., Patel, D., Skordis-Worrall, J., Sniehotta, F. F., Steegers-Theunissen, R., Vogel, C., Woods-Townsend, K., & Stephenson, J. (2018). Intervention strategies to improve nutrition and health behaviours before conception. *Lancet (London, England), 391*(10132), 1853–1864. 10.1016/S0140-6736(18)30313-1

Barker, R. (2001). *The mighty toddler: The essential guide to the toddler years*. Pan Macmillan Australia.

Barrett, K. C., Zahn-waxler, C., & Cole, P. M. (1993). Avoiders vs. amenders: Implications for the investigation of guilt and shame during toddlerhood? *Cognition and Emotion, 7*(6), 481–505. https://doi.org/10.1080/02699939308409201

Barth, R. P., Courtney, M., Berrick, J. D., & Albert, V. (2017). *From child abuse to permanency planning: Child welfare services pathways and placements*. Routledge. 10.4324/9780203791424

Beaudoin, C., Leblanc, É., Gagner, C., & Beauchamp, M. H. (2020). Systematic review and Inventory of theory of mind measures for young children. *Frontiers in Psychology, 10*, 2905. 10.3389/fpsyg.2019.02905

Beebe, B., & Steele, M. (2013). How does microanalysis of mother–infant communication inform maternal sensitivity and infant attachment? *Attachment & Human Development, 15*(5–6), 583–602. 10.1080/14616734.2013.841050

Behrens, K. Y. (2010). Amae through the eyes of Japanese mothers: Refining differences and similarities between attachment and amae. In P. Erdman & K.-M. Ng (Eds.), *Family therapy and counseling series: Attachment: Expanding the cultural connections* (pp. 55–69). Routledge/Taylor & Francis Group.

Berger, L. M., & Font, S. A. (2015). The role of the family and family-centered programs and policies. *The Future of Children, 25*(1), 155–176. 10.1353/foc.2015.0007

Beyond Pesticides. (n.d.). *Pesticide-induced diseases database*. Retrieved August 30, 2021, from https://www.beyondpesticides.org/resources/pesticide-induced-diseases-database/birth-defects

Boundless. (n.d.). *What is DACA? Everything you need to know*. Retrieved August 30, 2021, from https://www.boundless.com/immigration-resources/what-is-daca

Bowlby, R., & King, P. (2004). *Fifty years of attachment theory: Recollections of Donald Winnicott and John Bowlby*. Karnac Books.

Brazelton, T. B., & Nugent, J. K. (1995). Neonatal behavioral assessment scale (no.137). Cambridge University Press.

Brigano, M. O. (2011). Parallel play. In: S. Goldstein, & J. A. Naglieri (Eds,), Encyclopedia of child behavior and development. Springer. https://doi.org/10.1007/978-0-387-79061-9_2073

Burbidge, A. (2017). *Bedsharing, breastfeeding, and the risk of SIDS. La Leche League*. https://www.laleche.org.uk/bedsharing-breastfeeding-risk-sids/

Campbell-Yeo, M. L., Disher, T. C., Benoit, B. L., & Johnston, C. C. (2015). Understanding kangaroo care and its benefits to preterm infants. *Pediatric Health, Medicine and Therapeutics*, 15. 10.2147/PHMT.S51869

Centers for Disease Control and Prevention. (2019). *DCHS data brief*. Retrieved August 30, 2021, from https://www.cdc.gov/nchs/data/databriefs/db352-h.pdf

Centers for Disease Control and Prevention. (2020, November 16). *National center on birth defects and developmental disabilities: Data and statistics on ADHD*. Retrieved August 30, 2021, from https://www.cdc.gov/NCBDDD/adhd/data.html

Centers for Disease Control and Prevention. (2021, February 4). *National center on birth defects and developmental disabilities: Data and statistics, prevalence of FASD*. Retrieved August 30, 2021, from https://www.cdc.gov/ncbddd/fasd/data.html

Cervantes, J. M. (2010). Mestizo spirituality: Toward an integrated approach to psychotherapy for Latina/OS. *Psychotherapy (Chicago, Ill.)*, 47(4), 527–539. 10.1037/a0022078

Charpak, N., Tessier, R., Ruiz, J. G., Hernandez, J. T., Uriza, F., Villegas, J., Nadeau, L., Mercier, C., Maheu, F., Marin, J., Cortes, D., Gallego, J. M., & Maldonado, D. (2017). Twenty-year follow-up of Kangaroo mother care versus traditional care. *Pediatrics*, 139(1), e20162063. 10.1542/peds.2016-2063

Chasnoff, I. J. (1989). Drug use and women: Establishing a standard of care. *Annals of the New York Academy of Sciences*, 562, 208–210. 10.1111/j.1749-6632.1989.tb21019.x

Chasnoff, I. J., Anson, A., Hatcher, R., Stenson, H., Iaukea, K., & Randolph, L. A. (1998). Prenatal exposure to cocaine and other drugs. Outcome at four to six years. *Annals of the New York Academy of Sciences*, 846, 314–328. 10.1111/j.1749-6632.1998.tb09748.x

Chasnoff, I. J., Barber, G., Brook, J., & Akin, B. A. (2018). The child abuse prevention and treatment act: Knowledge of health care and legal professionals. Child Welfare, 96(3), 41–58.

Chasnoff, I. J., Landress, H. J., & Barrett, M. E. (1990). The prevalence of illicit-drug or alcohol use during pregnancy and discrepancies in mandatory reporting in Pinellas County, Florida. *The New England Journal of Medicine*, 322(17), 1202–1206. 10.1056/NEJM199004263221706

Chasnoff, I. J., McGourty, R. F., Bailey, G. W., Hutchins, E., Lightfoot, S. O., Pawson, L. L., Fahey, C., May, B., Brodie, P., McCulley, L., & Campbell, J. (2005). The 4P's Plus screen for substance use in pregnancy: Clinical application and outcomes. *Journal of Perinatology*, 25(6), 368–374. 10.1038/sj.jp.7211266

Chasnoff, I. J., Wells, A. M., & King, L. (2015). Misdiagnosis and missed diagnoses in foster and adopted children with prenatal alcohol exposure. *Pediatrics*, 135(2), 264–270. 10.1542/peds.2014-2171

Chen, S.-Y., Roller, K., & Kottman, T. (2021). Adlerian family play therapy: Healing the attachment trauma of divorce. *International Journal of Play Therapy*, 30(1), 28–39. 10.1037/pla0000146

Children's Defense Fund. (n.d.). *The state of America's children 2020*. Retrieved August 30, 2021, from https://www.childrensdefense.org/policy/resources/soac-2020-gun-violence

Children's Hospital of Philadelphia. (2020, December). *Center for violence prevention*. Retrieved August 30, 2021, from https://violence.chop.edu/types-violence/gun-violence/gun-violence-facts-and-statistics

Christensen, D. L., Maenner, M. J., Bilder, D., Constantino, J. N., Daniels, J., Durkin, M. S., Fitzgerald, R. T., Kurzius-Spencer, M., Pettygrove, S. D., Robinson, C., Shenouda, J., White, T., Zahorodny, W., Pazol, K., & Dietz, P. (2019). Prevalence and characteristics of autism spectrum disorder among children aged 4 years - early autism and developmental disabilities monitoring network, seven sites, United States, 2010, 2012, and 2014. *Morbidity and Mortality Weekly Report. Surveillance Summaries (Washington, D.C), 68*(2), 1–19. 10.15585/mmwr.ss6802a1

Cleaveland, C., & Kirsch, V. (2020). "They took all my clothes and made me walk naked for two days so I couldn't escape": Latina immigrant experiences of human smuggling in Mexico. *Qualitative Social Work, 19*(2), 213–228. https://doi.org/10.1177/1473325018816362

Cleveland, L., Hill, C. M., Pulse, W. S., DiCioccio, H. C., Field, T., & White-Traut, R. (2017). Systematic review of skin-to-skin care for full-term, healthy newborns. *Journal of Obstetric, Gynecologic & Neonatal Nursing, 46*(6), 857–869. 10.1016/j.jogn.2017.08.005

Clifford, T., & Gorodzinsky, F. (2000). Toilet learning: Anticipatory guidance with a child-oriented approach. *Paediatrics & Child Health, 5*(6), 333–335. https://doi.org/10.1093/pch/5.6.333

Comas-Díaz, L. (2006). Latino healing: The integration of ethnic psychology into psychotherapy. *Psychotherapy, 43*(4), 436–453. 10.1037/0033-3204.43.4.436

Committee on the Science of Children Birth to Age 8: Deepening and Broadening the Foundation for Success; Board on Children, Youth, and Families; Institute of Medicine; National Research Council. (2015). *Transforming the workforce for children birth through age 8: A unifying foundation*. National Academies Press (US). Child Development and Early Learning, 4. https://www.ncbi.nlm.nih.gov/books/NBK310550/

Crawley, D., Zhang, L., Jones, E. J. H., Ahmad, J., Oakley, B., San José Cáceres, A., Charman, T., Buitelaar, J. K., Murphy, D. G. M., Chatham, C., den Ouden, H., Loth, E., Ramus, F., & the EU-AIMS LEAP group. (2020). Modeling flexible behavior in childhood to adulthood shows age-dependent learning mechanisms and less optimal learning in autism in each age group. *PLOS Biology, 18*(10), e3000908. 10.1371/journal.pbio.3000908

Crittenden, A. N., & Marlowe, F. W. (2013). Cooperative child care among the Hadza: Situating multiple attachment in evolutionary context. In N. Quinn & J. M. Mageo (Eds.), *Attachment reconsidered: Cultural perspectives on a Western theory*. Palgrave.

Crosby, S., Laird, K., & Younie, S. (2019). Interactive health-hygiene education for early years: The creation and evaluation of learning resources to improve understanding of handwashing practice. *International Journal of Early Years Education, 27*(4), 374–390. 10.1080/09669760.2019.1628010

Crouter, A. C., & Booth, A. (Eds.). (2003). *Children's influence on family dynamics: The neglected side of family relationships*. Routledge.

Danese, A. J., & Lewis, S. (2017). Psychoneuroimmunology of early-life stress: The hidden wounds of childhood trauma? *Neuropsychopharmacology, 42,* 99–114. https://doi.org/10.1038/npp.2016.198

Dawson, N. K. (2018). From uganda to baltimore to alexandra township: How far can Ainsworth's theory stretch? *South African Journal of Psychiatry, 24,* 1137. 10.4102/sajpsychiatry.v24i0.1137

de Arellano, M. A., Andrews, A. R., Reid-Quiñones, K., Vasquez, D., Doherty, L. S., Danielson, C. K., & Rheingold, A. (2018). Immigration trauma among Hispanic youth: Missed by trauma assessments and predictive of depression and PTSD symptoms. *Journal of Latina/o Psychology, 6*(3), 159–174. 10.1037/lat0000090

DeGruy, J. (2017). Post traumatic slave syndrome. Uptone Press.

Dennis, C.-L., Fung, K., Grigoriadis, S., Robinson, G. E., Romans, S., & Ross, L. (2007). Traditional postpartum practices and rituals: A qualitative systematic review. *Women's Health,* 487–502. https://doi.org/10.2217/17455057.3.4.487

Dennis, T. (2006). Emotional self-regulation in preschoolers: The interplay of child approach reactivity, parenting, and control capacities. *Developmental Psychology, 42*(1), 84–97. 10.1037/0012-1649.42.1.84

Department of Labor Bureau of International Labor Affairs. (n.d.). *Child labor, forced labor, and human trafficking*. Retrieved August 30, 2021, from https://www.dol.gov/agencies/ilab/our-work/child-forced-labor-trafficking

Diamond, J. (2012). Best practices for raising kids? Look to hunter-gatherers. Newsweek. https://www.newsweek.com/best-practices-raising-kids-look-hunter-gatherers-63611

Ding, H. T., Taur, Y., & Walkup, J. T. (2017). Gut microbiota and auMicrobiota and Autism: Key concepts and findConcepts and Findings. *Journal of Autism and Developmental Disorders, 47*(2), 480–489. https://doi.org/10.1007/s10803-016-2960-9

Dmitrieva, J., Gibson, L., Steinberg, L., Piquero, A., & Fagan, J. (2014). Predictors and consequences of gang membership: Comparing Gang Members, Gang Leaders, and non-gang-affiliated adjudicated youth. *Journal of Research on Adolescence, 24*(2), 220–234. 10.1111/jora.12111

Dong, B., & Krohn, M. D. (2016). Escape from violence: What reduces the enduring consequences of adolescent gang affiliation? *Journal of Criminal Justice, 47*, 41–50. 10.1016/j.jcrimjus.2016.07.002

Dunst, C. J., & Kassow, D. Z. (2008). Caregiver sensitivity, contingent social responsiveness, and secure infant attachment. *Journal of Early and Intensive Behavior Intervention, 5*(1), 40–56. 10.1037/h0100409

Edwards, F., Lee, H., & Esposito, M. (2019). Risk of being killed by police use of force in the United States by age, race-ethnicity, and sex. *Proceedings of the National Academy of Sciences of the United States of America, 116*(34), 16793–16798. 10.1073/pnas.1821204116

Ellis, K. (2019). *Race and poverty bias in the child welfare system: Strategies for child welfare practitioners.* https://www.americanbar.org/groups/public_interest/child_law/resources/child_law_practiceonline/january---december-2019/race-and-poverty-bias-in-the-child-welfare-system---strategies-f/

Erin's Law. (n.d.). Retrieved August 30, 2021, from http://www.erinslaw.org

Evertz, K., Janus, L., & Linder, R. (2021). *Handbook of prenatal and perinatal psychology.* Springer International Publishing. 10.1007/978-3-030-41716-1

Feldman, R., Gordon, I., Influs, M., Gutbir, T., & Ebstein, R. P. (2013). Parental oxytocin and early caregiving jointly shape children's oxytocin response and social reciprocity. *Neuropsychopharmacology: Official Publication of the American College of Neuropsychopharmacology, 38*(7), 1154–1162. 10.1038/npp.2013.22

Felitti, V. J., & Anda, R. F. (2010). The relationship of adverse childhood experiences to adult medical disease, psychiatric disorders and sexual behavior: Implications for healthcare. In L. Ruth, E. Vermetten, & C. Pain (Eds.), *The impact of early life trauma on health and disease* (pp. 77–87). Cambridge University Press.

Fisher, P. A., Kim, H. K., Bruce, J., & Pears, K. C. (2012). Cumulative effects of prenatal substance exposure and early adversity on foster children's HPA-axis reactivity during a psychosocial stressor. *International Journal of Behavioral Development, 36*(1), 29–35. https://doi.org/10.1177/0165025411406863

Fleming, T. P., Watkins, A. J., Velazquez, M. A., Mathers, J. C., Prentice, A. M., Stephenson, J., Barker, M., Saffery, R., Yajnik, C. S., Eckert, J. J., Hanson, M. A., Forrester, T., Gluckman, P. D., & Godfrey, K. M. (2018). Origins of lifetime health around the time of conception: Causes and consequences. *Lancet (London, England), 391*(10132), 1842–1852. 10.1016/S0140-6736(18)30312-X

Fontenelle-Tereshchuk, D. (2021). 'Homeschooling' and the COVID-19 Crisis: The insights of parents on curriculum and remote learning. *Interchange, 52*(2), 167–191. 10.1007/s10780-021-09420-w

Fowlie, G., Cohen, N., & Ming, X. (2018). The perturbance of microbiome and gut-brain axis in autism spectrum disorders. *International Journal of Molecular Sciences, 19*(8), 2251. 10.3390/ijms19082251

Fox, N. (1977). Attachment of Kibbutz infants to mother and metapelet. *Child Development, 48*(4), 1228. 10.2307/1128480

Garcini, L. M., Galvan, T., Peña, J. M., Klonoff, E. A., Parra-Medina, D., Ziauddin, K., & Fagundes, C. P. (2019). "A high price paid": Migration-related loss and distress among undocumented Mexican immigrants. *Journal of Latinx Psychology, 7*(3), 245–255. 10.1037/lat0000127

Gil, E. (2006). *Helping abused and traumatized children: Integrating directive and nondirective approaches.* Guilford.

Gilliland, A. L., Verny, T. R., & Psych, D. (1999). The effects of domestic abuse on the unborn child. *Journal of Prenatal & Perinatal Psychology & Health*, 13(3/4), 235.

Goldstein, J., Cohen, J. E., Mareckova, K. M., Holsen, L., Whitfield-Gabrieli, S., Gilmann, S., Buka, S. L., & Hornig, M. (2021). *How we handle stress at 45 linked to prenatal exposure*. The Harvard Gazette. https://news.harvard.edu/gazette/story/2021/04/how-we-handle -stress-at-45-linked-to-prenatal-exposure/

Gouze, K. R., Hopkins, J., Bryant, F. B., & Lavigne, J. V. (2017). Parenting and anxiety: Bi-directional relations in young children. *Journal of Abnormal Child Psychology*, 45(6), 1169–1180. 10.1007/s10802-016-0223-z

Hasanjanzadeh, P., & Faramarzi, M. (2017). Relationship between maternal general and specific-pregnancy stress, anxiety, and depression symptoms and pregnancy outcome. *Journal of Clinical and Diagnostic Research*, 11(4), VC04–VC07. 10.7860/JCDR/2017/24352.9616

Heidarzadeh, M., Hosseini, M. B., Ershadmanesh, M., Gholamitabar Tabari, M., & Khazaee, S. (2013). The effect of kangaroo mother care (KMC) on breastfeeding at the time of NICU discharge. Iranian Red Crescent Medical Journal, 15(4), 302–306. https://doi.org/10.5812/ircmj.2160

Herman, J. L. (2018). Shattered shame states and their repair. In *Shattered states* (pp. 157–170). Routledge.

Herzog, J. I., & Schmahl, C. (2018). Adverse childhood experiences and the consequences on neurobiological, psychosocial, and somatic conditions across the lifespan. *Frontiers in Psychiatry*, 9, 420. 10.3389/fpsyt.2018.00420

Hewitt, L., Kerr, E., Stanley, R. M., & Okely, A. D. (2020). Tummy time and infant health outcomes: A systematic review. *Pediatrics*, 145(6), e20192168. 10.1542/peds.2019-2168

Holmes, R. M., Romeo, L., Ciraola, S., & Grushko, M. (2015). The relationship between creativity, social play, and children's language abilities. *Early Child Development and Care*, 185(7), 1180–1197. https://doi.org/10.1080/03004430.2014.983916

Hong, Y. R., & Park, J. S. (2012). Impact of attachment, temperament and parenting on human development. *Korean Journal of Pediatrics*, 55(12), 449. https://doi.org/10.3345/kjp.2012.55.12.449

Hunziker, U. A., & Barr, R. G. (1986). Increased carrying reduces infant crying: A randomized controlled trial. *Pediatrics*, 77(5), 641–648. https://doi.org/10.1542/peds.77.5.641

Iftikhar, N. (2020). *Dunstan baby language: What is it and does it work?*. https://www.healthline .com/health/baby/dunstan-baby-language

Jawaid, A., Roszkowski, M., & Mansuy, I. M. (2018). Transgenerational epigenetics of traumatic stress. *Progress in Molecular Biology and Translational Science*, 158, 273–298. https://doi.org/10.1016/bs.pmbts.2018.03.003

Jenco, M. (2020). In-hospital formula linked to earlier weaning from breastfeeding. American Academy of Pediatrics. https://www.aappublications.org/news/aapnewsmag/2020/06/09/formulafeeding060920.full.pdf?eType=EmailBlastContent&eId=4793e9bc-c33c -41c3-8333-c4aeaf0d92ce

Jin, M. K., Jacobvitz, D., Hazen, N., & Jung, S. H. (2012). Maternal sensitivity and infant attachment security in Korea: Cross-cultural validation of the strange situation, Attachment & Human Development, 14(1), 33–44. https://doi.org/10.1080/14616734.2012.636656

Johnson, S. (2019). *Attachment theory in practice: Emotionally focused therapy with individuals, couples, and families*. Guilford.

Jonson-Reid, M., Drake, B., Kohl, P., Guo, S., Brown, D., McBride, T., Kim, H., & Lewis, E. (2017). What do we really know about usual care child protective services? *Children and Youth Services Review*, 82, 222–229. https://doi.org/10.1016/j.childyouth.2017.09.019

Kapoulitsas, M., & Corcoran, T. (2015). Compassion fatigue and resilience: A qualitative analysis of social work practice. *Qualitative Social Work*, 14(1), 86–101. https://doi.org/10.1177/1473325014528526

Karp, H. (2002). The happiest baby on the block. Bantam Books.

Keller, H., Voelker, S., & Yovsi, R. D. (2005). Conceptions of parenting in different cultural communities: The case of West African Nso and Northern German Women. *Social Development*, 14(1), 158–180. https://doi.org/10.1111/j.1467-9507.2005.00295.x

Kid Sense. (n.d.). *Gross Motor Activites*. Retrieved August 30, 2021, from https://childdevelopment.com.au/resources/child-development- charts/gross-motor-developmental-chart

Kim, S., Kwok, S., Mayes, L. C., Potenza, M. N., Rutherford, H., & Strathearn, L. (2017). Early adverse experience and substance addiction: Dopamine, oxytocin, and glucocorticoid pathways. *Annals of the New York Academy of Sciences, 1394*(1), 74–91. https://doi.org/10.1111/nyas.13140

Kim, S., & Strathearn, L. (2017). Trauma, mothering, and intergenerational transmission: A synthesis of behavioral and oxytocin research, The Psychoanalytic Study of the Child, 70(1), 200–223, https://doi.org/10.1080/00797308.2016.1277897

Klassen, R. M., Usher, E. L., & Bong, M. (2010). Teachers' collective efficacy, job satisfaction, and job stress in cross-cultural context. The Journal of Experimental Education, 78(4): 464–486. https://doi.org/10.1080/00220970903292975

Klassen, R. M., Wilson, E., Siu, A. F. Y., Hannok, W., Wong, M. W., Wongsri, N., Sonthisap, P., Pubilchol, C., Buranachaitavee, Y., & Jansam, A. (2013). Preservice teachers' work stress, self-efficacy, and occupational commitment in four countries. European Journal of Psychology of Education, 28, 1289–1309. https://doi.org/10.1007/s10212-012-0166-x

Klosterkotter, J., Schultze-lutter, F., Bechdolf, A., & Ruhrmann, S. (2011). Prediction and prevention of schizophrenia: What has been achieved and where to go next? *World Psychiatry, 10*(3), 165–174. https://doi.org/10.1002/j.2051-5545.2011.tb00044.x

Koerner, S. S., Shirai, Y., & Pedroza, R. (2013). Role of religious/spiritual beliefs and practices among Latino family caregivers of Mexican descent. *Journal of Latina/o Psychology, 1*(2), 95–111. https://doi.org/10.1037/a0032438

Kolb, B., & Gibb, R. (2011). Brain plasticity and behaviour in the developing brain. *Journal of the Canadian Academy of Child and Adolescent Psychiatry, 20*(4), 265–276.

Koralek, D. (1992). *Caregivers of young children: Preventing and responding to child maltreatment.* U.S. Department of Health and Human Services Administration for Children and Families Administration on Children, Youth and Families National Center on Child Abuse and Neglect.

Krassner, A. M., Gartstein, M. A., Park, C., Dragan, W. Ł., Lecannelier, F., & Putnam, S. P. (2017). East–west, collectivist-individualist: A cross-cultural examination of temperament in toddlers from Chile, Poland, South Korea, and the US. *European Journal of Developmental Psychology, 14*(4), 449–464. https://doi.org/10.1080/17405629.2016.1236722

Kratzer. (2019). *Harsh Nazi parenting guidelines may still affect German children of today.* https://www.scientificamerican.com/article/harsh-nazi-parenting-guidelines-may-still-affect-german-children-of-today1

Kringelbach, M. L., Stark, E. A., Alexander, C., Bornstein, M. H., & Stein, A. (2016). On Cuteness: Unlocking the Parental Brain and Beyond. *Trends in Cognitive Sciences, 20*(7), 545–558. https://doi.org/10.1016/j.tics.2016.05.003

Kung, K. T. F., Li, G., Golding, J., & Hines, M. (2018). Preschool gender-typed play behavior at age 3.5 years predicts physical aggression at age 13 yeGender-Typed Play Behavior at Age 3.5 Years Predicts Physical Aggression at Age 13 Years. *Archives of Sexual Behavior, 47*(4), 905–914. https://doi.org/10.1007/s10508-017-1005-6

Lai, Y.-H., & Carr, S. (2018). A critical exploration of child-parent attachment as a contextual construct. *Behavioral Sciences, 8*(12), 112. https://doi.org/10.3390/bs8120112

Latini, G., Del Vecchio, A., Massaro, M., Verrotti, A., & DE Felice, C. (2006). *Current Medicinal Chemistry, 13*(21), 2527–2534. 10.2174/092986706778201666

Lehrner, A., & Yehuda, R. (2018). Cultural trauma and epigenetic inheritance. *Development and Psychopathology, 30*(5), 1763–1777. https://doi.org/10.1017/S0954579418001153

Leung, A. K., & Hon, K. L. (2019). Gastroesophageal reflux in children: An updated review. *Drugs in Context, 8*, 1–12. https://doi.org/10.7573/dic.212591

Levine, E., & Tamburrino, M. (2014). Bullying Among Young Children: Strategies for Prevention. *Early Childhood Education Journal, 42*(4), 271–278. https://doi.org/10.1007/s10643-013-0600-y

Levine, P., & Kline, M. (2008). Trauma-proofing your kids. North Atlantic Books.

Lewin, A. B. (2019). *Innovations in CBT for childhood anxiety, OCD, and PTSD: Improving access and outcomes* (pp. 313–331). Cambridge University Press. https://doi.org/10.1017/9781108235655.015

Lewin, A. B., & Piacentini, J. (2010). Evidence-based assessment of child obsessive compulsive disorder: Recommendations for clinical practice and treatment research. *Child & Youth Care Forum, 39*(2), 73–89. https://doi.org/10.1007/s10566-009-9092-8

Lewis, T., Amini, F., & Lannon, R. (2001). A general theory of love. Vintage.

Li, J., Wang, W., Yu, J., & Zhu, L. (2016). Young children's development of fairness preference. *Frontiers in Psychology, 7,* 1274. https://doi.org/10.3389/fpsyg.2016.01274

Liu, Y.-Z., Wang, Y.-X., & Jiang, C.-L. (2017). Inflammation: The common pathway of stress-related diseases. *Frontiers in Human Neuroscience, 11,* 316. https://doi.org/10.3389/fnhum.2017.00316

Lobmaier, S. M., Müller, A., Zelgert, C., Shen, C., Su, P. C., Schmidt, G., Haller, B., Berg, G., Fabre, B., Weyrich, J., Wu, H. T., Frasch, M. G., & Antonelli, M. C. (2020). Fetal heart rate variability responsiveness to maternal stress, non-invasively detected from maternal transabdominal ECG. *Archives of Gynecology and Obstetrics, 301*(2), 405–414. https://doi.org/10.1007/s00404-019-05390-8

Lundström, J. N., Mathe, A., Schaal, B., Frasnelli, J., Nitzsche, K., Gerber, J., & Hummel, T. (2013). Maternal status regulates cortical responses to the body odor of newborns. *Frontiers in Psychology, 4,* 597. https://doi.org/10.3389/fpsyg.2013.00597

Lyons-Ruth, K., Dutra, L., Schuder, M. R., & Bianchi, I. (2006). From infant attachment disorganization to adult dissociation: Relational adaptations or traumatic experiences? *The Psychiatric Clinics of North America, 29*(1), 63–86, . https://doi.org/10.1016/j.psc.2005.10.011

Madigan, S., Browne, D., Racine, N., Mori, C., & Tough, S. (2019). Association between screen time and children's performance on a developmental screening test. *JAMA Pediatrics, 173*(3), 244. https://doi.org/10.1001/jamapediatrics.2018.5056

Madore, C., Leyrolle, Q., Lacabanne, C., Benmamar-Badel, A., Joffre, C., Nadjar, A., & Layé, S. (2016). Neuroinflammation in Autism: Plausible role of maternal inflammation, dietary omega 3, and microbiota. *Neural Plasticity, 2016,* 1–15. https://doi.org/10.1155/2016/3597209

Mah, B. L., Bakermans-Kranenburg, M. J., Van IJzendoorn, M. H., & Smith, R. (2015). Oxytocin promotes protective behavior in depressed mothers: A pilot study with the enthusiastic stranger paradigm. *Depression and Anxiety, 32*(2), 76–81. https://doi.org/10.1002/da.22245

Main, M. (1990). Cross-cultural studies of attachment organization: Recent studies, changing methodologies, and the concept of conditional strategies. *Human Development, 33*(1), 48–61. https://doi.org/10.1159/000276502

Mamane, A., Raherison, C., Tessier, J.-F., Baldi, I., & Bouvier, G. (2015). Environmental exposure to pesticides and respiratory health. *European Respiratory Review, 24*(137), 462–473. https://doi.org/10.1183/16000617.00006114

Marcin, A. (2019). Guide to baby wearing: Benefits, safety tips, and how to. Healthline. https://www.healthline.com/health/parenting/baby-wearing#takeaway.

Mayo Clinic. (2021, March 25). *Language development: Speech milestones for babies.* Retrieved August 30, 2021, from https://www.mayoclinic.org/healthy-lifestyle/infant-and-toddler-health/in-depth/language-development/art-20045163

McCarthy, N. (2017, January 18). *Which countries send and receive the most migrants? Statista.* Retrieved August 30, 2021, from https://www.statista.com/chart/7636/which-countries-host-and-send-the-most-migrants

McGowan, P. O., & Matthews, S. G. (2018). Prenatal stress, glucocorticoids, and developmental programming of the stress response. *Endocrinology, 159*(1), 69–82. https://doi.org/10.1210/en.2017-00896

Mckee, C., Stapleton, P., & Pigeon, A. (2018). History of pre and perinatal (PPN) parenting education: A literature review. Journal of Prenatal & Perinatal Psychology & Health, 32(3), 191–219. https://birthpsychology.com/journal/article/history-pre-and-perinatal-ppn-parenting-education- literature-review

McNaughton, M. J. (1997). Drama and Children's Writing: A study of the influence of drama on the imaginative writing of primary school children. *Research in Drama Education, 2*(1), 55–86. https://doi.org/10.1080/1356978970020105

Mesman, J., Van Ijzendoorn, M. H., & Sagi-Schwartz, A. (2016). Cross-cultural patterns of attachment. In *Handbook of attachment: Theory, research, and clinical applications* (pp. 852–877).

Metin Aslan, Ö. (2018). Turkish and American preschoolers' play, aggression and victimization behaviours in play context. *Early Child Development and Care, 190*(3), 348–363. https://doi.org/10.1080/03004430.2018.1472088

Migration Data Portal. (n.d.). *International data.* Retrieved August 30, 2021, from https://www.migrationdataportal.org/international-data?i=stock_abs_&t=2020

Mlynek, A. (2019). *6 magical ways that breastmilk changes to meet your baby's needs, Today's Parent.* https://www.todaysparent.com/baby/breastfeeding/magical-ways-breastmilk-changes-to-meet-your-babys-needs/

Monk, C., Spicer, J., & Champagne, F. A. (2012). Linking prenatal maternal adversity to developmental outcomes in infants: The role of epigenetic pathways. *Development and Psychopathology, 24*(4), 1361–1376. https://doi.org/10.1017/S0954579412000764

Montenovo, L., Jiang, X., Rojas, F. L., Schmutte, I. M., Simon, K. I., Weinberg, B. A., & Wing, C. (2020). Determinants of disparities in covid-19 job losses (no.w27132). National Bureau of Economic Research.

Mueller, N. T., Bakacs, E., Combellick, J., Grigoryan, Z., & Dominguez-Bello, M. G. (2015). The infant microbiome development: Mom matters. *Trends in Molecular Medicine, 21*(2), 109–117. https://doi.org/10.1016/j.molmed.2014.12.002

Murfin, C. (2012). Lying in: Why laying low for first few weeks after birth is good for you both. Seattle's Child.

Murray, D. (2020). The composition of breastmilk. Verywell Family. https://www.verywellfamily.com/whats-in-breast-milk-4047820

Nader, K., Dubrow, N., & Stamm, B. H. (2013). *Honoring differences: Cultural issues in the treatment of trauma and loss.* Routledge. https://doi.org/10.4324/9780203778005

Nelson, C. A. (2020). The implications of early adversity even before birth. *JAMA Network Open, 3*(1), e1920030. https://doi.org/10.1001/jamanetworkopen.2019.20030

Novak, I. (2019). Why neuroplasticity is the secret ingredient for kids with special needs. Cerebral Palsy Alliance. https://cerebralpalsy.org.au/sstposts/StoryId1575590115573

Occupational Therapy for Children. (n.d.). *Dominance-hand dominance.* Retrieved August 30, 2021, from https://occupationaltherapychildren.com.au/dominance-hand-dominance/

Odom, S. L., Hall, L. J., & Suhrheinrich, J. (2020). Implementation science, behavior analysis, and supporting evidence-based practices for individuals with autism. *European Journal of Behavior Analysis, 21*(1), 55–73. https://doi.org/10.1080/15021149.2019.1641952

Office of Juvenile Justice and Delinquency Prevention. (2017). *National estimates of missing children: Updated findings from a survey of parents and other primary caretakers.* Retrieved August 30, 2021, from https://ojjdp.ojp.gov/sites/g/files/xyckuh176/files/pubs/250089.pdf

Office of the Surgeon General. (n.d.). *Call to action to support breastfeeding.* https://www.hhs.gov/surgeongeneral/reports-and-publications/breastfeeding/index.html

Oxfam. (2016). *Unearthed: Land, power and inequality in Latin America.* https://www.oxfam.org/en/research/unearthed-land-power-and-inequality-latin-america

O'Hara, K. L., Sandler, I. N., Wolchik, S. A., Tein, J. Y., & Rhodes, C. A. (2019). Parenting time, parenting quality, interparental conflict, and mental health problems of children in high-conflict divorce. Journal of Family Psychology, 33(6), 690. https://doi.org/10.1037/fam0000556

Peden, M., Oyegbite, K., Ozanne-Smith, J., Hyder, A. A., Branche, C., Rahman, A., Rivara, F., & Bartolomeos, K. (2008). *World report on child injury prevention.* World Health Organization. https://pubmed.ncbi.nlm.nih.gov/26269872/

Pediatric Autoimmune Neuropsychiatric Disorders Associated with Streptococcal Infections Network. (2018). *Statistics: 1 in 200 children may have PANDAS/PANS.* Retrieved August 30, 2021, from http://pandasnetwork.org/statistics/

Pergamit, M. R. (2010). On the lifetime prevalence of running away from home. Urban Institute (NJ1).

Perreira, K. M., & Ornelas, I. (2013). Painful passages: Traumatic experiences and post-traumatic stress among immigrant latino adolescents and their primary caregivers. *The International Migration Review, 47*(4), 976–1005. https://doi.org/10.1111/imre.12050

Perroud, N., Rutembesa, E., Paoloni-Giacobino, A., Mutabaruka, J., Mutesa, L., Stenz, L., Malafosse, A., & Karege, F. (2014). The Tutsi genocide and transgenerational transmission of maternal stress: Epigenetics and biology of the HPA axis. *The World Journal of Biological Psychiatry, 15*(4), 334–345. https://doi.org/10.3109/15622975.2013.866693

Perry, B. D. (2006). Applying principles of neurodevelopment to clinical work with maltreated and traumatized children: The neurosequential model of therapeutics. In N. B. Webb (Ed.), Social work practice with children and families: Working with traumatized youth in child welfare (pp. 27–52). Guilford Press.

Pew Trust. (2016). *States struggle to provide housing for migrant farmworkers.* https://www.pewtrusts.org/en/research-and-analysis/blogs/stateline/2016/05/02/struggle-to-provide-housing-for-migrant-farmworkers

Pilch, D. (2015). The influence of birth modus on the emotional state of the mother, bonding, and the newborn's neurobehavioural state. Pomeranian Journal of Life Sciences, 61(3), 249–256.

Pineda, A. M. B., Pineda, R. C. L., Pinos, H. O., Rirao, L. B., Rivera, R. J. B., Rodil, K. A. C., Roque, M. C. P., Sabate, R. J. C., Sanchez, S. F., Santos, J. L. M., Santos, J. M., & Brizuela, G. E. (2016). The efficacy of Dunstan baby language in decreasing the parenting stress levels of housewives with 0-2 month old infants: A quasi-experimental study. UERM Health Sciences Journal, 5(1).

Polanczyk, G., Moffitt, T. E., Arseneault, L., Cannon, M., Ambler, A., Keefe, R. S. E., Houts, R., Odgers, C. L., & Caspi, A. (2010). Etiological and Clinical Features of Childhood Psychotic Symptoms. *Archives of General Psychiatry, 67*(4), 328. https://doi.org/10.1001/archgenpsychiatry.2010.14

Porges, S. W., Davila, M. I., Lewis, G. F., Kolacz, J., Okonmah-Obazee, S., Hane, A. A., Kwon, K. Y., Ludwig, R. J., Myers, M. M., & Welch, M. G. (2019). Autonomic regulation of preterm infants is enhanced by Family Nurture Intervention. *Developmental Psychobiology, 61*(6), 942–952. https://doi.org/10.1002/dev.21841

Putignani, L., Del Chierico, F., Petrucca, A., Vernocchi, P., & Dallapiccola, B. (2014). The human gut microbiota: A dynamic interplay with the host from birth to senescence settled during childhood. *Pediatric Research, 76*(1), 2–10. https://doi.org/10.1038/pr.2014.49

Raballo, A., Poletti, M., Preti, A., & McGorry, P. (2020). Clinical high risk for psychosis in children and adolescents: A meta-analysis of transition prevalences. *Schizophrenia Research,* S0920-9964(20)30174-2. https://doi.org/10.1016/j.schres.2020.03.063

Rafferty, J. (2018, September 18). *Gender identify development in children.* Healthy Children.org. https://www.healthychildren.org/English/ages-stages/gradeschool/Pages/Gender-Identity-and- Gender-Confusion-In-Children.aspx

Ragusa, A., Svelato, A., Santacroce, C., Catalano, P., Notarstefano, V., Carnevali, O., Papa, F., Rongioletti, M. C. A., Baiocco, F., Draghi, S., D'Amore, E., Rinaldo, D., Matta, M., & Giorgini, E. (2021). Plasticenta: First evidence of microplastics in human placenta. *Environment International, 146,* 106274. https://doi.org/10.1016/j.envint.2020.106274

Repo, L., & Sajaniemi, N. (2015). Bystanders' roles and children with special educational needs in bullying situations among preschool-aged children. *Early Years: An International Journal of Research and Development, 35*(1), 5–21. https://doi.org/10.1080/09575146.2014.953917

Reynolds-Miller, R. L. (2016). Potential Therapeutic Benefits of Babywearing. *Creative Nursing, 22*(1), 17–23. https://doi.org/10.1891/1078-4535.22.1.17

Rhodes, M., Cardarelli, A., & Leslie, S.-J. (2020). Asking young children to "do science" instead of "be scientists" increases science engagement in a randomized field experiment. *Proceedings of the National Academy of Sciences, 117*(18), 9808–9814. https://doi.org/10.1073/pnas.1919646117

Robb, C. (2006). This changes everything: The relational revolution in psychology. Picador.

Roberts, B., DelVecchio, W., & Wendy, F. (2000). The rank-order consistency of personality traits from childhood to old age: A quantitative review of longitudinal studies. *Psychological Bulletin, 126*(1), 3–25. https://doi.org/10.1037/0033-2909.126.1.3

Roberts, J. R., & Karr, C. J. (2012). Pesticide exposure in children. In Council on Environmental Health. *Pediatrics, 130*(6), e1765–e1788. https://doi.org/10.1542/peds.2012-2758

Ross, E. J., Graham, D. L., Money, K. M., & Stanwood, G. D. (2015). Developmental consequences of fetal exposure to drugs: What we know and what we still must learn. *Neuropsychopharmacology, 40*(1), 61–87. https://doi.org/10.1038/npp.2014.147

Rothbaum, F., & Kakinuma, M. (2004). Amae and attachment. Human Development, 47(1), 34–39. https://doi.org/10.1159/000075368

Rowhani-Rahbar, A., & Moe, C. (2019). School Shootings in the U.S.: What Is the State of Evidence? *The Journal of Adolescent Health, 64*(6), 683–684. https://doi.org/10.1016/j.jadohealth.2019.03.016

Rubin, K. H., Hemphill, S. A., Chen, X., Hastings, P., Sanson, A., Coco, A. L., Zappulla, C., Chung, O.-B., Park, S.-Y., Doh, H. S., Chen, H., Sun, L., Yoon, C.-H., & Cui, L. (2006). A cross-cultural study of behavioral inhibition in toddlers: East–West–North–South. *International Journal of Behavioral Development, 30*(3), 219–226. https://doi.org/10.1177/0165025406066723

Ruhrmann, S., Schultze-Lutter, F., Salokangas, R. K. R., Heinimaa, M., Linszen, D., Dingemans, P., Birchwood, M., Patterson, P., Juckel, G., Heinz, A., Morrison, A., Lewis, S., von Reventlow, H. G., & Klosterkötter, J. (2010). Prediction of psychosis in adolescents and young adults at high risk: results from the prospective European prediction of psychosis study. *Archives of General Psychiatry, 67*(3), 241–251. https://doi.org/10.1001/archgenpsychiatry.2009.206

Russell, B. S., Hutchison, M., Tambling, R., Tomkunas, A. J., & Horton, A. L. (2020). Initial Challenges of Caregiving During COVID-19: Caregiver Burden, Mental Health, and the Parent-Child Relationship. *Child Psychiatry and Human Development, 51*(5), 671–682. https://doi.org/10.1007/s10578-020-01037-x

Sagi, A. (1990). Attachment Theory and Research from a Cross-Cultural Perspective. *Human Development, 33*(1), 10–22. https://doi.org/10.1159/000276499

Sakala, C., Belanoff, C., & Declercq, E. R. (2020). Factors Associated with Unplanned Primary Cesarean Birth: Secondary Analysis of the Listening to Mothers in California Survey. *BMC Pregnancy and Childbirth, 20*(1), 462. https://doi.org/10.1186/s12884-020-03095-4

Saracho, O. N. (2017). Bullying prevention strategies in early childhood education. *Early Childhood Education Journal, 45*(4), 453–460. https://doi.org/10.1007/s10643-016-0793-y

Scatliffe, N., Casavant, S., Vittner, D., & Cong, X. (2019). Oxytocin and early parent-infant interactions: A systematic review. *International Journal of Nursing Sciences, 6*(4), 445–453. https://doi.org/10.1016/j.ijnss.2019.09.009

Schore, A. N. (1991). Early superego development: The emergence of shame and narcissistic affect regulation in the practicing period. Psychoanalysis and Contemporary Thought, 14(2), 187–250.

Schrock, M., & Woodruff-Borden, J. (2010). Parent-Child Interactions in Anxious Families. *Child & Family Behavior Therapy, 32*(4), 291–310. https://doi.org/10.1080/07317107.2010.515523

Schwarze, C. E., Mobascher, A., Pallasch, B., Hoppe, G., Kurz, M., Hellhammer, D. H., & Lieb, K. (2013). Prenatal adversity: A risk factor in borderline personality disorder? *Psychological Medicine, 43*(6), 1279–1291. https://doi.org/10.1017/S0033291712002140

Scott, G. (2021). "Never grow weary of doing good:" Expressions of emotional labor and the presence of burnout and compassion fatigue in child welfare system employees and volunteers [Doctoral dissertation, Angelo State University].

Seng, J., & Taylor, J. (2015). Trauma-informed care in the perinatal period. Dunedin Academic Press.

Serpeloni, F., Radtke, K., de Assis, S. G., Henning, F., Nätt, D., & Elbert, T. (2017). Grandmaternal stress during pregnancy and DNA methylation of the third generation: An epigenome-wide association study. *Translational Psychiatry, 7*(8), e1202–e1202. https://doi.org/10.1038/tp.2017.153

Sharkey, J. D., Shekhtmeyster, Z., Chavez-Lopez, L., Norris, E., & Sass, L. (2011). The protective influence of gangs: Can schools compensate? *Aggression and Violent Behavior*, *16*(1), 45–54. https://doi.org/10.1016/j.avb.2010.11.001

Sharma, D., Murki, S., & Oleti, T. P. (2018). Study comparing "Kangaroo Ward Care" with "Intermediate Intensive Care" for improving the growth outcome and cost effectiveness: Rrandomized control trial. *The Journal of Maternal-Fetal & Neonatal Medicine*, *31*(22), 2986–2993. https://doi.org/10.1080/14767058.2017.1359832

Sheftall, A. H., Asti, L., Horowitz, L. M., Felts, A., Fontanella, C. A., Campo, J. V., & Bridge, J. A. (2016). Suicide in elementary school-aged children and early adolescents. *Pediatrics*, *138*(4), e20160436. https://doi.org/10.1542/peds.2016-0436

Shonkoff, J. P., & Phillips, D. A. (Eds.). (2000). From neurons to neighborhoods: The science of early childhood development. National Academies Press.

Simmons, R. T., Coker, K., Hanks, B. B., Sheperis, D. S., & Bohecker, L. (2021). Mothering identity experiences: A backwards glance. *The Family Journal*, *29*(4), 401–409. https://doi.org/10.1177/10664807211023927

Singh, M. M., Parsekar, S. S., & Nair, S. N. (2014). An epidemiological overview of child sexual abuse. *Journal of Family Medicine and Primary Care*, *3*(4), 430. https://doi.org/10.4103/2249-4863.148139

Sivberg, B. (2003). Parents' detection of early signs in their children having an autistic spectrum disorder. *Journal of Pediatric Nursing*, *18*(6), 433–439. https://doi.org/10.1016/S0882-5963(03)00139-8

Solomon, E. P., & Heide, K. M. (1999). Type III Trauma: Toward a more effective conceptualization of psycholoMore Effective Conceptualization of Psychological Trauma. *International Journal of Offender Therapy and Comparative Criminology*, *43*(2), 202–210. https://doi.org/10.1177/0306624X99432007

Solomon, E. P., & Heide, K. M. (2005). The biology of trauma: Implications for treatment. *Journal of Interpersonal Violence*, *20*(1), 51–60. https://doi.org/10.1177/0886260504268119

Srikantha, P., & Mohajeri, M. H. (2019). The possible role of the microbiota-gut-brain-axis in autism spectrum disorder. *International Journal of Molecular Sciences*, *20*(9), 2115. https://doi.org/10.3390/ijms20092115

Stephenson, J., Heslehurst, N., Hall, J., Schoenaker, D. A. J. M., Hutchinson, J., Cade, J. E., Poston, L., Barrett, G., Crozier, S. R., Barker, M., Kumaran, K., Yajnik, C. S., Baird, J., & Mishra, G. D. (2018). Before the beginning: Nutrition and lifestyle in the preconception period and its importance for future health. *The Lancet*, *391*(10132), 1830–1841. https://doi.org/10.1016/S0140-6736(18)30311-8

Stiles, J., & Jernigan, T. L. (2010). The basics of brain development. *Neuropsychology Review*, *20*(4), 327–348. https://doi.org/10.1007/s11065-010-9148-4

Strand, P. S., Vossen, J. J., & Savage, E. (2019). Culture and child attachment patterns: A behavioral systems synthesis. *Perspectives on Behavior Science*, *42*(4), 835–850. https://doi.org/10.1007/s40614-019-00220-3

Sudland, C. (2020). Challenges and dilemmas working with high-conflict families in child protection casework. *Child & Family Social Work*, *25*(2), 248–255. https://doi.org/10.1111/cfs.12680

Talge, N. M., Neal, C., & Glover, V. (2007). Antenatal maternal stress and long-term effects on child neurodevelopment: Hhow and why? *Journal of Child Psychology and Psychiatry*, *48*(3–4), 245–261. https://doi.org/10.1111/j.1469-7610.2006.01714.x

Tarmure, S., Alexescu, T. G., Orasan, O., Negrean, V., Sitar-Taut, A. V., Coste, S. C., & Todea, D. A. (2020). Influence of pesticides on respiratory pathology – a literature review. *Annals of Agricultural and Environmental Medicine*, *27*(2), 194–200. https://doi.org/10.26444/aaem/121899

Tellis, G. (2010). Kids overimitate adults, regardless of culture. Science. https://www.sciencemag.org/news/2010/05/kids-overimitate-adults-regardless-culture#:~:text=The%20findings%20suggest%20that%20overimitation,was%20a%20human%2Dspecific%20quirk.

Terr, L. C. (2003). Childhood Traumas: An outline and overview. *FOCUS*, *1*(3), 322–334. https://doi.org/10.1176/foc.1.3.322

Terrizzi Jr., J. A., & Shook, N. J. (2020). On the origin of shame: Does shame emerge from an evolved disease-avoidance architecture? *Frontiers in Behavioral Neuroscience, 14*, 19. https://doi.org/10.3389/fnbeh.2020.00019

Thayer, Z. M., Wilson, M. A., Kim, A. W., & Jaeggi, A. V. (2018). Impact of prenatal stress on offspring glucocorticoid levels: A phylogenetic meta-analysis across 14 vertebrate species. *Scientific Reports, 8*(1), 4942. https://doi.org/10.1038/s41598-018-23169-w

The Imprint. (2020). *Who cares? A national county of Foster homes and families*. Retrieved August 30, 2021, from https://www.fostercarecapacity.com/data/youth-in-care

Thiel, F., Iffland, L., Drozd, F., Haga, S. M., Martini, J., Weidner, K., Eberhard-Gran, M., & Garthus-Niegel, S. (2020). Specific relations of dimensional anxiety and manifest anxiety disorders during pregnancy with difficult early infant temperament: a longitudinal cohort study. *Archives of Women's Mental Health, 23*(4), 535–546. https://doi.org/10.1007/s00737-019-01015-w

Torjesen, I. (2020). Covid-19: Mental health services must be boosted to deal with "tsunami" of cases after lockdown. *BMJ*, m1994. https://doi.org/10.1136/bmj.m1994

Tremblay-Perreault, A., & Hébert, M. (2020). Uncovering the associations between child sexual abuse, peer victimization and behavior problems using child, parent and teacher report. *Journal of School Violence, 19*(3), 336–348. https://doi.org/10.1080/15388220.2019.1697276

Trent, M., Dooley, D. G., Dougé, J., & AAP Section on Adolescent Health, AAP Council on Community Pediatrics, AAP Committee on Adolescence. (2019). The impact of racism on child and adolescent healImpact of Racism on Child and Adolescent Health. *Pediatrics, 144*(2), e20191765. https://doi.org/10.1542/peds.2019-1765

Tuthill, S-R. (2021). Can a parent lose their right to a child while in prison? Law Info. https://www.lawinfo.com/resources/child-custody-lawyers/can-parental-rights-be-terminated-when-a-pare.html

Umer, M., & Elliot, D. L. (2021). Being hopeful: Exploring the dynamics of post-traumatic growth and hope in refugees. *Journal of Refugee Studies, 34*(1), 953–975. https://doi.org/10.1093/jrs/fez002

University of Notre Dame. (2010). Child rearing practices of distant ancestors foster morality, compassion in kids. *ScienceDaily*. Retrieved October 29, 2020, from www.sciencedaily.com/releases/2010/09/100921163709.htm

University of Southern California. (2017). Swings in dad's testosterone affects the family -- for better or worse -- after baby arrives. *ScienceDaily*. Retrieved April 30, 2021, from www.sciencedaily.com/releases/2017/09/170905145535.htm

van Ijzendoorn, M. H., & Sagi-Schwartz, A. (2008). Cross-cultural patterns of attachment: Universal and contextual dimensions. In J. Cassidy & P. R. Shaver (Eds.), *Handbook of attachment: Theory, research, and clinical applications* (pp. 880–905). Guilford Press.

Van Lancker, W., & Parolin, Z. (2020). COVID-19, school closures, and child poverty: A social crisis in the making. *The Lancet. Public Health, 5*(5), e243–e244. https://doi.org/10.1016/S2468-2667(20)30084-0

van Reenen, S. L., & van Rensburg, E. (2013). The influence of an unplanned caesarean section on initial mother-infant bonding: Mothers' subjective experiences. *Journal of Psychology in Africa, 23*(2), 269–274. https://doi.org/10.1080/14330237.2013.10820623

Verny, T. R. (1984). Prenatal psychology: Implications for the practice of medicine. *Canadian Family Physician Medecin de Famille Canadien, 30*, 2115–2118.

Verny, T. R. (1989). The scientific basis of pre-and peri-natal psychology-Part 1. Pre- and Peri-Natal Psychology Journal, 3(3), 157–170. https://doi.org/10.2307/25605540

Verny, T. R. (1996). Isolation, rejection and communion in the womb. International Journal of Prenatal and Perinatal Psychology and Medicine, 8, 287–294.

Verny, T. R. (2014). What cells remember: Toward a unified field theory of memory. Journal of Prenatal & Perinatal Psychology & Health, 29(1), 16.

Vesper, H. W., Wang, Y., Vidal, M., Botelho, J. C., & Caudill, S. P. (2015). Serum total testosterone concentrations in the US household population from the NHANES 2011-2012 study population. *Clinical Chemistry, 61*(12), 1495–1504. https://doi.org/10.1373/clinchem.2015.245969

Walker, A. (2010). Breast milk as the gold standard for protective nutrients. *The Journal of Pediatrics, 156*(2 Suppl), S3-7. https://doi.org/10.1016/j.jpeds.2009.11.021

Weissenberger, S., Ptacek, R., Klicperova-Baker, M., Erman, A., Schonova, K., Raboch, J., & Goetz, M. (2017). ADHD, lifestyles and comorbidities: A call for an holistic perspective - from medical to societal intervening factors. *Frontiers in Psychology, 8*, 454. https://doi.org/10.3389/fpsyg.2017.00454

Weissinger, D., West, D., Smith, L. J., & Pitman, T. (2014). Sweet sleep. Pinter & Martin.

World Health Organization. (2011). *Exclusive breastfeeding for six months best for babies everywhere.* Retrieved August 30, 2021, from https://www.who.int/news/item/15-01-2011-exclusive-breastfeeding-for-six-months-best-for-babies-everywhere

World Health Organization. (2021). *Breastfeeding.* Retrieved August 30, 2021, from https://www.who.int/health-topics/breastfeeding#tab=tab_1

Yang, I., Corwin, E. J., Brennan, P. A., Jordan, S., Murphy, J. R., & Dunlop, A. (2016). The infant microbiome: Implications for infant health and neurocognitive development. *Nursing Research, 65*(1), 76–88. https://doi.org/10.1097/NNR.0000000000000133

Young, M. A., & Gonzalez, V. (2013). Getting out of gangs, staying out of gangs: Gang interventions and desistence strategies. National Gang Center Institute for Intergovernmental Research.

Youth.gov. (n.d.a.). *Youth topics/Gang involvement prevention.* Retrieved August 30, 2021, from https://youth.gov/youth-topics/preventing- gang-involvement/federal-data

Youth.gov. (n.d.b.). *Youth topics/LGBT.* Retrieved August 30, 2021, from https://youth.gov/youth-topics/lgbtq-youth/health-depression- and-suicide

CHAPTER **5**

Developmental Theories of Infancy Through Early Childhood

LEARNING OBJECTIVES

Upon completion of this chapter, students will be able to:

1. Identify the stage of lifespan development known as "early childhood."
2. Describe key theories impacting this stage of development.
3. Paraphrase key research impacting this stage of development.
4. Recognize future directions for research and understanding of children and families in early childhood.

INTRODUCTION

Childhood development was the first area of focus for human development theorists. While development clearly unfolds across the lifespan, our earliest years lay the foundation for how our bodies, brains, nervous systems, beliefs, and expectations get set as a baseline from which we make meaning about ourselves and our place in the world. Understanding the situations in which our clients were conceived, gestated, birthed, and raised helps demystify why they react as they do in a variety of circumstances, especially when non-optimal contexts challenge access to developmental needs such as safety and belonging being fulfilled in good timing. Infancy and early childhood are also extremely demanding on caregivers, more so when caregivers are not sufficiently supported, so the relational caregiving context of early childhood is also centered in these theories.

CASE STUDY 5.1: THE CASE OF XQUENDA

Xquenda's family is raising two children who are 6 years apart. The elder daughter Nayeli's gestation and early childhood were spent on family lands in a nearly homogeneous cultural environment with low conflict over values, norms, and beliefs, with shared context of experience that allowed for a sense of continuity in belonging, responsibility, role differentiation, and an available network of support for all members of the family, in addition to enjoying food and housing security throughout this earliest formative stage (though we know these last components

of security began to erode as Nayeli grew). Xquenda's gestation and early childhood have been spent force-migrating to colonized land in crowded co-housing, in a heterogeneous rural residential neighborhood with more conflict over values, norms, and beliefs, without as much shared context of experience, and without an available network of support for all members of the family, in addition to ongoing exposure to chemical and toxic stress, economic stress, and acculturation stress.

Though sharing much genetic inheritance, Xquenda and Nayeli's early childhood epigenetic experiences are vastly different, and this has implications for their physical, emotional, relational, and cognitive development. Furthermore, the bi-directional development that occurs between caregivers and their charges can be quite different between parents and their children due to a variety of impacts on goodness of fit (Newland & Crnic, 2017; Simmons et al., 2021). For instance, Inda Jani and Surem have consistently felt more successful and at ease with their first child than they have with their second based on differences in the children's temperaments and the relative demands placed upon the parents to provide for and attune to the children's needs, as they arrived in vastly different moments in the parents' life cycles. The relative stress each has had to carry in attending to each child has ongoing impacts on their relationships, which they are all navigating together as their life cycles unfold.

A major variable that is shared between the children is the cohesive relationship of the biological parents being committed to their children and doing everything in their power to ensure their children have their needs met under ever-changing circumstances, while maintaining a strong relationship between themselves and those with whom they interact. The parents' shared expectations for how they will treat each other and their children helps mitigate some of the loss and ongoing stressors they are processing, though the long adult memory still creates a tendency to compare the easier past with the more demanding current phase of life. The parents cannot help but wonder why they are having so much more difficulty with Xquenda than they did Nayeli, even when they account for how little support they have now.

INFANCY THROUGH EARLY CHILDHOOD

The founders of human developmental theory began with birth and the early years. They aimed to make sense of the physical and emotional needs of newborns, infants, toddlers, and young children from their frames of reference. The following early theorists emphasized sensory experience, emotions, and meaning-making that result from repeated experience in response to caregiving. While each theorist honed in on different aspects of a young person's earliest development as it influences identity formation, all acknowledged in their theories that caregivers have a tremendous, lasting impact on how babies and children experience safety, belonging, respect, connection, worth, power, and other embodied birthrights. We will explore more deeply the widely misunderstood father of psychoanalysis, Sigmund Freud, and then move on to some of his more influential successors.

Freud's Psychosexual Stages

Freud's *libidinal phases of development*, the psychosexual stages known as *oral, anal, phallic, latency,* and *genital libido* phases, mostly operate beneath our conscious awareness.

They are ancient, inborn, sexually reproductive social mammal needs that give rise to bonding behaviors when they are met well, and aggressive or depressive behaviors when they are not (Freud, 1936). Having a disruptive pattern of needs from any stage going unmet leads to *fixation* on, or *regression* to,that stage, and gives rise to predictable personality traits and defenses that point to traumas and unresolved conflicts emblematic of the work of that phase. Core beliefs and somatic self-states formed about self and others during these early developmental stages give rise to *transference* and *projections* of emotion/expectation onto subsequent *objects* of potential relationship, which Freud explored through *free association* in order to increase patient insight into their root causes and bring to resolution (Brill, 1938). The general therapeutic goal was making the unconscious conscious by integrating the *id* and *superego* into the *ego*, so that one could resolve *neuroses*. Dreamwork and letter-writing were also incorporated to make sense of the unconscious symbolism pointing to the internal wishes and fears (Brill, 1938). Themes around safety, belonging, power, and fulfillment thread throughout all the psychosexual stages.

RELATIONAL–CULTURAL CONSIDERATIONS

Bruno Bettleheim's *Freud and Man's Soul* (1982) importantly revisits the cultural context in which Freud worked with patients and wrote to share his findings and theories, while clarifying problematic losses in translation of his work from Viennese German to English that persist to this day. Victorian Vienna was a sexually repressive society within the realm of the rising Third Reich as Freud's impact was becoming more widespread and hard to control (Gruber, 1987). The meth-addicted Gestapo (Ohler, 2017) eventually arrested Freud's daughter Anna, burned many of his books, and murdered several of his sisters in concentration camps in the wake of forcing him to ex-patriate and write a statement in support of their reign (Gay, 1988; Jones, 1957; Roudinesco & Porter, 2016). In the years leading up to the invasion, a high degree of social control was exhibited by the elite ruling and professional class, and patriarchal abuse of power was normative.

Modern social media fans may consider that many of Freud's patients could have been part of the #metoo movement, and his writings had a similar effect of creating a social revolution requiring accountability and reparation (Danil, 2017). Freud's psychoanalytic patients were often the daughters of his contemporaries (what would now be considered a major conflict of interest, if not a dual relationship), many of whom were reporting molestation and incest (Brill, 1938). Freud was trying to find a way to address this scourge without getting himself killed or his financially dependent patients disowned from their powerful families, and thus his presentations and writing were delivered in a coded manner, with hints of how trauma was being perpetrated by his influential peers (Bettelheim, 1982). Empathizing with his lived experience, one may have compassion for how he veiled his controversial findings while engaged in the talking cure.

Bettleheim's linguistic understanding of Freud's original writings demystifies some of the main suppositions behind Freud's efforts to make the unconscious conscious. The *id*, that animalistic part of us driven by raw impulse to consume, fornicate, attack, and do whatever is necessary to survive, means the *it* within us, that raw body desire ruled by the reptilian and lower mammalian parts of the brain whose sole job is to keep us alive and moving forward as an individual and a species. This portion of the brain is present in the neurotypical neonate. The *ego* is the *I*, that upper limbic and rational mammalian portion of the brain containing the reptilian/lower mammalian *id/it*; if I can tolerate it, I can let you see it, and this layer of awareness is the intermediary between what is underneath and above it, further developed from birth through about age 7. The *superego* is the *over-I*; it is the internalized parental or authority figure, exemplified by the neo- and prefrontal cortex, that watches over the *I* and governs its conduct so that my *it* doesn't take over and destroy me in society (Bettelheim, 1982). This portion of the brain also needs to be constructed from about school age through to age 26, and then is continually organizing itself across the lifespan (U.S. Department of Health and Human Services, 2021, February 22). These notions will be explored a bit more in the updated neuroscience research that follows.

As Freud's developmental and cultural context necessarily informed his identity and meaning-making, he could not imagine what early childhood development might be like in cultures that were more collectivistic, healthfully sex-positive for all genders and consensual adult relationships, focused on emotional proximity, and including children in the group's daily activities. Furthermore, because he was inadvertently uncovering relational and developmental trauma in his early patients in an abusive patriarchal society (Brill, 1938), and presumably comparing their functionality to his own children's experiences, his observations were specific to a group that was largely culturally homogeneous, but may have been demonstrating some in-group variance around early relational/developmental trauma (assuming his own children were not abused and/or neglected).

Looking at birthing and early parenting practices around the world, we know that Victorian Vienna was a comparatively uptight and individualistic culture compared to many others, in a prodromal transcrisis on the verge of a massive collective trauma when Freud was discovering unsavory realities about the behavior of some of his intellectually elite peers and trying to make sense of how to help without putting himself, his family, or his patients in greater danger (City of Vienna, n.d.). With that in mind, let us remember that all human babies are social mammals born with the same universal needs for safety and belonging in proximity and soothing, nourishment and attention, positive predictability and encouragement (Otto & Keller, 2014). What tends to vary between cultures and individuals is not the needs themselves, but the strategies to get those needs met (Main, 1990; Puddledancer press, 2021). If the strategies to meet needs are well attuned and delivered in good timing, the end result will be more time spent in positive affect, which is beneficial for both individuals and their relationships (Johnson, 2019). Much mental health intervention is prescribing specific strategies to get needs met; culturally responsive intervention requires that clinicians be sensitive to what strategies work for whom, when, how, and why (Seponski et al., 2012).

For instance, if we look to various countries in Asia, the Middle East, Africa, and Latin America, as well as among the U.S. Amish, it is common whenever possible to have a *lying in*, or postpartum confinement process for the birth parent and newborn baby, ranging from 30 to 100-days. During *lying in*, the birth parent is protected to heal from being ripped open in giving birth, and is not expected or encouraged to go out into the world, but rather to focus on bonding with the baby and building up their immune systems before interfacing with the world outside while receiving "mothering" from mostly female elders within the family and trusted community (Dennis et al., 2007). Such an endeavor means birth is a highly social and organized event for a family and community, which can reduce the risk of postpartum depression and overwhelm in an otherwise too-isolated birth parent. Such practices, if truly well supported, can increase the likelihood of a baby getting their initial needs met without having to scream in protest or collapse in despair during the early oral phase, thus facilitating greater ease, calm, and well-being as byproducts of early biological and emotional needs being co-regulated in good timing. This would theoretically lower the risk for disruptions to oral gratification, assuming the birth parent has access to the help necessary to meet the demands of this phase, resulting in a general sense of trust within the babies. Conversely, when babies' needs are not responded to quickly, when they must expend a lot of energy protesting to get the nourishment of attention, holding, and food, the negative affect and resulting stress neurochemistry generates embodied tension and a sense of mistrust, which appear in factor analysis research on Freud's oral phase to create "a heightened preoccupation with being supported and nurtured and with seeking oral gratification in terms of over-eating, the abuse of alcohol, and verbosity" (Fisher & Greenberg, 1996, as cited in DelMonte, 1998, p. 39), and can also manifest as depression (Desmet, 2013).

The Oral Phase

CASE STUDY 5.2

Inda Jani and Surem were surrounded by family and friends when Nayeli was born. Inda Jani was able to lay in and rest for weeks after giving birth to Nayeli, and she was tended to by her mother, grandmother, aunties, and lifelong friends, in addition to Surem during breaks from the fields throughout the day. Because Inda Jani was not solely responsible for managing the household, or an outside job, and she had this support network helping welcome the new member, she was able to get some self-care during this demanding phase, which helped with mood stability amid the new stressors. When Nayeli *rooted* on the breast as an infant, or fussed, she was able to nurse for as long as necessary, while Inda Jani sang songs that had come through the family line for generations. When Inda Jani needed a break to bathe, nap, or go for a little walk by herself, she had multiple willing caregivers she trusted to hand the baby to, who would swaddle and sing to her between feedings, and Inda Jani was able to return to bonding refreshed and ready to engage. She recalls this time with a wan smile: "It was the happiest time in my life. Tiring, but happy, hopeful." From a Freudian perspective, Nayeli would presumably not be fixated on getting support or nurturing, or filling up physically and emotionally; Nayeli would presumably trust that her basic needs will be met if at all possible, in good timing, and the result is a basic sense of ease about ingestion and trust in connection.

Xquenda's sister Nayeli was naturally home-birthed and worn by her mother in the first year of life, enjoying on-demand breastfeeding and the comfort of physical and emotional proximity during this vulnerable formative period. Nayeli spent the majority of her infancy soothed and relaxed, with ease of access to her needs being met in a timely manner, without having to compensate with unpreferred substitutions, and this allowed her nervous system and brain to develop optimally, with soft muscles and an emotional openness to connect with attentive others, while not needing to seek attention from overly burdened, distracted or dismissive caregivers. From a Freudian perspective, further developed by Melanie Klein into *object relations*, Nayeli would be expected to perceive her parents as *good objects*, who were physically and emotionally available and responsive to her, allowing her to avoid splitting her perception of her caregivers as good versus bad (Petot, 1991; Westen, 1991).

Xquenda's gestational experience primed him for more prolonged experiences of elevated heart rate when upset, and more difficulty bringing his heart rate back down to a resting baseline (Chiera et al., 2020; Lobmaier et al., 2019); overwhelm can be experienced as shocks to the electrical rhythm of the heart, and these shocks can be held as a "freeze" response in the heart, which needs to be sobbed, trembled, and touched/caressed through the skin to resolution (Heller & LaPierre, 2010; LaPierre, personal communication, Feb. 2021; Stupica et al., 2019). The emergency C-section and subsequent antibiotics further upset his fragile digestive tract; the resulting colic, difficulty latching, and the hospital's protocol of not offering a lactation consultant coalesced in Xquenda being put on formula in the hospital, and thus he did not get the same skin-to-skin contact, baby-specific enzymes and immune-boosting antibodies (Kotlen, 2020; Mlynek, 2019: Murray, 2020; Walker, 2010; World Health Organization, 2011), and relaxed access to immediate, cozy, holistic nourishment as his sister, which may have left him more frustrated and aggravated around being able to receive and take in what he needs from the world, in addition to simply not developing the microbiome necessary to optimally digest stress neurochemistry and rest in a positive baseline mood (Mueller et al., 2015; Putignani et al., 2014; Robertson et al., 2018; Yang et al., 2016).

Furthermore, because his parents suffered multiple stresses and were relatively unsupported emotionally during Xquenda's first year, their ability to respond with ease to his basic first year needs was much more intermittent than for his sister (Stupica et al., 2019). His oral phase development led to much frustration, with long hours of crying, shorter and shallower naps, and a quicker startle response that was tougher to soothe. Both his parents spent much of this year wishing he would sleep better, be more calm and quiet, and be satisfied with the attention they could give him; they also secretly worried about what was "wrong" with their second child.

Inda Jani and Surem were in a new and alien place, without their beloved support system to help them, when Xquenda was born. There was no time for a laying in; Inda Jani took 2 weeks unpaid leave off work, as she had no paid family medical or maternal leave with her fieldwork job. Though the housemates did offer to share food and help with some laundry, Inda Jani and Surem were concerned about becoming a burden, so Inda Jani managed household responsibilities and the baby, and tried not to bother anyone with the crying. Xquenda's difficulty latching and gastrointestinal reflux disorder made him loudly uncomfortable and cranky; he did not root or suckle for comfort, as Inja Jani's milk dried up from not nursing in the hospital. Sometimes Xquenda could settle enough to take formula from a bottle, but sometimes he refused it angrily, reducing Inda Jani to tears. Very much against her wishes, she returned to work 2 weeks after Xquenda was born to keep her job on which the family depended, and left him with a neighbor lady who ran a daycare out of her apartment. Xquenda often refused the bottle there in frustrated, crying protest, and sometimes cried himself back to sleep. From a Freudian perspective, Xquenda would presumably be fixated on oral gratification due to the pattern of disrupted satisfaction in this first psychosexual phase. It would be expected that he would be concerned with getting support and nurturance, getting his turn and attention, getting comfort through food, and being heard. It is also expected he would be at higher risk than Nayeli for falling into depression when relationships aren't going the way he wants, even though their shared genetic and parental inheritance affords them some significant similarities.

THE ANAL PHASE

Subsequent focus around the world on toileting practices suggests that the further from the Equator one is raised, the more toilet-training is delayed; climate, economics, and maternal educational attainment all appear to impact the amount of time babies are permitted to simply follow organicallyarising biological rhythms rather than assert some discipline and self-control over urinating and defecating in a particular place at a particular time (Howard, 2017). Medical data show that about 99% of all people achieve and maintain continence until about 60 years old unless trauma, medical, and/or developmental difficulties interrupt it, and so toileting practices around the world work for the vast majority of us who are medically capable (World Health Organization, 2017). From a Freudian perspective, the main question would be how much stress, tension, and shame one carries because of the messages and even punishment one received about how well we met the parental and societal expectations placed upon us while trying to gain mastery over toileting functions, and to what degree the power and control dynamics inherent in the socialization of our toilet training continue to have a deleterious impact on our day-to-day functioning (Brill, 1938). As stated by Fisher and Greenberg (1996) in relation to their factor analysis, power struggles between the developing toddler and their caregivers over toileting appears to increase risk for "the anal triad-consisting of orderliness, parsimony, and obstinancy. The anal personality is thus confirmed of being concerned with issues of control" (DelMonte, 1998, p. 39).

CASE STUDY 5.3

Nayeli moved through the anal phase living closer to the Equator than her brother, but her parents did not come from a culture where there was pressure to do consistent *elimination communication* in order to teach babies to control urination and defecation on a schedule (Xu et al., 2021). Because she was in arms during so much of her infancy, her cues to go potty were often noticed, and she was supported to go potty in a bowl or outside, but not required to do potty training early. She spent little time uncomfortable in a diaper, and as she became a toddler, was free to run around undiapered much of the time, self-directing to appropriate places to go potty without much stress (Dewar, 2020; Jordan et al., 2020). From a Freudian perspective, Nayeli did not experience power struggles through the Anal Stage. She did not have to assert herself obstinately as she became capable of more continence and decided whether or not to make a mess adults would have to clean, so presumably, she is not overly concerned ("fixated-regressed") about how much control she has in a situation, represented by imbalances or reactivity around personal assertion, personal productivity, tidiness issues, and general movement toward a focus on others, rather than herself (Combalbert et al., 2006; Juni & Cohen, 1985).

Xquenda moved through the Anal Phase living farther from the Equator, where cultural norms do not generally allow for elimination communication due to work requirements away from home (Dewar, 2020). Because his caregivers were not realistically able to have him in arms most of the time during his infancy, his cues for needing to urinate and defecate were not tracked as closely, and he lived in a diaper to make general care and cleanliness more manageable. When he became a toddler and was physically able to remove his own diaper, he sometimes did so out of frustrated desperation to get focused attention at daycare and, realizing this worked, he began to do it at home on occasion, too. His parents became very concerned he would defecate on the host family's furniture or carpet, and began to monitor him with more stress as he asserted his budding independence. From a Freudian perspective, Xquenda's oral fixation bled into an anal fixation, where his unfulfilled need to be nourished and nurtured was then exacerbated by power struggles around where, how, when, and even why he eliminated when and where he did. This was experienced as obstinacy by his caregivers.

STUDENT REFLECTION 5.1

What would your clinical judgment suggest would be a natural difference between Nayeli and Xquenda with regard to their sense of ease around holding and letting go as developmentally appropriate? How do you think the parents and school can best help Xquenda navigate these pressures at home and school? How would you use supervision, consultation, and collaboration with school-based community partners to come up with satisfactory strategies to empower Xquenda so that he is not embarrassed by accidents at school? How could you use child-centered and family play with preferred activities and objects to empower him to hold and let go with more facility, and help anchor those gains to his ego development in relationship?

The Phallic Stage

Sociological research on child-rearing practices of preschool-aged children also reveals meaningful variation in how much young children are incorporated into the daily rhythms of the family of origin, extended kinship, and community, which would theoretically have an impact on emotional and relational integration of developmental needs and changes during Freud's Phallic Stage (Kulic et al., 2019; Roopnarine & Davidson, 2015). Sleeping arrangements, bathing practices, errands, food preparation, how much access to which caregivers, expectations to perform academically, which impulses and emotions are permissible to express (plus when and how) are all culturally informed, and children must learn to survive and cope within the systems where they find themselves.

While language, gross and fine motor skills, cognitive, and gender identity development all explode on the scene for most children during the Phallic Stage, it is not as clear across the globe that all children are universally having to navigate a deep-seated desire to eliminate their rival parent to have sexual access to their preferred parent, or that fear of losing one's genitalia is common outside of cultures where genital mutilation is widely practiced or a realistic concern (Campbell et al., 2009; Mpinga et al., 2016; Wilson & Roehrborn, 1999; World Health Organization, 1997). What is evident is that preschool age children are generally aware of their genitalia, what that means about their assigned sex, possibly whether or not that accords with their subjective sense of gender, some expectations of gender roles within the society where they live, and whether or not they are safe in their bodies at home and outside (Healthy Children, 2019). Traumatology would suggest that precocious overtly and accurately sexualized behavior may very well be a trauma response, while innocent curiosity and questions of peers (e.g., "playing doctor") and adults are normative and not necessarily something to worry about (Levine, 2003; Rady Children's Hospital, 2014).

CASE STUDY 5.4

Both Nayeli and Xquenda were affirmed in their need for affection and attention from both their parents through the Phallic Stage, leaving both of them free of fixation or regression on the Oedipal/Electra complex and resulting residue of a phallic personality (Brill, 1938). Neither was exposed to dismissive or invasive attitudes about their self-expression with regard to inborn sexuality or gender identity, nor forced to submit to sexual attention or touch. Both have enjoyed uninterrupted and safe co-sleeping in the family bed, and the parents have been organized about how and when to privately maintain their sexual relationship without over-stimulating or rejecting the children in their developmental needs. While Nayeli was nestled in kinship care with beloveds who honored her body boundaries and self-expression, Xquenda also was blessed with non-kinship caregivers that fundamentally respected his body and identities, and allowed him free expression without over-stimulating him or requiring his affection in exchange for his needs to be met. Nayeli's name is strictly feminine, derived from a Zapotec phrase that means "I love you," but also the word "open," in addition to the Nahuatl word for "princess"; thus far, her name appears to be syntonic with her identities, and not a subject of resistance. Xquenda's name is androgynous in Zapotec for "spirit, soul, essence," which signals his parents' culturally syntonic openness to fluid sexual and gender identity and expression (at least for Xquenda), in resistance to missionary colonialism (Estrada, 2003; Indian Health Service, n.d.; Nicolas, 2018; Ristock et al., 2010); no matter where Xquenda lands on the gender identity spectrum, the name is gender-fluid.

From a Freudian perspective, both Nayeli and Xquenda appear to have navigated the Phallic Stage without circumstances adding tension regarding their developing sense of gender and sexual identity, inborn attractions, need for parental love and affection, or safety in their developing sexual self. Had sexual boundary violations, emotional rejections, or other significant traumas occurred during the Phallic Stage, it would be expected there would be added acting out or acting in related to body boundaries and expression of affection and attraction, possibly resulting in eventual sexual compulsivity and/or promiscuity (Jerkovic & Berberovic, 2012).

Updated Research

Neuroscience has become the new darling of modern psychological research, and *neuropsychoanalysis* is revisiting Freud's original suppositions with the benefit of

STUDENT REFLECTION 5.2

When children have been molested directly or over-exposed to sexual behavior, it is not unusual for them to demonstrate precocious sexualized behavior with peers or adults. How do you think this might show up in the classroom or play yard, and how would you use supervision and consultation to navigate these sensitive issues therapeutically?

technologies unavailable in his day (McGowan, 2014). Neuroscience power brokers Antonio Damasio, Joseph LeDoux, Jaak Panksepp, V. S. Ramachandran, and Eric Kandel have all taken Freud's theories to investigative task. Kandel, a Nobel Prize-winning neuroscientist, affirmed in *The Age of Insight* (2012) Freud's view that the majority of our mental and emotional life,

> is unconscious at any given moment....(and) that the instincts for aggressive and sexual strivings, like the instincts to eat and drink, are built ... into our genome....normal mental life and mental illness form a continuum (Owen, 2017, para. 7).

Multiple imaging techniques of the last decades have differentiated the triune (three-layered) brain, with various types of scans demonstrating that the three layers do not always talk to each other fluently, but work in neural networks, and develop in response to repeated experience, thus creating functional variance between individuals (Music, 2018; Turnbull et al., 2019). Traumatology neuroscience shows that rather than an elevator smoothly moving up and down between the layers across the lifespan when under duress, our blood flow and electricity tend to drop from the upper layers, once they have been built in adolescence and early adulthood, way down into the basement of the reptilian brain when our attempts to use the social-engagement system do not resolve a threat, or when we are otherwise presented with rapid threat stimuli that trigger a historical trauma response (Kozlowska et al., 2015; Schimmenti & Caretti, 2016). Furthermore, when "we are placed under extreme stress, the memory-forming hippocampus is bypassed, and experience registers in the fear center of the amygdala, creating what LeDoux in 'Psychoanalytic Theory: Clues from the Brain' (1999) called an 'unconscious memory'" (Owen, 2017). Much of modern traumatology works with these implicit, embodied memories as they show up in repetitive holding, movement and behavior, sometimes working to make them explicit, but sometimes not (Schimmenti & Caretti, 2016).

Neuroscience is now corroborating much of Freud's conceptualization of how our various developmental capacities as a species are brought online and made dominant in response to maturation within circumstances, what is now called *experience-dependent learning*, and that with consistent patterns, our grey matter thickens and synapses neurologically wire together in response to the demands and gifts of the environment (Costandi, 2014; Fields, 2020). Thus, for babies and small children who are well-supported and whose developmental needs are met consistently, the early-developing lower layers of the brain do not need to grow larger or more reactive for survival, and the blood flow and electricity can afford to go up the elevator, focusing growth on the later developing cortex and neocortex, and resulting organization of higher executive functions as those developmental capacities naturally unfold (Lewis et al., 2000). However, for babies and small children who are exposed to toxic stress, including neglect and/or abuse, the blood flow and electricity must necessarily stay focused on the survival activities mediated by the reptilian brain, and thus a more reactive fight-flight-freeze-fawn-flop response is a predictable outgrowth of that lived experience, as can be blocks to explicit recall of overwhelming events that initiate a self-protective or aggressive reaction to stress (Bracha, 2004; Hambrick et al., 2019).

Neuroscience is therefore normalizing the biological and physiological underpinnings of psychological beliefs and resulting behavior under both calm and stressful developmental (trait) and momentary (state-specific) conditions, aligning with Freud's *Project for a Scientific Psychology*, with various approaches being more or less reductionistic, more or less focused on the brain (objective material) versus the mind (subjective meaning-making; Bassiri, 2013; Khalsa et al., 2018). This ongoing research highlights the nature of nurture, that epigenetic exposure turns on or off inherited genetic potentials, resulting in both individual and cultural beliefs, with free-floating anxiety being channeled in ways that can be both culturally syntonic or dystonic (Campbell & Garcia, 2009; Lende & Downey, 2012). So while Freud's theories are not all universally applicable, they are not all universally inaccurate, either. As Cieri and Esposito (2019) note, the free energy principle is:

> *the royal road* in the dialogue between neuroscience and psychoanalysis, *the bridge* between mind and brain (as an) adaptive biological system, connecting psychological sciences, neurosciences and related fields in perfect confluence and synergy with psychoanalytic concepts. (para. 12)

Subsequent developmental theorists who built upon Freud's foundation sometimes needed to jackhammer open a few holes to go underneath it, as well as cantilever out from it before erecting their walls; that they were able to do so meaningfully is owed to the solid slab he laid down for them.

STUDENT REFLECTION 5.3

From an updated Freudian lens, what would your budding clinical judgment tell you regarding how much tension versus ease each child of Inda Jani and Surem has had to hold and process? Since it requires biological and emotional labor to digest stress neurochemistry and body-based tension, which of the two children is likely to be spending more time and effort stressed? How do you imagine that stress might show up behaviorally as the children move through developmental stages? How might that stress affect the family, educational professional, and peers around the child? How would you as a mental health professional soothe yourself to regulate reactivity to that stress?

CASE STUDY 5.5

Xquenda is having difficulties incorporating the developmental tasks of the Oral and Anal Stages during the entry to school, with echoes of the unresolved work showing up in frustrated aggression when he is not able to access what he needs, or when he can't control an interaction with relaxed ease that it will resolve in his favor. Luckily, he does not have added anxiety, inhibition, and shame from traumatic interruptions during the Phallic Stage, thus there is some holding capacity to work through earlier frustrations and grief as he moves toward formal school entry and the latency phase. Because he is not also caught up in fight-flight-freeze-fawn-flop from ongoing traumatic interruptions in current time, and he is supported by a secure base in his parents, it is possible to do titrated exposure to that which causes him small amounts of stress and work to build his window of tolerance with that activation, while aiming to deliver the emotional and physical supplies he needed but did not always get as a fetus, neonate, infant, and toddler to down-regulate that activation in increasingly age-appropriate ways.

Clinicians aware of the subconscious stress that may be held over from gestation and birth through to school entry may gently assess through the parents how baby's ingestion and toilet training was navigated, listening for themes of tension, negative affect, or other parenting difficulty, and helping to process through age-appropriate child-centered and family play therapy (Ray & McCullough, 2016) the patterns that show the child is stuck trying to gain mastery yet from those phases, while also working with holistically oriented medical practitioners to help build the biological health necessary for positive mood and easeful behavior. Freud's *repetition compulsion* (Brill, 1938) of stuck patterns that need working through can help clarify what stage of early development has been thwarted and merits therapeutic attention, and family counseling with sensitivity to perinatal and early developmental themes can facilitate the processing of grief and relational disconnection from behavior that arose out of overwhelming emotions (Lieberman et al., 2020).

Reich (c. 1920–1957)

Wilhelm Reich was a star pupil of Freud's, both having medical and psychoanalytic education to inform their ongoing studies of the mind–body connection, in a shared cultural experience, developing their theories among the Vienna Psychoanalytic Society before having to escape the Nazis. Reich took Freud's psychosexual work one step further (Reich, 1927) and stirred up even more controversy and professional ostracization in the process, as he migrated over Europe looking for a safe place to research and practice out of the reach of the Gestapo. Reich's life work of experimentation and research was originally centered on White, European, presumably cisgender, heterosexual adults, resulting in his development of sexual health policies he was trying to extend down into adolescence through public health clinics, to his own peril (Sharaf, 1983, 1994). Homosexuality was much maligned under fascism, and socialist reactions to fascism (Gruber, 1987; Reich, 1933b), and thus much that might have been written about same-sex relationships and psychological development was likely burned (Kinsey Institute, 2017, Nov. 28); however, Reich appeared to be a product of his environment in his belief that homosexuality was a neurosis or aberration to be aligned with Nazism (Oosterhuis, 1995). He ultimately emigrated to America in hopes of finding a more receptive environment for his research, but suffered an even worse fate of ex-communication than Freud, ultimately dying of heart failure in prison shortly after his books were burned in the United States (Hale, 1974; Today in Civil Liberties History, n.d.).

Reich is credited with being the godfather of a sexual revolution in his day (Bramwell, 2018). His student Fritz Perls went on to found the most widely recognized body-inclusive modality, Gestalt therapy (Fischer, 2012; Totally History, n.d.), while many other modern body-inclusive therapies also root their origin stories in Reich's work (Marlock et al., 2015). The Beat Generation artists often referenced Reich's experimental devices and their experiences in them (Antonic, 2019), thus he enjoyed an influential following at his peak.

Biographical research on Reich (Sharaf, 1983, 1994) suggests that he likely had a significant Type II and III trauma history; specifically, a sexual abuse history with a trusted nanny; exposure to his mother's sexual relationship with her private tutor; his mother's suicide upon discovery of the affair by her husband when Reich was 12; surviving life in the trenches; and living under the pressing specter of fascism throughout his early childhood and early career. In reflection on losing his mother, he wrote the "joy of life [was] shattered, torn apart from [his] inmost being for the rest of [his] life!" (Sharaf, 1983, 1994, p. 43); his tutor was sent away, and then his father soon after died of unceasing pneumonia and tuberculosis. Reich spent his late teens in the trenches in a horrendous war, his family home destroyed, family fortune vanished; he arrived in Vienna shell-shocked, penniless, and without family (Reich, 2005). The details of these suppositions are acknowledged in his private journal entries (Reich, 2013), and if taken at face value through a trauma-informed lens, normalize some of the ways he reportedly comported himself sexually and relationally across his lifespan (Barnum & Perrone-McGovern, 2017). As formal codes of ethics were still in the formative stages during the early development of psychoanalysis, modern reflection on the boundary blurring and abuse of power that occurred between practitioner and patient highlights how the projected trauma of toxic patriarchy informed the need for laws and regulations with regard to patient rights; Reich became sexually involved with a patient whom he later married, and may have aborted his child with another patient (New World Encyclopedia, n.d.).

ORGONE AND VEGETOTHERAPY

For the purposes of this chapter, we will focus on the components of Reich's *orgone* and *vegetotherapy* theory that are relevant for young children's development (Reich, 1983, 1984), while situating his work in the larger cultural milieu and resulting theory development. Reich's investigations into the inborn lifeforce, which he dubbed *orgone* (derived from *organic* and *orgasm*, similar to Freud's *libido*) (Reich, 1942, 1963, 1973), led him to further incarnate Freud's and Jung's depth psychology theories on how chronic social impingements and threats infringe upon the embodied being, both individual and sociocultural, breaking down our ability to love fully and resulting in the rise of evil and violence (Reich, 1933b, 1953).

CHARACTER ARMOR

Rather than just affecting how we think and emote in the moment in response to our internal desires versus the expectations placed upon us by family and society, Reich posited that the stress of these assaults on our natural needs for empathy and embodied connection and expression left behind residue of muscular tension defenses he called *muscular* or *character armor* (1933b), that shows in how one holds oneself in, up, down, or back; blocks against emotional or physical exposure; and aims to protect from future hurt. This character armoring expanded clinical body-based awareness from Freud's erogenous libidinal zones to the muscles we use to fight or flee, freeze, fawn, or flop (aka fright or faint; Bracha, 2004; Kozlowska et al., 2015), while Reich's work on adolescence and adulthood encouraged the healing powers of complete orgasmic release both as a measure of how free one's lifeforce was flowing, and as a way to heal these historical embodied blocks (1942, 1973).

CHARACTER STRUCTURE AND ANALYSIS

Reich considered character armor to be our subconscious defenses erected to protect us when we were too young and small to do so effectively with other behavior, and this muscular tension was theorized to organize itself in particular segmented body patterns based on survival and coping mechanisms, which he categorized into *character structures*. The tension can result in a depletion of energy, resulting in a slumping,

FIELD NOTES 5.1

From a general practice standpoint, I (Roller) have found that at least some components of Reich's character armor theory are self-evident when comparing two very disparate groups of infants. As a volunteer holding babies born addicted to crack while their birth parents participated in recovery treatment, this author has felt the stuck holding and tactile withdrawal from touch that is common in babies with this form of in utero substance exposure and neonatal abstinence syndrome (Addiction Center, 2021, 2021, March 24). Their arching of the back, rigid bellies, clenched fists, and general inability to relax from prolonged unsootheable crying makes these babies' muscles very tense, and the diaphragm particularly reactive to rubbing. Their movement patterns are thus gripping and sharp, and their lower weight simply does not rest down comfortably into the support of being held. They simultaneously need, but cannot be soothed by touch. It is clear the nervous system is more highly reactive and less easily down-regulated, and that contact with the world is generally overwhelming due to the lack of endogenous painkillers and feel-good neurochemistry they generate.

However, in many other babies without in-utero exposure I've held as a babysitter, family clinician, allo-parent, and parent, particularly babies who are breastfeeding and being worn a lot, those babies tend to allow their heavier weight to sink down trustfully into the supportive holding arms, lean heavily against the caregiver's torso, melt their muscles in relaxation when it is time to rest, and demonstrate more fluid, easeful movement when they are awake, while being peacefully responsive to both soothing and playful touch. These safer, calmer, happier babies don't generally resist touch, or hold defensive tension in their bodies, but instead engage in mutual enjoyment of touch and proximity.

withdrawn, flaccid stance on one end of the spectrum, and an uptight, rigid, aggressive stance on the other end. Reich experimented with touch and pressure to release this held over muscular tension or depletion, and facilitate emotional expression and liberation in his clients, as well as in building devices to try to collect and direct this orgone for self-healing, or facilitate clients' self-care and release of this tension through self-applied pressure in postures to access and breathe through the armoring (Reich, 1933a, 2004), much like yoga asanas.

Reich's Character Analysis (1933a) is continuing to be revisited and studied using methods more aligned with updated codes of ethics (Anthi, 2020; Bodynamic International, n.d.; Energetics Institute, n.d.; Lothane, 2017; Sletvold, 2011). In reflecting on his core principles regarding a universal life force that brings human life into being through the orgasm, and how that life force continues to seek expression in directional and receptive movement in order that life be sustained and sent forth, one may appreciate how Reich's rational fear of the rigidly controlling SS soldiers would help shape his beliefs that love and evil could not be embodied simultaneously, but would necessarily split during early character formation, and that these basic setpoints for worldview would have biological expression in myriad ways. Reich was critiquing prevailing Nazi parenting practices that actually encouraged intentional neglect of infant's needs to make babies less able to attach, which may have contributed to the widespread de-sensitization and lack of empathy that made their genocide possible, and may have ongoing transgenerational effects (Kratzer, 2019).

Among Reich's legacy desires was to change the way parenting and educational practices embraced and fostered the health of all children, to protect their inherent wholeness and freedom, while leading to a more gentle and loving world (Reich, 1983, 1984). As he stated in the most recent biopic "Love, Work, and Knowledge: The Life and Trials of Wilhelm Reich" by Kevin Hinchey,

> "… we have to … derive our whole … criticism of society from the needs of the living in the child … hope that (they) will be able to influence … society from the standpoint of the living, not … party, state, church, … culture."

The Wilhelm Reich Infant Trust is a museum and bookstore that offers resources and training for the use of his "pioneering contributions to psychoanalysis, scientific study of human sexuality, and body psychotherapy, as well as his decades of scientific work developing an energetic understanding of medicine, biology, sociology" (Wilhelm Reich Museum, n.d., para. 2).

Relational–Cultural Considerations

Like Freud, Reich's life and work cannot be separated from the White, Eurocentric, industrialized, patriarchal, cis-heteronormative society with which he identified and within which he enjoyed many more visible and invisible privileges of ableism, citizenship, dominant language facility, educational attainment, financial status, and professional identity, plus all the social collateral those privileges bring. Significantly countering these privileges were his traumatic relational losses, complex trauma of multiple deployments, and the fascist threat and genocide occurring throughout much of his development, although less so for him than those who did not have his protective privileges and freedom of movement to escape.

Though he was able to hold a critical lens to that which caused *him* harm and traumatic stress, Reich did not demonstrate that he was as sensitized to the harm and stress that did not affect those who looked or lived like him directly; his privilege as a White cis and heterosexual able-bodied man informed his biases as he worked toward some semblance of sexual, emotional, and political liberation for those with whom he identified. That Reich's parents were Galician and Bukovina Jews, but opted not to raise him Jewish or speak Yiddish (presumably for fear of persecution), may have further protected him from the Holocaust well enough that he was able to escape and complete the work that he did (Sharaf, 1983, 1994).

Having to deny or be cut off from parts of one's ancestral heritage can mean an irreversible loss that one must find a way to integrate, which is a traumatic pattern in place for millions of people today; this pain of loss can initially sensitize one to that loss in others, unless it becomes pervasively traumatizing, in which case capacity for empathy in others' suffering may be reduced (Hofmeyer et al., 2020). Using his own theory, one could posit that Reich had developed *character armor* in response to the pervasive threat that his parents knew loomed and would require skillful navigation to escape, compounded by his early sexualization by his nanny, and the traumatic death of his mother, loss of his tutor, and then death of his father, and that this embodied tension resulted in shaping his worldview and perception in ways he was trying to work through much of his life.

Reich's character armor work was deeply influenced by movement specialist Elsa Gindler; her role in the development of his vegetotherapy allowed the field of somatics to receive White cisgender able-bodied heterosexual feminist input, and initial attempts at diversification in thought and research (Geuter et al., 2010). His character armor work is also widely credited with inspiring his contemporary Anna Freud's *The Ego and the Mechanisms of Defence* (1936), which then allowed an initial branching out of embodied psychoanalytic theory generation and research through White cisgender women. This preliminary diversification began a practice of applying the White Western scientific method to embodied wisdom and healing traditions from around the world, which is still in the beginning stages of generating peer-reviewed research outcomes (Matlock et al., 2015), a necessary ingredient for legitimacy in the eyes of Western managed care so that interventions may be applied with a Western science evidence base.

CASE STUDY 5.6

Xquenda's gestation, infancy, and early childhood appear to be devoid of outright abuse, but may have tinges of occasional unintentional neglect resulting in held frustration and reactivity due to the toxic stressors the entire family was having to navigate during his most formative stages, reducing their capacity to focus on regulating his needs and temperament. It is likely he holds more tension than Nayeli in the large muscles of the legs, chest, arms, and along the diaphragm. The brain cannot be relaxed when the muscles are constantly tensed, so finding age-appropriate ways to release this tension through play, movement, and attuned parental touch will be necessary to help fulfill his needs for peace and ease.

Updated Research

There are a few neo-Reichian researchers who continue to adhere to his original lines of inquiry with updated ethics and methods (DeMeo, 2011; DeMeo et al., 2012; Strick, 2015), however most subsequent body-inclusive psychoanalysts and clinical practitioners have used his premises more as stepping-stones than end-games, and have instead mined Reich's articulation of incarnated childhood trauma to help prevent or resolve character armor (Matlock et al., 2015).

There are now several dozen distinct body-inclusive psychotherapies and somatic approaches, a significant subset of which focus their treatment on the embodied echo of early childhood developmental disruptions that continue to impact people's sense of safety in connection, in resolving held patterns that restrict neurophysiological signs of ease, and in dissolving states of shock that impede effective grieving in order to re-engage fully (Matlock et al., 2015). Though this body of published work is increasingly cross-cultural and beginning to be led by LGBTQ + and BIPOC practitioners and researchers around the world, the written work has historically been rooted in White-centered and financially privileged educational and training institutions, even though many of the wisdom traditions from which it draws have long oral histories and traditions that made the theories available for Western scientific method application in the first place. Thus,colonization of thought and practice is therefore also evident here, and much more diversification of leadership within and outside of academia will be necessary before meaningful outcomes will be generated for underrepresented and marginalized groups and individuals who cannot access therapeutic services but must work through the methods approved by managed care.

The evolution of somatics is currently allowing for both increased differentiation and prioritization between the three main foci (awareness, touch, and movement), as well as integrated approaches that honor common factors (Matlock et al., 2015). Work underway is beginning to utilize neurophysiological and other quantitative measures, in addition to a history of qualitative inquiry, to assess mixed-methods outcomes over various treatment modalities (The Traumatic Stress Research Consortium, 2020, September).

Among somatic approaches focused on preventing character armor and resulting dysregulation and disconnection in babies and children, or aiming to resolve character armor defenses from these early developmental phases through body-inclusive interventions for youth and adults are: Biosynthesis (Boadella, 1987, 2015; Boadella & Boadella, 2006); Body–Mind Centering (Cohen, 2017); Body–Mind Integration (Aposhyan, 2004); Bodynamics (Frazer, 2014; Isaacs & Isaacs, 2001; Suvorov, 2020); Cranio-Sacral Therapy (Exner-Pirot et al., 2018); Dialectical Behavioral Therapy (Bohus et al., 2020; Krüger et al., 2014: Linehan et al., 2006); Gestalt Therapy (Brownell, 2019; Fischer, 2012; Wagner-Moore, 2004); Mindful Parenting (Townshend & Caltabiano, 2019); NeuroAffective Relational Model (Heller & LaPierre, 2010); NeuroAffective Touch (LaPierre, 2021); Nurturing Resilience (Kain & Terrell, 2018); Sensory Awareness (Khalsa et al., 2018; Selver, 1999); Somatic Experiencing (Carleton & Ho, 2009; Levine, 2017, 2019); Sensorimotor Psychotherapy (Ogden & Fisher, 2015); and Trauma Releasing Exercises (Edwards, 2019; Herold, 2015; Lynning et al., 2019; Salmon, 2013), to name a few. While purely Reichian approaches center most of their practice and research on individual or group work to resolve past trauma, Reich's work has also inspired methods that center attachment relationships as the unit of treatment to enhance felt security in proximity (Carleton & Padolsky, 2012; Isaacs & Isaacs, 2001; LaPierre, 2021; Townshend & Caltabiano, 2019).

Reich's research on character armor is rooted in what would later become known as Types II and III trauma. We will focus on Type II (aka, attachment/relational/developmental) trauma in our next section. From The National Child Traumatic Stress Network (n.d.), current validated measures that assess for Type III trauma include: Child Behavior Checklist (CBCL); Posttraumatic Stress Disorder Semi-Structured Interview and Observation Record; Posttraumatic Symptom Inventory for Children (PT-SIC); Preschool Age Psychiatric Assessment (PAPA); PTSD Symptoms in Preschool Aged Children (PTSD-PAC); Traumatic Events Screening Inventory-Parent Report Revised (TESI-PRR); Trauma Symptom Checklist for Young Children (TSCYC); Violence Exposure Scale for Children-Preschool Version (VEX-PV); Violence Exposure Scale for Children-Revised Parent Report (VEX-RPR).

Bowlby (c. 1907–1990)

John Bowlby's social location and personal development predictably informed his theory development. Like Wilhelm Reich, Bowlby was originally trained in Freud's psychoanalytic approach (1939, 1940), but he subsequently grounded the prevailing White, educated, industrialized, rich, cis-, and heteronormative intrapsychic exploration of subconscious processes by incorporating biological patterns found in the animal kingdom (Bowlby, 1953), to which humans belong. He was also deeply impacted

STUDENT REFLECTION 5.4

Many of the historical and ongoing stressors experienced by Xquenda and his family have long-term biological implications if left unaddressed, which then give rise to mood and behavior difficulties. Not all family stress is resolved through psychotherapeutic clinical interventions alone. What referrals, linkage, and holistic interventions may be necessary to help Xquenda and his family begin to find more health, ease, and well-being, so that the byproducts of his mood and behavior can begin to calm and stabilize, and he can more deeply benefit from family play therapy and other clinical support?

by Hungarian psychoanalyst Sandor Firenzi, who broke with Freud over how to work with childhood sexual abuse (Stanton, 1991), and Scottish psychiatrist Ian Suttie's sociological study of parental love and expressed tenderness as central to the ability to love (Suttie, 1935). His personal life and times may be evident in the patterns he was exposed to, which prioritized his clinical research attention; his body of work (Bowlby, 1940, 1951, 1969, 1973, 1980, 1982, 1988; Bowlby & King, 2004) continues to be replicated and diversified.

Bowlby's early childhood was culturally syntonic with a privileged London-based family in service to an imperial reign; his biological parents were focused on their high profile work and societal prominence, believing too much parental attention resulted in spoiling the children, thus he was emotionally raised by nannies and nursemaids in a hierarchy (Van Dijken, 1998). Bowlby asserted upon reflection that when his main attachment figure, nursemaid Winnie, left the family at his tender age of 4, this was as devastating as losing a mother (Bowlby & King, 2004). He was then sent away to boarding school at age 7, and subsequently lost his beloved godfather (Van Dijken, 1998). These losses, grafted onto his parents' minimal bonding behaviors, likely sensitized him to the pain suffered by the many war-orphaned children with whom he worked who ended up living in institutions that were designed to be dismissive of children's emotional needs (Karen, 1998), and probably led to his formulations around the distress of *maternal deprivation* (1953) from the position of first-hand experience in both culturally syntonic and traumatic ways (Van Dijken, 1998).

After his foundational studies in psychology and psychoanalysis, Bowlby worked with maladjusted and delinquent children; this inspired him to become a psychiatrist. During his psychiatry training, he was introduced to the work of Melanie Klein, founder of play therapy, but came to feel her work focused too much on the imaginal world of the kids, and not enough on their family and caregiving relationships and environments. He was asked by the World Health Organization to write a report on homeless children, and in it, he centered the loss of attachment figures (Bowlby, 1951). Happily, he went on to marry Ursula Longstaff, and they had four children (Holmes, 1993); this author hopes he came to enjoy earned secure attachment with her and all his children.

Embedded in the Bowlby family history is a professional *attachment network* which was paid to meet the emotional needs of the children, and Bowlby's life work could be viewed as having tried to make sense of the effects of absent and dismissive parents, while both appreciating the protective effects of substitute long-term, consistent caregivers, and mourning the loss of that continuity of care across critical periods (Bowlby, 1940, 1951, 1969, 1973, 1980, 1982, 1988). While there was fervent peer critique against these original suppositions (Karen, 1998), ongoing psychological research has borne out how protective *secure attachment* with at least one consistent caregiver is, and how much relational and biobehavioral effort is required to move from *insecurely attached* to *earned secure attachment* in order to confer security when that was not originally given to one as a child (Izard et al., 1991; Roisman et al., 2003; Saunders et al., 2011).

Bowlby established the Tavistock Clinic in 1948 to systematically study parent–child relationships (Polat, 2017). There he identified "three phases of response: protest, despair, and detachment," when an infant's primary caregiver leaves (Ainsworth, 1992, p. 1). Noticing that there were also patterns that arose upon reunion, experimental approaches to assess parent–child relationships began to be formulated (Polat, 2017). Generative collaboration between Bowlby and his dissertating student, Mary Ainsworth, began under these circumstances.

Ainsworth (c. 1913–1999)

Mary Ainsworth's social location and personal development also informed her theory development. Ainsworth was born in Ohio in 1913 (moving to Canada in 1918) to White, middle-class, college-educated parents in a cis-heterosexual marriage, the eldest of three daughters, and grew up surrounded by expectations for high academic achievement; she reflected that her father was more affectionate and attentive than her mother, and that there seemed to be emotional tensions with her mother due to that (Gale, 2017). Ainsworth's doctoral studies occurred under security theory founder Blatz (1966); van Rosmalen et al., 2016), and her 1940 dissertation focused on adjustment as a function of family as a *secure base* (Main, 1999). As protegé and lauded attachment researcher Mary Main reported upon reflection of their long mentorship, Ainsworth herself went through a "long, radically enjoyed personal psychoanalysis" prior to her life-altering move to Uganda with her husband, Leonard Ainsworth (1999, p. 2), which appears to have sharpened her focus on the impact of the mother–child relationship in deeply impactful ways (Ainsworth, 1962, 1969; Ainsworth & Boston, 1952; Ainsworth et al., 1956).

Ainsworth's original naturalistic observations and detailed note taking of infant–mother dyads in the community and at home in Uganda showed that children moved freely between allo-parents in search of attention and interaction, but when distressed, evidenced preferential attention-seeking for the birth mother (Ainsworth, 1967). Within that preference, half the children were immediately soothed upon reunion with the birth mother and in response to her physical affection, verbal reassurance, and attuned attention to their bids for connection (Ainsworth, 1967). About one quarter of them continued to cry whether attended to by mother or not, and another quarter demonstrated flat affect and lack of upset whether with mother or not (Ainsworth, 1967). These *quality of care* observations led to Ainsworth's "'tripartite' classification system of 'avoidant,' 'secure,' and 'ambivalent' (aka resistant) infant–mother attachment relationships" (van Ijzendoorn & Sagi-Schwartz, 2008, para. 1). These observations spawned replication studies in her "Baltimore" research at Johns Hopkins, creating the Strange Situation, which later was applied at the Tavistock Clinic, in order to test whether these categories appeared to hold across cultures and relational configurations (Ainsworth & Bell, 1970). Mary Main and Jude Cassidy subsequently differentiated "disorganized" attachment, which is highly correlated with more serious long-term pathology (Beebe et al., 2012; Main & Solomon, 1986; Reisz et al., 2018; van

Ijzendoorn et al., 1999). Some researchers have begun to re-conceptualize attachment security as on a spectrum, rather than discrete categories (Fraley & Spieker, 2003).

From these observations and experiments, Ainsworth developed the "Sensitivity–Insensitivity to Infant Signals and Communications Observational Scale" (Ainsworth et al., 1974). Ainsworth stated that rather than "warmth" (which was relatively universal among the Ugandan mothers), it was "the amount of caregiving for the baby, and the mother's excellence as an informant about the baby" that created "a pattern of proximity and availability, interest in the baby, perceptiveness about the baby's needs, and prompt responsiveness to the baby's signals" (Mesman & Emmen, 2013; Mesman et al., 2016). Subsequent research highlighted the contingent responsivity central to *maternal sensitivity*, and its role in fostering secure attachment, which confers lifelong health and social–emotional protective factors for children; Ainsworth's body of research (Ainsworth, 1962, 1967, 1969; Ainsworth & Boston, 1952; Ainsworth et al., 1956, 1974, 2015) continues to be replicated and expanded upon around the world.

Relational–Cultural Considerations

Non-violent communication would say that though all humans do have the same basic needs represented in Maslow's hierarchy, and the same basic positive and painful emotions when those needs are and are not getting met; what varies between cultures and individuals (and indeed puts people in conflict) is the *strategies* for getting those needs met (Rosenberg, 2005). While all human beings are born as if covered in glue (Goldberg, personal communication, 2015), primed to stick to whomever they are given, and unable to judge the worthiness of those to whom they are given (Lewis et al., 2000), the ways in which cultures, communities, and families meet those needs varies (Domínguez Duque et al., 2010; Sagi, 1990). Babies and children must learn to survive and cope with whomever people and whichever strategies are available in their caregiving (Lai & Carr, 2018), and their development is deeply influenced by the strategies into which they are born, by the "accident of their birth" (Johnson, personal communication, 2010).

In the communal culture of the West African Nso, birth mothers consider it disadvantageous for their children to attach too much to them, because the risk that the primary parent will not live long enough or be regularly available when needed means that it serves their children better to seek out the bulk of their caregiving from a wide variety of available community members (Keller et al., 2005). Among the many underlying threads this protective parenting strategy reveals is the core survival connection between birth parent and child; if birth parent is not available, how will this child get along (because dependence on birth parent is self-evident) if they do not willingly respond to care from available sources?

The Nso have collectively devised a strategy to reduce the risk that a child would not survive or would be too neglected and devastated if they lost their primary caregiver, and there arose a shared responsibility that all caregivers look out for each others' children as if they are their own (Keller et al., 2005), in a broad attachment network. Such a strategy also translates into specific parenting practices that require effort to uphold; when children come looking for their primary parent, the primary caregiver will often intentionally redirect the child away to any other caregiver, to break the child's habit of looking for them. Other communal cultures with higher earlier mortality rates around the world have similar practices, even if the timing or circumstances of pressing the children away varies (van Ijzendoorn & Sagi-Schwartz, 2008). I (Roller) see that as a reflection of how instinctively driven human children are to have an abiding connection with their birth parent, and how much effort is required to overcome that desire for both parent and child if indeed the birth parent is raising them.

Cross-sectional studies of babies raised in Israeli kibbutzim also revealed the monotropy of the birth mother over the (more primarily involved surrogate) caregiver (van Ijzendoorn et al., 1992), in particular with regard to the rate of down-regulation of distress when each attachment figure returned (Fox, 1977). van IJzendoorn and Kroonenberg (1988) found in their meta-analysis of 2000 Strange Situation classifications from eight countries that "A (avoidant) classifications emerge as relatively more prevalent in Western European countries and C (resistant) classifications as relatively more frequent in Israel and Japan," and that "intracultural variation was 1.5 times the cross-cultural variation" (p. 1). In their cross-cultural research, Grossman and Grossman (1990) found that because cultural differences "may exist in terms of frequency and difficulty of potentially conflicting challenges imposed on individuals ... (attachment research must) consider both ... the universal and the culture-specific, when testing the full potential of attachment theory from a life course perspective" (p. 1). Subsequent meta-analysis of data from "various African cultures, the People's Republic of China, Israel, Japan, and Indonesia ... suggest a balance between universal trends and contextual determinants" factor into how insecure attachment rates and patterns vary between cultures when considering the "universality, normativity, sensitivity, and competence hypotheses (that) constitute the core hypotheses of attachment theory" (van Ijzendoorn & Sagi-Schwartz, 2008, p. 1).

Strategies to meet needs appear to arise out of necessity and opportunity while navigating the demands placed upon a family and community system in context, and sociological conditioning powerfully informs the messages sent and received about whether caregivers are using approved strategies, thus *neuroanthropology* studies how culture informs brain development, and vice versa (Campbell & Garcia, 2009; Domínguez Duque et al., 2010; Lende & Downey, 2012, 2020), while biobehavioral studies are beginning to show how the extended nervous system of caregiving aptitude informs the developing nervous system of one's charges (Perry et al., 2017; Porges, 2006; Townshend & Caltabiano, 2019).

Factoring into the bidirectional processes leading to attachment outcomes is whether there is *goodness of fit* between the caregivers' and child's *temperaments* (Sravanti, 2017), and to what degree parental attachment and developmental trauma history (Bretherton, 1990, 1999; Kerns & Brumariu, 2014; Scharpf et al., 2020; Wadsworth et al., 2018), parental stress, problematic coping mechanisms, and/or child developmental delays (Dagan & Sagi-Schwartz, 2018; Finzi et al., 2000; Newland & Crnic, 2017; Scharpf et al., 2020) complicate goodness of fit. In a multiple stress sample it was determined that "for temperamentally difficult children, unresponsive parenting exacerbates risks for behavior problems, but responsive parenting can effectively buffer risks conferred by temperament" (Kochanska & Kim, 2013). Another multifactorial study found that perception of difficult temperament was correlated with insecure maternal attachment and maternal developmental trauma history, suggesting that intervention to reduce risk really must begin before pregnancy and continue through at least the first year of baby's life to help moderate for suboptimal parental history (Wadsworth et al., 2018).

Of further consideration is that variation in relational priorities across cultures arise in how parents direct their children's attention after they have down-regulated in response to caregiver attention after an upset, which can factor into how researchers perceive relative security through culturally syntonic or dystonic lenses (Fivush, 2006). For instance, while the secure base function of attachment thus far appears to be universal, there are "cultural variations" in how "an infant and mother achieve (that)." In Western cultures, mothers are more likely to separate from their infant and encourage independent exploration. When the infant becomes distressed, infants generally are the ones to seek proximity (Jin et al., 2012). However, Jin and team noted that, "Korean and Japanese mothers encourage their infants to stay physically close. After a separation, the mothers are more likely to approach the infant immediately and stay near even after the infant's distress is no longer present" (p. 42). Such patterns result in different expectations being built for children regarding what happens once one is feeling secure again (i.e., stay connected in proximity and play, or go off on your own to focus on play projects). Jin's team noticed that, "once proximity is achieved, regardless of how it is achieved, the majority of infants across cultures are able to receive comfort and are able to return to their exploration and play" (p. 42). This *amae*, also known as *maternal dew,* or emotional interdependence, is commonly practiced in more collectivistic societies, thus Western assessors might over-attribute anxious "enmeshment" to parent–child dyads engaging in relational patterns more typical of collectivistic cultures (Behrens, 2010; Rothbaum & Kakinuma, 2004; Yamaguchi, 2004).

It has been demonstrated that group-sustaining preferences for individualistic or collectivistic patterns drive group member choices with regard to the reinforcement schedule of bonding behaviors that impact attachment as desired by the primary caregiver (Strand, 2020), and that "behavioral predispositions concerned with security-seeking versus novelty-seeking, established during childhood, hedge interdependent choice behavior in culture-consistent ways and serve as a deep source of cultural stability" (Strand et al., 2019, para. 33). Even when children could not have yet been "exposed to the contingencies that define the adult social world, children behave in ways that are consistent with the contingencies and values of the societies into which they are born" (Strand et al., 2019, para. 32). Thus the internalized cultural messaging a primary caregiver lives out in attending or not to their child's bids for securing attention serve to shape how much that child seeks the reduction of stress from that (and other) caregivers, and how much that child learns to value weak versus strong social ties.

Secure Attachment Benefits

One key element that does appear to hold across cultures is how primary or continuous secure attachment leads to increased ability to form a subsequent attachment network once children begin moving out into the world (Riggs & Riggs, 2011; Rosenthal & Kobak, 2010), which creates a tiered system for seeking support across the lifespan, and more positive academic and social outcomes across various domains (Balenzano, 2010; Carli et al., 2019; Gillath et al., 2019). It also appears that optimal *plasticity* in how that network is achieved and maintained is correlated with the more initial security one is afforded (Gillath et al., 2019; Joseph, 1999; Kobak et al., 2005; Mundo, 2006; Schore, 1994, 2001, 2003a, 2003b, 2013). This appears to be true for neurotypical children, as well as those on the autism spectrum (Teague et al., 2017).

To help achieve these optimal outcomes, natural generation of *oxytocin*, the "bonding hormone," appears to deeply influence empathy, sensitive attunement to baby, and parental enjoyment of soothing, nursing, and other caregiving behaviors in biological females, and in activating play behaviors in biological males (Feldman et al., 2013; Mah et al., 2015; Scatliffe et al., 2019; Strathearn et al., 2012). Tragically, it appears so far that there is a critical window in infancy and early childhood to develop the endogenous ability to produce and respond to oxytocin, with all its stress and trauma-mediating effects, and that taking oxytocin intranasally to try to gain the same benefits can paradoxically decrease stress coping and caregiving-related memories and behaviors (Kim & Strathearn, 2017). Thus, interventions to interrupt the transgenerational transmission of trauma really must occur prenatally whenever possible (van IJzendoorn et al., 1995), to increase the baby's possibility of generating the neurological capacity to produce oxytocin for lifelong protective benefits. To do so reduces the risk of parents transmitting their insecure attachment, which in its most severe form can become reactive attachment disorders and problematic coping that result from inadequate caregiving environments, and morph into two basic clinical presentations: an emotionally withdrawn/inhibited phenotype, and an indiscriminately social/disinhibited phenotype (Kim et al., 2017; Zeanah & Gleason, 2015).

There will be many circumstances in which clinicians will not be able to intervene prenatally, and must find ways to support children and families to experience the benefits of parental bonding behaviors even after critical windows for building neurological protective factors may be closing on the child. Currently, 40% of infants assessed in the United States do not meet criteria for secure attachment, with 25% avoiding parents and the other 15% resistant to their intervention, because the parents are more agitating than regulating (Huber, 2014).

Children in foster care will have among the highest rates of insecurity, but they too can demonstrate gradual movement toward earned secure attachment once they are placed in a stable home and can begin to count on identified caregivers, though this is more likely for avoidant/withdrawn children than indiscriminately attached children (Lehmann et al., 2020; Smyke et al., 2012; Zimmermann & Soares, 2019). Because it gets harder to find a forever home the longer a child is institutionalized or in the foster care system, it is even more critical to try to find goodness of fit in permanent placement for children as soon as possible, for the long-term deleterious effects of reactive attachment disorder come to have generally global negative effects on a person's quality of life (Chase Stovall & Dozier, 1998; Humphreys et al., 2017; Pritchett et al., 2013). What does not appear problematic about attachment is the sex or gender of the caregivers (Ahnert & Schoppe-Sullivan, 2020; Gutierrez et al., 2018; Manning et al., 2014; Salinas-Quiroz et al., 2018; Trub et al., 2016) so long as they are engaging in secure base provision (Woodhouse et al., 2009, 2020).

Secure Base Provision

Secure base provision (SBP) appears to be the key takeaway for lifelong relational satisfaction and epigenetic protections from all attachment research to date (Woodhouse et al., 2009). SBP includes soothing a crying baby to a "fully calm and regulated state while in chest-to-chest contact … (so the) infant learns … whether the caregiver can be counted on to be available as the infant achieves a calm state or whether (they) typically must stop crying alone" (Woodson et al., 2019, para. 14). Such patient and regulated soothing and attending tends to morph into securing co-regulation that facilitates culturally syntonic toddler development and play (Alcock, 2013), which then allows for securing support for early childhood explorations into adolescence (Jones & Cassidy, 2014). These patterns tend to hold over adulthood, with regression toward insecurity less likely the more primary security one had (like old money). Thus, clinical efforts that cannot be directed at prenatal resolution of trauma and toxic stress may need to focus on the development of secure base provision in spite of past risk factors, as a history of insecure attachment increases the risk of not knowing how to provide a secure base for one's children (Feeney et al., 2013; Grossmann et al., 2006). Therefore, for clinicians to proactively help their clients move toward greater earned security, no matter the clinician's theoretical orientation, the greater likelihood humanity will move toward peace, ease, safety, respect, connection, love, and healthier longevity.

Treatment Modalities

In addition to the Reichian approaches that center attachment relationships, there is a growing evidence base of practices that have developed specifically for the evolution of attachment theory, with a focus on preventing insecurity, or fostering earned security. FirstPlay Infant Storytelling (aka Kinesthetic) Massage teaches caregivers how to gently approach the baby's space, read their cues, make sensitive and soothing contact, and coherently narrate their emotional state, while validating and normalizing their feelings in response to the various experiences they have throughout the day (Baldwin, 2020; Courtney & Nolan, 2017). Theraplay, a dyadic child and family therapy, has been "recognized by the Association of Play Therapy as one of seven *seminal psychotherapies for children*. Developed over 50 years ago ... practiced around the world," Theraplay aims to foster secure attachment for "lifelong good mental health as well as the mainstay of resilience in the face of adversity" (The Theraplay Institute, n.d.). Theraplay teaches clinicians and caregivers how to assess what their toddler to young child is needing, when and why, and fosters four essential qualities found in healthy parent–child relationships: structure, nurture, engagement, and (appropriate) challenge. Emotion-Focused Therapy has expanded from focusing on attachment in couples to working with family attachment patterns in many relational constellations (Johnson, 2019). And any family or systems-inclusive approach that brings secure base provision and emotional attunement as central to the work is likely to help nudge clients along toward greater earned security.

FUTURE DIRECTIONS

The Adverse Childhood Experiences Scale (ACES) is among the most widely recognized measures to capture events of Type II (attachment/relational/developmental) trauma that have been shown to have lifelong effects on medical and mental health; extensive collaborations and program planning are now funded by ACES-related federal funds due to the billions of dollars of loss longitudinal ACES effects have on the U.S. economy. The ACES does not yet assess for Type III (hate-based targeting and other public threat) traumas, or for subjective response to traumatic developmental events; those nuances are better captured in the Childhood Trauma Scale (S. Porges, personal communication, April 21, 2021), though there is not currently significant funding available for program development around this measure. The Adverse Early Experiences and Resiliency Survey aims to capture trauma and protective response during the pre- and perinatal period, to enhance opportunities for prevention and reduce the need for later, much more expensive and labor-intensive attachment-based intervention.

Polyvagal-informed therapies are leading the way with biobehavioral feedback measures tracking response to attunement and connection, while noting the various deleterious effects of disconnection (Cherland, 2012; Flores & Porges, 2017; Porges, 2009; Porges & Buczinsky, n.d.), to assess what fosters co-regulation for mutual satisfaction in counseling and therapy in a variety of client constellations (Porges & Dana, 2018). Polyvagal theory emphasizes that the range of social behavior is "limited by physiological state ... mobilization and immobilization behaviors may be adaptive strategies to a challenged (e.g., frightened) individual. Thus ... creating states of calmness and (regulating) brainstem structures may potentiate positive social behavior by stimulating ... the social engagement system" (Porges, 2006, p. 52). This research can help operationalize what clinicians may do in session to co-regulate clients while avoiding compassion fatigue, and provide effective psychoeducation to loved ones to help extend the benefits of therapy that aims to resolve attachment trauma and move clients toward earned security.

CASE STUDY 5.7

Xquenda and his sister Nayeli have been blessed with attentive and responsive parents who do all they can to foster secure base provision in spite of the multiple stresses they have faced with forced migration, loss, and acculturation adjustments over the last several years. Xquenda's temperament requires more biobehavioral effort to regulate, so due to these factors complicating goodness of fit, attachment-based family play therapy would be indicated to help the whole family find more ease and enjoyment together, giving him the best future possible.

PERSPECTIVES FROM THE FIELD: PODCAST

Access this podcast at http://connect.springerpub.com/content/book/978-0-8261-8279-1/part/part02/chapter/ch05

The goals of this chapter are to: provide you with an initial understanding of how developmental theories of infancy and early childhood conceptualize these most formative stages; expose you to their seminal concepts; encourage your critical thinking about their own context; and introduce you to clinical research and applications of these developmental theories. I invite you now to listen once again to Dr. Judyth Weaver, this time speaking about how she might start applying Freudian, Reichian, and attachment principles to her work with Xquenda and his family.

SUMMARY

Freud, Reich, Bowlby, Ainsworth, Main, and hundreds of subsequent child developmental researchers around the world have traveled from the infant's erogenous zones and projections of their minds, to their soft animal bodies, to their extended nervous system of caregiver co-regulation, to the varied context in which children are born and grow and learn about themselves in relationship to their immediate families, their families' support systems, their eventual peer relationships, and their ultimate families of choice, situated within their cultures of origin and migration. What all have pointed out is how sensitive and vulnerable children are to the impact of developmental trauma, such as abuse and neglect, and how the quality of their caregiving may mediate for that risk in myriad ways. They all forwarded methods to recognize, prevent, and work with this traumatic stress through clinical intervention, education, or policy work. Their collected body of work gives clinicians and clients of varying constitutions and cultural preferences various roads inward to help resolve the anxiety and depression that come from not having a reliably secure base. Their collected body of work also shows that, though our species may have walked and re-planted all over this planet, we all fundamentally do better and find life more manageable when we have at least one receptive and responsive heart to call a stable home.

REFERENCES

Addiction Center. (2021, March 24). *What is neonatal abstinence syndrome?*. https://www.addictioncenter.com/addiction/neonatal-abstinence-syndrome

Ahnert, L., & Schoppe-Sullivan, S. J. (2020). Fathers from an attachment perspective. *Attachment & Human Development, 22*(1), 1–3. https://doi.org/10.1080/14616734.2019.1589054

Ainsworth, M., & Bell, S. M. (1970). Attachment, exploration, and separation: Illustrated by the behavior of one-year-olds in a strange situation. *Child Development, 41,* 49–67. https://doi.org/10.2307/1127388

Ainsworth, M., Boston, M., Bowlby, J., & Rosenbluth, D. (1956). The effects of mother-child separation: A follow-up study. *The British Journal of Medical Psychology, 29*(3–4), 211–247. https://doi.org/10.1111/j.2044-8341.1956.tb00915.x

Ainsworth, M. D. (1962). The effects of maternal deprivation: A review of findings and controversy in the context of research strategy. *Public Health Papers, 14,* 97–165.

Ainsworth, M. D. (1969). Object relations, dependency, and attachment: A theoretical review of the infant-mother relationship. *Child Development, 40*(4), 969–1025. https://doi.org/10.2307/1127008

Ainsworth, M. D., & Boston, M. (1952). Psychodiagnostic assessments of a child after prolonged separation in early childhood. *The British Journal of Medical Psychology, 25*(4), 169–201. https://doi.org/10.1111/j.2044-8341.1952.tb00419.x

Ainsworth, M. D. S., Bell, S. M., & Stayton, D. J. (1974). Infant-mother attachment and social development: "Socialisation" as a product of reciprocal responsiveness to signals. In P. M. Richards (Ed.), *The integration of a child into a social world* (pp. 99–135). Cambridge University Press.

Ainsworth, M. D. S., Blehar, M. C., Waters, E., & Wall, S. N. (2015). *Patterns of attachment.* Routledge.

Ainsworth, M. S. (1967). *Infancy in Uganda: Infant care and the growth of love.* Johns Hopkins Press.

Ainsworth, M. S. (1992). John Bowlby (1907–1990): Obituary. *American Psychologist, 47*(5), 668–668. https://doi.org/10.1037/0003-066X.47.5.668

Alcock, S. (2013). Toddlers' complex commuComplex Communication: Playfulness from a secure baSecure Base. *Contemporary Issues in Early Childhood, 14*(2), 179–190. https://doi.org/10.2304/ciec.2013.14.2.179

Anthi, P. R. (2020). Wilhelm Reich's character analysis revisited. *The Scandinavian Psychoanalytic Review, 43*(1), 40–49. https://doi.org/10.1080/01062301.2020.1797436

Antonic, T. (2019). Genius and genitality: William S. Burroughs Reading Wilhelm Reich. *Humanities, 8*(2), 101. https://doi.org/10.3390/h8020101

Aposhyan, S. (2004). *Body-mind psychotherapy: Principles, techniques, and practical applications.* Norton.

Baldwin, K. (2020). *An examination of adolescent maternal-infant attachment relationship outcomes following a FirstPlay therapy infant storytelling-massage intervention: A pilot study.* Capstone project for Florida Atlantic University.

Balenzano, C. (2010). The transfer of attachment functions outside the family: The role of romantic attachment. *Psicologia Clinica Dello Sviluppo, 14,* 597–608. https://doi.org/10.1449/33632

Barnum, E. L., & Perrone-McGovern, K. M. (2017). Attachment, self-esteem and subjective well-being among survivors of childhood sexual trauma. *Journal of Mental Health Counseling, 39*(1), 39–55. https://doi.org/10.17744/mehc.39.1.04

Bassiri, N. (2013). Freud and the matter of the brain: On the rearrangements of neuropsychoanalysis. *Critical Inquiry, 40*(1), 83–108. https://doi.org/10.1086/673227

Beebe, B., Lachmann, F., Markese, S., & Bahrick, L. (2012). On the origins of disorganized attachment and internal working models: Paper I. A dyadic systems approach. *Psychoanalytic Dialogues, 22*(2), 253–272. https://doi.org/10.1080/10481885.2012.666147

Behrens, K. Y. (2010). Amae through the eyes of Japanese mothers: Refining differences and similarities between attachment and amae. In P. Erdman & K.-M. Ng (Eds.), *Family therapy and counseling series. Attachment: Expanding the cultural connections* (pp. 55–69). Routledge/Taylor & Francis Group.

Bettelheim, B. (1982). *Freud and man's soul.* Random House.

Blatz, W. E. (1966). *Human security: Some reflections.* University of Toronto Press. https://doi.org/10.3138/9781442632134

Boadella, D. (1987, 2015). *Lifestreams: An introduction to biosynthesis.* Routledge. https://doi.org/10.4324/9781315737713

Boadella, D., & Boadella, S. S. (2006). Basic concepts in biosynthesis. *International Body Psychotherapy Journal, 5*(1), 18–21.

Bodynamic International. (n.d.). *Developmental model and character structures.* https://www.bodynamic.com/theory/the-seven-developmental-stages

Bohus, M., Kleindienst, N., Hahn, C., Müller-Engelmann, M., Ludäscher, P., Steil, R., Fydrich, T., Kuehner, C., Resick, P. A., Stiglmayr, C., Schmahl, C., & Priebe, K. (2020). Dialectical Behavior Therapy for Posttraumatic Stress Disorder (DBT-PTSD) Compared With Cognitive Processing Therapy (CPT) in complex presentComplex Presentations of PTSD in women survivors of childhood abWomen Survivors of Childhood Abuse: A randomized clinical triRandomized Clinical Trial. *JAMA Psychiatry, 77*(12), 1235–1245. https://doi.org/10.1001/jamapsychiatry.2020.2148

Bowlby, J. (1940). The influence of early environment in the development of neurosis and neurotic character. *International Journal of Psycho-Analysis, 21,* 154–178.

Bowlby, J. (1951). *Maternal care and mental health.* World Health Organisation.

Bowlby, J. (1969, 1982). *Attachment: Attachment and loss.* Basic Books.

Bowlby, J. (1973). *Separation: Anxiety and anger.* Basic Books.

Bowlby, J. (1980). *Loss: Sadness and depression.* Basic Books.

Bowlby, J. (1988). *A secure base: Parent-child attachment and healthy human development.* Routledge.

Bowlby, R., & King, P. (2004). *Fifty years of attachment theory: Recollections of Donald Winnicott and John Bowlby.* Karnac Books.

Bracha, H. S. (2004). Freeze, flight, fight, fright, faint: Adaptationist perspectives on the acute stress response spectrum. *CNS Spectrums, 9*(9), 679–685. https://doi.org/10.1017/S1092852900001954

Bramwell, D. (2018). The godfather of the sexual revolution? *The British Psychological Society, 31,* 84–87.

Bretherton, I. (1990). Communication patterns, internal working models, and the intergenerational transmission of attachment relationships. *Infant Mental Health Journal, 11*(3), 237–252. https://doi.org/10.1002/1097-0355(199023)11:3<237::AID-IMHJ2280110306>3.0.CO;2-X

Bretherton, I. (1999). Updating the "internal working model" construct: some reflections. *Attachment & Human Development, 1*(3), 343–357. https://doi.org/10.1080/14616739900134191

Brill, A. A. (Ed.). (1938). *The basic writings of Sigmund Freud.* Random House.

Brownell, P. (Ed.). (2019). *Handbook for theory, research, and practice in Gestalt therapy.* Cambridge Scholars Publishing.

Campbell, B. C., & Garcia, J. R. (2009). Neuroanthropology: Evolution and emotional embodiment. *Frontiers in Evolutionary Neuroscience, 1*(4), 4. https://doi.org/10.3389/neuro.18.004.2009

Campbell, G., Miers, S., & Miller, J. C. (2009). *Children in slavery through the ages.* Ohio University Press. https://doi.org/10.1353/book.8948

Carleton, J. A., & Ho, E. (2009, October). *Somatic treatment of attachment issues: Applying neuroscientific and experimental research to the clinical situation. Canadian Society for Psychotherapy Research.* http://www.jacquelineacarletonphd.com/text/pdfs/somatictreatmentofattachmentissues.pdf

Carleton, J. A., & Padolsky, I. (2012). Wilhelm Reich's theoretical concept of mother–infant attachment as the origin of self-regulation: A neurophysiological perspective. *Body, Movement and Dance in Psychotherapy, 7*(2), 89–100. https://doi.org/10.1080/17432979.2011.592395

Carli, L. L., Anzelmo, E., Pozzi, S., Feeney, J. A., Gallucci, M., Santona, A., & Tagini, A. (2019). Attachment networks in committed couples. *Frontiers in Psychology, 10,* 1105. https://doi.org/10.3389/fpsyg.2019.01105

Chase Stovall, K., & Dozier, M. (1998). Infants in foster care. *Adoption Quarterly, 2*(1), 55–88. https://doi.org/10.1300/J145v02n01_05

Cherland, E. (2012). The polyvagal theory: Neurophysiological foundations of emotions, attachment, communication, self-regulation. *Journal of the Canadian Academy of Child and Adolescent Psychiatry, 21*(4), 313–314.

Chiera, M., Cerritelli, F., Casini, A., Barsotti, N., Boschiero, D., Cavigioli, F., Corti, C. G., & Manzotti, A. (2020). Heart rate variability in the perinatal period: A critical and conceptual review. *Frontiers in Neuroscience, 14,* 561186. https://doi.org/10.3389/fnins.2020.561186

Cieri, F., & Esposito, R. (2019). Psychoanalysis and neuroscience: The bridge between mind and brain. *Frontiers in Psychology, 10,* 1790. https://doi.org/10.3389/fpsyg.2019.01983

City of Vienna. (n.d.). *Vienna under the Nazi regime.* https://www.wien.gv.at/english/history/overview/nazi.html

Cohen, B. B. (2017). *An introduction to body-mind centering.* Preuzeto s. https://www.bodymindcentering.com/files/an_intro_to_body-mind_centering.pdf

Costandi, M. (2014). Freud was a pioneering neuroscientist. The Guardian. https://www.theguardian.com/science/neurophilosophy/2014/mar/10/neuroscience-history-sciencE

Courtney, J. A., & Nolan, R. D. (2017). FirstPlay® infant massage storytelling: Facilitating corrective touch experiences with a teenage mother and her abused infant. In J. A. Courtney & R. D. Nolan (Eds.), *Touch in child counseling and play therapy: An ethical and clinical guide.* Routledge. https://doi.org/10.4324/9781315628752

Dagan, O., & Sagi-Schwartz, A. (2018). Early attachment network with mother and father: An unsettled issue. *Child Development Perspectives, 12*(2), 115–121. https://doi.org/10.1111/cdep.12272

Danil, L. R. (2017). *Freud the socialist, Freud the revolutionary.* Verso. https://www.versobooks.com/blogs/3964-freud-the-socialist-freud-the-revolutionary

DelMonte, M. (1998). Freud scientifically reappraised: Testing the theories and therapy. Fisher, S. & Greenberg, R.P. New York: John Wiley & Sons, 1996. *Irish Journal of Psychological Medicine, 15*(1), 39–40. https://doi.org/10.1017/S0790966700004742

DeMeo, J. (2011). *Heretic's notebook: Emotions, protocells, ether-drift and cosmic life-energy, with new research supporting Wilhelm Reich.* Natural Energy Works, Orgone Biophysical Research Lab.

DeMeo, J., Albini, A., Aronstien, W., Bingham, A., Vecchieti, A., Del Giudice, E., Haralick, R. M., Herskowitz, M., Heiman, M., Hillman, H., Kavouras, J., Koblenzer, J., Maluf, N., Maglione, R., Mazzochi, A., Musenich, S., Odent, M., Okuma, P., Pollack, G., ... Tosi, M. (2012). In defense of Wilhelm Reich: An open response to Nature and the scientific/medical community. *WATER, 4,* 72–81.

Dennis, C.-L., Fung, K., Grigoriadis, S., Robinson, G. E., Romans, S., & Ross, L. (2007). Traditional postpartum practices and rituals: A qualitative systematic review. *Women's Health, 3*(4), 487–502. https://doi.org/10.2217/17455057.3.4.487

Desmet, M. (2013). Some preliminary notes on an empirical test of freud's theory on depression. *Frontiers in Psychology, 4*, 158. https://doi.org/10.3389/fpsyg.2013.00158

Dewar, G. (2020). *Fast-track" toilet training techniques: An evidence-based review. Parenting Science.* http://parentingscience.com/toilet-training-techniques

Domínguez Duque, J. F., Turner, R., Lewis, E. D., & Egan, G. (2010). Neuroanthropology: A humanistic science for the study of the culture-brain nexus. *Social Cognitive and Affective Neuroscience, 5*(2–3), 138–147. https://doi.org/10.1093/scan/nsp024

Edwards, L. (2019). *The potential role of trauma releasing exercises (TRE) in the treatment of trauma, PTSD and its co-morbid conditions including anxiety, depression and somatoform disorders.* https://traumaprevention.com/wp-content/uploads/2019/10/Trauma-Releasing-Exercises-TRE-for-PTSD41.pdf

Energetics Institute. (n.d.). *Reich's segmental armoring theory.* https://www.energeticsinstitute.com.au/characterology/reichs-segmental-armouring-theory

Estrada, G. S. (2003). An Aztec two-spirit cosmology: Re-sounding Nahuatl masculinities, elders, femininities, and youth. *Frontiers: A Journal of Women Studies, 24*(2), 10–14. https://doi.org/10.1353/fro.2004.0008

Exner-Pirot, H., Norbye, B., & Butler, L. (Eds.). (2018). *Northern and indigenous health and health care. Saskatoon, Saskatchewan: University of Saskatchewan.* openpress.usask.ca/northernhealthcare

Feeney, B. C., Collins, N. L., Van Vleet, M., & Tomlinson, J. M. (2013). Motivations for providing a secure base: Links with attachment orientation and secure base support behavior. *Attachment & Human Development, 15*(3), 261–280. https://doi.org/10.1080/14616734.2013.782654

Feldman, R., Gordon, I., Influs, M., Gutbir, T., & Ebstein, R. P. (2013). Parental oxytocin and early caregiving jointly shape children's oxytocin response and social reciprocity. *Neuropsychopharmacology, 38*(7), 1154–1162. https://doi.org/10.1038/npp.2013.22

Fields, R. D. (2020). *The brain learns in unexpected ways: White matter, the insulation around our neural wiring, plays a critical role in acquiring knowledge.* https://www.scientificamerican.com/article/the-brain-learns-in-unexpected-ways

Finzi, R., Cohen, O., Sapir, Y., & Weizman, A. (2000). Attachment styles in maltreated children: A comparative study. *Child Psychiatry and Human Development, 31*(2), 113–128. https://doi.org/10.1023/a:1001944509409

Fischer, S. (2012). The Gestalt research tradition: Figure and ground. *Gestalt Review, 16*(1), 3–6. https://doi.org/10.5325/gestaltreview.16.1.0003

Fisher, S., & Greenberg, R. P. (1996). *Freud scientifically reappraised: Testing the theories and therapy.* John Wiley & Sons.

Fivush, R. (2006). Scripting attachment: Generalized event representations and internal working models. *Attachment & Human Development, 8*(3), 283–289. https://doi.org/10.1080/08912960600858935

Flores, P. J., & Porges, S. W. (2017). Group psychotherapy as a neural exercise: Bridging polyvagal theory and attachment theory. *International Journal of Group Psychotherapy, 67*(2), 202–222. https://doi.org/10.1080/00207284.2016.1263544

Fox, N. (1977). Attachment of kibbutz infants to mother and metapelet. *Child Development, 48*(4), 1228–1239. https://doi.org/10.2307/1128480

Fraley, R. C., & Spieker, S. J. (2003). Are infant attachment patterns continuously or categorically distributed? A taxometric analysis of strange situation behavior. *Developmental Psychology, 39*(3), 387–404. https://doi.org/10.1037/0012-1649.39.3.387

Frazer, S. (2014). Body encyclopedia: A guide to the psychological function of the muscular system. *Body, Movement and Dance in Psychotherapy, 9*(3), 189–191. https://doi.org/10.1080/17432979.2013.862570

Freud, A. (1936). *The ego and mechanisms of defense.* International Universities Press.

Gale. (2017). *A study guide for psychologists and their theories for students: Mary Salter Ainsworth.* Cengage Learning.

Gay, P. (1988). *Freud: A life for our time.* Norton.

Geuter, U., Heller, M. C., & Weaver, J. O. (2010). Elsa Gindler and her influence on Wilhelm Reich and body psychotherapy. *Body, Movement and Dance in Psychotherapy, 5*(1), 59–73. https://doi.org/10.1080/17432971003620113

Gillath, O., C Karantzas, G., & Lee, J. (2019). Attachment and social networks. *Current Opinion in Psychology*, *25*, 21–25. https://doi.org/10.1016/j.copsyc.2018.02.010

Grossmann, K. E., Grossmann, K., & Waters, E. (Eds.). (2006). *Attachment from infancy to adulthood: The major longitudinal studies*. Guilford Press.

Gruber, H. (1987). Sexuality in "Red Vienna": Socialist party conceptions and programs and working-class life, 1920–34. *International Labor and Working-Class History*, *31*, 37–68. https://doi.org/10.1017/S0147547900004105

Gutierrez, D., Gamboni, C., Wojciak, A., & Frazier, A. (2018). Parent attachment, relationship quality, and gender influence of adults with parents with past same-sex relationships. *The Family Journal*, *26*(2), 166–173. https://doi.org/10.1177/1066480718785915

Hale, N. (1974). *Wilhelm Reich vs. the USA*. The New York Times. https://www.nytimes.com/1974/08/11/archives/wilhelm-reich-vs-the-usa-the-discoverer-of-the-orgone-byjerome.html#:~:text=In%20a%20childish%20auto%20da,prison%20for%20contempt%20of%20court

Hambrick, E. P., Brawner, T. W., & Perry, B. D. (2019). Timing of early-life stress and the development of brain-related capacities. *Frontiers in Behavioral Neuroscience*, *13*, 183. https://doi.org/10.3389/fnbeh.2019.00183

Healthy Children. (2019, April 1). *Sexual behaviors in young children: What's normal, what's not?*. https://www.healthychildren.org/English/ages-stages/preschool/Pages/Sexual-Behaviors-Young-Children.aspx

Heller, L., & LaPierre, A. (2010). *Healing developmental trauma: How early trauma affects self-regulation, self-image, and the capacity for relationship*. North Atlantic.

Herold, A. (2015). Neurogenic tremor through TRE tension, stress and trauma releasing exercises according to D. Berceli in the treatment of post-traumatic stress disorder PTSD. *Psychological Counseling and Psychotherapy*, *2*(1–2), 76–84.

Hofmeyer, A., Kennedy, K., & Taylor, R. (2020). Contesting the term 'compassion fatigue': Integrating findings from social neuroscience and self-care research. *Collegian (Royal College of Nursing, Australia)*, *27*(2), 232–237. https://doi.org/10.1016/j.colegn.2019.07.001

Holmes, J. (1993). *John Bowlby and attachment theory*. Routledge.

Howard, J. (2017). *How the world potty trains: Parenting without borders*. CNN Health. https://www.cnn.com/2017/10/31/health/potty-training-parenting-without-borders-explainer/index.html

Huber, B. R. (2014). *Four in 10 infants lack strong parental attachments*. Woodrow Wilson School of Public and International Affairs. https://www.princeton.edu/news/2014/03/27/four-10-infants-lack-strong-parental-attachments

Humphreys, K. L., Nelson, C. A., Fox, N. A., & Zeanah, C. H. (2017). *Signs of reactive attachment disorder and disinhibited social engagement disorder at age 12 years: Effects of institutional care history and high-quality foster care*. Cambridge University Press.

Indian Health Service. (n.d.). *Two-Spirit*. https://www.ihs.gov/lgbt/health/twospirit

Isaacs, A., & Isaacs, J. (2001). Body psychotherapy with couples. *Journal of Couples Therapy*, *10*(2), 75–90. https://doi.org/10.1300/J036v10n02_08

Izard, C. E., Porges, S. W., Simons, R. F., Haynes, O. M., Hyde, C., Parisi, M., & Cohen, B. (1991). Infant cardiac activity: Developmental changes and relations with attachment. *Developmental Psychology*, *27*(3), 432–439. https://doi.org/10.1037/0012-1649.27.3.432

Jerkovic, I., & Berberovic, D. (2012). Sexual compulsivity, promiscuity and phallic stage of psychosexual development fixation. *Health & Medicine: Journal of the Health and Medicine Policy Research Group*, *6*(5).

Jin, M. K., Jacobvitz, D., Hazen, N., & Jung, S. H. (2012). Maternal sensitivity and infant attachment security in Korea: Cross-cultural validation of the Strange Situation. *Attachment & Human Development*, *14*(1), 33–44. https://doi.org/10.1080/14616734.2012.636656

Johnson, S. M. (2019). *Attachment theory in practice: Emotionally focused therapy (eft) with individuals, couples and families*. The Guilford Press. ISBN 978-1462538287

Jones, E. (1957). *Sigmund Freud: Life and work* (Vol. 3). Hogarth Press.

Jones, J. D., & Cassidy, J. (2014). Parental attachment style: Examination of links with parent secure base provision and adolescent secure base use. *Attachment & Human Development*, *16*(5), 437–461. https://doi.org/10.1080/14616734.2014.921718

Jordan, G. J., Arbeau, K., McFarland, D., Ireland, K., & Richardson, A. (2020). Elimination communication contributes to a reduction in unexplained infant crying. *Medical Hypotheses*, *142*, 109811. https://doi.org/10.1016/j.mehy.2020.109811

Joseph, R. (1999). Environmental influences on neural plasticity, the limbic system, emotional development and attachment: A review. *Child Psychiatry and Human Development*, *29*(3), 189–208. https://doi.org/10.1023/a:1022660923605

Karen, R. (1998). *Becoming attached: First relationships and how they shape our capacity for love.* Oxford University Press.

Keller, H., Voelker, S., & Yovsi, R. D. (2005). Conceptions of parenting in different cultural communities: The case of West African Nso and Northern German women. *Social Development*, *14*(1), 158–180. https://doi.org/10.1111/j.1467-9507.2005.00295.x

Kerns, K. A., & Brumariu, L. E. (2014). Is insecure parent-child attachment a risk factor for the development of anxiety in childhood or adolescence? *Child Development Perspectives*, *8*(1), 12–17. https://doi.org/10.1111/cdep.12054

Khalsa, S. S., Adolphs, R., Cameron, O. G., Critchley, H. D., Davenport, P. W., Feinstein, J. S., Feusner, J. D., Garfinkel, S. N., Lane, R. D., Mehling, W. E., Meuret, A. E., Nemeroff, C. B., Oppenheimer, S., Petzschner, F. H., Pollatos, O., Rhudy, J. L., Schramm, L. P., Simmons, W. K., Stein, M. B., … Zucker, N. (2018). Interoception and mental health: A roadmap. *Biological Psychiatry: Cognitive Neuroscience and Neuroimaging*, *3*(6), 501–513. https://doi.org/10.1016/j.bpsc.2018.04.007

Kim, B.-R., Chow, S.-M., Bray, B., & Teti, D. M. (2017). Trajectories of mothers' emotional availability: Relations with infant temperament in predicting attachment security. *Attachment & Human Development*, *19*(1), 38–57. https://doi.org/10.1080/14616734.2016.1252780

Kim, S., & Strathearn, L. (2017). Trauma, mothering, and intergenerational transmission: A synthesis of behavioral and oxytocin research. *The Psychoanalytic Study of the Child*, *70*(1), 200–223. https://doi.org/10.1080/00797308.2016.1277897

Kinsey Institute. (2017, November 28). *Kinsey Institute: Untold stories "debuts Dec. 3 in Miami. Indiana University Press.* https://kinseyinstitute.org/news-events/news/2017-11-28-untold-stories.php

Kobak, R., Rosenthal, N., & Serwik, A. (2005). The attachment hierarchy in middle childhood: Conceptual and methodological issues. In K. A. Kerns & R. A. Richardson (Eds.), *Attachment in middle childhood* (pp. 71–88). The Guilford Press.

Kochanska, G., & Kim, S. (2013). Difficult temperament moderates links between maternal responsiveness and children's compliance and behavior problems in low-income families. *Journal of Child Psychology and Psychiatry, and Allied Disciplines*, *54*(3), 323–332. https://doi.org/10.1111/jcpp.12002

Kotlen, M. (2020). *Overview of the enzymes in breastmilk.* Verywell Family. https://www.verywellfamily.com/enzymes-in-breast-milk-431797

Kozlowska, K., Walker, P., McLean, L., & Carrive, P. (2015). Fear and the defense cascade: Clinical implications and management. *Harvard Review of Psychiatry*, *23*(4), 263–287. https://doi.org/10.1097/HRP.0000000000000065

Kratzer. (2019). *Harsh Nazi parenting guidelines may still affect German children of today.* https://www.scientificamerican.com/article/harsh-nazi-parenting-guidelines-may-still-affect-german-children-of-today1

Krüger, A., Ehring, T., Priebe, K., Dyer, A. S., Steil, R., & Bohus, M. (2014). Sudden losses and sudden gains during a DBT-PTSD treatment for posttraumatic stress disorder following childhood sexual abuse. *European Journal of Psychotraumatology*, *5*, 1. https://doi.org/10.3402/ejpt.v5.24470

Kulic, N., Skopek, J., Triventi, M., & Blossfeld, H.-P. (2019). Social background and children's cognitive skills: The role of early childhood education and care in a cross-national perspective. *Annual Review of Sociology*, *45*(1), 557–579. https://doi.org/10.1146/annurev-soc-073018-022401

Lai, Y.-H., & Carr, S. (2018). A critical exploration of child-parent attachment as a contextual construct. *Behavioral Sciences*, *8*(12), E112. https://doi.org/10.3390/bs8120112

LaPierre, A. (2021). *Research updates on NeuroAffective Touch. Board meeting of the United States Association for Body Psychotherapy/International Association for Somatic Psychology.* CA.

Lehmann, S., Monette, S., Egger, H., Breivik, K., Young, D., Davidson, C., & Minnis, H. (2020). Development and examination of the reactive attachment disorder and disinhibited social engagement disorder assessment interview. *Assessment, 27*(4), 749–765. https://doi.org/10.1177/1073191118797422

Lende, D. H., & Downey, G. (2020). *Neuroanthropological perspectives on culture, mind, and brain.* Cambridge University Press.

Lende, D. H., & Downey, G. (Eds.). (2012). *The encultured brain: An introduction to neuroanthropology.* MIT press.

Levine, P. (2003). *Sexual healing: Transforming the sacred wound.* Sounds True.

Lewis, T., Amini, F., & Lannon, T. (2000). *A general theory of love.* Vintage.

Lieberman, A. F., Diaz, M. A., Castro, G., & Oliver Bucio, G. (2020). *Make room for baby: Perinatal child-parent psychotherapy to repair trauma and promote attachment.* Guilford.

Linehan, M. M., Comtois, K. A., Murray, A. M., Brown, M. Z., Gallop, R. J., Heard, H. L., Korslund, K. E., Tutek, D. A., Reynolds, S. K., & Lindenboim, N. (2006). Two-year randomized controlled trial and follow-up of dialectical behavior therapy vs therapy by experts for suicidal behaviors and borderline personality disorder. *Archives of General Psychiatry, 63*(7), 757–766. https://doi.org/10.1001/archpsyc.63.7.757

Lobmaier, S. M., Müller, A., Zelgert, C., Shen, C., Su, P. C., Schmidt, G., Haller, B., Berg, G., Fabre, B., Weyrich, J., Wu, H. T., Frasch, M. G., & Antonelli, M. C. (2019). Fetal heart rate variability responsiveness to maternal stress, non-invasively detected from maternal transabdominal ECG. *Archives of Gynecology and Obstetrics,* 1–10. https://doi.org/10.1007/s00404-019-05390-8

Lothane, H. Z. (2017). Wilhelm Reich Revisited: The role of ideology in character analysis of the individual versus character analysis of the masses and the Holocaust. *International Forum of Psychoanalysis, 28*(2), 104–114. https://doi.org/10.1080/0803706X.2017.1347710

Lynning, M., Nissen, M., Lorenzen, K., & Skovgaard, L. (2019, June). Perceived benefits of tension and trauma releasing exercises (TRE) among people with multiple sclerosis–qualitative results from a pilot study. *Multiple Sclerosis Journal, 25*(7), 1049.

Mah, B. L., Bakermans-Kranenburg, M. J., Van IJzendoorn, M. H., & Smith, R. (2015). Oxytocin promotes protective behavior in depressed mothers: A pilot study with the enthusiastic stranger paradigm. *Depression and Anxiety, 32*(2), 76–81. https://doi.org/10.1002/da.22245

Main, M. (1990). Cross-cultural studies of attachment organization: Recent studies, changing methodologies, and the concept of conditional strategies. *Human Development, 33*(1), 48–61. https://doi.org/10.1159/000276502

Main, M. (1999). Mary D. Salter ainsworth: Tribute and portrait. *Psychoanalytic Inquiry, 19*(5), 682–736. https://doi.org/10.1080/07351699909534273

Main, M., & Solomon, J. (1986). Discovery of a new, insecure-disorganized/disoriented attachment pattern. In M. Yogman & T. B. Brazelton (Eds.), *Affective Development in Infancy* (pp. 95–124). Ablex.

Manning, W. D., Fettro, M. N., & Lamidi, E. (2014). Child well-being in same-sex parent families: Review of research prepared for american sociological association amicus brief. *Population Research and Policy Review, 33*(4), 485–502. https://doi.org/10.1007/s11113-014-9329-6

Marlock, G., Weiss, H., Young, C., & Soth, M. (2015). *The handbook of body psychotherapy and somatic psychology.* North Atlantic Books.

McGowan, K. (2014). The second coming of Sigmund Freud. Discover. https://www.discovermagazine.com/mind/the-second-coming-of-sigmund-freud.

Mesman, J., & Emmen, R. A. G. (2013). Mary Ainsworth's legacy: A systematic review of observational instruments measuring parental sensitivity. *Attachment & Human Development, 15*(5–6), 485–506. https://doi.org/10.1080/14616734.2013.820900

Mesman, J., Van Ijzendoorn, M. H., & Sagi-Schwartz, A. (2016). Cross-cultural patterns of attachment. In *Handbook of attachment: Theory, research, and clinical applications* (pp. 852–877).

Mlynek, A. (2019). *6 magical ways that breastmilk changes to meet your baby's needs. Today's Parent*. https://www.todaysparent.com/baby/breastfeeding/magical-ways-breastmilk-changes -to-meet-your-babys-needs

Mpinga, E. K., Macias, A., Hasselgard-Rowe, J., Kandala, N.-B., Félicien, T. K., Verloo, H., Bukonda, N. K. Z., & Chastonay, P. (2016). Female genital mutilation: A systematic review of research on its economic and social impacts across four decades. *Global Health Action, 9*(1), 31489. https://doi.org/10.3402/gha.v9.31489

Mueller, N. T., Bakacs, E., Combellick, J., Grigoryan, Z., & Dominguez-Bello, M. G. (2015). The infant microbiome development: Mom matters. *Trends in Molecular Medicine, 21*(2), 109–117. https://doi.org/10.1016/j.molmed.2014.12.002

Mundo, E. (2006). Neurobiology of dynamic psychotherapy: An integration possible? *The Journal of the American Academy of Psychoanalysis and Dynamic Psychiatry, 34*(4), 679–691. https://doi.org/10.1521/jaap.2006.34.4.679

Murray, D. (2020). *The composition of breastmilk. Verywell Family*. https://www.verywellfamily .com/whats-in-breast-milk-4047820

Music, G. (2018). *Nurturing children: From trauma to growth using attachment theory, psychoanalysis, and neurobiology*. Routledge.

New World Encyclopedia. (n.d.). *Wilhelm Reich*. https://www.newworldencyclopedia.org/ entry/Wilhelm_Reich

Newland, R. P., & Crnic, K. A. (2017). Developmental risk and goodness of fit in the mother-child relationship: Links to parenting stress and children's behaviour problems. *Infant and Child Development, 26*(2), e1980. https://doi.org/10.1002/icd.1980

Nicolas, B. (2018). Behind the mask: Gender hybridity in a Zapotec community. *Latino Studies, 16*(2), 274–276. https://doi.org/10.1057/s41276-018-0119-x

Ohler, N. (2017). *Blitzed: Drugs in the Third Reich*. Houghton Mifflin.

Oosterhuis, H. (1995). The"Jews" of the antifascist lAntifascist Left. *Journal of Homosexuality, 29*(2–3), 227–257. https://doi.org/10.1300/J082v29n02_09

Otto, H., & Keller, H. (Eds.). (2014). *Different faces of attachment: Cultural variations on a universal human need*. Cambridge University Press.

Owen, M. M. (2017). *Can neuroscience rehabilitate Freud for the age of the brain? Aeon*. https://aeon .co/essays/can-neuroscience-rehabilitate-freud-for-the-age-of-the-brain

Perry, R. E., Blair, C., & Sullivan, R. M. (2017). Neurobiology of infant attachment: Attachment despite adversity and parental programming of emotionality. *Current Opinion in Psychology, 17*, 1–6. https://doi.org/10.1016/j.copsyc.2017.04.022

Petot, J.-M. (1991). Melanie Klein. In *The ego and the good object, 1932-1960. (C. Trollope, Trans)* (Vol. 2). International Universities Press, Inc.

Polat, B. (2017). Before attachment theory: Separation research at the tavistock clinic, 1948-1956. *Journal of the History of the Behavioral Sciences, 53*(1), 48–70. https://doi.org/10.1002/ jhbs.21834

Porges, S. (2006). The role of social engagement in attachment and bonding: A phylogenetic perspective. In C. S. Carter, L. Ahnert, K. E. Grossmann, S. B. Hrdy, M. E. Lamb, S. W. Porges, & N. Sachser (Eds.), *Attachment and Bonding: A New Synthesis*. MIT Press.

Porges, S. W. (2009). The polyvagal theory: Nnew insights into adaptive reactions of the autonomic nervous system. *Cleveland Clinic Journal of Medicine, 76 Suppl 2*, S86-90. https://doi .org/10.3949/ccjm.76.s2.17

Porges, S. W., & Buczinsky, R. (n.d.). *The polyvagal theory for treating trauma: A teleseminar session*. The National Institute for the Clinical Application of Behavioral Medicine. https:// static1.squarespace.com/static/5c1d025fb27e390a78569537/t/5cce03089b747a3598c5794 7/1557005065155/porges_nicabm_treating_trauma.pdf

Porges, S. W., & Dana, D. (2018). *Clinical applications of the polyvagal theory: The emergence of polyvagal-informed therapies*. WW Norton & Company.

Pritchett, R., Pritchett, J., Marshall, E., Davidson, C., & Minnis, H. (2013). Reactive attachment disorder in the general population: A hidden ESSENCE disorder. *TheScientificWorldJournal, 2013*, 1–6. https://doi.org/10.1155/2013/818157

Puddledancer press. (2021). *Non-Violent Communication Research.* https://www.nonviolentco
mmunication.com/learn-nonviolent-communication/research-on-nvc

Putignani, L., Del Chierico, F., Petrucca, A., Vernocchi, P., & Dallapiccola, B. (2014). The human
gut microbiota: A dynamic interplay with the host from birth to senescence settled
during childhood. *Pediatric Research, 76*(1), 2–10. https://doi.org/10.1038/pr.2014.49

Rady Children's Hospital. (2014, October). *Understanding early sexual development.* https://www
.rchsd.org/health-articles/understanding-early-sexual-development

Ray, D. C., & McCullough, R. (2016). *Evidence-based practice statement: Play therapy (Research
report).* Retrieved from Association for Play Therapy website. http://www.a4pt.org/?
page=EvidenceBased

Reich, W. (1927). *Genitality in the theory and therapy of neuroses.* Internationaler Psychoanalytischer
Verlag.

Reich, W. (1933a). *Character analysis.* Farrar, Straus and Giroux.

Reich, W. (1933b). *The mass psychology of fascism.* Farrar, Straus and Giroux.

Reich, W. (1942, 1973). The discovery of the orgone vol. 1. In *The function of the orgasm; sex-
economic problems of biological energy.* Orgone Institute Press.

Reich, W. (1953). *History of the development of the life energy.* Orgone Institute Press.

Reich, W. (1963). *Wilhelm Reich - selected writings: An introduction to orgonomy.* Farrar, Straus &
Giroux.

Reich, W. (1983). *Children and their mothers.* Farrar, Straus & Giroux.

Reich, W. (1984). *Children of the future: On the prevention of sexual pathology.* Farrar, Straus & Giroux.

Reich, W. (2005). *Passion of youth: An autobiography, 1897-1922.* Farrar, Straus & Giroux.

Reich, W. (2013). *American odyssey: Letters & journals, 1940-1947.* Farrar, Straus & Giroux.

Reisz, S., Duschinsky, R., & Siegel, D. J. (2018). Disorganized attachment and defense: Eexploring
John Bowlby's unpublished reflections. *Attachment & Human Development, 20*(2), 107–134.
https://doi.org/10.1080/14616734.2017.1380055

Riggs, S. A., & Riggs, D. S. (2011). Risk and resilience in military families experiencing deployment: The role of the family attachment network. *Journal of Family Psychology, 25*(5), 675–
687. https://doi.org/10.1037/a0025286

Ristock, J., Zoccole, A., & Passante, L. (2010). *Aboriginal two-spirit and LGBTQ migration, mobility
and health research project.* Winnipeg.

Roisman, G. L., Padrón, E., Sroufe, L. A., & Egeland, B. (2003). Earned-secure attachment status in retrospect and prospect. *Child Development, 73*(4), 1204–1219. https://doi.org/
10.1111/1467-8624.00467

Roopnarine, J. L., & Davidson, K. L. (2015). Parent-child play across cultures: Advancing play
research. *American Journal of Play, 7*(2). https://files.eric.ed.gov/fulltext/EJ1053428.pdf

Rosenberg, M. (2005). *Raising children compassionately: Parenting the nonviolent communication
way.* Puddledancer.

Rosenthal, N. L., & Kobak, R. (2010). Assessing adolescents' attachment hierarchies:
Differences across developmental periods and associations with individual adaptation. *Journal
of Research on Adolescence, 20*(3), 678–706. https://doi.org/10.1111/j.1532-7795.2010.00655.x

Rothbaum, F., & Kakinuma, M. (2004). Amae and attachment. Human Development, 47(1),
34-39.

Roudinesco, E., & Porter, C. (2016). *Freud in his time and ours.* Harvard University Press.

Sagi, A. (1990). Attachment theory and research from a cross-cultural perspective. *Human
Development, 33*(1), 10–22. https://doi.org/10.1159/000276499

Salinas-Quiroz, F., Rodríguez-Sánchez, F., Costa, P. A., Rosales, M., Silva, P., & Cambón, V. (2018).
Can children have ordinary expectable caregiving environments in unconventional con-
texts? Quality of care organization in three mexican same-sex planned families. *Frontiers in
Psychology, 9,* 2349. https://doi.org/10.3389/fpsyg.2018.02349

Salmon, M. (2013). Interim research report. Pilot TRE research program with Chrysalis Academy
students, Cape Town, South Africa.

Saunders, R., Jacobvitz, D., Zaccagnino, M., Beverung, L. M., & Hazen, N. (2011). Pathways to
earned-security: The role of alternative support figures. *Attachment & Human Development,
13*(4), 403–420. https://doi.org/10.1080/14616734.2011.584405

Scatliffe, N., Casavant, S., Vittner, D., & Cong, X. (2019). Oxytocin and early parent-infant inter-actions: A systematic review. *International Journal of Nursing Sciences*, 6(4), 445–453. https://doi.org/10.1016/j.ijnss.2019.09.009

Scharpf, F., Mkinga, G., Neuner, F., Machumu, M., & Hecker, T. (2020). Fuel to the fire: The esca-lating interplay of attachment and maltreatment in the transgenerational transmission of psychopathology in families living in refugee camps. Development and Psychopathology, 1-14. 10.1017/S0954579420000516

Schimmenti, A., & Caretti, V. (2016). Linking the overwhelming with the unbearable: Developmental trauma, dissociation, and the disconnected self. *Psychoanalytic Psychology*, 33(1), 106–128. https://doi.org/10.1037/a0038019

Schore, A. N. (1994). *Affect regulation and the origin of the self: The neurobiology of emotional develop-ment*. Lawrence Erlbaum Associates.

Schore, A. N. (2001). Effects of a secure attachment relationship on right brain development, affect regulation, and infant mental health. *Infant Mental Health Journal*, 22(1–2), 7–66. https://doi.org/10.1002/1097-0355(200101/04)22:1<7::AID-IMHJ2>3.0.CO;2-N

Schore, A. N. (2003a). *Affect regulation and the repair of the self*. Norton & Co.

Schore, A. N. (2003b). *Affect dysregulation and disorders of the self*. Norton & Co.

Schore, A. N. (2013). Bowlby's "environment of evolutionary adaptedness": Recent studies on the interpersonal neurobiology of attachment and emotional development. In D. Narvaez, J. Panksepp, A. N. Schore, & T. R. Gleason (Eds.), *Evolution, early experience and human devel-opment: From research to practice and policy* (pp. 31–67). Oxford University Press. https://doi.org/10.1093/acprof:oso/9780199755059.001.0001

Selver, C. (1999). *Sensory awareness and our attitude toward life*. Sensory Awareness Foundation.

Seponski, D. M., Bermudez, J. M., & Lewis, D. C. (2012). Creating culturally responsive family ther-apy models and research: Introducing the use of responsive evaluation as a method. *Journal of Marital and Family Therapy*, 39(1), 28–42. https://doi.org/10.1111/j.1752-0606.2011.00282.x

Sharaf, M. R. (1983, 1994). *Fury on earth: A biography of Wilhelm Reich St*. Martin's Press.

Simmons, R. T., Coker, K., Hanks, B. B., Sheperis, D. S., & Bohecker, L. (2021). Mothering iden-tity experiences: A backwards glance. *The Family Journal*, 29(4), 401–409. https://doi.org/10.1177/10664807211023927

Sletvold, J. (2011). "The reading of emotional expression": Wilhelm Reich and the his-tory of embodied analysis. *Psychoanalytic Dialogues*, 21(4), 453–467. https://doi.org/10.1080/10481885.2011.595337

Smyke, A. T., Zeanah, C. H., Gleason, M. M., Drury, S. S., Fox, N. A., Nelson, C. A., & Guthrie, D. (2012). A randomized controlled trial comparing foster care and institutional care for children with signs of reactive attachment disorder. *American Journal of Psychiatry*, 169(5), 508–514. https://doi.org/10.1176/appi.ajp.2011.11050748

Sravanti, L. (2017). Goodness of fit. *Indian Journal of Psychiatry*, 59(4), 515. https://doi.org/10.4103/psychiatry.IndianJPsychiatry_423_17

Stanton, M. (1991). *Sandor Ferenczi: Reconsidering active intervention*. Jason Aronson Publishers Lanham.

Strand, P. S. (2020). The security-seeking impulse and the unification of attachment and culture. *Psychological Review*, 127(5), 778–791. https://doi.org/10.1037/rev0000194

Strand, P. S., Vossen, J. J., & Savage, E. (2019). Culture and child attachment patterns: A behav-ioral systems synthesis. *Perspectives on Behavior Science*, 42(4), 835–850. https://doi.org/10.1007/s40614-019-00220-3

Strathearn, L., Iyengar, U., Fonagy, P., & Kim, S. (2012). Maternal oxytocin response during mother–infant interaction: Associations with adult temperament. *Hormones and Behavior*, 61(3), 429–435. https://doi.org/10.1016/j.yhbeh.2012.01.014

Strick, J. E. (2015). *Wilhelm Reich, Biologist*. Harvard University Press. https://doi.org/10.4159/9780674286863

Stupica, B., Brett, B. E., Woodhouse, S. S., & Cassidy, J. (2019). Attachment security priming decreases children's physiological response to threat. *Child Development*, 90(4), 1254–1271. https://doi.org/10.1111/cdev.13009

Suttie, I. D. (1935). *The origins of love and hate*. K. Paul, Trench, Trubner.

Suvorov, B. (2020). The development of body-oriented psychotherapy in Russia. *International Body Psychotherapy Journal, 19*(1), 122-125.

Teague, S. J., Gray, K. M., Tonge, B. J., & Newman, L. K. (2017). Attachment in children with autism spectrum disorder: A systematic review. *Research in Autism Spectrum Disorders, 35*, 35–50. https://doi.org/10.1016/j.rasd.2016.12.002

The National Child Traumatic Stress Network. (n.d.). *Screening and Assessment*. https://www.nctsn.org/what-is-child-trauma/trauma-types/early-childhood-trauma/screening-and- assessment

The Theraplay Institute. (n.d.). *What is theraplay?*. https://theraplay.org/what-is-theraplay

The Traumatic Stress Research Consortium. (2020, September). *Newsletter*. https://kinseyinstitute.org/pdf/TSRC_Newsletter.2020.9.pdf

Today in Civil Liberties History. (n.d.). *Stamp out orgasms! Government seizes and burns the work of Dr Wilhelm Reich*. https://todayinclh.com/?event=stamp-out-orgasms

Totally History. (n.d.). *Fritz Perls*. https://totallyhistory.com/fritz-perls

Townshend, K., & Caltabiano, N. J. (2019). The extended nervous system: Affect regulation, somatic and social change processes associated with mindful parenting. *BMC Psychology, 7*(1), 41. https://doi.org/10.1186/s40359-019-0313-0

Trub, L., Quinlan, E., Starks, T. J., & Rosenthal, L. (2016). *Discrimination, internalized homonegativity, and attitudes toward children of same-sex parents: Can secure attachment buffer against stigma internalization?*. https://doi.org/10.1111/famp.12255

Turnbull, A., Wang, H.-T., Schooler, J. W., Jefferies, E., Margulies, D. S., & Smallwood, J. (2019). The ebb and flow of attention: Between-subject variation in intrinsic connectivity and cognition associated with the dynamics of ongoing experience. *NeuroImage, 185*, 286–299. https://doi.org/10.1016/j.neuroimage.2018.09.069

U.S. Department of Health and Human Services. (2021, February 22). *Child Development*. https://www.cdc.gov/ncbddd/childdevelopment/early-brain-development.html

Van Dijken, S. (1998). *John Bowlby: His early life: A biographical journey into the roots of attachment theory*. Free Association Books.

van IJzendoorn, M. H., Juffer, F., & Duyvesteyn, M. G. (1995). Breaking the intergenerational cycle of insecure attachment: A review of the effects of attachment-based interventions on maternal sensitivity and infant security. *Journal of Child Psychology and Psychiatry, and Allied Disciplines, 36*(2), 225–248. https://doi.org/10.1111/j.1469-7610.1995.tb01822.x

van IJzendoorn, M. H., & Kroonenberg, P. M. (1988). Cross-cultural patterns of attachment: A meta-analysis of the strange situation. *Child Development, 59*(1), 147–156. https://doi.org/10.1111/j.1467-8624.1988.tb03202.x

van Ijzendoorn, M. H., Sagi, A., & Lambermon, M. W. E. (1992). The multiple caretaker paradox: Data from Holland and Israel. *New Directions for Child and Adolescent Development, 1992*(57), 5–24.

van Ijzendoorn, M. H., & Sagi-Schwartz, A. (2008). Cross-cultural patterns of attachment: Universal and contextual dimensions. In J. Cassidy & P. R. Shaver (Eds.), *Handbook of attachment: Theory, research, and clinical applications* (pp. 880–905). The Guilford Press.

van Ijzendoorn, M. H., Schuengel, C., & Bakermans-Kranenburg, M. J. (1999). Disorganized attachment in early childhood: Mmeta-analysis of precursors, concomitants, and sequelae. *Development and Psychopathology, 11*(2), 225–249. https://doi.org/10.1017/s0954579499002035

van Rosmalen, L., van der Horst, F. C. P., & van der Veer, R. (2016). From secure dependency to attachment: Mary Ainsworth's integration of Blatz's security theory into Bowlby's attachment theory. *History of Psychology, 19*(1), 22–39. https://doi.org/10.1037/hop0000015

Wadsworth, P., Degesie, K., Kothari, C., & Moe, A. (2018). Intimate partner violence during the perinatal period. *The Journal for Nurse Practitioners, 14*(10), 753–759. https://doi.org/10.1016/j.nurpra.2018.08.009

Walker, A. (2010). Breast milk as the gold standard for protective nutrients. *The Journal of Pediatrics, 156*(2 Suppl), S3-7. https://doi.org/10.1016/j.jpeds.2009.11.021

Westen, D. (1991). Social cognition and object relations. *Psychological Bulletin, 109*(3), 429–455. https://doi.org/10.1037/0033-2909.109.3.429

Wilhelm Reich Museum. (n.d.). *Home.* https://wilhelmreichmuseum.org/about/the-wilhelm -reich-infant-trust

Wilson, J. D., & Roehrborn, C. (1999). Long-term consequences of castration in men: Lessons from the Skoptzy and the eunuchs of the Chinese and Ottoman courts. *The Journal of Clinical Endocrinology and Metabolism, 84*(12), 4324–4331. https://doi.org/10.1210/jcem.84.12.6206

Woodhouse, S. S., Dykas, M. J., & Cassidy, J. (2009). Perceptions of secure base provision within the family. *Attachment & Human Development, 11*(1), 47–67. https://doi.org/ 10.1080/14616730802500792

Woodhouse, S. S., Scott, J. R., Hepworth, A. D., & Cassidy, J. (2020). Secure Base Provision: A New Approach to Examining Links Between Maternal Caregiving and Infant Attachment. *Child Development, 91*(1), e249–e265. https://doi.org/10.1111/cdev.13224

World Health Organization. (1997). *Female genital mutilation. A joint WHO/UNICEF/UNFPA Statement.* https://apps.who.int/iris/bitstream/handle/10665/41903/9241561866.pdf

World Health Organization. (2011). *Exclusive breastfeeding for six months best for babies everywhere.* https://www.who.int/news/item/15-01-2011-exclusive-breastfeeding-for-six-months -best-for-babies-everywhere

Xu, P. C., Wang, Y. H., Meng, Q. J., Wen, Y. B., Yang, J., Wang, X. Z., Chen, Y., He, Y. L., Wang, Q. W., Wang, Y., Cui, L. G., Sihoe, J. D., Franco, I., Lang, J. H., & Wen, J. G. (2021). Delayed elimination communication on the prevalence of children's bladder and bowel dysfunction. *Scientific Reports, 11*(1), 12366. https://doi.org/10.1038/s41598-021-91704-3

Yamaguchi, S. (2004). Further clarifications of the concept of amae in relation to dependence and attachment. *Human Development, 47*(1), 28–33. https://doi.org/10.1159/000075367

Yang, I., Corwin, E. J., Brennan, P. A., Jordan, S., Murphy, J. R., & Dunlop, A. (2016). The infant microbiome: Implications for infant health and neurocognitive development. Nursing Research, 65(1), 76–88. https://doi.org/10.1097/NNR.0000000000000133

Zeanah, C. H., & Gleason, M. M. (2015). Annual research review: Attachment disorders in early childhood--clinical presentation, causes, correlates, and treatment. *Journal of Child Psychology and Psychiatry, and Allied Disciplines, 56*(3), 207–222. https://doi.org/10.1111/ jcpp.12347

Zimmermann, P., & Soares, I. (2019). Recent contributions for understanding inhibited reactive attachment disorder. *Attachment & Human Development, 21*(2), 87–94. https://doi.org/ 10.1080/14616734.2018.1499207

CHAPTER 6

Cultural and Contextual Factors of Middle Childhood Through Adolescence

LEARNING OBJECTIVES

Upon completion of this chapter, students will be able to:

1. Identify the stage of lifespan development known as "middle childhood through adolescence."
2. Recognize key cultural factors impacting this stage of development
3. Recognize key contextual factors impacting this stage of development.
4. Analyze counseling considerations for the case of "Dev."
5. Infer from our podcast expert, Dr. Stacee Reicherzer, how to work with clients in this stage of life.

CASE STUDY 6.1: THE CASE OF DEV

Dev is a 13-year-old transgender boy living at home with his parents and older brother. "Dev," the shortened version of his female birth name, Devya, is Indian and Muslim. Dev began questioning his gender identity early in life, reflecting that his male-ness never seemed in question for him, although he struggled with people's responses to this acknowledgment and quickly learned to limit his outward expressions of it: "I was a boy. I knew I was a boy like my brother. It was just that no one else could see it or could understand it." Shy and often reserved as a child, Dev sought comfort in isolation when he felt he was being misunderstood, rejected, or shamed. In his room, alone, he felt safe to play, dress, and live in his world as a boy. However, in the presence of anyone other than his brother, Aarav, Dev felt self-conscious and fearful.

Dev's parents, both first-generation immigrants who came to the United States as young children, were divided in their early responses to Dev. His father, Sanjiv, was initially more accepting and indulged Dev in what he initially thought was just a sincere affection for, and imitation of, Aarav. His mother, Kavya, was less accepting and struggled with how to explain his behaviors and reactions to her family and friends.

Though, as a family, they were less traditional than their immigrant parents, Kavya felt a sense of shame and embarrassment in Dev's assertions, and struggled with the loss of the daughter she believed she had. As Dev continued to grow and maintain his male identity, conversations on the topic often became heated or resulted in a collective avoidance of the issue, by both parents, altogether. Over time his parents have agreed to refer to him as "Dev" but have not yet begun to use his preferred gender pronouns of *him* or *his*.

School and peer interactions have been challenging as well. Though a good student who often uses school and academics as a means of avoidance, Dev faced considerable social rejection from his peers at an early age. He noted that "boys didn't see me as a boy and girls were doing things I had no interest in." As he matured and his identity further solidified, he began to struggle with what this meant for his developing sexuality. He recognized that his outward female appearance only further complicated the fact that he was attracted to females. This often left him with no sense of connection with male peers, mislabeled as a lesbian, and ridiculed for both. Dev acknowledges, "The hardest part of school is knowing I am not me and that I can't even be who I am not. I am either a girl who likes girls or some freaky girl trying to pretend I'm a boy. People don't get it and they make fun of me either way."

As Dev has continued to age, his struggle with *gender dysphoria*, the discomfort and stress associated with a gender identity that does not align with his sex-related physical characteristics, has intensified. His feelings of isolation and rejection have largely shifted to a place of depression and anxiety that are compounded by hormonal changes and a significant fear of what will happen when his body only further develops in ways that don't align with who he feels he is. Using the internet for research and connection to social media, Dev has found himself in a new place of optimism and challenge—he feels he can more firmly identify with being transgender and is finding social support for those like him, and, yet, he struggles with how to transition in the face of family opposition, peer rejection, and the impending hormonal changes he is facing. He has convinced his family to bring him to see you, a clinical social worker. Their goal is that he will see you and work through this "stage" he is in. His goal is that you can convince them of who he truly is and that you will help advocate for hormone blockers to assist in the suppression of puberty.

MIDDLE CHILDHOOD THROUGH ADOLESCENCE

The developmental trajectory of middle childhood through adolescence is perhaps one of the most complex and critical of the entire lifespan. Though limited to slightly more than 10 years, the developmental stages of middle childhood (ages 6 through 11) and adolescence (ages 12 through 17) can easily be broken down into smaller subsets of development based entirely on the variations in cognitive, physical, and social and emotional development achieved in these swaths of time (Centers for Disease Control and Prevention [CDC], 2020a, 2020b, 2020c, 2020d). Children in this phase of life are rapidly developing the mental and emotional skill sets to foster independence as well as engage more deeply with others in their lives. Likewise, their bodies are in near-constant transition. This begins with continued height and weight growth from early childhood followed by the hormonal, neurological, and physiological changes that stem from the puberty process (Del Giudice, 2014; Susman & Dorn, 2013). Add to this the complicating factors of social influence and sexual development, and it makes sense that this phase of life is often perplexing and so pivotal to the broader lifespan development process.

Middle childhood through adolescence is often associated with the push and pull of individual identity development paralleled with an increased desire for peer and intimate relationships. As children move through this phase they meander between their families, friends, and their own growing sense of themselves in a much broader world. Peer relationships take on new significance, which can lead to peer pressure, experimentation, and the expression and adoption of varied identities (Dumas et al., 2012). Parents, though still critical to a developing sense of self, progressively have less overt influence (Blaževic, 2016). Cognitive developments that occur during this period of life foster greater insight and self-awareness, as well as the ability to see outside points of view and to think more critically (Mah & Ford-Jones, 2012). While significant, these moments can be fleeting or masked by the equally significant egocentricity bias that can occur during this time (Riva et al., 2016). Development at this stage of life is complicated, empowering, frustrating, and fundamental to the foundation of adulthood.

Table 6.1 provides a high-level overview of the primary physical, cognitive, and social–emotional changes that are associated with these stages of development for individuals in Western societies (CDC, 2020a, 2020b, 2020c, 2020d). Though years are assigned to these developmental milestones and reflect typical development, as this chapter will demonstrate, the developmental process is highly individualized and context driven. This is important to keep in mind as you consider the developmental theories and stages laid out in this chapter and the chapter to follow.

The shared experiences of middle childhood and adolescence are significant and, while varied for each person experiencing them, often overlap. This can be a difficult time in the developmental process, but also one full of opportunity, growth, and experiences that shape a lifetime. Other portions of this text focus on developmental theories that speak to the milestones noted in Table 6.1. The remainder of this chapter allows us to further explore the cultural and contextual factors that may differentiate this experience for individuals moving through the middle childhood and adolescent stages of life.

CULTURAL FACTORS: MIDDLE CHILDHOOD THROUGH ADOLESCENCE

To truly understand the development of middle childhood we have to consider the child within the context of their cultural identities. What may be true for some children at this age is that they do not yet have a good understanding of their cultures or what their culture represents to them in their lives (Aguayo et al., 2021). Perhaps, at minimum, they cannot overtly voice this in the manner that we understand the term "cultural identity" to mean. However, children at this stage of development are highly embedded in varied cultural groups that can have a significant impact on who they are, how they operate, what opportunities they have, and how they interact with the world around them. Just like you or me, a child's culture reflects their "way of life" and the associated beliefs, values, and customs associated with being a member of that group. Common examples of this include family culture, religion or spirituality, identity, ethnicity, and race (Aguayo et al., 2021).

Table **6.1** Middle Childhood and Adolescence

	MIDDLE CHILDHOOD (6–8 YEARS)	MIDDLE CHILDHOOD (9–11 YEARS)	ADOLESCENCE (12–14 YEARS)	ADOLESCENCE (15–17 YEARS)
Physical	Demonstrate a slower but continuous growth rate and advances in gross and fine motor development and coordination	Become increasingly aware of their developing body prior to puberty	Reflect significant physical and hormonal changes as a result of puberty	Most girls will be physically mature and have completed puberty while boys may still be maturing
Cognitive	Show rapid development in mental abilities including an increased ability to express thoughts and feelings	Demonstrate increased attention span and perspective-taking ability	Develop a stronger sense of right and wrong and a heightened ability for complex thinking.	Can better express themselves and their reasons for doing things. Demonstrate more future planning and concern for what lies ahead
Social–emotional	Demonstrate independence from parents and begin to emphasize friendships. Begin to understand their place in the larger world	Develop deeper and more complex peer relationships, particularly with those of the same sex. Increasingly become more independent from the family	Demonstrate increased emotionality and self-focus. Preference for peers over family continues to increase as well as peer influence	Engage in more romantic relationships and have heightened sexuality. Peer relationships are more intimate and primary. Parent–child relationships may improve

Source: Adapted from Centers for Disease Control and Prevention. (2020a, March 6). *Middle childhood (6–8 years of age).* U.S. Department of Health and Human Services. https://www.cdc.gov/ncbddd/childdevelopment/positiveparenting/middle.html; Centers for Disease Control and Prevention. (2020b, March 6). *Middle childhood (9–11 years of age).* U.S. Department of Health and Human Services. https://www.cdc.gov/ncbddd/childdevelopment/positiveparenting/middle2.html; Centers for Disease Control and Prevention. (2020c, March 6). *Teenagers (15–17 years of age).* U.S. Department of Health and Human Services. https://www.cdc.gov/ncbddd/childdevelopment/positiveparenting/adolescence2.html; Centers for Disease Control and Prevention. (2020d, December 2). *Young teens (12–14 years of age).* U.S. Department of Health and Human Services. https://www.cdc.gov/ncbddd/childdevelopment/positiveparenting/adolescence.html

What is different about children's cultural identities is that, unlike some cultural identities for adults, children often do not choose their cultural groups. These more often reflect the cultural identities of parents or caregivers and may or may not ultimately be adopted by the child at various future stages of life. This is a critical consideration, as culture plays a significant role in how we are raised and how we come to view the world. When we consider development, we have to understand that milestones and "typical" experiences of a developmental period can be heavily impacted by forces outside of our own control—some highly protective and positive and others that can create unique challenges to that developmental stage of life.

Ethnic and Racial Identity Development

The ethnic and racial groups to which we belong are an important part of our identity development and can take on different levels of meaning depending on our maturation and the developmental period we are in. As children move through early and middle childhood they begin to recognize and take part in ethnic–racial identification and labeling of themselves and others (Umaña-Taylor et al., 2014). As they continue to age and move into adolescence their increased cognitive capacity and socio–emotional development allow for greater insight and analysis of what those identities really mean. During this time their *ethnic and racial identity* (ERI) begins to form. Our ERI not only reflects the racial and ethnic identities to which we belong, but the beliefs we hold relative to those ethnic and racial groups as well as how they are formed across time (Umaña-Taylor et al., 2014).

As we consider our case study, Dev, we want to keep in mind that he is a member of a South Asian family of Indian descent and that his parents were first-generation immigrants. The fact that his parents moved to the United States as young children likely shaped their worldviews and had an impact on their ERI development during this stage of their lives. As a result, they may have varying levels of cultural connection tied to their South Asian heritage as well as their new American culture that are reflected in who they are and how they parent. This can be reflected in their family values, food choices, style of dress, acceptable expressions of gender identity and gender roles, hopes for the future generation in terms of expectations of educational and professional attainment, and clear preferences for how youth choose future mates (e.g., some version of arranged marriage is still practiced in various cultures around the world, which can lead to increasing schisms as subsequent generations acculturate away from their ancestors' influence). It can also be tied to views they hold about concepts like autonomy and parental authority for significant life choices (Jensen & Dost-Gözkan, 2015).

The beliefs that Dev's parents hold related to their ethnic or racial identities can influence their understanding of Dev along with expectations they have for him during this and future periods of development. Similarly, as Dev develops and begins to understand his ERI, he may find he aligns closely with the identity of his parents, or that he adopts only parts of this identity that are meaningful to him. His ERI will also likely be impacted by social influences at school and within his broader community. Just as with many elements of our cultural identities, our understanding and adoption of ethnic and racial identity can change and evolve with time. It can also highly impact or be impacted by other forms of identity that we hold, the social and contextual factors of the time, and our cognitive and emotional development. Racial and ethnic identity will be explored more deeply in other chapters, but it is an important consideration to bear in mind as we look further into Dev's case study and the impact of multiple converging identities.

Religion

Just as with cultural identity, and sometimes as an interrelated part of it, religious beliefs can greatly influence the developmental process. They can impact our beliefs on right and wrong, provide reason and rationale to events in our lives, and offer comfort and guidance in times of challenge. Depending on the guardians, the religion, and the adherence to beliefs associated with the religion, children can be highly or minimally influenced by religion in their lives. Where religious beliefs are strong and highly influential, they can frame many experiences within the middle childhood and adolescent stages of development including social interactions, relationships to parents, drinking, dating, sexual activity, and other behaviors associated with these stages of development.

Children first begin discerning and categorizing different religions in the middle childhood years between the ages of 8 and 11 (van der Straten Waillet & Roskam, 2012). Similar to what we see with ethnic and racial identity, children are able to identify with their own religion at younger ages, but require a heightened cognitive capacity to discern differences between religious groups and ideological belief systems that go beyond physical traits such as the color of someone's skin. This ability to discern and make distinctions between religious groups comes earlier for children of minority religions and those who attend schools with diverse religious beliefs (van der Straten Waillet & Roskam, 2012). That is, the more exposure children have to religious beliefs outside of their own, the more aware they are of them by contrast. Similarly, when children belong to families of a minority religion there can be greater effort placed on educating children about differences in an effort to help prepare them and to help them cope with social situations (van der Straten Waillet & Roskam, 2012).

Religious beliefs, particularly in the childhood and adolescent years are largely shaped and influenced by the religion of the parents. This can be especially true for Muslim minority children. Phalet et al. (2018) found that levels of religious identification tend to be higher for Muslim minority youth when compared to other minority and majority youth. Additionally, as Muslim youth moved into adolescence, their religious identification remained stable or further increased. Over time, this religious identification also held steady with less religious decline across generations compared to other minority and majority youth (Phalet et al., 2018). One consideration tied to this finding is the strong influence of family, culture, and shared friendships that are associated with the Muslim religion. According to Phalet et al. (2018), Muslim youth are more likely to self-select co-ethnic and co-religious peer groups as opposed to those of differing religions or ethnicities, which continues to reinforce their religious identity.

As we consider Dev and his developing identity, we would want to be mindful of the impact of his Muslim faith in our understanding of who he is. We would first want to look at this through the lens of age and cognitive capacity, recognizing that this may differ for him depending on where he is in the maturation process. From there we might consider questions that allow us greater insight into his beliefs and how they impact his worldview. Does he identify as Muslim, and what does this mean to him? Further, what does this look like in his home, with his parents, and with his extended family? Are his friends co-ethnic or co-religious and does that shape his beliefs and understanding of his world around him? How does his religion view gender identity and roles? Does he feel a sense of acceptance from others based on his religion or does this create a barrier from him? Does his religion serve as a protective factor for him or is it creating challenges in the developmental process? When we view Dev's development with these considerations in mind, we begin to get a more holistic perspective of the challenges and benefits tied to his Muslim faith and how they may ultimately impact current and future development.

Transgender Identity Development

The term *transgender* is an umbrella term that refers to situations where a person's felt or identified gender does not align with their gender assigned at birth. Various identities fall underneath this broader term and can impact a child's developing sense of gender identity. These include those who are gender non-conforming, gender non-binary, gender fluid, gender creative, and gender expansive, among others (Bernardini, 2017). While research on transgender identity development continues, a significant number of studies demonstrate that gender identity is, at least in part, hereditary and associated with innate biological factors including genes (Polderman et al., 2018).

For children in the middle childhood phase, the concept of gender identity is starting to solidify. Having a sense of oneself as a particular gender or identity begins to take on specific meaning and has implications for how a child dresses, engages socially, and develops both emotionally and physically, depending on where they are in their transgender identity development. This process only expands and grows more complex as children move into adolescence where the physical changes of the body, the emphasis on social groups, and the culturally defined norms related to maturing into a young adult bear significant weight. As transgender children move into adolescence, gender identity is something that they may both be identifying as well as expressing outwardly for the first time (Singh, 2017).

In Dev's case, gender identity is one of the most salient cultural identities forming for him. From his case study, we see that he has questioned his gender identity from a young age—not from an internal perspective that he is male, but in terms of the highly complex situation that stems from having a physical and socially prescribed identity that does not align with who he sees himself as being. As a result of this, and the multitude of contextual and cultural factors surrounding him, he may have moved through one or more identity formation stages specific to his transgender identity in his middle childhood and adolescent years.

TRANSSEXUAL OR TRANSGENDER IDENTITY FORMATION MODEL

To better understand an individual's identity development process, it is important to consider their transgender identity and how this ties back to, informs, and is interwoven with the developmental milestones of each phase of life. Devor (2004) outlines a 14-stage model of Transgender and Transsexual Identity Formation shown in Table 6.2. While a stage model of transgender development is a valuable tool for beginning to understand this experience, Devor (2004) clarifies that this model of identity formation is highly individualized, meaning individuals may move through all or only some stages and can move quickly or slowly between and among them. Further, Devor (2004) notes this model was developed specific to a Euro-American experience

Table 6.2 Devor's Stages of Transsexual or Transgender Identity Formation

STAGE	CHARACTERISTICS AND ACTIONS OF EACH STAGE
1. Abiding Anxiety	• **Characteristics:** Unfocused gender and sex discomfort • **Actions:** Preference for other gender activities and companionship
2. Identity Confusion About Originally Assigned Gender and Sex	• **Characteristics:** First doubts about suitability of originally assigned gender and sex • **Actions:** Reactive gender and sex conforming activities
3. Identity Comparisons About Originally Assigned Gender and Sex	• **Characteristics:** Seeking and weighing alternative gender identities • **Actions:** Experimenting with alternative gender-consistent identities
4. Discovery of Transsexualism or Transgenderism	• **Characteristics:** Learning that transsexualism or transgenderism exists • **Actions:** Accidental contact with information about transsexualism or transgenderism
5. Identity Confusion About Transsexualism or Transgenderism	• **Characteristics:** First doubts about the authenticity of own transsexualism or transgenderism • **Actions:** Seeking more information about transsexualism or transgenderism
6. Identity Comparisons About Transsexualism or Transgenderism	• **Characteristics:** Testing transsexual or transgender identity using transsexual or transgender reference groups • **Actions:** Start to disindentify with originally assigned sex and gender. Start to identify as transsexed or transgendered
7. Tolerance of Transsexual or Transgender Identity	• **Characteristics:** Identify as probably transsexual or transgender • **Actions:** Increasingly disidentify with originally assigned gender and sex
8. Delay Before Acceptance of Transsexual or Transgender Identity	• **Characteristics:** Waiting for changed circumstances. Looking for confirmation of transsexual or transgender identity • **Actions:** Seeking more information about transsexualism or transgenderism. Reality testing in intimate relationships and against further information about transsexualism or transgenderism
9. Acceptance of Transsexual or Transgender Identity	• **Characteristics:** Transsexual or transgender identity established • **Actions:** Tells others about transsexual or transgender identity
10. Delay Before Transition	• **Characteristics:** Transsexual identity deepens. Final disidentity as original gender and sex. Anticipatory socialization • **Actions:** Learns how to do transition. Saves money. Organizes support systems

(continued)

Table 6.2 Devor's Stages of Transsexual or Transgender Identity Formation *(continued)*

STAGE	CHARACTERISTICS AND ACTIONS OF EACH STAGE
11. Transition	• **Characteristics:** Changing gender and sex • **Actions:** Gender and sex reassignments
12. Acceptance of Post-Transition Gender and Sex Identities	• **Characteristics:** Post-transition identity established • **Actions:** Successful post-transition living
13. Integration	• **Characteristics:** Transsexuality mostly invisible • **Actions:** Stigma management. Identity integration
14. Pride	• **Characteristics:** Openly transsexed • **Actions:** Transsexual advocacy

Source: Data from Devor (2004). Witnessing and mirroring: A fourteen stage model of transsexual identity formation. *Journal of Gay & Lesbian Psychotherapy, 8*(1/2), 41–67. doi:10.1300/J236v08n01_05

and perspective with research largely on adult White males. As a mental health professional, these are essential limitations to bear in mind as you choose and begin applying identity or development theories to a client.

The first nine stages of the Transsexual or Transgender Identity Formation model are tied explicitly to identity development—recognizing, identifying with, and accepting oneself as transgender (Devor, 2004). They emphasize the emotional, cognitive, and behavioral responses individuals may go through when they begin to unpack their experiences and recognize that they are transgender and begin the social transitioning process. These stages include significant self-reflection as well as considerations and responses made in reaction to people in their lives. Specific to middle childhood and adolescence, these stages reflect the need to seek safety while also having to absorb the shock of rejection and ostracization that can come with a developmental stage centered on belonging to peer groups and continued support of family. Many of these may be positive, such as when they experience another transgender person and recognize they are not alone. However, others may feel deeply shameful or challenging, such as when they have to let go of relationships or parts of themselves tied to their assigned birth gender. These experiences can accumulate as forms of trauma and increase risk for anxiety, depression, and resulting behaviors.

The final five stages reflect a continuation of the transgender identity formation process where there is an emphasis on the physiological transitioning, including the use of hormones or sexual reassignment surgery to match the affirmed gender identity (Devor, 2004). The complexities of these stages are significant. They account for financial considerations as well as continued emotional, cognitive, and behavioral changes as the individual more overtly expresses their transgender identity in daily life. It is important to note that not all transgender individuals can or will choose to complete the steps associated with a physiological transition as part of their identity formation process, and yet this in no way diminishes their felt sense of who they really are.

The stages of transition can be more or less challenging for individuals based on the gender to which they are transitioning (Devor, 2004). For example, female-to-male individuals will likely experience less social stigma in the child and adolescent years, as the concept of being a "tomboy" carries with it some social acceptance (Coyle et al., 2016). They can also carry this benefit into the physical transitioning process where the use of testosterone can facilitate a deepening of the voice, provide hair growth, and result in increased muscle mass that allows them to more easily conform to a male physique (Devor, 2004). Depending on when the physical transitioning process occurs, this benefit is often not afforded to male-to-female transitioning individuals because estrogen supplements are not able to counteract the effects of early testosterone and secondary sex characteristics that develop in puberty (Devor, 2004).

TRANSGENDER IDENTITY DEVELOPMENT IN MIDDLE CHILDHOOD

Keeping all of this in mind, let us now consider how this ties back to the stage of middle childhood. In this stage of development, children have an increased awareness of their physical bodies, particularly as they move closer to puberty. As you might imagine, this can be a more complicated experience for transgender children because they are challenged to not only consider physical changes into an adult body, but also changes that reflect an adult body that does not align with who they view themselves as being. Children in this stage of life have also developed more cognitive capacity that allows them to empathize and take others' perspectives, thereby also making them more keenly aware of others and themselves. For transgender children this awareness may foster a heightened sense of difference or fear that are not understood by others because of those differences. Further, in middle childhood social relationships with same-sex children have become key, as parents begin to lose emphasis within the child's social circle. This can be particularly challenging for transgender children when their peers do not recognize or accept them as their affirmed gender identity, leaving them with limited options for peer relationships or having to alter their behavior to accommodate those relationships. This can also lead to harassment, bullying, or discrimination at school or in play experiences with other children (Singh & Eaker, 2017).

One important consideration is the role parents and family systems play during this time of development. In order for healthy gender identity formation to occur children need a safe and affirming environment that allows them to express a true understanding of themselves and their preferences (Singh & Eaker, 2017). Parents who are accepting and supportive of their transgender children can buffer some of the negative consequences and offer added support during this time. According to Singh (2017), family acceptance of transgender and gender non-conforming children is a major protective factor and can reduce the risks of negative mental health outcomes for their children. However, that is not always the case as many parents are grappling with what this change means to them and may face stigma and harassment from others in their lives as well (Bernardini, 2017). This disenfranchised grief can be very complex for parents to process, and merits sensitive therapeutic support and linkage.

When we consider our case study client Dev, and where he was in his transgender identity formation in middle childhood, we might expect him to fall into one of the beginning stages of transgender identity formation in the Devor (2004) model. What we know of Dev's early development is that he recognized his differing identity relatively early in life. Although he may not have had a name for it or understood the larger implications, this is not necessarily atypical for children. By middle childhood, most children have a relatively strong awareness of their sex and gender and the associated social meanings ascribed to them, including the fact that changes in dress or length of hair do not change the underlying gender or sex of the person (Pardo & Devor, 2017). We see this in Dev's responses to his social environment. He clearly recognizes that he prefers to dress and play as a boy, but he has already discovered these behaviors are viewed as atypical or not acceptable and he must therefore hide them. It is likely that he continues to demonstrate assigned gender behavior in social settings in order to maintain a sense of acceptance by his parents or peers, because belonging and care from the group serves as a protective factor. However, doing so comes with a cost. At this stage of development, Dev may be questioning himself and feeling guilt and shame associated with why he is the way he is. Likewise, he may have anger or frustration at his parents or peers for not accepting him for who he feels he is on the inside. Most likely, this is a highly confusing and lonely time for Dev, as he moves into a space of heightened desire for peer interaction and is unable to find acceptance socially or within his own home.

As a mental health provider, your challenge in working with someone at this stage of development is in recognizing the levels of support that exist around the child and working to create a buffer by fostering a sense of safety and validation of their experience that may or may not be present in other relationships in their lives. When transgender identity issues are in question, it can also be important to try and understand the child's own understanding of their identity and how this manifests in the home and in social settings. As the clinical social worker working with Dev in his middle childhood years, you might have an initial conversation such as the following:

SESSION EXCERPT

Clinical Social Worker: I am so glad you came in to talk to me today. I am happy to meet you and to get to spend a little time learning about you. Over the next little bit I am hoping we can talk some and you can help me understand a little more about how things are going for you. Does that sound okay?

Dev: Yes.

Clinical Social Worker: Okay, good. So, your parents tell me that you are spending a lot of time in your room lately. Is that true?

Dev: Yes.

Clinical Social Worker: I sometimes like to be alone in my room as well. Will you tell me a little bit about what you like about being in your room?

Dev: I like that I can play in my room and do things I like.

Clinical Social Worker: Ah, yes, getting to play is so much fun. What types of things do you like to play?

Dev: I like to play with my brother's Pokémon cards a lot.

Clinical Social Worker: Nice! There are so many different and cool Pokémon characters, aren't there? I don't know a lot about them, but I do know that much. What do you like about playing Pokémon?

Dev: I like learning about all the Pokémon and pretending I am them in battle.

Clinical Social Worker: Oh, so you play out some of the scenes from the cards or from what you know of them?

Dev: Yes, just in my room.

Clinical Social Worker: Got it. That sounds like it is fun for you. Do you ever play Pokémon outside of your room or with other people?

Dev: Sometimes I play with my brother. He collects the cards and plays the video games with his friends. He will share them with me and sometimes play with me, too.

Clinical Social Worker: That's nice. It sounds like your brother is fun to play with.

Dev: Yeah, most of the time.

Clinical Social Worker: Do you and your brother play together a lot?

Dev: Not a lot. My parents don't like me to play Pokémon. They say it is a game for boys and I should find other things to do with my time and leave my brother alone.

Clinical Social Worker: I see. I can imagine that is hard for you.

Dev: Yeah, I don't like doing other things they think I should be doing like playing with dolls or the girls on my street.

Clinical Social Worker: Those are just not things you are interested in.

Dev: No. Everyone wants me to play and act like a girl all the time. I hate it. I don't like to wear dresses or play with girl things. I just want to be me.

Clinical Social Worker: Right, you just want to be you. And you feel like you can do this when you are home in your room?

Dev: Yes, when I am alone. If no one is watching or looking I can wear what I want and play what I want.

Though incomplete, this initial interaction gives you a sense of how Dev identifies himself in terms of behavior and social relationships at this stage of middle childhood development and transgender identity formation. It demonstrates, at minimum, that he is feeling a lack of acceptance from his parents and that he struggles with a pressure he feels to conform to outside standards of behavior and dress. This early conversation reflects one of many situations that could be occurring for Dev right now, many of which would not necessarily mean he is transgender. For example, Dev may be *gender non-conforming*. If this were the case, Dev could still identify as female and use "she/her/they" pronouns, but may not act or behave in ways that adhere to others' stereotyped beliefs of female gender. The point is not that the clinical social worker identifies or names the experience in the first interaction, or that they expect Dev will. The reality may be that he is not at a place where he understands what all of this means for him or his family, on whom he depends, and that the terminology does not yet exist for that type of response. Instead, what we see in this interaction is the clinical social worker building rapport and offering a safe place for Dev to explore his experiences.

As a mental health provider for someone presenting with questions around gender identity formation in middle childhood, the important piece to consider is how development is shaped by experiences at home, with peers, within the broader social structure, and with the child's own developing sense of identity. Being able to explore and probe for the child's impressions and understanding of what is occurring for them is key to this process. As you are able to work with the child to more fully understand their experience, you will be able to determine next steps in supporting them and their family in whatever additional needs exist relative to their identity development and possible transitioning journey.

TRANSGENDER IDENTITY DEVELOPMENT IN ADOLESCENCE

Just as it did in middle childhood, transgender identity formation can be highly impacted by the social, emotional, physical, and cognitive developments that occur in the adolescent years. In fact, depending on where the child was in their transgender identity formation in middle childhood and how much support they had in those years, the adolescent years can be that much more challenging and critical. As children age and move into their teenage years, there is an even greater emphasis on same-sex peer relationships that can be coupled with a newly forming desire for romantic and sexual relationships. For transgender adolescents, the initial challenge in forming and maintaining peer relationships may abate as they move more fully into a socially transitioned experience and find acceptance among other peer communities within the LGBTQ +population (Bernardini, 2017). However, this is not always the case, and can lead to further ridicule by peers and an increased sense of shame and self-isolation, including an increased risk of parasuicidal and suicidal ideation and behaviors (Pardo & Devor, 2017). This is particularly concerning given that suicide rates grew roughly 7% each year from 2013 to 2017 and was the second leading cause of death for persons aged 10 to 14 and 15 to 19 in 2017 (Curtin & Heron, 2019).

The physical development associated with adolescence can be particularly challenging. For some transgender adolescents, the concept of being transgender has not fully cemented or been accepted. This can result in anxiety or general malaise associated with the physical and hormonal changes that accompany this developmental stage (Singh, 2017). For other transgender teens who have affirmed their gender identity and have begun the social transition process, the physiological changes of this stage can be terrifying because their bodies are only further betraying their sense of gender identity. It is for this reason that many transgender adolescents seek medical care to delay the puberty process (Singh, 2017). This step can prevent secondary sex characteristics from forming and allow transgender teens additional time to process and further explore their gender identity. This is also an age where non-medical manipulation of secondary sex characteristics, through binding and tucking, may be practiced to present themselves more closely aligned with the preferred gender (Holman & Goldberg, 2006; Tran Ngoc et al., 2020). Further, questions around romantic relationships and sexual activity can be complicated for transgender teens who are both working out the physiological changes to their own bodies as well as how this impacts how they are perceived and how who they are attracted to is perceived by others. Like most teenagers, sexual identity development is also a consideration in this phase of life, and is only more complicated by the fact that a transgender teenager may not yet have socially or physically transitioned.

When we look back at our case study Dev, and consider his situation through the lens of adolescence, we can see many of these issues playing out for him. First, he is isolated. He has limited social support beyond his brother and has found that he is not accepted by peers in school or at home by his parents. He has begun developing social interactions online, which have helped solidify his understanding and belief in his transgender identity. Considering this, we might expect him to be in stages 8 or 9 of the Transexual or Transgender Identity Formation model, where he has been further investigating transgender identity and has begun to accept himself as transgender (Devor, 2004). While this can be a positive experience for him, the challenge of others not accepting his transgender identity can cause further feelings of anxiety or depression that his clinical social worker would want to consider. We also know that he is considering the physical changes occurring for him. Given that his assigned gender is female and he is now in his early teenage years, he is likely experiencing the growth of secondary sex characteristics that are adding to his growing urgency to address this with his parents and to seek out help from the clinical social worker.

As a mental health professional, it is critical to consider the full range of social, emotional, cognitive, and physiological changes going on for your adolescent clients. In particular, when working with transgender adolescents, the complexities are significant and compounded by the levels of social support available in the home, with peers, in the school, and online. Exploring these and understanding the varied interplay between them will assist in helping the client gain the support necessary to move forward, while reducing risk of emotional cut-off from family and peers that can be life-threatening for youth. At this stage of development, you might expect a conversation between Dev and his clinical social worker to look like this:

SESSION EXCERPT

Clinical Social Worker: Dev, I appreciate your willingness to come in and meet with me. I understand that there has been a lot going on for you lately. Can you tell me a little bit about that?

Dev: I don't know. I am not really sure what to say or how to say it.

Clinical Social Worker: I get that. Sometimes it is hard to put things into words—how we feel or what we think.

Dev: Yeah.

Clinical Social Worker: Okay, well, let's start with what you came in wanting to talk about. Your parents mentioned that coming to see me was partly your idea.

Dev: Yeah, it was. I was hoping you could help me with something.

Clinical Social Worker: Okay, let's talk about that. What are you looking for help with?

Dev: I think that I may be transgender. I mean, I think that I am. I've kind of known for a long time that I was different and that I didn't ever feel like I was a girl. I just feel like I am a boy. My parents think I'm crazy and don't want to talk about it, but I found some people online who talk about feeling the same way. And I've seen shows on TV and read about other trans people. So, I mean, I guess I am.

Clinical Social Worker: So, watching TV and seeing other people online has really helped you to recognize that you are transgender.

Dev: Yes. For a long time I haven't really known how to say it or what it was. I thought I was just unhappy as a girl.

Clinical Social Worker: But this feels like it is more than that?

Dev: Yes. I have always liked doing boy things and dressing as a boy. I just saw myself as a boy. Even when I was little. It just wasn't something my family would talk about. It made my mom upset and my parents would fight about it, so I stopped bringing it up.

Clinical Social Worker: But you always felt that way and it hasn't changed?

Dev: Yeah, it never changed. As I got older, I thought about it all the time. I thought maybe something was just wrong with me, but I couldn't stop.

Clinical Social Worker: So, you've been doing a lot of work trying to figure this out.

Dev: Yeah. I mean I think I've known it for a long time. Just being able to research it and find other people online has really helped. I don't have a lot of friends at school. Everyone thinks I am weird, so I just keep to myself. But online there are a lot of people like me.

Clinical Social Worker: Tell me more about that.

This dialogue demonstrates a shift from where Dev was in his middle childhood years. We can see from this exchange that he has more cognitive understanding of what is occurring for him and has moved into a place of personal acceptance and acknowledgment of his transgender identity. There are implications for him around social interactions and how this transgender identity will manifest for him. For example, how comfortable will he be in expressing this to others? What will the impact be for him and his family? Is he ready or willing to make a social or physical transition? Similarly, working with families of transgender children and adolescents is important and can have a significant impact on how the transition process goes. Part of your work as a mental health provider will be to help assist your client in the identity formation process as well as consider ways you can advocate with family, schools, and medical professionals to support the needs of your adolescent client.

STUDENT REFLECTION 6.1

The Transsexual and Transgender Identity Formation model outlined by Devor (2004) centers on the concepts of mirroring and witnessing. According to Devor (2004), as social beings we experience *witnessing* when we are seen for who we are by those external and objective or separate from us. When this occurs, it provides validation that we are who we think we are and that this is recognizable to others who have an objective perspective. At the same time, we yearn to experience *mirroring*, the concept that we get to see ourselves in the eyes of others who are like us (Devor, 2004). In this regard, we get validation through experiencing connection and affiliation with people who understand and relate to us and our experiences. Being understood for who we believe ourselves to be and finding connection with those like us offer a form of self-acceptance and grounding in our identities. Devor (2004) asserts that both processes are necessary for healthy development in all people but can be critically important for transgender individuals because it means that they are seen and understood in an identity that often contradicts physical characteristics or prior social experiences of the other gender.

Witnessing is a particularly important part of our work as mental health providers. When we can serve as a mirror or witness to the people we work with, we validate who they are and reinforce their identity development. Assuming you were the mental health professional working with Dev, how might you serve as a witness to his developing trans identity? What would this look like in your interactions with him and in your responses to his family? How might your responses change based on his stage in the transitioning process?

CONTEXTUAL FACTORS: MIDDLE CHILDHOOD THROUGH ADOLESCENCE

Just as culture is intimately tied to an experience of development, so, too, is the context in which it occurs. This makes a lot of sense if we consider it at face value. For example, if it is a cold day outside and you are walking around in shorts and a t-shirt, you are likely to be uncomfortable and could respond poorly to a stressful situation as a result of your physical discomfort. Alternatively, if you were dressed for cold weather and appropriately warm, you may be in a better mood and respond in a completely different way to even the most difficult of challenges. Though this example is simplistic, it sets the tone for the considerations we must bear in mind when we look at experiences of development. Each experience, for each individual experiencing it, will be impacted by the situational and contextual factors that shape the experience at that time. These contextual factors, some of which we can control and many that we cannot, are critical to consider when we overlay them with the lifespan development process.

Theories of development often fold specific awareness of context into the theoretical model. However, they can also largely assume a shared experience and overlook the influence that a specific set of circumstances, social or relational connections, or set of life events can have on an individual in a given developmental period. In particular, social interaction and peer influence take on great significance in middle childhood and adolescence. When we look at Dev, for example, we are mindful that he is coming to terms with his own transgender identity development in the midst of a school and home environment where he does not feel supported and where peer relationships and influence are heightened. The social spheres in which Dev lives can have a significant impact on how he perceives the experiences of development, both in terms of typical maturation, but also relative to the cultural factors we noted earlier. In this way context and culture weave together and create the foundation for which Dev's physiological, cognitive, and emotional development occur. Therefore, they are vastly important to our understanding of his development.

Sociocultural Theory

One developmental perspective that specifically accounts for the impact of context on development is that of Sociocultural theory. Developed through the work of Russian theorist, Lev Vygotsky, Sociocultural theory is a cognitive development theory that emphasizes social and cultural influences on individual development (see Vygotsky, 1962, 1978; Vygotsky et al., 1997). Central to Sociocultural theory is the recognition that individual development cannot not be understood without acknowledging the broader social system within which it is encased (McLeod, 2020). As a counterpoint to more behavioral developmental models of the time, which largely emphasized individualism, Vygotsky began researching cognitive development with a specific focus on the influence of society, culture, and context (Jovanović, 2020). Though its origins are dated, Sociocultural theory is considered an emerging theory in psychology given its emphasis on the interaction among people, cultures, and the learning process.

Perhaps the most significant consideration of Sociocultural theory we need to consider for this chapter is the emphasis on culture. While all of the concepts of Sociocultural theory reflect the social interaction required for learning to occur, Vygotsky was also mindful that these experiences were grounded in cultures in which people lived. This means, of course, that what we learn is shaped by the values and beliefs of the cultures we exist in—the tools, language, social interactions we use in our daily lives reflect that which we were exposed to and for which there is cultural value. Vygotsky also noted that within each culture there are *tools of intellectual adaptation* that are strategies for problem-solving used to promote learning and higher order thinking (McLeod, 2020). These tools are culturally determined and include such things as the memory strategies we develop.

To better understand this concept, let's consider the example of shoe laces. For cultures of people who wear laced shoes, learning to tie them is part of a developmental experience that often occurs around age 6 or 7. This can include demonstrations, shoe lace tying songs or rhymes, and step-by-step methods that may have been passed down through generations. It may be taught at home, in school, or some combination of the two, but the goal is to teach the child how to tie their shoes, given the significance of laced shoes in the culture. Alternatively, if a child were to grow up in a family system or culture where there were no laced shoes, the concept of learning to tie a shoe would never present itself or be a particularly important learning task. It would never be a skill the child needed to develop because it was not relevant to the family or culture in which the family was embedded. This is a somewhat simplistic example, but it does demonstrate that children are influenced by the environments in which they are raised and that influence ultimately impacts learning and thinking.

So, what does all of this mean relative to Dev? Sociocultural theory helps us understand the cognitive developments Dev is experiencing within the framework of his social and cultural experiences. Within his home, school, and cultural communities, Dev is being exposed to thoughts and ideas that shape his understanding of the world. Take, for example, his avoidance behaviors. Dev has learned, as a product of the experiences he has had with his parents, that in order to maintain a sense of safety and avoid family conflicts he has to keep discussions of his gender identity to himself. Within the school setting he has also learned that academic success fosters a sense of acceptance and also preserves that space of avoidance he feels he needs as a result of peer rejection. Dev is learning, through interactions with others around him, what is valued and what is not, what is deemed appropriate and what is not, what can be said out loud and what cannot. His cognitive development and understanding of the world is being directly shaped by the social and cultural influences around him. Further, this is occurring during a period of development that emphasizes more complex peer relationships and a stronger sense of right and wrong. The process of taking in social experiences and internalizing meaning from them can have significant impact at this stage of development. What he is learning now will have a direct impact on how he views himself, the world around him, and future development moving forward.

Knowing this, it is helpful to turn back to the clinical social worker in our case study and consider how they might work with Dev using a Sociocultural theory lens to explore how his developmental experience is tied to his familial and ethnic cultures.

SESSION EXCERPT

Clinical Social Worker: Dev, as we've talked through your situation you've shared a lot about your family and the struggles they have had in accepting you for who you are. You've noted, for example, that you really hate hearing your parents argue about your transition to being a boy and generally avoid conversations about it. I can imagine that is pretty hard on you.

Dev: Yeah, it is. I wish they could be more understanding or that they just didn't look at me like they hate me. It's like they don't even know what to do with me. So, they either avoid talking about it or start arguing. I hate it.

Clinical Social Worker: Yeah, I can see why you would. It can be pretty painful when our families don't accept us for who we are or when we feel like they are fighting because of us. Sometimes we even tell ourselves that is our fault. I'd like to talk a little bit more about that. I know you've shared with me that your parents are immigrants and that this transition is not something that is acceptable in your culture. Share with me more about that.

Dev: For my mom it is just super hard. She still thinks of me as her daughter, and there are very clear expectations for girls in my culture. Part of me gets that, but then I wonder why it matters. I mean, I am still her kid whether I am a girl or boy. I wish she could just see me for who I am and be supportive. But, she's stuck in her ways. She is afraid what other people will think or say, especially my family in India.

Clinical Social Worker: So, you feel like it is less about how she might really feel about you than it is her fear of how others might see you or her, in response?

Dev: I think it is both. My mom was raised in a very traditional Indian household. Even though she and my father have changed a lot and are more American, she has strong beliefs about her role in our family and what sons and daughters should do and who they should be. She has struggled with me not conforming for a long time. But adding a desire to physically transition is just too much for her. It's like she sees me as a failure and she is afraid her family will judge her for raising me all wrong … or something like that.

In the portion of the preceding session we see how important the cultural experiences of Dev are to his understanding of himself, his transition process, and the relationships he holds with his mother. As a teenager, who Dev is and how he sees himself is largely shaped by the perspectives he has in relationship to his parents, brother, and peers. He is in a developmental period where social influence is at its height and where having parental support, while not something teens may overtly seek, is still highly important (Bhatt & Pujar, 2020). Further, while many adolescents deal with shifting emotions and physical changes that come with this developmental period, Dev has the added layer of working through a transition experience that may require hormone treatment or elective surgery. In this regard, he needs parental support more than most, from both a financial and emotional development standpoint. However, that may or may not be what his cultural and social experiences offer. As mental health providers, it is our job to maintain an awareness of these factors and understand how the nuances of each individual's lived experiences shape their developmental process and trajectory. In addition, we must ensure we ethically manage our own biases so that we do not harm our clients or the relationships on which they depend for survival and well-being. It is when we do this that we can begin to understand how significantly developmental milestones are shaped by the world in which they are embedded.

Social Media

Regardless of developmental stage it is hard to overlook the impact and influence social media has on people today. It allows for a sense of connection with those we know well and those we may not know at all. It also provides direct access to information, experiences, and groups of people who may share interests or identities that are part of our own and those that are nothing like us. For children in middle childhood and adolescence, the impact of social media can be particularly significant when we consider the influence of peers and the identity development process. It also poses an interesting reflection on how much children and teens are now shaped by these experiences when those of generations past did not have social media to engage with. As we consider the development of children and teens today, we should be mindful of the trajectory of cognitive, social, emotional, and even physical development has shifted across time, and with increased access to these forms of information, connection, and identity expression.

Research in this area continues, but we do have some initial findings to help us understand the impact on this stage. Social competence, for example, is a key consideration for the childhood development process. As children gain access to and engage with social media there have been shifts in how this construct plays out in online interactions. Reich (2017) found that while components of social competence like adaptability, attractiveness, social skills, prosocial behaviors, absence of aggression, and likeability continue to present similar to offline interactions, other components such as popularity and direct friendships do not. That is, how many friends one has, who they are online friends with, and how popular they are in an online venue do not always translate equally in offline interactions. Additionally, due to the format of online interactions in social media, children have to modify elements of communication like timing (asynchronous or real time) and rely on other elements of representation such as avatars, emojis, and responses from "friends" as part of their developing social competence (Reich, 2017). In other words, the sense of who they are and how they are perceived by others can manifest in very different ways.

In a literature review conducted by Best et al. (2014), impact findings for online technology reflected mixed results or no effect on adolescent well-being. Some noted benefits included increased self-esteem, perceived social support, safe identity experimentation, and increased opportunities for self-disclosure (Best et al., 2014). As we consider Dev's situation, this might explain why he is seeking out information and connection online. In interacting with others in the online trans community, Dev may be receiving a level of social support and an opportunity to begin safely expressing his trans identity with others who will acknowledge and accept him. According to Singh and Eaker (2017), the internet and social media provide transgender and gender non-conforming youth with opportunities to express themselves openly, connect with other transgender and cisgender peers, engage in broader social justice movements, and learn how adolescence and gender identity is experienced across the world.

For all the positives that social media can offer middle school and adolescents, there are risks and drawbacks to consider as well. These include increased social isolation, depression, exposure to triggering or abusive content, and cyberbullying (Best et al., 2014). While some research suggests that cyberbullying among adolescents is less prevalent than face-to-face bullying (e.g., Juvonen & Gross, 2008; Lapidot-Lefler & Dolev-Cohen, 2015), the intensity of attacks and the severity of the outcomes can be more damaging due to perceived anonymity, or lack of boundaries, and greater diffusion that online interactions can provide (Lapidot-Lefler & Dolev-Cohen, 2015). While we do not know if Dev has directly experienced cyberbullying or other negative outcomes as a result of his online experiences, we do know he is feeling socially isolated and has feelings of depression. Recognizing where those feelings are coming from and when and how the social media interactions play a role in this would be important to discern in work with him.

Poverty and Household Structure

It is not likely to surprise you that family income and structure can have a significant impact on the development of children and teens. However, this contextual element of our lives can be easily overlooked in broader discussions of developmental theory which do not always factor in the considerable role they play. The amount of money a family has directly influences accessibility to primary resources like food, clothes, and shelter. It can also lead to wide disparities in areas such as educational experiences and outcomes, stress and psychological distress of family members, childcare, and supplementary social and learning activities (Duncan et al., 2017). According to the U.S. Census Bureau (2020), the poverty line in the United States is defined as $26,246 for a family of four with two children. For families living in poverty, access to employment may be limited or require work hours that minimize opportunities for family interaction. This, in turn, can lead to significant psychological stress for caregivers who are trying to manage household bills and engage in meaningful ways with their children. Additionally, high stress levels and long or overnight work hours can negatively impact parenting skills and ultimately lead to stress in children (Heinrich, 2014). This has critical implications for young children and their cognitive and emotional development. Neuropsychological research indicates chronic or elevated psychological distress in children has an effect on brain development and puts these children at risk for poor stress response management and self-regulation in the future (Duncan et al., 2017).

The impact of poverty on children, just like all of the other elements of culture and context we have discussed, is not a uniform experience. There are many variables that can put one child or teen at higher risk for impact than others. Similarly, within the United States, poverty and the associated risks are not uniformly distributed across ethnic and racial groups, with children of color more likely than White children to experience poverty (Haider, 2021). Roy and Raver (2014) evaluated the key risk factors of *deep poverty* (defined as income at or below .50 of the poverty line), residence in a single-parent household, residential crowding, caregiver depression, and stressful life events to evaluate both the combined impact of these risk factors as well as their overall contribution to behavioral concerns and performance. In general they found that the more poverty-related risks children are exposed to in their preschool years, the more behavior problems and the lower performance they had in third grade. In particular, children who fared the worst were those with "nonnuclear" family structures who lived in crowded households, experienced deep poverty, and had multiple life stressors (Roy & Raver, 2014).

On the flip side, there can be distinct benefits of family economic advantage for children in middle childhood and adolescence. In homes where access to resources are available there are often opportunities for tutoring, extracurricular activities, learning resources, and scheduled social play that may increase social and cognitive development during these phases of life. When evaluating family income on distinct phases of development, Duncan et al. (2017) found direct correlations that linked increases in family income to increased academic achievement in middle childhood and higher academic attainment in adolescence. That is to say, having increased resources during the middle childhood and adolescent years resulted in better educational experiences and overall performance.

Looking back at Dev and his family, we see some indicators of family income we would need to consider in our work with him. For example, he lives at home with both parents. Based on the information we have, we also know that he has his own room or, at most, shares his room with his older brother. Similarly, we know he had toys as a child, seems to be thriving academically, and has access to the internet. Though we do not know if his parents could afford to support him in the medical costs associated with hormone treatment or elective surgeries, we do know he has some belief that they can. And, finally, we know they have brought him to see a clinical social worker. They may or may not be paying for these services, but we do know they have some awareness of and willingness to seek mental health services. So, what does this mean in terms of the financial impact on Dev's specific development? While we do not know all of the impacts this might have, we do know Dev has some financial advantages that may support or create buffers for him and that his financial risk factors are fairly low. This, of course, does not mean that Dev will thrive in this stage of development or be protected from other challenges he faces during this time. It simply means we have an additional piece of contextual information to help us understand who he is and the environment in which he is developing.

STUDENT REFLECTION 6.2

Within this chapter we have discussed contextual factors that might serve to support or otherwise create challenges for Dev as he transitions through the stages of middle childhood and adolescence. We noted, for example, that Dev was likely not dealing with poverty as an added contextual consideration in his life. However, assume that was not the case. How might Dev's developmental trajectory be impacted if he lived below the poverty line, with only his mother and brother as a means of familial support? Consider also what it might be like for Dev to have a strong support network at school with a highly supportive teacher and two close friends who accepted and protected him. What might be different for him and how would that impact his developing sense of self? Finally, what might Dev's experience and transitioning process entail if he were deaf? When you consider his levels of support, resource access, and identity development, how might being differently abled shift the way you offer support and your role in providing him and his family services?

As you consider Dev and how shifting the contextual variables in his life may alter his developmental pathway, also consider your own. What were the contextual situations and factors that impacted your development in middle childhood and adolescence? Have they continued to impact you and shape you into adulthood? Finally, how can you use this knowledge to support your future work in the helping profession?

CLIENTS IN MIDDLE CHILDHOOD AND ADOLESCENCE: CLINICAL CONSIDERATIONS

The case study of Dev is a good illustration of the varied cultural and contextual considerations we must bear in mind as mental health professionals. Every individual we will work with in our professional roles is a composite of cultural and contextual experiences that have shaped the development process. Recognizing this is critical to understanding developmental models as well as how and when they apply differently to each person. It also helps us to understand why, for example, some people move through various stages of development while others do not, or why the speed of those transitions can differ between the individuals experiencing them. These also become important factors when we want to avoid pathologizing or making faulty assumptions around why those we work with respond in particular ways.

There are other considerations to factor in as well. Just as we have clarified that social influence is key to the adolescent and middle childhood years, it is important to recognize the way it shapes the models and theories we apply to our understanding of them. You have already been presented with several theories in this text and will continue to read more in the chapters to come. While they each have merit and help us to better understand the experiences of those we will work with in our professional lives, they are also a product of social understanding and responses of a set period of time. Vygotsky offers us a great example of this. While his work offers us valuable insight into understanding social influence and the value of context and culture in our lives, this theory was largely impacted by his own contextual understanding of life after the October Revolution of 1917 and the subsequent socialist society (Vasileva & Balyasnikova, 2019). The world he was embedded in emphasized a political and economic system of social organization, so the awareness of its influence was everywhere.

In a similar vein, consider the societal shifts within American culture related to knowledge, understanding, and acceptance of transgender experiences even since the Transexual and Transgender Identity Formation model (Devor, 2004) was first published. We now have new language around gender identity, an understanding that gender is non-binary or fluid for some individuals, and increased exposure to trans and gender non-conforming individuals in our communities, online, and in media. This rapid change in scientific, social, and public visibility of gender diversity is changing the landscape of development for newer generations and may date prior models and research. For example, updated research in this area emphasizes that younger individuals and those who have been exposed to more socially accepting or knowledgeable communities are often better equipped and able to identify gender feelings quickly, face less stigma, and find more support (Pardo & Devor, 2017). Though this is not always the case for every young trans person, it can result in a faster or truncated transitioning process than is experienced by older adults or as was reflected in the original Devor (2004) model.

So, why is this important? It means that society, context, and culture have an impact, both on individuals in a set period of time, but also on the collective. As we continue to evolve and grow, the ways in which we function and understand our functioning also evolve. This is why your work as a mental health provider will always require evaluating the cultural and contextual factors of your clients' lives and will mandate on-going education and engagement in the professional research literature. As a mental health professional working with children in middle childhood and adolescence you will want to ensure a strong awareness of the developmental milestones tied to cognitive, physical, social, emotional, and moral development. This will provide you an important foundation for level-setting expectations for children of this age group. In addition to that, you will want to consider the variations of culture and context that overlay that foundation. Even the slightest variances in experience can shift the way the developmental process lays out. When we think about Dev, we can see multiple factors at play and any number of ways that his story could unfold. Your challenge in supporting him and his family will be in understanding the uniqueness of his story and how those elements of his identity foster support and create barriers for him within the purview of any developmental theory or model you are using.

PERSPECTIVES FROM THE FIELD: PODCAST

Access this podcast at http://connect.springerpub.com/content/book/978-0-8261-8279-1/part/part02/chapter/ch06

The goal of this chapter is to provide you an initial understanding of how middle childhood and adolescence are shaped by the experiences, contexts, and cultures in which they are embedded. As we prepare to move into the next chapter and dig more deeply into additional theories and models specific to this age of development, we invite you to listen to Dr. Stacee Reicherzer speak more directly to the cultural and contextual considerations we should bear in mind when working with a client like Dev. Dr. Reicherzer is a transgender licensed professional counselor, consultant, educator, and author of The Healing Otherness Handbook.

STUDENT REFLECTION 6.3

In our podcast you had the opportunity to listen to Dr. Stacee Reicherzer share her story of growing up as a trans woman in San Antonio, Texas, and the particular influence her family, context, and the culture played in this experience. She also gave us some important insights relative to understanding Dev and how his journey may be impacted due to his cultural, familial, and contextual upbringing. As you consider the content from this chapter and the expertise offered in this podcast discussion, what do you feel like you have learned? As you compare their stories of development, paying particular attention to the time of development and the various levels of cultural and contextual support, or not, what stands out to you? How might you expect Dev's experience to parallel that of Dr. Stacee's and what might be different for him?

SUMMARY

This chapter was designed to provide initial exposure to the developmental experiences associated with middle childhood and adolescence, with a specific emphasis on the cultural and contextual factors that can influence development during this span of life. Within this chapter we began to unpack the developmental phase of middle childhood and adolescence that runs from ages 6 to 17. We started with a basic orientation to the physical, cognitive, and social developmental milestones that are often associated with these years of development. Then, using a case study client named Dev, we explored what these years of development might look like when factoring in his unique situations, experiences, and identities.

Through an evaluation of Dev's case study, we looked at the influence of cultural factors such as Dev's South Asian heritage, his Muslim faith, and his developing transgender identity. As part of this review, we spent some time with the Transgender Identity Formation model (Devor, 2004) and paid particular attention to where Dev likely fell within this model, as well as the various contextual factors that may have impacted his unique transitioning and identity development process. Throughout our discussion of cultural factors, we also evaluated your role as a helping professional and how key considerations relative to these cultural identities should be part of your on-going work in supporting future clients.

Similarly, we spent some time evaluating how context shapes the middle childhood and adolescent years. We began with a review of Vygotsky's Sociocultural Theory that emphasizes an awareness of culture and context in the developmental process (see Vygotsky, 1962, 1978; Vygotsky et al., 1997). Again, returning to Dev's case study, we evaluated how a clinical social worker might use this theory to begin assessing and engaging in a clinical session with Dev. In addition to this theoretical framework, we looked at other contextual factors that may have shaped Dev's experiences including his interactions with social media and how poverty and family structure framed his experiences and may impact these years of development for others as well. As we moved through these sections we continued to emphasize the importance of context in the understanding of people's lives and development, as well as how you, in your future work, will use these to better understand the unique needs of those you work with.

The chapter wrapped up with an insightful and informative discussion of middle childhood development with our podcast expert Dr. Stacee Reicherzer. In our discussions we explored her development as a transgender female growing up in San Antonio, Texas, noting the influence of culture and context on her developmental trajectory. We also discussed our case study Dev, and Dr. Stacee offered us some critical considerations for understanding how to use cultural and contextual understanding to help us view and come to better understand those we work with.

In the next chapter we build off of the information we learned about culture and context and further explore developmental theories that align specifically with the middle childhood and adolescent years. It will be important for you to carry over the information you learned in this chapter and continue analyzing the ways in which culture and context shape development, theory generation, and individuals like Dev.

REFERENCES

Aguayo, L., Hernandez, I. G., Yasui, M., Estabrook, R., Anderson, E. L., Davis, M. M., Briggs-Gowan, M. J., Wakschlag, L. S., & Heard-Garris, N. (2021). Cultural socialization in childhood: Analysis of parent-child conversations with a direct observation measure. *Journal of Family Psychology, 35*(2), 138–148. https://doi.org/10.1037/fam0000663

Bernardini, S. (2017). Transgender children. In K. L. Nadal (Ed.), *The SAGE Encyclopedia of Psychology and Gender* (pp. 1693–1695). SAGE Publications. https://doi.org/10.4135/9781483384269.n576

Best, P., Manktelow, R., & Taylor, B. (2014). Online communication, social media and adolescent wellbeing: A systematic narrative review. *Children and Youth Services Review, 41*, 27–36. https://doi.org/10.1016/j.childyouth.2014.03.001

Bhatt, M., & Pujar, L. (2020). Influence of self-concept and parenting on adolescents identity development. *IAHRW International Journal of Social Sciences Review, 8*(4–6), 158–160.

Blaževic, I. (2016). Family, peer and school influence on children's social development. *World Journal of Education, 6*(2), 42–49. https://search-ebscohost-com.ezproxy.snhu.edu/login.aspx?direct=true&db=eric&AN=EJ1158301&site=eds-live&scope=site

Centers for Disease Control and Prevention. (2020a, March 6). *Middle childhood (6–8 years of age)*. U.S. Department of Health and Human Services. https://www.cdc.gov/ncbddd/childdevelopment/positiveparenting/middle.html

Centers for Disease Control and Prevention. (2020b, March 6). *Middle childhood (9–11 years of age)*. U.S. Department of Health and Human Services. https://www.cdc.gov/ncbddd/childdevelopment/positiveparenting/middle2.html

Centers for Disease Control and Prevention. (2020c, March 6). *Teenagers (15–17 years of age)*. U.S. Department of Health and Human Services. https://www.cdc.gov/ncbddd/childdevelopment/positiveparenting/adolescence2.html

Centers for Disease Control and Prevention. (2020d, December 2). *Young teens (12–14 years of age)*. U.S. Department of Health and Human Services. https://www.cdc.gov/ncbddd/childdevelopment/positiveparenting/adolescence.html

Coyle, E. F., Fulcher, M., & Trübutschek, D. (2016). Sissies, mama's boys, and tomboys: Is children's gender nonconformity more acceptable when nonconforming traits are positive? *Archives of Sexual Behavior, 45*(7), 1827–1838. https://doi.org/10.1007/s10508-016-0695-5

Curtin, S. C., & Heron, M. (2019). *Death rates due to suicide and homicide among persons aged 10–24: United States, 2000–2017 (NCHS Data Brief no.352)*. U.S. Department of Health and Human Services. https://www.cdc.gov/nchs/data/databriefs/db352-h.pdf

Del Giudice, M. (2014). Middle childhood: An evolutionary-developmental synthesis. *Child Development Perspectives, 8*(4), 193–200. https://doi.org/10.1111/cdep.12084

Devor, A. H. (2004). Witnessing and mirroring: A fourteen stage model of transsexual identity formation. *Journal of Gay & Lesbian Mental Health, 8*(1/2), 41–67. https://doi.org/10.1080/19359705.2004.9962366

Dumas, T. M., Ellis, W. E., & Wolfe, D. A. (2012). Identity development as a buffer of adolescent risk behaviors in the context of peer group pressure and control. *Journal of Adolescence, 35*(4), 917–927. https://doi.org/10.1016/j.adolescence.2011.12.012

Duncan, G. J., Magnuson, K., & Votruba-Drzal, E. (2017). Moving beyond correlations in assessing the consequences of poverty. *Annual Review of Psychology, 68*, 413–434. https://doi.org/10.1146/annurev-psych-010416-044224

Haider, A. (2021). *The basic facts about children in poverty*. Center for American Progress. https://www.americanprogress.org/issues/poverty/reports/2021/01/12/494506/basic-facts-children-poverty/#:~:text=Child%20poverty%20rates%20have%20fluctuated%20over%20the%20last%20decades%20but%20remained%20relatively%20steady&text=In%202019%2C%2014.4%20percent%20of,below%20the%20official%20poverty%20measure

Heinrich, C. J. (2014, January). Parents' employment and children's wellbeing. *The Future of Children, 24*(1), 121–146. https://doi.org/10.1353/foc.2014.0000

Holman, C. W., & Goldberg, J. M. (2006). Ethical, legal, and psychosocial issues in care of transgender adolescents. *International Journal of Transgenderism*, 9(3–4), 95–110. https://doi.org/10.1300/J485v09n03_05

Jensen, L. A., & Dost-Gözkan, A. (2015). Adolescent-parent relations in asian indian and salvadoran immigrant families: A cultural-developmental analysis of autonomy, authority, conflict, and cohesion. *Journal of Research on Adolescence*, 25(2), 340–351. https://doi.org/10.1111/jora.12116

Jovanović, G. (2020). How lost and accomplished revolutions shaped psychology: Early Critical Theory (Frankfurt School), Wilhelm Reich, and Vygotsky. *Theory & Psychology*, 30(2), 202–222. https://doi.org/10.1177/0959354320917216

Juvonen, J., & Gross, E. F. (2008). Extending the school grounds?--Bullying experiences in cyberspace. *The Journal of School Health*, 78(9), 496–505. https://doi.org/10.1111/j.1746-1561.2008.00335.x

Lapidot-Lefler, N., & Dolev-Cohen, M. (2015). Comparing cyberbullying and school bullying among school students: prevalence, gender, and grade level differences. *Social Psychology of Education*, 18(1), 1–16. https://doi.org/10.1007/s11218-014-9280-8

Mah, V. K., & Ford-Jones, E. L. (2012). Spotlight on middle childhood: Rejuvenating the "forgotten years." *Paediatrics & Child Health (1205–7088)*, 17(2), 81–83. https://doi.org/10.1093/pch/17.2.81

McLeod, S. (2020). *Lev Vygotsky's sociocultural theory*. Simply Psychology. https://www.simply-psychology.org/vygotsky.html

Pardo, S. T., & Devor, A. H. (2017). Transgender and gender nonconforming identity development. In K. L. Nadal (Ed.), *The SAGE Encyclopedia of Psychology and Gender* (pp. 1689–1692). SAGE Publications. https://doi.org/10.4135/9781483384269.n575

Phalet, K., Fleischmann, F., & Hillekens, J. (2018). Religious identity and acculturation of immigrant minority youth: Toward a contextual and developmental approach. *European Psychologist*, 23(1), 32–43. https://doi.org/10.1027/1016-9040/a000309

Polderman, T. J. C., Kreukels, B. P. C., Irwig, M. S., Beach, L., Chan, Y.-M., Derks, E. M., Esteva, I., Ehrenfeld, J., Heijer, M. D., Posthuma, D., Raynor, L., Tishelman, A., Davis, L. K., & International Gender Diversity Genomics Consortium. (2018). The biological contributions to gender identity and gender diversity: Bringing data to the table. *Behavior Genetics*, 48(2), 95–108. https://doi.org/10.1007/s10519-018-9889-z

Reich, S. M. (2017). Connecting offline social competence to online peer interactions. *Psychology of Popular Media Culture*, 6(4), 291–310. https://doi.org/10.1037/ppm0000111

Riva, F., Triscoli, C., Lamm, C., Carnaghi, A., & Silani, G. (2016). Emotional egocentricity bias across the life-span. *Frontiers in Aging Neuroscience*, 8, 74. https://doi.org/10.3389/fnagi.2016.00074

Roy, A. L., & Raver, C. C. (2014). Are all risks equal? Early experiences of poverty-related risk and children's functioning. *Journal of Family Psychology*, 28(3), 391–400. https://doi.org/10.1037/a0036683

Singh, A. A. (2017). Transgender and gender nonconforming adolescents. In K. L. Nadal (Ed.), *The SAGE Encyclopedia of Psychology and Gender* (pp. 1686–1688). SAGE Publications. https://doi.org/10.4135/9781483384269.n574

Singh, A. A., & Eaker, R. (2017). Gender identity and adolescence. In K. L. Nadal (Ed.), *The SAGE Encyclopedia of Psychology and Gender* (pp. 668–670). SAGE Publications. https://doi.org/10.4135/9781483384269.n225

Susman, E. J., & Dorn, L. D. (2013). Puberty: Its role in development. In R. M. Lerner, M. A. Easterbrooks, & J. Easterbrooks (Eds.), *Handbook of psychology, Volume 6: Developmental Psychology* (2nd ed, pp. 289–320). Editor-in chief: I. B. Weiner. Wiley.

Tran Ngoc, M.-A., Greenberg, K., Alio, P. A., McIntosh, S., & Baldwin, C. (2020). 165. Nonmedical body modification (Body-Mod) strategies among transgender and gender diverse (TG/GD) adolescents and young adults. *Journal of Adolescent Health*, 66(2), S84. https://doi.org/10.1016/j.jadohealth.2019.11.168

Umaña-Taylor, A. J., Quintana, S. M., Lee, R. M., Cross, W. E., Rivas-Drake, D., Schwartz, S. J., Syed, M., Yip, T., Seaton, E., & Ethnic and Racial Identity in the 21st Century Study Group. (2014). Ethnic and racial identity during adolescence and into young adulthood: an integrated conceptualization. *Child Development, 85*(1), 21–39. https://doi.org/10.1111/cdev.12196

van der Straten Waillet, N., & Roskam, I. (2012). Developmental and social determinants of religious social categorization. *The Journal of Genetic Psychology, 173*(2), 208–220. https://doi.org/10.1080/00221325.2011.600356

Vasileva, O., & Balyasnikova, N. (2019). (Re)Introducing Vygotsky's thought: From historical overview to contemporary psychology. *Frontiers in Psychology, 10*, 1515. https://doi.org/10.3389/fpsyg.2019.01515

Vygotsky, L. S. (1962). *Thought and language*. MIT Press.

Vygotsky, L. S. (1978). *Mind in society: The development of higher psychological processes*. Harvard University Press.

Vygotsky, L. S., Rieber, R. W., & Wollock, J. (Eds.). (1997). *The collected works of L. S. Vygotsky, Vol. 3. Problems of the theory and history of psychology* (R. van der Veer, Trans.). Plenum Press.

CHAPTER **7**

Developmental Theories of Middle Childhood Through Adolescence

LEARNING OBJECTIVES

Upon completion of this chapter, students will be able to:

1. Recognize the stage of lifespan development known as "middle childhood through adolescence."
2. Distinguish key theories impacting this stage of development.
3. Evaluate updated research impacting this stage of development
4. Identify future directions for research and understanding of people in middle childhood and adolescence.

CASE STUDY 7.1: THE CASE OF DEV

In the previous chapter we met Dev, a transgender Muslim boy moving through middle childhood and entering the early years of adolescence. In this process Dev has taken many steps in his own transgender identification process and has also faced many challenges, most notably that of navigating these changes amid a family who hasn't supported him and a social sphere that doesn't understand him. As a result of his continued and regular sessions with his clinical social worker, Dev has grown more confident in his identity and found validation in sharing and talking through his experiences at home, in school, and in his growing interactions online. He has also seen a shift in support from his parents, Sanjiv and Kavya, who have also benefited from interactions with the clinical social worker. Holding multiple sessions with Sanjiv and Kavya alone, the clinical social worker has provided psychoeducation on the transgender development process and connected them with outside resources, including some specific to their Muslim faith. While reservations, questions, and grief remain present in their interactions with Dev, they have grown open to accepting him and have started using his preferred pronouns within their immediate family system.

In spite of noted progress with his family, Dev continues to face significant shame and frustration associated with his developing female body. He hates the high pitch of his voice and the growing curviness of his body. As a result, he has started binding his chest and has begun wearing loose fitting clothes in an attempt to hide the physical manifestations of his birth sex. While Dev's parents are growing more supportive of him, neither are willing to consider the use of hormone blockers that would prevent the physical development of adolescence. As a result, Dev reports that he "feels trapped" in a body that is "betraying" him and remains acutely aware of his physical body in nearly all interactions.

Socially, Dev has found growing acceptance in a small group of LGBTQ+ students at school, some of whom he first met online—a space that continues to be a source of information and support for him. He is grateful for this change but remains shy and uncomfortable in most social gatherings, continuing to battle most people's preference to view him as a gender non-conforming girl rather than a transgender boy. Now that Dev has some increased support in his home life, his most recent work with the clinical social worker has centered on the social arena of school and how Dev wants to assert his male identity there. Dev acknowledges fears of rejection by female friends he has been close to in childhood as well as the girls he is now finding himself initially attracted to. As a developing teenager, with real and significant feelings of shame and fear, Dev struggles to name his experience and understand how to cope in a world of growing social influence and pressure.

MIDDLE CHILDHOOD THROUGH ADOLESCENCE

The years of middle childhood and adolescence are roughly considered to begin at age 6 and end just before early adulthood begins around age 18. As you might imagine this stage of development is full of change, growth, and advancement. Whereas the physical changes of middle childhood are slower and less prominent than the infant and toddler years or the adolescent years to follow, these years offer significant neurological changes that allow us to control impulses, reason, focus, and plan ("The wonder years; Science highlights the powerful cognitive events of middle childhood, 2012"). They also offer opportunities for increased social development and learning. As children move from middle childhood into adolescence, the changes in their physical, cognitive, social, and emotional development only increase. Here, developmental tasks like puberty, sexual development, abstract thinking, peer influence, and personal identity play an important and expanding role in the lives of teens (Christie & Viner, 2005).

To help us best understand the unique and overlapping elements of development, we can use development theories and models to guide us. Developmental theories offer us the ability to frame certain milestones within the context of age, maturation, and area of development. They give us a broad template to understand how humans grow and are shaped over time and can offer the benefit of some baseline metrics for understanding ourselves and those we work with in the mental health professions. This allows us to make comparisons, evaluate influences, and understand barriers to progress that may manifest in our work with clients in the field. In this way, they are a valuable tool for the mental health professions. As our text has also pointed out, broad and context-driven theories can also be limited in their frame of reference or application. In this way, developmental theories may only highlight partial experiences, neglect key considerations, or over-generalize to populations for whom the theory was not developed. While they have significant utility, this is important to keep in mind as you consider their use and application to your future profession.

As we consider the stage of middle childhood through adolescence and move through the remainder of the chapter, you will be exposed to some of the most critical developmental theories specific to middle childhood and adolescence. You will be challenged to consider the cognitive changes associated with this period of time, evaluate identity development specific to children and teens, and consider the way that psychosocial development occurs in this highly socially driven period of the life cycle. Writing a lifespan development text can be challenging in that there is much to cover and it can be hard to know what to include and leave out. That said, we have chosen very specific theories to present in this chapter to expose you to some of the most fundamental developmental tasks associated with this period of time. It is important to keep in mind that these theories span other developmental stages and are only a few of the many theories that may be applicable to middle childhood and adolescence. It is also important to consider that each theory has its strengths, value, and weaknesses and that all development, regardless of stage, is contextually and culturally dependent. We will explore much of this as we move forward.

PIAGET'S COGNITIVE DEVELOPMENT THEORY

When we consider child and adolescent development we often think of this in terms of cognitive development. This is for good reason. During middle childhood and into adolescence the brain changes in significant ways and a child's capacity to think and process thought expand dramatically (Widjojo, 2018). While there are many theories of cognitive development, one of the first, and perhaps the most famous, is Jean Piaget's Cognitive Development theory. Piaget was a Swiss psychologist who was born in 1896 and spent much of the first half of the 20th century researching childhood development in search of the question "How do we know what we know?" (Mallon, 1976, p. 28). Piaget believed the answer to that question came from an understanding of how children develop, think, process language, interact with, and actively manipulate materials in the world.

The Four Stages of Cognitive Development

Piaget's Cognitive Development theory is a stage theory that assumes learning is predicated on prior experiences and capabilities that occur over time in a step-like fashion (Flavell, 1996; Mallon, 1976). Movement through one stage offered a specific set of skills and learning that represented both a neurological ability, paired with opportunities to engage and manipulate elements in the environment, resulting in learning and cognitive development. In this way, Piaget believed the child was the active agent in their own learning (Isaacs, 2015). Piaget also recognized the influence of biological processes tied to learning and development. His stage theory reinforced that neurological development and specific biological capabilities, known as *cognitive structures*, must first be in place before specific learning could occur (Flavell, 1992). Once present, increased intelligence and more complex understanding would follow (Mallon, 1976). That is to say, Piaget did not believe children simply accumulated more knowledge over time, but that there was a fundamental shift in how they thought, relative to time,

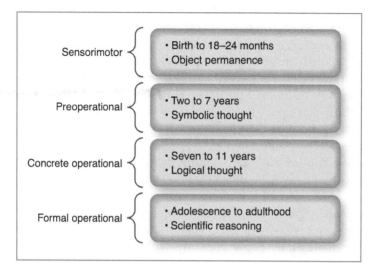

Figure 7.1 Piaget's stages of cognitive development.

Source: Adapted from Isaacs (2015). *A brief introduction to Piaget: The growth of understanding in the young child and new light on children's ideas of number.* Algora Publishing.

age, and development that laid the foundation for his four stages. For the purposes of this chapter we will explore the last two stages that align with middle childhood and adolescence (Figure 7.1).

THE CONCRETE OPERATIONAL STAGE

The concrete operational stage of cognitive development occurs between the ages of 7 and 11. This stage is characterized by an increase in logical and organized thought. While children in this stage are generally considered to persist in concrete thinking, they are better able to perspective-take and begin to understand hat their experiences, thoughts, and feelings may be unique to them and not necessarily shared by others in the same situation. This is also the stage in which children begin to develop an under-standing of *conservation,* the idea that a mass, distance, number, and so on, remains constant regardless of how it is subdivided (Isaacs, 2015). That is to say, they can now understand that a cup of water poured into a tall and skinny glass is the same amount of water if poured into a wide and short cup. This form of logical thinking is a key milestone for the concrete operational stage.

THE FORMAL OPERATIONAL STAGE

The formal operational stage of cognitive development occurs at approximately age 12. This final stage of cognitive growth is marked by the development of abstract thought. According to Piaget, it is in this stage that children are capable of deductive reasoning and demonstrate increased logical thinking. In addition, they are able to see multiple solutions to problems and reason out hypothetical situations (Mallon, 1976). This is also a stage in which Piaget believed children could engage and rea-son through moral, social, and ethical situations for the first time because they now have the necessary theoretical and abstract thinking ability required for this depth of thought.

Cognitive Development Theory: The Stages of Middle Childhood and Adolescence

When we look specifically at the years of middle childhood and adolescence, we see that they largely overlap with the concrete operational and formal operational stages of Piaget's development theory. These are the stages where thinking really expands from a concrete and logical frame of reference in middle childhood to the more nuanced, abstract, and analytical thought associated with adolescence. This growth in cognitive capacity allows for increased perspective-taking such that children can begin understanding points of view and circumstances outside of their own. When we consider the shifting of peer influence and growing social relationships associated with this stage of development, we can begin to understand why this might occur. As children move from *parallel play* (i.e., playing independently alongside one another in early childhood) to playing with each other and having the capacity to logically reason, empathize, and analyze situations, their ability to engage and form peer relationships grows. In addition to better understanding others, this higher level of cognitive capacity allows for more self-insight and awareness and sets the stage for a heightened social consciousness in later years.

Bearing this in mind, let's return to our case study client, Dev. When we evaluate Piaget's stages of development, we see that Dev has now entered into the formal operations period. He has increased abstract and analytical thought; we see this in how he is processing his experiences with his clinical social worker. He has an acute awareness of the social implications for his transitioning process and is working to balance what he logically knows will happen to his physical body with how he is feeling emotionally. Dev is mindful of the perspectives of others, including his parents and peers, and also recognizes that his social situation is far more complex and challenging than others may be experiencing. Just a few years earlier, when he was in the middle childhood phase of concrete operations, we would likely have seen Dev in a more logical space. He may have found frustration in how his physical body did not align with his sense of himself as a boy; however, he was likely less attuned to the social implications. Dev may have understood that his parents were upset by his identification as a boy, and yet he may not have had the ability to really understand why—not recognizing the significant implications of culture, religion, and normative expectations of society. Similarly, he would likely have felt rejection or shame in peer interactions—not always or fully understanding why other boys did not want to play with him or why he didn't want to play with the girls in his social sphere.

One of the most important considerations mental health professionals should have in working with children and adolescents is recognizing their cognitive capacity and development. Because Dev is a bright child who is not demonstrating altered mental capacities, we would expect that the clinical social worker would be targeting his approach to work with Dev bearing in mind his ability to reason, think logically, and demonstrate some initial abstract thinking. The social worker would be using this knowledge to help Dev process through the new experiences he is facing in his early adolescent years.

In this session vignette, we see Dev's clinical social worker trying to gauge Dev's cognitive level. They are working to determine how much self-insight Dev has and also to capitalize on his ability to perspective-take. In creating the opportunity to foster empathy for Kai, the social worker is hoping that Dev can create a parallel experience for himself—using some of that analytical thought and abstract reasoning that accompanies Piaget's formal operations stage to create a new perspective for Dev. Because Dev is still relatively young in his adolescence, we can also see a bit of the concrete

SESSION EXCERPT 7.1

Clinical Social Worker: It sounds like you have been getting some good support from your new friends at school.

Dev: Yeah, it's nice to have people to be with who accept me and don't act all weird all the time.

Clinical Social Worker: But I think I also hear you say that you still don't feel comfortable with your classmates in the rest of school. Do I have that right?

Dev: No (head drops down). Nobody knows what to do with me. People still sometimes call me Devya, and either make fun of me or ignore me. I sometimes wish I could just curl up and hide, especially now that my body is changing. I hate it!

Clinical Social Worker: So, you are in that really hard spot of knowing your body is changing due to puberty and not wanting it to. And then everyone else is going to see it and know it as well.

Dev: Yes! It's like I just started to get a few friends who know me as a boy. And now I'm going to get boobs. They won't get it. I wish I could just cut them off. I wish my parents would let me get the hormones and stop all of it. That would fix everything. Then people would like ... well, they would like just get me.

Clinical Social Worker: I know we've talked about the physical changes and how much you wish you could stop them. I guess I am wondering a little more about the ability for your friends to accept you even if you can't.

Dev: I just don't think they will.

Clinical Social Worker: Okay, well, let's talk about that a little bit. Why don't you tell me a little more about your new friends?

Dev: They are all pretty cool. But, I hang out mostly with Kai. He's pretty shy like me. But he gets me. We do the same things for fun and our parents are kind of the same.

Clinical Social Worker: Is Kai trans like you?

Dev: No, he's gay. He came out about a year ago. I think it was pretty hard for him. He had to go live with his aunt. He said his parents couldn't accept him for religious reasons.

Clinical Social Worker: That sounds like it was pretty rough. It also sounds like you accept him.

Dev: Well, yeah. He's, um, well, he just is who he is. He's nice.

Clinical Social Worker: So I guess I am just wondering if you can accept him for who he is, why he can't accept you for who you are?

Dev: (Sigh) I don't know. Maybe he can. But what if he doesn't?

thinking still at play—his sense that he can only be a boy and be accepted as such if he has the hormones or that no one can understand him because they haven't experienced his issues. As he continues to grow, mature, and develop cognitively, we would expect to see this starting to change as well.

PERSONS WITH DIFFERING ABILITIES

Piaget's theory of Cognitive Development is largely articulated in reference to age, thereby associating stages with ages of development. Understandably, though, there are those for whom numerical age will not translate directly with their corresponding cognitive developmental stage. Research indicates individuals with special needs (e.g., hearing loss, mild intellectual disabilities, speech and language disabilities) can progress more slowly and reflect lower values of general development on Piaget's developmental task experiments than children without special needs (Zamfirov, 2019). Alternatively, gifted children may demonstrate cognitive development beyond their numerical age but have unique cognitive development needs as well. While they may meet intellectual learning tasks with ease, they may grow bored with developmental tasks and subsequently lose their desire to learn without opportunities for creativity and challenge in areas of interest (Ribeiro Piske et al., 2017).

As you consider your future work in the mental health field, it is important to remember the impact of differing abilities on those with whom you will work. Some individuals will fall within "normative" ages and stages and correspond accordingly. However, many others will not. Recognizing where any one person is on the cognitive development spectrum is important to not only understand who they are, but how you will work with them and those around them. As you consider this information, look back to our case study, Dev. Knowing he is intellectually advanced, how might this affect his cognitive development and the issues he is grappling with in his life? How might it impact the work you do with him and how you approach that work? As you continue to read forward in this chapter, keep these questions in mind. One thing that is critical to understanding client experiences is knowing the interplay between cognitive and psychosocial development. What might work for one area may not encapsulate the full needs of development. To that end, it is helpful to understand and consider all developmental implications in our work.

Critical Analysis of Piaget's Cognitive Development Theory

One of the recognized benefits of Piaget's work is the simple stage model and broad framework he provided for how children develop higher-order thinking across time. Proponents of his work argue that Piaget's descriptions of each stage are easy to understand, memorable, encompassing, and hold some truth regarding the specific cognitive capacities and thought processes of each stage (Flavell, 1996; Siegler, 2016). Others highlight Piaget's constructivist educational philosophy and emphasis on the individual as an active learner as his most significant contributions to Cognitive Developmental theory and part of why his work remains so important to this day

(Flavell, 1996; Matusov & Hayes, 2000). In spite of this, research conducted after Piaget's rise in the 1970s suggests there are many flaws with his proposed theory of Cognitive Development that are important to consider for any future use of his theory in your work as a mental health professional.

Let's begin with cultural application. Piaget, not unlike other White, male theorists of the 20th century, produced a theory of Cognitive Development that reflected his own Western, middle-class cultural background (Babakr et al., 2019; Matusov & Hayes, 2000). He devised his theory using children, including his own, from his own cultural background and to whom he had direct access. So, while he developed a universal theory of cognitive development he believed was applicable to all humanity, his research participants were significantly limited. This resulted in a deficit model for cultures and communities where values, beliefs, and opportunities for varied experiences were different than what he was observing and researching in his own culture and community (Babakr et al., 2019; Matusov & Hayes, 2000). For example, in a society where educational opportunities or requirements are not centered on the development of critical thinking, the formal operational stage may not be met, thereby making it seem those individuals are not as advanced.

Piaget's theory of Cognitive Development also assumes a universal experience of linear and uniform intellectual growth based on the concepts of adaptation, accommodation, assimilation, and equilibration. According to Khabbache et al. (2020), this resulted in errors of oversimplification and overgeneralization. In terms of oversimplification, Piaget is considered to have neglected the significant impact of interpersonal dynamics on the learning process (Khabbache et al., 2020). That is to say that, yes, children learn through engaging with and manipulating objects on their own, but they also learn through interacting with and watching others and through the guidance provided in modeling and teaching (Babakr et al., 2019; Matusov & Hayes, 2000). In terms of overgeneralization, Piaget assumed all individuals, regardless of context or cultural variability, would develop the same (Khabbache et al., 2020). However, research indicates cultural and contextual considerations play a significant role in cognitive development (Babakr et al., 2019).

Recent Research on Cognitive Development Theory

In the years since Piaget's initial work and publications there has been a growing body of research in the area of cognitive development, including advancements in neuroscience and sociology. This has led to enhanced understanding of the learning process as well as the development of new models of cognitive development. Where we once appreciated Piaget for a broad and rather all-encompassing, albeit flawed, perspective of cognitive development, we now have a very detailed understanding of the vast and complex contribution of factors that shape the learning experience. According to Siegler (2016), "In moving on to newer theories, we have traded a rough, sometimes inaccurate depiction of the forest for innumerable, more accurate depictions of specific trees (and often their branches, twigs, leaves, and chloroplasts)" (p. 132). In the sections that follow we will look more deeply into newer research and one model that has come out of our increased understanding of cognitive development.

PLURALISTIC AND COALITIONAL MODEL

As its name implies, the Pluralistic and Coalitional model (PCM) recognizes psychological development as a multifaceted, fluid, nonlinear, and open system based on five pillars: (a) psychological subject, (b) poly-variability, (c) multi-pathways of cognitive development, (d) poly-mechanisms of cognitive functioning, and (e) cognitive flexibility and self-organization due to the dynamics of coordination between several processes and sub-cognitive system (Khabbache et al., 2020). The term *psychological subject* is used to reflect the individual nature of each person and the micro-developmental variability unique to each of us that occurs in relation to our specific developmental contexts (Khabbache et al., 2020). In other words, PCM recognizes that cognitive development is impacted by our individual contexts, and therefore our learning experiences are shaped accordingly.

In a similar vein, PCM considers multiple forms of variability that can exist between individuals in the cognitive development process. Whereas Piaget's theory of Cognitive Development assumed the lone form of variability to be the cognitive structures that differentiated in children as a result of age, PCM assumes that many forms of variability can exist specific to cognitive development. These include variability within ourselves (*intra-personal variability*), between us and others (*inter-individual variability*), those resulting from the specific contexts in which we live (*inter-contextual*), and those specific to the cultures that we belong to (*inter-cultural variability*; Khabbache et al., 2020).

While PCM recognizes the linear pathway of cognitive development that Piaget proposed, it also emphasizes this is one path among many (Khabbache et al., 2020). Research conducted on many of Piaget's learning tasks indicate that the pathway for learning often reflects a distinctly non-linear depiction and can even reflect reversibility or regression once skills have been achieved (Khabbache et al., 2020). This emphasis on *multi-pathways* helps explain why some people learn concepts before others, why some concepts come easier for the same person than others, and why regression can occur. Even within the same individual, learning can progress, regress, come quickly, slow down, and start all over again depending on what is being learned and their experiences with it.

For Piaget, learning centered on the two key mechanisms of assimilation and accommodation. However, advancements in neuroscience have afforded us the opportunity to look more deeply at the structures of the brain and the mechanisms that support the learning process. Through this effort researchers have found that there are multiple or *poly-mechanisms* of cognitive development (Khabbache et al., 2020) that occur in the learning process that are often dictated by the specifics of the tasks being performed. In such instances there can be multiple mechanisms at play at the neuronal level—some that build off one another, some that inhibit functioning, and some that integrate into others. PCM asserts that these unique neuronal differences significantly impact how learning is achieved from individual to individual and from task to task (Khabbache et al., 2020).

The final element of PCM reflects two sub-systems of human cognition that work together and are innately present. This includes a practical/procedural system that is designed to process information gathered from the external environment, as well as a conceptual/abstract system that is used to control, contextualize, and regulate the activities of the procedural subsystem (Khabbache et al., 2020). Whereas Piaget found conceptualization and the ability to think abstractly come later in the development process, this component of PCM speaks to how abstract thought is present at earlier ages and supports the developing child with concepts like self-representation, self-concept, self-regulation, self-modification, and self-initiative at very young ages (Khabbache et al., 2020).

NEW RESEARCH SPECIFIC TO AGE AND STAGE

More recent research on the ages linked to Piaget's stages of cognitive development demonstrate inaccuracies as well. In a literature review on Piaget's key constructs, Babakr et al. (2019) reviewed updated studies in all four stages of development, noting issues with each. In the pre-operational stage Babakr et al. (2019) found infant cognitive development emerges earlier, faster, and often more innately than Piaget asserted. Similarly, children in the pre-operational stage of development were found to perspective-take and demonstrate less egocentrism at an earlier age than Piaget proposed (Babakr et al., 2019; Matusov & Hayes, 2000). There were also issues noted with how Piaget tested specific constructs such as conservation in the concrete operational stage. Research indicates when children were given tasks that were more appropriate to their understanding or with which they had some experience, they could apply the concept of conservation at earlier ages (Babakr et al., 2019; Siegler, 2016). Children in this stage were also found to be able to understand more complex and multi-faceted problems than Piaget believed (Babakr et al., 2019). Alternatively, Piaget seems to have overestimated the capacity for all children to think logically and abstractly or even reach the formal operational stage (Babakr et al., 2019; Siegler, 2016).

When we consider Dev's transitioning experience and the specific levels of self-insight and perspective-taking he demonstrated at young ages, this would seem to fit. There is a growing body of research that indicates trans children are aware of their trans identity at earlier ages and can identify the associated feeling more easily, particularly when exposed to more socially accepting communities of support (Pardo & Devor, 2017). Dev initially understood his male-ness at a very young age when he would have been in the pre-operational stage of development. Though he struggled with societal, cultural, and familial dynamics around this, he seemed to have a fairly astute ability to understand both who he was as well as how he had to modify his behavior to accommodate those around him. This would appear to reflect some of the key cognitive capacities that Piaget associated with the more advanced stages of development.

ERIKSON'S PSYCHOSOCIAL DEVELOPMENT

Another important facet of our development includes how we engage with those around us and how this ultimately impacts our individual identity and personality development. For Erik Erikson, this concept of identity formation was particularly important for children and adolescents and contributed to his broader theory of psychosocial development (Erikson, 1950). This was due, in large part, to his own experiences in childhood and adolescence and the fact that he never knew his biological father. Erikson's mother never revealed who Erikson's father was, resulting in his life-long struggle with his own identity (Elkind, 2015). As a result, the key underpinning of Erikson's writings focus on the development of identity throughout the lifespan and the associated identity crises that can occur if specific developmental tasks are not achieved.

The Eight Stages of Psychosocial Development

Much like many other theorists, Erikson developed a stage theory that was founded on the belief in *epigenetics*, or the idea that people's personalities are developed across time through a particular sequence of prescribed developmental milestones (Maree, 2020). The milestones in focus in this theory tie specifically to personality development and how this is shaped through our interactions with others and with specific tasks tied to our agency at that time. Depending on how we are able to navigate those—positively, negatively, or not at all—we ultimately develop strengths or face a developmental identity crisis that can plague us in future stages.

Unlike other stage theories that require particular success in a stage before progressing forward, the expectation is that persons progress based roughly on age and expected adherence to the milestones associated with that age and stage. Failure to effectively deal with the developmental tasks of a particular stage will not prevent progression but will likely result in those "problems" resurfacing in later stages (Maree, 2020). Alternatively, if we are able to successfully navigate the developmental task at each stage, we foster personality strengths that will aid in our identity development and carry over into our future interactions and stages. In this way, Erikson's stages should be viewed as a broader continuum of development where optimal psychological health is achieved through successfully addressing the crises of each stage (Table 7.1; Dunkel & Harbke, 2017).

There is much to each stage of Erikson's Psychosocial Development theory and the impact on the collective lifespan. In fact, you will see this theory presented in several future chapters as well. For now, we focus specifically on the application to middle childhood and adolescence.

Psychosocial Development Theory: The Stages of Middle Childhood and Adolescence

Whereas developmental theorists like Freud and Piaget emphasized the importance of early childhood, particularly the first 6 years of life, Erikson believed the critical developmental period for psychosocial development was tied to the years that followed. It is in these years, and during the third, fourth, and fifth stages when children transition from childhood through adolescence and into emerging adults, where identity formation is at its peak and ultimately begins to consolidate (Erikson, 1968; Maree, 2020).

In the fourth stage, industry versus inferiority, children are developing their competence and expanding their capabilities in carrying out culturally important skills and tasks on their own (Dunkel & Harbke, 2017; Maree, 2020). Through this process they start to gain a sense of what they can achieve and where their talents lie. As they are able to experience success with various initiatives they grow in their capabilities and confidence and ultimately develop a sense of industry—that they can achieve and be successful at tasks on their own. The end result of successful movement through the developmental tasks of industry versus inferiority is a growing sense of competence that they can achieve and succeed in life (Dunkel & Harbke, 2017). On the other hand, if a child struggles with task achievement and fails to have opportunities for success in daily life, they can ultimately experience feelings of inferiority (Karkouti, 2014). These feelings of inferiority can persist long after movement out of this stage of development and are often tied to the work we do in the mental health professions.

Table 7.1 Erikson's Psychosocial Stages of Development

AGE	STAGE	DEVELOPMENTAL TASK	CRISIS	PSYCHOSOCIAL STRENGTH
1–2 Years: Infancy	Basic Trust vs. Mistrust	Infants interact with caregivers and begin to visualize and develop trust related to attaining needs	Infants create a feeling of distrust due to a disruption in the caregiving pattern	Hope
2–4 Years: Early Childhood	Autonomy vs. Shame and Doubt	Children start exploring their environment and begin distinguishing themselves from others	An identity crisis occurs when parents punish their children for not accomplishing expected tasks (e.g., toilet training)	Will
4–5 Years: Preschool Age	Initiative vs. Guilt	Children begin interacting with peers, distinguish between right and wrong, and complete certain tasks successfully on their own	Children who try to exert too much power experience disapproval, resulting in a sense of guilt	Purpose
5–12 Years: School Age	Industry vs. Inferiority	Children start to build their own social networks and become more competent and adept at carrying out increasingly complex tasks	Children develop a sense of inferiority if their performance is not appreciated	Competence
13–19 Years: Adolescence	Identity vs. Role Confusion	Individuals start developing their belief system, values, sense of self, and goals as they grow more independent and self-confident	Individuals who fail to accommodate both external recognition and self-satisfaction ultimately struggle with developing their sense of self	Fidelity
20–40 Years: Emerging Adulthood	Intimacy vs. Isolation	Young adults decide whether they will establish, maintain, and promote intimate relationships with people they trust	Individuals refrain from creating friendships and resort to emotional stress and isolation	Love
40–65 Years: Adulthood	Generativity vs. Stagnation	Individuals begin giving back to their social system, focus on their professional life, and are concerned about raising children	Stagnation will prevail leading to disengagement in productive life activities	Care
65+: Maturity	Ego Integrity vs. Despair	Individuals re-evaluate their lives and reflect on their achievements as they confront the idea of dying and their mortality	Individuals who feel they have failed to seize opportunities in their lives enter a state of despair and surrender to frustration	Wisdom

Source: Adapted from Dunkel, C. S., & Harbke, C. (2017). A review of measures of Erikson's stages of psychosocial development: Evidence for a general factor. *Journal of Adult Development, 24*(1), 58–76. https://doi.org/10.1007/s10804-016-9247-4; Karkouti, I. M. (2014). Examining psychosocial identity development theories: A guideline for professional practice. *Education, 135*(2), 257–263; Maree, J. G. (2020). The psychosocial development theory of Erik Erikson: Critical overview. *Early Child Development and Care.* https://doi-org.ezproxy.snhu.edu/10.1080/03004430.2020.1845163.

Erikson's concept of industry versus inferiority speaks to the opportunities we each have for success and failure as we begin taking more initiative and are given more responsibility in childhood. As you consider this stage, think back to your own development and the ages 5 to 12. What were these years like for you? Do you remember trying new things or being able to do something new you had not been able to do before? Maybe it was riding a swing on your own, opening a bottle for the first time, or learning a new concept at school. What did that success feel like for you, and how do you think it shaped you as you grew older? Similarly, did you ever have feelings of failure or experiences where you could not achieve something you tried on your own? What did this experience mean to you, and how has it contributed to your views of your own competence or inferiority where you are now?

These types of exercises are valuable to helping us know ourselves and from where our strengths and limitations may have originated. Similarly, they help us in our work within the helping professions. As we have greater perspective of what shapes people's identity development, we can better understand who they are, how they see themselves, and how they interact with others in their lives.

As important as the fourth stage is to identity development, the fifth stage, identity versus role confusion, is considered the most important in Erikson's theory of Psychosocial Development (Dunkel & Harbke, 2017). In this stage of development adolescents are challenged to develop a sense of self and understand who they are as individuals as they explore the roles around them and those they will occupy as an adult. This is the time, for example, when adolescents begin to question what they believe, what their values and goals are, and how those differ from or align with significant others around them. This is a period of increased independence and questioning of "Who am I?" (Dunkel & Harbke, 2017). As adolescents move through this stage and find support and affirmation with their noted belief systems, they gain a sense of self-confidence and self-continuity (Karkouti, 2014). In these instances identity formation leads to the psychosocial strength of *fidelity*, or the ability to commit to and accept others in spite of ideological differences (McLeod, 2018). Alternatively, when adolescents are unable to effectively manage the discrepancies between others' belief systems and their own, they can fail to develop a strong sense of self or their place in society (Karkouti, 2014; McLeod, 2018). In Eriksonian terms, this leads to *role confusion*.

In a nutshell these two stages allow us, at least to the extent applicable to our cultures and contexts, to develop our sense of agency and competence as children and then move into adolescence where we can begin solidifying our sense of self. These two phases are the precursors to who we will be when we "grow up" and allow us to navigate the challenging waters of success, failure, acceptance, rejection, and overall sense of who we are. When we add in the fact that children in these stages are moving into more complicated social circles of school and community, we can see why the social emphasis of family, peers, and role models are so important and how they tie into our overall personality development.

As we consider all of this, let's return to our case study client, Dev. As he is now an adolescent he would land in the stage of identity versus role confusion. We have clearly seen Dev working out much of his identity already—those parts tied to his parallel and intertwined trans identity development. He has a growing awareness of gender roles, which are already creating challenges for him. Similarly, he has a deepening discomfort with the physical changes to his body which represent him as female when he is not. While adolescents in this stage are often grappling with figuring out who they are, Dev seems to have at least some parts of his identity worked out. The *identity crisis* Dev is experiencing is the fact that he is not sure where he exists in his place in society. Because this stage requires both a developing sense of individual identity, coupled with a level of acceptance and understanding by peers and communities, we can appreciate how challenged Dev is in his current experience. Not only does he have to figure out all of the typical adolescent identity elements expected of those in Western societies—future career goals, relationships, beliefs—but he has to do so with the added layer of his trans identity. This has implications for how he views and accepts his religious beliefs, who and how he interacts with his peers in friendship and romantic relationships, and what opportunities he sees available to him in terms of future goals.

What can also be hard for trans children in this stage is the fact that it is often associated with a time of "trying on" or experimenting with various beliefs or lifestyles (McLeod, 2018). While necessary and important for many aspects of adolescent identity development, trans adolescent experiences can often be minimized or overlooked as a form of typical experimentation rather than a true sense of identity. It is, in part, the role of the mental health professional to ensure a validating experience for teens who are trans and to work with associated parents and community members to support the same. If this is not effectively supported by Dev's clinical social worker, Dev could be left with feelings of role confusion and a significant challenge in developing a strong sense of self.

SESSION EXCERPT 7.2

Clinical Social Worker: You've been juggling a lot lately, trying to balance who you are in a space that doesn't feel very accepting of it.

Dev: Yep. It super sucks. I mean, I feel like I've worked really hard to get to this point and to a place where I can even have my parents accept me. But now there are so many other things going on. Ugh. (Head drops.) It's like just when I figure one thing out then something else pops up that makes me question myself all over again.

Clinical Social Worker: So, talk to me about those other things. What is weighing on you the most right now?

Dev: Well, right now I guess I would say it's my religion. The way I feel about it. The way it doesn't accept me for who I am. I don't even know what I believe, but it feels like I am wrong for even being me.

Clinical Social Worker: So you are starting to question some things?

Dev: Yeah, being Muslim is really hard. My parents are important to me and I know how important that is to who we are. It's everything to them and has been everything to who I am growing up. It's my family. It's how we dress. It's what we believe. It's just been so much a part of me I sometimes didn't notice. It's just ... I guess it just feels different now. Like, I met someone through my new LGBTQ+ group at school and we were just talking. It made me think more about religion and what it means. I guess I just don't know what I believe anymore.

Clinical Social Worker: It sounds like you are feeling a little guilty about having those questions.

Dev: I don't know. I guess so. I've never thought about me being a boy as a choice. It's never felt like something I picked to do. I really wasn't sure how my being trans even mattered to being Muslim. I just knew my parents were upset that I wasn't doing what girls were supposed to do and that it wasn't "acceptable." But now, I guess I'm just learning more. I feel like it does. And then it makes me question what that means about me. Am I right or wrong? Are my parents right? Have they been right this whole time? I don't know. It's just a lot.

In this session excerpt we are given some insight into one of the areas of identity exploration going on for Dev. According to Erikson's stages of development, Dev is now in a place where he is contemplating his own beliefs around his Muslim faith and how these align or differ from his parents. There are broad and complex implications for Dev resulting from these questions and how he is able to reconcile them for himself. Understanding this, Dev's clinical social worker is allowing a safe place for some of that exploration and questioning to occur. The clinical social worker is aware of the significance of this issue for Dev and his family and is using probing questions and reflections to support the exploration process. Ultimately, Dev will have to work out how his belief systems around his Muslim religion and transgender identity shape his sense of self. However, it is his social worker's role, and your future role as a helping professional, to understand the implications of this stage of development on one's sense of self and to offer opportunities for supportive exploration.

Critical Analysis of Psychosocial Theory

There are a great many strengths to Erikson's theory of Psychosocial Development. For example, Erikson was the first theorist to build a framework for identity development from early adolescence through adulthood (Karkouti, 2014). Perhaps even more significantly, his theory accounts, in some part, for social and contextual underpinnings and how cultural and environmental factors influenced the developmental process (Sorell & Montgomery, 2001). This can be seen in his work with the Sioux and Yurok tribes where he emphasized that social and behavioral norms are culture dependent and that what is considered normal, neurotic, or appropriate to a phase in life is specific to the individual culture (Syed & Fish, 2018). In this way, Erikson recognized the unique elements of our social and contextual environments and how this may alter the experiences of each stage of development. Yet, in spite of these strengths, there have been critiques of Erikson's work as well.

Erikson's research, like many other psychodynamic researchers, suffered from methodological concerns and relied largely on case studies as the foundation for theory development (Maree, 2020). This resulted in overgeneralization to cultures for whom particular developmental crises or milestones were not as applicable. Particular criticism has been noted relative to gender differences, with Erikson criticized for being androcentric and developing his stages to align more closely with male tasks and identity development (triumph and independence) than those stereotypically associated with females (connectedness; Karkouti, 2014; Rattansi & Phoenix, 2005; Sorell & Montgomery, 2001). According to Sorell and Montgomery (2001), within the Eriksonian framework "most modern females and others without societal privilege, are either ignored or, when acknowledged, are seen as following a different developmental pathway from that specified as normal, healthy, or ideal" (p. 118).

While Erikson did expand his developmental theory beyond childhood, critics also argue that too much emphasis was placed on the childhood and adolescent years and not enough focus was given to later adulthood (Rattansi & Phoenix, 2005). One area in which this has been noted as a particular concern is in the alignment between physiological change and psychosocial change. While Erikson's early childhood and adolescent stages of development recognize the impact of biological and physical development on relationships and psychosocial functioning in the early stages of development, Sorell and Montgomery (2001) argue that Erikson failed to consider the physical changes that occur as individuals progress through the decades after physical maturity. In particular, they note that experiences of increasing physical frailty and dependency on others ultimately impact psychosocial development in later stages and are not appropriately addressed in Erikson's theory.

One additional consideration and criticism of Erikson's work is that it is limited to a largely Western, privileged developmental experience and that the construct of the personal sense of identity is not something afforded to everyone (Sorell & Montgomery, 2001). For example, there are people in the world who are being persecuted, suffer severe economic limitations, struggling to meet basic survival needs, or who live in political upheaval and are not afforded the types of identity development experiences that Erikson's theory prescribes. Because Erikson's stages hinge on autonomy, trust, and experiences for growth, those with restricted environments or opportunities for these experiences may never reach the self-development noted in Erikson's psychosocial stages of development (Sorell & Montgomery, 2001).

Recent Research on Psychosocial Theory

Erik Erikson is arguably one of the most well-known and significant contributors to developmental theory and his work on psychosocial development has spawned significant additional research in the years that followed his original work. This updated research highlights gaps in Erikson's psychosocial theory and also asks us, as professionals, to consider applicability to unique populations as we consider psychosocial development. As feminist scholars, Sorell and Montgomery (2001) put it: "Can a theory that ties individual development to a biological ground plan, thus emphasizing a certain uniformity of experience, offer guidance for investigations of identity as it is constructed in a rapidly changing, multicultural context?" (p. 99). This is our question to answer. In the sections that follow we will explore recent research and theoretical perspectives on elements of psychosocial development that can help us better address this question and understand the strengths and limitations of Erikson's original work.

CULTURAL IMPLICATIONS FOR IDENTITY VERSUS ROLE CONFUSION

As noted, one of the criticisms of Erikson's model of psychosocial development is the fact that he overemphasized the adolescent stage and the culminating crisis of identity versus role confusion. While some may move out of this stage having fully explored various elements of who they are and with a fully solidified sense of identity, current research indicates that some cultural groups require additional time and experiences to feel as though they have a fully formed sense of identity development due to the complexity of their developmental experiences (Brocious, 2017).

Brocious (2017), for example, conducted research on transnational adoptees, paying particular attention to how ethnic identity development and cultural belonging tied into overall identity development using Erikson's stages of development. To do so, Brocious (2017) conducted 10 qualitative interviews with participants who ranged in age from 19 to 34 and were adoptees to the United States from four different countries. Themes from the research indicated birth country travel, friendships with other adoptees, and learning the birth country language all had implications for participants' ethnic identity development. Additionally, results from this study indicated that many of the participants felt they needed or longed for additional opportunities to explore their birth culture as a means of fostering their self-identity (Brocious, 2017). That is to say, participants did not feel as though they had completed exploration of this element of their identity within adolescence and found they needed more exposure or exposure in later life to fully appreciate the way in which their birth culture and their adoptive culture ultimately impacted their sense of identity. Specific to this population, Brocious (2017) also argued that the concept of "resolution" may not fit as the culmination to a developmental stage as much as it is an on-going process of self-understanding that requires continued exploration across the lifespan.

Similar results were found in research on LGBTQ-persons of color (POC). Enoch Leung used an autoethnographic approach to evaluate his coming out experiences as a Canadian Chinese man in Western society and how these aligned, or did not, with Erikson's stages of psychosocial development (2021). Using diary entries, documented conversations, interviews, social media interactions, a personal drawing, and blogs which spanned from 2006 to 2020, Leung sought to understand the very specific intersectionality of his LGBTQ identity with that of his POC identity and how this differed from research focused on LGBTQ-White populations. Two key findings from his research were (a) intersectionality complicates and extends the developmental process of identity development beyond Erikson's adolescent years into emerging adulthood, and (b) this resulted from the challenge of consolidating his internal identity with external expectations that stemmed from stereotypes and cultural expectations associated with being an LGBTQ-POC (Leung, 2021). More specifically, Leung found himself able to explore and integrate his various identities internally, but found that he was particularly challenged to do so when external expectations dictated what society found acceptable or not for him as a gay Canadian Chinese man. Because of this, he found himself "compelled to 'throw' or dissociate one part of my identity" (Leung, 2021, p. 6). While his study was singularly focused and therefore cannot be generalized to larger populations of LGBTQ-POC, it does highlight the need for more focused research on intersectionality of LGBTQ-POC and how Erikson's stages may not be applicable across all cultures or contexts. This experience also seems to mirror some of what we see Dev experiencing in his identity development as an LGBTQ-POC.

NEW THEORETICAL PERSPECTIVES

Perhaps stemming from the cultural research in the preceding discussion and the recognition of societal change on the developmental process, new theoretical perspectives and models are expanding Erikson's work. Crocetti et al. (2008), for example, proposed the Three-Factor Identity model to account for the dynamic ways in which our identities develop and are revised over time. Emphasizing that identity development is an iterative process, the Three-Factor Identity model outlines a dual-cycle of identity formation and identity maintenance that accounts for three identity processes: (a) *commitment*—the choices individuals make about various developmental domains and the confidence resulting from those choices; (b) *in-depth exploration*—active thought, reflection, and data gathering specific to the commitments that have been made; and (c) *reconsideration of commitment*—comparing current commitments with alternatives when the original commitments no longer feel fulfilling. Crocetti (2017) ultimately argues that adolescents begin Erikson's stage of identity versus role confusion with some level of commitment in various domains in their lives based on childhood experiences and understanding of their social worlds. They then spend time focusing on in-depth exploration of those domains and ultimately confirm or modify parts of their identities. This moves them from an identity formation period to a time of identity maintenance, wherein they are stable in their chosen identities. When changes occur and in-depth exploration leads to reconsidering of commitments, individuals can move back to the identity formation cycle. According to Crocetti (2017), a stable sense of self and identity is largely tied to adolescent psychosocial functioning and well-being. Where these do not exist, there may be increased or prolonged role confusion across time.

Kerpelman and Pittman (2018) have also expanded on Erikson's work, looking specifically at the relationship between attachment theory and the relational context of Erikson's stages of identity development. Emphasizing the critical nature of our closest relationships in the developmental process, these authors propose that identity formation is not fixed and ultimately varies in the ways it emerges and is expressed, based on relational factors. Further, they argue that attachment and caregiver–child interactions serve as a precursor to identity development (Kerpelman & Pittman, 2018). In attachment theory, *security* is the key underpinning of a well-developed and healthy attachment to a caregiver. That is to say, a child feels comfort, safety, and a desire to be close to their caregiver (Cherry, 2020). According to Kerpelman and Pittman (2018), the attachment framework is important in understanding the Eriksonian stage of identity development because of the risk associated with identity exploration. Depending on the level of security and subsequent attachment that formed in infancy and early childhood, individuals can have increased or decreased levels of comfort with identity exploration and the commitments resulting from them. Similarly, because identity development occurs within the context of a family, parenting styles and subsequent parent–child interactions are likely to impact levels of safety and security in identity formation (Kerpelman & Pittman, 2018). As we consider Dev's situation, this theoretical perspective helps us to understand the influence and importance Dev's parents played in his early childhood years as well as why their perspectives are so critical to his identity exploration process.

PERSPECTIVES FROM THE FIELD: PODCAST

Access this podcast at http://connect.springerpub.com/content/book/978-0-8261-8279-1/part/part02/chapter/ch07

In this podcast we return to our discussions with our expert in the field, Dr. Stacee Reicherzer. Building on the information on culture and context from the previous chapter, Dr. Stacee highlighted how developmental theory can be used in understanding lifespan development, but also where there may be gaps and misalignment for many people along the way. She ends this podcast emphasizing the need for you to "grapple with" developmental and psychotherapeutic theories and to also "trust that your experience is powerful pedagogy." Bearing this in mind, what has stood out for you as making sense or fitting with your understanding of your own development? Where have the theories in this chapter and beyond not seemed to connect for you or those you know? Finally, consider how you will use this information, along with your own understanding of life and development, to guide your future work as a mental health professional.

SUMMARY

This chapter explored two key developmental theories that are frequently associated with the middle childhood and adolescent years: Piaget's Cognitive Development theory and Erikson's Psychosocial theory. Building on the cultural and contextual considerations from the chapter before, this chapter gave an overview of each theory, with specific focus on the developmental stages tied to middle childhood and adolescence. Using our case study, Dev, we considered the implications of each theory and how these might play out in his experiences at school, home, and in his work with his clinical social worker.

We also looked at each theory from a critical lens—considering both the strengths of each theory as well as noted imitations that should be considered when evaluating and applying these developmental theories in practice. In addition, we explored some of the newer research on cognitive and psychosocial development and how this expands upon or differs from the original theoretical perspectives of Piaget and Erikson. Developments in neuroscience and ever-evolving shifts in social and cultural experiences were highlighted.

We ended this chapter with our podcast expert, Dr. Stacee Reicherzer. In her discussions she shared the significance of using developmental theory as a framework for understanding clients we work with. Reflecting on her own experiences as a transgender woman, she also noted the challenges that come about when individuals within certain developmental periods do not "fit" milestones or elements of development that these theories espouse. She ended the podcast segment with the recommendation for students to recognize and honor their understanding of development and use this to guide their understanding of theories and those that are yet to come.

In the following chapter you will move from middle childhood and adolescence into the years and developmental period of early and emerging adulthood. As you did with Dev, you will be provided a case study to begin conceptualizing those developmental years and will have opportunities to continue your exploration of developmental theory with some cultural and contextual considerations to bear in mind relative to those years of life. As you continue your progression forward, remember to keep these theories in mind and consider how they may ultimately shape or impact future developmental periods of the new case studies you review. Also continue to keep Dev in mind. As you read additional chapters and get exposed to additional developmental theories, consider how you might conceptualize Dev across the years and through those new theoretical lenses.

REFERENCES

Babakr, Z. H., Mohamedamin, P., & Kakamad, K. (2019). Piaget's cognitive developmental theory: Critical review. *Education Quarterly Reviews, 2*(3), 517–524. https://doi.org/10.31014/aior.1993.02.03.84

Brocious, H. (2017). Erickson's identity theory and the importance of ethnic exploration for transnational adoptees. *Journal of Human Behavior in the Social Environment, 27*(4), 321–333. https://doi.org/10.1080/10911359.2017.1284029

Cherry, K. (2020). *The different types of attachment styles.* Verywell Mind. https://www.verywellmind.com/attachment-styles-2795344

Christie, D., & Viner, R. (2005). Adolescent development. *BMJ (Clinical Research Ed.), 330*(7486), 301–304. https://doi.org/10.1136/bmj.330.7486.301

Crocetti, E. (2017). Identity formation in adolescence: The dynamic of forming and consolidating identity commitments. *Child Development Perspectives, 11*(2), 145–150. https://doi.org/10.1111/cdep.12226

Crocetti, E., Rubini, M., & Meeus, W. (2008). Capturing the dynamics of identity formation in various ethnic groups: Development and validation of a three-dimensional model. *Journal of Adolescence, 31*(2), 207–222. https://doi.org/10.1016/j.adolescence.2007.09.002

Dunkel, C. S., & Harbke, C. (2017). A review of measures of Erikson's stages of psychosocial development: Evidence for a general factor. *Journal of Adult Development, 24*(1), 58–76. https://doi.org/10.1007/s10804-016-9247-4

Elkind, D. (2015). *Giants in the nursery: A biographical history of developmentally appropriate practice.* Redleaf Press.

Erikson, E. H. (1950). *Childhood and society.* Norton.

Erikson, E. H. (1968). *Identity: Youth and crisis.* Norton.

Flavell, J. H. (1992). Cognitive development: Past, present, and future. *Developmental Psychology, 28*(6), 998–1005. https://doi.org/10.1037/0012-1649.28.6.998

Flavell, J. H. (1996). Piaget's legacy. *Psychological Science, 7*(4), 200–203. https://doi.org/10.1111/j.1467-9280.1996.tb00359.x

Isaacs, N. (2015). *A brief introduction to piaget: The growth of understanding in the young child and new light on children's ideas of number.* Algora Publishing.

Karkouti, I. M. (2014). Examining psychosocial identity development theories: A guideline for professional practice. *Education, 135*(2), 257–263.

Kerpelman, J. L., & Pittman, J. F. (2018). Erikson and the relational context of identity: Strengthening connections with attachment theory. *Identity, 18*(4), 306–314. https://doi.org/10.1080/15283488.2018.1523726

Khabbache, H., Ouazizi, K., Bragazzi, N. L., Watfa, A. A., & Mrabet, R. (2020). Cognitive development: Towards a pluralistic and coalitional model. *Cosmos and History: The Journal of Natural and Social Philosophy, 16*(2), 245–265.

Leung, E. (2021). Thematic analysis of my "coming out" experiences through an intersectional lens: An autoethnographic study. *Frontiers in Psychology, 12*, 1–15. https://doi.org/10.3389/fpsyg.2021.654946

Mallon, E. J. (1976). Cognitive development and processes: Review of the philosophy of Jean Piaget. *The American Biology Teacher, 38*(1), 28–47. https://doi.org/10.2307/4445437

Maree, J. G. (2020). The psychosocial development theory of Erik Erikson: Ccritical overview. *Early Child Development and Care.* https://doi-org.ezproxy.snhu.edu/10.1080/03004430.2020.1845163

Matusov, E., & Hayes, R. (2000). Sociocultural critique of Piaget and Vygotsky. *New Ideas in Psychology, 18*(2–3), 215–239. https://doi.org/10.1016/S0732-118X(00)00009-X

McLeod, S. A. (2018, May 3). *Erik Erikson's stages of psychosocial development.* https://www.simplypsychology.org/Erik-Erikson.html

Pardo, S. T., & Devor, A. H. (2017). Transgender and gender nonconforming identity development. In K. L. Nadal (Ed.), *The SAGE encyclopedia of psychology and gender* (pp. 1689–1692). SAGE Publications. https://doi.org/10.4135/9781483384269.n575

Rattansi, A., & Phoenix, A. (2005). Rethinking youth identities: Modernist and postmodernist frameworks. *Identity, 5*(2), 97–123. https://doi.org/10.1207/s1532706xid0502_2

Ribeiro Piske, F. H., Stoltz, T., de Camargo, D., Blum Vestena, C. L., Machado, J. M., de Freitas, S. P., Dias, C. L., & dos Reis Taucei, J. (2017). Creativity in gifted education: Contributions from Vygotsky and Piaget. *Creative Education, 06*(1), 64–70. https://doi.org/10.4236/ce.2015.61005

Siegler, R. S. (2016). Continuity and change in the field of cognitive development and in the perspectives of one cognitive developmentalist. *Child Development Perspectives, 10*(2), 128–133. https://doi.org/10.1111/cdep.12173

Sorell, G. T., & Montgomery, M. J. (2001). Feminist perspectives on Erikson's theory: Their relevance for contemporary identity development research. *Identity, 1*(2), 97–128. https://doi.org/10.1207/S1532706XID0102_01

Syed, M., & Fish, J. (2018). Revisiting Erik Erikson's legacy on culture, race, and ethnicity. *Identity, 18*(4), 274–283. https://doi.org/10.1080/15283488.2018.1523729

The wonder years; Science highlights the powerful cognitive events of middle childhood. (2012, January 7). *Spectator [Hamilton, Ontario].* https://link.gale.com/apps/doc/A276498518/GIC?u=nhc_main&sid=bookmark-GIC&xid=c34661d8

Widjojo, K. (2018). The adolescent brain: Changes in learning, decision-making and social relations in the unique developmental period of adolescence. *Journal of Youth and Adolescence, 47*(8), 1789–1793. https://doi-org.ezproxy.snhu.edu/10.1007/s10964-018-0890-x

Zamfirov, M. Z. (2019). Application of Jean Piaget's cognition development tasks on students with special educational needs. *European Journal of Special Education Research, 5*(2), 79–93.

CHAPTER 8

Cultural and Contextual Factors of Emerging Adulthood Through Early Adulthood

LEARNING OBJECTIVES

By the end of this chapter, readers will be able to:

- Recognize how culture impacts the primary developmental tasks of emerging and early adulthood.
- Recognize the ways context impacts the primary developmental tasks of emerging and early adulthood.
- Explain the impact of culture and context on the development of emerging and early adults.
- Explain how culture and context impact the experience of career, family, and home commitment in emerging and early adulthood.
- Recognize the intersection of diverse salient identities on emerging and young adult development

CASE STUDY 8.1: THE CASE OF BI'LAL

Bi'lal is a 28-year-old African American man who is in a relationship with Mystic. Bi'lal has two bachelor's degrees: one in business, and one in political science. However, he has never worked a professional job. He has made a living in a series of part-time jobs like food delivery, working with a food truck, and driving for rideshare services. Whenever he can, Bi'lal performs with a group of African drummers, and he has performed at festivals in and out of his city. Until very recently, he primarily lived with his mother or his sister and, for a while, he and his girlfriend Mystic lived with her mother and grandmother. He and Mystic travel often and they proudly say  they have traveled to eight countries. Travel is a source of pride and he and Mystic feel it distinguishes them from other people, especially many friends their age.

Bi'lal has not been monogamous throughout the duration of his relationship with Mystic and that has caused tension. One night he and Mystic got into a very heated argument when he wanted to go out with friends. Mystic was suspicious that he was going to be with another woman and demanded to know why she could not go with him if he was only going to be out with friends. He resented her questions and refused to answer her. He eventually told her he excluded her because she had already made plans with her friend who was in their sitting room waiting for her. Mystic did not believe him and tried to physically stop him from leaving the room by blocking the door with her body. He asked her several times to move and when she would not move, he pushed her aside and she fell, hitting her mouth on the side of a piece of furniture and knocking down a lamp on the bedside table. Mystic was angry and screamed and her friend called the police when she heard the crash. Bi'lal was arrested as a suspect in a domestic violence incident. Bi'lal was immediately remorseful that things escalated to that degree and as soon as he was released from police custody, he contacted Mystic to apologize.

Bi'lal has worked hard to get Mystic to forgive him for the incident, and he knows that her willingness to resume the relationship has caused a significant rift for her with her friends and her mother. Mystic doesn't blame him, but he knows she has lost a lot because of him. He doesn't really know how to help with that because his relationship with his own mother is strained. He is happy that Mystic has started a new business selling clothing, but he is anxious that he is not as certain about what he is going to do with his own life. As a matter of fact, when he sees what his other friends and acquaintances are doing with their lives, he is feeling even more pressure to find his path.

For now, Bi'lal is continuing to work his jobs and he is supporting Mystic in her new urban wear business, but he is getting much more engaged in the community.

EMERGING ADULTHOOD

In the spring of 2020, as the world tried to understand the right response to a public health crisis called coronavirus disease-19, the United States was also dealing with the public health crisis of racism, a side effect of which was inequities in public safety and criminal justice for African Americans, highlighted by the killing of George Floyd and Breonna Taylor and the shooting of Jacob Blake by police officers. It is difficult to identify words that lend themselves to objectivity and impartiality, because depending on your perspective of the world, specifically your experiences in the world and the general narrative about your rights, access, and privilege, you may not interpret and speak about these events in the same way. And that perspective very profoundly shapes how you see yourself and what your expectations are of the world.

However, what we know is that the experiences and perceptions of Black men have been complicated, at best. In this chapter, we examine the cultural and contextual factors of emerging adulthood from the perspective of an African American man. Critical to this conversation that explores the impact of the sub-optimal context of racism, discrimination, low expectations, fear, disproportionality in poverty and criminalization, and other risks for African American men is the exploration of strengths that arise from the cultural contexts during emerging and early adulthood.

In this chapter, you will be introduced to Bi'lal in great depth, and you will get a brief introduction to Mystic, Bi'lal's companion. The two people are introduced here because there is significant interrelatedness to their developmental experiences. You will learn more about Mystic in Chapter 9. You will also hear from two experts from the fields of psychology and social work who will explore emerging and early adulthood. Additionally, you will have the opportunity to get a glimpse of Bi'lal's work with a clinical social worker, Therapist James, who has worked with mental health courts in the past. Mental health courts are programs within the court system designed to connect offenders with the needed mental health support and keep them out of the prison system (Warnke, 2020).

EMERGING ADULTHOOD AND EARLY ADULTHOOD

The modern study of adult development was more than 40 years old when Jeffrey Arnett introduced a theory of emerging adulthood to explain the development of people between approximately 18 and 25 years (Arnett, 2000). Arnett felt that it was necessary to describe this time in the lifespan differently, because he believed that in industrialized societies there had been changes for that age group that affected development. Arnett, 2000 observed that because people were committing to life partners and careers later, participating in education longer, and having less stability in where they lived, they were spending more time in exploration and were not as committed to adult roles. Arnett (2000) identified this time as transitional and referred to it as emerging adulthood. While Bi'lal is outside the age range initially described as the time of emerging adulthood, Arnett (2006) allows for variability by cultural and social experience. You will learn that both Bi'lal's cultural and contextual experiences contribute to the timing of his emergence from emerging adulthood to early adulthood.

The language around the time period of emerging adulthood, which can last into the late 20s, and the time period that follows, which spans from the late 20s through the 30s, can be confusing. For example, the time period being described here as emerging adulthood is also referred to as early adulthood or young adulthood, and there are often no distinctions made between the time period of the 30s and other stages of adulthood. Arnett (2012) makes the point that referring to the time of 18 to 25, and sometimes the time between 18 and 29 (Arnett, 2003) as young adulthood suggests that the person has already reached adulthood, and he proposes that the time period between 30 and f40 is actually young adulthood. However, for this text, we refer to the period between the late 20s and 40 as early adulthood, taking into account the subjective nature of the word "young" and accounting for the early stage of adulthood post transition.

Early adulthood differs from emerging adulthood in that it is marked by having made a long-term commitment and investment in love, work, and community (Eriksson et al., 2020). Arnett (2012) refers to this time as role immersion, noting that the person's commitment to work, parenting, love, and community is more substantial than at any time before or after. There is substantially less research about this time period than there is for emerging adulthood (Arnett, 2012).

Our task is centered on understanding the development and developmental task of a client like Bi'lal. Clients like Bi'lal do not neatly fit in one or the other area, primarily because as a 28-year-old male who is highly educated, he is most likely moving beyond the transitional stage of emerging adulthood in most areas of his life. Additionally, his race and ethnicity are mediators to his development. Arnett and Brody (2008) point out that for an African American emerging adult, the development tasks are not only related to understanding their own identity with regard to love, work, community, and values, but to determine how to navigate racist systems that limit their opportunities and overcome negative attitudes and prejudices people have about African American people. Phinney (2006) notes in addition to the contextual challenges people belonging to ethnic minorities may face in emerging adulthood, there are also cultural strengths, like the interdependent relationships with family.

Bi'lal is struggling to appropriately manage his emotions, be monogamous in his relationship, and establish a professional identity; however, he is engaging in purposeful activities designed to help others and build up his community. In this chapter, we closely examine the cultural and contextual experiences that shape Bi'lal's ability to emerge from this transitional stage after adolescence to early adulthood. We focus on psychosocial identities like racial identity, ethnic identity, and explore some personality traits or experiences that are emerging as significant to understanding individuals, like race-related stress, resilience, and post-traumatic slave syndrome. Of course, the purpose of the discussion is not to comprehensively address all aspects of identity development in emerging adulthood and early adulthood that are shaped by culture and context. The goal is to help you, as the emerging helping professional, understand the complexities of identity development and to understand why it is so important to develop a therapeutic relationship that allows your client to inform you of how the pieces of identity come together to form the whole person. In that process, you will recognize that the paths, the road maps, the tools toward actualization are varied and no one path should be designated as optimal, particularly in light of diversity in culture and context.

You will also bear witness to Bi'lal's time with Therapist James. Therapist James is an African American male who has been practicing for 16 years. He has worked in both drug and mental health courts in the past. Bi'lal is not a part of either program, but Therapist James's experience with these courts allows him to engage in an approach that is respectful of the cultural dynamics that exist and reflective of the premise that community interventions can be very impactful for people who are engaged in the criminal justice system (Tyuse & Linhorst, 2005).

CULTURAL FACTORS: EMERGING ADULTHOOD

As we were planning for this book, we were intentional in addressing culture and context, not as add-ons to a conversation that assumes normal development is reflective of only Western culture and values and middle-class people with dominant group membership. We wanted to challenge helpers to understand the relevance of a person's social location and cultural background and how that impacts everything from family relationships, understanding of the world and their role in that world, values, goals, and a host of other things, particularly resources to be productive and resilient. We also wanted our readers to understand the impact of context on human development. The world impacts how each person develops or, more importantly, what tasks the person has to achieve in order to develop in a healthy way. There are times when it is not easy to distinguish between culture and context, because responding to the context is informed by one's cultural experiences. However, we will try to present a cultural orientation that illuminates our understanding of Bi'lal that begins with a discussion about the African American family.

African American Family

A major asset that should not be overlooked for an African American client is the African American family. It is easy to be distracted by the contexts of racism, environmental stressors, and socioeconomic stressors common to African Americans and start to see the African American experience only from a deficit. Bell-Tolliver and Wilkerson (2011) specifically warn new practitioners about providing services only through the lens of deficits when clients present with their primary concerns. What a clinician who is unfamiliar with the cultural context of a client might see as suboptimal or a major issue for a client, may not be an issue in the client's opinion. Clients should be the informants about how to categorize their concerns and assign value to them, which will result in the client being the leader in goal setting.

Bi'lal was not particularly interested in therapy and is mistrustful of therapists in general. The following is an excerpt from his first session with Therapist James. Notice that Therapist James establishes early that Bi'lal's perceptions of things are more important than Therapist James.

SESSION EXCERPT

Therapist James (after initial intake): Mr. Bi'lal W, it's nice to meet you. Mr. Bi'lal, the chosen one, what brings us here together? May I call you Bi'lal?

Bi'lal: (Nods.) You know the meaning of my name? Most people don't and they definitely don't say it right. (Sighs.) I'm here because I messed up and it seems that everything is a mess.

Therapist James: You're alive and walked in here on your own accord, so from where I sit everything is not a mess. But my opinion doesn't matter as much as yours right now. So why don't you start from the beginning and tell me about the things you want to address in our time together and we can talk about how we might work together to manage these things that seem like a mess to make them neater and less messy. But first, tell me how you feel about being here right now.

Bi'lal: I wasn't really feeling it and I don't know what to expect. I don't want anyone head-shrinking me or just giving me pills.

Therapist James: I wouldn't know where to start with head-shrinking and I don't know enough to know if you might need medication at some point, but I am sure that this process won't be any more or less than you put in it. It is yours to own.

Therapist James's description of Bi'lal's ownership of the therapy process is important because it establishes that Therapist James believes that Bi'lal has the maturity to direct the course of the sessions. As they continue to address Bi'lal's decisions and the influences on his decisions, it will be important to acknowledge the possibility of an orientation reflective of interdependence with family (Arnett, 2003). This interdependence is not an indication that the client is less mature developmentally. The African American culture is a collectivist culture where the family is the focus more than the individual (Bell-Tolliver & Wilkerson, 2011). While family may be blood relatives, the relationships between extended family members and *fictive kin*, people who are not actually related by blood but are in the role of family, are as significant as the identified nuclear family. These family members are relied on for financial and emotional support. As helpers, it is imperative that we examine our clients' familial relationships to uncover the strengths and assets the client has for healthy and productive living (Bell-Tolliver & Wilkerson, 2011).

There are five major strengths or characteristics of African American families. Those strengths are: (a) strong education and work ethic; (b) egalitarian and adaptable family roles; (c) extended family kinship networks; (d) flexible and strong coping skills; and (e) strong religious orientation (Bell-Tolliver & Wilkerson, 2011). These are assets that should be assessed and accessed when working with a client like Bi'lal. We mention that the assets should be assessed, because while these strengths are common to African American families, they do not always exist for African American people. As a matter of fact, having a family that does not reflect some of these strengths can sometimes be a source of marginalization for an African American person within the community.

One of the major tasks for African American families is supporting their children in mediating the impact of racism in their lives. It is very common for African American parents to adopt an authoritative style where children are expected to quickly comply with parents' directives and expectations regarding behavior (McCallum, 2016). African American families know that normal childhood pranks and misconduct can come with consequences that are extremely high for African American children and young adults. While often seen as a suboptimal parenting style, this style of parenting is a protective factor common to African American culture. In addition, even as African American emerging adults leave home, parents maintain a significant presence in their lives around everything from work, education, extracurricular activities, and religious practice, making clear the expectation that the emerging or young adult stay connected to the family and community of origin (McCallum, 2016). It is quite common for African American families to make significant financial sacrifices to make sure that their emerging adults are able to have the best opportunities, like a college education. McCallum (2016) also points out that siblings, other extended family members, and fictive kin also invest significantly in the academic success especially of African American young adults, providing not only moral support, but often financial support, as well.

African American Mothers and Sons

Crucial to understanding a client like Bi'lal, a male African American most likely nearing the end of his time in emerging adulthood and on the cusp of early adulthood, is understanding the relationships between African American mothers and their sons. About 65% of African American children live in single-parent households. Annie

E. Casey Foundation (2020) and Bush (2004) indicate that over 50% of Black households are headed by African American mothers. One major difference in how African American mothers parent their sons in comparison to their White counterparts is that African American mothers must parent in the context of racism, which makes it sometimes very difficult to distinguish between what is cultural and what is contextual (McCallum, 2016). African American mothers devote significant attention to protecting their sons from racism, but they also want them to mediate the impact of racism (Bush, 2004). One common cultural feature of the mother–son dynamic is that African American mothers provide their sons with examples of male relatives and ancestors who have overcome adversity, providing male role models to their sons through these narrative accounts.

African American mothers often focus on supporting their sons' development in ways that are neither traditionally masculine nor traditionally feminine and focus on their sons having respect for their mothers, a strong sense of responsibility, a sense of responsibility for the family and community, and being compassionate and honest. These are the traits that are reflective of being a man or being an adult (Bush, 2004). Bush (2004) conducted an investigation of the role African American mothers play in their sons' development of manhood and masculinity. Results indicated that while African American mothers were able to teach their boys about sexuality and the African American male experience, for example, the mothers themselves expressed concerns and doubts about their abilities to help their sons' development in these areas.

Black Otherfathering

One phenomenon that is quite common to the African American community is this experience of otherfathering. Otherfathering is when a male presents as a significant role model to a person who is not his birth child (Brooms, 2017). These otherfathers are often coaches, scout leaders, teachers, or religious leaders who provide the person with more than just knowledge about the event or activity they are leading, but also provide the person with life coaching, nurturing, or support that creates a climate for growth and improved self-actualization.

Bi'lal has joined with a group of men in his community who are mentoring young African American males by exposing them to a variety of cultural activities and providing them with guidance related to Blackness and maleness. Bi'lal invited some of his friends to a session to teach the boys about the African drums. Under normal circumstances, the group of men meet with their mentees twice a month, but many of the boys in the group have expressed interest in the Black Lives Matter protests around their city, so the men in the group have decided to start focusing on helping the young boys in developing a social justice agenda and engaging in advocacy. Bi'lal is not leading these activities, but he is learning a lot and realizing that many of the lessons these boys are learning are things he might have learned if his father had been around. Many of the mentors are fathers and he notices that there are noticeable differences in how the fathers interact with the mentees. Sometimes he feels like he is behaving like their pal; other times he has really high expectations of the boys and gets impatient when he feels they are acting immaturely.

Bi'lal is recognizing that he is benefitting from being around these other African American men. However, he is also aware that the other men, because of their parental roles, behave less like peers to the mentees and more like otherfathers.

Connection and Home-Leaving for African American Emerging Adults

From the perspective of the dominant group culture, leaving home is a common experience of early adulthood. In many parts of Western culture, there is the belief that not leaving home by the mid-20s is an indication that adulthood is delayed in some way and marks a failure to achieve a developmental milestone (Wilson et al., 2017). But not leaving home before the late 20s to early 30s is increasingly more common. In general, emerging adults are leaving home later and when the emerging adult leaves the family of origin, it is a major event in the experience of the entire family (Wilson et al., 2017).

Until recently, Bi'lal never lived entirely on his own. He primarily lived with his mother or his sister and, for close to a year, he lived in the small apartment of his girlfriend Mystic and her mother. Even now, he and Mystic are living in a home his grandmother owns, so they do not have to pay as much rent as they would renting from another non-related landlord, but they are responsible for the small rent and utilities.

Wilson et al. (2017) found that it was hard for the African American emerging adults they interviewed to leave home and that they often struggled with the desire to be independent but maintain their sense of responsibility to their families. They also found that African American young adults felt that a distinction between them and other young adults was the privilege to live independently, a situation they felt was associated with financial advantages. Their perception was that there was little opportunity for mistakes because there was less family support and fewer opportunities to recover from those mistakes. Additionally, while the participants in the Wilson et al. (2017) study were excited about the prospect of leaving home and saw it as necessary for growth, there was also fear and anxiety associated with leaving home.

This example is interesting because it demonstrates the blurring of culture and context; what looks like a cultural phenomenon is highly influenced by context, such as socioeconomic status.

Ethnic Identity Development

Ethnic identity refers to the degree to which one develops a sense of affiliation and identification with one's ethnic group. As discussed in Chapter 3, the four identity statuses are diffused, foreclosed, moratorium, and achieved, each describing a different combination of exploration and commitment to the identity. Phinney (2006) indicates that most people are not identity achieved by the end of adolescence and the person who never leaves the community of origin or pursues activities that afford opportunities for exploration could remain identity foreclosed for a long time, committing to an identity that has never been fully explored. The identity-achieved person has engaged in both exploration and commitment and understands what it means to be a part of the ethnic group. Bi'lal appears to have an achieved ethnic identity. He has interacted enough with people who are not members of his racial, cultural, or ethnic group to understand where there are differences, and he understands what he has in common with people with whom he shares an ethnic identity. Additionally, he is engaged in activities like mentoring, drumming, and justice-promoting that reinforce his ethnic identity.

McClain et al. (2016) found, in their study of Black college students, that ethnic identity is a significant positive predictor of mental health. Phinney (2006) describes ethnic heritage, racial phenotype, and cultural background as the three aspects of ethnic identity, emphasizing that three parts of ethnic identity can overlap. Unfortunately, identity development at this period is largely dependent on context and cannot be neatly described. For example, mediators like immigration status, ethnic background, generation of immigration, socioeconomic status, and education experience, all interact to create a new set of opportunities and crises for the emerging adult's developmental process (Phinney, 2006). Additionally, not all parts of the individual identity are salient in every context, which also complicates matters. Phinney (2006) maintains that for those individuals belonging to ethnic minority groups, developing cultural, ethnic, and racial identities are crucial to their development toward adulthood.

According to Phinney (2006), ethnic identity in emerging adulthood must be understood in context. For example, one of the things we know about Bi'lal, the experiences, some witnessed firsthand, and others witnessed through media with regard to police violence against African American men, impact behavior and can result in fear that the consequences of a police call could be deadly. While Bi'lal may not have had these fears as an adolescent, he is more aware of his vulnerability to death at the hands of the police as a young man. It should be noted that stressful contexts may find a person functioning in a stage of identity development that appeared achieved in less stressful situations or contexts. For example, college students who have successfully navigated their ethnic identity in high school with the support of their family of origin, may find themselves more vulnerable in those environments that they must navigate independently.

Phinney (2006) describes two common pathways of African American college students at predominantly White institutions. Those students may either develop a stronger ethnic identity, immersing themselves in culturally affirming activities, or may experience a weakening of their identity. The latter is most common for those who do not have a strong ethnic identity when they enter college. These students are often surprised at the prevalence of discriminatory experiences and the experiences of being isolated in these environments. Phinney (2006) also indicates that for those who do not want to identify with their ethnic group, they may face the disapproval of that group for not connecting with the group.

As cognitive development increases, the emerging adult can evaluate circumstances and experiences in a way they may not have been able to as an adolescent. Lewis et al. (2018) assert that a strong sense of ethnic identity could result in having self-efficacy in a variety of areas including career decision-making. Rollins and Valdez (2006) maintain that ethnic identity is a greater predictor of career self-efficacy than other contextual factors. This suggests that a primary responsibility of any mental health provider serving emerging adults is to support healthy exploration of ethnic identity to facilitate fulfillment of career goals in this transformative developmental stage.

CONTEXTUAL FACTORS: EMERGING ADULTHOOD

Joseph et al. (2020) reported that African Americans experience racial discrimination more than any other group. While most of the research regarding racism focuses on the impact it has on the mental well-being of an emerging adult, it should be noted that the context of racist experiences and a racist environment can be disruptive to the overall developmental process of emerging adults by challenging a positive sense of self, confidence in peer groups, and any sense that an individual has the ability to control the outcome of situations for themselves (Joseph et al., 2020). This is not to discount the emotional, psychological (Joseph et al., 2020), and physical impact (Gupta, 2021) of daily racist interactions which serve to deplete the resources an individual has to cope with daily life (Joseph et al., 2020).

However, the respondents in the Wilson et al. (2017) study also reported that they expected to have limited opportunities because of the low expectations larger society has of African Americans. Some of these expectations or stereotypes are that they would have children without being married, have children with multiple different partners, and would have large families with the expectation that other people would be responsible for the care of those families. The African American men in the Wilson et al. (2017) study indicated that they were only valued for their athletic and physical ability and that this would have an impact on their career opportunities. Bi'lal has two bachelor's degrees, but he has never had a professional job. It is possible Bi'lal has been overlooked as a well-qualified candidate in some jobs for which he has applied or that he has been the victim of name bias in the application process (Amrani, 2019). This may result in anxiety or a pessimistic attitude about applying for professional positions in his field based on his experiences of being dismissed by those in a position of authority.

Race Socialization as an Orientation to the Culture

Next, we explore psychosocial identity development theories around racial identity development and other constructs such as race socialization, post-traumatic slave syndrome, and race-related and minority status stress. Again, we maintain that there are some experiences that are so common to the context of African American male identity that the resulting responses or coping strategies becomes cultural. African American male children are disproportionately sentenced as adults and there is a prevalence of the "adultification" of African American males by those in the criminal justice system which results in more severe responses to them when they are suspected of crimes than their White counterparts (Harris & Amutah-Onukagha, 2019). It is estimated that one in 1000 Black males will be killed by the police. As a result, a significant part of the culture of Black people is to educate Black males about how to respond to police. This education is called *race socialization*.

The race socialization process usually focuses on egalitarianism, preparation for bias, or promotion of mistrust (Harris & Amutah-Onukagha, 2019). The egalitarian approach might also be described as fostering a raceless identity and is centered around helping children thrive in dominant culture by developing in ways that are valued in the dominant culture. One example of this approach is teaching young people how to dress professionally according to the standards of dominant society. The preparation for bias approach is focused on giving children skills to deal with discrimination. Most African American adults will recount being taught to always get a bag and receipt from a merchant even when making a small purchase, especially in a convenience store, as a protective measure in the likelihood that someone will think a Black person has stolen something. In recent years, it has become quite common for the preparation for bias messages to extend to preparing African American adolescents and young adults for encounters with police, by emphasizing the need to not resist arrests or argue back and essentially "just get home." The promotion of mistrust, however, rooted in the myriad of experiences African Americans have had where they have been mistreated and undervalued, does not provide any prescriptive guidance about how to respond to racism. African American mothers assume a very prominent role in the race socialization of their children and tend to place greater emphasis on this race socialization process for their sons, especially with regard to law enforcement, than they do their daughters (Harris & Amutah-Onukagha, 2019).

Racial Identity Development

While writing this chapter, we considered whether models related to racial identity should be paired with other models related to cultural and ethnic identity. After all, the ethnic identity development model discussed previously accounts for the impact of race on identity development. However, to emphasize the ideas that race is a social construct, and that racial identity develops in response to the context of attitudes about race, systemic oppression, racial prejudice, racism, and racist violence, we have included racial identity in this section. Discussing race as a social construct allows us to emphasize that race has been used to classify people for the purposes of social and political advantage, but it is neither scientific nor immutable (Pierce, 2014). Additionally, it is important to understand that race and culture are not synonymous. It could be said that we are taking dramatic license by so emphatically separating racial identity development from ethnic identity development. That is likely and it is your responsibility to think critically about this argument and take a position. After all, the consequence of your position could be the difference between thinking that a person's circumstances and behaviors are predetermined or that everyone has the same potential for actualization or that behaviors vary according to context.

According to Sellers et al. (1998) racial identity describes the extent to which an individual is aware of and interprets lived experiences through their racial group. We do not have conclusive evidence that racial identity positively or negatively contributes to well-being. What is consistent is that racial identity contributes to an individual's well-being (McClain et al., 2016). While some people use the terms *racial identity* and *ethnic identity* interchangeably, they are not the same. Racial identity is that identity that results from those experiences in the world that are responses to immutable phenotype characteristics like skin color and hair texture, but ethnic identity might best be explained more broadly as beliefs and behavioral cultural identity. It is possible that a person does not have the skin color or hair texture we associate with a specific race and still have the same ethnic identity as those who do. Often the ethnic identity can also accompany a group of people who have race in common. Both racial identity and ethnic identity are sociocultural identities, however (McClain et al., 2016). This means they are both cultural and contextual.

STUDENT REFLECTION

Reflect on your own experience of the differences between racial identity and ethnic identity. Do you think one is cultural and the other is contextual? Why? Why would this matter to a practitioner or a client?

Chapter 3 provides an in-depth discussion of racial identity development and, specifically, the Cross Racial Identity Development Model. We will use that to try to understand Bi'lal's development. There are a few important behavioral clues that suggest Bi'lal's identity is that of the Black Nationalist with internalization attitudes. Bi'lal is very interested in other cultures and has traveled all over the world.

Bi'lal has been very angry about the socio-political climate for African American men in the United States, and the angrier he has become, the more reactive he has become. As a matter of fact, he insisted that a shared ride passenger leave his car when the passenger insistently engaged him in a conversation where the passenger proclaimed that he was not a supporter of the Black Lives Matter movement because all lives, especially blue lives, matter. This resulted in a horrible review from the passenger, a situation that he suspects is impacting customers' willingness to accept him as their shared ride driver. Bi'lal frequently suggests he believes the world is out to get him and he often remarks that he does not know if he will live to see 30. He is very angry with Mystic's friend who called the police, feeling that Mystic's friend knew that he could have potentially lost his life at the hands of the police.

While he is also frustrated by being underemployed, Bi'lal is starting to identify ways that he can act powerfully and create his own path in the world. He is finding ways to provide service, help others, and share his culture with other people. His volunteer service as a mentor for the boys, teaching drumming to the boys, and participating in the civil rights activities all suggest that his racial identity is internalized. However, Worrell (2008) examined racial identity development across adolescence, emerging adulthood, and adulthood, and the findings supported previous research that suggest racial identity is not developmental in nature. Bi'lal's evolution may be more closely aligned with Black Male Identity Development.

Black Male Identity Development

Bi'lal and Mystic's arguments have been more heated lately, but it was not his intention to hurt Mystic when he shoved her out of the way. In hindsight, he realizes that pushing her away as forcefully as he did could have had horrible consequences.

SESSION EXCERPT

Therapist James: Bi'lal, tell me about the incident that happened between you and Mystic on the night you were arrested.

Bi'lal: I'm not sure where to start. Sometimes I wonder how things got to this point. You know?

Therapist James: You were surprised about how things turned out?

Bi'lal: Yeah, I guess. I know I had been feeling hemmed in for weeks and I was getting tired of her questioning me about every move. It's as if she was always suspicious of everything.

Therapist James: Suspicious how? What did she suspect you of?

Bi'lal: You know it was like every time I got a text, she was on alert. Every time I left, she was questioning me asking me where I was going and who I was going to be with. She was always accusing me of being with somebody else.

Therapist James: Did she have a reason to be suspicious?

Bi'lal: You know? In the past, there were other females I was seeing. Yeah. She had reason in the past to feel that way.

Therapist James: And now or, more importantly, then—the night of the incident?

Bi'lal: Nah. You know, once we knew we were going to move in together, I decided that was it. (Laughs.) You know I knew it was going to be harder to step out if we were living together. Seriously, you know I was tired of that. I wasn't getting anything out of it and I knew that I really wanted to be with Mystic.

Therapist James: But on the night you were arrested for domestic battery, you were not going to see another woman and you could not convince her.

Bi'lal: Nah. I was really going to hang out with my boys.

Therapist James: And when you told her that, she didn't believe you?

Bi'lal: I didn't tell her where I was going. I just didn't feel like answering her. That's what I mean. I don't know why I didn't just tell her. It would have been simple. I know that I've given her reasons to be suspicious, but I …I don't know. (Pauses.) It's like I know I'm ready to be all in, but I'm not sure if I'm ready for her to know that I'm ready to be all in and … that night I felt hemmed in with no way out. It's like there were so many thoughts going on through my mind at once.

Therapist James: Like what?

Bi'lal: I was already feeling pressed. Like, how were we going to do this? You know? We were living together and she didn't really have a good job and I felt like it was all on me. What if I couldn't handle it? And she and her mom were not on good terms when she left. Her mom told her she could always come back if it didn't work out. Like her mom wasn't expecting it to work out. Like I was going to let Mystic down somehow. She planted doubt in her head when she said that. Mystic was probably stressed about all of that, too. She's really close to her mom. But it was like she had too much riding on me and I felt that it was all on me. I guess I just wasn't sure I could step up and I was looking for a way out.

Committing to a romantic relationship is a major task of emerging adulthood. The benefits of which include support and nurturing resulting in the reduction of risk behaviors, better mental health, and a focus on career and vocational development (Bae & Kogan, 2020). Intimate relationships are as important for men as they are for women (Simon & Barrett, 2010). The stressors that impact African American men's abilities to establish significant relationship bonds are based in socioeconomic and childhood stressors.

Bae and Kogan (2020) conducted a study of the relationship habits of African American men with a low socioeconomic status, living in rural communities with high rates of poverty, and limited education and vocational opportunities (Bae & Kogan, 2020). They specifically sought to uncover how the relationships of these African American men changed over time during emerging adulthood. The researchers focused on three aspects of functioning in romantic relationships: conflict, support, and dyadic trust. The context of not having adequate resources like housing, food, and healthcare can make people vulnerable to stress, frustration, depression, and anger, resulting in relationship stress and conflict. It can be difficult for individuals to find the support they need in the context of the relationship. These circumstances may also impact the person's confidence that another person can be supportive of them in those circumstances. Finally, there is the issue of dyadic trust, which is essentially the belief that a partner can be counted on and will demonstrate care and concern. One conflict that is common among African American couples is that there is a high rate of incarceration and unemployment for African American males, decreasing the number of available African American men to date. One outcome of the reduction in available mates is that African American men are more likely to have concurrent sexual partners (Bae & Kogan, 2020).

Bi'lal is demonstrating the attitudes of someone who is nearing the end of emerging adulthood. In his conversation, he communicates that he wants to be in a monogamous, committed relationship with Mystic and he is also keenly aware of his responsibility in the relationship and the consequences of his behavior, not just on his relationship with Mystic, but Mystic's relationship with her mother.

Minority Status Stress

As Therapist James continues to work with Bi'lal, he starts to realize that in addition to the pressures Bi'lal felt with his new adult responsibility of being and having a live-in companion, Bi'lal's anxiety on the night of the arrest is also rooted in his fear that he will never be able to get the opportunities he's worked for and that being a partner to Mystic, and even having a family, are things that will be difficult for him as a Black man in America. We are going to explore two socio-cultural constructs that Bi'lal may also be experiencing: minority status stress and post-traumatic slave syndrome.

Minority status stress is used to describe being stressed because of the persistent experiences associated with the individual's nondominant group membership such as racism, discrimination, or microaggressions like insensitive comments, being excluded from opportunities, or being made to feel like an outsider (McClain et al., 2016). The experiences can make a person in the minority feel isolated and impact the person's ability to adjust to or function in the environment (Smedley et al., 1993).

Post-Traumatic Slave Syndrome

Post-traumatic slave syndrome is the effect of multigenerational oppression suffered by enslaved African Americans (Womack, 2016). It is based on the irrefutable premise that chattel slavery in the United States was traumatic for those who were held in captivity, forced to work as free labor, beaten, mutilated, and raped with no consequences for their abusers, rapists, or murderers. Additionally, Black people in America have continued to be subjected to unjust laws, unethical medical practices and misguided discriminatory theories about their intellect, ability, and morality.

DeGruy (2005), in theorizing this syndrome, offered that many of the behaviors and beliefs that are common to African American people in contemporary times are legacies from a time when they adopted those behaviors to survive. The result is a kind of internalized oppression or internalized racism where African American people can have low expectations for themselves, their children, and other members of their race or ethnic group. These experiences show up in Black people's distrust of medical professionals whom they suspect will treat them as human subjects for the sake of medical discoveries that will benefit their White patients (Womack, 2016). There is a history of African American people not getting mental or physical treatment because of this distrust. In the case of Bi'lal, he does not trust the mental health provider and, only when faced with the possibility of going to jail, does he even consider this option.

Other Contextual Realities of Emerging Adulthood

There are other contextual realities of emerging adulthood that impact the individual, such as social media, globalization, and the impact of the COVID-19 pandemic. We cannot explore all of them, but we can implore you to continue your educational process by recognizing the dynamic nature of our society and critically evaluating how those realities impact your clients. Two more that are reflective of the dynamic nature of society and very relevant to Bi'lal's experiences emerging adulthood are living at home and underemployment.

LIVING AT HOME

According to the Pew Research Center, 17.8% of adults ages 25 to 34 lived with their parents in 2019 and nearly half of 19- to 29-year-olds in the United States were living with one or both or their parents in March 2020 (Creamer et al., 2020). By July of 2020, this was up to 52%, a rate that has never been that high since the Great Depression (Fry et al., 2020). We can only assume that as the pandemic progressed, it had an impact on emerging and young adults who often do not have significant funds in reserve to maintain their living responsibilities without daily work. However, the rate of young adults living with at least one parent has been rising since the 1960s, primarily because young people are acquiring more education and are, consequently, less likely to have jobs that allow them to live independently (Arnett, 2020).

UNEMPLOYMENT OR UNDEREMPLOYMENT

African American men have the lowest employment rate of any group by race or gender, and we know that low employment or underemployment impacts lifetime earnings. Presently African American men are experiencing less upward mobility and more downward mobility than previous generations. Since the 1970s, there has been a steady decrease in unskilled manufacturing jobs (Raley et al., 2015). There are many factors that are contributing to unemployment and underemployment, not the least of them being discrimination, lower work experience, lower marriage rates, and crime and incarceration (Holzer, 2021). As recently as the early part of the 21st century, for those African American men who did not attend college, more than one third had been incarcerated (Raley et al., 2015). While we could certainly expect lack of education and a record of incarceration to impact the ability to be gainfully employed in today's economy, Bi'lal's underemployment is curious and requires more attention to the structural discrimination that takes place in today's labor market. Our limited experience of Bi'lal is that he is well educated, but under-experienced, a fact that will be even more complicated if he is convicted of the crime for which he has been charged. He has had jobs that were less likely to lead to career opportunities. One strength Bi'lal has is that he is creating his own experiences that might lead to more opportunities for him. Additionally, his service activities are more likely to create a professional network with other African American men that can lead to opportunities. Encouraging Bi'lal's sense of empowerment in this regard will be critical in his therapeutic process.

CULTURAL FACTORS: EARLY ADULTHOOD

Eriksson et al. (2020) define early adulthood as the period between the late 20s through the 30s where people are focused on love, work, and being a contributing member of society. While there are generous amounts of literature focused on emerging adulthood, there is significantly less that focus on early adulthood and even less that describe the specific developmental needs of those who have non-dominant group membership. Additionally, what we know about this group is largely dependent on context. For example, the context for most people who fall in this category now, those people commonly referred to as millennials born between 1981 and 1996, is an economic crisis where people's wages have not grown to match the cost of living, particularly the cost for necessities like housing and childcare (Seligson, 2019). The timing of millennials' emerging adulthood was the middle of a recession in the United States, so many were in debt before they ever started to commit to expensive ventures like children and mortgages. Over half of millennials receive financial assistance or receive some free services from their parents. The most common free service is childcare. The implications are great because this dependence on their parents may result in early adults not being able to make decisions independent of their parents. Additionally, they may find that they are not able to offer support to their parents when they need it.

Bi'lal, like a lot of early adults, finds that he is still largely dependent on his parents, or in his case, his grandmother, for financial support. The experience of many African Americans in early adulthood, however, is that they have more financial capital than their parents and, because of technology, can communicate more widely with people who share common interests. Where previous generations of African Americans have been White referent because the prevailing media images were White, African Americans in early adulthood have been able to connect with each other through social media to bring worldwide attention to the social and political issues that matter to them. Additionally, this group has significant spending power and has been able to get the attention of businesses who want them as customers. The resulting experience is that many African Americans, partcularly those in early adulthood, are navigating a world unfamiliar to many of their parents. Even though many of them have more financial capital than their parents, it does not necessarily translate into being able to do as well as their parents. Like millennials of other groups, African American millennials make less money, have less free time, and have minority status stress—a combination offered as an explanation for why depression is on the rise for this group (Villines, 2020).

Some of Bi'lal's actions are reflective of someone who is in the later stages of emerging adulthood and entering early adulthood. For example, he has committed to Mystic as his only companion. Additionally, while Bi'lal is unsure about what he wants to do professionally, he has made a commitment to his community by volunteering with the boys in the mentoring group and teaching them about African drumming. His commitment to therapy is also important. Initially, he entered therapy because he was motivated to minimize the repercussions of the domestic battery arrest. Now he is interested in finding better ways of problem-solving with Mystic. He is also very concerned about helping Mystic repair her relationship with her mother. In this way, Bi'lal is placing community and family as a priority.

Bi'lal's work with the boys in the mentoring group is also important to his own development. As a mentor to the boys, he is assuming the role of otherfather. Being able to assume the role of otherfathers is culturally very important for African American men, especially those in the early adulthood years. Bi'lal can use his personal trials and struggles to inform and support the boys he mentors. Through the otherfathering role, there is both role-modeling and accountability around the expected behaviors and responsibilities of men for themselves and their families and communities. Additionally, having the opportunity to connect with other men who are successful in their professional, service, and family lives gives him access to multiple blueprints he can use as a reference point as he customizes his own idea of successful adulthood.

Bi'lal frequently suggests he believes the world is out to get him and he often remarks that he doesn't know if he will live to see 30. Black males are almost 8 times as likely to have someone close to them murdered than White males (Singletary, 2020). Bi'lal grew up with three other friends who were like brothers to him. He is the only one of the four living freely, but he feels vulnerable all the time. He is very angry with Mystic's friend who called the police, feeling that Mystic's friend knew that he could have potentially lost his life at the hands of the police. Exposure to traumatic events can have a long-term impact on a person depending on the level of exposure to the trauma and the protective factors, like family support and stability in relationships and resources, that might exist as mediators to the impact of trauma (Singletary, 2020).

As Therapist James learns more about Bi'lal's cumulative trauma, he has a clearer understanding of Bi'lal's irritability and aggression. Therapist James is supporting Bi'lal in unpacking his feelings and his fears and, as they continue their work together, he will focus on identifying new ways to manage fear, vulnerability, and frustration. However, he is laying the foundation by reinforcing Bi'lal's strengths and introducing him to the idea of getting support or otherfathering for himself.

SESSION EXCERPT

Therapist James: Tell me about your volunteer work mentoring the young boys. How did that come about?

Bi'lal: I know this guy who was doing it and he suggested that I come with them to check it out, and I think.... Well I've lost a few friends to the streets—three actually. They were like brothers to me. Two of them were killed. One while he was playing basketball over a pick-up game and the other one was shot when someone thought he robbed a convenience store. The other one is in prison with a 20-year sentence. I'm really the only one left. Some days, I don't know why I made it and some days I just feel that my number hasn't come up yet.

Therapist James: So are you helping the boys you mentor or are they helping you?

Bi'lal: I guess a little of both. I don't want to die. It's just hard to think I'm going to live long with the world being the way it is for Black men. But while I'm here I want to help some kids if I can. My friends and I only had the streets. We all wanted to go to college, but we were still in the streets. There's a lot in this world we didn't know about. There were a lot of things we didn't know Black people did.

Therapist James: What do you mean?

Bi'lal: Well, we didn't know to dream about traveling all over the world. We didn't know that we could do some of the things like African drumming. We didn't go to the arts festivals or things like that. We knew basketball and some music like hip-hop and (laughs) maybe gospel when I was at my grandma's, but the things I've learned about have opened up a whole new world for me.

Therapist James: So you want to give that to these boys?

Bi'lal: Yeah. It's important that they know the world is bigger.

Therapist James: How are they helping you?

Bi'lal: That's funny. I've been thinking about that a lot. One of the kids told me that he really looked up to me. I'm not sure anyone ever told me that before. This job thing did not go like I thought it would when I went to college. But, when I'm with the kids, I feel like I'm using my education and it feels really good to share what I know with someone else.

Therapist James: It sounds like even though you haven't been able to get going with your professional goals in the way that you planned, you have found another way to use what you've learned and you've found a way to use it to benefit others.

Bi'lal: Yeah, they make me feel like a grown-up and what they think about me matters. That's why this whole thing is messed up. I don't want to disappoint them.

Therapist James: How about the other men who are mentors? Have you talked with any of them about what you have going on?

Bi'lal: Not a lot, because, you know, I was worried that they may not want me to be a part of the group. Plus, it feels like it makes me stand out even more.

Therapist James: Tell me more about standing out.

Bi'lal: I mean some of these guys are doing their thing—lawyers, doctors, judges.... Sometimes I don't feel that I measure up; like I'm the only one not doing big things. But I'm learning a lot from them and it's kind of making me hopeful about what I can do as a Black man. Like, for the first time, I'm thinking that there really might be something to this music thing.

Therapist James: Well, it seems that your friend who suggested you join the group had respect for what you are doing but tell me about your ideas about music. You think you want to be a musician full time?

Bi'lal: Well not exactly. But there's some real talent in this group I play with. Sometimes, I feel that I'm just tagging along. But in this area, they are in high demand and I think we could tap into a market in other cities this size and do well, especially at the festivals. I've been thinking that I might be able to use my business degree to do some marketing for them and possibly manage them. It would be a small operation, at first.

Therapist James: It definitely sounds like being around this group of men, even if you do feel that your accomplishments don't yet measure up to theirs, has given you some ideas about how to direct your own career.

Bi'lal: I mean if I don't bet on myself, who else will?

Therapist James: How does it feel to start to see a place where you can make things happen for yourself?

Bi'lal: It feels good. It feels new, too. I think about it a lot and I talked to the group. They're all in. One of the guys told me, if I could travel the world on the hustle I have now, he believed I could make anything happen.

Therapist James: Sounds like you are on your way to being the next Matthew Knowles. Bi'lal, you get really excited when you talk about this. Does this all make you more optimistic about your future?

Bi'lal: In a lot of ways, yeah. But there are still fears there. You know, I thought I was kind of aging out of the stuff that happened to my friends like going to jail or getting killed for no reason. But then, you know, George Floyd was killed and a few weeks later I was arrested for the first time in my life.

Therapist James: (Nods.) I get you. George Floyd was only 1 year younger than I am. I've thought about that a lot. You do start to believe that maybe you age out of some of the things that Black men experience in this society. So how did you deal with that revived sense of vulnerability about your life as a Black man?

Bi'lal: I don't know. I don't know if I did deal with it. I mean it wasn't new, not really, but the timing of it. I was not driving as much and the food truck had completely shut down. So my cash was dwindling every day. Mystic and I had already committed to moving in together and I wasn't sure that I was going to be able to pull my weight. Plus, I wasn't sure when I would ever get the marketing and managing thing going. It felt like so much and I was feeling like I was just really getting my feet wet with mapping out a plan for my life.

Therapist James: How did these feelings or uncertainty about your financial future and the situation you were seeing with Black people and the police impact you on the night of the incident where you were arrested?

Bi'lal: Yeah….

Therapist James: (Says nothing but waits.)

Bi'lal: (Laughs.) It's not funny, the situation I mean. But I guess you're getting me thinking. I didn't want to feel vulnerable, as you say, especially not with Mystic. I mean she's taking a chance with me because I haven't done her right in places and her mom knows it. I felt like she was trying to make me be what she wanted me to be at that moment. Even though I was trying, I just couldn't give her what she needed right then. I didn't know how to tell her that her feelings were important, but I needed to get with my boys because I was feeling things I didn't know how to talk about with her. I didn't think she would understand. She just kept pushing and I was getting angrier because she was all wrong about why I wanted to get away.

Therapist James: How did it feel to want to escape that situation and feel hemmed in. (Bi'lal doesn't speak for several moments. He is obviously a little overwhelmed and Therapist James looks down at his notes.)

Bi'lal: I honestly felt like I couldn't breathe and I just wanted to get out of that room.

CONTEXTUAL FACTORS: EARLY ADULTHOOD

One of the ways we can understand early adulthood is by contrasting the tasks of emerging adulthood with the developmental tasks of early adulthood. While emerging adulthood is focused on exploration before commitment, early adulthood is really marked by significant commitment and responsibility, most likely predicated by the relationships one assumes personally. It is marked by a time when people fully establish themselves as members of a community, find ways to make significant contributions in the world of work, in their families, and in their communities. It is also a time marked by contributing to the development of others. While this may start in the person's own home, it could also be extended to other people, as well. As Bi'lal starts to leave emerging adulthood, we find that he is finding more ways to use his drumming and connection to musicians to generate income and he is thinking about ways he can contribute to others at the center.

The context of African American men is very important to understanding their developmental task (Table 8.1). One critical task of this time is learning optimal ways of managing stress. The context of discrimination, environmental stressors, and economic hardship causes significant psychological stress. This psychological stress can have an impact on an individual's physical health and particularly contribute to heart disease, the onset of type 2 diabetes, and high blood pressure (Barr et al., 2018).

We see that Bi'lal's responses to stress most assuredly impact his relationship with Mystic, but there are other contextual factors at play in this relationship as well, not the least of which is the experience of African American women and men in romantic relationships with each other and the contextual factors that impact their individual and interpersonal development. Bi'lal has more dating options than Mystic, because in their age group, there are about 100 dating African American women to 84 dating African American men. Previous studies suggest that this results in a power imbalance between African American men and African American women (Simons et al., 2021). Bi'lal acknowledges that he has not complied with the expectation of monogamy in the relationship and he will share that he has been taught that he should sow his proverbial oats. Bi'lal, however, is not an island and the context of his world is met with the context of Mystic's.

The Context of African American Women and Heterosexual Partnerships

In the United States, African American women marry later with a median age of first marriage being 30 years, but many do not marry at all. Ninety percent of White women and 80% of Hispanic women have been married at least once by the age of 40, but less than 70% of African American women had been married by the age of 40 (Raley et al., 2015). This pattern started to emerge in the 1960s, a time which also saw the increase in the numbers of people generally who were continuing to live at home and an increase in the pursuit of higher education (Arnett, 2020). In comparison to White women who have ever married of whom 60% are likely to be married in their 40s, only 45% of African American women who have married once are likely to be married in their 40s (Raley et al., 2015).

There is speculation that this change is because of the changing ideas about family dynamics (Simons et al., 2021). However, the state of African American men contributes greatly to the likelihood of marriage for African American women who are less likely than any other group to marry outside of their racial or ethnic group (Baars, 2009). By contrast, African American men are more likely to marry interracially and the African American men who marry interracially are usually well educated with higher levels of

Table 8.1 Cultural and Contextual Identity Development Models for Emerging and Early Adulthood

THEORY	THEORIST	MAJOR CONCEPTS
Theory of Emerging Adulthood	Arnett	• Transitional time between 18 to 25 • Allows for variability for age range by cultural and social experiences • Distinct from adolescence and early adulthood • Marked by exploration and low commitment to relationships, career, living arrangements, and other adult roles
Model of Ethnic Identity Development	Phinney	• Describes the degree to which one develops a sense of affiliation and identification with one's ethnic group • Includes four identity statuses: diffused, foreclosed, moratorium, and achieved • Each status is defined by the degree to which an individual has engaged in exploration and commitment to identity
Black Male Moral Development	Wood and Hilton	• Examines how Black male identity is influenced by Black culture • Focused on connectedness and responsibility; focused on justice and care • Describes moral development occurring throughout the lifespan • Multidimensional, not linear • Includes five stages: moral externality, moral experiment, moral consequence, moral negotiation, moral internality • Individuals move from an individualistic orientation to socially conscious orientation • Morality is influenced by gender roles and racial identity development

income (Baars, 2009). A decrease in the availability of marriageable African American men, a fact mediated by high mortality rates and incarceration and institutionalized racism, is a contextual dynamic in early adulthood for African American heterosexual women. Bi'lal, as an educated African American man, has more opportunities for potential mates than Mystic. However, his opportunities are not as great as someone who is more gainfully employed. We have included a discussion about moral development in this chapter, because in the context of relationships between heterosexual African American couples, moral development in the context of social realities contribute greatly to the success of these relationships.

Black Male Moral Development Model

In the next chapter, we focus on moral development, but to delve into the socio-cultural implications for Bi'lal's development, we examine the context that impacts Bi'lal's moral development here. Wood and Hilton (2013) proposed the Black Male Moral Development model to explore how a Black male's identity is influenced by the collectivist nature of Black culture which is focused on connectedness and responsibility to the community, as well as justice and care. Wood and Hilton (2013) assert that considerations of moral development for Black males must account for the intersection of multiple identities in someone with agency in their moral decision-making. Wood and Hilton (2013) created a non-linear development model to accommodate multiple identities of African American men. Wood and Hilton (2013) identified five stages of morality: moral externality, moral experiment, moral consequence, moral negotiation, and moral internality. In the following excerpt from a therapy session, we see that Bi'lal is starting to consider the consequences of his behavior on his relationship with Mystic and he is deciding to act in ways that are not stereotypically ascribed to African American males. Bi'lal's behavior seems most reflective of the moral consequence stage where he is adjusting his perspective about what it means to be Black and male and re-evaluating the choices he made in the past (Wood & Hilton, 2013).

SESSION EXCERPT

Therapist James: Bi'lal, why the change in your attitude about monogamy in your relationship with Mystic?

Bi'lal: I am not sure if my attitude changed. I mean, I always thought that it was right to be monogamous in my relationship with her once we agreed on it. I guess, I was just doing what I could do?

Therapist James: What does that mean: What you could do?

Bi'lal: It's not like I was out there like that. But I did deal with other women and they knew about Mystic. Nobody was catching feelings or anything, at least I don't think they were. We were just having a good time and I was thinking that I probably would settle down at some point, so why not have fun now?

Therapist James: So did it feel like you were having fun?

Bi'lal: Yeah, sometimes it was fun. But it was never the same with them as it was with Mystic. It was carefree, but those other women were never like my girl. That's Mystic. It just kind of felt like that was what I was supposed to do.

Therapist James: Are you saying that you felt you were supposed to be involved with other women when you and Mystic had an agreement that you were in a monogamous relationship?

Bi'lal: Yeah. I guess.

Therapist James: How did you learn that?

Bi'lal: I don't guess anybody close to me said it, but you know I guess the old heads and, my boys, you know. I guess that's what I heard from them. Have your fun while you're young. Have your fun while you can.

Therapist James: And where did Mystic's feelings come in in the face of what these other people expected of you?

Bi'lal: I definitely didn't want to hurt Mystic and I didn't want to lose her. I never want to lose her. But she was hurt. She was really hurt.

Therapist James: So that's when you stopped seeing the other women? When you found out you were hurting Mystic?

Bi'lal: No. Not at first.

Therapist James: What was it about what the older men and your friends said that made it worth risking Mystic?

Bi'lal: I guess ... I guess it felt like they were telling me I was supposed to cheat. I felt like they were saying those are the things a man is supposed to do.

Therapist James: Did it feel right or good to you?

Bi'lal: I started to see what she really meant to me and I was feeling empty with the other women. I was also feeling that I didn't have to listen to those other men.

Therapist James: I think it's good that you are starting to decide for yourself the price you want to pay for your decisions. At every turn, you have to do what you think you should be doing and think about how it impacts the people who matter to you.

The next stage that could be used to describe Bi'lal's moral development is the moral negotiation stage. In this stage the person starts to consider ways of being that have been previously rejected, even if these new considerations are not aligned with previously held ideas about what was either Black or masculine behavior. For example, while Bi'lal has an aversion to therapy and talking to someone about his problems, he is not only participating in individual therapy, but also starting to believe that therapy might be a useful resource for him and Mystic in their relationship.

STUDENT REFLECTION

If you were Bi'lal's therapist, what strengths would you bring to the therapeutic environment? What would be some of your limitations in working with Bi'lal? How will you compensate for those limitations?

CLIENTS IN EMERGING AND EARLY ADULTHOOD: CLINICAL CONSIDERATIONS

There are many African American men with untreated mental health concerns, concerns that often are the result of systemic and systematic oppression (Stare & Fernando, 2019). Additionally, many of these men are in communities where there is not adequate access to the mental health support they need. Adding to that the mistrust and concerns about mistreatment from mental health providers, there are significant barriers to African American men getting mental health treatment or support when they need it. Stare and Fernando (2019) examined the mental health treatment of Black men ages 18 to 41 who were participating as mandated by mental health courts. Concerned that therapeutic interventions were skewed significantly toward medication, they wanted to better understand their participants' experiences. Through their interviews with study participants, the researchers were able to identify treatment factors, cognitive dissonance, and treatment barriers.

The participants in the study reported internal growth, relational growth, and behavioral growth because of participation in the mental health court and they indicated that their perceptions and attitudes shifted, and they were receptive to the information they garnered through the program. This was like Bi'lal's experience. While he was distrustful of going to therapy, his incentive was that itherapy might be favorable for him when he did go to court to have his case heard, but the experience with his therapist opened him up to the possibility of entering couple's therapy with Mystic. One experience of the therapeutic process for the participants in the Stare and Fernando (2019) study was the normalization of the participants' experiences and the stigma removal. Some participants indicated that working with the therapists in the program gave them a sense of relief. They also reported increased self-esteem and confidence in how they related to others.

Additionally, the participants reported experiencing relational growth with their providers and their peers. Critical to their experience was the perception of racial equality and understanding. Participants also reported behavioral growth as evidenced by greater personal awareness and self-control.

The participants in this study also experienced cognitive dissonance. For example, the participants reported being distrustful of the criminal justice system and therapists, but found that their experience was positive and challenged their previously held beliefs. While some reported having positive experiences, they also indicated that it did not change their attitudes about the criminal justice system or therapists overall. They indicated that they were still reserving some distrust. The participants also acknowledged that the medications they were taking were helpful for regulating mood, but they were not happy with having to take the medications (Stare & Fernando, 2019).

The researchers also identified treatment barriers that were categorized by two themes: factors of marginalization and interpersonal barriers. The participants in the Stare and Fernando (2016) study described experiences of racism and oppression by agents of institutions like law enforcement; stigmatization around their mental health within the Black community; and experiences of poverty and basic distrust of systems.

Therapist James

It was important to introduce Therapist James to this chapter because as an African American man, he is familiar with some of the experiences Bi'lal has had regarding career development, socialization around romantic relationships, and racism, in particular. Unfortunately, the number of African American male helpers is not very large (Harper et al., 2009). In 2013, it was reported that only 5.3% of the psychology workforce was Black or African American, but we do not know how many of those are male (American Psychological Association Center for Workforce Studies, 2015). It is estimated that 7% of all licensed social workers are African American, but there is no information about the percentage of male African American social workers (Morris-Compton, 2007). This means that other helpers need to be prepared to work with clients like Bi'lal.

Connecting With Client

From his first meeting with Bi'lal, there were a few things that are notable, particularly in light of the concerns Bi'lal has. The first thing was that he addressed Bi'lal as "Mister Bi'lal W." and asked Bi'lal's permission to call him by his first name. This demonstrates respect for Bi'lal and it establishes that Therapist James is recognizing Bi'lal as an adult. This is also establishing an egalitarian relationship between the two.

Therapist James also acknowledges Bi'lal's name, which is not common among dominant groups in America, but is not uncommon in the African American community. By acknowledging the meaning of Bi'lal's name, Therapist James is once again demonstrating respect and high expectations for Bi'lal. This is important in a society where pervasive stereotypes lead to low expectations of African American males.

A therapist working with Bi'lal should try to give Bi'lal an opportunity to describe his lived experience and talk about the way those experiences may cause him stress. Anyone working with Bi'lal should also acknowledge his intersecting identities, particularly as they relate to being an African American person, a man, an emerging or early adult, a partner, community member, and a person who is trying to define who he is with regard to work. These different roles are all interrelated and should not be dealt with separately, because doing so is a disservice to the African American male in the therapeutic experience (Hannon & Vereen, 2016). As Bi'lal talks about feeling vulnerable after George Floyd was killed, Therapist James shares his own feelings about the events and his ability to relate to Bi'lal's expectations that he would be less vulnerable to violence as he got older. His expression of empathy around this helped establish the feelings as normal. Therapist James was also able to probe to see how this race-related stress and the crisis around additional adult responsibility in the face of reduced income because of COVID-19 manifested the night that he was arrested for domestic battery.

Therapist James sought to discover how Bi'lal made meaning of his experience as a role model to the African American boys and how his legal situation impacted identity. Bi'lal expresses doubt that his accomplishments are as significant as others who are mentoring the boys. In his work with Bi'lal, Therapist James focuses on the importance of the work Bi'lal is doing with the boys, but he also validates that someone else, his friend who recommended the program to him, saw him as valuable to the program.

Bi'lal's experience with the mentoring group, especially what he is learning as he works with the mentoring group, is important because African American men are more likely to use informal support than they are to use professional services (Woodward et al., 2011). In evaluating Bi'lal's resources, the therapist should acknowledge his work with the mentoring group as a significant source of support. Bi'lal is learning from the men in the mentoring group and they are making him feel that he may be able to take control of his own career.

While not explicitly stated in the interactions described here, Therapist James is aware that there are influences on Bi'lal's career opportunities over which he has no control. For example, with two degrees, there might be the expectation that Bi'lal could readily be gainfully employed. However, even equipped with those degrees, Bi'lal's opportunities are influenced by racist systems, marginalization with regard to access to opportunities, and social misconceptions about who he is and what he can do (Vereen et al., 2017). As Bi'lal expresses an interest in managing the scheduling and marketing for the music group, Therapist James makes a comparison between him and Matthew Knowles, the famed manager of the successful music group Destiny's Child. This comparison to Bi'lal and this notable African American man is intended to be inspirational to him and help him see the possibilities for an African American man. Hopefully, this will contribute to Bi'lal's development and sense of self-efficacy.

It is important that the helping professional working with Bi'lal operates within a strengths-based approach (Hannon & Vereen, 2016). For example, in addition to the fact that Bi'lal is working with the group mentoring African American boys, he has completed two degrees, he is employed, he continues to develop his skills with African drumming and is finding ways to share that with others. Additionally, in the context of American society, another strength is that until now, Bi'lal has never been arrested and has no criminal history. In doing this, the helping professional is acknowledging the context of Bi'lal's life and acknowledging his ability to make progress in that context of socially constructed barriers (Hannon & Vereen, 2016). Furthermore, he wants to be trustworthy and reliable for the female role models in his life, and he speaks of loved ones with care and concern, which along with his service to the young boys in his community, shows his gift of empathy and engagement in the greater good.

Meaning of Life

In the case of Bi'lal, we have an example of multiple aspects of identity developing. He is trying to identify the meaning of life. Steger et al. (2006) define the meaning of life as the "sense made of, and significance felt regarding, the nature of one's being and existence" (2006, p. 81). He is trying to determine who he is regarding his career. He is also questioning who he has been in his relationship. He is developing a better understanding of himself in relationship to Mystic and is examining how his behavior impacts her relationships with people who matter to her. Additionally, he is trying to understand that he is still vulnerable to the violence of racism and he is looking for a way to contribute to others.

Bi'lal is at a transitional stage in life where he is questioning old patterns of behavior and ways of being and he is trying to find more purpose or understand the meaning of life. However, he may be limited in his ability to engage in this exploration without assistance, and while he was not trusting of a therapist initially, he is starting to recognize that this may be an opportunity for him. Therapist James established an egalitarian relationship with Bi'lal where it is clear that Bi'lal will be responsible for the outcome of the process. He also demonstrated respect for and acknowledgment of who Bi'lal is culturally. As they continue to work together, Therapist James will work to help Bi'lal build confidence and help him see that he already has strengths. Therapist James taps into the vulnerabilities James has as an African American man and helps him see how that identity intersects with his career identity and his identity as a partner.

PERSPECTIVES FROM THE FIELD: PODCAST

Access this podcast at http://connect.springerpub.com/content/book/978-0-8261-8279-1/part/part02/chapter/ch08

We invited two clinicians to explore Bi'lal's contextual and cultural strengths to support him in the therapeutic environment. In addition, they speak to the impact of trauma common to African American men in emerging and young adulthood and share how they are responding to the trauma of clients like Bi'lal. Both guests use their knowledge of African American traditions and cultural context as tools to encourage and support clients like Bi'lal. These two men prompt us to further explore how history, family, and community shape identity and provide insight to how they have worked with clients like Bi'lal in their clinical practice.

Dr. Brian Ragsdale is a licensed clinical psychologist in the State of Illinois and is Director of Student Success in the Office of Academic Affairs at Walden University. For the past 25 years, his research, teaching, and clinical work have examined identity development, the impact of structural racism, and family developmental concerns.

Dr. Emmett R. Roberts, Jr., is a licensed clinical social worker as well as a licensed alcohol and drug counselor who has the position of a Core Faculty member of the Barbara Solomon School of Social Work. Dr. Roberts has over 25 years of experience in working with adolescent males, primarily those of color, in making the successful transition to adulthood.

SUMMARY

This is the first chapter focused on adult development in the lifespan. You were introduced to the case of Bi'lal as a vehicle to understanding the cultural and contextual implications for development during emerging and early adulthood. As you will see in the next chapter, Bi'lal's development is not a diversion from what you will see of other theories about development, but his cultural identity and the context in which he lives are both important mediators for his development. We also make the case that it is sometimes difficult to make the distinction between the cultural and the contextual, because over time, what appears to be cultural is a response to prolonged context.

Including the excerpts from his work with Therapist James and the Perspectives From the Field were attempts to familiarize you with how practitioners apply the knowledge described in this and other chapters about lifespan development. In the next chapter, you will learn a little more about Mystic, but we are not abandoning Bi'lal. Where relevant, we will highlight how the next theorists amplify our understanding of Bi'lal. If you have not done so already, go back to the sidebars to give serious consideration to how you will practice in a way that is inclusive of culture and context.

REFERENCES

American Psychological Association Center for Workforce Studies. (2015, July). *Demographics of the U.S. psychology workforce.* https://www.apa.org/workforce/publications/13-demographics#:~:text=Racial%2Fethnic%20minority%20groups%2C%20including,16.4%20percent%20of%20active%20psychologists.&text=F

Amrani, I. (2019). Is your name holding you back? *Raconteur.* https://www.raconteur.net/hr/diversity-inclusion/ethnic-name-bias/gure%206

Annie E. Casey Foundation. (2020). *Kids count data center.* https://datacenter.kidscount.org/data/tables/107-children-in-single-parent-families-by-race#detailed/1/any/false/37,871,870,573,869,36,868,867,133,38/10,11,9,12,1,185,13/432,431

Arnett, J. J. (2000). Emerging adulthood. A theory of development from the late teens through the twenties. *The American Psychologist, 55*(5), 469–480. https://doi.org/10.1037/0003-066X.55.5.469

Arnett, J. J. (2003). Conceptions of the transition to adulthood among emerging adults in American ethnic groups. *New Directions for Child and Adolescent Development, 100,* 63–75. https://doi.org/10.1002/cd.75

Arnett, J. J. (2006). Emerging adulthood: Understanding the new way of coming of age. In J. J. Arnett & J. L. Tanner (Eds.), *Emerging adulthood in America: Coming of age in the 21st century* (pp. 3–19). American Psychological Association.

Arnett, J. J. (2012). New horizons in research on emerging and young adulthood. In A. Booth, S. L. Brown, N. S. Landale, W. D. Manning, & S. M. McHale (Eds.), *Early adulthood in a family context. National Symposium on Family Issues* (Vol. 2, pp. 221–265). Springer.

Arnett, J. J. (2020, October 13). *Yes, more and more young adults are living with their parents-but is that necessarily bad.* The Conversation US, Inc. https://theconversation.com/yes-more-and-more-young-adults-are-living-with-their-parents-but-is-that-necessarily-bad-146979

Arnett, J. J., & Brody, G. H. (2008). A fraught passage: The identity challenges of African American emerging adults. *Human Development, 51*(5–6), 291–293. https://doi.org/10.1159/000170891

Baars, M. (2009). Marriage in Black and White: Women's support for law against interracial marriage. *Intersections, 10*(1), 219–238.

Bae, D., & Kogan, S. M. (2020). Romantic relationship trajectories among young African American men: The influence of adverse life contexts. *Journal of Family Psychology, 34*(6), 687–697. https://doi.org/10.1037/fam0000645

Barr, A. B., Simons, L. G., Simons, R. L., Beach, S. R. H., & Philibert, R. A. (2018). Sharing the burden of the transition to adulthood: African American young adults' transition challenges and their mothers' health risk. *American Sociological Review, 83*(1), 143–172. https://doi.org/10.1177/0003122417751442

Bell-Tolliver, L., & Wilkerson, P. (2011). The use of spirituality and kinship as contributors to successful therapy outcomes with African American families. *Journal of Religion & Spirituality in Social Work: Social Thought, 30*(1), 48–70. https://doi.org/10.1080/15426432.2011.542723

Brooms, D. R. (2017). Black Otherfathering in the Educational Experiences of Black Males in a Single-Sex Urban High School. *Teachers College Record, 119*(11), 1–46. https://doi.org/10.1177/016146811711901102

Bush, L. (2004). How Black mothers participate in the development of manhood and masculinity: What do we know about Black mothers and their sons? *The Journal of Negro Education, 73*(4), 381. https://doi.org/10.2307/4129623

Creamer, J., Shrider, E., & Edwards, A. (2020, September 15). *More young adults lived with their parents in 2019.* U. S. Department of Commerce. https://www.census.gov/library/stories/2020/09/more-young-adults-lived-with-their-parents-in-2019.html#:~:text=Estimated%2017.8%25%20of%20Adults%20Ages,Their%20Parents'%20Household%20Last%20Year&text=A%20Pew%20Research%20Center%20report,their%20parents%20in%20March%202020

DeGruy, J. (2005). *Post traumatic slave syndrome: America's legacy of enduring injury and healing.* Uptone Press.

Eriksson, P. L., Wängqvist, M., Carlsson, J., & Frisén, A. (2020). Identity development in early adulthood. *Developmental Psychology, 56*(10), 1968–1983. https://doi.org/10.1037/dev0001093

Fry, R., Pasel, J. S., & Cohn, D. (2020). A majority of young adults in the U.S. live with their parents for the first time since the Great Depression. *Pew Research Center.* https://www.pewresearch.org/fact-tank/2020/09/04/a-majority-of-young-adults-in-the-u-s-live-with-their-parents-for-the-first-time-since-the-great-depression

Gupta, S. (2021, February). Racial trauma and your health. *GoodRx, Inc.* https://www.goodrx.com/blog/how-racial-trauma-affects-mental-health

Hannon, M. D., & Vereen, L. G. (2016). Irreducibility of Black male clients: Considerations for culturally competent counseling. *The Journal of Humanistic Counseling, 55*(3), 234–245. https://doi.org/10.1002/johc.12036

Harper, F. D., Terry, L. M., & Twiggs, R. (2009). Counseling strategies with Black boys and Black men: Implications for policy. *Journal of Negro Education, 78*(3), 216–232.

Harris, A., & Amutah-Onukagha, N. (2019). Under the radar: Strategies used by Black mothers to prepare their sons for potential police interactions. *Journal of Black Psychology, 45*(6–7), 439–453. https://doi.org/10.1177/0095798419887069

Holzer, H. J. (2021, March 1). *Why are employment rates so low among Black men?*. The Brookings Institution. https://www.brookings.edu/research/why-are-employment-rates-so-low-among-black-men

Joseph, N. T., Peterson, L. M., Gordon, H., & Kamarck, T. W. (2020). The double burden of racial discrimination in daily-life moments: Increases in negative emotions and depletion of psychosocial resources among emerging adult African Americans. *Cultural Diversity & Ethnic Minority Psychology, 27*(2), 234–244. https://doi.org/10.1037/cdp0000337

Lewis, J. A., Raque-Bogdan, T. L., Lee, S., & Rao, M. A. (2018). Examining the role of ethnic identity and meaning in life on career decision-making self-efficacy. *Journal of Career Development, 45*(1), 68–82. https://doi.org/10.1177/0894845317696803

McCallum, C. M. (2016). "Mom made me do it": The role of family in African Americans' decisions to enroll in doctoral education. *Journal of Diversity in Higher Education, 9*(1), 50–63. https://doi.org/10.1037/a0039158

McClain, S., Beasley, S. T., Jones, B., Awosogba, O., Jackson, S., & Cokley, K. (2016). An Examination of the Impact of Racial and Ethnic Identity, Impostor Feelings, and Minority Status Stress on the Mental Health of Black College Students. *Journal of Multicultural Counseling and Development, 44*(2), 101–117. https://doi.org/10.1002/jmcd.12040

Morris-Compton, D. J. (2007). Wanted: African American men in social work. *Social Work Today, 7*(1), 24.

Phinney, J. S. (2006). Ethnic identity exploration in emerging adulthood. In *Emerging adults in America: Coming of age in the 21st century* (pp. 117–134). American Psychological Association. https://doi.org/10.1037/11381-000

Pierce, J. L. (2014). Why teaching about race as a social construct still matters. *Sociological Forum, 29*(1), 259–264. https://doi.org/10.1111/socf.12079

Raley, R. K., Sweeney, M. M., & Wondra, D. (2015). The growing racial and ethnic divide in U.S. marriage patterns. *The Future of Children, 25*(2), 89–109. https://doi.org/10.1353/foc.2015.0014

Rollins, V. B., & Valdez, J. N. (2006). Perceived racism and career self-efficacy in African American adolescents. *Journal of Black Psychology, 32*(2), 176–198. https://doi.org/10.1177/0095798406287109

Seligson, H. (2019, March 2). The new 30-something: Have you or haven't you cut the financial cord with your family? *New York Times.* https://www.nytimes.com/2019/03/02/style/financial-independence-30s.html

Sellers, R. M., Smith, M. A., Shelton, J. N., Rowley, S. A. J., & Chavous, T. M. (1998). Multidimensional model of racial identity: a reconceptualization of African American racial identity. *Personality and Social Psychology Review, 2*(1), 18–39. https://doi.org/10.1207/s15327957pspr0201_2

Simon, R. W., & Barrett, A. E. (2010). Nonmarital romantic relationships and mental health in early adulthood: Does the association differ for women and men? *Journal of Health and Social Behavior, 51*(2), 168–182. https://doi.org/10.1177/0022146510372343

Simons, L. G., Sutton, T. E., Landor, A. M., Barr, A. B., Bryant, C. M., & Granberg, E. M. (2021). Gender differences in the dating experiences of African American young adults: The challenge of forming romantic relationships within the context of power imbalance. *Youth & Society, 53*(1), 3–25. https://doi.org/10.1177/0044118X19828097

Singletary, G. (2020). Beyond PTSD: Black male fragility in the context of trauma. *Journal of Aggression, Maltreatment & Trauma, 29*(5), 517–536. https://doi.org/10.1080/10926771.2019.1600091

Smedley, B. D., Myers, H. F., & Harrell, S. P. (1993). Minority-status stresses and the college adjustment of ethnic minority freshmen. *The Journal of Higher Education, 64*(4), 434. https://doi.org/10.2307/2960051

Stare, B. G., & Fernando, D. M. (2019). Black American men's treatment experiences in mental health court: A phenomenological analysis. *Journal of Addictions & Offender Counseling, 40*(1), 17–35. https://doi.org/10.1002/jaoc.12054

Steger, M. F., Frazier, P., Oishi, S., Kaler, M., Frazier, P. A., & Kaler, M. E. (2006). Meaning in Life Questionnaire. *Journal of Consulting and Clinical Psychology, 74*(5), 859–869.

Tyuse, S. W., & Linhorst, D. M. (2005). Drug courts and mental health courts: Implications for social work. *Health & Social Work, 30*(3), 233–240. https://doi.org/10.1093/hsw/30.3.233

Vereen, L. G., Wines, L. A., Lemberger-truelove, T., Hannon, M. D., Howard, N., & Burt, I. (2017). Black existentialism: Extending the discourse on meaning and existence. *The Journal of Humanistic Counseling, 56*(1), 72–84. https://doi.org/10.1002/johc.12045

Villines, Z. (2020, July). What to know about depression in Black communities? *Medical News Today*. https://www.medicalnewstoday.com/articles/black-depression#treatment

Warnke, A. (2020). Mental health courts: The silver bullet made of rubber. *Kansas Journal of Law & Public Policy, 29*(2), 256–276.

Wilson, N. N., Sailor, J. L., Calix, S. I., & Carney, W. (2017). Leaving home for African Americans in the emerging adulthood era: A phenomenological study. *The Qualitative Report, 22*(2), 527–541. https://doi.org/10.46743/2160-3715/2017.2517

Womack, S. (2016). I know I can't: The negative effects of post traumatic slave syndrome on the well-being of African American college students. *Vermont Connection, 37*, 119–125.

Wood, L. J., & Hilton, A. A. (2013). Moral Choices: Towards a conceptual model of Black male moral development (BMMD). *Western Journal of Black Studies, 37*(1), 14–27.

Woodward, A. T., Taylor, R. J., & Chatters, L. M. (2011). Use of professional and informal support by Black men with mental disorders. *Research on Social Work Practice, 21*(3), 328–336. https://doi.org/10.1177/1049731510388668

Worrell, F. C. (2008). Nigrescence attitudes in adolescence, emerging adulthood, and adulthood. *Journal of Black Psychology, 34*(2), 156–178. https://doi.org/10.1177/0095798408315118

CHAPTER 9

Developmental Theories of Emerging Adulthood Through Early Adulthood

LEARNING OBJECTIVES

Upon completion of this chapter, students will be able to:

1. Identify various theoretical explanations of lifespan development in emerging adulthood.

2. Identify various theoretical explanations for lifespan development in early adulthood

3. Apply various models of lifespan development to respond to client presentations.

4. Identify future directions for research and understanding of people in emerging adulthood and early adulthood.

CASE STUDY 9.1: THE CASE OF MYSTIC

Mystic is a 28-year-old African American female living in the inner city. Mystic has no children and is living with her boyfriend of 3 years, Bi'lal. Prior to that, Mystic lived with her mother and her grandmother in a one-bedroom apartment. Until a year ago, Mystic was enrolled full-time as a college student with a 3.8 GPA. However, her college closed and she has not resumed her studies elsewhere. She has attempted higher education four times and changed her major at each attempt. Mystic did have non-relative roommates when she attended the first college, but she has mostly lived with her mother and her grandmother.

About 3 months ago, Mystic and Bi'lal had a verbal altercation that made Mystic feel very unsafe and she shared it with her mother and best friend, so when her best friend heard a heated argument between the two of them followed by the loud sound of something breaking, she called the police. Mystic, against the advice of her mother and her friends, decided to move in with her boyfriend. She cares deeply for him and feels that he is a much better prospect than other men she's dated. Even though the previous situation was significant and alarming, she generally feels safe with her boyfriend and feels that the relationship is a loving one.

Mystic has started a redesign wear business and is experiencing great success with this. She continues to work another full-time job but has high hopes that one day she will be able to support herself and her future family from her business. Mystic would like to have children one day, but she and Bi'lal are enjoying other aspects of their lives and have not seriously discussed adding children to their lives.

No doubt, Bi'lal and Mystic are complex individuals and that complexity influences their relationship. We cannot delve into every presenting issue for the individuals or the couple, but there are a few things that we will consider as we progress through the chapter. First, the crisis for Bi'lal and Mystic that results in them both seeking help is the situation that led to Bi'lal's arrest. The prevailing issue was that Mystic did not trust what Bi'lal was saying about where he was heading. Mystic's concern at that moment was about the relationship. Bi'lal had a series of frustrations at the time of the argument, but he was reliving trauma and started to feel suffocated by Mystic's refusal to allow him to leave the room. It could be argued that they were both reacting to trauma. Second, Mystic has had some false starts professionally, but she is still very focused on her relationship with Bi'lal, her relationship with her mother, and her desire to start a family. Bi'lal is concerned with his career primarily, and his safety as an African American man. However, he has mentally and emotionally recommitted to his relationship with Mystic. Finally, the two of them have just entered a living arrangement that could be long-term for the first time in either of their lives. As you continue to read, consider how you think the theorists described in this chapter would identify Mystic and Bi'lal's development.

INTRODUCTION TO ADULT DEVELOPMENT THEORY

In the remaining chapters, we focus on adult development theory. Adult development theory is a subset of developmental psychology (Kjellström & Stålne, 2017). This area of focus is important, because even if you have chosen to work only with children, you should get to know the adults who are nurturing, providing for, teaching, and mentoring them. The first theory of adult development was created in 1908, but the application of adult development stage theories used to inform practice, education, and workplace dynamics is a practice of the last half century (Kjellström & Stålne, 2017). Adult development theory describes development that occurs after adolescence, resulting from the interaction between the internal and external environment. Adult development is generally referred to as a sequential growth process of transitions through adulthood and how the individual makes meaning of or reasons about events. An important feature of adult development theory is that as the person matures, characteristics of earlier stages remain. Additionally, the more mature person can recall, behave, and make meaning of the reasoning of the earlier self, but the earlier self cannot reason at the level of the more mature self (Kjellström & Stålne, 2017).

While there are different theories regarding adult development, we notice patterns of development and see that as people become more mature, there is increased depth in observation, communication, decision-making, autonomy, and ability to tolerate ambiguity. However, these stages do not happen for everyone at the same time and there is no guarantee that everyone will achieve every stage of development (Kjellström & Stålne, 2017).

Well into the 20th century, the attention paid to adult development was limited or deficient in comparison to child development. The influence of Freud on Psychosocial Identity Development theory is the first reason adult identity development was ignored (Hoare, 2006). Freud and those theorists influenced by Freud felt that there was no significant development that took place in adults. The premise of Freud's theory was that psychosocial identity development ended at adulthood and his theories "adultify" children's development. In addition, Freud saw adults as the complete product of the development that occurred in childhood. Another deficiency of the adult development focus was that it was only conceptualized in a linear way, not accounting for differences in experiences, contexts, and culture. Additionally, in previous generations, the lifespan of the average adult was too short to sufficiently study adult development over a meaningful period of time and there were few opportunities to access a population of adults to study outside of college and university campuses (Hoare, 2006).

Emerging Adult and Early Adult Development Theory

The first part of this discussion about adulthood focuses on emerging adulthood and early adulthood. Often, the terms early adulthood, young adulthood, and emerging adulthood are used interchangeably to describe the time between age 18 and the mid to late 30s. These time periods will be discussed as different times in a person's life marked by different tasks, different relationships with family, different levels of exploration and commitment, and different attitudes about family, work, relationships, religion, values, and lifestyles. The term *emerging adulthood* was not coined until the end of the 20th century by Arnett (2000), even though other theorists speak to a transitional time from adolescence to adulthood: Erikson speaks to a prolonged adolescence (Arnett, 2000), and Levinson speaks to the early adult transition that takes place in a time between 17 and 25 (Levinson, 1978). Many of the theorists discussed in this chapter do not specifically define the age at which a person is at each stage of development. While it may initially feel frustrating, not having a prescribed or definite time for each stage allows the practitioner to consider that other factors like culture, socioeconomic status, parenting styles, ability, and geography, just to name a few, can influence the onset of development. It also decreases the likelihood that the practitioner would lead to the conclusion that variations in development in adulthood suggest delay or pathology.

For example, one thing that both Bi'lal and Mystic share is that there has been much change in their residential status prior to our introduction to them. They both have lived with parents or older relatives at different points in the earliest parts of their adulthood, a behavior that is indicative of emerging adulthood (Arnett, 2000), but when you consider that they are living in a large, urban community with a very high cost of living, we must consider other aspects of their development to fully understand how the theories and approaches described in this chapter might be applicable to them.

For the sake of developing an in-depth understanding of individuals in context, within an industrial society we will define emerging adulthood as those people who are 18 to 25, but it is possible that a person could be in this stage between adolescence and early adulthood until the late 20s. We will define the period of early adulthood as that time between the mid to late 20s to the late 30s, possibly early 40s. At the end of the chapter, you will be introduced to a new term called established adulthood that is used to describe the period we are referring to as early adulthood.

Reflect on your own life and your observations of your friends. What kinds of challenges do you all seem to be navigating? Are there any commonalities in the criteria for decision-making? What factors account for the differences? Write down two or three questions you would like to have answered that might explain these commonalities and differences.

There was much debate in my (Dixon-Saxon) mind about whether to use the term *established adulthood* instead of *early adulthood*. The term *early adulthood* is maintained here to acknowledge the heterogeneity of this time. While 30 to 45 could be a time of established adulthood for some people, for some groups because of sociocultural factors like racism and socioeconomic status, individuals are not established in some areas of their lives at this time (Mehta et al., 2020). We implore you to think critically about what you are reading and allow the introduction to these theorists be the beginning of your exploration of adult development. Is the information shared throughout this chapter congruent with what you have observed about adult development?

It has probably been quite interesting reflecting on the early stages of development. You may have enjoyed reflecting on your own behavior as a child or made comparisons between what you are reading and hearing with what you have observed of the children in your life. But as we continue to explore adult development, you will start to reflect on your adult experiences and those of your friends, partner(s), and even parents. As you progress through this chapter, we explore a variety of theorists who have tried to explain this time in life. This is not an exhaustive list of theorists who have studied and conceptualized how adults develop. Our charge to you is to read about these theorists through a critical lens and to seek your own answers to the questions that may not be answered about the differences in development for people who have disabilities, people who are gender non-conforming, people raised in the southern United States, people who decide not to marry, people in indigenous communities, and a whole host of other individuals who have experiences of life, family structure, access, education, culture, socioeconomic status, trauma, gender identity, career, and wellness that serve as mediators to how they develop. While all these aspects of identity influence identity and human development, it is interesting to note that there are commonalities in how most humans develop. As you become a more critical reader, practitioner, and advocate, it is important to consider developmental theory and theorists, their orientation to the world, and how they thought about, or, in some cases dismissed, large segments of society.

In this chapter, we review adult development theory as explained by Carl Jung, Erik Erikson, Daniel Levinson, and Jeffrey Arnett. We will also consider how useful each theorist is for better understanding of Bi'lal or Mystic individually and as two people intimately connected with each other trying to navigate the world.

You will also be introduced to Therapist Rasheeda. Therapist Rasheeda is a social worker at a non-profit organization that provides marriage, couples, and family counseling to people in the community where Bi'lal and Mystic live. Therapist James recommended her to Bi'lal when Bi'lal told him he thought they needed some help in moving forward as a couple. When Therapist James asked Bi'lal if he had any preferences regarding a therapist, Bi'lal said that he would prefer an African American woman.

SESSION EXCERPT 9.1

Therapist Rasheeda (After initial intake, where Therapist Rasheeda has learned a little about the status of Mystic and Bi'lal's relationship.) Why are you in this place at this time?

(Bi'lal reaches for Mystics hand and squeezes it gently.)

Mystic (Nodding at Bi'lal.) You go first. You wanted to come here.

Bi'lal: I've been seeing a therapist by myself and it's helping me. I got in some trouble and I really needed to see someone. I was hoping it would help me with my case, but now I'm understanding things about me and the world and figuring out how I might operate in it without feeling so scared and angry all the time and I realized I sometimes feel like that in our relationship. I'm not sure what Mystic feels and, sometimes, it's hard for us to communicate about the hard stuff. When I mentioned that to Therapist James, he suggested maybe we should learn how to talk about the hard stuff and figure out ways to communicate what we feel to each other. He thought we might need help learning how to work together for the life we want. He thought couples counseling could help us with that.

Therapist Rasheeda: Mystic, why are you here with Bi'lal?

Mystic: (Shrugs.) He asked me to come. I think we have stuff to work on, but all couples do. But if he thinks this could help, I'm game. I didn't know he was feeling scared and angry in our relationship. I'm interested to hear more about that. I don't know what I did to make him angry.

Therapist Rasheeda: And you, Mystic? What kinds of feelings come up for you when you think about your relationship with Bi'lal? (Mystic is quiet, but she has tears in her eyes. Therapist Rasheeda is silent and Bi'lal is rubbing Mystic's hand while he looks down at her hand.)

Mystic: Lonely.

Therapist Rasheeda: Are there things you think we might work together on here to help you feel less lonely?

Mystic: Maybe.

Therapist Rasheeda: What would you like to work on or change to make your relationship with Bi'lal better?

Mystic: I want to feel like I can be myself in our relationship and I want to figure out if we really have a future together.

Therapist Rasheeda: So you don't feel like you are yourself? You are talking about being authentic. Do you feel that being authentic will in any way impact the future you and Bi'lal will have?

Mystic: Sometimes I feel that if he knew the real me, he would be bored, and he wouldn't want to be with me. We're very different.

Therapist Rasheeda: Bi'lal, what's your perspective on this? How are your differences impacting your relationship?

Bi'lal: Well, I'm not sure what I don't know about Mystic. Hopefully, I can learn more. I want to know who she really is. I'm kind of hurt ... disappointed to think that she doesn't feel she can be who she really is with me or that she thinks I wouldn't want to be with her if she was her real self. I know that we are different. I'm way more social than she is. That's been a problem for us in the past. But I think that's minor. I think that's something we can work through. But I think that we have some of our biggest arguments when it's time to decide about things. (Looks at Mystic.) Do you agree?

Mystic: Yeah, he follows his gut and wants me to trust his gut. But he gets angry when I ask a lot of questions so that I know the details. Things need to make sense to me. He trusts his gut, but that's a lot harder for me.

Bi'lal is obviously more comfortable with therapy now than he was at the start of his time with therapist James, but Therapist Rasheeda has been able to quickly launch us into our discussion about adult development. What Mystic and Bi'lal are trying to understand is how the differences in their personalities might impact their relationship with each other. Personality is essentially the pattern of behaviors, attitudes, thinking, and feeling a person demonstrates (Randall et al., 2017). One of the first theorists to delve into understanding development beyond childhood was Carl Jung and his primary contribution to understanding adults was his notion of the mask(s) we wear, or *persona,* to cope with people and the world (Hudson, 1978).

CARL JUNG AND PERSONALITY THEORY

Carl Jung is often referred to as the father of analytic psychology and Levinson referred to Carl Jung as the "father of the modern study of adult development" (Levinson, 1978, p. 4). This is notable, because for years, Jung's work was considered too intrapsychic and abstract, not rooted in science, and mystical (Jones, 2013). Another criticism of Jung's work was that it could not be scientifically tested (Jones, 2013). Jung, however, was one of the earliest of the 20th century theorists to focus on development beyond childhood.

Jung, unlike Freud, believed there was substantial development that took place throughout the lifespan (Crain, 2003). He felt, like other humanistic theorists, that a significant part of the second part of adulthood or that time after 35 or 40 was spent finding meaning to life and being more spiritually oriented (Moraglia, 1994). Jung also diverged from Freud's focus on pathology and intrapsychic process only. Jung felt that development was also influenced by social and cultural factors. Regarding the time between 20 and 40, Jung believed that this was an in-between time where the individual was still experiencing some of the emotional upheaval of childhood while trying to navigate new adult roles like partner, parent, community member, and worker (Levinson, 1978). Jung's ideas about personality and learning continue to influence a variety of disciplines beyond psychology like business and education.

Personality

Essential to Jung's understanding of development was understanding the *psyche*. The psyche has been used to refer to both the mind and the soul (Becker, 2020) and, as conceptualized by Jung, psyche is synonymous with personality. At the root of Jung's theory is the idea of individuation, the understanding of self (Webb, 1990). According to Jung, this search for individuation does not start until mid-life when the person starts their search for meaning (Engelmann et al., 2019). Jung conceptualized personality around the conscious, the unconscious, and the collective unconscious. The conscious aspect of the personality was referred to as the ego (Engelmann et al., 2019). Jung indicated that our psyche is composed of unconscious and conscious opposites. These opposites correspond with the conscious ego, which gives the person an understanding of who the person is, or the unconscious shadow (Chappell et al., 2019). Like Freud, Jung gave most attention to the unconscious parts of the personality (Engelmann et al., 2019).

Attitude and Functions of Personality

Helson (1982) refers to Jung's theory of personality as a structural theory that does not describe any differences culturally in thinking. However, Jung felt that differences were rooted in the cognitive–affective style or the way the individual's thinking interacts with situations. Because, as Helson (1982) asserts, it is a theory about the differences in the way individuals process information and make decisions, it is useful to understand more as we further conceptualize Mystic and Bi'lal as two adults living with each other.

EXTRAVERSION AND INTROVERSION AS ATTITUDES

Foundationally, Jung believed that our differences are based on our way of processing information and how we approach decision-making (Webb, 1990). According to Jung, we each have preferences in this information processing and decision-making that predispose us to be either introverted or extroverted, sensing or intuiting, thinking or feeling, and judging or perceiving. He also believed these differences would impact our energy flow, our perceptions, judgments, and lifestyle (Webb, 1990).

Jung used opposite pairs to describe the energy flow in these four different aspects of personality (Wilde, 2011). The first way that Jung organized personality identification was around the attitudes of extraversion and introversion. Extraversion describes psychic energy flow that goes outward and introversion is used to describe psychic energy flow that goes inward (Wilde, 2011). One of these attitudes is predominant in a person's behavior (Crain, 2003). The person with the propensity toward extroversion is more likely expressive, sociable, engaging (Wilde, 2011), and highly relational (Crain, 2003). These are people who like fast-moving environments and can be impatient at times (Crain, 2003). The person more inclined to introversion is likely reserved and likely to enjoy solitary activities or in activities in smaller groups. We are disinclined here to label a person as an introvert or an extrovert, because Jung later recognized that psychic energy flow in this domain could change based on the person's role in each situation (Wilde, 2011). Based on what we know about Bi'lal and his collection of jobs, his professional interests, and his service activities, it appears that Bi'lal is someone with an extraversion attitude. Mystic favors small group activities and her design business is largely solo work. As a matter of fact, she sells her clothing at street fairs and usually asks Bi'lal to accompany her since he is the more gregarious of the two.

SENSING AND INTUITING AS FUNCTIONS

The second area of focus were the psychological functions of which there are three pairs: sensing and intuitive, thinking and feeling, and perceiving and judging. Jung theorized that perception was based on a person using either their senses or their intuition. The sensing person collects information using the senses, gathering information through the sensing organs of the body (Wilde, 2011). This person understands the world according to observable facts, and their understanding of the world is based on evidence and personal experience (Crain, 2003). The person whose perceptions are based on intuition gathers information through the unconscious (Wilde, 2011). The intuitive person focuses on meaning and possibilities and might indicate that perceptions are based on a "gut feeling" or a "sixth sense." Because of both Mystic and Bi'lal's interests in creative activities, we could assert that they are both intuitive people. Mystic observes that Bi'lal relies on his gut more heavily for decision-making.

THINKING AND FEELING AS FUNCTIONS

Jung believed that people either make judgments informed by their thinking or by their feelings. The person who is inclined to make judgments based on thinking relies on principles and objectivity to make judgments. The person making judgments informed by feelings makes judgments motivated by relational dynamics, caring, and warmth towards another (Crain, 2003).

PERCEPTION AND JUDGMENT AS FUNCTIONS

Regarding judgment, Jung felt that people made decisions informed by either their thinking based on intellect-informed conclusions (judgment) or through their subjective feelings about a situation (perception; Wilde, 2011).

Typology of Personality

From the attitude and three functions emerged eight different personality types, four of which were extraverted types and the other four introverted. Jung believed that while each person can demonstrate aspects of both extraversion and introversion, individuals would have difficulty when they encountered the opposite type. Jung believed that understanding the personality types could be useful for couples and families, but he expressed regret that typology was being overused in therapy to lock an individual into a way of being and treatment techniques (Galipeau, 2013).

Criticism of Jung

One of the greatest criticisms of Jung's body of work was related to the failing of the man himself. It has been largely asserted that Jung was guilty of an over-reliance on the colonial and racist attitudes of the late 19th and early 20th century and caused specific harm to people of African and Asian descent (Bair et al., 2018). Specifically, about people of African descent, Jung alleged that their brains were inferior to White people, and that they were primitive and incapable of the same emotional and psychological functioning as White people. In 2018, Bair et al. called for the field of analytic psychology to denounce theories that further marginalized and caused harm to other groups of people.

Another criticism of Jung's work is that it is too abstract and is therefore difficult to test (Helson, 1982). However, one of the most used personality assessments, the Myers-Briggs Type Indicator, is based on Jung's theory of personality. The Myers-Briggs is used in a variety of settings like business and education to assess individual personality types as a way of determining how groups of people might work together and how personality types might impact communication. There are 16 possible personality types that can be identified through the Myers-Briggs. The premise of the Myers-Briggs is that a person has a preference in the attitude and three functions described by Jung, and the combination of preferences can be used to identify likely patterns for individuals in decision-making and communication (Randall et al., 2017). Randall et al. (2017) conducted a meta-analysis of studies examining reliability and construct validity. Their collection of studies indicated test/retest reliability and construct validity. However, the results were limited because of the small numbers of studies included and these were mostly examining the personalities of college student subjects. This punctuates another consideration for using personalities to explain intergroup dynamics. Personality can change with context (Dweck, 1996) and time.

PSYCHOSOCIAL IDENTITY DEVELOPMENT THEORY

As we more closely examine the individual experiences and development of Bi'lal and Mystic, it is obvious that their social and cultural lives are impacting both the psychological and the behavioral. We therefore turn our attention to models of psychosocial identity development to better understand how Erikson's, Levinson's, and Arnett's models of psychosocial identity inform our understanding of emerging and early adulthood generally, and how each might be specifically applied to Bi'lal and Mystic. Simmermon and Schwartz (1986) offer that psychosocial identity development "takes into account that individual's relationships with institutions, traditions, family, occupation, and sociological situations, as well as internal images and mental life." (Simmermon & Schwartz, 1986, p. 405). One of the main premises of psychosocial identity development is that it is a lifelong process (Simmermon & Schwartz, 1986, p. 405).

Erik Erikson and Emerging and Early Adulthood

Before we address those stages of Erikson's Psychosocial Identity Development model that are relevant to emerging and early adulthood, we need to consider the premises of identity development according to Erikson that might further our understanding of both Bi'lal and Mystic. The first premise is that if there are negative outcomes or development in previous stages, those issues can be rectified in later stages. The second premise is that regression, usually precipitated by life events, is possible (Lineros & Fincher, 2014).

Erikson considered the impact of culture, race, and ethnicity on identity. One aspect of Erikson's work in this area was to examine identity in context and he understood the role of culture on identity development. He spent significant time observing the Sioux, now referred to as the Lakota and Dakota, and the Yurok and, as a result, maintained that development reflects each person's social context (Syed & Fish, 2018).

Erikson acknowledged that within a culture, there are specific expectations unique to that cultural group around development. Interestingly, about African Americans, Erikson noted that the history of colonialism and slavery have had residual influences on African American people's development resulting in people either finding a way to assimilate or resist oppressive forces. In this context, the developmental challenge is to "assert their personhood, agency, and value" (Syed & Fish, 2018, p. 279).

As we consider the context of Bi'lal and Mystic, two African American young adults, we must consider that some negative aspects of their socio-cultural experience may undermine their development and cause them to regress to earlier stages. Consequently, we could assume that the regression could result in delayed movement to other stages. It will be years before we know the full impact of the social crises this generation of young African American men has witnessed, but we might expect that the threat of bodily harm, loss of life, and discrimination around access and opportunity could slow down a person's willingness to take chances in life beyond a perceived comfort zone. There is the possibility that young African American men, like Bi'lal, will not move through the stages that Erikson describes in the time he describes or that they might regress to previous stages. The other consideration is that there may be differential development in different parts of identity.

Let us consider the previous chapter's discussion of race socialization that is a common part of the cultural experience of African American men. We might assume that Bi'lal is struggling with the idea that the world is a safe place, and he may experience dissonance or a crisis of mistrust based on the police killings of Black men and his perception that, as a Black man, he is being discriminated against in the job market. There is the distinct possibility that Bi'lal does not expect things to be just or fair for him. As a matter of fact, his race socialization may have included specific messages designed to manage his expectation of systems that were not going to operate in his favor or operate consistently according to the stated rules. It is possible that the renewed crisis and controversy in 2020 around the killing of African American men by police could spur a regression. Although this regression does not look like the trust versus mistrust of infancy, there is the possibility that Bi'lal has regressed to an earlier stage of development. Bi'lal is concerned about his welfare, in general, but especially as it relates to the police and his inability to find employment that matches his education.

Another thing that may have been taught in the race socialization Bi'lal experienced in childhood is that the consequences of mistakes are very high. You may recall that Bi'lal is afraid to tell the other mentors that he is in legal trouble. We would probably agree that he should be forthcoming and allow the organizers to handle the situation appropriately. Because he has not been convicted of a crime, it is possible that the organizers could manage the situation and Bi'lal would still have an opportunity to participate in the mentoring program. However, the consequences of not disclosing this information may result in him being removed as a mentor. Additionally, he has not disclosed to Mystic that he lived with someone else before, because he does not want to accept the consequences of her having that information. We will look at Erikson's description of adolescence and young adulthood and see if it provides any insight that might help Therapist Rasheeda in her work with Mystic and Bi'lal.

Erikson uses discrete age ranges to describe each stage of development. According to Erikson's model of lifespan identity development, the latter part of adolescence and young adulthood coincides with the time that we are identifying as emerging and early adulthood. Adolescence and young adulthood are stages five and six, respectively, of Erikson's nine-stage model of lifespan identity development. Erikson acknowledged that there could be substages of development at each stage. He proposed that organizing adulthood in two stages provided for a broader application of the theory (Erikson, 1997).

LATE ADOLESCENCE AS EMERGING ADULTHOOD

As described by Erikson, the fifth stage of development is focused on adolescence, the period of late school age to college years or 13 to 19 years of age. As a reminder, adolescence is the time of identity versus identity confusion. Erikson (1997) described adolescence as the time when an individual searches for a personal identity. He also described this period as one of moratorium because the person has not had experiences of work and relationship that lead to value and preference clarification, and, consequently, self-awareness. According to Erikson's psychosocial development model, adolescence is a time of idealism and the time when an individual discovers what is possible in life. This is the stage most ripe for cognitive and emotional development. It is where the individual engages in a significant process of evaluating and comparing what one has been taught with new experiences and decoding (Erikson, 1997).

The adolescent person is ideological and most wary of any confusion about who they are and what their interests and values are. During adolescence, the individual, through experimentation, confirms or repudiates what has been accepted as true until this time. The individual starts to commit to an identity that is a combination of taught values and ideologies, personal preferences, and natural responses to the people and society, talent, and potential. However, it is the role repudiation that can feel like the greatest risk in adolescence because it results in significant questioning and feeling separate from previous ideals or informants of those ideals. It is through role repudiation that the person starts to resist ideologies, roles, and values that are incongruent with how the individual sees self. While role repudiation can result in a lack of self-confidence, rebelliousness, or a negative sense of self, role repudiation is a necessary part of identity formation.

This struggle of identity versus identity confusion that Erikson describes in adolescence is very closely aligned with our understanding of emerging adulthood. We explore the theoretical framework for emerging adulthood more later. But simply stated, this time of the individual deciding what is important separate from what has been taught is one of the characteristics of emerging adulthood. Prior to adolescence, guidance in previous years has only come from parents and families. Adolescence marks a time when the person becomes more group referent and, in the beginning of adolescence, parents may have difficulty with this new dynamic. As the person struggles with the push and pull of influences by the two forces, the individual relies heavily on the ideology that starts to emerge independent of experience and circumstance.

This is a challenge for Mystic at 28 years of age. The relationship between Mystic and her mother is strained because Mystic has chosen to continue her relationship with Bi'lal. Not surprisingly, Mystic's mother is concerned about her daughter's welfare after the situation occurred where Bi'lal was arrested. But the tension about their relationship existed before the incident.

The transition from adolescence to adulthood marks the emergence of the strength of fidelity. Fidelity refers to the development of being trusting, trustworthy, and loyal (Erikson, 1997).

YOUNG ADULTHOOD AS EMERGING ADULTHOOD

The sixth stage of development focuses on young adulthood. The age range of early adulthood, according to Erikson, is 19 to 40. This period covers both emerging and early adulthood. Young adulthood, according to Erikson (1997), is a time when the individual is seeking to share life with a partner, work, and friends who complement the individual. This period, referred to as intimacy versus isolation, is a stage where the person longs to be affiliated with other people and for mutual intimacy. For the sake of intimate relationships, young adulthood is marked by making sacrifices and compromises.

The isolation of young adulthood refers to the fear of being alone and unconnected. Erikson suggests that the sense of and fear of isolation can result in feeling excluded or rejected. The task of young adulthood is the successful resolution of the conflict between intimacy and isolation. When the conflict is resolved, love emerges. This love is described as mutual and mature devotion.

MARCIA'S IDENTITY STATUSES

For nearly 40 years, Marcia and his students worked to both validate and illuminate Erikson's theory (Marcia, 2002). Using interviews to better understand psychosocial identity, Marcia did not just seek confirmation for each stage of development, as described by Erikson, but he asked participants to describe their experiences at each stage of development. As a result, Marcia conceptualized statuses that, while acknowledging the polarities of crisis resolution at each stage of development, suggested a range of alternative resolutions of each psychosocial crisis. Marcia also proposed that it was possible for a person to move from status to status within each stage of development, but he agreed with Erikson that there was a pattern of development for adults (Marcia, 2002).

Within Erikson's stage of identity versus identity confusion, Marcia indicated that there were four statuses focused on exploration and commitment. Those four statuses are foreclosure, diffusion, moratorium, and identity achievement. We expect that a person at the beginning stages of adolescence is in a foreclosed status of development because this person is committed to an identity based on the identity and commitment of others, most likely parents, family, and community; but this person has not explored other possibilities regarding personal identity. The person in the identity diffusion status has not committed to an identity or explored the possibilities regarding those things that contribute to understanding self and developing an identity. Moratorium describes the status of a person who is most likely transitioning to achievement, because this person is engaged in significant exploration, but has not yet committed to an identity. Where identity diffusion is marked by low commitment and low exploration, identity achievement describes the person who has engaged in exploration around values and identity and has made a commitment based on that exploration. The emerging adults largely demonstrate exploration and commitment reflective of the moratorium and achievement statuses. However, for individuals in the diffusion status during emerging adulthood this could contribute to an inability to connect with or care for others later in life and result in significant isolation (Marcia, 2002).

To further illuminate Erikson's ideas about identity development, Orlofsky et al. (1973) focused on intimacy. As you recall, the stage in Erikson's theory reflective of what we are defining as early adulthood is the stage referred to as intimacy versus isolation. Orlofsky et al. (1973) studied the intimacy statuses that were reflective of depth and commitment in relationships (Marcia, 2002). They identified five intimacy statuses: isolated, stereotyped, pseudo-intimate, pre-intimate, and intimate. The isolated status is the identity status of a person who avoids relationships altogether. The stereotyped status describes the relationship paradigm for the person who has relationships, but those relationships are generally superficial relationships not marked by any real commitment of ideals or values in the context of the relationship. People referred to as pseudo-intimate are people whose relationships are committed relationships with no real intimacy or depth. Pre-intimate people understand the depth they want in relationships but are not able to commit or have chosen not to commit to relationships. The intimate person is the person who values depth in relationships and has the capacity to commit to relationships.

SESSION EXCERPT 9.2

Therapist Rasheeda: Have either of you lived with a partner before?

Mystic: No ... well, we sort of lived together when I was living at my mom's, but this is the first time we are officially living together and I've never lived with anyone else.

Bi'lal: I lived with someone once for about 6 months when I was around 22. (Mystic turns to him with a look of surprise, but Bi'lal only makes eye contact with Therapist Rasheeda.)

Therapist Rasheeda: Mystic, you seem surprised by what Bi'lal just said. (Mystic nods.)

Therapist Rasheeda: Does it matter to you that you didn't know that Bi'lal lived with someone else? (Mystic nods again.)

Therapist Rasheeda: Would you like to tell me how it matters?

Mystic (shrugs): I thought we were doing this for the first time together. It feels less special knowing he's done this before and I feel like he knew I would feel this way, which is why he never told me.

Bi'lal: I knew you would feel that way, but I didn't tell you because it didn't mean that much to me. I didn't want it to be a big deal. Besides, you have had other more serious relationships than I have.

Mystic: Maybe, but you know about them and I've never lived with anyone. Never even came close.

The relationship with the previous partner with whom Bi'lal cohabitated most likely predates his relationship with Mystic, but this exchange is important as Therapist Rasheeda starts to understand who Mystic and Bi'lal are as individuals and as a couple. For example, it will be important to understand what it means to both to live together in the present, because Bi'lal did not see living together as a serious commitment when he was 6 years younger, and Mystic feels that living together is a special commitment.

There is evidence that Bi'lal, like many emerging adults, was in a pre-intimate stage when he lived with another woman when he was younger and for much of his relationship with Mystic. However, Mystic and Bi'lal appear to be in similar places regarding the intimacy versus isolation time in their lives and they both appear to be in the intimacy status. They both have mutual affection for each other and they have strong affiliations with other friends and peers whose interests complement their own. Mystic and Bi'lal have a lot in common themselves, for instance, their love of travel and their appreciation of art. However, there are stark differences in some areas and, while Bi'lal feels that he has changed his attitude about some things, like honoring the commitment he has made to Mystic, Mystic is not as confident that he is different. The challenge for Therapist Rasheeda will be helping each person in the couple accommodate changes in development. For example, while not discussed yet, you will see that Mystic has some different attitudes about having children than she did at the beginning of her relationship with Bi'lal. In that area, Bi'lal has not changed.

STUDENT REFLECTION BOX 9.1

Based on what you have observed so far of Mystic and Bi'lal, what do each person's behaviors and attitudes tell us about each person's identity development and how might that inform our understanding of the two of them as a couple? What kinds of questions might you ask of Mystic and Bi'lal to help them understand each other better? In what ways are your questions reflective of how you are conceptualizing each person's development?

Daniel Levinson and Adult Development Theory of Life Structure

While Jung and Erikson focused on development across the lifespan, Levinson (1978) focused on adult development only, concentrating on early and middle adulthood. Levinson's theory of adult development, which he referred to as the theory of Life Structure, built on the work of Erikson and other theorists (Levinson, 1978) and is a theory of psychosocial identity development (Aktu & Ilhan, 2017). His work focuses on the person in the world or the person in context (Levinson, 1978) and is based on the premise that development is orderly and consists of periodic change at transitional periods (Aktu & Ilhan, 2017). The basis of the theory is that at each period of adult development, the person must accomplish development tasks that have implications for later development (Roberts & Newton, 1987).

Levinson's assertion was that to understand adult development, you must understand the nature of both the individual and society. He maintained that history and culture and social institutions influence development. The life cycle in Levinson's theory of life structure was conceptualized in eras and stages (Levinson, 1996). Notably, eras and stage are conceptualized differently. There are stages within an era in the theory of Life Structure. Early and middle adulthood are separate eras of the life cycle and Levinson theorized that the transition from one era to the next takes about 4 or 5 years and it is during this transition that one era ends and the next era begins. According to Levinson (1996), termination, individuation, and initiation are parts of every transitional phase. Each of these transitional phases marks the end of one stage and the beginning of the next.

Each life cycle is defined in about 25-year eras. However, adolescence lasts until a person is about 22 and Levinson defines early adulthood as somewhere between 17 and 45 (Levinson, 1978). The beginning of early adulthood is the early adult transition and during this transition, the individual stops doing the things that were common to childhood and individuates by assuming more adult roles and responsibilities. As a new initiant into adulthood, the individual tests the waters trying different things and different relationships to determine what is pleasing and congruent with identity, lifestyle, and values. According to Levinson, the time between 35 and 45 is the mid-life decade and the end of early adulthood is marked by a mid-life transition. Levinson theorized that the life changes that occur around the time a person is 40 are significant enough to require attention separately.

MEN AND THE THEORY OF LIFE STRUCTURE

While Levinson studied the differences in adult development for both men and women (Levinson, 1996), he still maintained that there were not significant differences in the eras and stages of development for men and women. However, one might assume that because he initially studied men (Aktu & Ilhan, 2017), his ideas about women's development are not independent of his ideas about men's development. This section starts with a discussion of Levinson's ideas about men's adult development.

Pre-Adulthood.　The time prior to adulthood, ages 17 to 22, is referred to as pre-adulthood. It is the time when the pre-adulthood era ends and the early adulthood era begins. During pre-adulthood the man reaches sexual maturity. This time is referred to as the adult transition. It is notable that Levinson does not refer to this time as adolescence.

Early Adulthood.   Early adulthood, according to Levinson, is the second era of life and it is divided into four phases. This is the time when the adult male is physically and biologically at his peak. It is also the time when the male is at peak intelligence, memory, abstract thought, and problem-solving ability. This remains relatively unchanged until the adult male reaches about 40 years of age, when the male tries to define his place in society. For the adult male this is a time of stress and satisfaction because it is also the time when the adult male makes the most significant contributions to work, family, and community. Committing to partnership, career, and lifestyle during this time, the adult male moves from being new and less confident in adult roles to being more senior in all adult roles including work, family, and community. At the end of the early adulthood era, the individual starts to experience emotional losses like children leaving home or becoming more independent. This is also the time when the adult male moves from trying to get parents to see him as an equal to starting to take care of the parents.

The first phase or Early Adult Transition of early adulthood takes place between 17 and 22 years. During this early adult transition, the person starts to explore the possibilities and, in the process, starts developing an adult identity and test choices. The second phase is referred to as Entering the Adult World. This phase occurs between 22 and 28 years and here the person continues to explore and test choices around work, peer groups, love, values, and lifestyle. This is the time, according to Levinson, that the person usually finds a home of his own. The tasks of this stage are twofold. The person must explore all the possibilities and keep options open, but he must also create a stable life with direction and more responsibility. Most of this time is spent in exploration and the objective is to avoid committing too quickly.

The next transition or phase of this era is Changing the First Life Structure. The age of this transition is 28 to 33 and it is a transition focused on self-improvement and reflection. Life, at this stage, is becoming more serious and there is significant self-evaluation that takes place. As a result, this can be a time of significant crisis if the choices are incongruent with dreams, talents, and interests.

STUDENT REFLECTION BOX 9.2

Mystic and Bi'lal have continued therapy and one of their conflicts is whether they will become parents. Mystic decided long ago that if she was ever going to have children, she would do so by the time she was 30. It is not that motherhood is something she longs for and she knows it would be challenging given she has just started her business, but she is concerned that there will never be a good time and she is not getting any younger. Bi'lal thinks he wants to be a father one day, but he thinks that this timing is not at all right. He would really like to be more secure professionally and financially. He is hopeful that he and Mystic will be ready to become parents in about 5 years and Mystic thinks the time is now or never. How can you support Bi'lal and Mystic in navigating this impasse?

The first three phases of adulthood are referred to as the novice phases. There are four primary tasks of the novice phase. The first task is forming a dream and giving it a place in the structure of life. The second task is forming a mentor relationship. The third task is forming an occupation and the final task is forming an enduring love relationship with a special person and usually a committed contractual relationship that leads to marriage and family (Roberts & Newton, 1987).

The Dream.   According to Levinson, the dream is the vision a person has for their life that motivates and activates the person and he also felt that the dream was necessary for future development (Levinson, 1978). It is the dream that prepares the individual man for the final phase of early adulthood or the Second Life Structure: Settling Down. This phase happens between 30 and 40 years of age and this is the phase where the person has launched, is achieving goals, and is established in work, family, and community identity. The person is clearer about their own identity and demonstrates this clarity consistently and confidently.

LEVINSON AND WOMEN'S DEVELOPMENT

One of the questions researchers asked was whether Levinson's model of adult development was applicable to women's development (Roberts & Newton, 1987). Consequently, Levinson spent 15 years studying the life course of women because he felt that there had not been adequate attention focused on the development of women. He studied women from the late teens to the mid-40s and studied women who were occupied as homemakers, corporate financiers, and academics (Levinson, 1996). Pointedly, he felt that it was important to not study women in a way that was referent to or compared women to men. His research was centered around two questions: (a) Is there a human life cycle? and (b) What is the significance of gender in women's lives?

At the completion of his study of women, Levinson determined that the framework for the life structure was the same generally and he felt that the framework could be used to explain cultural, gender, class, and other differences between individuals. But he noted that he was surprised to see that the differences between men and women were so stark that he really needed to better understand how gender influenced both women's and men's development (Levinson, 1996). Central to understanding the differences in women's and men's development was the idea of gender splitting, which refers to the sharp contrast in women's and men's ways of being and identity. It refers to the feminine in comparison to what is masculine and what is male in comparison to what is female. Levinson asserted that the differences in men's and women's social worlds impacted the differences in development and he examined four forms of splitting. The first area was the domestic sphere and the public sphere as the spaces or domains of society. The domestic sphere describes the work that is related to taking care of the home and family. The public sphere includes the economy, the government, and other activities that are not related to the family. Traditionally women's lives were centered around the domestic sphere and men's lives were centered around the public sphere (Levinson, 1996).

Levinson's second area of focus as he progressed in his study of women was the Traditional Marriage Enterprise and the resulting split between the female homemaker and the male provider. Third, there was a focus on the split between what is identified as women's work and men's work. Finally, there was a focus on gender identity and how a person thinks about what is feminine and what is masculine (Levinson, 1996).

One of the most important differences between men and women was the dream. Men's dreams focused on occupation, but women had greater conflict in defining their dreams and most women in Levinson's study were unable to form a vital dream or secure a mentor in the early stages of adulthood. For more traditional women, their goal was marriage and they were concerned about their role in their husband's dream.

EXTENDING LEVINSON'S IDEAS ABOUT LIFE COURSE

Levinson defines the eras and phases of adulthood in discrete age ranges, but there is a rejection of the universality of these periods (Roberts & Newton, 1987). For example, there is concern that Levinson did not account for variations that might be attributed to race, class, culture, and history.

Levinson's ideas about life course were not evergreen. There have been societal changes like increases in the numbers of women who pursue higher education and careers and choose not to have children early in life. These sociocultural changes have influenced women's dreams and their access to mentors. In a Roberts and Newton (1987) study, the researchers found that about 15% of the women in their study were unable to form a dream; about 15% formed relational dreams; about 15% formed individualistic dreams; and over 50% had dreams that were individualistic and relational.

While not a specific critique of Levinson's work, another criticism of life course theory, in general, is that he largely explored what are considered normative paths of behavior and does not account for the heterogeneity of experiences (Kneale & French, 2018). Most of these theories focus on five transitions to adulthood in some capacity. Those five transitions are reflective of the end of the formal education process, starting a career or full-time work, leaving the childhood home, getting married, and caring for children. However, these theories do not account for the fact that these markers are different for some groups of people, especially people in the LGBT community and people with lower socioeconomic status. For example, while entry into the workforce and formal education for non-heterosexual emerging adults is like heterosexual emerging adults, the age of first parenthood for this population is 3 years later than their heterosexual peers (Kneale & French, 2018). The other criticism of these theories is that people who belong to these groups may have a developmental course that is considered deviant because it does not follow the pattern of dominant groups.

Emerging Adulthood and Arnett

In the latter part of the 20th century, Jeffrey Jensen Arnett began to theorize that there was a period of development distinct from adolescence and early adulthood for people in industrialized nations. Arnett's impetus for focusing on this time and identifying it as a stage of post-adolescent development was the recognition that there had been a generational shift where people were pursuing education longer, starting careers and family later, and remaining at least partially dependent on their parents longer. He noticed a societal shift where, because of the changing attitudes about gender roles and sexuality, increased globalization, and changes in communication, there was no one prescribed pathway for people at this time of life (Gilmore, 2019). He also felt that by identifying it as a specific stage of development, there would be a greater likelihood that researchers would study this time separately from other stages of adult develop-ment (Arnett, 2000).

Arnett maintained that there were three features of this time that made it distinct, and he felt it was worth investigating, because he felt that previously developed the-ories did not appropriately capture this period (Arnett, 2000). His first premise of distinction was that emerging adulthood was distinct demographically. Unlike other periods, when most of the people during that time are doing similar things, there was greater variability in what people during this time were doing. He also maintained that emerging adulthood is distinct from other stages subjectively, meaning that people in this stage generally have ambiguous feelings about whether they are an adolescent or an adult and the feelings about this status are situational (Arnett, 2000). For most peo-ple in this stage, they have not decided where they will maintain long-term residence; they have not committed to a relationship; and they may be pursuing higher education and vocational training, but not fully ensconced in a career. An additional feature of this time is identity exploration and instability. It is during this time that emerging adults test a variety of possibilities regarding love, friendships, work, family, spiritual-ity, and lifestyle to identify what they value and how they want to live (Arnett, 2000).

Arnett identified five distinguishing features of emerging adulthood; he indicates that emerging adulthood is the time of identity exploration, instability, self-focus, feel-ing in-between, and having a lot of possibilities.

AGE OF IDENTITY EXPLORATION

Like Erikson's ideas that there was a prolonged adolescence in industrialized societies where the individual engaged in great exploration, Arnett (2000) proposed that this is a time where the individual explores around love, work, and developing a greater understanding of self. This is the time when the person starts to live a life indepen-dent of parents, but the person has not yet made any long-term commitments about work, family, partnership, or parenting. This lack of commitment gives the person that opportunity to explore a variety of things. A significant feature of this identity explora-tion is the individual starting to understand self. It is this time that the person explores likes and dislikes and values and beliefs.

AGE OF INSTABILITY

Emerging adulthood is marked by frequent changes in where a person works and lives, how and where a person is educated, and who the individual loves or engages with sexually. Regarding living, the person who leaves the parental home for college may live in a residence hall or apartment during the college years, sometimes return-ing to the parental home during school breaks or at other transitional points. It is also likely that an individual in emerging adulthood may live with a romantic partner. Most of these cohabitation relationships end within 5 years. Some emerging adults move to several different places to pursue job opportunities, as well.

TIME OF SELF-FOCUS

This time in the life of a young adult is not to be confused with the selfishness that is characteristic of adolescence. The emerging adult is self-focused and concerned about others. The person at this point is likely to express deep care and concern for par-ents but is most likely not responsible for the welfare of their parents. Additionally, this person does not have the attachment or commitments of partners or children that require either their complete devotion, time, or attention. Many emerging adults find this a carefree time marked by flexibility and mobility (Arnett, 2006).

IN-BETWEEN TIME

The ambiguous time of emerging adulthood is considered an in-between time, because while most at this time are not obligated to follow their parents' rules and are not mandated to participate in school, in industrialized societies most individuals have not fully transitioned into roles common to later adulthood like parenthood and home ownership or residential stability (Arnett, 2006). For most people in emerging adulthood, the markers of being a full adult are the ability to accept responsibility for oneself, the ability to make independent decisions, and being financially independent (Arnett, 2000, 2006). Most individuals start to feel like an adult most of the time by their late 20s or early 30s, and by the mid-30s nearly all people feel that they are firmly in adulthood (Arnett, 2006).

TIME OF POSSIBILITIES

Emerging adulthood is a time of great optimism and the individual's strong belief that life goals will be achieved. In addition, emerging adulthood allows the person who has experienced a difficult life growing up around which there was little control to pursue a different way of living with the expectation that life will be better by doing so.

ADDITIONAL THOUGHTS ON EMERGING ADULTHOOD

Arnett (2006) cautions that there is great diversity in this time because emerging adulthood is a time of great exploration and there are so many combinations of relationship status, job and career status, parental status, and educational status that can exist at this time. But he also argues that the same holds true for any other time in the lifespan, as well.

There are researchers who are skeptical about acknowledging this relatively new addition to how we understand adult development, particularly because it is a stage of development explained by culture (Gilmore, 2019; Hendry & Kloep, 2010) and social institutions (Hendry & Kloep, 2010). Hendry and Kloep (2010) were critical that Arnett prescribes to a discrete age range for which we would identify a person as an emerging adult in Western culture and they portend that the theory is based on the experience of traditional-aged college students who still largely come from middle-income socioeconomic status. They argue that being in moratorium or a place of high exploration and low commitment, a hallmark of much of emerging adulthood, is not an option for some people. For example, they interviewed people in this age group who did not go to college. Through interviews with participants, they discovered that many of them not only felt like adults in their late teens and very early 20s, they were also already committed to work, family, and partners. They also determined significant exploration in emerging adulthood usually is associated with having access to financial support from family during that time and that it is possible for a person to achieve adulthood at different times in different aspects of the person's life.

Hendry and Kloep (2010) also maintain that many of the characteristics and experiences of emerging adulthood are not confined to a specific time and are likely to be the experience of adults at any point of transition in the lifespan. It is their assertion that there are a variety of possibilities for normal development within industrialized societies for people between 18 and –29. The most significant concern of these researchers is that any developmental process outside of Arnette's description of normal development could be considered deviant and they maintain that development in this age group is contextual.

Emerging Adults With Disabilities. Meyer et al. (2015) offer additional support for contextual considerations about development in the years between 18 and 29 in their specific focus on the development of emerging adults with disabilities. They were specifically interested in understanding the differences in developmental milestones for people with disabilities in comparison to people who are in the ability majority. They examined the likely development of people with disabilities in each of the five principles of Arnette's theory of emerging adulthood. Regarding self-exploration as identity development, Meyer et al. (2015) indicate that emerging adults with disabilities are likely to require more time in identity development because of the tasks required around their identity as a person with a disability. In addition to emerging adulthood being a time of self-exploration, it is also a time of self-acceptance, advocacy, and social integration for a person with a disability. There is time required for the two identities to successfully merge, as well. Meyer et al. (2015) recognize that more study is devoted to understanding the influence of community and family support and the significance of the disability.

Regarding uncertainty, there are laws that protect or guarantee equal access and opportunity for persons with disabilities. These laws are designed to increase the independence people with disabilities have about accessible living and inclusion around housing, transportation, and employment, for example. Therefore, we could expect similarities in emerging adulthood for persons with disabilities and people who do not have a disability. Four years after high school, a little over 67% of adults with disabilities lived with their parents compared to about 69% of all adults in that age group living with their parents (Meyer et al., 2015). However, by 30, twice as many adults with disabilities live with their parents in comparison to adults overall. The dynamic between the adult with a disability and the parents depends on the significance of the disability and the level of additional care and support the individual needs, the person's education, the family's resources, and the degree to which the living arrangement between the parents and the adult child changes. While the uncertainty of this time is comparable to that of other people in emerging adulthood, there may be additional layers of support needed for the person to feel more certain about pursuits like work and home (Meyer et al., 2015).

The developmental tasks related to the principles of self-focus and feeling in-between do not differ significantly for a person with a disability than for the person who does not have a disability. As a matter of fact, in many ways, emerging adults with disabilities have more support in moving beyond feeling in-between, especially about career development. Both people with disabilities and people without disabilities fare better with support and experience in this area. In the area of self-focus, the developmental opportunity for the emerging adult with a disability is to develop a sense of self-determination. Self-determination allows the person to self-advocate and consequently become more self-sufficient. Success in this area requires developing skills in decision-making, problem-solving, and goal setting. Self-focus usually includes developing significant interpersonal skills. Meyer et al. (2015) suggest that more research is needed to understand the principle of optimism, in general, for emerging adults.

ESTABLISHED OR EARLY ADULTHOOD

To connect all the disconnected ideas and research about the task associated with the time of life between 30 and 45, Mehta et al. (2020), a group that includes Jeffrey Arnett, developed a model for conceptualizing established adulthood in line with Arnett's conceptualization of emerging adulthood. They decided to use the term *established adulthood,* because there is no one way to refer to the period referenced. The researchers felt that established adulthood was the least investigated time, but, in contemporary society, it is a time of significant growth, commitment, and development. It is also a time of significant responsibilities like work, partnership, and family and, according to Mehta et al. (2020), the period sets the stage for the rest of a person's life.

Mehta et al. (2020) do not conceptualize universal stages for this period, because they maintain that there is variation based on history, culture, and context. People in this age range generally have a healthier lifestyle than emerging adults and are less likely to take unnecessary risk. Established adulthood is a time when people can demonstrate expertise in their jobs and advance in their careers. As a matter of fact, this is the case for both professional and blue-collar workers (Mehta et al., 2020).

Mehta et al. (2020) also speak to the competing demands of this period and refer to the phenomenon as a crunch. Notable crunches of established adulthood are the career and care crunch used to describe the challenge to balance work and parenting responsibilities. They note, however, this crunch could extend to caring for parents or other older relatives for some people. There is also a push and pull with romantic partnerships and other responsibilities like child rearing, and women are more likely to feel the crunch than men, especially women in heterosexual relationships, because there is an uneven expectation for child-rearing and household management between men and women where women have more responsibilities in both areas than men.

As mentioned earlier, the term *early adulthood* has been used to refer to this period, because it is very possible that a person could reach this approximate time and not be established. This is particularly true of marginalized groups who traditionally experience high unemployment and high underemployment. This is the case of Bi'lal and Mystic, and we see that they are having difficulty getting established professionally and with their family goals (Table 9.1).

SESSION EXCERPT 9.3

Therapist Rasheeda: You both seem to be interested in starting a family, but you both seem to feel that optimally you'd be more settled professionally before you start a family.

Mystic: If I was younger, I definitely would not want to have kids now. There are a lot of things I want to do. I want to travel more and I want to make sure my business is solid before I have children. I mean, right now, I have to work a full-time job and focus on my business afterward. I can't see where a kid would fit in. I would have to let something go if I had a kid. I love my business, but I need paid employment for now. If we had a child, I would probably have to stop my business.

Therapist Rasheeda: It seems like time dictates your feelings about having a child now.

Mystic: Most definitely. My biological clock is ticking and if I don't have a child by 30, I'm not going to have one.

Therapist Rasheeda: It sounds like that's non-negotiable. Why is a child before 30 so important?

Mystic: It's just what I always imagined. I don't want to be an old mother.

Bi'lal: I don't understand that. I mean 30 is less than 2 years away and I think we both need time to get our careers going and we need to purchase our own home instead of renting from my grandmother.

Therapist Rasheeda: Bi'lal, it sounds as if you think about having children in the future, but you think you both need to make some progress in other areas before you think about adding to your family.

Bi'lal: Yes. I think we will be ready in about 5 years.

Therapist Rasheeda: Bi'lal and Mystic, you both seem to have similar ideas about when to expand your family. It sounds like you both think that you will have the opportunity to pursue some very important goals if you wait a few years to have children. But it also seems that you, Mystic, have a long-held belief that you should have children at a certain time and you have some concerns that you don't have an indefinite number of child-bearing years.

(Bi'lal and Mystic both nod.)

Therapist Rasheeda: You both have some legitimate points that should be considered. How might we use this discussion to explore the vision you both have for this relationship, so you can see where children, career, and travel fit into that picture?

CLIENTS IN EMERGING AND EARLY ADULTHOOD: CLINICAL CONSIDERATIONS

In the session excerpts provided in this chapter, you see the therapist trying to uncover the presenting issues for the couple in therapy and also trying to understand the personalities and identities of the individuals who make up this couple and help the individuals understand their dynamics as a couple. Her knowledge of adult development

Table 9.1 Identity Development Theory Applicable to Emerging and Early Adulthood

THEORY	THEORIST	MAJOR CONCEPTS
Theory of Personality	Jung	• Development influenced by social and cultural factors • Psyche essential to understanding personality • Personality conceptualized around conscious, unconscious, and collective conscious • Established four aspects of personality and eight personality types
Stages of Psychosocial Identity Development	Erikson	• Uses discrete age ranges • End of adolescence (identity vs. identity confusion) and first half of young adulthood comparable to emerging adulthood • End of young adulthood (intimacy vs. isolation like early adulthood)
Adult Development Theory of Life Structure	Levinson	• Significant aspect is the dream • Only relevant to adult development • Development depicts as orderly • Requires understanding of both individual and society • Conceptualized in eras, stages, and transitions • Eras last approximately 25 years
Theory of Emerging Adulthood	Arnett	• Occurs between 18 and 25, possibly to 29 • Period between adolescence and early adulthood • Five distinguishing features: exploration, instability, self-focus, feeling in-between, having lots of possibilities
Established Adulthood	Mehta, Arnett, Palmer, & Nelson	• Time between late 20s and 30s • Marked by significant growth, commitment, and development • Marked by adult responsibilities • Has no universal stage • Varies based on history, culture, and context

theory not only allows her to understand them individually, but it helps her facilitate interactions in therapy that allow them to understand each other in a way that is reflective of the individuals' developmental capabilities. Therapist Rasheeda has obviously determined that Mystic and Bi'lal have committed to their relationship and they are not exploring other options regarding intimate partners. In this regard, it seems as if Mystic and Bi'lal are identified as early adults and not emerging adults. Additionally, they both seem to have committed to a career identity, even though Mystic has made more progress in securing an opportunity reflective of her values. However, the couple seems vulnerable to mistrust and differences in personality. The couple's instability with their home and the individuals' self-focus regarding their careers suggest that they are not yet fully established as adults.

Therapists Rasheeda will most likely help them understand how differences in personalities also impact their communication styles and their decision-making. Noticeably, Therapist Rasheeda has uncovered some things that are causing problems for them; however, she has decided to focus instead on understanding the couple's broad ideas about their goals and vision of their relationship. To this point, we have not examined how Therapist Rasheeda addresses what has become known as "the incident" with Bi'lal and Mystic. What do you think will happen in that session? What are some of the cultural considerations that need to be addressed? See this final excerpt from a session.

SESSION EXCERPT 9.4

Therapist Rasheeda: Bi'lal, it seems that you described feeling caged in on the night of the incident. What were the actual feelings?

Bi'lal: Yeah, I did. I felt so many things. I was feeling trapped and anxious. I had been spending so much time watching the news about George Floyd and his murder. I just wanted to get away, get with my boys, and just see how everyone was doing. It was all so heavy. I felt it in my chest. She was asking me so many questions like she didn't trust me. I felt like we had moved past that. I thought she knew that I was really committed to us. I just felt hemmed in.

Therapist Rasheeda: I understand that you were feeling anxious and you were disappointed that Mystic might not trust you. Mystic, what were you feeling that night?

Mystic: I guess there was a part of me that was concerned that he was going to see another woman, but there was also a part of me that just wanted to know where he was going and when he was going to get back. I worry every time he leaves. I am constantly afraid that something will happen to him and he will never make it back home.

The challenge for Therapist Rasheeda, as she continues to work with Mystic and Bi'lal, will be to understand how context and culture impact how they operate as a couple and make distinctions between less mature development and appropriate responses in their context. The session excerpt illustrates that an individual's culture and context can require developmental tasks that may not be a requirement of another person's context. Very importantly, in addition to having common interests and similar thinking, Mystic and Bi'lal appear to genuinely care for each other and both are committed to their relationship. Additionally, Mystic and Bi'lal seem to be closely aligned developmentally and we can expect that in the different aspects of their lives as early adults they are focused on similar things. These are great foundations for Therapist Rasheeda's work with them.

PERSPECTIVES FROM THE FIELD: PODCAST

Access this podcast at http://connect.springerpub.com/content/book/978-0-8261-8279-1/part/part02/chapter/ch09

Listen to two clinicians talk about their clinical considerations for working with Mystic and Bi'lal. Our guests explore the interpersonal dynamics between Mystic and Bi'lal, the cultural expectations for women in young adulthood in the African American community, and the relevance of clinicians understanding clients in a variety of contexts or spaces and times. Each of them also shares how theory impacts and guides how they work with a client like Mystic.

Dr. Stephanie J. W. Ford is a licensed psychologist who specializes in clinical and counseling psychology. She is a professor in the Counselor Education and Family Studies department at Liberty University, co-owner of Psychology of the Western Reserve, LCC, and has provided psychological services to adolescents and young adults in community agencies as well as college and university counseling centers.

Dr. Chenobia Webster-Hill, LCSW, DSW, is a core faculty member at Walden University and a licensed clinical social worker with almost 20 years of experience in the field of social work. Her practice experience includes specialties of clinical licensure, understanding the DSM and its application in clinical practice, anxiety and depression with an emphasis on adjustment to college, healthy relationships, diversity, and developing mental health outreach programming.

SUMMARY

This chapter included an exploration of the earliest stages of adulthood, emerging adulthood, and early adulthood. Included in this discussion were Jung's theory of personality and the psychosocial development theories of Erikson, Levinson, and Arnett. Throughout this chapter was the continued exploration of Bi'lal and Mystic and their work with a couple's therapist. The intention was to emphasize the interdependency between the individual client and others or significant others in their lives. Of course, this is a relevant concern across the lifespan, but the transitions relevant to selection and commitment to a partner in early adulthood have significant implications for the rest of the lifespan.

We also examined some contemporary thoughts about Jung, Erikson, and Levinson and we explored how Arnett is joining with others to extend his ideas about the earliest phases of adult development to focus on established adulthood. We notice throughout that the challenge is to consider the dynamic nature of personality and to understand there are significant differences in development based on culture and context. The challenge of human services professionals is to take the heterogeneity of people and development into consideration and not over-rely on predominant group references to explain the development of everyone.

REFERENCES

Aktu, Y., & Ilhan, T. (2017). Individual life structures in the early adulthood period based on Levinson's theory. *Educational Sciences: Theory and Practice, 17*(4), 1383–1403.

Arnett, J. J. (2000). Emerging adulthood: A theory of development from the late teens through the twenties. *American Psychologist, 55*(5), 469–480. https://doi.org/10.1037/0003-066X.55 .5.469

Arnett, J. J. (2006). Emerging adulthood: Understanding the new way of coming of age. In J. J. Arnett & J. L. Tanner (Eds.), *Emerging adulthood in america: Coming of age in the 21st century.* American Psychological Association.

Bair, D., Beebe, J., Brewster, F., Brooke, R., Carta, S., Duckworth, M., Flowers, B. S., Formaini, H., Franco, L. A., Hejinian, C., Heuer, B., Heuer, G. M., Holifield, B., Lanfranchi, A. K., Kimbles, S., Luci, M., Maitra, B., Mills, J., Morgan, H., & Zoja, L. (2018). Open letter from a group of Jungians on the question of Jung's writings on and theories about 'Africans.' *British Journal of Psychotherapy, 34*(4), 673–678. https://doi-org.ezp.waldenulibrary.org/10 .1111/bjp.12408

Becker, J. L. (2020). The autonomous psyche. *Journal of Heart Centered Therapies, 22*(2), 73.

Chappell, S., Cooper, E., & Trippe, G. (2019). Shadow work for leadership development. *Journal of Management Development, 38*(5), 326–335. https://doi.org/10.1108/JMD-08-2018-0216

Crain, W. (2003). Jung. *Encounter, 16*(3), 2.

Dweck, C. S. (1996). Capturing the dynamic nature of personality. *Journal of Research in Personality, 30*(3), 348–362. https://doi.org/10.1006/jrpe.1996.0024

Engelmann, J. B., Schmid, B., De Dreu, C. K. W., Chumbley, J., & Fehr, E. (2019). On the psychology and economics of antisocial personality. *Proceedings of the National Academy of Sciences of the United States of America, 116*(26), 12781–12786. https://doi.org/10.1073/pnas .1820133116

Erikson, E. H. (1997). *The life cycle completed: Extended version with new chapters on the ninth stage of development by Joan M. Erikson.* W. W. Norton & Company.

Galipeau, S. (2013). The red book and Jung's typology. *Psychological Perspectives, 56*(1), 34–49. https://doi-org.ezp.waldenulibrary.org/10.1080/00332925.2013.758522

Gilmore, K. (2019). Is emerging adulthood a new developmental phase? *Journal of the American Psychoanalytic Association, 67*(4), 625–653. https://doi.org/10.1177/0003065119868680

Helson, R. (1982). Critics and their texts: An approach to Jung's theory of cognition and personality. *Journal of Personality and Social Psychology, 43*(2), 409–418.

Hendry, L., & Kloep, M. (2010). How universal is emerging adulthood? An empirical example. *Journal of Youth Studies, 13*(2), 169–179. https://doi.org/10.1080/13676260903295067

Hoare, C. H. (2006). *Handbook of adult development and learning. [electronic resource].* Oxford University Press. https://doi-org.ezp.waldenulibrary.org/10.1002/j.1556-6676.1994 .tb00932.x

Hudson, W. C. (1978). Persona and defence mechanisms. *The Journal of Analytical Psychology, 23*(1), 54–62. https://doi.org/10.1111/j.1465-5922.1978.00054.x

Jones, R. A. (2013). Jung's "Psychology with the Psyche" and the behavioral sciences. *Behavioral Sciences (Basel, Switzerland), 3*(3), 408–417. https://doi.org/10.3390/bs3030408

Kjellström, S., & Stålne, K. (2017). Adult development as a lens: Applications of adult development theories in research. *Behavioral Development Bulletin, 22*(2), 266–278. https://doi.org/ 10.1037/bdb0000053

Kneale, D., & French, R. (2018). Examining life course trajectories of lesbian, gay and bisexual people in England - exploring convergence and divergence among a heterogeneous population of older people. *Longitudinal and Life Course Studies, 9*(2), 226–244. https://doi.org/10.14301/llcs.v9i2.425

Levinson, D. J. (1978). *The seasons of a man's life*. Ballentine Books.

Levinson, D. J. (1996). *The seasons of a woman's life*. Ballentine Books.

Lineros, J. V., & Fincher, M. (2014). Erikson's development crises: Applying developmental theory to adult learning. *Learning & Performance Quarterly, 2*(3), 35–48.

Marcia, J. E. (2002). Identity and Psychosocial Development in Adulthood. *Identity, 2*(1), 7–28. https://doi-org.ezp.waldenulibrary.org/10.1207/S1532706XID0201_02

Mehta, C. M., Arnett, J. J., Palmer, C. G., & Nelson, L. J. (2020). Established adulthood: A new conception of ages 30 to 45. *American Psychologist, 75*(4), 431–444. https://doi.org/10.1037/amp0000600

Meyer, J. M., Hinton, V. M., & Derzis, N. (2015). Emerging adults with disabilities: Theory, trends, and implications. *Journal of Applied Rehabilitation Counseling, 46*(4), 3–10. https://doi.org/10.1891/0047-2220.46.4.3

Moraglia, G. (1994). C. G. Jung and the psychology of adult development. *Journal of Analytical Psychology, 39*(1), 55–75. https://doi.org/10.1111/j.1465-5922.1994.00055.x

Orlofsky, J. L., Marcia, J. E., & Lesser, I. M. (1973). Ego identity status and the intimacy versus isolation crisis of young adulthood. *Journal of Personality and Social Psychology, 27*(2), 211–219. https://doi.org/10.1037/h0034787

Randall, K., Isaacson, M., & Ciro, C. (2017). Validity and reliability of the Myers-Briggs Personality Type Indicator: A systematic review and meta-analysis. *Journal of Best Practices in Health Professions Diversity: Education, Research & Policy, 10*(1), 1–27.

Roberts, P., & Newton, P. M. (1987). Levinsonian studies of women's adult development. *Psychology and Aging, 2*(2), 154–163. https://doi.org/10.1037/0882-7974.2.2.154

Simmermon, R., & Schwartz, K. M. (1986). Adult development and psychotherapy: Bridging the gap between theory and practice. *Psychotherapy, 23*(3), 405–410. https://doi.org/10.1037/h0085631

Syed, M., & Fish, J. (2018). Revisiting Erik Erikson's legacy on culture, race, and ethnicity. *Identity: An International Journal of Theory and Research, 18*(4), 274–283. https://doi.org/10.1080/15283488.2018.1523729

Webb, B. (1990). Type casting: Life with Myers-Briggs [Cover story]. *Library Journal, 115*(11), 32–37.

Wilde, D. J. (2011). Jung's qualitative personality theory. In D. J. Wilde (Ed.), *Jung's personality theory quantified*. Springer.

CHAPTER 10

Cultural and Contextual Factors of Middle Adulthood

LEARNING OBJECTIVES

Upon completion of this chapter, students will be able to:

- Identify the stage of lifespan development known as "middle adulthood."
- Identify key cultural factors impacting this stage of development.
- Identify key contextual factors impacting this stage of development
- Review counseling considerations for the case of "Ellen."
- Analyze how to work with clients when you listen to an expert, Dr. Donna Sheperis, on counseling women in middle adulthood.

CASE STUDY 10.1: THE CASE OF ELLEN

Ellen is a 57-year-old cisgender White female who recently separated from her husband, Clark. Ellen has a 22-year-old son, Rusty, who is in his last year of college. She also is finding herself more involved in her aging mother Frances's care. Ellen spent most of her adult life as a homemaker and stay-at-home mom for Rusty. She went to college for 1 year, but then met Clark, a graduating senior, married him after her freshman year, and dropped out of school to move with him to the suburbs of Chicago where he had gotten a lucrative job in a chemical company. Ellen threw herself into managing her home and raising her son. She describes this time in her life of being a wife and mom as "mostly happy" though sometimes "boring and monotonous." When Rusty left for college, Ellen plunged into a state of grief that was, as she describes, "unexpected." She did not realize how much of her identity was being a mom. Ellen also started to notice that she and Clark were just drifting apart. She said that there was a lack of intimacy, communication, and interest between her and her husband. To her surprise, when she brought this up with Clark, he agreed with her assessment and suggested a separation. Just as Clark moved out to an apartment in downtown Chicago, Ellen found herself once again in a caretaker role as her 83-year-old mother, Frances, had just moved in with her. Frances was living in an apartment by herself but recently had a fall, breaking her wrist and fracturing her hip. Instead of exploring assisted living facilities, Ellen offered for Frances to come stay with her as she recuperates. Ellen describes the relationship with her mother as "tense," but says she feels guilty about even suggesting a nursing home or assisted living situation to her. She is seeking individual counseling for the first time in her life because she "just doesn't know who she is anymore and what is next in her life." She says to you, her counselor, "I guess I'm just having one of those midlife crises you hear about."

MIDDLE ADULTHOOD

As with other stages of development across the lifespan, the period of middle adulthood is not one that has received a great deal of attention. One reason for this is that people generally are living longer. According to the World Health Organization (WHO), the life expectancy for both men and women in the United States is 78.5 years (2016). One hundred years ago, the average life expectancy in the United States was about 47 years so this period of "middle life" did not even exist. We consider this stage of life to be between about 40 and 65 years of age (Newton & Stewart, 2010; Overstreet, n.d.), but some research has suggested that this phase of life can extend even into the early to mid 70s. This may be one of the least studied periods of life as well as one of the most varied.

Individuals in the time of life referred to as middle adulthood often find themselves sandwiched between preparing to launch emerging adult children and beginning to transition into a role of caretaker for aging parents. They are settling into long-term marriages or partnerships, or questioning their relationships and seeking a change. They wrestle with still feeling like their 30-year-old self, but are faced with a different image when they look in the mirror. Middle adults also experience significant physical transitions (e.g., menopause, declining testosterone, weight gain due to hormonal changes), career transitions (e.g., moving up the ranks, being laid off and replaced by younger workers, moving into retirement, starting a brand new career), and identity changes (being an "empty nester," re-examining romantic relationships, beginning to face mortality and striving for a sense of purpose and meaning).

CULTURAL FACTORS: MIDDLE ADULTHOOD

Culturally anchored theories of development usually identify how an aspect of development is experienced through a particular identity. The experiences of a Black male at 57 years old will be presumably different from the experiences of a White female at 57 years old based on differences in the social constructs of race and gender. If we also add identifiers like sexual orientation, socioeconomic status, education, disability, religion, and nationality, the lens through which we explore the middle adulthood phase shifts even more. The importance of developing a multicultural framework for working with clients from diverse backgrounds is vital. When meeting a new client like Ellen, the mental health professional takes the time to learn her story from her experiences and frames of reference. The culturally humble and competent clinician will listen with open curiosity, a lack of assumption, and a sincere desire to understand all facets of Ellen's life that are relevant to understanding her issues. The acronym "ADDRESSING" is a good reminder of the points of intersectionality that a client like Ellen might bring to the table for counseling.

ADDRESSING Issues of Diversity

According to Hays (2016), when we think about "culture," many different facets of who we are come into play. Mental health professionals in training should focus on their own multiple identities and consider how these identifiers influence their sense of self. Similarly, understanding the varied identities of our clients can also give some indication of what factors to explore more, what factors are central to a client's own identity, and what factors represent points of challenge and conflict. Table 10.1 shows Hays's ADDRESSING framework for understanding different points of identity.

The components of the model are represented with the acronym, ADDRESSING. *A* stands for *Age and generational influences* on identity. This includes cultural, societal, and familial influences on one's sense of self based on their age or identified generation (e.g., baby boomers, generation X). *DD* represents *Developmental or other disabilities*. Disabilities can be cognitive, developmental, physical, or psychological. Some individuals are born with disabling conditions (e.g., blindness, fetal alcohol syndrome), some individuals develop a disability at some point during their lifetime (e.g., accident, illness). Many people with an identified disability consider themselves as part of a cultural group or community. The *R* in the model stands for *Religion and spiritual orientation*. Depending on where in the world, country, region, or community a person lives, their religious affiliation can represent a minority or majority status. In the United States, for example, minority religious groups include Muslim, Jewish, Hindu, and Buddhist (Hays, 2016).

The letter *E* stands for *Ethnic and racial identity*. Individuals who belong to an identified ethnic and racial cultural group such as Asian, South Asian, Pacific Islander, Latin-x, Black, and African American are part of a nondominant or minority group

Table 10.1 ADDRESSING Framework

CULTURAL CHARACTERISTIC	POWER	LESS POWER
Age and generational influences	Adults	Children, adolescents, elders
Developmental disability	Temporarily able-bodied	Individuals with disabilities
Disability acquired later in life	Temporarily able-bodied	Individuals with disabilities (e.g., multiple sclerosis or dementia caused by stroke)
Religion and spiritual orientation	Christians	Non-christian
Ethnicity/race identity	White or Caucasian	Persons of color
Socioeconomic status	Owning home and middle class (access to higher education)	People of lower status because of occupation, education, income, or rural habitat
Sexual orientation	Heterosexuals	Gay, lesbians, and bisexual people
Indigenous heritage	Non-native	Native
National origin	U.S. born	Immigrants, refugees, and international students
Gender	Male	Women, transgender, and intersex people

Source: Adapted from Hays, P.A. (2016). *Addressing Cultural Complexities in Practice: A Framework for Clinicians and Counselors (3ʳᵈ. ed.).* American Psychological Association

in North America. A Caucasian individual living in Japan, however, would be considered part of a nondominant or minority group in that country. Ethnic and racial identity is potentially one of the most salient cultural identity factors as well as the factor that can often garner the most experiences with privilege and oppression. The first S represents *Socioeconomic status* which can include one's education, occupation, and income. Those with limited formal education, those living in areas of poverty (e.g., rural communities, inner cities), and those in occupations that pay a lower wage may have a disadvantaged socioeconomic status and identity (Hays, 2016).

The second S in the model stands for *Sexual orientation* or those belonging to sexual minority groups. Individuals who identify as lesbian, gay, bisexual, transgender, queer, intersex, or assexual (LGBTQIA) often share a broader identity as a sexual minority, but there are specific identities related specifically to gender which is discussed in the following. *I* stands for *Indigenous heritage* and is considered in a separate category from ethnic and racial identity because many people who identify as having an indigenous heritage (e.g., Aboriginal, Native) identify themselves as part of a larger, world-wide culture who have shared interests and concerns around land and water rights, sovereignty, and specific cultural traditions (Hays, 2016).

The *N* in the model represents *National origin* and can include components such as country of origin if different from the country where someone is living, immigrant status, refugees, international students, and second-language learners and workers. Individuals who immigrated to the United States from another country, for example, may retain many of the cultural, familial, and social rules, norms, traditions, and language of their homeland. There may also be a strong relationship with other ADDRESSING domains such as ethnic and racial identity and indigenous heritage. The last letter in the acronym is *G* representing *Gender identity*. In most parts of the world, females are more likely to experience a minority or oppressed status based on their gender. Other gender identities also increasingly represent the potential for oppression in most societies including transgender, transsexual, intersex, gender-questioning, and other gender-nonconforming identities (Hays, 2016).

The ADDRESSING model is rooted in a Western framework consistent with clients in the United States and Canada, so "majority" and "minority" groups should be adjusted accordingly for other countries. Consistent with Collins's work on intersectionality (see *Black Feminist Thought: Intersectionality*), the ADDRESSING model presents different points of identity as being aligned with "power" or "less power." People typically experience some of their cultural characteristics as a representation of power or privilege, and other characteristics as representations of less power, discrimination, oppression, or racism/sexism/ageism. For example, Ellen might identify her gender and age roles as representing less power in her world, but might also acknowledge that being a White woman living in a higher socioeconomic bracket brings her more power. Ellen's lack of formal education, however, might threaten her sense of power based on socioeconomic status if she must now consider ways to make money differently since she is separated from the primary breadwinner in her home and now has added responsibilities of caring for her own mother.

SESSION EXCERPT

As Ellen's counselor, it is important that you, too, engage in an exploration of your own cultural characteristics and identities so you can be on the lookout for how your individual framework might intersect with Ellen's. As a counselor, you might engage Ellen in a discussion that goes something like this:

Counselor: To say there has been a lot of change lately in your life is putting it mildly, Ellen! Before we get into some of the specific reasons you are here, it helps me to take a little time to get to know you and how you really see yourself. I hear you saying that you just don't know who you are any more, so let's start with that question. Who is Ellen?

Ellen: Well, I guess I would say I'm a "mom" first. Rusty is my main focus. I know he is an adult now and soon will be making his own way in the world, but I still think about him every day ... sometimes multiple times a day. I wonder how he is feeling. What he is doing. Who he is with. There was such a hole in my heart when he went to college. It was almost like a death that I still find myself grieving. I don't know, saying out loud makes me sound a little crazy and obsessive, doesn't it?

Counselor: I don't hear crazy, but what I do hear is that a big part of your identity is that of a mother. That being a mom, no matter Rusty's age, has always been and continues to be a core of who you are. Okay, so in addition to being a mom, who else are you?

Ellen: Well, until recently I would have said "I am a wife" but I don't even know how I feel about that one. Technically I still am as we are just in a trial separation, whatever that means, but it seems like that role is just getting fainter and fainter. I really thought Clark would have tried to do anything to work to improve our marriage, but I can't help but feel he is really enjoying being on his own in an apartment in the city. So now I rattle around this big house by myself, except for my mom now being here, of course.

Counselor: Yes, so two really important points, there. First of all, the identity of "wife" is one you occupied for a very long time, and now becoming something else. Maybe even fading from view. So part of what we may want to focus on is what takes that role's place in your life now? Second, you mentioned your mom. Now that Frances is living with you, I wonder if there is yet another role that you have taken on?

Ellen: Yes! Well of course I am still a "daughter" but now sometimes I feel like I am her mother. It is such a strange role reversal! Having to remind my mom to eat, to get dressed, even to help her bathe because she is in a cast feels, in some ways, just wrong; unnatural. She sometimes acts like a rebellious teenager! I don't think I imagined a time where I would be doing these kinds of things with her.

Counselor: So the role and identity of "mother" lives on! But now instead of just being that figure to Rusty, you are also occupying that space with Frances, your mother. What else? Are there other ways you define yourself and your roles? Other groups of people, or communities, or places that help to determine who you are?

Ellen: Well, I can't help but be aware of my age. I know mid-50s isn't old, but at the same time, I know I am moving into another time of life. I sometimes feel that people just treat me as old. Like offering to help carry my groceries. I was actually offered a senior citizen discount in the grocery store the other day. I couldn't believe it! I also used to belong to a church. It is where Clark and Rusty and I used to go, although I admit we were more the type of church goers who showed up on holidays and not every Sunday. I don't know, I've been thinking I might want to go back again, though. There are some women there I used to be friends with, but we kind of drifted apart. It might be nice to reconnect with them. Speaking of women, I am also noticing as now a single woman that I am aware of how others treat me. I had a repairman come to the house the other day to work on the heating unit. Clark kept promising to come fix it but never did. The repairman made me very uncomfortable. He kept asking where my husband was and seemed to talk to me as if I were a child and didn't understand anything. I also couldn't help but feel that he was staring at my breasts more than my face. It was all very off putting and embarrassing! Not to mention the fact that I was having hot flashes the entire time he was there. Sometimes I just feel so ridiculous! Like a young woman trapped in an old woman's body.

Through this discussion with Ellen, we can start to understand the parts of her identity that are important to her, that are uncomfortable to her, and that may be new and emerging for her. The role identifications of "mother" to a now-adult son and "caretaker" for her own mother have entered into new and confusing territory. Her identity as a "wife" is equally confusing and uncertain. She also notices that factors such as age and gender are playing a role in how she interacts with others and is perceived by and treated by others. You can also hear some possible strengths and resources in Ellen's discussion. How she might tap in to social relationships again, or make renewed spiritual connections are all possible avenues to explore.

Age, Gender, and Self-Concept

From a cultural perspective, the intersection of "age" and "gender" have developmental considerations for Ellen. There is a tendency in Western culture to de-value aging and aging identities (Barrett, 2005; Kornadt et al., 2013). By association, one's self-valuation based on age can be impacted by the social, institutional, environmental, and cultural definitions of "aging," "growing old," and "old age." According to Barrett (2005), the self-perceptions of aging are, in general, harsher for women than men even though women tend to retain a youthful identity longer than men. Barrett further articulated that other life roles in work, family, and health are associated with gender differences in age identity. For example, a role transition from "worker" to "retiree" may be a positive and significant marker for some individuals, representing opportunities for leisure, travel, a focus on children and grandchildren, and development of other hobbies and interests. But research identified by Barrett (2005) suggests that moving into retirement can for many be associated with worsening psychological outcomes due to a reduction in social support, financial stability, and sense of belonging and purpose.

As we see in the case of Ellen, family transitions tend to be more salient markers of aging and age status for women than for men. Women's movement into aging is also marked by their reproductive cycle. The movement into menopause can, for many women, be a marker of finality; that her role as parent or potential parent is forever changed. Women in the United States in middle age may be more likely to try to maintain a youthful identity to try to enhance their own sense of well-being and self-worth than men. This occurs as women in middle adulthood are also facing and sometimes embracing the emerging roles that come with this time of life including launching children, becoming grandparents, and caring for elderly parents. The juxtaposition of holding on to a youthful identity while dealing with very real role transitions during midlife can put a strain on self-concept and a positive age identity (Barrett, 2005).

As we move into a discussion of contextual factors impacting middle adulthood, continue to consider the case of Ellen and how familial and environmental factors impact her development.

CONTEXTUAL FACTORS: MIDDLE ADULTHOOD

The Social Ecology Model

As discussed in Chapter 3 of this book, a new way of thinking about human development was proposed by Urie Bronfenbrenner in 1979. In his seminal text entitled *The Ecology of Human Development*, Bronfenbrenner proposed that development is shaped by the way in which a person perceives and interacts with their environment (Bronfenbrenner, 1979). This ecological perspective of development identifies several systems that people interact with and are impacted by as they move through the course of their lives. At the center of Bronfenbrenner's model is the individual and the next closest system is the *microsystem*. This environment consists of those who are closest to the individual. Next in the model is the *mesosystem* which identifies interactions of the microsystems in a person's life with one another. The *exosystem* represents more indirect environments that may impact development, and the *macrosystem* includes additional cultural, societal, and contextual influences on the individual. The outer ring of the model, the *chronosystem*, adds the dimension of time acknowledging that any changes in the other systems over time will continue to impact the developmental cycle (Bronfenbrenner, 1979). While Bronfenbrenner's theory was initially intended for understanding development in children, it has been applied to a wider glimpse of development across the lifespan (Mitchell & Wister, 2015). We can look at the case of Ellen and make some initial assumptions about the impact of the different systems on her environment. Take a look at the Model of Ecological Development and apply this to what we know so far about Ellen (Figure 10.1).

We have already gotten to know Ellen a bit as an individual. The conversation between Ellen and her counselor shed light on her identities and how she defines

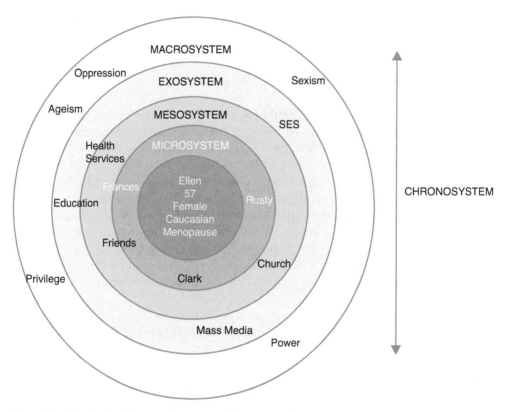

Figure 10.1 Ecological Systems Theory and case of Ellen.

Source: Data from Bronfenbrenner, U. (1979). *The Ecology of Human Development: Experiments by Nature and Design*. Harvard University Press.

her most salient roles. We know she is a Caucasian, middle-aged, cisgender female. We know that she is experiencing physical and hormonal changes because of her age. As we zoom out a bit on Ellen's ecological system, we see that her microsystem contains her immediate family including her son, Rusty, her mother, Frances, and even her husband, Clark, although they are currently separated. According to Bronfenbrenner (1979), individuals tend to experience their microsystem by those dyadic relationships that are central to their lives. In Ellen's case, these relationships are mother/son, daughter/mother, wife/husband. Even though each of these relationships is being redefined and reshaped, they are still the primary elements of Ellen's microsystem.

As we zoom out further, we can understand how Ellen the individual, through her primary dyadic relationships, experiences broader systemic attachments. The mesosystem helps us to understand the interactions of key figures in Ellen's life and how these interactions shape her development, and the exosystem is a reflection of broader, indirect environments that may be impactful. In other words, how do the different settings and contexts in Ellen's life function effectively (or not)? How does Ellen now reorganize around different experiences with her environment?

Ellen now has to take care of a home without the help of Clark. She has to interact with different healthcare providers to support Frances's recovery. She may be engaging with Rusty's college as he moves closer to graduation. She is considering widening her own social network through re-engagement with friends. She is also exploring re-establishing a relationship with her church community. All of these interactions among and between systems and people in Ellen's life have a direct impact on that primary question she brought to counseling: *Who am I now and what is next in my life?*

Ellen's macrosystem consists of those cultural and societal influences on her life. Ellen never finished college herself and faces a potentially uncertain financial future. What does this mean for her ability to manage her finances? Get a job? Start a business? Ellen is also seeing how being a "single" female as well as moving into middle age impacts how she is perceived by others and maybe even realizes for the first time her own experiences with privilege and oppression. All of these broader environmental experiences can have a ripple effect through Ellen's ecological context to directly impact who "Ellen" is at her core.

SESSION EXCERPT

So what does all of this mean for you, Ellen's counselor? From an ecology model perspective, it highlights the importance of understanding Ellen and her presenting concern in context. All of who she is, who she has been, and who she is becoming is shaped by her systemic interactions including herself, her primary dyads, her broader triads, and the direct, indirect, cultural, and societal influences on her life.

Counselor: One thing I am aware of, Ellen, is that change and transition seem to be key themes in your life right now. Consider the image of dropping a pebble in a pond and the ripples that move out from the pebble. Now imagine that you are that pebble; you are the catalyst for changes that impact your immediate relationships, your environments, and how you experience the world.

Ellen: That is a hard thing for me to picture. I've never seen myself as being the thing that has that much influence on what happens. I guess I've largely felt like my life just happened to me; that I just had to react and respond to what is going on around me. Like when Clark decided to move out. That wasn't my choice, but I figured out how to reorganize around his decision. I just had to pull myself together and make it work, you know?

Counselor: Yes, I can certainly understand how you have had to adapt to things beyond your control; like Frances's injury and Rusty moving out, and now Clark leaving. But as you look at yourself right now, in this moment, what are the ways in which you can impact these experiences in your life? These changes?

Ellen: One thing I've been thinking about is going back to college. I've been talking a lot to Rusty about his upcoming graduation and what he plans to do. He is so excited about putting his education to use in the real world! I've found myself feeling envious of him, and also a bit bitter, if I'm honest, against Clark because I dropped my own education to move here and start a life with him; to support him in his professional pursuits. But now here I am ... no real education, no real skills, and finding myself a bit scared by what could be a decrease in financial support from Clark. And honestly, I would love to not even need his support! I am ready to stand on my own two feet and show him and everyone else that I can be a strong, independent woman.

Counselor: So what I'm hearing from you, Ellen, is that while you certainly feel that your current experiences are shaped by your environment and the people in your life, you also are starting to see ways that you can also do things to shape and change those experiences. There are still some things you have to continue to adjust to, like Rusty growing into adulthood and starting his own journey, but I also see that you are starting to broaden your own thinking about who you are and who you now can become.

The Multicontextual Lifecycle

Another way to understand development during midlife is by looking at how a family moves through developmental stages. McGoldrick (2016) presented the *Multicontextual Lifecycle Framework* which posits that, as we age, grow, and develop over time, our development process is directly impacted by our families as well as our sociocultural context. This developmental view encourages us to focus on all ages and stages of development though a systemic and familial lens; that we think, for example, about *families* during midlife instead of *individuals* during midlife. According to Preto and Blacker (2016), people at midlife face a confluence of changing roles; sometimes seemingly all at once. From changes in partner relationships (separated, divorced, remarried, widowed), to the realities of aging (hormonal changes, physical changes, reassessment of mortality), to the impact of social location and other cultural and contextual factors (socioeconomic status, race and ethnicity), this time of midlife represents a myriad of possibilities to reassess ones' life role, reinvent oneself, and to renegotiate relationships. The lifecycle perspective of development invites exploration of pivotal events and milestones through the interactions among and between people in families, in friendships, and in society. Ellen, our fictional client, is in the process of renegotiating several key relationships; with her mother, her husband, her friend group, and her child. Ellen's ability to effectively engage in this renegotiation could both normalize her experiences and lead to a sense of resolution.

SESSION EXCERPT

Counselor: Ellen, let's talk a bit more about Rusty. I know you are very close! I have also heard you talk about how hard it was when he went to college, and even now as he is planning to graduate, there seems to still be quite a struggle for you as you envision his continued absence.

Ellen: (Sighs deeply.) I just don't know how to explain it. It feels both totally normal and abnormal at the same time. I want him to move on from college, to start living his own life. I want him to continue to work through what it means to be an adult, so I know that means that I have to continue to find ways to "let go." But on the other hand, I still just miss him so much. I miss waking him up at the crack of dawn and making him breakfast before high school. I miss running around like a crazy woman getting him to soccer practice, then to chorus, then having all of his friends come to our house for snacks after the game. It feels like I can't quite figure out what our relationship is anymore, either. It is just weird to try to now have an adult relationship with him. I sometimes don't even know what to say, and even though I try to stop myself, inevitably I will start saying "Mom stuff," as he calls it. Things like, "Are you eating well?" or "How are you sleeping?" or "Did you study for that test?" It is just so strange that even now with him almost 4 years away at college I still can't quite put my finger on who I am to him and who he needs me to be.

THE EMPTY NEST

The concept of the "empty nest" is one that has largely been anchored to Western, industrialized countries (Mitchell & Wister, 2015). Launching young adult children is seen as a normative developmental milestone for both children and parents as children begin to fulfill their "adult" roles and make their way in the world. In more collectivist societies, there may be different expectations, ideas, and emotions tied to the movement into adulthood and the impact on the family system. For example, multigenerational living may be typical in families with a collectivist focus. Adult children can contribute to the financial well-being of the family system. They can take on more responsibilities for helping with younger siblings or aging parents or grandparents. They may also be given more room and space to move into adulthood with different familial ideas about the "timetable" for becoming an adult (Mitchell & Wister, 2015). Similarly, families who are poor or working class often rely on their adult children's added resources for ongoing support, so the notion of a "clean break" from the family is not necessarily expected, even though it may be a cultural norm (Preto & Blacker, 2016). In Western, industrialized society and particularly in families who occupy the middle or upper class, however, there is often an expectation that the "launch" of adult children carries with it some finality; that as young adults fly from the nest, their parents now have to generate new meanings and expectations around the role of "Mom" or "Dad."

Just as we see with Ellen, many parents who are in the phase of launching adult children feel bewildered and unsure as to how to navigate this change in the family system (Preto & Blacker, 2016). In addition, it is not uncommon for parents in mid-life with adult children to experience the failed launch, or *boomerang effect*. According to a study conducted by the Pew Research Center (2019), most Americans (64%) believe adult children should achieve financial independence by the time they are 22 years old. The reality, however, is that only 24% of 22-year-old Americans are financially independent. In fact, as much as six in 10 parents indicate they have provided some level of financial help to their adult children who are between 18 and 29 years of age (Pew Research Center, 2019). Adult children who return home or otherwise rely on their parents into adulthood can be an added stress for parents who may have anticipated having more financial freedom as their children entered the world of adulthood and independence.

There are other cultural and contextual factors impacting the movement of children into adulthood for their parents in midlife. Parents who might themselves be less acculturated to the dominant culture but who have children who are more acculturated to the dominant culture can experience added stress and conflict around launching. According to Preto and Blacker these parents might even experience their adult child's wish to leave home as "… a failure on their part, and as their children's lack of loyalty" (2016, p. 326). In addition, those parents in midlife who have a more collectivist cultural framework may not even experience an "empty nest" syndrome as described here since their adult children are likely to remain active, engaged, and involved in the overall family unit. Regardless of when, how, or whether adult children leave the nest, the movement into adulthood itself will likely have a profound impact on the roles and function of adult parents in midlife.

THE SANDWICH GENERATION

Another key renegotiation of roles many adults in midlife experience is being caught between parenting adolescent or emerging adults while also beginning to play a more active role in the care of aging parents. As stated at the start of this chapter, the stage of development known as middle adulthood is a relatively recent phenomenon as people are, in general, living longer. There is a ripple effect on the roles of family members; couples are waiting longer to have children so children are therefore reaching adulthood as their grandparents are entering a phase of life potentially impacted by physical and mental challenges. This means that the middle-aged adult can be squarely sandwiched between renegotiating both parenting roles and child roles with aging parents (see Figure 10.2).

Figure 10.2 Sandwich generation.

Source: iStock

SESSION EXCERPT

Ellen: (To her counselor during their fifth session.) You just wouldn't believe what my weekend was like! Remember how I was so sad that Rusty would be moving on after college? Well he came home this weekend and told me he wanted to move back home until he could figure out his next move! You would think that I would have been thrilled by this, right? But actually, I found myself feeling frustrated with him and a little scared.

Counselor: That is news! Tell me a bit about those feelings of "frustration" and "fear." What do you think is causing those to bubble up?

Ellen: Well, I've been trying to figure that out, too. I mean, I have been talking about how hard it has been to let go of Rusty, but I realize that it has been hard to let go of Rusty, my little boy; my busy adolescent. I am not sure I feel prepared to now take care of Rusty, the grown man. I'm just not sure what he even expects, frankly. I talked to Clark about it last night and he said that if Rusty moves back into the house we need to have some strict rules, like he has to get a job in a certain amount of time, and he has to pay rent or bills or something. Of course that is easy for Clark to say! I will be the one having to enforce whatever rules or boundaries we set; and with a grown man! It reminds me of what I am already having to do with my mother … she is just so belligerent sometimes and won't do the things she should be doing to get better. Yesterday I caught her in the kitchen on a stool trying to reach something from the top cabinet. I was so surprised I just yelled at her, which of course made her very upset. Now I have to think about how to keep dealing with Mom while also dealing with Rusty at home. It just feels very overwhelming!

As we can see, Ellen is facing some challenging renegotiations of multiple family roles. Midlife can be fraught with family contradictions, resolving old issues with children and parents, and dealing with new conflicts around roles and expectations (Preto & Blacker, 2016). An added complication for these sandwiched adults is that many young adult children in today's society expect that their parents will continue to provide financial and emotional support into adulthood. The Pew research study on young adult financial independence found that a majority of young adults (65%) say their parents are doing the "right amount" of financial support for them and 77% indicate that they rely on their parents either "a lot" or "some" for emotional support (Pew Research Center, 2019).

THE COUPLE IN MIDLIFE

Not only is Ellen faced with renegotiating the "parent/child" relationship with Rusty and the "child/parent" relationship with Frances, her mother, she is also renegotiating her marital relationship with Clark. This third level of renegotiation can lend to the overall emotional challenges Ellen is facing as all of her attachment ties are being upended (Mitchell & Wister, 2015). While the divorce rate in the United States has been steadily declining since the 1990s, it has almost doubled for those over the age of 50 (Preto & Blacker, 2016).

Separation and Divorce.   In 2004, The American Association for Retired Persons (AARP) conducted a survey with adults who had gone through a divorce in their 40s, 50s, or 60s. A total of 1,148 people responded to the survey. Interestingly, more women (66%) than men initiate divorce. While some notable reasons for asking for a divorce included instances of verbal, physical, or emotional abuse (34%), a difference in values or lifestyles (29%), or issues such as cheating (27%), about one in four reasons for divorce were because one or both members of the couple had simply fallen out of love (AARP, 2004). Since separations or divorces in midlife tend to follow longer term marriages (96% were married for 10 years or longer), they potentially have more impact on the immediate and extended family, the social circle, and the financial stability of the family unit (AARP, 2004). Many divorces in midlife occur because one or both of the partners dreads facing a future prospect of being alone with the same person the rest of their life, especially if children have launched, one or both members of the couple have retired, and/or a new reckoning with mortality or the time that is left motivates a change. Whatever the impetus, the decision to end a long partnership is often very difficult and painful (Preto & Blacker, 2016).

SESSION EXCERPT

Counselor: I know you told me, Ellen, that Clark's decision to move out came as a bit of a surprise to you, even though you were the one who let him know you were dissatisfied with how the marriage was going. I wonder if you could share a bit of what things have looked like between you both since he's been gone? I know you are coming up on almost 6 months since he moved into an apartment in the city. What are the primary changes you have noticed in that time?

Ellen: Well, it hasn't been easy, that's for sure. A lot of what has been hard, though, is more the practical stuff. Like I told you I had to call the repairman to come fix the heater, and I usually never had to do that kind of thing. I've also had to figure out how to work the riding lawn mower and do more of the yard work because that was always Clark's thing. Of course money is a worry … he is still paying the mortgage and the bills, and I get some money each month from him for groceries and things, but I know the time is coming where I am going to have to figure out my own finances.

Counselor: Yes, that does sound like a lot of practical changes you have had to make. What about emotionally? How has it felt since he's been gone?

Ellen: That is hard to say. Some days I miss him and it is just strange that he isn't there, sitting in the family room with the newspaper or bursting into the house after his morning run. Other days I don't even think much about him honestly; I just go about my day doing what I've always done: go grocery shopping, cook a meal, clean up the house. I guess I am just aware that we just started to drift apart, probably for a long time now. We were in such a routine, maybe even some would say a rut. So in some ways it almost felt like the natural thing to do. I'm pretty sure this is heading for divorce, which I think I am okay with. It is just figuring out the practical stuff that is still scary.

Relationship Satisfaction.   Of course many long-term marriages and relationships endure into midlife and beyond. For many couples, there can be a rediscovering of one another that is a joyful and exciting phenomenon. Launching children and moving into retirement have also been correlated with higher marital satisfaction (Preto & Blacker, 2016). For some couples in midlife, the marriage or partnership may be characterized as a deepening friendship, a sense of companionship, a feeling of increased tolerance and equality, and a movement toward discovering shared interests (Cordova, 2014).

For these couples, the renewed investment in the relationship can enhance a sense of intimacy and increase sexuality as a couple. It is also not uncommon, however, for sexual activity to decrease as couples move through midlife; not necessarily as a byproduct of anything being "wrong" in the relationship, but perhaps because sex in a relationship does not represent the same urgency it once did. According to Nichols (2005), for example, while sex may be less frequent among gay and lesbian couples in midlife, it is also reported to be more satisfying. Navigating physical and hormonal changes for both women and men in midlife can lead to a need to renegotiate the sexual relationship and intentionally identify other forms of intimacy.

Being Single in Midlife.   It is also important to note that many people in midlife are living happy, fulfilled lives as purposefully single adults. Whether divorced, separated, widowed, or never married/coupled, the well-adjusted single adult in midlife is typically able to participate meaningfully and fully in relevant and important relationships with family, friends, and coworkers. According to McGoldrick (2016), some women in midlife who find themselves uncoupled actually experience a new sense of confidence and self-esteem. In addition, close friendships in midlife have been shown to be a primary factor in overall well-being. Positive social networks outside of the marital unit have even been shown to reduce the number of physical impairments experienced by women as they age (McGoldrick, 2016). Understanding how to help clients like Ellen establish or re-establish meaningful relationships even as her marriage may be ending is an important factor in helping her establish balance and well-being.

SESSION EXCERPT

Counselor: You mentioned in an earlier session, Ellen, that you are thinking some about yourself and what you might like to do. It can be difficult sometimes for people, especially women, who are used to being caretakers for others to begin to think a little selfishly about possible next steps. You had mentioned things like reconnecting with some of your women friends, possibly getting involved in your church again, and even going back to school. Could you talk a bit about any one of these ideas and what it might take to make it happen?

Ellen: Yes, all of those are things I've been thinking about. You had asked me when we first started meeting about how I defined myself, and I talked about being a "wife" and a "mother" and a "daughter." That is all about other people! I do find myself day-dreaming more and more about doing something that is just about me, but that word you used, "selfish," has a nasty ring to it. I still have to take care of my mom, Rusty is moving home, and I'm still trying to figure out what Clark and I are going to do. But I do miss having girlfriends to hang out with.

Counselor: I think it can be particularly difficult for women, sometimes, to consider doing something for themselves and not feel guilty about it! The truth is that we are often better for others when we feel fulfilled ourselves. It seems to me that with Rusty moving home, you now also have an opportunity to have him assist with the care of his grandmother. This might allow you to free up some time to take a look at connecting with friends, or look at taking a class or two.

Ellen: That is a good idea. I have been trying to think of ways for Rusty to earn his keep when he moves back home. My cousin Katherine contacted me last week, actually. She said she belongs to a book club with women from the church I used to go to. She asked me to come to the next meeting. I don't know, maybe I should think about it. I also did pick up a brochure at the community college last week. I'm really good with numbers, you know, and once upon a time I thought I'd be a good accountant. It really does feel a little exciting to think about some new possibilities; also a little scary!

CLIENTS IN MIDLIFE: CLINICAL CONSIDERATIONS

Throughout this chapter, we have examined cultural and contextual factors, theories, and models of development at midlife. Ellen, our fictional client, has assisted us in anchoring this discussion through possible interactions with her counselor. Notice throughout this chapter, these interactions have been focused primarily on Ellen's stage in life, on her relationships, and on the changes she is experiencing as a woman in her 50s. Clinicians who incorporate their knowledge of key developmental considerations into their work with clients will be more likely to convey an understanding of their client's cultural and contextual factors through a developmental lens. Regardless of the psychotherapy theory or approach, the developmentally focused mental health professional is able to contextualize client concerns in a more robust way. A key part of working with clients from a culturally responsive and competent stance includes a mental health professional's ability to examine their own multiple cultural identities, biases, and blind spots. Clinical strategies for helping clients in midlife explore the role that their developmental stage plays, culturally and contextually, in their identified issues can be used to help the mental health professional increase their overall understanding of the client and their concerns.

Cultural Considerations in Counseling

The intersectionality of roles and identities are salient factors in understanding a client's experiences with power, privilege, and oppression. The mental health professional who takes the time to explore both stable identities and changing/evolving identities may be better able to conceptualize the client's concern through a culturally aware and sensitive approach. Using acronyms like ADDRESSING can remind clinicians to take the time to explore with open curiosity and cultural humility the client's intersectionality and its impact on both development and presenting issues (Hays, 2016). Engaging clients in activities to identify their own identities while also engaging in a self-exploration of cultural identities can bolster the mental health professional's efficacy in bringing cultural consideration to the forefront of their counseling relationship.

STUDENT REFLECTION 10.1

Cultural Considerations and Ellen

Using the ADDRESSING framework in Table 10.1, write down your key cultural characteristics and identities. Then identify whether each characteristic/identity represents a position of "power" or "oppression." Now do the same exercise for our fictional client, Ellen. Imagine you are the mental health professional working with her. Based on your own identities and those of Ellen, what are some cultural considerations to keep in mind when working with her? What are some potential blind-spots, prejudices, or assumptions you need to be mindful of when working with a client like Ellen? Finally, what are those areas of your own identity that could be challenging for future clients, and how can you engage in a discussion with clients about their cultural characteristics and identities?

Contextual Considerations in Counseling

When working with people in midlife, mental health professions should consider the impact of other contextual factors on the developmental process. Exploring the client's interactions with different systems and the systems' interactions with each other can widen the clinician's understanding of the contextual variables impacting their identified issues. Considering a systemic view of development can also be helpful in framing the client's primary concerns in their familial and sociocultural contexts. Two strategies that can be used to help clients explore the impact of their different ecological, social, and familial systems are the *Ecomap* and the *Genogram*.

THE ECOMAP

The Ecomap is a visual representation of the client or client family's relationships to different existing or potential support systems (Correa et al., 2011; McCormick et al., 2008). Based in Bronfrebrenner's Social Ecology model, the Ecomap exercise is a way for clients to map their support systems in relation to themselves and/or their family unit. Circles are used to identify the primary system (i.e., self, partner, child/children, parent/parents), and then lines are drawn from the primary system to extended family members, friends, coworkers, community members, school members, church members, or anyone who could be considered an actual or potential source of social support. The lines can be coded to identify if the relationship is strong or lacking.

In a study of Puerto Rican mothers of children with disabilities, Correa et al. (2011) used the Ecomap as one tool to learn about the strengths and reciprocities of support relationships between the mothers and members of their network. The results of the study found that mothers identified strong and supportive relationships with family members including grandmothers, aunts, uncles, and cousins. While their child's father was often identified as a potential source of support, the lines on the Ecomap showed that often these relationships are complicated by conflictual interactions. Results also highlighted the importance of friendships to the women participants. In particular, female friends who were also Latina and those who also had children with disabilities were shown to offer strong support (Correa et al., 2011). Other important relationships identified on the Ecomaps included teachers, social workers, case managers, and doctors.

The Ecomap can be used in clinical settings to quickly aid in the identification of existing and potential sources of support. It is important for clinicians to also suggest that they also are a source of support that can be identified on the Ecomap. Clients are also encouraged to think beyond the obvious and existing sources of support and to consider potential and new sources of support to add to their network. Clients are also able to examine the nature of relationships, and to see when even those relationships that are existing and sometimes supportive can also be fraught with conflict.

THE GENOGRAM

Similar to an Ecomap, the Genogram is a way to create a diagram of relationships. The Genogram is typically focused on the family and includes intergenerational relationships. Genograms can be used to understand how a family works, what patterns of behavior exist in a family, and the interdependent relationships among and between family members (Galindo et al., 2016).

Genograms are typically co-created by the mental health professional and the client or client family. Shapes (squares for males, circles for females, and additional symbols for inter-sex, transgender, and gender fluid individuals) are used to depict individuals within a family, and lines are used to identify relationships between members of the family. There are several resources clinicians can use to assist in creating a Genogram including Galindo et al.'s *A Family Genogram Workbook* (2016) and software programs like *GenoPro* (genopro.com). The construction of a genogram can in and of itself be a therapeutic endeavor. Clients who are able to identify and articulate family rules, family rituals, family problems such as addiction or abuse, transgenerational trauma, and the nature of family relationships, past and present, can begin to see key multigenerational patterns emerge and can examine themselves in context to these patterns.

STUDENT REFLECTION 10.2

Contextual Considerations and Ellen

What are your social and familial relationships? How do they represent support in your life? What are key patterns in your family that impact the ways in which you interact with the world? Using one of the following resources, develop either an Ecomap or Genogram for yourself. Consider how either your social relationships represented in an Ecomap or your familial relationships represented in a Genogram potentially impact the ways in which you will work with clients in a mental health setting.

Ecomap Resource: https://app.creately.com/diagram/gecrWopwVq9/edit

Genogram Resource: https://genopro.com/

PERSPECTIVES FROM THE FIELD: PODCAST

Access this podcast at http://connect.springerpub.com/content/book/978-0-8261-8279-1/part/part02/chapter/ch10

Before we move into an exploration of other theories and models of development we might consider when working with clients who are in the developmental stages of middle adulthood, let's talk to Dr. Donna Sheperis to discuss some important developmental considerations when working with a client like Ellen. Dr. Sheperis is a Licensed Professional Counselor (LPC) in Texas and a professor at Palo Alto University. We sat down with Dr. Sheperis and asked her to consider the case of "Ellen" and how she might approach working with this client within the context of Ellen's stage of development. We also asked Dr. Sheperis to consider other relevant cultural and contextual factors to consider when working with clients in this developmental stage.

STUDENT REFLECTION 10.3

You have considered the case of Ellen and listened to Dr. Sheperis discuss working with women in midlife. Dr. Sheperis talked about being a woman in midlife herself, and therefore having to be mindful of not imposing her identity onto her clients in midlife. From a clinical perspective, how might you work to encourage exploration of your midlife clients' intersecting identities? What are the main cultural and contextual considerations you will apply to your work with clients in midlife? How does this understanding inform your treatment plan and clinical approach?

SUMMARY

In this chapter, we introduced the phase of life called middle adulthood. As we have seen so far in this book, there are generally no hard and fast age markers that we attribute to a particular stage of life, so this span of time we consider middle adulthood could be anywhere from the early 40s into the 60s and beyond. In Western civilizations, people are living longer and longer, so we can anticipate that our idea of middle adulthood could continue to shift.

To orient our discussion, we met Ellen, a cisgender White female in her mid 50s. Ellen's circumstances represent what we might often see of clients in this phase of life. She is dealing with launching her adult child (empty nest) while also facing his potential return home (boomerang effect). She is caring for her mother who has suffered a recent injury (sandwich generation) and also navigating the changing nature of her relationships with her husband from whom she is separated. Ellen is aware of key physical changes such as menopause and changes to her appearance, and she is also rethinking and redefining who she wants to be as she considers new and rekindled friendships, spiritual connections, and educational pursuits.

We considered our clinical work with Ellen from both cultural and contextual perspectives. Using the ADDRESSING acronym, we identified the salient identities of our client and ourselves as mental health providers. Understanding the intersectionality of these identities, both within the client and ourselves and between the client and ourselves, helps to inform ways to connect with clients in midlife from a culturally responsive approach.

The consideration of clients in midlife from a social ecological framework assists in understanding how one's primary roles impact and are impacted by relationships with others in their microsystem, macrosystem, mesosystem, and exosystem, keeping in mind the cultural chronosystem that threads through all of these layers. The use of an Ecomap can assist mental health professionals in understanding their clients' potential sources of support and barriers to that support.

As all clients have families; whether families of origin, families by marriage, or families of choice, the understanding of the developmental process in context to family relationships is another helpful process in which to engage. The Multicontextual Lifecycle Framework of development encourages this examination of how all of the salient interactions and roles in a family impact the life transitions and experiences of our clients. Using a Genogram to help clients trace their multigenerational relationships and family patterns can help clients to better navigate their key developmental milestones.

Our podcast expert, Dr. Donna Sheperis, helped us to understand how working with someone like Ellen reminds us of the importance of holding space for clients to truly share their intersecting identities and how we as clinicians can learn from our clients through engagement in open curiosity and cultural humility. We look forward to further exploration of this phase of life in the next chapter.

REFERENCES

American Association of Retired Persons. (2004). *The divorce experience: A study of divorce at midlife and beyond*. Author. https://assets.aarp.org/rgcenter/general/divorce.pdf

Barrett, A. E. (2005). Gendered experiences in midlife: Implications for age identity. *Journal of Aging Studies, 19*(2), 163–183. https://doi.org/10.1016/j.jaging.2004.05.002

Bronfenbrenner, U. (1979). *The ecology of human development: Experiments by nature and design*. Harvard University Press.

Cordova, J. V. (2014). *The marriage checkup practitioner's guide: Promoting lifelong relationship health*. American Psychological Association.

Correa, V. I., Bonilla, Z. E., & Reyes-MacPherson, M. E. (2011). Support networks of single Puerto Rican mothers of children with disabilities. *Journal of Child and Family Studies*, 20(1), 66–77. https://doi.org/10.1007/s10826-010-9378-3

Galindo, I., Boomer, E., & Reagan, D. (2016). *A family genogram workbook*. Educational Consultants.

Hays, P. A. (2016). *Addressing cultural complexities in practice: A framework for clinicians and counselors* (3rd ed). American Psychological Association. https://doi.org/10.1037/14801-000

Kornadt, A. E., Voss, P., & Rothermund, K. (2013). Multiple standards of aging: gender-specific age stereotypes in different life domains. *European Journal of Ageing*, 10(4), 335–344. https://doi.org/10.1007/s10433-013-0281-9

McCormick, K. M., Stricklin, S., Nowak, T. M., & Rous, B. (2008). Using eco-mapping to understand family strengths and resources. *Young Exceptional Children*, 11(2), 17–28. https://doi.org/10.1177/1096250607311932

McGoldrick, M. (2016). Women and the family life cycle. In M. McGoldrick, N. G. Preto, & B. Carter (Eds.), *The expanded family life-cycle: Individual, family, and social perspectives* (5th ed). Pearson.

Mitchell, B. A., & Wister, A. V. (2015). Midlife challenge or welcome departure? Cultural and family-related expectations of empty nest transitions. *The International Journal of Aging & Human Development*, 81(4), 260–280. https://doi.org/10.1177/0091415015622790

Newton, N., & Stewart, A. J. (2010). The middle ages: Change in women's personalities and social roles. *Psychology of Women Quarterly*, 34(1), 75–84. https://doi.org/10.1111/j.1471-6402.2009.01543.x

Nichols, M. (2005). Sexual function in lesbians and lesbian relationships. In I. Goldstein, C. Meston, S. Davis, & A. Traish (Eds.), *Women's sexual functions and dysfunction: Study, diagnosis, and treatment*. Taylor & Francis.

Overstreet, L. (n.d.). *Introduction to middle adulthood*. https://courses.lumenlearning.com/suny-lifespandevelopment2/chapter/introduction-to-lesson-9-middle-adulthood

Pew Research Center. (2019, October). *Majority of Americans say parents are doing too much for their young adult children*. https://www.pewsocialtrends.org/2019/10/23/majority-of-americans-say-parents-are-doing-too-much-for-their-young-adult-children

Preto, N. G., & Blacker, L. (2016). Families at midlife: Launching children and moving on. In M. McGoldrick, N. G. Preto, & B. Carter (Eds.), *The expanded family life-cycle: Individual, family, and social perspectives* (5th ed). Pearson.

World Health Organization (2016). Global health estimates: Life expectancy and healthy life expectancy. https://www.who.int/data/gho/data/themes/mortality-and-global-health-estimates/ghe-life-expectancy-and-healthy-life-expectancy

CHAPTER **11**

Developmental Theories of Middle Adulthood

LEARNING OBJECTIVES

Upon completion of this chapter, students will be able to:

1. Identify the stage of lifespan development known as "middle adulthood."
2. Identify key theories impacting this stage of development.
3. Examine key research impacting this stage of development.
4. Identify future directions for research and understanding of people in middle adulthood.

Analyze how to work with clients in this stage of life while listening to an expert on counseling women in middle adulthood, Dr. Donna Sheperis,

CASE STUDY 11.1: THE CASE OF ELLEN AND CLARK

Ellen is a 57-year-old cisgender White female who recently separated from her husband, Clark. Ellen has an adult son, Rusty,
who has recently moved back home after finishing college. She is
also caring for her mother, Frances, who has been living with her
since an accident that has required ongoing rehabilitation. Since
we started working with Ellen in counseling, she has started
taking classes in accounting at the local community college, has
joined a book club, and has begun volunteering at her church.
Ellen, Rusty, and Frances seem to have found a good balance
of supporting one another, contributing to the household, and
finding time for themselves and their own interests. Ellen has recently been reporting
to her counselor that she is feeling better about herself, her many life roles, and the
direction her life is taking. Her counselor has been moving toward termination with
Ellen as a client, but in her last session she comes in with new information. Ellen's husband Clark, from whom she has been separated for almost a year, took her to dinner
last week and begged her to take him back. He said to her that his life has felt "empty"
and "meaningless" without her, that as he is getting ready to retire from his job at the
chemical company where he has worked for almost 30 years, he doesn't have any idea
of what he will do next and is very afraid of growing old alone. He told Ellen that
he "would do anything" for her to consider taking him back. Ellen's counselor has
referred Ellen and Clark for couples therapy so they can work together on figuring

out a possible way forward. In their first session their marriage therapist learns about Ellen, introduced in the last chapter and about Clark, a 61-year-old cisgender White male. Clark shares that his looming retirement has caused him to be "terrified" and has also forced him to begin looking at himself and his own mortality. "I don't know what I was thinking, asking Ellen for a separation," he tells their therapist. "My life has been so empty and lonely, and she seems to have just blossomed into someone new. I need to do whatever I can to get her back. I sure hope you can help me."

MIDDLE ADULTHOOD

The stage of middle adulthood is between about 40 and 65 years of age (Newton & Stewart, 2010; Overstreet, n.d.), but some research has suggested that this phase of life can extend even into the early to mid 70s. This may be one of the least studied periods of life as well as one of the most varied. Middle adulthood represents a unique time of life for many people. It can be a time of new beginnings as children launch and workers move into retirement. It can be a time of loss of older parents and other family members. It is a time also marked by key cognitive and physical changes as "development" is sometimes better characterized by "decline." Changes in personality can occur as people engage in self-reflection of concepts such as worth, meaning, and achievement. It is not uncommon for adults in this phase of life to face existential questions: Who am I? What have I contributed to my family, to society? What does it mean to have more years behind me than ahead of me (Newton & Stewart, 2010)?

In this chapter, we discuss and critique specific developmental theories that seek to explain this phase of life from the perspectives of personality development, ego development, and moral development. We also use the case of Ellen and Clark to explore some ways in which these different development milestones and challenges can impact the client/counselor relationship. We examine recent and emerging research on this phase of life and how these inquiries help us to continue to understand the experiences of people in midlife.

PERSONALITY DEVELOPMENT IN MIDDLE ADULTHOOD

Many theories of development focus on the development of the personality. What exactly does one's *personality* represent, and what does it mean in the context of development during middle adulthood? According to Loevinger and Knoll (1983), personality can include key constructs such as morality, empathy, and a sense of self, or ego. Some theories of personality development focus on the individual, so cognitive development and self- and ego-development are central factors to consider. Other theories focus on self in relation to others and the world around them, so moral, ethical, and social development are viewed as relevant facets of personality. Most traditional theories of personality development follow a stage model and seek to explain the process of development in children and adolescents, suggesting that the development of personality is determined by the time one enters adulthood. More recently, there has been a focus on the ongoing developmental process of adults. Many lifespan developmental theories postulate that growth development and change can and does occur at every phase of life (Mitchell, 2021).

PSYCHOSOCIAL DEVELOPMENT

Perhaps one of the best known stage theories of development across the lifespan is Erik Erikson's theory of Psychosocial Development. Erik Erikson was a German-born American psychologist who developed his theory of psychosocial development based largely on his own experiences in his clinical practice. Erik Erikson, along with his wife, Joan, continued to refine their theory into their 90s; even adding a ninth stage of development for the very old (i.e., 80s and 90s) where people revisit each of the earlier stages and resolve the previous conflicts in new ways. As with many theories of human development, the Psychosocial Development theory was developed in the 20th century by a middle-aged, affluent White man, so we know that it is rooted in presumptions of "normative" development based largely on White, male, and affluent cultural premises (Mitchell, 2021). For Erikson, each developmental stage of life, from birth to death, was marked by a development crisis to resolve. If the crisis is successfully resolved, the individual continues along the path of the development of a healthy personality and sense of self.

Erikson originally conceived eight stages of psychosocial development that people pass through starting in childhood and ending with the final stage of life. At each stage, individuals are theorized to grapple with two competing constructs that lead to the formulation of our emerging identity. As noted, Joan Erikson was a key contributor to her husband's work, and published their conceptualization of a ninth stage in *The Life Cycle Completed* in 1997, which will be discussed in a future chapter in more detail. Table 11.1 shows each of the stages of the Psychosocial Development theory and the conflict to be resolved at each stage.

At its core, the Psychosocial Development model is a strengths-based framework for understanding how individuals, within their social contexts, struggle with the antithesis of each stage (trust versus mistrust, autonomy versus shame, initiative versus guilt, industry versus inferiority, identity versus confusion, intimacy versus isolation, generativity versus stagnation, and integrity versus despair). If children, adolescents, and adults are able to resolve the conflict of the stage, they emerge with psychosocial strengths (hope, will, purpose, competency, fidelity, love, care, and wisdom) that bolster their sense of self and identity (Erikson & Erikson, 1997).

Generativity Versus Stagnation

For those in midlife, the primary conflict to resolve is *generativity* versus *stagnation*. Generativity is, fundamentally, about care. For women, that can mean caring for others (children, parents), caring for community and society, and even a renewed sense of self-interest (Mitchell, 2021). For men, generativity can manifest as a desire to maintain productivity related to work, to society, and to family. For all people in midlife, a sense of purpose can be called into question as one begins to consider one's contributions to others and the world around one. Stagnation can occur when there is an experience of rejectivity, or an unwillingness to extend care and focus to others (Erikson & Erikson, 1997). For the crisis of stagnation, there can be a sense of not caring to care; of selectively rejecting family, friends, and co-workers. Consider how Clark and Ellen's marriage therapist, using the lens of generativity versus stagnation, seeks to uncover Clark's motives for wanting to move back home after leaving Ellen.

Table 11.1 Psychosocial Development Model

APPROXIMATE AGE	PSYCHOSOCIAL CRISIS/TASK	WHAT HAPPENS AT THIS STAGE?	VIRTUE DEVELOPED
Infant–18 Months	Trust vs. Mistrust	If needs are met, infants develop a sense of basic trust	Hope
18 Months–3 Years	Autonomy vs. Shame/Doubt	Toddlers learn to exercise will and do things for themselves or they'll doubt their abilities	Will
3–5 Years	Initiative vs. Guilt	Preschoolers learn to initiate tasks and carry out plans, or they feel guilty about efforts to be independent	Purpose
5–13 Years	Industry vs. Inferiority	Children learn the pleasure of applying themselves to tasks, or they feel inferior	Competency
13–21 Years	Identity vs. Confusion	Teenagers work at refining a sense of self by testing roles and integrating them to form a single identity, or they become confused about who they are	Fidelity
21–39 Years	Intimacy vs. Isolation	Young adults struggle to form close relationships and to gain the capacity for intimate love, or they feel socially isolated	Love
40–65 Years	Generativity vs. Stagnation	The middle-aged adult discovers a sense of contributing to the world usually through family and work, or they may feel a lack of purpose	Care
65–80	Integrity vs. Despair	When reflecting on their lives, the older adult may feel a sense of satisfaction or failure	Wisdom
80–End of Life	All Previous Stages	Oldest adults experience all previous stages as they struggle to maintain the virtues of previous stages	Gerotranscendence

Source: Adapted from Erikson, E., & Erikson, J. M. (1997). *The life cycle completed: Extended version with new chapters on the ninth stage of development.* W. W. Norton & Company.

SESSION EXCERPT

Marriage Therapist: You shared with me, Clark, that your goal is to "get Ellen back" at all costs. I wonder if we could spend a little time talking about what drove you apart in the first place?

Clark: I don't know why you want to talk about that. I am just ready to get back together, and I know she thinks the way to do that is for me to talk to you and then for both of us to talk to you together. So can't you just tell me what I should do or say to make that happen?

Ellen: I think it is important, Clark, that you really use this time to not just look at us but to look at you. That really helped me with my last counselor.

Marriage Therapist: Thanks for that, Ellen. I hear, Clark, that there is a sense of urgency on your part—to just figure out how to fix things and get on with it already. What I do know, however, is that this process usually takes some willingness to really engage in some reflection and to invest in understanding yourself, understanding Ellen, and your relationship so you can consider a new beginning. So if you'll indulge me a bit in getting to know you better, that will help me to get a sense of who you are. Are you also okay, Ellen, with us spending a little time on Clark here?

Ellen: Yes, fine with me. I'm also really interested to hear his response to this.

Clark: (Sighing heavily.) Okay. I get it. So what did you want to know? ... Oh yeah, what caused me to leave in the first place. Well, it was a little over a year ago now. Rusty had been away at college for a couple of years and it was just Ellen and I, rattling around in that big house. I knew it really hit her hard having Rusty leave. I mean, I remember, Ellen, that it was like your whole identity of being a mom got totally upended. (Ellen nods in agreement.) It was easier for me, I think, as I still could throw myself into work, so my day-to-day life didn't change too much. But Ellen was just so restless, and bored, and seemed like she just got pissed off with me all the time for this or that. I guess she thought I should be investing more in her or us, or whatever. The truth is, if I'm honest, I had just been getting bored myself. Bored with our routine, bored with our relationship, just even bored with Ellen. (Clark shoots her a guilty glance.) I know that sounds terrible, but that is how I felt. So when she actually brought it up that she felt things weren't good between us, I saw that as a way to get out of the boredom and try something new, so I'm the one who suggested we separate. I know that hurt you and surprised you, Ellen, and I feel bad about that. I just had this weird excitement about being on my own again, in the city. Looking back on it, I see how selfish that was.

Marriage Therapist: I really appreciate that context, Clark. So for you, Ellen's admission of feeling a lack of closeness with you was, at the time, an opportunity to leave instead of an opportunity to work on the marriage, is that right?

Clark: Yeah, that is pretty much it in a nutshell. I guess I also just felt like my time at my job was closer to coming to an end since I'm about to retire. As I think about it now I was feeling pretty desperate. Seeing that my youth was behind me, that I only had getting older to look forward to, and that I had to do something for myself that was just about me. But I realize over the past several months that as Ellen seemed to use this time to reinvent herself and to really thrive, I have just hunkered down in my little apartment; just going to work and back and eating a lot of takeout. I haven't even spent much time with Rusty or any of my old friends in the neighborhood. All my coworkers seem to just get younger and younger, and I really have no interest, I realized, in dating anyone or anything. (Turns to Ellen.) I just miss you, Ellen, and I miss our life. I am afraid, though, that it just won't be the same even if you do take me back. You just seem to be blossoming while I feel like I have just been shrinking.

In this exchange, Clark is identifying how he has engaged in rejectivity of his marriage, his son, his other relationships and has slipped into a stage of stagnation. In contrast, Ellen has invested in exploring her possible selves and has increased her generativity in her care for her mother, in having Rusty back in the home, and in engaging in social, spiritual, and educational pursuits. While Ellen is on her way to solidifying the virtue of care, Clark has increasingly been experiencing isolation and self-rejection. Clark's therapist, therefore, can help him examine the task of generativity and identify strategies that can help Clark create a sense of contribution beyond himself through his reinvestment in his marriage, his family, and other potentially meaningful relationships. As Clark nears retirement, creating a sense of generativity and purpose will be especially important as he begins to navigate the next phase of life marked by the conflict of integrity versus despair.

Critical Analysis of Psychosocial Development Theory

Part of your job as an emerging, master's-level helper is to engage in critical analysis of the literature that informs our understanding of human development, recognized theories, and approaches and interventions with clients. Part of our job as authors of this textbook is to provide both information about foundational and relevant developmental theories, and also to encourage you to seek additional information about the potential limitations of these theories. No theory is perfect and no theory perfectly fits every client.

It is important to note that some theories discussed in this chapter and in this book that focus on personality, ego, or other individual development are fundamentally presumed to describe a male, Western, White, hetero-normative experience. Assumed affluence is another overlay of typical theories of development, whereby an individual has their basic needs cared for in such a way that they can focus on resolving, for example, tasks of identity versus role confusion where optimal development is establishing a sense of independence and autonomy—a very Western, White, male attribute. According to Mitchell (2021), developmental theories and theorists often presume meanings about family through a White cultural premise and may miss the relevance of collectivist influences on the developing personality.

Consider our fictional client Clark. As an affluent, educated, White male in Western society, Clark appears to fit nicely into Erikson's model of development. Since money is not a factor for him, Clark is able to use his "mid-life crisis" to explore the conflict of generativity versus stagnation by moving out of his house and being able to support two households, live for a time independently, and then engage with Ellen in a counseling process to explore ways to enhance his contributions to his family and society. He works in a job that will allow him to fully retire with ongoing financial stability, further creating space for Clark to move into the next phase of Erikson's model—Integrity versus Despair—where he will strive to make meaning of his life and contributions. While the Psychosocial Developmental theory does include some stages, particularly those in adulthood and later life, an increased focus on family, legacy, society, and earlier stages of development are marked by a striving for autonomy, independence, and a sense of self as an individual. Remembering that not all individuals, families, cultures, and societies value such attributes as optimal is an important consideration when examining the potential application of Erikson's theory.

Even the Eriksons themselves, in the last edition of *The Life Cycle Completed*, discussed the concept of "I" and "we" in the context of Erikson's developmental theory. Erikson and Erikson (1997) suggested that, "... each person is a center of awareness in a universe of communicable experience, a center so numinous that it amounts to a sense of being alive and, more, of being the vital condition of existence. At the same time, only two or more persons who share a corresponding world image and can bridge their languages may merge their 'I's into a 'we.'" (p. 96). The Eriksons go on to suggest that the developmental context within which development occurs is significant to understanding each person's journey.

While Erik Erikson's contributions to our understanding of the developmental process are noteworthy and still being discussed and studied today, there are limitations related to generalizability of these tenets to people from different cultural backgrounds, to people who are older, and to women (Mitchell, 2021).

Recent Research on Generativity and the Psychosocial Development Theory

Many of the theories discussed in this textbook were developed decades ago with a focus on a specific population or group; often Western-society White boys and men. It is important, therefore, that ongoing research be conducted on development theories to help us understand how (and if) these theories stand the test of time when examined through the lenses of different variables including gender, age, race, ethnicity, and other cultural factors. An examination of newer research helps us to understand how we can generalize theories and models to other groups and think about how to apply this learning to our work with future clients.

Several studies have examined the prevalence of generativity in middle-aged adults. In general, research supports that generativity, especially as it relates to parenting, is perceived by women to be most prominent in middle age (Stewart et al., 2001) and that it can peak and then level-off for women in their 60s (Newton & Stewart, 2010; Zucker et al., 2002). Since the concept of generativity is primarily about care, it is not surprising that for many women, a focus on guiding and enriching their children toward adulthood is paramount. For both men and women, middle age represents a time where there are significantly higher levels of generativity than in both younger and older adults, although the types of generativity displayed can vary by age and gender. According to Newton and Baltys (2014), generativity does not just include the care of children, but can also include the care of parents, grandchildren, or can be reflected in the context of careers (i.e., younger employees, students, or colleagues) and in other social roles and settings.

GRANDPARENTING AND GENERATIVITY

Sometimes research focuses on addressing a gap in our understanding of a particular phenomenon. A significant gap in the literature related to the experiences of generativity in midlife includes a lack of focus on those not in parenting roles, for example, as caregiving grandparents or non-parents, as well as a lack of studies that examine race differences in levels of generativity (Newton & Baltys, 2014). As we have established so far in this book, our conceptualization of "the lifespan" continues to shift as people, at least in developed and Western countries, continue to live longer. It stands to reason, then, that grandparenthood could occur for many people in the stage of life still considered midlife.

In addition, different cultures may have alternative frameworks for the role that grandparenting plays in the care of children. Some grandparents are directly involved in the emotional and even financial care of grandchildren. African American grandparents, for example, often play pivotal roles in families which can include becoming direct caregivers to their grandchildren. African American grandmothers, in particular, may occupy a more central role taking on responsibilities of caring for and even raising grandchildren, and experience this responsibility as less of a burden than do White grandmothers (Pruchno & McKenney, 2002). Another interesting phenomenon is the increase in the numbers of grandparents caring for their grandchildren because of the opioid crisis (Anderson, 2019). When parents are not able to care for their children due to addiction and other factors, grandparents often step in to take on primary caregiving responsibilities, which can certainly impact their generativity.

Active involvement as grandparents may also fend off stagnation in the stage of midlife and contribute to a successful transition into later stages of life. As generativity is represented by a sense of intentionality around contributions made to future generations, the knowledge imparted from a grandparent to their grandchildren can foster a sense of significance and purpose (Newton & Baltys, 2014).

RACE AND GENERATIVITY

While studies of psychosocial development of individuals from other racial backgrounds are lacking, some studies have examined the phenomenon of generativity in midlife among African American adults (see Hart et al., 2001; Jones & McAdams, 2013; Versey & Newton, 2013; as cited in Newton & Baltys, 2014). In general, findings suggest that African American and White women and men approach midlife roles in different ways. African American, middle-aged adults often consider their roles within an "... expanded radius of care" including immediate family, extended kin, and community circles (Newton & Baltys, 2014, p. 175). African American parents are more likely to view themselves as direct role models to their children and African American men in midlife are more likely to take on role modeling, or "otherfathering" for all young people, particularly young men, in their communities than are White men (Newton & Baltys, 2014).

Newton and Baltys (2014) conducted a study of generativity by parent status within race by using narratives collected through a *life-story interview* where participants were asked to describe key experiences in their life story as well as their thoughts about their future selves. Three questions of interest asked for descriptions of the next chapter in participants' lives, the hopes for the future, and whether participants had a life project of importance.

In qualitative research, the investigators will often develop a coding system to capture the main themes and insights gained from responses of participants. The researchers for this study used coding of generative themes across the participant narratives. Four primary themes were identified by the researchers. *General generativity* was marked by experiences of giving time and direct guidance to children, grandchildren, students, or mentees. *Productive generativity* was represented by statements that focused on the creation or development of products, art, or ideas that will exist in the future and contribute to future generations. *Generative caring* expressions included concern over one's capacity to care for others, including both younger and older generations and people. *Generative need to be needed* was captured by statements expressing an inner need to be needed or to be of use to others (Newton & Baltys, 2014).

The researchers in this study were surprised by some of the findings. They hypothesized, for example, that non-parents in midlife would have higher levels of productive generativity than parents, but this hypothesis was not supported by the results across the sample. In addition, the hypothesis that grandparents would show higher levels of generative need and generative caring was not only not supported, but results showed that parents and non-parents expressed more of these themes (Newton & Baltys, 2014). Significant findings of this study included that grandparenting was similar to parenting as a generative role for both African American and White participants and that African American men who were not parents demonstrated higher levels of generative caring than did White men who were not parents and African American women who were not parents (Newton & Baltys, 2014).

As with all research you may read during your graduate program, results should always be interpreted with caution. Every study has limitations that researchers should highlight in their articles. In the Newton and Baltys study, for example, issues with measurements used, sample size, and age of participants were identified. The study used several measures of generativity, but identified that we still need studies that help operationalize that concept in terms of what it looks like for people in different social roles and across different cultural identities. While the sample size was reasonably representative of the population of interest, it also was relatively small, meaning that the results cannot be generalized to the larger population. Finally, by using a limited age range (55–58 years), the sample of focus was further limited and did not include those who typically are included in the group of individuals in midlife (40–65 years; Newton & Baltys, 2014). Even with limitations, research that is conducted on theories of development representing different social and family roles, different cultural backgrounds, and different ages help to expand our understanding of how these theories can be understood and applied in our work with clients now and in the future.

EGO DEVELOPMENT

There are other theories of development impacting the phase of life called middle adulthood that are worthy of exploration. One is the theory of Ego Development developed by Jane Loevinger. Loevinger was an American psychologist who postulated a theory of ego development. According to Loevinger, the ego is the lens through which individuals perceive their world (Sias & Lambie, 2008). Loevinger's early research focused exclusively on women and led to the identification of stages that, when resolved, led to the development of the self (Loevinger & Knoll, 1983; Mitchell, 2021). Optimal ego development results in self-fulfillment, interpersonal awareness, self-regulation, and integration. See Table 11.2 for Loevinger's stages of ego development.

Loevinger did not anchor her stages in specific ages or phases of life, but instead suggested that each of the stages is hierarchical and tends to occur in a sequential order. Instead of considering personality and our sense of self as a fixed construct, Loevinger theorized that there is considerable, ongoing development of personality for those who continue to move through the stages of ego development (Mitchell, 2021). Individuals can, however, essentially "stop" at a particular ego development level and not develop further. For example, some adults may become *conformist* in their sense of self, and may have a general respect for rules and social acceptances.

Table 11.2 Levels of Ego Development

STAGE	PRIMARY DESCRIPTORS
Impulse	Physical needs and impulses Simple dichotomies (e.g., good or bad)
Self-Protection	Opportunistic and exploitive Typically adhere to rituals and traditions
Conformist	Respect for rules and social acceptance Perceive self in the simplest concrete terms (e.g., I am a nice person)
Self-Aware	Increased self-awareness and reflection Decreased stereotyping, but still does not see individual differences
Conscientious	Significant developmental transition marked by increased perspective taking Development of internalized standards and personal choice and responsibility
Individualistic	Increased sense of individuality and awareness of own incongruence and empathy Greater appreciation of differences, empathy, and mutuality
Autonomous	Increased respect for others, their choices, and their need for autonomy Greater understanding of interdependence and striving for self-fulfillment
Integrated	Individuality, autonomy, congruence, and self-actualization (few individuals achieve this level of social–cognitive development)

Source: Adapted from Hy, L. X., & Loevinger, J. (1996). *Measuring ego development* (2nd ed.). Lawrence Erlbaum Associates.

These individuals tend to perceive the self in more simple and direct terms and may view the world in more dichotomous ways (i.e., right and wrong, good and bad). Conformist adults may, for example, live out the rest of their days with a conformist ego and regard the world in this more concrete way and not move into stages of increased self-awareness or conscientiousness. Loevinger's research to validate her stages included test/retest correlation studies using sentence completion tests to identify the ego levels of individuals at different ages. Her research concluded that among 18- to 25-year-olds, for example, the most frequently occurring ego level is somewhere between the *conformist* and *conscientious* (Loevinger & Knoll, 1983). What prompts us to move from one level or stage to the next is usually an introduction of new information or experiences that we cannot make sense of in the context of our current stage or level. This phenomenon results in developing the next ego stage where we then refine our thinking about our sense of self and who we are. Even though some individuals may plateau at a particular stage, often for many years, a shift or change in the environment and people within it can lead to an alteration of self-concept and a new ego identity (Sias & Lambie, 2008).

We see this play out in our fictional clients, Ellen and Clark, in different ways. While Ellen may have been largely moving through life in a *conformist* level of ego development, the changes in her world marked by her separation from Clark, Frances, her mother, moving backinto the home, and Rusty's boomerang effect of leaving the nest then flying back to it, has fostered a shift in how Ellen now perceives herself. One could argue that these changes in her life have led to an increased sense of *self-awareness* where she is less likely to view her role in historical and stereotypical ways. She also is gaining a *conscientious* and *individualistic* framework marked by new awareness of her own personal choices and an increased sense of individuality.

For Clark, the upheaval in his life marked by leaving the marriage and moving by himself to the city were rooted in more *impulsive* and *self-protective* senses of self, resulting in almost a regression from a more stable *conformist* framework. Clark now has the task of activating a sense of *self-awareness* and *conscientiousness* if he hopes to "catch up" to where Ellen is in her new ego structures. If Clark and Ellen can together explore the experiences that now shape their current state of ego development, they have the potential to expand their capacity for respect for each other's differences, appreciation and empathy for one another, and understanding of their shared interdependence.

From an Ego Development framework, Clark and Ellen's marriage therapist is encouraging them both to examine ways in which their sense of self has been impacted by their separation and other factors in their lives. Loevinger believed that adults generally stay in a particular stage until they encounter new information or new experiences that they cannot make sense of with that stage's system of meaning (Mitchell, 2021). When people grapple with external factors that conflict with their current Ego Development level, they shift into a higher (or even lower) level to adjust around that change. For Ellen and Clark, this awareness can potentially assist them in examining both their new and emerging egos as well as the interplay of these shifts on one another and their future relationship. Both Ellen and Clark could arguably be entering the *autonomous* level of ego development as a couple if they are able to develop increased respect for one another, their choices, and their needs for autonomy (Sias & Lambie, 2008).

SESSION EXCERPT

Marriage Therapist: I have an observation I'd like to check out with you both if I may. (Clark and Ellen nod.) Your recent separation was an event that caused changes in the way both of you view yourselves in pretty significant ways, but for each of you, those changes were pretty different. So for you, Ellen, your ideas about your roles of "wife, mother, daughter" have all been upended by the changes in your family, seemingly happening all at once. These shifts really caused you to expand the way you viewed these roles from a more concrete perspective of what they meant to a broader experience of seeing yourself as an individual beyond those roles. Is that a fair observation?

Ellen: I do think that is true. It was really scary at first; I honestly didn't know who I was if I wasn't a wife to Clark or having to mother Rusty. But with Rusty away at college, Clark off in the city, and then Mom moving in with me, I had to put on my big-girl pants and figure some things out. Part of that was trying to connect again with me, with Ellen. Maybe even the Ellen I was before I met Clark, that young woman who had goals to be bold, to be unique, to be my own person. It was really kind of exciting, if I'm honest, to find a way to really connect with the person I am. I kind of like this person now. (Turns to Clark.) That is why I am a little wary, Clark, of getting back together. I don't want to let go of my new-found independence and autonomy, and I don't see myself going back to the same housewife I was before, doing all those things that I was "supposed" to do.

Marriage Therapist: Thank you, Ellen, for sharing that. Clark, I'll give you a chance to respond, but let me share some of my observations of how you have described this shift in how you see yourself since the separation. For you, the opportunity to make a break for it to the city when Ellen told you she wasn't happy was in some ways a regression of your sense of who you are. It was an impulsive act that was motivated, in part, by seeing a new opportunity to be independent and, as you've described it, a bit selfish. During the time you were apart, however, you started to develop a new perspective about your role as husband and father, realizing that you now had a new appreciation for your family and your potential new way of being a husband and father. Does that seem right?

Clark: I agree with part of that. I certainly was impulsive and selfishly motivated when I decided to leave and not stay and work on the marriage at that time. I see that now. (Turns to Ellen.) I also have no desire, Ellen, to take away anything that you have cultivated over these past months. If anything, I love this new you and I respect the choices you have made and I also respect your new-found independence. I am just worried that my realization is too little, too late; both for you to be willing to give me another shot and for me to now figure out who I am in the same way you have been able to do that for yourself.

Critical Analysis of Ego Development Theory

Loevinger herself offered a critique of her own theory by acknowledging that since the Ego Development framework was conceptualized in females-only studies, it might reflect a sexual bias (Loevinger & Knoll, 1983). Since subsequent research has been conducted on both males and females and Loevinger has long-since expanded her database, this particular critique may be moot. An interesting consideration with the Ego Development theory, however, is that since it has been widely studied, research has consistently shown that adults tend to plateau at or below the *self-aware* ego stage which involves basic self and interpersonal awareness (Manners et al., 2004). This finding across several studies of Ego Development calls into question, then, whether this theory can truly account for ongoing development in adulthood.

Part of the problem is that much of the research conducted on the theory with adults has been limited to studying college students. These studies have generally supported the theory that ego development continues into adulthood, but has also challenged the hypothesis that ego development is progressive (i.e., people move up in stages of ego development; Manners & Durkin, 2001). One study conducted on ego development in college-age adults, for example, showed that for 61% of the sample, their ego development stage stayed stable after a 1 year period whereas 22% progressed in their ego stage and 17% actually regressed (Adams & Fitch, 1982, as cited in Manners & Durkin, 2001).

Furthermore, Loevinger found it difficult to describe the final *integrated* stage and even suggested that most individuals never reach this level of ego development (Mitchell, 2021). In fact, studies have been conducted to specifically look at whether ongoing ego development is experienced by adults, particularly into the advanced stages of development. Some studies have examined interventions that could, if experienced, move adults into more advanced stages of ego development. Empathy training, transcendental meditation experiences, effective communication strategies, and emotional engagement are all interventions that have been studied as ways to encourage movement from the *self-aware* stage of ego development to *conscientious* or even higher stages of development (Manners et al., 2004).

Recent Research on Ego Development Theory

Loevinger is credited with the development of an assessment of ego development that has been widely researched and utilized. The Washington University Sentence Completion Test (WUSCT) is often used in studies of ego development to track whether adults are able to move into higher levels of ego development after experiencing new information that helps them to integrate new understandings of themselves and others. Manners et al., for example, had adult participants between the ages of 22 and 53 take the WUSCT before participating in a study of advanced ego development and then again once the study was completed (2004). The researchers found that adults at the *self-aware* stage who undergo a 10 week intervention program entitled, "Building Better Relationships" did experience a stage transition into the *conscientious* ego stage, while participants in the control group who did not go through the intervention program did not advance into higher stages of development. The findings of Manners et al., therefore, support the idea that ongoing ego stage development is possible in adults, and is often experienced after some new learning, new information, or new experiences that cause them to shift their thinking about who they are and their place in the world.

EGO DEVELOPMENT IN CROSS-RACIAL RELATIONSHIPS

Bakken and Huber conducted an interesting study on ego development among Black men and White women in cross-racial relationships in 2005. The researchers were interested in knowing if partnership in a cross-racial relationship impacted the ego development of each individual in the relationship in any significant way. In other words, what does ego development look like for dyads who have "... crossed the color line" (Bakken & Huber, 2005, p. 63). According to the researchers, there was a general lack of research, or a gap, when it came to understanding the development of identity in individuals who are also engaged in cross-racial relationships. Literature exists that examines the identity development of Black men, for example, whereby being Black itself is a crucial variable in forging an identity (Cross, 1991, as cited in Bakken & Huber, 2005). Studies have also been done on identity development of European American women which suggests that identity formation among females cannot be understood in the context of male-focused models. The general consensus is that "identity" is understood differently for women, and involves resolving both intrapersonal and interpersonal issues (Bakken & Huber, 2005).

What Bakken and Huber wanted to know was whether White women and Black men who were involved in relationships would have higher stages of ego development. The participants in the study (12 Black men who were in relationships with White women and 9 White women who were in relationships with Black men) completed the WUSCT instrument and participated in individual interviews and focus groups. Bakken and Huber (2005) found that the participants in the study were able to describe both thoughtful and complicated reasons for their cross-racial relationships and demonstrated their ability to reflect and analyze perceptions of themselves and others, indicating a high level of ego development. In addition to individual interviews of the participants, they also completed the WUSCT, Loevinger's instrument to measure levels of ego development. All participants showed higher levels of ego development at the self-aware stage and beyond, and the majority (83% of the Black males and 89% of the White females) demonstrated complex differentiated and integrated stages of ego development.

What is interesting about this research is that it helps us to consider how ego development might occur relationally and culturally, adding a layer of depth to our understanding of this theory.

MORAL DEVELOPMENT

If the ego represents the self, then morality represents how the self operates and moves through the world. Other theories of development have paid particular attention to the development of the moral compass and how our sense of right and wrong informs who we are.

When you hear the word "morality" what does that mean to you? Are you a moral person? If so, how do you know? Do you think morality is something that can continue to develop and evolve over time, even into adulthood? What does morality say about who we are as people? These are some of the questions that theorists have focused on to understand a key aspect of human development. We will focus on two theorists who identified moral development as fundamental to human development: Lawrence Kohlberg and Carol Gilligan.

Kohlberg was the first to build on Piaget's theory of cognitive development to add a specific focus on cognitive development through the lens of moral reasoning. Gilligan was an early critic of Kohlberg's theory, however, largely because Kohlberg focused on the development of moral reasoning through the resolution of moral dilemmas in boys and men. His theory, therefore, was predicated on the Western male ideals of universal rules or principles of morality that Kohlberg identified as *conventional* morality leading to a sense of individualized *justice* (McLeod, 2013). Gilligan developed her own theory of moral development for women focused on an ethic of *care* instead of *justice*. Gilligan argued that girls and women were more likely to prioritize connection and would therefore resolve moral quandaries with a focus on how actions impacted others, not just on a universal principle of justice (Mitchell, 2021).

Kohlberg's Theory of Moral Reasoning

Kohlberg initially developed his theory of moral reasoning in the late 1950s during his doctoral studies, and continued defending and testing his theory until his death in the late 1980s. Kohlberg contended that structures of moral judgment were developed over time through a series of stages. These stages operate within three levels: the pre-conventional level, the conventional level, and the post-conventional level (Table 11.3; Kohlberg & Hersh, 1977).

Similar to most stage theorists of development, Kohlberg felt that moral development was sequential (each stage occurs at particular points in development and leads to the next stage) and that they were not regressive (that we don't fall back into older stages). He also indicated that for most children, specifically male children since this is the group he primarily studied, conventional levels of morality are typically in place by the time someone enters adulthood. So what are the implications of Kohlberg's theory, therefore, on the middle adulthood stage? According to Kohlberg, adults continue to explore and develop their moral identity and sense of justice and fairness well into adulthood, and it is through continued interactions with society that their thinking about morality may evolve (Kohlberg & Hersh, 1977).

Let us consider Clark, the spouse of Ellen, who is now trying to save his marriage. As Clark confronts his own beliefs that led him to suggest a separation in the first place, he is increasingly understanding how his actions have had a ripple effect on his wife, his son, and himself. You can see from the exchange that follows that Clark has been rooted pretty firmly in the *conventional* level, but that he is beginning to consider how he needs to shift his thinking about what is right for his wife which may begin to move him into a *post-conventional* level of moral reasoning.

Consistent with Kohlberg's ideas, Clark considers his actions and their moral implications through lenses of fairness, justice, and a sense of right and wrong. If we contrast this view of morality with a more *care*-oriented theory, we can see that there are other ways to think about moral development in adults.

Table 11.3 Stages of Moral Development

LEVEL AND AGE	STAGE	WHAT DETERMINES RIGHT FROM WRONG?
Pre-Conventional Morality (Up to About Age 9)	**Stage 1:** Punishment and Obedience Orientation	Child is "good" to avoid being punished. Punishment equals being "wrong."
	Stage 2: Instrumental–Relativist Orientation	Child begins to understand elements of fairness and reciprocity but this is based on a physical, pragmatic understanding ("You scratch my back and I'll scratch yours").
Conventional Morality (Most Adolescents and Adults)	**Stage 3:** Interpersonal Concordance (Good Boy/Nice Girl Orientation)	Individual seeks approval of others and wants to be viewed as "good." Behavior is often judged by intention ("She means well").
	Stage 4: Law and Order Orientation	Individual is aware of wider rules of society so moral judgments include obeying rules of law.
Post-Conventional Morality (20s and Beyond)	**Stage 5:** Social Contract and Legalistic Orientation	Individual is aware that there are times when rules and laws work against the interests of particular individuals, and sometimes the moral action is to work to change unjust laws and rules.
	Stage 6: Universal–Ethical Principle Orientation	Individuals develop their own set of moral guidelines that they feel apply to everyone including justice, equality, and the rights of individuals.

Source: Adapted from Kohlberg, L., & Hersh, R. H. (1977). Moral development: A review of the theory. *Theory Into Practice*, *16*(2), 53–59. https://doi.org/10.1080/00405847709542675

SESSION EXCERPT

Marriage Therapist: Clark, you've talked about how your decision to leave the marriage felt "right" at the time, but now somehow feels "wrong." Can you talk more about that?

Clark: Well, I guess I've always felt like I've done what was "right" in my life, or at least what was expected of me as a husband and a father. I've always done my duty to my family, I think, and have tried to be a good citizen and good worker. I guess I was just tired of always shouldering the burden of doing what I was supposed to do as a provider. It also felt at the time that it was my right to see what life could be like if I wasn't always in those roles.

Marriage Therapist: So for you, Clark, there was a sense that you had spent years upholding your moral obligations, and that you deserved to have some different experiences. That this choice did not feel to you at the time like a wrong choice to make. Is that right?

Clark: Yes, that is right, for sure. (Turns to Ellen.) I of course know now, Ellen, that just because it seemed like a logical choice to make given the trouble you and I were having, that I didn't really consider the impact of that choice on you and on Rusty. Sometimes what might seem right to me at a given moment might not be right at all; especially when I consider how that way of thinking just wasn't fair to you or our family.

Gilligan's Theory of Moral Development for Women

While at Harvard University, Carol Gilligan served as a research assistant for Lawrence Kohlberg. Kohlberg's methods for evaluating moral development using his model consistently identified girls and women as lacking in moral development. Gilligan vehemently and vocally criticized Kohlberg's assertions and his theory for being biased against women and how they develop and navigate their worlds. His privileged and male-centric view of moral development was, in Gilligan's estimation, not applicable to our understanding of moral development, particularly in girls and women (Jorgensen, 2006). Gilligan has largely rejected stage theories as being the best way to understand development, but in order to compare her paradigm to Kohlberg's, she used his identified levels of development to anchor her description of moral development in women. According to Gilligan, the levels of *pre-conventional, conventional,* and *post-conventional* could be marked by levels and transitions instead of stages (Figure 11.1).

Gilligan agreed with the notion that for young children, an innate survival instinct drives moral reasoning, but that for most girls and women in Western society, the orientation then shifts from one of individual justice to a sense of ethical care. As women continue to develop, they transition from selfishness to responsibility for others leading to a *conventional* level or morality marked by a willingness to self-sacrifice for the good of others. Another transition then occurs from goodness to truth, marked by a new understanding of the validity of one's own needs and the importance of caring for one's self. This transition leads to the *post-conventional* level marked by a morality of non-violence; that one's own actions should not hurt self or others and should promote fairness and equity for all (Gilligan, 1993).

In a 2003 interview with Gunnar Jorgensen, Gilligan indicated that she had great respect for the work of "Larry" Kohlberg, and that there is a certain logic to his theory, but that her work and research demonstrated that for people, including women, moral development has much more to do with context, culture, and personal histories than with a universally accepted edict on truth and justice. Kohlberg, for his part, did not reject Gilligan's work as contradictory to his own, but seemed to instead feel that her contributions were additive to our understanding of how moral development can and does occur (Jorgensen, 2006). It is interesting to consider this concept of moral development as it applies to women and men. If we consider our fictional client, Ellen, and her journey during this phase of midlife to transition from a place of self-sacrifice to a place of knowing and experiencing her own truth, we can see how she has moved from a *conventional* to *post-conventional* level of moral development using Gilligan's model.

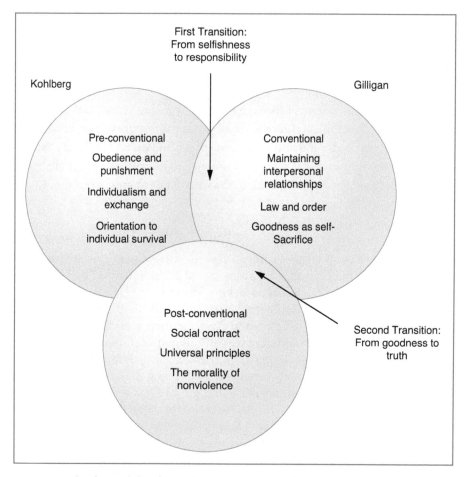

Figure 11.1 Levels of moral development: comparison of Kohlberg and Gilligan.

Source: Adapted from https://edu.glogster.com/glog/kohlberg-and-Gilligan/2t1kigfa3b7

SESSION EXCERPT

Ellen: (To Clark) It is so interesting, Clark, to hear you talk about your ideas of right and wrong. I always thought my role as your wife and Rusty's mom was what I was supposed to do. After all, my mom showed me the value of taking care of others, sometimes at the expense of yourself. I'm not saying I didn't enjoy those roles and even embrace them, but I have been able over these past months to see what it is like to value myself as an individual while also still thinking about how that balances with my responsibilities to others. I guess I now feel that it is important going forward for me to be very intentional about doing what I think is right, which is to really care for myself while I also continue to work to care for other people.

Clark: I understand that, I think. I guess I never realized how much of what you did for me, for us, really was a sacrifice in that you just never put yourself first. That really does seem unfair. If we are able to try again, I pledge to you that I will change the way I think about our marriage and work to come up with a new agreement with you about how we do things. There needs to be a just and equitable balance for both of us.

Marriage Therapist: That was a great exchange, you two. I can really hear how you both are trying to come to a new understanding of who you are for yourselves and for each other as you consider your next steps as a couple. I'll just make one observation that might be helpful. Clark, I hear that you are really thinking about what is just, fair, and right as you move forward. Ellen, you seem to be trying to understand the balance between taking care of others and yourself and doing no harm in the process. Clark, you might benefit from seeing if you focus a bit less on fairness and a bit more on how you and Ellen might truly connect with one another, as husband and wife.

It is clear in this exchange that both Clark and Ellen continue to view their own moral development from more "male" (Kohlberg) and "female" (Gilligan) perspectives. According to Mitchell (2021), Gilligan's third level of development may be particularly salient for women in midlife as they reconsider the responsibility they have for themselves and their own happiness after living a life largely in service to others. Increasingly, the field of moral reasoning and cognitive psychology have suggested that moral development may not be so clearly anchored in gender differences, and in fact there are certainly men who value caring over justice, women who value justice over caring, and plenty of people who value both as central to moral reasoning (Jorgensen, 2006).

CRITICAL ANALYSIS OF MORAL DEVELOPMENT THEORIES

As we have considered both Kohlberg's and Gilligan's theories of moral development, we will explore critiques of these theories in tandem. Gilligan was, of course, a main critic of Kohlberg's theory, which in many respects led to the development of her own theory. Gilligan has suggested that her primary critique was with Kohlberg's methodology. Kohlberg developed "The Heinz Dilemma" to help determine levels of moral development in a sample of 78 males, ages 10 to 16. See Student Reflection 11.1 for a description of The Heinz Dilemma as used in Kohlberg's research.

STUDENT REFLECTION 11.1

The Heinz Dilemma

Lawrence Kohlberg used storytelling techniques to involve his subjects in responding to moral dilemmas. Kohlberg would present the following story and ask his subjects, boys ages 10 to 16, the question, Should Heinz have stolen the drug? It is through this research that he developed his Theory of Moral Development. Read the story and answer the question for yourself.

Consider what factors impact your responses. Does your age make a difference in how you think about the dilemma? How about your gender or cultural background? How might our fictional client, Ellen, respond? How about her husband, Clark?

Heinz's wife was dying from a particular type of cancer. Doctors said a new drug might save her. The drug had been discovered by a local chemist, and Heinz tried desperately to buy the drug, but the chemist was charging ten times what it cost to make the drug, and this was much more than Heinz could afford. Heinz tried and tried, but even with the help of family and friends could only raise half of what the chemist was demanding for the drug. He explained to the chemist that his wife was dying, and asked if he could please have the drug for cheaper or pay the rest of the money later. The chemist refused, saying that he had discovered the drug and was going to make money from it, no matter what! Heinz was desperate to save his wife, so one night he broke into the chemist's lab and stole the drug.

1. Should Heinz have stolen the drug?
2. Would it change anything if Heinz did not love his wife?
3. What if the person dying was a stranger, would it make any difference?
4. Should the police arrest the chemist for murder if the woman died?
(McLeod, 2013).

Gilligan was working with Kohlberg as a research assistant, and started to see how the singular focus on boys and their moral reasoning was not adequate to put forward a "universal" theory of moral development. In addition, Kohlberg's focus on moral *justice* as the apex of moral reasoning was not consistent with what Gilligan began seeing when she embarked on research of moral development in girls. Instead, Gilligan saw that girls tended to show patterns of moral development based on relationships and feelings of care and responsibility for others (McLeod, 2013). Kohlberg's theory has also been criticized for being too individually oriented rather than community or context oriented (Rest et al., 2000). This idea further highlights the Western White male orientation of this theory; that optimal moral development is seen through the lens of a universal idea of moral justice built upon individualistic ideas of right, duty, social order, and reciprocity instead of cross-cultural considerations that might be relative (Rest et al., 2000).

Gilligan's theory of moral development has also been criticized for potential gender bias. Rest et al., 1999 (as cited in Jorgensen, 2006) suggested that there may not be as large a difference between moral development between men and women, and that the dichotomous focus on *justice* and *care* as two different types of moral reasoning between the genders does not hold up to empirical scrutiny. Rest and his colleagues used the Defining Issues Test (DIT) to analyze moral development by having subjects recognize moral arguments. Since several of Rest et al.'s studies on moral development using the DIT did not show significant differences between men and women, they concluded that education and exposure to new information is a more powerful predictor of moral development than is gender.

RECENT RESEARCH ON MORAL DEVELOPMENT

Kohlberg's and Gilligan's respective theories may have originally been conceptualized as very different theories of moral development based on perceived gender differences of moral reasoning, but newer research on this aspect of development has increasingly shown that moral development likely occurs on a continuum and in overlapping ways for people of different genders. Recent research has included a deeper dive into the construct of *gender* itself. We increasingly understand how the social construct of gender is, for some individuals, experienced along a continuum instead of as the dichotomous "male" or "female." While Kohlberg postulated that children can recognize their own gender by about age 2 years, he did not account for circumstances where children, adolescents, and adults are transgender, gender non-conforming, or otherwise non-binary in their gender expression (Katz-Wise et al., 2017). This notion further challenges ideas about how dichotomous gender identities may be linked to moral development.

In addition, considerations of moral reasoning as a complex phenomenon that occurs within relevant cultural contexts is of increased interest in the development field. Gilligan herself often argued that the primary difference between her theory and Kohlberg's was that she viewed the process of moral development as layered, complex, and impacted by relationships and social experiences (Jorgensen, 2006).

Morality and Prejudice.   Rutland and Killen (2015) introduced a developmental science approach to examine the complex nature of moral development and reasoning focused on the development of prejudice and negative attitudes that can lead to social exclusion. Rutland and Killen (2015) suggested that both moral reasoning based on a sense of what is "right" and "wrong" occurs in children at around the same time as the development of an awareness of "in group" and "out of group" differences. They examined literature to provide a framework for understanding the overlaps of moral development and prejudice and social exclusion based on differences in group identities. In other words, when does prejudice develop? How is it influenced by an emerging moral compass? What tips the scale towards either intergroup bias or mutual respect?

The authors concluded that social interactions in childhood impact both moral reasoning and prejudice based on differences such as race and gender. If exclusion is socially condoned, individuals can reason that this exclusion is acceptable and therefore not immoral. For example, if a boy is invited to join a chess club at his middle school and there are no girls in the club, he might reason that "Girls don't like chess anyway so it is okay that there are no girls in this club." If, on the other hand, exclusion is blatantly based on identified differences such as gender and race, children and adolescents are more likely to question and even reject that exclusion. So the same boy asked to join the chess club who is told, "We don't let girls in our club" has direct information supporting exclusion that may cause him to question or reject that exclusion.

Why is this interplay of moral reasoning and the development of prejudice important as we consider adults in middle age? Rutland and Killen (2015) suggest that adults often use the reasoning they developed in childhood to either reject or condone exclusion based on factors such as gender and race. Clark, for example, might belong to a country club that only has White members. If Clark has developed a social and moral reasoning that allows him to condone this reality, he might justify this to himself through statements like, "I'm sure if a Black person wanted to join our club they could, they just must not be interested." If, however, Clark had a well-developed moral and social reasoning that aligned with his awareness of bias, prejudice, and exclusion, he might instead actively advocate for membership in the country club to be extended to individuals of different racial and ethnic backgrounds.

It is clear that a development of moral reasoning, while initiated in childhood, has long-standing implications for how we interact with our social circles in adulthood. Rutland and Killen (2015) offer that an integrated approach to focusing on the social and moral development of children can enable them to actively engage in reasoning about their social environments and therefore their sense of intergroup fairness and equity, which can, theoretically, persist into adulthood.

OTHER FACTORS IMPACTING DEVELOPMENT IN MIDDLE ADULTHOOD

The theories we have discussed in this chapter focus on how our cognitive development is impacted as we age. Psychosocial development, ego development, and moral development depend on our abilities to reason; to make sense of our place in the world. There are, of course, other aspects to development experienced by middle adults. Physical development such as body changes (i.e., decrease in muscle mass, menopause and hormonal changes, vision and hearing loss, weight gain), heath changes (i.e., onset of illness and disease), and sexual changes (decreased sex drive, vaginal wall thinning and dryness, decreased sperm count and less frequent erections) can all impact middle adults (Ford & Ford, 2016).

Physical Changes in Middle Adulthood

Many physical changes in middle adulthood can be managed through minor adjustment as long as individuals have access to healthcare and the ability to adjust lifestyles to include a healthy diet and activity level. Most adults in this phase of life will invariably notice declines in overall physical well-being and will become aware of the emerging consequences of aging including weight gain that is harder to lose, more aches and pains, trouble with vision or hearing, and feeling less able to do the things that used to come easy (Ford & Ford, 2016). On a recent skiing trip, I (Coker), who is in the phase of middle adulthood commented to her sister, also in this phase of life, that it is humbling to have a brain that tells you that you can still ski as well as you ever did, but a body that somehow doesn't seem to agree!

Sexual Changes in Middle Adulthood

Zheng et al. (2020) took a look at the prevalence of low sexual desire in adult women and the distress it can cause. In their study of women in Australia, ages 18 to 79, they found that women in midlife tended to have lower sexual desire with around 70% of the women in the study representing this group. Interestingly, the older women got, the less distressed they were about having lower sexual desire. This seems to suggest that for women like Ellen, while it may be normal that her sex drive could decrease with age, she is likely to be less anxious about this decline. Marriage therapists working with couples in midlife should take the time to explore attitudes about sex, sexual activity, and any stress or anxiety associated with sexual activity and behavior to assist couples in developing health and realistic sexual relationships.

Cognitive Changes in Middle Adulthood

Some research on cognitive development over the lifespan has shown that individuals in middle adulthood experience improvements in cognition, especially as it relates to the ability to engage in empathic understanding, moral reasoning, and the mental state of themselves and of others. Spenser et al. (2020), for example, conducted a study where they looked at how these attributes of cognitive development change over time. They measured differences in cognitive attributes of personality among adolescents, young adults, and middle adults. Their results demonstrated that overall, those in middle adult groups showed age-related improvements in empathic understanding and moral reasoning. The researchers reasoned that as adults mature and experience new environments, people, and situations, they are able to further develop their cognitive understanding of their world and the people in it. This seems to suggest that for adults, continued access to new situations, new information, and new contexts and cultures can deepen their cognitive processing and understanding (Spenser et al., 2020).

Certainly some adults in middle adulthood can begin to experience some level of cognitive decline. Cognition can be impacted by trauma, by physical impairment, mental health issues, and by genetic factors and predispositions (Ford & Ford, 2016). Clinicians can conduct assessments such as the Mental Status Exam (MSE) and a full biopsychosocial assessment with middle adult clients to help identify any potential cognitive impairments that may impact treatment.

PERSPECTIVES FROM THE FIELD: PODCAST

Access this podcast at http://connect.springerpub.com/content/book/978-0-8261-8279-1/part/part02/chapter/ch11

In the last chapter, you heard Dr. Donna Sheperis, Licensed Professional Counselor (LPC) in Texas and a professor at Palo Alto University, discuss how cultural and contextual factors impact work with clients in middle adulthood. Here, we continue our conversation with Dr. Sheperis to consider how we integrate our understanding of their developmental age and stage to inform clinical decisions and direction.

STUDENT REFLECTION 11.2

Now that you have read this chapter and heard Dr. Sheperis discussing developmental considerations for people in midlife, what do you think are some of the key strengths of the theories presented? What are some of the weaknesses and limitations of these theories as they apply to working with clients in midlife? What theories resonate with you as you consider your own development and the development of those in your life who might be in this phase of life?

SUMMARY

We have, over the last two chapters, explored the phase of life called middle adulthood. We have seen that during this period in the lifespan (between about 45 and 65 years of age) people do, in fact, continue to grow, change, and develop. We know that when adults experience new circumstances it can cause an evaluation of the self: Who am I?

What do I believe? What do I want? This existential questioning can be a catalyst for movement into a new stage of development. Ellen and Clark have experienced such an upheaval. Through a separation, launching of their oldest child and his return to the home, and welcoming Ellen's mother, Frances, into their home, they have had to reconsider their own sense of who they each are as individuals and as a couple. So do Ellen and Clark get back together? That is the big question. Some of this might depend on how well they reconcile the conflict of *generativity* versus *stagnation*, if they are able to move from a *conformist* to a *conscientious* ego development framework, and if they develop from a *conventional* to a *post-conventional* stage of moral reasoning. Notice that whether we consider middle adult development through the lens of psychosocial development, ego development, or moral development, we are suggesting that positive movement is marked by an awareness of how one's actions impact others, how able one is to consider others' perspectives, and how better one is at considering concepts of justice, care, and what is right and wrong. If Ellen and Clark are able to sustain this movement as individuals and as a couple, we can have reasonable hope that their developmental progress will lead to reconciliation and a new appreciation for one another.

What do you think? Imagine you are the marriage therapist who has been working with Ellen and Clark. Based on the theories discussed in this chapter, where do you imagine they both are in their development? What do you think either Ellen or Clark would need to consider from a developmental perspective to lead to growth as individuals and as a couple? Use the Student Reflection that follows to come up with your own ending to Ellen and Clark's story.

STUDENT REFLECTION 11.3

DEVELOPMENTAL CONSIDERATIONS OF ELLEN AND CLARK
Based on what you have learned about individual development in this chapter and the presented case of Ellen and Clark, how would you assess each of their developmental progress? What impact do you believe their respective stage of development has on their ability to work through the challenges in their marriage? If you were their marriage therapist, what homework might you give each of them to further investigate their own psychosocial, ego, and/or moral development?

REFERENCES

Adams, G. R., & Fitch, S. A. (1982). Ego stage and identity status development: A cross-sequential analysis. *Journal of Personality and Social Psychology*, 43(3), 574–583. https://doi.org/10.1037/0022-3514.43.3.574

Anderson, L. (2019). *States with high Opioid prescribing rates have higher rates of grandparents responsible for grandchildren*. United States Census Bureau. https://www.census.gov/library/stories/2019/04/opioid-crisis-grandparents-raising-grandchildren

Bakken, L., & Huber, T. (2005). Ego development at the crossroads: Identity and intimacy among Black men and White women in cross-racial relationships. *Journal of Adult Development*, 12(1), 63–73. https://doi.org/10.1007/s10804-005-1322-1

Cross, W. E. (1991). *Shades of Black*. Temple University Press.

Erikson, E., & Erikson, J. M. (1997). *The life cycle completed: Extended version with new chapters on the ninth stage of development*. W. W. Norton & Company.

Ford, A. E., & Ford, L. A. (2016). Middle adulthood: Physical and cognitive development. In D. Capuzzi & M. Stauffer (Eds.), *Human growth and development across the lifespan: Applications for counselors*. John Wiley & Sons.

Gilligan, C. (1993). *In a different voice*. Harvard University Press.

Hart, H. M., McAdams, D. P., Hirsch, B. J., & Bauer, J. J. (2001). Generativity and Social Involvement among African Americans and White Adults. *Journal of Research in Personality*, *35*(2), 208–230. https://doi.org/10.1006/jrpe.2001.2318

Jones, B. K., & McAdams, D. P. (2013). Becoming Generative: Socializing Influences Recalled in Life Stories in Late Midlife. *Journal of Adult Development*, *20*(3), 158–172. https://doi.org/10.1007/s10804-013-9168-4

Jorgensen, G. (2006). Kohlberg and Gilligan: duet or duel? *Journal of Moral Education*, *35*(2), 179–196. https://doi.org/10.1080/03057240600681710

Katz-Wise, S. L., Budge, S. L., Fugate, E., Flanagan, K., Touloumtzis, C., Rood, B., Perez-Brumer, A., & Leibowitz, S. (2017). Transactional pathways of transgender identity development in transgender and gender nonconforming youth and caregivers from the trans youth family study. *The International Journal of Transgenderism*, *18*(3), 243–263. https://doi.org/10.1080/15532739.2017.1304312

Kohlberg, L., & Hersh, R. H. (1977). Moral development: A review of the theory. *Theory Into Practice*, *16*(2), 53–59. https://doi.org/10.1080/00405847709542675

Loevinger, J., & Knoll, E. (1983). Personality: Stages, traits, and the self. *Annual Review of Psychology*, *34*(1), 195–222. https://doi.org/10.1146/annurev.ps.34.020183.001211

Manners, J., & Durkin, K. (2001). A critical review of the validity of ego development theory and its measurement. *Journal of Personality Assessment*, *77*(3), 541–567. https://doi.org/10.1207/S15327752JPA7703_12

Manners, J., Durkin, K., & Nesdale, A. (2004). Promoting advanced ego development among adults. *Journal of Adult Development*, *11*(1), 19–27. https://doi.org/10.1023/B:JADE.0000012524.32002.8d

McLeod, S. (2013). Kohlberg's stages of moral development. *Simply Psychology*. www.simplypsychology.org/kohlberg.html

Mitchell, V. (2021). The aging woman worker in a lifespan developmental context. In E. Cole & L. Holis-Sawyer (Eds.), *Older women who work: Resilience, choice, and change*. The American Psychological Association.

Newton, N. J., & Baltys, I. H. (2014). Parent status and generativity within the context of race. *International Journal of Aging & Human Development*, *78*(2), 171–195. https://doi.org/10.2190/AG.78.2.e

Newton, N., & Stewart, A. J. (2010). The middle ages: Change in women's personalities and social roles. *Psychology of Women Quarterly*, *34*(1), 75–84. https://doi.org/10.1111/j.1471-6402.2009.01543.x

Overstreet, L. (n.d.). *Introduction to middle adulthood*. Lumen Learning. https://courses.lumen-learning.com/suny-lifespandevelopment2/chapter/introduction-to-lesson-9-middle-adulthood

Pruchno, R. A., & McKenney, D. (2002). Psychological well-being of Black and White grandmothers raising grandchildren: Examination of a two-factor model. *The Journals of Gerontology. Series B, Psychological Sciences and Social Sciences*, *57*(5), 444–452. https://doi.org/10.1093/geronb/57.5.p444

Rest, J., Narvaez, D., Bebeau, M. J., & Thoma, S. J. (1999). *Postconventional moral thinking: A neo-Kohlbergian approach*. Psychology Press.

Rest, J. R., Narvaez, D., Thoma, S. J., & Bebeau, M. J. (2000). A neo-Kohlbergian approach to morality research. *Journal of Moral Education*, *29*(4), 381–395. https://doi.org/10.1080/713679390

Rutland, A., & Killen, M. (2015). A developmental science approach to reducing prejudice and social exclusion: Intergroup processes, social-cognitive development, and moral reasoning. *Social Issues and Policy Review*, *9*(1), 121–154. https://doi.org/10.1111/sipr.12012

Sias, S. M., & Lambie, G. W. (2008). An integrative social-cognitive developmental model of supervision for substance abuse counselors-in-training. *Journal of Teaching in the Addictions*, 7(1), 57–74. https://doi.org/10.1080/15332700802072282

Spenser, K., Bull, R., Betts, L., & Winder, B. (2020). Underpinning prosociality: Age related performance in theory of mind, empathic understanding, and moral reasoning. *Cognitive Development*, 56, 1–19. https://doi.org/10.1016/j.cogdev.2020.100928

Stewart, A. J., Ostrove, J., & Helson, R. (2001). Middle aging in women: Patterns of personality change from the 30s to the 50s. *Journal of Adult Development*, 8(1), 23–37. https://doi.org/10.1023/A:1026445704288

Versey, H. S., & Newton, N. J. (2013). Generativity and Productive Pursuits: Pathways to Successful Aging in Late Midlife African American and White Women. *Journal of Adult Development*, 20(4), 185–196. https://doi.org/10.1007/s10804-013-9170-x

Zheng, J., Islam, R. M., Bell, R. J., Skiba, M. A., & Davis, S. R. (2020). Prevalence of low sexual desire with associated distress across the adult life span: An Australian cross-sectional study. *The Journal of Sexual Medicine*, 17(10), 1885–1895. https://doi.org/10.1016/j.jsxm.2020.07.007

Zucker, A. N., Ostrove, J. M., & Stewart, A. J. (2002). College-educated women's personality development in adulthood: Perceptions and age differences. *Psychology and Aging*, 17(2), 236–244. https://doi.org/10.1037//0882-7974.17.2.236

CHAPTER 12

Cultural and Contextual Factors of Late Adulthood Through End of Life

LEARNING OBJECTIVES

Upon completion of this chapter, students will be able to:

1. Identify the stage of lifespan development known as "later adulthood."
2. Identify key cultural factors impacting this stage of development.
3. Identify key contextual factors impacting this stage of development.
4. Identify counseling considerations for the case of "Rose."
5. Relate comments from an expert in supporting clients with dementia to inform how to work with clients in this stage of life.

CASE STUDY 12.1: THE CASE OF ROSE

Meet Rose, a 77-year-old Black woman of Jamaican descent who was referred for counseling after a neurological assessment concluded she is in the early stages of dementia. Rose has no living children, as her only son died from a heart attack 6 years ago. Rose has recently lost her long-term partner and wife, Ruth, to cancer. Rose moved into an assisted living facility called The Gardens when Ruth was still alive and is still able to live semi-independently in a small apartment on the premises. Rose is physically healthy and still active. She engages socially with other residents at the facility and she has a good sense of humor and a dry wit. Rose migrated from Jamaica to the United States with her parents in 1950 where they settled in New York City. Rose's father made a modest but comfortable living as a maintenance worker at Brooklyn College. In 1962, Rose married Roberto, a Puerto Rican American from her neighborhood who had been wounded in the Korean War. Rose and Roberto had one son in 1964: Marcos. Soon after Marcos's birth, Rose asked Roberto for a divorce. Rose had known for many years that she was not attracted to men. After her divorce, Rose and Marcos lived with her parents and Rose enrolled in community college to earn her associate degree

in nursing. She then got a job at the University Hospital in Brooklyn where she met a fellow nurse, Ruth. Rose and Ruth secretly became a couple in 1970. They lived as "single roommates" for many years, largely hiding their romantic relationship except with a few close and trusted friends. The couple began coming out to more and more people and lived as an "out" lesbian couple starting in the 1990s. Happily, Rose's son, ex-husband, and trusted friends all embraced her union with Ruth. Rose and Ruth finally married in June of 2011 when New York became the seventh U.S. jurisdiction to legalize gay marriage with the *Marriage Equality Act*. In the summer of 2015, when Marcos was 51 years old, he died of a heart attack. It was around this time that Ruth started noticing that Rose would forget where she put things, would repeat things she had already said, and couldn't remember the names of some friends and acquaintances. Rose was diagnosed with dementia but Ruth felt confident that she could, at least for a time, keep Rose at home and care for her needs. It was only after Ruth was diagnosed with acute myeloid leukemia that the couple decided to move together to The Gardens. With the help of the staff at the facility, Rose helped to care for Ruth until she died about 6 months ago. Rose is seeking individual counseling with a therapist in private practice. She is provided transportation by the assisted living facility to her appointments, and also has some appointments via tele-mental health sessions. Rose is working with her therapist on a few different concerns. She is still grieving the loss of her wife, Ruth, and her son, Marcos. She is grappling with the frustration of her early stage dementia and is dealing with depression and anxiety. Her therapist, Marva, is a Black, married woman who is 50 years old. She has two adult children of her own and, as a certified rehabilitation counselor (CRC), often works with clients who have some form of disability. She contracts with Rose's assisted living facility and provides face-to-face and tele-mental health sessions with clients.

LATE ADULTHOOD

Aging is, for all intents and purposes, the degeneration of our bodies, minds, and ultimately, lives. It sounds depressing, but every year we are alive leads us closer to our death. As we age into what is considered "old" age, around 65 to 75 years, and "old-old" age, 75 years and older, we experience that degeneration in almost every aspect of our functioning. Our skin loses its elasticity. Our motor functions get slower. Muscle strength and bone density diminish. Hearing and vision become impaired. The human brain loses neurons as we age, impacting cognitive functioning such as memory and potentially leading to neurocognitive disorders such as dementia (boundless.com, n.d.).

There is, however, something quite fascinating that happens in this stage of life. There is evidence to suggest that for today's older adults, not only are they more cognitively fit than the older adult from 20 years ago, but they also tend to be happier and more satisfied with their lives (Gerstorf et al., 2020). This phenomenon is called the *Flynn effect* and represents that, over time, cohorts of older adults will show improvements in many areas of function over cohorts from decades past. One way to think about the Flynn effect is that the 75-year-old of today functions like the average 56-year-old did 20 years ago (Gerstorf et al., 2020). These results have occurred in samples across North America and Western Europe and have been evident across different cognitive measures including "... spatial abilities, inductive reasoning, cognitive speed, memory, and crystallized abilities" (Gerstorf et al., 2020, p. 526). In addition, age-related dementia has declined over the last 25 years in Western societies. Other subjective factors of psychological functioning such as happiness and a sense of well-being, life satisfaction, a sense of personal control over self, and feeling less lonely have all been demonstrated in studies of the Flynn effect in older adults (Gerstorf et al., 2020). In short, while older adults today are certainly still experiencing the natural declines that come with aging, they are, in general, experiencing them later in life than generations that came before, and can live happily and fully well into "old old" age.

As we consider the cultural and contextual factors that impact the development of older adults, it is important to remember that, as we have suggested in earlier chapters of this book, human functioning and development are very much shaped by sociocultural contexts. We will explore these factors within the experiences of our case study, Rose, and how she is navigating grief and loss, her own cognitive impairment, and her experiences of being a gay Black woman entering the "old-old" phase of life.

CULTURAL FACTORS: LATE ADULTHOOD

When we examine cultural factors impacting development, we often look through the lens of intersectionality. As a reminder, intersectionality is the exploration of differences within and between social groups and individuals (Cronin & King, 2010). Examining and striving to understand clients' identities can aid mental health professionals in considering the potential inequalities, marginalization, and disempowerment experienced by individuals they serve, which is a central feature of providing sensitive, trauma-informed care. Consider our fictional client, Rose, who has just started seeing her new counselor, Marva. As it is early in their counseling relationship, Marva plans to spend some time understanding the intersecting identities that Rose has experienced in her life.

During this exchange, we can see how Marva is getting a sense of Rose's intersecting identities and how they inform who she is and how she sees herself. The ADDRESSING model introduced earlier in this book can serve as a reminder to clinicians as to other significant identities (Table 12.1). According to Hays (2016), taking the time to explore and understand the complex, multiple identities that frame a client's sense of self, sense of place, and sense of belonging and exclusion can inform the clinical understanding of identities that represent "less power" and those that represent "more power."

Intersection of Age and Sexual Orientation

For older adults, the aging process itself can represent a new identity variable that may play a significant role in their intersectionality experience. Ageism is a common form of discrimination, particularly in Western cultures and societies, where "old age" can hold negative views and stereotypes. Ageism can be experienced by people of all genders, ethnicities, sexual orientations, and abilities. What we understand about intersectionality, however, is that those who have multiple minority identities are more likely to experience the effects of ageism. In their exploration of diversity and intersectionality among older lesbian, gay, bisexual, transgender (LGBT) adults, Cronin and King (2010) caution clinicians to not fall into the trap of assuming a "homongonized" identity of LGBT adults. Instead, an awareness that there can be many within-group differences and there are between group differences with older LGBT adults is important to cultivate. In other words, Marva will want to be attuned to the likelihood that

SESSION EXCERPT

Marva: It is very nice to be able to sit down with you in person, Rose. I appreciate you meeting with me last week for the first time over the computer. Now that some of the COVID restrictions have eased, I hope you feel comfortable with a face-to-face conversation.

Rose: Oh, I was happy to come. To be honest, I have gotten so sick of staring at the walls in my apartment. This lockdown has been terrible for everyone! We've had a few losses at The Gardens, that's the name of our facility, as I'm sure you know. I certainly hope the worst is behind us. Also, I really hate that computer! It never seems to do what I ask of it. So yes, sitting here with you in person is a treat.

Marva: So, Rose, even though we had that conversation over the computer where we went over the paperwork and got to know each other at least a little, I really would love to spend our time today getting to know each other even more. Would that be okay with you? (Rose nods.)

Marva: Wonderful. So if asked the question, "Who is Rose?," how would you answer that?

Rose: Well, that answer could certainly take a very long time! I guess you know I am a woman who loves women instead of men. So a lesbian. Maybe I'll start with that. Although as I understand from the younger folks who work at The Gardens, that's the name of the facility where I live, we don't really say lesbian anymore, so I'll say I'm gay.

Marva: Well, that is certainly a good place to start, Rose. I imagine that since you started there, that your first descriptor of who you are is as a lesbian, that this is an important part of your identity.

Rose: Oh, most definitely! It always has been, if I can remember. But it is funny ... even though it is such a core of who I am, for so many years, I never could even say that out loud! Not even to people I loved and who loved me. (Rose shakes her head.) The world really is a different place in a lot of ways, isn't it? But really, in other ways, it isn't.

Marva: What do you mean, Rose?

Rose: Well, I'm sure you know. You are a Black woman, too. So there are two other parts of who I am, being Black and being a woman, that has shaped me, and that still shapes me. But just like being gay, they come with challenges. Now I was a nurse in a hospital that was in a very diverse neighborhood, so that helped me to belong. After all, being a nurse was a perfectly acceptable career for a woman. And most of my neighbors and patients were either African American, or Latino, or Asian, or an Islander, like me. It seems we were all from somewhere else, you know? But even there, we had prejudice. We were not immune.

Marva: Yes, you bring up a good point, Rose. You and I have some parts of who we are in common; we are both women of color, for example. There are also some key ways we are different, and the more I understand about both of those things, the better able I will be to help. Does that make sense?

Rose: Oh yes, I understand for sure. For example, you are not old! At least, not to me. And I bet your brain works better than mine. I'm sure they told you about my dementia? Also, unless you've lost a child and a spouse, you probably can't know what that is like. I never really thought about how many ways I think about myself.

Marva: You do bring to the table so many layers of yourself and your experiences, Rose. One more question about this if you don't mind. As you said, you've recently experienced the loss of your wife, and I know you also lost your son a few years ago. So can you tell me, who are the people in your life now who help to make up your community? Who is your family now, whether they are by blood or choice?

Rose: (With tears in her eyes.) Yes, it has been so hard ... so hard to lose Ruth. She was my rock for so long, and when she got sick, I didn't know what I would do if I lost her. I didn't think I wanted to live, either. But I do have people, yes I do. My niece Rochelle for one. She lives the closest and is really good about coming to see me, and now that we are able, to even take me places. We went out to eat last week ... I think it was last week? There's also the girls. Just a small group of us at The Gardens, that's the name of the facility where I live. There's Mary, and Rebecca, and ... oh, there's another one but I don't have her name on the tip of my tongue right now. Anyway, I taught them all how to play dominoes. None of them knew how! Can you imagine? It was the most popular game in Jamaica. My Daadie, my father, taught me to play when I was a girl. So I guess the girls at The Gardens are my, what did you call it? Family by choice. In many ways, we have each other. (Rose leans in and whispers.) They even know about me being a lesbian! After all, Ruth and I moved in together as a married couple, so it isn't like it is a secret.

Marva: I love hearing about Rochelle and the girls! It sounds like you really do have those people in your life who are there for you and who you are also there for.

Rose's experiences as a Jamaican-born woman of color who is also an older lesbian with dementia will be different from other people who may be a part of one or more of those broader identities.

Take, for example, the intersection of age and sexual orientation. It is possible that Rose may experience ageism from other LGBT individuals, and she may also experience discrimination for being LGBT herself among other older residents in her assisted living facility. According to Copper (2015), older lesbians are susceptible to experiencing ageism within the lesbian community. Copper, a lesbian feminist who died in 1988, suggested that the fear of becoming "old" and all that this brings can impact the ways in which younger women treat older women in the LGBT community. In addition, the expectation that older women's primary roles in families and other groups

Table 12.1 ADDRESSING Framework

CULTURAL CHARACTERISTIC	POWER	LESS POWER
Age and generational influences	Adults	Children, adolescents, elders
Developmental disability	Temporarily able-bodied	Individuals with disabilities
Disability acquired later in life	Temporarily able-bodied	Individuals with disabilities (e.g., multiple sclerosis or dementia caused by stroke)
Religion and spiritual orientation	Christians	Non-Christian
Ethnicity/race identity	White or Caucasian	Persons of color
Socioeconomic status	Owning a home and middle class (access to higher education)	People of lower status because of occupation, education, income, or rural habitat
Sexual orientation	Heterosexuals	Gay, lesbian, and bisexual people
Indigenous heritage	Non-native	Native
National origin	U.S. born	Immigrants, refugees, and international students
Gender	Male	Women, transgender, and intersex people

Source: Adapted from Hays, P.A. (2016). *Addressing Cultural Complexities in Practice: A Framework for Clinicians and Counselors* (3rd. ed.). American Psychological Association.

is to be the listener, the nurturer, and the less assertive, "little old lady" can reinforce the avoidance, bias, and even contempt that younger women may have for their older counterparts (Copper, 2015).

Sexuality itself can become a conduit to ageism. The erasure of older lesbians as sexual beings, for example, can cause a shift in how older women are perceived in the LGBT communities they occupy. Copper offered that instead of "ageism" we might consider the phenomenon of "daughterism," where older women get turned into mother figures for their younger peers, whether they want this role or not. This phenomenon can, in turn, lead to an exploitation of older women in the lesbian community. For the mental health provider working with older lesbian women, it is important to acquaint oneself with the issues and experiences of women in this older age bracket, and not assume characteristics that fit a stereotype or preconceived notion of who she is.

STUDENT REFLECTION 12.1

CULTURAL CONSIDERATIONS AND ROSE

Consider the emerging counseling relationship between Rose and Marva. If you were Marva, which of Rose's identities would you relate to and why? Which would you need to learn more about to understand the intersectionality of Rose's identities and the intersection of her identities with yours?

Intersection of Age, Ethnicity, and Sexual Orientation

"For many Black lesbians in the U.S. culture, becoming older or being perceived as old marks the beginning of another chapter of oppression" (Woody, 2015, p. 50). This powerful opening statement in an article describing a qualitative study that examined the narratives of older, Black lesbians highlights the layers of complexity that exist with multiple intersecting identities. Minority stress theory posits that individuals who are part of a group that is marginalized are exposed to additional stress because of their stigmatized positions (Woody, 2015). Sexual minority stress can be experienced as an added and compounding stressor for women of color who are also older.

One way to conceptualize these intersecting experiences is to also consider them individually. So, for Rose, she may feel a sense of belonging with her older peers at her assisted living facility because a shared identity is being old. She and her "girls" can talk about what it is like getting older and experiencing physical changes that come with aging and commiserate about how they are now viewed and treated differently because they are old. Rose and her fellow residents of The Gardens have a shared experience of ageism, and likely experience it regularly; whether it is being talked to like they are children, or viewed as feeble, or chastised for outdated beliefs and ideas. Woody (2015) found that for many older people, a shared experience is of invisibility. So even people who have other marginalized experiences based on ethnicity or sexual orientation often share a new experience of feeling invisible when they become old.

When Rose was growing up in Brooklyn and working at the hospital, she was immersed in a community with rich diversity and different cultural experiences. Rose's relatives and possibly some close friends of the family shared her Jamaican heritage, and could share traditions, histories, colloquialisms, and other common features of coming from Jamaica. But being Black in America takes many forms, and it is also possible that Rose experienced a lack of shared experiences and understanding with African American neighbors and friends. Colin Powell, deceased four-star General and former U.S. Secretary of State, wrote about his experiences of being a child of Jamaican immigrants in his autobiography. He described the chilly reception he received from his future wife's family when they discovered that he was not African American but was of West Indian descent (Fullwood, 1995). A culture of competition between African Americans and Black Americans of Caribbean descent was described in a *Los Angeles Times* article where differences in the Black experience were noted between these groups (Fullwood, 1995). For example, some African Americans whose descendants came to the United States as enslaved people have, for many generations, been engaged in struggles for equality and opportunity. One perception of immigrants from the Caribbean is that they are willing to come to the United States, work closely with White Americans, and potentially take opportunities away from African Americans. While Black Americans whose descendants are from West Indian islands certainly experience racism, discrimination, and are subject to oppression, their willingness to assimilate into the dominant culture can be seen as an affront to other Black Americans (Fullwood, 1995). How might have Rose experienced belongingness in the Black community in Brooklyn, particularly when she was in the company of African American people who did not share her Caribbean heritage?

Now let us consider Rose's sexual orientation identity. Even if Rose felt a kinship with others in her community due to her ethnic and cultural identity, she still may have felt a sense of alienation because of her sexual minority status. In Woody's (2015) study of the voices of older, Black, lesbian women, women who otherwise felt a sense of kinship and belonging with other Black women still experienced isolation and depression for the alienation they experienced because they were gay. Rose and Ruth lived for many years as "roommates" to hide their relationship and sexual minority status. Safety is a primary consideration for LGBT people and being closeted and denying one's sexual orientation can be a key survival mechanism for living in a sexist and racist world (Woody, 2015).

Intersectionality is the exploration and understanding of sociocultural factors that often intersect to impact potential inequities and disparities (Thierry et al., 2021). As we develop our competence as future mental health professionals, keeping in the forefront of our work a willingness to engage with our clients around their multiple, intersecting identities and recognizing that just as one identity might represent opportunity, other identities can reinforce oppression. It is the complex interplay of this phenomenon that can assist in understanding our clients' experiences.

Intersection of Age, Ethnicity, and Cognitive Functioning

There is no typical way that cognitive functioning changes as people age. Two things that can impact cognitive changes in late adulthood are neighborhood characteristics and dementia.

NEIGHBORHOOD CHARACTERISTICS

The communities in which individuals live can also play a part in their experiences of privilege and oppression. Thierry et al. (2021) conducted a study where they looked at the potential relationship between neighborhood perceptions and cognitive functioning of older adults and whether this relationship would vary across intersections of race/ethnicity, education, and gender. The authors considered neighborhood perceptions to include factors such as cleanliness, safety, and level of social cohesion. One reason for looking at neighborhood perceptions is because in previous studies, older adults who live in lower socioeconomic status (SES) communities have experienced health disparities as compared to older adults in higher SES communities (Thierry et al., 2021). An anticipated experience of older adults is some level of physical and cognitive decline but understanding other sociocultural factors including social determinants of health that might propagate those experiences can increase understanding of these potential barriers. Thierry et al. identified people 65 years of age and older representing non-Hispanic White, non-Hispanic Black, and Mexican American populations. Several measures were used to try to capture the significant intersections of cognitive functioning, neighborhood perceptions, and health characteristics that were assessed through self-report measures (Thierry et al., 2021).

They found that overall, older adults who reported worse neighborhood perceptions did have worse cognitive functioning. Specifically, lower ratings of cleanliness, safety, and social cohesion were associated with lower cognitive functioning (Thierry et al., 2021). Using intersectionality as a framework, the researchers found that neighborhood perceptions were associated with education level, but that this interaction was different across race/ethnicity. For example, White older adults with lower education levels experienced a negative association between cognitive functioning and worse neighborhood perceptions, but White older adults with higher education were less likely to have their cognitive functioning impacted by less than favorable neighborhood conditions. Older Black adults with less education levels still had better cognitive functioning even when reporting negative neighborhood perceptions, versus older Black adults with more education who showed a higher correlation between lower cognitive functioning and negative neighborhood perceptions. Thierry et al. (2021) suggested older Black individuals may have stronger cognitive functioning even with adverse neighborhood characteristics because of enhanced *cognitive reserve*, or the ability to draw on protective cognitive resources and extra vigilance. Finally, Mexican American older adults with lower education levels experienced a less pronounced negative association between negatively perceived neighborhoods and cognition.

So, what can we glean from Thierry et al.'s study? Overall, the study highlights that there is some noticeable relationship between neighborhood characteristics and cognitive functioning; that if older adults are in environments that they deem unsafe, unclean, or lacking in social cohesion, they are more likely to experience lower cognitive functioning. When we look at other factors such as race/ethnicity, SES, and education, we see that this relationship can be either stronger or weaker. When we stack up multiple factors that can impact experiences of racial disparities and social injustices, such as lower SES and lower education and poorer neighborhood conditions, the impact on cognitive functioning can be even greater. As we work with older adults in our clinical practices, being mindful of how multiple, intersecting identities and circumstances can impact either protective factors or risk factors is valuable information.

DEMENTIA AND DEVELOPMENT

Another important phenomenon as we consider the case of Rose is the role her dementia is playing in her development process. Dementia, or neurocognitive disorder, is distinct from normal cognitive decline in aging brains. Alzheimer's disease is the most common form of neurocognitive disorder, accounting for about 50% to 70% of cases (Boundless Psychology, n.d.). As discussed from the Thierry et al. study, there can be many factors—environmental, psychological, and biological—that contribute to neurocognitive disorders and cognitive decline. Understanding each client's unique cultural and contextual factors can assist mental health professionals in understanding the role that this may play in the client's experience.

Biddle et al. (2020) conducted a study that demonstrated an association between widowhood in older adults and cognitive decline. In a sample of previously unimpaired older adults (mean age of 73.5), being widowed was associated with accelerated development of an Alzheimer pathogen protein. While this is still a new area of research needing more investigation, these startling conclusions speak to the potential impact of significant relationships on cognitive well-being.

Westwood (2014) wrote about intersectionality to include experiences of dementia. Given that persons living with dementia will engage with the healthcare system, and many, like Rose, will find themselves in assisted living or nursing home care, it is important to understand the barriers to inclusive and accessible care for those with multiple intersecting identities. The added dimension of having a neurocognitive disorder that usually requires medical support means that those with other minority status identities, such as sexual orientation, are likely entering systems and facilities that are heteronormative at best and even homophobic at worst (Westwood, 2014). Those working in facilities that serve LGBT persons have a responsibility to create inclusive environments that actively support their patients' intersecting identities.

MODEL OF DISABILITY IDENTITY DEVELOPMENT

For many older adults, a new component of their intersecting identities is developing and living with disability. Models of disability identity development attempt to characterize the personal and intrinsic experiences of people with a disability. Some individuals are born with disability, while others develop disability at different stages of life. According to Forber-Pratt et al. (2017), however one experiences disability, it is a unique phenomenon that shapes ways in which individuals see themselves, experience their bodies, and interact with and relate to their worlds. In general, the literature is lacking when it comes to empirically examined models of disability identity development. People can be born with a disability or can develop one at some point over their lifespan. Disabilities can be hidden or visible. Because of these and other complexities, our understanding of disability identity development is in its infancy (Forber-Pratt & Zape, 2017). One model of disability identity development was identified by Gibson (2006) to describe the three stages that individuals with disabilities experience (Figure 12.1).

The model is predicated on a developmental cycle for people with life-long disabilities that may begin in childhood and progress through adolescence, young adulthood, and adulthood. In the model, the first stage is characterized by a *passive awareness* of being disabled. During this stage, the individual may find themselves in situations or settings where they are the only person they know with a disability, where they have no real role models of people with disabilities, where they may be taught to hide or even be embarrassed by their disability, and where they generally shy away from any attention that might also spotlight their disability (Gibson, 2006). The second stage is *realization*, where the disabled individual begins to more strongly identify as someone living with a disability. This realization can be experienced by people through a concern about how others perceive them, and with a more focused awareness of having a disability. This stage can also be accompanied by feelings of self-hate, anger (why me?), and a sense of needing to be "Superman/Superwoman" and prove oneself worthy and capable. Finally, Gibson described the stage of *acceptance*, where individuals who are differently abled will embrace their disability as part of who they are, will shift their perception of "being different" from a negative light to a positive one, will begin to incorporate others with disabilities into their lives, and will even engage in activism and advocacy (Gibson, 2006). While Gibson's model offers a framework for understanding the possible stages of change that someone with disabilities might experience, it is limited in a couple of fundamental ways. First, *acceptance* as the final stage suggests that for each person with a disability, there is an assumption of coming to terms with an experienced disability that leaves little room for future growth. Second, there is an individualized lens through which disability identity development is understood which does not consider the importance of community and belongingness as key factors (Forber-Pratt & Zape, 2017).

For older adults who develop physical or cognitive disability in later life, their movement through phases of disability identity development may be more sudden and are likely to also be experienced alongside other emerging intersectional experiences

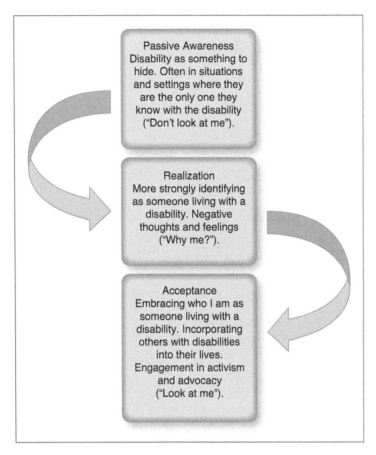

Figure 12.1 Gibson's Model of Disability Identity Development.

Source: Adapted from Gibson (2006). Disability and clinical competency: An introduction. *The California Psychologist, 39*, 6–10.

already discussed, such as aging and widowhood. For Marva, our rehabilitation counselor, keeping in mind these different and even emerging intersecting identities will be an important part of her work with Rose.

SESSION EXCERPT

Marva: I wondered, Rose, if we could talk about your dementia. What is your understanding of your diagnosis?

Rose: (Looks down and picks at her dress.) Ruth first noticed it I think; even before me. At first it was just what you would expect ... forgetting little things like where I put things and turning left when I should turn right. But then it was more like I would forget words, or even entire phrases. I would look at something simple, like a coffee pot or a throw rug or a book, and not know what to call it. Ruth is the one who got me to go for an evaluation; you know, where they make you draw the clock and remember the three words and other tests like that. (Rose shrugs and looks up at Marva.) I don't know, it made me feel really dumb, if I'm honest. What my Daadie used to call a "foofool"

Marva: I imagine that was pretty scary for you and Ruth both! Dementia has nothing to do with intelligence as I believe you know, Rose, but I certainly understand how you could feel that way; like somehow you were missing pieces of what you know, maybe even feeling like you were missing pieces of yourself.

Rose: Yes; hard times, hard times. Ruth ... Ruth was there, though, all the time. She said, "Rose, we've been through worse than this, so we'll just get through this, too, one step at a time." It was her idea to move into The Gardens, you know, the facility where I live? She thought she could help me, of course, but then she could get help, too. Then she got sick ... I don't know ... what are we talking about again, dear?"

Marva: Yes, I hear that. Hard times for sure. So, you were saying that it was you and Ruth, facing your diagnosis head on together, but then you got thrown another curve ball because then she got sick.

Rose: Yes! That is it! Then the tables, they turned. It was me who took care of her. All the while I'm trying to remember the important things. Of course we both had help. God bless the good people at The Gardens, and my niece ... my niece is.... (Rose trails off.)

Marva: Yes, your niece, Rochelle. She comes to get you to take you to lunch, sometimes. So, Rose, just one more question because I am sure this isn't easy to talk about, and you are doing great! For some people who develop a condition like dementia, there is a process of learning how to reorganize around the condition; kind of like finding a way to accept it, but at the same time trying to learn some skills for dealing with it, with help from others, of course. I'd love to be someone who you can talk to about that, and I'd also be happy for Rochelle to join us sometimes, if you like, so she can also learn more about ways to be helpful. How does that sound?

As we can see from this exchange, Rose is still able to engage in a conversant manner and follow Marva's questions. She is also able to reflect on her neurocognitive disorder, which shows that her decline is more gradual, and while it is impacting her daily life, she is still able to function with a level of independence. Marva's questions shed light on how Rose is dealing both with the loss of her wife and her cognitive decline, as well as how other potential sources of support can be leveraged for Rose's benefit.

According to Gibson's model of Disability Development, we might place Rose in the stages of *realization*, marked by her understanding of her condition as well as the negative feelings (i.e., "feeling dumb"). Initially, Rose may have had a *passive awareness* of her dementia, where she may have tried to hide or mask her forgetfulness. As Marva continues to work with Rose, she can try to foster a sense of *acceptance* as Rose and others in her life learn to employ coping strategies, communication strategies, and activities such as physical exercise and cognitive and behavioral therapies.

Another consideration for Marva is that, given that Rose's disability was acquired later in life, she may struggle with identifying her decline as a "disability." According to Kelley-Moore et al. (2007), a high proportion of adults who may classify as disabled still do not consider themselves disabled. Importantly, a person's subjective experience of their own health status can impact that perception of that person as disabled or not. Kelley-Moore and colleagues sought to understand the perceptions of older adults who have an identified disability but who may have different perceptions of themselves as disabled persons. In a longitudinal study of subjective perceptions of disability among community-dwelling older adults, the researchers found that persons in the poorest health with more experienced physical and cognitive symptoms were more likely to label themselves as having a disability. In contrast, those who still functioned with a level of independence, autonomy, and freedom of movement and mobility were less likely to classify themselves as disabled, even when their conditions warranted this label. Another finding was that older adults with disabilities who have a strong and intact support network (e.g., family, peers, caregivers) and who are able to tap into this network in meaningful ways tended to have a higher self-perception of health, even when a disability was present. This finding bears repeating and is seen in similar research: There is a recognized, positive relationship between subjective perceptions of health and strong and meaningful social networks (Kelley-Moore et al., 2007).

CONTEXTUAL FACTORS: LATE ADULTHOOD

Both culture and context are complex entities when trying to understand development. Why, you ask? Because both culture and context can intersect to influence lifespan identity of an individual and there can be intersecting cultural and contextual domains. Let us recap those aspects of Rose's identity, of which we are aware, that may be salient. Rose is an older Caribbean African American female with dementia and a recently widowed lesbian who was once in an interracial heterosexual marriage to which a son, who died as an adult, was born. We also know that Rose was a caretaker for her partner. She was also a professional person. For a short period of time, she was a single mother who relied on her extended family for support. You will notice some of the things on the list describe the conditions of her past. Those things are included because as we consider how a person's context or situation impacts development, we need to understand that the context of the person's life in the past impacts how the individual shows up in the present. Johnson and Favreault (2004) examined the economic health of women aged 65 to 75 who raised children as a single parent for at least 10 years. Twenty-six percent of those women lived below the poverty level during that time compared to 5% of the women that age who were continuously married. The context of single parenting impacted the context of those women's lives later in life. Historical contexts significantly impact a person's expectations of the present and the future (Hughes, 2009).

As we continue to discuss the contextual factors of Rose's life today, we should look back at the context of Rose's life. For example, Rose has seen a major shift in mainstream society's attitudes about people in the LGBT community, and most importantly, she has borne witness to a change in the civil rights of the LGBT community, but she notes that she was not always open about her sexuality and she shares that the younger people at The Gardens are encouraging her to use different language to describe herself. Rose and Ruth moved to a community where they were obviously accepted as a couple, but for most of their relationship, Rose and Ruth could not be legally recognized as a couple. Her ability to support Ruth as her legal spouse during Rose's illness would have represented an entirely new context for Ruth, but we would expect that, even now, she has not shed the expectations that she might experience some discrimination from others because she is a lesbian. Research indicates that being open about one's sexuality makes a person more psychologically healthy (Van Wagenen et al., 2013), however, older LGBT people sometimes continue to have the burden of past discriminations and may be hesitant to be open or demand fair, nonheterosexist treatment.

As an older person who is experiencing diminishing cognitive function and possibly diminishing physical abilities, we should understand Rose's previous context and what impact that has on her development and mental health now. To this point, was Rose a very active person? Did she take long walks every morning? Did she fly fish? How has changing her environment by moving to The Gardens impacted her ability to live actively and independently?

A significant portion of this conversation will focus on the context of health and the social determinants of health because the future of their health is one of the greatest concerns of older people (Hughes, 2009). The social determinants of health are the social, economic, and environmental factors that can impact a person's health (Alzheimer's Association, 2021; Hughes, 2009). We will start with overall health and healthcare. Throughout this section, you will see references to successful aging as one of the most critical tasks of the lifespan. There are some aspects of the aging process that are universal, but at this juncture, we want to describe the contextual factors that contribute to the successful aging for African American women, older LGBT people, and older people with dementia.

STUDENT REFLECTION 12.2

Before you read further, take a moment to think about your own future as an older person. Imagine what your life will be like. Based on the way you are planning today, do you think you will be safe? Do you think you will be cared for? Do you expect to have adequate resources? How do you think you will contribute to society? What aspects of your sociocultural identity are likely to be unduly influenced by context? Consider what you need to do to ensure that you have the greatest opportunity to successfully age. Are those things around which you have control? Use the "A Day in Your Life at 75" worksheet that follows to record how you imagine your life in late adulthood. Consider how context like a chronic illness or inadequate resources like housing or healthcare might change your vision of your own late adulthood.

A DAY IN YOUR LIFE AT 75

The following activity provides you the opportunity to create a blueprint for how you are likely to live as an older adult. Fill out a day in your life when you are 75 years old. For each hour of the day, describe the activity that you expect to engage in on a typical Tuesday. Once you complete this activity, reflect on the benefit this kind of activity might have in the therapeutic setting

HOUR	ACTIVITY	OUTCOME	HOW ARE YOU PREPARING TODAY FOR THIS ACTIVITY?	WHAT ARE YOU DOING TODAY THAT MIGHT PREVENT YOU FROM ENGAGING IN THIS ACTIVITY AT 75?
Example 7 AM–8 AM	Eat a balanced breakfast	I will not be hungry, and I will be energized for the rest of my day.	Developing good eating habits and learning as much as I can about nutrition; making sure I have sufficient financial resources to be able to access healthy food.	I sometimes skip breakfast now even though I know it's the most important meal of the day. That could be a habit that I find hard to break as I get older.
7 AM–9 AM				
8 AM–9 AM				
9 AM–10 AM				
10 AM–11 AM				
11 AM–12 Noon				
12 Noon–1 PM				
1 PM–2 PM				
2 PM–3 PM				
3 PM–4 PM				
4 PM–5 PM				
5 PM–6 PM				
6 PM–7 PM				

Successfully Aging

One of the most popular public figures during the COVID-19 pandemic has been comedian, actor, and author, Leslie Jordan. Each day, Jordan regales his nearly 6 million followers with chronicles from each day in quarantine. His followers watch him exercise, sing hymns on Sunday morning, cut a country music album, start a new television series, and write a *New York Times* best seller. Jordan is a 66-year-old man who each day provides a blueprint for someone who is successfully aging or aging well through his acquisition of new skills, using technology to develop relationships, and making the necessary adjustments when circumstances change.

It has been argued that the definition of successful aging can be elitist and ageist (Van Wagenen et al., 2013). Aging successfully is subjective and individually defined. However, for the sake of this discussion about the last stages of lifespan development, we will refer to the person who aging successfully as the person who is able to make the necessary psychological and physical adjustments to remain socially engaged, maintain a family life (Fredriksen-Goldsen et al., 2015), and continue to learn (Van Wagenen et al., 2013) under the circumstances of declining mental and physical ability. We may use terms like aging well or aging successfully they are synonymous with the idea of successfully aging.

There is a myriad of protective factors for aging well or successfully aging like socioeconomic status, living conditions, social support, connection with family, ability and sense of independence. However, depending on how favorable or unfavorable the circumstances are in each of these areas, they can also be risk factors. For example, the person who has strong ties with friends and has the opportunity to engage regularly with family and friends is more likely to be identified as someone who is successfully aging in comparison to a person who is alone most of the time but prefers to be connected to others. The person who feels safe both inside and outside of the home is more likely to be identified as aging successfully than the person who lives in a community where there is high crime and there is a high likelihood that the person will be victimized either inside or outside the home.

As you see, context plays a significant role in aging well and identity impacts context. For example, an elderly African American woman might feel very safe and well respected by the people in her predominantly African American urban community, but an older African American gay male may feel unsafe because of past victimization and physical threats he has experienced on the same street. Our responsibilities as helpers are to understand how the person interacts with the environment and how the different environments respond to the person so that we can support the individual in living, aging, and even dying well.

SOCIAL COGNITIVE LEARNING AND AGING

When my (Dixon-Saxon) daughter was about 2 years old, she decided that she was going to stop wearing pull-up diapers and would immediately start wearing "big girl" underwear. We had not had great success with toilet training to that point, so I was concerned about her abrupt halt in using this transitional support system. We had just returned from a vacation with extended family where she witnessed her slightly older cousin going to the bathroom with "big girl" underwear. My niece was repeatedly rewarded with a smile and a "good job" every time she went to the bathroom, adjusted her own clothing, and washed her hands on her own. My daughter, having witnessed this, decided she could do the same thing. She had observed her cousin's behavior and she had seen how adults (the environment) responded to my niece. She was motivated by that same kind of response from the environment and because she is the kind of person who is also motivated by a sense of independence in all things, she decided to imitate my niece's behavior as soon as she got the opportunity. She decided that her best course of action to get a similar response was to stop wearing pull-up diapers and start wearing "big girl" panties. Once she made the decision, she never had a bathroom accident in her "big girl" panties. This brief anecdote is a real-world example for Albert Bandura's Social Cognitive Learning theory, which asserts that there is a continuous interaction between the individual's behavior, the environment, and cognitive activities (Harinie et al., 2017).

Bandura's theory was initially a social learning theory proposed to broaden our understanding of behavior. At the heart of the Social Cognitive Learning theory is observational learning and agency or the agentic perspective (Bandura, 2001). Bandura maintained that human beings are not just acted on by the environment, but they are actors who influence the environment. According to Bandura, the human mind does not just react, but it can create different actions and execute a different course. Observational learning, a key feature of social cognitive learning, allows the person to identify behavior that gets the desired result to imitate. One of the considerations for Marva in her work with Rose will be identifying new ways of doing things as abilities and memory decline because she may struggle to do this on her own.

The core features of agency, according to Bandura, are intentionality, forethought, self-reactiveness, and self-reflectiveness (Bandura, 2001). *Intentionality* describes the motivations for behavior to yield the intended outcome. It is referred to as the overall goal or plan. *Forethought* is essentially the blueprint that provides the details of the plan with consideration of the actions needed. The key informant of forethought is observation of people and the environment and the interaction between the two. My daughter, at years old, did not understand that the pull-up diapers were not an impediment to her behavior, but she had the forethought to consider all the details that might get her the desired outcome which was praise from the environment and she considered that "big girl" underwear was a necessary component of her plan. Forethought allows the individual to consider unintended consequences and adjust for those.

Self-reactiveness describes the ability to execute the plan. Self-reactiveness requires monitoring behavior, thoughts and feelings, and the environment's response to the behavior. The thoughts and feelings are related to pride, satisfaction, purpose, and self-worth. The individual will most likely try to avoid those behaviors and environmental responses that make the person feel dissatisfied or that diminish self-worth. *Self-reflectiveness* is the cognitive ability to reflect on self, thoughts, and actions. It is this self-reflection process that allows us to focus on our values and the meaning of life (Bandura, 2001). However, this self-reflective process is affected by the mental health and cognitive ability of the individual (Bandura, 2001).

At the core of Social Cognitive Learning theory is self-efficacy and the individual's belief in their ability to manage their own behavior and influence the environment (Figure 12.2; Bandura, 2001). As we think about successful aging, we should consider what we are observing and what our older adult clients have observed regarding aging and aging successfully. Do we see media images of happy people who are treated with dignity in late adulthood? While the older adult has the task of aging well or successfully aging, mental health providers should consider our role in creating environments where older adults feel valued and supported.

Health and Healthcare

You probably know, or at least have heard, that there are overall health differences for poor people and people who have adequate financial resources; people of color and White people in the United States; people in rural communities and people living in urban areas; and, of course, people who are younger and older people. There are so many different aspects of Rose's identity that have already been discussed, let us now examine health and healthcare for people with similar socio-cultural identities as Rose.

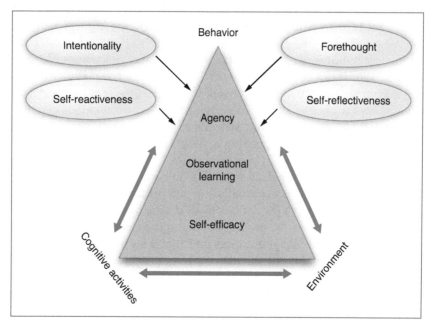

Figure 12.2 Bandura's Social Cognitive Theory.

Source: Adapted from Bandura (2001). Social cognitive theory: An agentic perspective. *Annual Review of Psychology, 52*(1), 1-26.

HEALTHCARE AND AFRICAN AMERICAN WOMEN

Historically, people of color and poor people struggle with accessing healthcare (Alzheimer's Association, 2021). Racial disparities in healthcare are a part of the context of African American women's lives.

Distrust of Medical Providers.   For African American women, there may be concerns that a provider is not familiar with their cultural orientation or will apply stereotypes to them. One concern is that providers do not expect African American women to accurately relay health concerns. Another concern is that medical providers may not be working with the patient's best interests in mind and may treat or may overprescribe medication to patients for the sake of the medical providers best interests like incentives from pharmaceutical companies or to advance medical science (Stevens, 1998).

Pain Management and Diagnosis.   One of the greatest concerns is that medical providers' failure to attend to African American women's pain and suggestions that their complaints of pain are a ruse intended to get them access to narcotics (Stevens, 1998). The attention paid to healthcare disparities increased because of the COVID-19 pandemic and the escalated conversation around social injustices (Alzheimer's Association, 2021). This was the case for Dr. Susan Moore, an African American woman and medical doctor hospitalized for complications from COVID-19 in late 2020 (Elignon, 2020). Dr. Moore videotaped herself in her hospital room describing the difficulties she had in getting the appropriate treatment even though, because of her professional experience, she was able to communicate the appropriate medical treatment. Her complaints of pain were not adequately addressed and she indicated that she was prematurely discharged. She was admitted to another hospital where she later died (Elignon, 2020).

There is the erroneous belief among some White medical providers that biologically Black patients are stronger than White patients and can take more pain. This belief in the biological differences between Black and White people goes back to slavery to justify treating Black people in inhumane ways (Hoffman et al., 2016). Therefore, Black people are less likely to receive pain medication and this includes pain medication for things like fractures and cancer.

Cultural Barriers.   There are also cultural barriers that influence the healthcare context (Alzheimer's Association, 2021). One phenomenon older African American women experience is a failure to get timely healthcare. Sobel and Mannis (2003), in examining the healthcare trends of older African American women in Delaware, reported that African American women have a higher mortality rate for breast cancer than 11 other racial and ethnic groups, primarily because of the delays in screening. In examining some of the reasons for postponing screening, it was determined that in addition to the expectation that the procedure would be painful, the women were more likely to be concerned about and be engaged in addressing the health needs of others and there is a general avoidance of wanting to hear bad news.

PATIENT–PROVIDER RELATIONSHIPS

A good patient–provider relationship directly affects the patient's health. After all, while the medical provider has some expectations of the outcomes of treatments like physical therapy, dietary changes, and medications, the patient must inform the provider if there are any mediators to the effectiveness of these approaches that might change the outcome.

Critical to the relationship between a patient and the patient's medical provider is the understanding of who the patient is and how the patient lives. Stevens (1998) interviewed 45 lesbians to understand their experiences of healthcare. At least half of the women interviewed were women of color and about 20% of them were African American. Stevens (1998) asserted, based on the results of a qualitative study, that most providers were unaware of the power and privilege that exists between people with multiple marginalized identities and their healthcare providers. Another assertion was that today's managed care systems limit the opportunity for relationship building between the provider and the patient and, consequently, providers have very little time to understand how clients are perceiving the interaction. The women in Stevens (1998) study reported feeling like they were stereotyped in the interactions with their providers. For example, some of the African American women reported that they were treated as if they were ignorant about their own health history or that their experiences of pain were indicators that they were lazy or of poor psychological health. They also reported that providers treated them like they were promiscuous and needed to be lectured about family planning. The women shared that they were talked down to by providers and they had the impression that providers associated poverty with ignorance (Stevens, 1998).

Living Environment

The most significant context is the living environment. Rose is in an assisted living facility, The Gardens, and she has made friends since Ruth's death, and she is even teaching them things like dominoes. There are many different places older people live and they live in so many different situations. Some people live with relatives, some live alone. Some people live in apartments in large cities and others live in wide open rural spaces. Some people live in environments surrounded by people from a variety of age demographics and they regularly see children waiting for school buses and commuters heading out to work. Others live in older established communities and most people around them are of similar ages. Each context has an impact on how satisfied the older person is with life. In this section, we only briefly describe some of the characteristics of rural and urban environments.

AGING IN RURAL AND URBAN COMMUNITIES

According to Evans (2009), the two indicators that a person is aging well are few depressive symptoms and a high level of satisfaction with life. Evans (2009) studied the differences between older adults in rural settings versus urban settings with regard to aging successfully in an effort to understand if there were environmental differences that impacted the quality of life for older adults. Rural settings are often lacking the formal support that can be found in urban settings (Evans, 2009). However, older adults in rural communities are more likely to have the support of relatives and friends and the support they receive is characterized by more intimate relationships giving them the opportunity for greater frequency in connections (Evans, 2009) and connections outside the parameters of a business hours schedule. While adults in rural communities are more likely to have lower incomes than older adults in urban settings, this is not a major factor in their satisfaction with life (Evans, 2009).

Van Kim et al. (2017) found that lesbians in rural areas had higher body mass indexes than lesbians in urban areas. Overall lesbians in rural communities are not as healthy as lesbians in urban areas because they are not as connected with their communities, often lack social support, and, consequently, engage in riskier behaviors. Many older LGBT people look for communities that are deemed gay friendly where they can receive the support services they need. Less than 5% of all LGBT people live in rural communities (Scher, 2019).

Older adults in urban settings report more depressive symptoms than older adults in rural communities. Evans (2009) speculates that this is likely because people's interactions in urban areas are less personal and more transitory. Additionally, older adults in urban areas have greater concerns about lack of income and social support than older adults in rural communities and the lack of those things have more negative psychological outcomes for older adults in urban communities. It is possible that there is a greater need to be self-sufficient in urban communities and that it is harder to access informal support networks in those communities. I (Dixon-Saxon) have an older friend living in New York City. Since her retirement 2 years ago, both her sisters have died and her daughter and granddaughter have moved away from the city. In addition, the bar she frequented daily only recently opened back up due the COVID-19 pandemic. She shared with me that she is lonely, but rarely tells her daughter that because she does not want to worry her. She said she has no one anymore, but she cannot imagine moving to the South with her daughter where you have to get in a car every time you want to go somewhere. She said, "Here, I go out in the morning with my shopping cart and go around the block. When I return, I have everything I need for the rest of the week."

Connection and Social Support

Social support and connection are other contributors to aging well. Social relationships aid in coping with stress and they can improve an individual's sense of self-worth. As people get older, they often rely on intergenerational relationships for connection and support (Mahne & Huxhold, 2015). Many older adults find this connection in their relationships with their grandchildren, particularly if they are not the custodial parent or the primary caregiver for those children. Sneed and Schulz (2019) report that non-custodial grandparents who provide only supplemental support for grandchildren or who spend time with their grandchildren when they choose have positive outcomes like better cognitive performance than other older adults.

However, many older LGBT people experience loneliness and isolation. There are various reasons that this is their experience. In the context of a heteronormative world, many older LGBT people are excluded from many of the activities in which older heterosexual people participate. Many do not have strong relationships with extended family members and older LGBT people are more likely to be single and childless and therefore are less likely to have immediate family support (Wilkens, 2015). As Rose mentions in her discussion about family of choice, however, many older LGBT adults have very supportive and connected relationships with friends and people they have chosen to identify as family (Van Wagenen et al., 2013); often these are others from the LCBT community (Wilkens, 2015).

Rose grew up in the United States, but she was born in Jamaica, a place known internationally for homonegative attitudes, behaviors, and laws (West, 2016). We might expect that, while Rose may not have experienced the structural discrimination LGBT people living in Jamaica might experience, Rose may have experienced this prejudice from friends and family in the United States with those values and she may be alienated from friends and family, especially family members who are her peers based on chronological age. She may not have strong relationships with her extended family. Again, the relationship with Rose's niece Rochelle is an important one for Rose's overall well-being.

Technology

When Rose and Marva meet face to face for the first time, Rose expresses her dislike for the computer. We do not know if Rose dislikes all technology, but her discomfort seems to be rooted in being uncertain about how to use the technology. Increasingly, there are smartphone applications designed to support older adults like technologies designed to aid in chronic care management. However, many of these technologies are not being used at a high rate and consequently they are not having the expected positive impact on older people's health. There is a myriad of reasons for the low use such as financial concerns, lack of knowledge about available technologies, and difficulty keeping up with the changing technology (Thielke et al., 2011). Another issue is the concern regarding privacy. I (Dixon-Saxon) purchased an artificial intelligence device for my parents that could be used in the event of an in-home emergency and they disconnected it for fear that the device was recording in-home conversations. In general, they are very skilled at using technology, but, like other older adults, are very sensitive to the ways that technological breeches can cause them harm.

The pandemic crisis, however, has increased technology use by older adults (DeAngelis, 2021) and reiterated the need for older adults to become more comfortable with technology. Fortunately, there have been advancements in designing technology that meets the needs of older adults. In the future, we expect there to be a host of new technologies designed to make homes safer for adults, thereby increasing their ability to age in place. In the summer of 2021, Elon Musk announced that personal in-home robots would be coming in the next year and many homes are already equipped with small robots to vacuum.

Discrimination and Heterosexism

Fortunately, Ruth and Rose lived in a time where they were eventually able to get married, but marriage equality in all states was not granted by the Supreme Court until 2015 (Alzheimer's Association, 2018a). The history of discrimination for LGBT older adults can impact their present circumstances. For example, many people, like older adults of color, have experienced significant experiences of discrimination in employment. The Alzheimer's Association (2018a) reports that in comparison to 36% of heterosexual older adults, 51% of older LGBT adults are concerned about having enough money through retirement. Even partnered, LGBT older adults have 37.4% less retirement savings than heterosexual married older adults and they are more likely to be working beyond retirement.

As they age, older LGBT adults need the support services offered to older adults like housing, transportation, and social activities, but they are less likely to seek that support for fear that they will be treated unfairly or that the personnel at agencies and facilities will provide support from a heteronormative perspective. In the United States, only about 8% of the services offered to older adults are specifically geared to older LGBT adults (Alzheimer's Association, 2018a). Does Rose feel that the staff at The Gardens is trained to support her specific needs? Did they respect her role as Ruth's primary caretaker? Were they supportive of her, as Ruth's widow when Ruth died? Personnel at agencies and facilities need the appropriate training to attend to the needs of older LGBT adults (Alzheimer's Association, 2018a).

Death and Dying

The longer one lives, the closer to the inevitability of death one becomes. The longer one lives, the more likely one is to be impacted by the deaths of others. While death is surely the greatest equalizer, it is still experienced, recognized, and ritualized in unique ways by different cultures, religions, and peoples. Mental health professionals who work with older adults should be prepared to address death and dying, mourning, grieving, and the role that spirituality plays in their clients' perceptions of and experiences with death.

MYTHS ABOUT MOURNING

What are you supposed to feel when someone close to you dies? How are you supposed to grieve, and how long are you supposed to grieve before you recover? What should your mourning rituals look like? According to Wortman and Silver (1989), people can hold strong assumptions about how others should respond to loss. There are expectations of the level of distress that should be experienced as well as about how long grieving is supposed to take place. The danger of these assumptions in the medical and mental health field is that experiences that fall outside of what is expected can be viewed as problematic or even pathological (Wortman & Silver, 1989).

As Marva continues to work with Rose, opportunities to talk through the significant losses in Rose's life will emerge. Understanding the variability with which grief can be experienced and linger will be an important consideration. Rose's dementia will also likely play a role in how Rose experiences the grief associated with the loss of her son, Marcos, and her wife, Ruth. As early as 1984, the Institute of Medicine reported that data suggest experienced loss can have a long-term impact on health issues. Changes in health maintenance behavior, removal of a primary source of social support, and a changed and altered worldview can all be byproducts of significant and traumatic loss of loved ones (Institute of Medicine Report on Bereavement, as cited in Wortman & Silver, 1989). In addition, the features and characteristics of neurocognitive decline can have an insidious impact on the experiences of grieving and mourning. As Rose's dementia becomes more severe, her ability to retain even the awareness of the loss of Marcos and Ruth will diminish. This may mean that there are times she believes Ruth is just in the next room, or Marcos is playing outside with friends. In these moments, Rose's awareness of experiencing a loss at all will be absent, but this certainly does not mean those losses are still not poignant and ever-present. In fact, if Rose's assumptions about Ruth being in the next room or Marcos playing outside are corrected, even by well-meaning individuals, the full force of her grief may be stronger than ever, and it could be as if she is experiencing the losses for the first time.

RITUALS OF LOSS

While grief can be individually experienced in different ways, mourning is a socio-cultural construct including traditions, rituals, and expectations. The practice of loss is impacted by spiritual beliefs, cultural values, and symbolic rituals. Mental health providers who take time to understand how mourning is experienced by their clients will have a fuller understanding of the ways in which beliefs about death and dying are shaped.

In Latin American culture, death is often experienced as a family event. *Familismo* represents deep feelings of loyalty, attachment, and reciprocity within families and between family systems (Shoulte, 2011). There is a preference for death to be experienced at home surrounded by family and close friends, when possible, and for the mourning process to flow from that event in the comfort of home with close kin. For many from Latin American backgrounds, religious and spiritual beliefs directly impact the grieving process, and care is taken to facilitate movement of loved ones into an afterlife where they can be at peace and rest. Care for those in mourning revolves around support of family, loved ones, a strong spiritual faith, and even an ongoing connection to the deceased through dreams, storytelling, keepsakes, and other remembrances (Schoulte, 2011).

For many African Americans, the ritual of death also involves strong support of family, extended family, and a faith community. For those in mourning who have a strong religious foundation, like Christianity, death is not viewed as an end as much as it is viewed as the beginning of a new afterlife (Schoulte, 2011). Christian funerals in the African American community are often not stoic affairs, but instead celebrations of a life well lived and an afterlife well deserved. Free expressions of grief, emotion, and love for the deceased and their family are often prominent markers of mourning.

In Jamaica, funerals are community-wide affairs that also are viewed as a celebration of life. One custom of mourning in Jamaica is "Nine Night," where on the ninth night after the death of a loved one, the family and community will come together with food, rum, dancing, and stories of remembrance. The ninth night after death is chosen because it was traditionally held that it would take nine nights for the spirit of the enslaved dead to make it back to Africa to find peace (May, 2021).

SPIRITUALITY AND LOSS

For many older adults, the inevitability of their own mortality reinforces their spiritual beliefs. Spiritual health is increasingly viewed as a key dimension of overall human health, and religious and spiritual well-being has been shown to positively impact other health dimensions (Abdolahrezaee et al., 2020). Some research on spirituality and overall health of elderly persons has shown that some environmental factors such as living in nursing homes and having a lower level of overall care can negatively impact spiritual well-being, which can, in turn, increase symptoms of depression, anxiety, and social dysfunction (Abdolahrezaee et al., 2020). Abdolahrezaee and colleagues conducted a study of 100 Iranian elderly persons to examine how their religious and spiritual well-being impacted other physical health measures. Overall, findings showed that those with higher scores on the spiritual well-being dimension also had lower levels of somatic symptoms. In addition, older adults who have a strong sense of existential well-being and spiritual health also experience more positive feelings of hope, forgiveness, and acceptance of death and dying.

CLIENTS IN LATE ADULTHOOD: CLINICAL CONSIDERATIONS

As suggested by participants in the Stevens (1998) study, Marva needs to understand all aspects of Rose's identity. It is also necessary for any clinician working with Rose to understand Rose's perception of her experience with the provider. Saulnier (2002), in her report of the results of focus groups with lesbians around their selection of providers, found that there is a continuum of responses that lesbians report from providers. Participants reported that they experienced homophobia and heterosexism which made them feel invisible. When selecting providers, the women in this study reported that they wanted providers who were knowledgeable about the specific care lesbians needed and were knowledgeable about how that care might change. The women also wanted providers who demonstrated comfort with lesbians and made them feel comfortable. Preferred providers would demonstrate tolerance, lesbian sensitivity, lesbian affirmative care, and respect their family dynamics, particularly their partners (Saulnier, 2002).

A mental health provider would need to ask questions to find out Rose's comfort with talking about issues related to sexuality because as an older woman, she may have experienced physical and mental health providers who were not lesbian affirming or may have even associated her lesbianism with mental illness. Additionally, it is important for the mental health provider to consider that Rose may still be a very sexual being and not think that because she is older, she is no longer interested in sexual expression (Alzheimer's Association, 2018a, Alzheimer's Association, 2018b; 2021).

Based on the report from the Alzheimer's Association (2021), patients with dementia and their caregivers also strongly desire providers who understand their background and experience. If she feels underprepared to support Rose, Marva should engage in some professional development that will allow her to understand not just who Rose is today, but how Rose's past cultural and contextual influences have impacted her. Marva should evaluate her own performance as Rose's therapist and reflect on whether her responses and support are reflective of implicit bias.

However, so far, Marva appears to be well prepared to support a client with dementia. Rose, like other people with dementia, is presenting with mild to moderate depression. Anxiety, irritability, and aggression can be quite common for people with dementia, as well (Farrand et al., 2017). The goal of Marva's work with Rose should be to make sure that Marva is engaged and participating in meaningful events if possible. People with dementia presenting with depression are less motivated to participate in activities and the less they participate in meaningful activities, the more disconnected they get from family and friends (Farrand et al., 2017).

Another part of the work with Rose should be designed to address the functional losses Rose might start to experience. In her work with Rose, Marva should either help Rose identify new activities to accomplish her goals or make modifications to old ways of doing activities. This process is referred to as the Selective Optimization and Compensation model (Farrand et al., 2017).

To compensate for the high cost to treat people with dementia and adjust for the lack of available professionals, a treatment strategy is being employed where people with dementia participate in a self-help, low-intensity cognitive behavioral therapy. These therapies are more effective when they are guided by a professional or a person with training in the technique like a non-professional or informal caregiver. This kind of therapy is appropriate for clients with mild depression and mild to moderate dementia (Farrand et al., 2017).

Those of us in the helping professions need to give serious thought to how we support our clients for a successful aging experience long before they get to this point. Successful aging requires planning for most people and it is far more challenging for people who do not have secure and adequate housing, family and community support, and healthcare earlier in their lives.

PERSPECTIVES FROM THE FIELD: PODCAST

Access this podcast at http://connect.springerpub.com/content/book/978-0-8261-8279-1/part/part02/chapter/ch12

Therapist and caregivers have important roles to play in supporting clients like Rose at the end of their lives and we thought it would be good to hear from two clinicians who have significant experience working with this population. In addition to being clinicians, Drs. Ramone Ford and Stephanie J. W. Ford have also been caregivers for a family member with dementia. As they discuss Rose, you will hear Dr. Ramone Ford share his orientation to reassuring his clients that their experiences are not abnormal; respecting his clients' values; creating an environment for his clients to feel empowered; and making sure that clients continue to use the skills and abilities they have for as long as they can. Dr. Ramone Ford is a licensed psychologist who has worked in hospital settings, community mental health, and geriatric mental health. He is also owner of his own private practice, Psychology of the Western Reserve. He has successfully worked with clients around depression and end-of-life issues.

We thought it beneficial to hear how clinicians might think about partnering with caregivers to provide the best support for their clients. One of Dr. Stephanie J. W. Ford's most significant roles in recent decades was her role as primary caregiver for a relative with dementia. She shares her cultural collectivist orientation to caring for older adults and even describes how she planned for this role in her early adulthood. Dr. Stephanie J. W. Ford has significant practice experience, as well. She is a licensed psychologist trained in both clinical and counseling psychology. She is a professor in counselor education and family studies at Liberty University.

SUMMARY

The purpose of this chapter was to use the case study of Rose to explore the cultural and contextual factors of late adulthood, the final stage of life. Throughout this chapter we have discussed the intersections of Rose's multiple identities and have given you a glimpse into the therapeutic setting through Rose's work with Marva. We have tried to help you gain a greater understanding of intersectionality and both the challenges and opportunities for successful aging. We have also shared that the contexts and previous stages of life greatly impact a person's experience of late adulthood. It is our hope that this chapter has increased your knowledge of people in late adulthood and made you think about how you might work with and advocate for this population in the future.

The very complex case of Rose serves to emphasize the need for mental health providers to develop good relationships with their clients that are reflective of a positive regard for the individual and the context and is free from bias. Of course, the most salient part of Rose's identity right now is that she is a person with dementia. As Marva continues to work with Rose, we hope Rose will be able to stay connected with her friends and stay engaged if possible, because we know that social connection and social support will positively impact her cognitive abilities.

We did not talk at length about the role of caregivers with older adults, but they are indeed our partners in supporting older clients toward successful aging. As a matter of fact, there were a host of other things we wanted to share with you throughout this chapter and this book, but we were unable to. However, we implore you to add to your knowledge by reading some of the articles we have emphasized in the reference list, especially the articles from the Alzheimer's Association.

Finally, we heard from Drs. Ramone Ford and Stephanie J. W. Ford about their perspectives on working with aging clients with multiple intersecting identities, including living with a disability. Drs. Ford and Ford shared their professional perspectives on working with aging clients as well as their personal experiences as caregivers of loved ones living with dementia. Their perspectives are reminders that no matter a client's age, they deserve to be treated with respect, reverence, humility, and through an ever-present cultural and contextual lens. In the next chapter, we continue to keep our client Rose in front of us as we consider developmental theories that inform the experiences of the "old old."

REFERENCES

Abdolahrezaee, N., Khanmohammadi, A., Dadfar, M., Rashedi, V., & Behnam, L. (2020). Prediction of hope, physical health, and mental health by mediating variable of religious spiritual well-being in elderly. *Mental Health, Religion & Culture*, 23(10), 928–940. https://doi.org/10.1080/13674676.2020.1819220

Alzheimer's Association. (2018a). *Issues brief: LGBT and dementia*. https://alz.org/media/Documents/lgbt-dementia-issues-brief.pdf?_gl=1*5zhh9g*_ga*NTY5OTMzNTYyL-jE2MzAwNjQzNzk.*_ga_9JTEWVX24V*MTYzMDA2NDM3OS4LjEuMTYzMDA2N-DQ5MC4w&_ga=2.204164436.516719336.1630064379-569933562.1630064379

Alzheimer's Association. (2018b, July 23). *First dementia prevalence data in lesbian, gay and bisexual older adults: Plus: Survival time for people with dementia is six years, regardless of age. And: prevalence of dementia increases with age, even in "oldest old"*. ScienceDaily. www.sciencedaily.com/releases/2018/07/180723142952.htm

Alzheimer's Association. (2021). *Special report: Race, ethnicity, and alzheimer's in America*. https://www.alz.org/media/Documents/alzheimers-facts-and-figures-special-report.pdf

Bandura, A. (2001). Social cognitive theory: An agentic perspective. *Annual Review of Psychology*, 52(1), 1–26. https://doi.org/10.1146/annurev.psych.52.1.1

Biddle, K. D., Jacobs, H. I. L., d'Oleire Uquillas, F., Zide, B. S., Kirn, D. R., Properzi, M. R., Rentz, D. M., Johnson, K. A., Sperling, R. A., & Donovan, N. J. (2020). Associations of widowhood and β-amyloid with cognitive decline in cognitively unimpaired older adults. *JAMA Network Open*, 3(2), e200121. https://doi.org/10.1001/jamanetworkopen.2020.0121

boundless.com. (n.d.). *Aging: Late adulthood*. https://courses.lumenlearning.com/boundless-psychology/chapter/aging-late-adulthood

Copper, B. (2015). Ageism in the lesbian community. *Journal of Lesbian Studies*, 19(1), 7–12. https://doi.org/10.1080/10894160.2015.972303

Cronin, A., & King, A. (2010). Power, inequality and identification: Exploring diversity and intersectionality amongst older LGB adults. *Sociology*, 44(5), 876–892. https://doi.org/10.1177/0038038510375738

DeAngelis, T. (2021, July 1). *Optimizing tech for older adults*. American Psychological Association. https://www.apa.org/monitor/2021/07/tech-older-adults

Elignon, H. (2020, December 23). *Black doctor dies od COVID-19 after complaining of racist treatment*. The New York Times. https://www.nytimes.com/2020/12/23/us/susan-moore-black-doctor-indiana.html

Evans, R. J. (2009). A comparison of rural and urban older adults in Iowa on specific markers of successful aging. *Journal of Gerontological Social Work*, 52(4), 423–438. https://doi.org/10.1080/01634370802609197

Farrand, P., Woodford, J., Small, F., & Mullan, E. (2017). Behavioural activation self-help to improve depression in people living with dementia: The PROMOTE treatment protocol. *New Zealand Journal of Psychology*, 46(2), 51–62.

Forber-Pratt, A. J., Lyew, D. A., Mueller, C., & Samples, L. B. (2017). Disability identity development: A systematic review of the literature. *Rehabilitation Psychology*, 62(2), 198–207. https://doi.org/10.1037/rep0000134

Forber-Pratt, A. J., & Zape, M. P. (2017). Disability identity development model: Voices from the ADA-generation. *Disability and Health Journal*, 10(2), 350–355. https://doi.org/10.1016/j.dhjo.2016.12.013

Fredriksen-Goldsen, K. I., Kim, H.-J., Chegshi, S., Goldsen, J., & Emlet, C. A. (2015). Successful aging among LGBT older adults: Physical and mental health-related quality of life by age group. *The Gerontologist, 55*(1), 154–168. https://doi.org/10.1093/geront/gnu081

Fullwood, S. (1995, November 25). *U.S. Blacks: A divided experience: Animosity clouds relations between Caribbean immigrants, native-born African Americans. Competition for jobs, differences in their dealings with whites are at the heart of the split.* Los Angeles Times. https://www.latimes.com/archives/la-xpm-1995-11-25-mm-6855-story.html

Gerstorf, D., Hulur, G., Drewelies, J., Willis, S. L., Schaie, W., & Ram, N. (2020). Adult development and aging in historical context. *American Psychologist, 75*(4), 525–539. https://doi.org/10.1037/amp0000596

Gibson, J. (2006). Disability and clinical competency: An introduction. *The California Psychologist, 39*, 6–10.

Harinie, L. T., Sudiro, A., Rahayu, M., & Fatchan, A. (2017). Study of the bandura's social cognitive learning theory for the entrepreneurship learning process. *Social Sciences, 6*(1), 1. https://doi.org/10.11648/j.ss.20170601.11

Hays, P. A. (2016). *Addressing cultural complexities in practice: A framework for clinicians and counselors* (3rd ed.). American Psychological Association. https://doi.org/10.1037/14801-000

Hoffman, K. M., Trawalter, S., Axt, J. R., & Oliver, M. N. (2016). Racial bias in pain assessment and treatment recommendations, and false beliefs about biological differences between blacks and whites. *Proceedings of the National Academy of Sciences of the United States of America, 113*(16), 4296–4301. https://doi.org/10.1073/pnas.1516047113

Hughes, M. (2009). Lesbian and Gay people's concerns about ageing and accessing services. *Australian Social Work, 62*(2), 186–201. https://doi.org/10.1080/03124070902748878

Johnson, R. W., & Favreault, M. M. (2004). Economic status in later life among women who raised children outside of marriage. *The Journals of Gerontology. Series B, Psychological Sciences and Social Sciences, 59*(6), S315-23. https://doi.org/10.1093/geronb/59.6.s315

Kelley-Moore, J. A., Schumacher, J. G., Kahana, E., & Kahana, B. (2007). When do older adults become "disabled"? Social and health antecedents of perceived disability in a panel study of the oldest old. *Journal of Health and Social Behavior, 47*(2), 126–141. https://doi.org/10.1177/002214650604700203

Mahne, K., & Huxhold, O. (2015). Grandparenthood and subjective well-being: Moderating effects of educational level. *The Journals of Gerontology. Series B, Psychological Sciences and Social Sciences, 70*(5), 782–792. https://doi.org/10.1093/geronb/gbu147

May, T. (2021). *The Jamaican funeral: A unique blend of traditions.* LovetoKnow Media. https://dying.lovetoknow.com/death-cultures-around-world/jamaican-funeral-unique-blend-traditions

Saulnier, C. F. (2002). Deciding who to see: Lesbians discuss their preferences in health and mental health care providers. *Social Work, 47*(4), 355–365. https://doi.org/10.1093/sw/47.4.355

Scher, A. (2019, April 12). *Gay in rural America: Up to 5 percent of rural residents are LGBTQ, report finds.* NBC News. https://www.nbcnews.com/feature/nbc-out/gay-rural-america-5-percent-rural-residents-are-lgbtq-report-n993936

Schoulte, J. (2011). Bereavement among African Americans and Latino/a Americans. *Journal of Mental Health Counseling, 33*(1), 11–20. https://doi.org/10.17744/mehc.33.1.r4971657p7176307

Sobel, E. R., & Mannis, C. (2003). Reporting the health quality improvement project for reducing the disparity in screening mammograms among senior African American women. *Journal of Health and Human Services, 26*(3), 350–362.

Stevens, P. E. (1998). The experiences of lesbians of color in health care encounters: Narrative insights for improving access and quality. *Journal of Lesbian Studies, 2*(1), 77–94. https://doi-org.ezp.waldenulibrary.org/10.1300/j155v02n01_06

Thielke, S., Harniss, M., Thompson, H., Patel, S., Demiris, G., & Johnson, K. (2011). Maslow's hierarchy of human needs and the adoption of health-related technologies for older adults. *Ageing International, 37*(4), 470–488. https://doi.org/10.1007/s12126-011-9121-4

Thierry, A. D., Sherman-Wilkins, K., Armendariz, M., Sullivan, A., & Farmer, H. R. (2021). Perceived neighborhood characteristics and cognitive functioning among diverse older adults: An intersectional approach. *International Journal of Environmental Research and Public Health, 18*(5), 1–14. https://doi.org/10.3390/ijerph18052661

Van Kim, N. A., Austin, S. B., Jun, H.-J., & Corliss, H. L. (2017). Physical activity and sedentary behaviors among lesbian, bisexual, and heterosexual women: Findings from the nurses' health study II. *Journal of Women's Health, 26*(10), 1077–1085. https://doi.org/10.1089/jwh.2017.6389

Van Wagenen, A., Driskell, J., & Bradford, J. (2013). "I'm still raring to go": successful aging among lesbian, gay, bisexual, and transgender older adults. *Journal of Aging Studies, 27*(1), 1–14. https://doi.org/10.1016/j.jaging.2012.09.001

West, K. (2016). Jamaica, Three Years Later: Effects of Intensified Pro-Gay Activism on Severe Prejudice Against Lesbians and Gay Men. *The Journal of Sex Research, 53*(9), 1107–1117. https://doi.org/10.1080/00224499.2016.1221028

Westwood, S. (2014). Dementia, women and sexuality: How the intersection of ageing, gender and sexuality magnify dementia concerns among lesbian and bisexual women. *Dementia (London), 15*(6), 1494–1514. https://doi.org/10.1177/1471301214564446

Wilkens, J. (2015). Loneliness and belongingness in older lesbians: the role of social groups as "community." *Journal of Lesbian Studies, 19*(1), 90–101. https://doi.org/10.1080/10894160.2015.960295

Woody, I. (2015). Lift every voice: voices of African-American lesbian elders. *Journal of Lesbian Studies, 19*(1), 50–58. https://doi.org/10.1080/10894160.2015.972755

Wortman, C. B., & Silver, R. C. (1989). The myths of coping with loss. *Journal of Consulting and Clinical Psychology, 57*(3), 349–357. https://doi.org/10.1037//0022-006x.57.3.349

CHAPTER 13

Developmental Theories of Late Adulthood Through End of Life

LEARNING OBJECTIVES

Upon completion of this chapter, students will be able to:

1. Identify the stage of lifespan development known as "late adulthood."
2. Identify key theories impacting this stage of development.
3. Identify key research impacting this stage of development.
4. Identify future directions for research and understanding of people in late adulthood.

CASE STUDY 13.1: THE CASE OF ROSE

In the last chapter, we met Rose, a 77-year-old Caribbean American lesbian in the early stages of dementia. Rose is a recent widow and mother whose adult son died 6 years ago. Rose lives in an assisted living facility and she is experiencing mild depression and anxiety. Rose has been working with a rehabilitation counselor, Marva, a 50-year-old cisgender female who is married with two adult children. Rose presented for counseling with issues of grief as well as declining cognitive functioning. As we consider the case of Rose throughout this chapter, we will be anchoring Marva's work with her from different developmental theories, models, and perspectives relevant to working with clients later in life.

LATE ADULTHOOD

Regardless of the cultural and contextual experiences of each of our lives, one thing we all have in common is that one day we will all die. Some of us will live full and long lives and others will never have the opportunity to achieve life expectancy. Does that sound bleak? That is not the intention. The intention is to understand that one of, if not, the most significant task of late adulthood is to end our time on Earth as a living being occupying a human body as well as we possibly can. Of course, there is variability in how we define living well, successful aging, and our final transition, and, like almost everything else, that is largely dependent on culture and context. While late adulthood is often marked by declines in physical wellness, significant changes in family roles and responsibility, and fewer financial resources (Nilsson et al., 2015), it is also a time where a person has more time for hobbies and service activities and offering wisdom and guidance gained from life experience to younger generations.

There are multiple theories about late adulthood. Elaine Cumming and W. E. Henry developed a theory of disengagement in the middle of the 20th century. On the basis of biological changes as one ages, Cumming and Henry asserted that older adults must go through a process of changing roles and reducing their interactions socially, instead focusing on a smaller circle of friends and relatives. This withdrawal or disengagement allows the old or older adult time for reflection and allows the person to prepare for the final transition, death, more peacefully (Nilsson et al., 2015). Cumming (1963) offered that this process of disengagement varies according to person and environments, proclaiming significant the interaction between the individual and the environment in the aging process.

In direct contrast to Cumming and Henry's disengagement theory was Robert Havighurst's argument that older adults who are more active are healthier and happier with greater satisfaction with life overall (Nilsson et al., 2015). Havighurst's activity theory of aging presented five tasks of aging for people 60 years and older (Zadworna-Cieślak, 2019). According to Havighurst, two of the tasks required of older adults are adapting to the changes in physical health and adapting to retirement and lowered income. A third task of late adulthood is coming to terms with the death of a spouse. Havighurst felt that older adults must also adjust to changing social roles and develop more relationships with people their age. The final task in this list is to make adequate living arrangements for this end of life stage (Zadworna-Cieślak, 2019).

John Rowe and Robert Kahn offered a theory of successful aging that maintains successful aging includes high cognitive and physical functioning in addition to a low likelihood for disease and disability and high engagement (Nilsson et al., 2015). Wagnild (2003) suggests that successful aging describes a time from middle adulthood through late adulthood where a person is healthy psychologically and physically and has a healthy spirit. She adds that it is marked by the person's ability to live independently and that a person who is aging successfully has strong social relationships and continues to be connected with and engaged in the community (Wagnild, 2003). While there are a variety of theories about successful aging, we will proceed with the assumption that successful aging is individually and culturally defined and highly influenced by context.

In this chapter, we discuss developmental theories of late adulthood. We also discuss updates and contemporary expansions or critiques of those theories and we will specifically explore how those theories can be applied to helpers' work with Rose.

While we did not title this chapter *gerontology*, the study of late adulthood is related to gerontology which is the study of all of the characteristics of older adults; the discovery of ways to address older adults' presenting mental, physical, and social concerns; and methods of preventing those things that might impede an older adult's ability to actively age or age well (Gerontological Society of America, n.d.). Between 2010 and 2019, the number of adults in the United States age 65 or older increased from 40 million to 54 million (U.S. Census Bureau, 2021). While the number and percentage of older adults is increasing, there is not significant interest in working with this older adult population and the number of academic programs and courses designed to prepare students to work with older adults has declined due to lack of interest (Maiden et al., 2010). The COVID-19 pandemic impressed upon us the service needs, particularly in-home service needs, of older adults (Gleckman, 2021). This is the last chapter of the text and we hope that you will consider how you will work with this population.

LIFESPAN DEVELOPMENT IN LATE ADULTHOOD

If there is anything we hope you have gained so far from this textbook, it is the idea that development is a life-long process. While it is true that many theories of development that you have read about focus primarily on development in children and adolescents, we have also introduced you to theories and models that extend our understanding of development beyond the accumulation of cognitive tasks and emerging personalities in earlier years of life to thinking about how we as adults navigate ongoing development, refine our sense of self, and integrate new and emerging knowledge and experiences into our understanding of who we are in relation to the world around us.

If we had to take a guess, it is likely that most of you reading this book are not in the stage of late adulthood (but if you are, kudos to you!). You likely have people in your life, however, who are in this phase of life: a parent, a grandparent, an aunt or great-uncle; maybe even just the older gentleman who lives in the apartment down the hall or the octogenarian who volunteers at your child's school. For many of us, we cannot yet know what it is like to be in this phase of life. What we do know is that, at the time of this writing, those in late adulthood, or 65 years of age or older, are the fastest growing age group in the United States. In fact, projections for older population growth are anticipated to steadily rise so that by the year 2030, one in five adults in the United States will be older than 65 and that by later in that decade, the percentage of older adults will be higher than the percentage of children for the first time in U.S. history (Vespa et al., 2020). For the mental health professional of the future, having expertise in meeting the mental health needs of older adults is paramount.

THEORIES OF LATE ADULT DEVELOPMENT

There are many physical and cognitive changes that occur throughout life, and in the late adulthood years, these changes often represent decline. Certainly there are studies that support the notion that older age is a time of loss of physical function, increased illness, and cognitive impairment and memory loss (Aichele et al., 2019), and that age-related functional decline is just a reality of getting old (Stibich, 2020). What is exciting, however, about theories of development that specifically look at adults in later life, is that the focus is often on what creates conditions for new growth, new learning, new relationships, and new understanding of the self in relation to contextual and cultural factors. Our intention in the presentation of some of these theories is to encourage you to think beyond the stereotypes of aging as a time of decline, and instead focus on aging as a time for continued growth and development.

Psychosocial Identity Development

You have read quite a lot about Erik Erikson in this textbook. One reason is that Erikson is one of the few developmental theorists whose stage model of development includes all ages across the lifespan. As you may recall, Erikson was a student of Sigmund Freud and actually based his stage model of development on Freud's psychosexual stages of development (Hoare, 2008). Whereas Freud conceptualized the adult years as largely void of new development and instead a time to continue to re-enact the instincts and neuroses of the past, Erikson saw development as a continual process informed largely by the social and contextual world (Hoare, 2008).

We have presented the stage model of development postulated by Erikson in other places in this book, so for this final chapter, we will simply remind you that Erikson suggested eight stages, and later his wife, Joan, postulated a ninth stage that individuals move through as they continue to develop. These stages each include a dichotomous psychosocial crisis to resolve, and that this resolution impacts the trajectory of development. In earlier writings, Erikson suggested that the final phase of development was marked by the polarity of *ego integrity* versus *despair* with successful resolution of this crisis leading to the virtue of *wisdom* (Erikson, 1950 as cited in Barnard, 2018). Later, Erikson and his wife revisited their stage model of development but now with their shared experience of being among the "old-old." It is worth noting that Joan Erikson was pivotal both in the development of the psychosocial theory of development and in its refinement and revision over the years. Erik Erikson admitted that at the time of his stage model construction, he was himself in his "middle years" and did not yet have the lived experience of being old (Erikson & Erikson, 1997). After her husband's death, Joan Erikson confirmed that their thinking about the final stage was based on an educated guess, at best, and that in truth, they should have talked to more old people (Gusky, 2012).

Originally, Erikson suggested that the stage of *ego integrity* versus *despair* starts around age 65 and extends to the end of life. In this final chapter of existence, older adults reflect back on their lives and determine whether it has been a life well lived, leading to a resolution of developed wisdom and a sense of integrity, or if they are left with a sense of confusion, or regret, or helplessness. The antithesis of *wisdom* is disdain, and the lack of resolution of the psychosocial crisis can leave the older adult wallowing in despair (Erikson & Erikson, 1997).

Erik and his wife themselves lived into their 90s (Erik died at age 91 and Joan updated *The Life Cycle Completed* when she was 93, one year before her death; Erikson & Erikson, 1997). Perhaps because they both bore witness to the actual experiences of the "old-old," they had the unique opportunity as developmental theorists to revise their much lauded theory on the basis of their own lives. In this later conceptualization of the psychosocial stages of development, Erikson re-envisioned his stage model from a linear perspective; moving in a straight line from one stage to the next, to more of a ladder conceptualization, with each subsequent stage being built upon and informed by the crises and values developed in previous stages (Erikson & Erikson, 1997). This allowed the Eriksons to determine that for the very old, the process of development is actually marked by a review and revisiting of every stage already experienced, creating a framework for a consideration of a ninth stage of development. Rather than being marked by a new crisis to resolve leading to a new virtue, this last stage is a recounting of earlier stages, crises, resolutions, and developed virtues. When Joan was 94, she was interviewed and shared an even more refined conceptualization of this latest stage of development; that it is more like a woven fabric than a ladder, and that the thread of life is woven back and forth throughout the other stages of development allowing individuals to revisit and re-evaluate their earlier resolutions (Gusky, 2012).

CRITIQUE OF PSYCHOSOCIAL DEVELOPMENT

You have read several critiques of Erikson's theory of development throughout this book. Hoare (2008) provided an overview of Erikson's theory and described the ways in which he and Joan updated and changed the theory over the years (and it is important to note that Joan played an active and pivotal role in the formulation and refinement of the theory throughout, but perhaps not surprisingly, she is rarely credited for her contributions). Hoare also pointed out that for Erikson himself, his theory was never one designed to be taken literally or to be a definitive way of understanding development. Erikson valued the process of ongoing inquiry, of questioning and questioning again the validity of his model over time. He also demonstrated an ongoing curiosity about the stages of development, especially as he himself passed into them and through them (Hoare, 2008). Certainly the point in time and limited scope through which Erikson developed his theory—during the mid-20th century with a focus on middle-class Western-European males—is worthy of ongoing critique. In addition, Erikson's theory is built on a fundamental idea that it is the developing ego that experiences stage-based crises that, if resolved, lead to virtues that persist and carry us into the next stage. But how does Erikson account for these very important contextual and cultural features? *Identity* versus *role confusion*, for example, can take on quite a different meaning for the transgender teenager who is faced with daily bullying and rejection from his family. Does Erikson's stage of *ego integrity* versus *despair* do justice to the experiences of a client like Rose, whose sense of who she is and who she has lost is experienced through the veil of encroaching dementia?

Hoare (2008) offers that we can consider Erikson's stage development model with a couple of important grains of salt. First, while today's adults might not mirror those adults Erikson formulated his theory around, we can still view his stages, crises, and virtues as experiences that adults may move through and between; maybe not in a linear or even ladder fashion, but anchored more to context than to age and stage. Second, we can view these stages as a jumping-off point to considering and understanding our clients. So if we have a general idea that for the very old, there can be tendency to look back over the landscape of their lives and wonder about who they have become (ego integrity) and that this can be juxtaposed with experiences of loss of people, of health, of faculties (despair), then we have a foundation from which to understand their experiences. Erik and Joan Erikson provided a final parting gift to the field with their book, *The Life Cycle, Completed* (1997), as they used this work to delve into the struggle between positive growth, awareness, and the satisfaction of a life well lived and the inevitability of decline. Erikson himself experienced many age-related illnesses including dementia in his later life (Agronin, 2013). Perhaps for this reason the final stages of development were conceptualized by Joan to bring, "... much sorrow to cope with plus a clear announcement that death's door is open and not so far away" (Erikson & Erikson, 1997, p. 113).

RECENT WRITING ON PSYCHOSOCIAL DEVELOPMENT AND THE OLD-OLD

Gusky (2012) provided a synopsis of Joan Erikson's writings about the woven fabric of development experienced by the "old-old." This is the re-experiencing of some of the earlier stages that older adults may go through as they reconcile the experiences of their lives in what is ultimately the final stage of their lives. For the stage of *mistrust* versus *trust*, older individuals are realizing that there are fewer things they may be able to trust because of the failings of their body and mind. For *guilt* versus *initiative*, the older adult may grapple with the idea of being able to do more than the body will allow. This author (Coker) thinks of her mother-in-law, who at 85, broke her wrist and fractured her hip because she was working in the yard and was knocked over by a neighborhood dog. I remember that she expressed some guilt and remorse because she then had to have surgery, go into the hospital, and into a rehabilitation center. The guilt was about feeling she should not have made the decision to push herself physically beyond her limits in the first place, even though no one could blame her for what the dog did! For *role confusion* versus *identity*, older adults may find themselves under the care of others, which can cause some questioning of who they are. Consider Rose, who now instead of being the caretaker for her son, or her wife, or even patients as a nurse, is now reliant on others for her well-being. Add to that the confusion that comes with dementia, and the crisis of identity can be experienced all over again. *Isolation* versus *intimacy* can be re-experienced for many older individuals who, through death and loss of loved ones or movement away of family members can find themselves increasingly isolated. For *stagnation* versus *generativity*, many older adults contend with whether to continue to engage, give back, and contribute to the well-being of others, or to increasingly withdraw into themselves. Joan Erikson's idea of the completed life cycle, therefore, consists of those in old age re-experiencing all of the psychosocial stages and conflicts from earlier life (Gusky, 2012).

SESSION EXCERPT 13.1

Marva: I wonder, Rose, what you remember about earlier times in your life. Would you like to talk about that for a bit?

Rose: (With a quizzical look on her face.) I can try ... some things are clearer than others, you know.

Marva: Of course! I will ask a few questions, and you can tell me if there is anything that comes to mind for you, Rose. No worries if not, though. Is that okay?

(Rose nods.)

Marva: Okay, what do you remember about being a little girl?

Rose: (Smiling.) Ah! The smells! Madda's rum cake! I could smell it all the way down the path. I'd run the last little way on my way home from playing when I could smell the rum cake, I tell you that. Madda says I was always running, running, running. I had to go fast everywhere! I would play with Amelia, and we would go everywhere together! Madda just let me go when we were still on the island. It is how I got to be so spunky so early ... that was all Madda's doing.

Marva: So for you, those early years really helped you to feel you could make some decisions for yourself and play with Amelia, and run all around, and come home and eat rum cake! I love that image of you, Rose! Sitting at your Madda's kitchen table with a big piece of rum cake in front of you! Once you and your family moved to Brooklyn, what do you remember about that time?

Rose: (Thinking.) Hmm ... let me think. (Rose closes her eyes.) That is blurry for me, a blurry time. I know that we were not as poor as some people, but we also did not have much. I know my Daadie worked hard and was gone a lot. I know I was busy all the time. Busy at school, busy with friends. Doing, doing, doing. My parents didn't worry about me, because I really did what I needed to do. I think they were proud, maybe, and felt that I would be okay. But I don't know ... what did you ask again, Precious?

Marva: You are telling me about Rose as a little girl in Brooklyn. That Rose is very busy, that her parents are proud of her and they don't need to worry about her. That she is able to feel competent in what she is doing, even as a little girl. You are doing such a great job sharing these parts of your life with me, Rose. What do you remember about your life with Ruth, your wife?

Rose: Ruth. Ruth is my life partner. We do everything together! She is someone who knows me. We really enjoy walking, and eating, and cuddling under the blanket to watch a movie. Is Ruth here?

Marva: Thank you for sharing a bit with me about Ruth, Rose. Ruth is not here. It is just you and me talking now. My name is Marva, and I am here to talk to you about whatever you would like to talk about.

Rose (Looking down at her hands.)

Marva: We don't have to talk any more today, Rose. I think your niece, Rochelle, is here to pick you up, so we can stop talking now.

As is typical with people with dementia, Rose is able to recall some memories anchored from her childhood, but has more difficulty organizing more recent memories and events. Cognitive decline initially attacks the part of the brain responsible for more recent memories, the hippocampus. Earlier recollections that are stored in other parts of the brain, the neocortex, take longer to be impacted by dementia (Alzheimer's Society, 2019). This is why Marva can do some exploration with Rose about earlier stages of life and understand a bit more about her developmental process. For Rose, her early years as a young child in Jamaica were marked by the ability to take *initiative* and establish a level of independence, also leading to the development of a sense of *purpose* as a virtue. When her family moved to the United States, her parents continued to support positive development through encouraging her *industry* which led to the development of a sense of *competence*. If we revisit these two stages of development through the lens of Joan Erikson's ninth stage, the tapestry of these early experiences woven together with who Rose is today could provide her rehabilitation counselor, Marva, the direction in counseling to help Rose, and, with the help of her niece, to establish activities that allow Rose to experience those feelings of purpose and competence. Also notice that when Rose becomes confused and starts talking about Ruth as if she is still alive, Marva does not dispute this belief, and simply states that Ruth is not here right now. Marva's approach can be linked to person-centered care, particularly for people with dementia. Based on the work of Carl Rogers, this approach promotes an ongoing focus on the therapeutic relationship, and the importance of creating a loving and supportive environment (Fazio et al., 2018). Clinical considerations for working with clients with dementia are covered later in this chapter. For now, we look at another theory of older adulthood, Gene Cohen's Human Potential Stages.

Theory of Human Potential Stages

Gene Cohen was an American psychiatrist born in Brockton, Maryland in 1944 and is one of the founders of the field of geriatric psychiatry (Agronin, 2013). Cohen started working with elderly individuals in 1973 and founded the American Association for Geriatric Psychiatry in 1978. Unique among theorists of his time, Cohen used his research in neuroplasticity and his experiences working with older adults living in public housing in Washington, D.C. to formulate a theory of development that *starts* in middle adulthood. Also unique in Cohen's conceptualization of development in older adulthood was that it was not just characterized by decline, but by new potentials including an expanding developmental intelligence, creativity, and an advanced cognitive stage of post-formal thinking (Agronin, 2013).

Cohen identified four phases of human potential development that starts in the mid to late 30s, or in mid-life, and continues into the late 70s and beyond (Figure 13.1). Cohen's conceptualization is more fluid than Erikson's in that individuals might experience them in different orders and in overlapping ways (Clarke, 2013). As Cohen described it, "The significance of these human potential phases is that they set the stage for a new creative thrust at different points in the life cycle" (Cohen, 1999, p. 2).

The first phase in Cohen's model is the *midlife re-evaluation phase*, which starts in the mid to late 30s and lasts until the mid 60s. Individuals in mid-life may re-evaluate their life journey so far, and make positive changes based on this assessment. Cohen referred to this positive movement in midlife as using "quest energy," and shares examples of people like Alex Haley, who used his quest to understand his African American heritage as the motivation to publish the book, *Roots*, at the age of 55 (Agronin, 2013). According to Cohen, not all people in middle age suffer the proverbial "mid-life crisis," but might instead experience a drive for new experiences and new learning; a quest that generates energy to aspire to something new (Cohen, 1999).

Phase two of the human potential model, the *liberation phase*, can overlap with phase one and may start anywhere between the mid 60s to mid 70s. The motto of this phase could be, *if not now, then when?* The clock is ticking, there is more time behind me than in front of me, and now might be the perfect time to tap into new avenues for creativity, for learning, for embracing the potential liberation of retirement, and reinventing oneself professionally. The inner push is toward innovation, experimentation, and even risk-taking (Clarke, 2013). For Cohen, it is primarily the freedom that comes with retirement that sets the stage for older adults to really thrive in their liberation phase; more time plus fewer financial concerns equal the opportunity to tap into

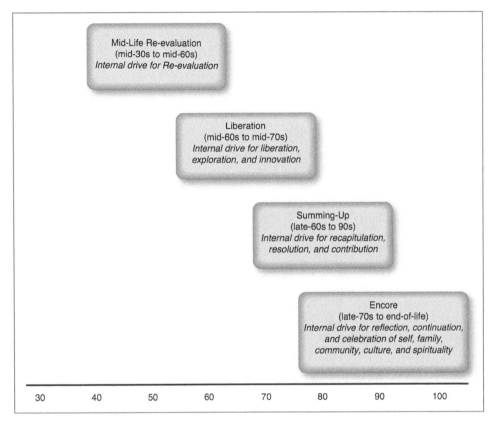

Figure 13.1 Human potential phases model.

Source: Adapted from Agronin, M. E. (2013). From Cicero to Cohen: Developmental theories of aging, from antiquity to the present. *The Gerontologist, 54* (1), 30-39.

creative potential that can have either broader implication for community and culture (Creativity with a "big C"), or more immediate impact on oneself and one's family (creativity with a "little c"; Cohen, 1999).

Summing up is a phase that occurs sometime between the late 60s and into the 90s. According to Cohen, this phase is when older adults reflect on their contributions to the world. Not unlike Erikson's stage of ego integrity versus despair, this assessment of contribution can lead to enhanced wisdom and a renewed desire to contribute to the world in some way. One example of this is Martha Graham, the dancer and choreographer who, after retiring at age 75, went back and choreographed several new ballets and dance pieces until her death at age 96 (Agronin, 2013). According to Cohen, this phase is often marked by a drive to create an *autobiography* that allows for reminiscing and reflecting on the stories of one's life. Whether through writing, or storytelling to others, or some other creative or visual expression, older adults in this phase of life often take on the role of *keepers of the culture* and are compelled to share their journey and wisdom with others (Cohen, 1999).

Cohen probably could have completed his model with the *summing up phase*, but instead he added one more phase that occurs in the late 70s to the end of life; the *encore phase*. This "final push" is characterized by an internal drive to engage in activities that celebrate major themes and experiences of one's life. This final taking stock can include an intentional effort to share with family, community, and friends important pieces of one's legacy and lessons learned (Agronin, 2013). Cohen originally called this phase the *swan song phase*, as it "... connotes the last act or final creative work of a person before retirement or death" (Cohen, 1999, p. 5).

CRITIQUE OF THE THEORY OF HUMAN POTENTIAL

Cohen's view of aging is refreshingly positive. Many other theories of adult develop-ment barely dip a toe in the water of development past middle age (e.g., Levinson) and those that do often do not paint a rosy picture (e.g., Erikson and Erikson). Cohen's strength-based approach encourages a different kind of consideration of what else there is to do, see, experience, and learn as we age. What makes Cohen's work even more poignant is that he was doing much of his research and writing on the potential, hopefulness, and expectations of aging adults while he engaged in a 13-year battle with prostate cancer (McFadden, 2017). During this time, Cohen, working with his wife Wendy, an art therapist, conducted a creativity and aging study. Their results demonstrated how older adults who engage in creative group activities can improve along both physical and mental health measures (Cohen, 2006).

A limitation of Cohen's theory, however, is that this ability to move into spaces of creative energy, liberation, risk-taking, and being keepers of the culture is more likely predicated on experiences where people have the financial resources to retire, have the physical health to explore, have the mental capacity to create, and have the social support network to thrive. Cohen himself acknowledged that in order for older adults to successfully navigate the *liberation phase* of human potential, a successful retirement that leads to freedom of time and freedom from financial constraints is what creates space for new creative energy to emerge (Cohen, 1999). Similarly, the risk-taking that can occur during this phase also assumes an absence of significant physical limitations or financial concerns (Cohen, 1999). As with many theories of development we have explored in this book, it is important to consider how the tenets of the theory may or may not fit a particular client or client family once we take into account relevant con-textual and cultural factors. For example, those with lesser privilege are less likely to enjoy these opportunities.

RESEARCH ON HUMAN POTENTIAL THEORY—THE CREATIVITY AND AGING STUDY

Cohen himself pointed to several studies conducted in the 1980s and 1990s that laid the foundation for his theory of human potential. He added to this research by examin-ing how psychological growth in the second half of life has led to new ways of under-standing the capacity for potential throughout the lifespan (Cohen, 2006). One area of interest to Cohen was looking at the realm of folk art. He noted that folk artists are, by and large, older people, who are using their later years to engage in creativity and performance. Cohen (2006) conducted research to demonstrate that even as we age, we have an inner drive to grow, experiment, create, and change, and that when we engage in these creative endeavors, we also experience physical and psychological health benefits.

The Creativity and Aging Study was conducted in the Fall of 2001 by Cohen at the George Washington University Center on Health, Aging and Humanities. This study used an experimental design with both a control group and a study group of adults ages 65 and older, with the average age of participants at around 80 years. The purpose of the study was to examine the impact of participatory art programs on the general health, mental health, and social activities of older people (Cohen, 2006). Cohen's rationale for his study was to build on existing and growing research that suggested aging can be viewed as a time of potential and not just a time of problems. He hypothesized that active and intentional participation in creative and artistic activities would enhance factors already demonstrated as positively impacting key health factors—a sense of control and social engagement.

Participants in the intervention group were engaged over a 2-year period in art-based programs conducted by professional artists and included concerts, exhibitions, and practice with ongoing artistic work. The control group for the study engaged in community activities, but not specifically art programs (Cohen, 2006). At the end of the 2-year period, all participants completed questionnaires designed to measure three domains of functioning: assessment of physical health issues; assessment of mental health issues including depression, morale and loneliness; and assessment of social activities. Several findings were significant between the control and study groups. For example, the control group reported a higher rate of visits to the doctor than the study group as well as an increase in medication usage. At the 1 year follow-up, the study group showed statistically significant improvements over the control group on the depression, morale, and loneliness scales. One remarkable finding was that 1 year into the study, the art group, in contrast to the control group, showed actual stabilization and improvement over time, even though many of these participants were at an advanced age that usually represented some kind of decline (Cohen, 2006).

Cohen felt that one of the most important impacts of his work was in consideration of how art can have a powerful effect on dementia and Alzheimer's disease. He noted that for those with dementia, it is often activities or experiences with art (e.g., painting, music, dance) that perseveres as a reserve skill (Cohen, 2006). At the time of this writing, there was a very poignant example of this remarkable phenomenon with a concert performed by Tony Bennet and Lady Gaga. Anderson Cooper of *60 Minutes* chronicled the preparation for this final joint performance. Bennett was 95 and dealing with Alzheimer's disease when his son and wife suggested to Lady Gaga, a long-time collaborator and friend, that they do a concert together at Radio City Music Hall (Cooper, 2021). While Tony had difficulty remembering people, places, and events, once he stood beside the piano and his pianist started playing song after song he had sung for years, he knew every word and every note of an hour-long set from memory. Bennett's neurologist explained that music stimulated several parts of the brain, so for those with dementia, it is a "whole brain activator" that allows those hard-wired parts of the memory to kick into high gear (Cooper, 2021). When Bennett rehearsed with Lady Gaga, he could not remember her name or who she was, but once they started singing, he was able to become the showman he has always been. Remarkably, during the Radio City Music Hall performance, when Lady Gaga came onto the stage to join Tony Bennett, he said, "Ladies and gentlemen, Lady Gaga!" It was the first time since they had been working on the show that he remembered who she was (Cooper, 2021).

Consider for a moment, if you will, how if we viewed the experiences of a client like Rose through the lens of human potential theory how we might be able to tap into her potential as someone who is still able to engage, create, teach, and fully participate in her life.

SESSION EXCERPT 13.2

Marva: It is so good to see you today, Rose. and I am happy that you brought your niece Rochelle with you today! How are you, Rochelle?

Rochelle: I am doing good. I'm glad to be here. I've been worried about Auntie, though. She seems to be more withdrawn when I've visited her lately at The Gardens. I also noticed that the last few times I visited I don't think she knows who I am; she just calls me "Sweets" or "Boonoonoonoos," never Rochelle.

Marva: (To Rose.) Rose, can you introduce me to who you've brought with you today? Who is this beautiful girl sitting beside you?

Rose: (Looks at Rochelle and smiles, takes her hand.) Sweetheart! She is my Boonoonoonoos.

Marva: So Rochelle is your niece, and your sweetheart. She is your loving niece, Rochelle.

Rose: Yes, this is my niece, Rochelle.

Rochelle: I suppose this is normal, right? I guess I just didn't think she would forget me ... at least not yet. Sometimes she seems like she is fine. She knows my name; she is excited for us to go out together to eat. The other week she wanted to dance, of all things, so we put on an old record of Tony Bennett and she sang along to all the songs while we danced!

Marva: I can see how difficult it is for you, Rochelle, when you can't really know what to expect when you see your auntie. Sometimes she seems like she is totally engaged and aware, and other times she seems to retreat and not really know you at all. It is one of the things that can make dementia just as hard on loved ones as on the person who has it. But the good news is, Rose still has the capacity to actively participate in her life! This selective engagement is one that we can help her to capitalize on. There is activity that I'd love to have you help with, Rochelle, if you are willing. (To Rose.) I think this could be something fun for you, too, Rose!

Rochelle: Sure, I'd love to be able to help Auntie have more of those times when she is engaged and happy.

Marva: Okay, great. So we are going to create for you, Rose, a social portfolio. This is a list of activities that Rochelle and I are going to help come up with that represent things that you, Rose, really like to do! The way we do this is to try to think back over your life, and to come up with those things that you really can still do. One thing I heard from Rochelle is that you like to dance, and you like to listen to music! I think we should put that in our portfolio. This means that Rochelle, or anyone else at The Gardens knows that sometimes dancing and singing are things that help you feel better and more engaged. What else could we add? What is something else, Rose, that helps you feel good?

Rose: I am the best at dominoes, I'll tell you that. I always beat the ladies I play with at The Gardens!

Rochelle: That is so true, Auntie! I've seen it with my own eyes! Auntie slays at dominoes. She also really likes to teach new people how to play. I think this is just so she can have more people to beat!

Marva: That is wonderful! Okay, let's add playing dominoes to your social portfolio as well....

STUDENT REFLECTION 13.1

The *social portfolio* is an activity proposed by Cohen that encourages older adults to create a list of vital activities that they can engage in both individually or in groups, along dimensions of low and high mobility, depending on level of physical and mental health (Agronin, 2013). Consider your own life for a moment. Engage in an active review of the vital activities you have participated in over the course of your life that bring meaning, purpose, and enjoyment. Think about your personal assets, strengths, and motivations for engaging in these activities. Now consider how this list of activities could inform and enhance your ability to selectively engage in one or more of these activities again. Some of them might be out of reach, some of them may have lost some appeal, but others could be employed, in a selective way, even in the face of some disability or loss.

Ecological Development Theory

In this next section, we look at ecological models of lifespan development. Ecological models focus on the conditions and processes that shape human development (Bronfenbrenner, 1995). Lawton felt that you cannot understand the person without an understanding of the individual's environment (Lawton & Nahemow, 1973). In this next section we explore the theories of Bronfenbrenner, Lawton, and Levy and discuss their application to understanding late adulthood.

THE BIOECOLOGICAL MODEL

You have already been introduced to the work of Uri Bronfenbrenner and, specifically, his Bioecological Systems model. This model is the most familiar and the most widely operationalized, but there were two other iterations of that model. The second iteration was the person-process-context model and the final iteration for a process-person-context-time or bioecological theory of human development (Xia et al., 2019).

Xia et al. (2019), refer to the bioecological model as a contextualist theory. According to Steenbarger (1991), contextualists emphasize process over outcomes. These models can be seen as a response to the shortcomings of the traditional stage models of human development, many of which have been discussed in this book. From the perspective of contextualists, the linearity of stage theories make no allowances for the diversity and complexity of human beings and the situational influences the individual experiences. There is the additional criticism that these stage theories are biased and do not account for diverse worldviews. Contextualists view development according to person-in-context interactions, asserting that the person influences the environment and the environment influences the person throughout the lifespan (Steenbarger, 1991). Bronfenbrenner (1995) refers to the bioecological theory as a lives-in-context theory that focuses on the interactions of the biopsychological person and the environment.

Process-Person-Context-Time Model.   There are four major components of this bioecological theory. Unsurprisingly, those components are process, person, context, and time. But we should begin this part of our discussion by providing clarity about how each component should be understood.

Proximal Processes.   Processes or, more accurately, proximal processes are mutually influential or reciprocal interactions between the developing individual and significant others, objects, or symbols in the immediate environment (Bronfenbrenner, 1995; Xia et al., 2019). These proximal processes allow the person to acquire knowledge, skills, and abilities (Xia et al., 2019) or they may provide opportunities to observe changes in these areas. The power of proximal processes is influenced by the intensity of and exposure to those processes (Cassells & Evans, 2020). The intensity of the process describes either the degree or amount of energy or pressure applied to a process.

Person.   Bronfenbrenner (1995) believed that a person impacts and is impacted by the environment. Through the regular and reciprocal interactions with the environment, the person becomes selective about how to get the desired response from the environment through the lifespan and develops developmentally instigative characteristics that allow the individual to influence the environment. As a person gets older, they have a more evolved understanding of the environment and they try to influence the environment in ways that are reflective of their values, beliefs, and interests. Bronfenbrenner (1995) maintained that human beings are different and many of those differences are the result of varying degrees of vulnerability to external environments. He argued that we should examine those differences instead of centralities and suggested that we study differences in development for people with different biopsychological characteristics in the same environments and proximal processes. The idea is that you can place the different individuals in the same environment and proximal process and get a different outcome. The biopsychological makeup includes temperament and personality, neurobiology and biochemistry, cognitive functioning, intelligence, and "academic achievement, self-concept, role expectations, self-efficacy, values, and goals" (Bronfenbrenner, 1995, p.633).

There are three types of person characteristics: force, resource, and demand. Force is used to describe those characteristics that allow proximal processes to start, continue, or be interrupted (Bronfenbrenner, 1995). Cassells and Evans (2020) describe the *force characteristics* as personal dispositions. Curiosity, self-efficacy, and persistence are referred to as force characteristics that are developmentally generative because they foster proximal processes. Developmentally disruptive force characteristics interfere with or prevent proximal processes. Examples of developmentally disruptive characteristics are impulsiveness and explosiveness or lack of self-confidence (Bronfenbrenner, 1995).

Resource characteristics are the assets the person brings to the environment. Resources may be biological like physical and mental abilities or they may be experiential. These resources interact with proximal processes (Bronfenbrenner, 1995). When we reflect on Rose, after her wife Ruth died, she used her knowledge of dominoes as a pathway or resource to develop new friendships at the assisted living facility.

The third category of person characteristics is *demand characteristics* (Bronfenbrenner, 1995) or physical characteristics (Cassells & Evans, 2020). These are the visible characteristics that invite or discourage interaction with the environment. Immutable characteristics like skin color and hair and indicators of physical ability like walkers and hearing aids also impact interactions with the environment. These are examples of demand characteristics.

Others.   Others or other people or significant others refer to the other people with whom the individual interacts and can include family, spouses, children, friends, or caregivers to name a few (Xia et al., 2019). As an individual gets older, the person may be influenced by the values and beliefs of those significant others or they may feel a loss of those from whom they may seek guidance (Bronfenbrenner, 1995). A common experience of individuals in late adulthood is a decrease in the number of significant others who can role model successful or active aging. While a person in late adulthood may expect to assume the role of wisdom and standard bearer in their community, they may experience dissonance around the shift in roles with children when their adult children become their advisors or caregivers.

Objects.   Objects refer to inanimate things that influence the person and that person's development. For a child objects that allow for either the demonstration of a child's development or fosters the child's development could be building blocks. For an older adult it could be a staircase, a toaster, the shower, or a pair of scissors that afford the same opportunity. Symbols are things like letters and numbers (Xia et al., 2019).

Context.   Consistent with previous iterations of his theory, Bronfenbrenner continued to focus on context. Context consists of the microsystem, the mesosystem, the exosystem, and the macrosystem. The microsystem is used to describe the immediate setting which could include places like home, the fitness center, or the person's place of worship. The mesosystem is used to describe the relationship between two settings. For example, in Rose's case, the relationship between her rehabilitation counselor and The Gardens, the assisted living facility where Rose lives, would be an example of a mesosystem; The

Gardens may not provide transportation for Rose to get to her visits with her counselor or it may not have resources or accommodations for the activities recommended by the therapist. In this way, the interactions between Rose's therapeutic system, specifically her therapeutic plan, and The Gardens's system, specifically the resources, would interact in a way that would impact Rose's development and well-being.

The exosystem is the third component of the context. While the exosystem is not a system with which the individual has interaction, it is the context of a significant other. In her own home, Rose's niece Rochelle may have a myriad of family responsibilities that impact her ability to spend time with and attend to Rose. This exosystem would have a great and potentially harmful impact on the kinds of social, emotional, and physical support Rose could expect from her niece Rochelle.

The final component of the context is the macrosystem. The macrosystem surrounds all other systems. The macrosystem may be one of the most important components of the contexts because it includes values, identity, opportunity, and access to the sociocultural group. Consider that Rose is a lesbian in an environment that, while gay friendly, is primarily a heteronormative environment. Rose may miss her community or family of choice that includes other gay people who do not require explanation about her life with Ruth and any specific concerns that relate to being a lesbian in late adulthood.

Time. There are three kinds of time in the process-person-context-time model. They are microtime, mesotime, and macrotime. *Microtime* refers to the continuity and discontinuity of proximal processes and what is happening during that time (Bronfenbrenner, 1995; Rosa & Tudge, 2013). Consider a person who through accident or illness has lost the capacity to take care of basic functions like bathing or getting dressed. That person may work with an occupational therapist to relearn how to do those things and may possibly need to learn new ways where the person and the therapist work to develop the skills necessary to bathe or get dressed. The proximal processes are the activities that the occupational therapist demonstrates or teaches the person with the intention of the person being able to bathe and get dressed independently.

Mesotime refers to the length of time proximal processes occur (Bronfenbrenner, 1995) or, specifically, the frequency with which the proximal processes occur (Rosa & Tudge, 2013). It is expressed in days, weeks, months, for example. Mesotime refers to the length of time that the person and the occupational therapists work together until the person has acquired the skills to bathe and get dressed independently. A patient who has had a massive stroke may work with an occupational therapist twice a day, an hour each session for the 6-week duration of the person's stay in the rehabilitation facility before the person learns how to bathe and get dressed independently.

Macrotime focuses on changes in larger society (Bronfenbrenner, 1995), possibly across generations (Rosa & Tudge, 2013). While Rose began her life with Ruth as a closeted lesbian, eventually she and Ruth were able to get married and live openly in the assisted living community. From the perspective of macrotime, there were changes in larger society that resulted in expansions of Rose's civil rights.

Propositions of the Process-Person-Context-Time Model

Bronfenbrenner's process-person-context-time model is based on two propositions. The first proposition is that proximal processes are interactions between the individual, significant others, objects, and symbols in the environment. These interactions are reciprocal and happen at regular intervals (Bronfenbrenner, 1995). Bronfenbrenner (1995) maintained that these interactions should become more complex over time and emphasized that the environment must remain relatively stable.

The second proposition is that the impact and nature of the proximal processes differ according to the person, the environment, and the kind of development taking place at a particular time (Bronfenbrenner, 1995). With regard to the latter for example, learning to navigate a staircase is different for a 3-year-old child, an active young adult, and an older adult who has had a stroke. The active young adult is most likely physically stronger with more physical endurance than the older adult. But the older adult is likely to use mental strategies in addition to other tools or objects to effectively navigate the stairs and other demands of the environment. A common mantra of older employees in a workplace with younger employees is to implore them to work smarter and not harder, suggesting that there are ways to navigate the work environment in ways that are not as physically taxing.

To understand Bronfenbrenner's process-person-context-time model, we should review the three principles of Bronfenbrenner's life course perspective. The first principle suggests that the individual's development is shaped by the contexts throughout the person's life and the context refers to the conditions and events in the historical period. One of the hardest things for contemporary African American young adults to understand is why people of African descent who were enslaved from the late 1600s to the late 1800s did not do more to resist bondage by physically fighting for their freedom and actively resisting the institution of slavery. Without the historical and pervasive context of beating, mutilation, castration, starvation and malnutrition, insufficient healthcare, overwork, forced illiteracy, and sexual assault, it is nearly impossible for present-day generations to understand a previous generation's response to an environment dictated by chattel slavery.

The second principle of life course is that human development is determined by the timing of biological and social transitions throughout life (Bronfenbrenner, 1995). Those social transitions are things like work, committed partnership, parenthood, career or job commitment, and commitment to wellness or lifestyle. A person who delays parenthood until the middle of young adulthood may have developed more skills for coping with the stress of managing a household, work, and family than someone who becomes a parent in emerging adulthood. The timing of this social and biological transition will result in the experience influencing each person's development throughout life differently.

The third and final life course principle is that there is an interdependent relationship between families and one family member's reaction to events or transitions impacts other family members, children, and potentially subsequent generations (Bronfenbrenner, 1995). Let us consider the person who becomes a parent early in life before that person has developed all the skills necessary for self-management and parenting. While the person may be able to teach these skills to the person's children as the person acquires them, there exists the likelihood that the children may never observe and learn those skills, decreasing the likelihood that the children will be able to teach those skills to the next generation of would-be parents in the family.

CRITIQUES OF THE BIOECOLOGICAL THEORY

The most significant critique of Bronfenbrenner's process-person-context-time model was that Bronfenbrenner did not test or operationalize his theory. Instead he used previous research conducted before he conceptualized this model to support the theory (Bronfenbrenner, 1995; Xia et al., 2019). One might assume that therefore scholars and practitioners refer primarily to the original ecological model. Another challenge was that Bronfenbrenner did not clearly define the terms used in this theory (Xia et al., 2019). Finally, it is difficult for researchers to operationalize the theory because several different variables must be considered at once and the relationship among these variables must be considered, as well (Xia et al., 2019).

Ecological Theory of Aging

M. Powell Lawton, like Bronfenbrenner, also focused on the interactions between the person and the environment that influence development (Greenfield, 2011). Lawton's work predates Bronfenbrenner's first publications of his bioecological theory by about 6 years. Lawton advocated for the elderly throughout his career with groundbreaking research on environmental psychology (Storandt, 2003). Recognizing that most older adults wanted to continue to age in place, Lawton attended to practical applications of his theory and research by informing the design of safe homes and communities for people in late adulthood (Pynoos et al., 2003). Lawton (1974) insisted that the effects of aging are often caused by the environment. As stated earlier, Lawton maintained that the only way to understand a person's life is to understand the person's behavior in context (Lawton et al., 1995). He offered that context impacts performance for people in late adulthood (Lawton, 1974). While many adults want to age in place so that they can continue to have control over all aspects of their daily living (Wahl et al., 2012), as early as the mid 1970s, Lawton lamented that technology and the creation of more urban areas were creating environments where the demands of the environment exceeded the older adult's resources (Lawton, 1974).

Lawton focused on the balance between environmental demands or environmental press and the individual's capacities (Izal et al., 2005). The outcome of an interaction between the person and the environment is determined by the person's competence and the demands of the environment (Izal et al., 2005). When the person's competence level allows the individual to meet the demands of the environment, then there are positive behavioral and affective outcomes (Izal et al., 2005).

Notably, environments that make excessively high demands on the individual or those where the environmental demands are particularly low both have negative outcomes for the individual (Izal et al., 2005). As people get older, family friends and community members require less of older people and include them less in activities (Lawton, 1974). Lawton also notes that as a person ages there are fewer rewards and incentives for the person professionally. The person is rarely encouraged to improve performance (Lawton, 1974).

ENVIRONMENT AND AGING

Lawton developed the Ecological Theory of Aging that is considered the seminal work on aging and the environment (Wahl et al., 2012). The theory is also referred to as the Ecological Model of Adaptation and Aging (Izal et al., 2005). The ecosystem of older adults is a dynamic environment that includes people, the physical environment, behavior, and quality of life (Zheng & Yang, 2019). A person's level of physical activity and social engagement indicates the quality of the person's life (Zheng & Yang, 2019).

He described the ecological system or behavioral system as interaction between the individual, the interpersonal environment, the suprapersonal environment, the social environment, and the physical environment. The interpersonal environment represents the environment in which significant others operate. The suprapersonal environment is used to describe the dictates of the dominant group. The social environment describes the social norms of the larger environment. A person's neighborhood is an example of a physical environment (Zheng & Yang, 2019).

Lawton argued that in late adulthood, there is significant sensitivity to the person–environment interaction (Wahl et al., 2012). He was a strong proponent of creating environments that increase functional competence or increase functioning (Lawton, 1974). He insisted that we consider elements of the environment like housing, neighborhoods, transportation, and technology (Wahl et al., 2012). Lawton and Nahemow (1973) developed the Ecological Model on Aging with the intention of informing the development of age-friendly communities (Zheng & Yang, 2019). The Ecological Theory of Aging model provides the framework for understanding the impact the environment has on older adults' actions (Zheng & Yang, 2019). The Ecological Model of Aging is based on the premise that aging well is dictated by the personal and environmental resources (Wahl et al., 2012). The level at which a person functions is based on the person's resources, the environment, and the compatibility of the person and the environment (Greenfield, 2011). If the environment's demands exceed the individual's biological, psychological, or social resources, the person is not able to function in that environment (Greenfield, 2011). The Ecology of Aging model maintains that old age or late adulthood is greatly influenced by the physical environment like housing, neighborhoods, transportation, and technology (Wahl et al., 2012).

Many adults want to age in place so that they can continue to have control over all aspects of daily living (Wahl et al., 2012). However, many adults and their families determine that, at some point, the person lacks the personal competence to continue to age in place. This personal competence refers to sensory ability, mobility, and cognitive ability (Wahl et al., 2012). Lawton (1974) offered that the perceived lack of competence in older adults is the result of most environments being designed for younger people and living in these environments reduces the performance of older adults. Lawton (1974) proposed that designing environments specifically for older adults could raise their functioning level.

The environment can present constraints and opportunities in late adulthood. For example, assisted living and technologies like artificial intelligence and emergency assistance notification technologies can greatly enhance how a person in late adulthood ages in place (Wahl et al., 2012).

It is also referred to as the Ecological Model of Adaptation and Aging (Izal et al., 2005). Lawton and Nahemow (1973) describe aging as the adaptation that the individual and the environment make in an organized way. They maintain that adaptation is required throughout the aging process. Both the individual and the environment foster the adaptation.

Noting the changes in sensory process, perception, and cognition as a person ages causes the person to experience a decreased ability to get information from the environment (Lawton & Nahemow, 1973). For example, there are decreases in vision, hearing, and the ability to smell. Additionally, there is a slowing down of how they process information (Lawton & Nahemow, 1973).

COMPONENTS OF THE ECOLOGY OF AGING MODEL

Lawton and Nahemow (1973) proposed a transactional Ecology of Aging model that describes how the aging individual interacts with the environment. The Ecology of Aging model is based on the assumption that the individual's biology and behavior interact with the physical, spatial, and technical aspects of the environment (Wahl et al., 2012) and that interaction determines how the person ages. While the person can certainly experience limited functions as a result of some characteristics of the environment, some environments have characteristics that can enhance the aging person's functioning. There are five components to this model (Table 13.1).

The first component is the degree of *individual competence*. This aspect does not address each aspect of ability separately but focuses on the combined parts of ability and how they contribute to individual competence. A person's cognitive and physical ability and physical and psychological health make up individual competence (Lawton & Nahemow, 1973).

The second component is the *environmental press* that describes the neutral experiences or forces that cause a behavior. Environmental press is also referred to as environmental demand (Lawton & Nahemow, 1973). While the experiences are neutral, the interaction between the person or the person's abilities (Lawton & Nahemow, 1973) and perception of the environment (Wahl et al., 2012) and the environment create the environmental press. For example, a set of stairs is a neutral aspect of the environment, but the environmental press associated with a set of stairs is determined by the abilities of the person trying to climb the stairs.

The third component, *adaptation*, refers to the outcome of the interaction between the person's competence and the environmental demands, and it basically describes how the person behaves in response to the environmental demands (Lawton & Nahemow, 1973). When a person experiences some loss in physical capacity that makes it difficult

Table 13.1 Ecology of Aging Model

PRIMARY ASSUMPTION: A PERSON'S LEVEL OF FUNCTIONING IS THE RESULT OF THE UNIQUE INTERACTION OF THE PERSON'S COMPETENCE AND THE ENVIRONMENTAL CHARACTERISTICS.	
Component	Description
Individual Competence	The level of an individual's physical, cognitive, and psychologicalfunctioning Also refers to technological functioning
Environmental Press	Interaction between the person's competence and the demands of the environment
Adaptation	The behavior that results from the interaction or transaction between the individual and the environment
Affective Responses	Personal meaning or emotional response given to the interaction between the person and the environment
Adaptation Level	The range of competence the individual has in response to environmental stimuli

Source: Adapted from Lawton, M. P., & Nahemow, L. (1973). Ecology and the aging process. In C. Eisdorfer and M. P. Lawton (Eds.) *The Psychology of Adult Development and Aging* (pp. 619–674) and Wahl, H., Iwarsson, S., & Oswald, F. (2012). Aging well and the environment: Toward an integrative model and research agenda for the future. *The Gerontologist, 52*(3), 306–316.

to climb a set of stairs without the use of some aid, the person may either decide to use some assistive device like a cane to navigate the stairs or find ways to get needs met in spaces that do not require navigation of stairs.

The fourth component is the *affective responses* which are the emotional reactions to the interaction between the environment and the person. A person who loses the ability to navigate a staircase without assistance may be frustrated or may be embarrassed about the changing abilities. Another person might feel a sense of triumph over finding ways to navigate the environment with changing abilities. Either response is affective and there are a host of other affective responses. However, we can see how affective responses to changes in the interaction between the person and the environment could contribute to the quality of life.

The fifth component is the *adaptation level*. According to Lawton and Nahemow (1973), each person has an adaptation level or range of competence and the environmental stimulus or challenge that the person experiences can increase or decrease around that adaptation level up to a certain point and still have a positive effect. However, a stimulus beyond that range in either direction can have a negative effect. High competence means you have a wider-ranged adaptation level and a wide range of ways to interact with the environment. A person with high competence can perform even when pushed beyond the adaptation level.

When we consider whether or not a person will age well, we must attend to both what we understand about the person (competence and adaptation level), what we know about the environment or the environmental demands, and what we observe about how the person responds to the environment (affective responses and adaptation). According to Lawton, aging well is the result of creating. What can be done to create harmony between Rose and her environment at The Gardens?

Research on the Ecology of Aging Model

Lawton made great contributions to our understanding of the ways the environment or, more importantly, support in the environment contributes to the quality of life for older people and enhanced our understanding of what is required for older adults to age in place.

In 2001, Lawton wrote about designing environments specifically for people with Alzheimer's disease as an additional focus in environmental gerontology with the intention of understanding how to favorably impact the quality of life for people with dementia. As dementia progresses so does the destruction of brain tissue, which makes it very difficult for these needs to be met. The person with dementia eventually loses the ability to evaluate the stimuli that might make the person feel good or bad and they lose the ability to identify stimuli that are relevant to them. Lawton wanted to understand the best way to identify how to design user-specific residential facilities for people who may have difficulty providing that information through evaluation, surveys, or interviews. He determined that the best way was through systematic qualitative observations and creating an extensive database that could be accessed by a large group of informants (Lawton, 2001). As a result of his research, he was able to identify four user needs that should be considered and provided for in the living space for people with dementia. Those four considerations or user needs are (a) decreasing disturbing behavior; (b) increasing social behavior; (c) increased activity; and (d) increasing positive feelings and decreasing negative feelings. Each of these areas should be areas of focus for Marva in her continued work with Rose.

CULTURAL FACTORS AND AGING

This author (Dixon-Saxon) visited Madrid, Spain, several years ago and I was really impressed with the presentation of the older women in the city. They frequently wore their hair long and loose and many of them had on low-neck, figure hugging clothes with beautiful jewelry like large dangling earrings. While tastefully dressed, many of them had on clothing I was only accustomed to seeing much younger women in the United States wearing. The other noticeable thing was that their posture and physical presentation suggested that they were courting their companions. These were merely my observations, but I kept thinking about the cultural differences in aging and the things that impact our perceptions of how an older person "should" act or dress. In this next section, we discuss culture and aging. There is not a wealth of information about cultural differences in aging, but we are able to include a more in-depth discussion of Levy's theory of stereotype embodiment.

Culture and Aging

The experience of aging and being cared for in late adulthood is not the same for all racial and ethnic groups. In the United States, over 20% of caregivers for older family members are African American compared to approximately 17% of caregivers being non-Hispanic White. Additionally, African American adults are less likely to be in long-term care facilities than non-Hispanic White older adults (Intrieri & Kurth, 2018). Both African American and East Asian cultures are oriented toward collectivism and filial piety, which is a high regard and respect for elders. In East Asian culture, greatly influenced by Confucianism, while this orientation toward filial piety continues, there is also tension, at times between older and younger women as the younger women struggle for independence from the influence and advice of older women (Intrieri & Kurth, 2018).

With the growing number of older adults come concerns about the availability of resources like healthcare, pensions, (Pew Research Center, 2014) and Social Security benefits. Pew Research Center (2014) indicates that most people in East Asia see the aging population as a major concern and that Americans are the least concerned. Notably the fastest growing aging population is in East Asia and Europe. Additionally, in East Asian cultures there is greater concern about the quality of life in old age. However, in countries where people tend to have more children like Indonesia, Pakistan, and Nigeria, there is less concern about the aging population. This seems to be a perfect illustration of the contextual nature of culture. Interestingly, in the United States people are less concerned about the growing number of aging people in the country because they expect individuals to take care of their own needs in old age and because the United States population is aging less rapidly than other countries.

There are many stereotypes that exist about older people, both positive and negative, and the research indicates that there exists the ability to change those negative stereotypes with additional education (Intrieri & Kurth, 2018). However, for some groups, culture and context may have a greater influence on attitudes about aging than knowledge. Intrieri and Kurth (2018) examined attitudes about aging and aging knowledge of African Americans and non-Hispanic White people predicting that more knowledge about aging would predict better attitudes about aging and less ageism. However, the results of the study indicated that increased knowledge about aging resulted in more positive attitudes about aging for the non-Hispanic White participants than African American participants and, while knowledge appeared to positively influence ageism attitudes, there were no statistically significant differences between the two groups. Given that the behaviors of the African American communities suggests very positive regard for older adults, they concluded that culture, specifically, the collectivist nature of African American families may be more influential on their attitudes toward aging than additional knowledge.

The United States, like other Western societies, has a historically dominant culture of being youth oriented. Unlike Eastern societies that are traditionally more oriented to collectivism and interdependence, the dominant culture of Western society reflects individualism and independence. In recent years there has been a perceived gap-closing in these attitudes between the two groups; a Vauclair et al. (2017) study indicates that people in Eastern cultures continue to hold the beliefs that older people should be honored and respected and have a higher regard for the competence of older people. At the same time, the sample from the Eastern culture of Taiwan also had contempt for older people, possibly rooted in the impact the aging population had on services and the pension system. Vauclair et al. (2017) indicated that they expected there to be greater negativity by the people sampled from the Western culture, in this case the United Kingdom, but found for both groups there were prevailing positive attitudes about older people.

THEORY OF STEREOTYPE EMBODIMENT

Levy (2009) suggested that age is more than the sum of physiological processes as evidenced in the way advancing age presents in different cultures. She hypothesized that an individual's beliefs about aging influence health more than health influences the beliefs and attitudes about aging. Levy et al. (2002) conducted a study over two decades with middle and late aged adults and found that participants with positive attitudes about aging had better health and lived over 7 years longer than participants with negative self-perception of aging. Based on research that positive and negative stereotypes impact cognitive and physical functioning, Levy offered that stereotypes impact the aging process (Levy, 2009).

Levy's theory of *Stereotype Embodiment*, similar to the concept of internalized oppression, proposes that stereotypes are embodied when the messages and attitudes in the culture are accepted and used to define how the person defines self, which in turn impacts health and the way a person functions. Levy's theory is based on four assumptions about stereotypes. Those assumptions are that (a) stereotypes are internalized across the lifespan; (b) age stereotypes operate unconsciously; (c) stereotypes are more salient when they have relevance to the individual or are self-relevant; and (d) stereotypes impact individuals through multiple pathways (Levy, 2009).

Stereotypes Internalized. The first assumption of Levy's (2009) theory is that stereotypes about old age occur throughout the lifespan and are messages that are transferred from society to the individual (Levy, 2009). If you reflect on fairy tales, cartoons, and movies from your childhood, you will recognize that many of the images of older people in those different media were stereotypical. We learn age stereotypes at an early age and we do not challenge them or defend against them when we are younger because they are not personally applicable before late adulthood. Additionally, when we are younger, we may gain some advantages in society from the stereotypes about late adulthood. For example, in the workplace we may gain benefits from people thinking that, unlike an older co-worker or applicant, a younger employee is more creative and energetic and has a wellspring of new ideas (Levy, 2009) and energy (Intrieri & Kurth, 2018). As the younger applicant, a person may accept the thoughts about older employees because it benefits that individual in the workplace. As we age, the stereotypes can have a negative impact on health. For example, age stereotypes that suggest we should expect to be less active as we age can result in adopting a more sedentary lifestyle which leads to chronic illness like cardiovascular disease (Levy, 2009).

Unconscious Stereotype Operationalization. We are continuously exposed to these stereotypes throughout our lives and we start to accept them. The stereotypes are all around us in our environment. As we age, positive and negative stereotypes can unconsciously influence the person in late adulthood on things like handwriting and state of mind.

In 1996, Levy produced the results of a study that examined the impact of implicit or unconscious stereotyping on cognitive aging. Levy theorized that even if people held positive beliefs about aging and actively resisted the negative stereotype, they could still be influenced by exposure to stereotypes of which they had no awareness (Levy, 1996). Those messages that society provides about aging early in the lifespan serve to prime stereotypes. The result of Levy's study supported the hypothesis that stereotypes about cognitive aging can influence memory and attitudes about aging (Levy, 1996).

Salience From Self-Relevance. The messages we get about aging when we are younger are rarely salient or relevant to our own lives. Those messages become more salient when we reach the time when societal markers of old age apply to us. Examples of those societal markers are when the aging individual receives an application from AARP that they can receive benefits through their organization or when the person becomes eligible for senior discounts at places like movie theaters and restaurants. For those in the workforce, there is usually a prescribed time for retirement that is only related to age. These social cues from the environment that we have aged trigger the self-relevance or salience of these age stereotypes for the older adult in late adulthood. The cues can come from the individual's interactions with other individuals or from institutions. The challenges for many people in late adulthood is that this oftentimes marginalized category of old age is new and they may not be prepared to optimally resist.

Multiple Pathways. Age stereotypes can influence psychological functioning, behavior, and physical wellness (Levy, 2009). An aging person who internalizes the stereotypes about aging may start to opt out of activities that society deems inappropriate for aging people. The person may stop or start activities, not because of any indications around physical capacity, but because of the stereotypes. They may also accept changes in physical and cognitive ability as inevitable and not engage in activities that could slow down these processes like making improvements in diet, engaging in physical exercise, or activities that improve and maintain cognitive functioning.

Relevant Recent and Emerging Research/Theories

Internalized stereotypes or stereotype embodiment can negatively impact relationships and sexual wellness in older adults. As mentioned before there are both positive and negative stereotypes about late adulthood. Some of the positive stereotypes are that older women are warm and nurturing and that older men are distinguished and stately (Intrieri & Kurth, 2018). Some of the negative stereotypes about late adulthood are that older adults are depressed, unwilling to learn new things, or are not interested in or able to engage in sexual activity (Dreer & Cox, 2019).

Late adulthood is a time when people have less sexual activity, but intimate activities like foreplay and hugging may increase in frequency. Syme and Cohn (2021) examined how age-based stereotypes impact attitudes about sex. They engaged in this research because being sexually active can result in a better quality of life, sense of well-being overall, and specifically sexual wellness. Syme and Cohn (2021) suggest that the reluctance or failure to address sex behaviors is rooted in stereotypes that older adults are unable to engage in sexual activity physically or that anything related to sexual activity and older adults is funny or disgusting.

Levy introduced the stereotype matching effect (SME) which is based on the idea that a stereotype is strongest when the content of the stereotype is related to the construct of interest (Syme & Cohn, 2021). In other words, stereotypes about sex and older adults will strongly impact sexual activity, but not necessarily have as strong an impact on intimacy.

Age-based stereotypes about sex often have more self-relevance for women. For example, older women who prioritize sexual wellness are often referred to as insatiable, indecent, or cougars. Additionally, in a youth-equals-beauty culture, older women may internalize the idea that they are not beautiful. In the Syme and Cohn (2021) study, the researchers examined whether sexual stigma would predict sexual engagement and they wanted to see if sexual stereotypes differentially predicted the sexual and intimate behaviors of women. They found that attitudes about sex or internalized stereotypes impact sexual behavior, but there was not a gender difference in either intimacy or sexual activity influence by aging sexual stereotypes (Syme & Cohn, 2021).

CONTEXTUAL FACTORS AND AGING

There are a host of contextual factors that could be explored around late adulthood like learning in late adulthood, the impact of socioeconomic status in late adulthood, aging-in-place, and living in rural versus urban communities. Readers are encouraged to engage in exploration of these very important aspects of context. The three contextual factors in this next section are technology use, social isolation and loneliness, and aging with or into disability.

Technology

While significant attention was already being given to the way technology in the environment improves the quality of life for people in late adulthood, the COVID-19 pandemic made this issue an even more pressing one. For those older adults who desire to age-in-place, technology can provide them with both support and autonomy (DeAngelis, 2021). Throughout the COVID-19 pandemic, older adults used technology for tele-health services and have used phone cameras to share pictures of physical problems like wounds or concerning skin conditions, aiding medical providers with information to make diagnoses and develop appropriate treatment plans. Technology is commonly used to monitor vital signs like blood pressure, blood sugar, weight, and oxygen levels because most of these monitoring devices are available for home use. In addition, cell phones, essentially handheld computers, have applications for logging in daily health information and applications to remind individuals about taking medications. During the pandemic, technology also served as a mediator for older adults who were isolated. While technology has significant advantages in late adulthood, using technology presents a challenge for some older adults.

BARRIERS TO USING TECHNOLOGY FOR OLDER ADULTS

Technology is only useful when people can access it and know how to use it. There is not equal access to technology and poor people and people in traditionally marginalized groups are not able to benefit from technology in the same way as others.

Comfort Using Technology.   Technology is often designed by younger people who may not be familiar with the needs of older people (DeAngelis, 2021). Many older adults have difficulty navigating the small screens, small keyboards, and small print with some of the handheld technologies because of poor eyesight and the physical dexterity required for using these devices (Moore & Hancock, 2020). Because using technology has not been a regular part of their lives, some older adults are hesitant or, in some cases, resistant to using new technology (Moore & Hancock, 2020). Frustration was a common experience for older adults who were trying to register for vaccinations during the COVID-19 pandemic (DeAngelis, 2021).

Concerns About Fraud.   Many older adults are skeptical about technology and concerned about the possibility of being victimized by scammers (Moore & Hancock, 2020). Older adults are often the target of people providing them with misinformation or people trying to access their financial resources. Interestingly, they are often more susceptible to being victimized by misinformation received through social media sites and on the internet, because they are not aware that the information is not being provided by credible authorities or journalists (Moore & Hancock, 2020).

Broadband Access.   The COVID-19 pandemic made broadband connectivity a major concern for people of all ages and in every community. Not only was it necessary to make sure that school children could continue to be educated, but it was critical to people accessing services, getting the appropriate healthcare, accessing resources like food and household supplies, and staying socially engaged. Over one third of older adults lack internet access and the majority of those people are older adults without a high school diploma and an annual income of less than $25,000. There is also a significant technological divide by race and ethnicity. Black and Latinx older adults are significantly less likely to have computer access (DeAngelis, 2021) and older adults in rural communities are 1.6 times more likely to not have internet access in their homes (Plunkett, 2021). It is estimated that over 40% of older adults were not able to access needed services during the COVID-19 pandemic because they lacked internet access in their homes (Plunkett, 2021).

OVERCOMING BARRIERS TO TECHNOLOGY USE

Older adults, if given the tools to know how to fact-check information on the internet and on social media sites, are more likely to engage in these fact checking activities because they have more time and tend to be more civically minded (Moore & Hancock, 2020). The government has a role in prosecuting scammers and placing greater regulations on misinformation on the internet.

Younger family members and friends are a great resource for helping older adults navigate technology, but many community-based organizations are providing older adults with training on technology. During the early days of the COVID-19 pandemic, I (Dixon-Saxon) provided teleconference training with churches that wanted to continue to connect with members and parishioners.

The government also has a role in improving the infrastructure by increasing access to internet service and by making available internet services more affordable. During the COVID-19 pandemic the federal government offered the Emergency Broadband Benefit that provided discounts for internet service and one-time discounts for laptops, desktops, and tablets (Plunkett, 2021). Technology companies should advance their research in providing technology that meets the needs of older adults by being more accessible and assistive (DeAngelis, 2021; Moore & Hancock, 2020). Additionally, technology companies can make technology more affordable.

Loneliness and Social Isolation in Late Adulthood

The references to the COVID-19 pandemic may feel excessive, especially when we are able to resume some normal semblance of life and, hopefully, when it is no longer a circumstance of pandemic proportions. But when that happens, we will be forever changed and one outcome will be increased sensitivity to the effects of loneliness and isolation as a result of the social distancing we all experienced during the pandemic.

Isolation and loneliness have been referred to as pandemics among older adults that existed before the COVID-19 pandemic (Laranjeira, 2021); about one quarter of all adults over 65 years of age can be considered lonely and isolated (Somes, 2021). *Loneliness* can be either social or emotional (Laranjeira, 2021) and is subjective (Somes, 2021). Social loneliness results from not having a substantial social network and emotional loneliness results in not having the desired quality of companionship. *Isolation* describes the condition of having few or no social contacts or interactions (Laranjeira, 2021) and is objective (2021).

ISOLATION

There are a variety of reasons older adults find themselves isolated like retirement, death of companions, decreased interactions with their adult children, limited mobility, and fewer financial resources to participate in social activities, for example (Somes, 2021). On the other hand, the older person's own stereotypes about aging and the stereotypes others have about aging can contribute to the person's sense of loneliness. In social settings, those in attendance may not engage with the older adult because they believe the person is uninterested or incapable of understanding what is happening in the environment (Somes, 2021). Fried (2020) suggests that the ageism informed by the stereotypes about people in late adulthood can result in devaluing people in late adulthood because people in the United States are generally valued for their functioning and performance ability. Ageism is the prejudice and discrimination against older people or people who are perceived to be old (Vauclair et al., 2017). As people get older they often move out of performance roles such as workers. The person may come to believe that they do not value-add in situations, or changes in the person's self-image can result in the person feeling less attractive, less interesting, and less able to contribute to those settings in a meaningful way.

In keeping with our earlier discussions about the environment, Fried (2020) also shares how communities have also contributed to the isolation some older adults experience. For example, some communities lack transportation resources or sidewalks that allow older adults to move safely through the community. Additionally, many communities consist primarily of homes that do not allow for community members to make a connection with each other or live interdependently or intergenerationally.

Moore and Hancock (2020) suggest that older adults are generally better able to deal with social isolation than younger people and had less difficulty with the social distancing required during the pandemic (Moore & Hancock, 2020) because they are more accustomed to spending time alone. However, Laranjeira (2021) maintains that human beings require social connection and there are significant health risks like hypertension, anxiety, depression, cardiovascular disease, and suicidal ideation associated with loneliness and isolation (Somes, 2021). Isolation also contributes to premature deaths of people in late adulthood (Plunkett, 2021). The relationships that Rose has with her niece Rochelle, the other residents and the employees at The Gardens are crucial to her well-being because they keep her engaged and connected socially.

LONELINESS

Fried (2020) offers that loneliness is a social construct and we can design communities that can eliminate loneliness through activities and design that includes older adults and not marginalize them. In addition to making recommendations about transportation, technology, and connected communities, Fried (2020) suggests that interventions for older adults should focus on connecting them with activities that allow them to serve others and activities that allow for intergenerational engagement. However, Fried (2020) warns that for the activities to have the desired effect, they must be sustained.

DIFFERENTLY ABLED BOX 13.1

BEING DIFFERENTLY ABLED: AGING WITH AND INTO DISABILITY

Important to the discussion of late adulthood is attending to the contexts of aging with disability and aging into disability. Aging with disability is the term used to describe the aging person who has experienced persistent functional problems for years, possibly a lifetime (Verbrugge et al., 2017). People with disabilities through a prolonged period are living longer because of medical advances. The person aging with a disability may develop more health difficulties as they age than the person who is not aging with disability (Clarke & Latham, 2014). For example, the person with a disability is more susceptible to organ failure in late adulthood and it is common for people aging with a disability to experience problems with limbs and joints that have been overused because of the disability (Dreer & Cox, 2019). The term aging into a disability is used to describe the aging person who has a chronic illness or injury that results in a disability in late adulthood (Dreer & Cox, 2019).

(continued)

RISK FACTORS

Dreer and Cox (2019) describe four risk factors for disability that increase with age. Those risk factors are comorbidities, sociodemographic factors, risks for falling, and obesity. Comorbidity has generally been a term used to describe the presence of more than one distinct chronic illness in an individual (Valderas et al., 2009) and impacts a person's quality of life physically and emotionally (Dreer & Cox, 2019). People aging with a disability are at a greater risk for comorbidity as they age.

Sociodemographic factors like living in rural areas, socioeconomic status, and race are all risk factors related to both age and disability (Dreer & Cox, 2019). The sociodemographic risk factors for disability impact the kinds of treatment people receive, the quality of care, and access to healthcare. One common feature of rural communities is not having adequate medical support (Dye et al., 2012) which can result in people not getting the attention to medical concerns in a timely way that can have the consequences of a person acquiring a disability or exacerbating the significance and impact of the disability. Health disparities because of race are a common occurrence for people with disabilities across the lifespan. Both people who are aging with or aging into disability can experience a double-bind related to the stereotypes about disabilities and late adulthood.

People with disabilities and people over 80 are at a greater risk for falls because of changes in their ability to balance, changes in mobility, changes in vision, problems like arthritis, and the effects of medication (Dreer & Cox, 2019). Falls can result in serious injuries that are difficult to recover from.

Obesity poses a risk for disability in late adulthood, much in the same way it does across the lifespan, and can increase a person's risk for stroke, diabetes, and heart disease. However, weight can be managed with diet and adaptive exercise in old age which results in slowing down or reducing the impact of chronic illnesses that may result from obesity (Dreer & Cox, 2019).

People can age successfully with chronic illness and disabilities. There are mediators and adjustments that have a positive impact on the quality of life for people aging with disability and people aging into disability. Resilience, social support, spiritual or religious beliefs, and healthy lifestyle all contribute to successful aging with disability or aging into disability (Dreer & Cox, 2019). Aging with or into disability can also be mediated by employing both physical and emotional mechanisms to compensate for losses associated with disability and that includes preparing for the end of life and having a positive attitude about this stage of life.

ATTITUDES AND KNOWLEDGE OF HELPERS

Those working with people aging with or into disabilities must acquire specific knowledge of the needs of this population and be trained to work with this specific population. They should also be aware of their own attitudes about people with disabilities and people in late adulthood and how those attitudes impact the service they provide to people in these populations.

It is not uncommon for us to have attitudes and preconceived ideas about individuals with a disability. Consider your own beliefs, assumptions, and stereotypes. What do you think when you see someone in a wheelchair? How about when someone with autism engages you in a conversation? What about when you meet someone who is visually impaired or hearing impaired? Try to seek out at least one person in your life who is living with a disability, and sit down with them to ask about their experiences. What can you learn that will inform your own work with clients living with disability?

CLINICAL CONSIDERATIONS

For Marva to successfully work with Rose, she must be trained to identify the concerns and needs that are specific to people in late adulthood and, specifically, a person in late adulthood who has aged into a disability. This requires being sensitive to the needs of older adults in addition to being sensitive to the myths and stigmas that exist about older adults that sometimes impact their ability to get timely care (Dreer & Cox, 2019). For example, a clinician who has adopted stereotypical attitudes about aging may not attend to depressed moods and limited cognitive functioning in late adulthood effectively because of the stereotypes that both are merely the result of aging.

Clinicians need to identify the older adult client's support system and determine if the person has adequate services, support, and caregiving. Clinicians should also attend to any indicators that the person in late adulthood is being subjected in any way to abuse or neglect by self or others. In most states, mental health professionals as well as medical professionals and other caregivers are mandated reporters, and are required to notify proper protective authorities if abuse or neglect is suspected (U.S. Department of Health & Human Services). With regard to loneliness and isolation, therapists and helpers can support their older clients to combat the subjective feelings of loneliness through cognitive behavioral therapeutic activities aimed at promoting positive thinking and by encouraging physical activities and breathing exercises (Somes, 2021). Another strategy is to guide clients through the use of technology designed to keep them connected to others (Somes, 2021) and to the activities that interest them (Laranjeira, 2021). There are specific therapies that have demonstrated effectiveness for clients with dementia. Two of them are reminiscence therapy and person-centered care.

Reminiscence Therapy and Dementia

In the first session excerpt in this chapter, Marva employs reminiscence therapy in her work with Rose. This therapy is a person-centered approach of looking back as a way to address Rose's emotional and psychological needs which are often left unattended for people with dementia (Macleod et al., 2021). Understanding Rose's past and her historical values informs this approach to addressing her mental health needs. There are three categories of reminiscence therapy: (a) autobiographical storytelling of personal memories; (b) a chronological life review that occurs over several sessions; and (c) life review therapy which involves cognitive reframing of previous life events (Macleod et al., 2021).

Person-Centered Care and Dementia

There is a growing call for anyone who works with individuals with dementia—from caregivers to nursing home staff to hospital staff to mental health providers—to employ a person-centered approach (Fazio et al., 2017; Fortinsky & Downs, 2014). This approach encourages a consistent focus on the interpersonal relationship and a commitment to always interact with clients and patients with dementia from a place of respect, understanding, and positive communication. Built on the Person-Centered Therapy model developed by Carl Rogers, this approach to dementia care emphasizes being attuned to an individual's current state of mind and state of being, moment by moment, and reacting and responding accordingly (Fazio et al., 2017). For example, there are times when Rose is in a state of relative well-being, and other times when she is in a state of ill-being. Marva's ability to read Rose's state of being and to interact with her from a place of love, support, understanding, and care will enhance their clinical relationship and create a condition for growth.

Another aspect of person-centered care for dementia involves using touch. Used appropriately, touch can enhance the sense of safety and well-being among older people with dementia (Geller, 2017). Even a short and gentle hand massage or foot massage has been shown to increase feelings of calm and reduce stress and anxiety. Skilled human touch, though sometimes controversial, can be an added strategy for working with individuals with dementia and is often included in comprehensive elder care models (Geller, 2017).

A Case for Well-Trained Helpers

In the United States, only about 5% of the need for geropsychologists, clinical psychologists who specialize in meeting the needs of older adults, is being met and most clinical psychologists have received very little training in working with this population. The same is true for social work, with less than 5% of social workers specializing in working with a geriatric population and very few social work programs offering training in this area (Maiden et al., 2010).

As Lawton and Nahemow (1973) observed, many young people find working in environments with older adults distasteful and as Levy noted, young children are exposed to stereotypes about older people very early. Maiden et al. (2010) offer that one of the efforts to combat this crisis should be grade school education about growing older.

PERSPECTIVES FROM THE FIELD: PODCAST

Access this podcast at http://connect.springerpub.com/content/book/978-0-8261-8279-1/part/part02/chapter/ch13

In this final chapter, you hear from two professionals from the field. Dr. Nina Nabors is an associate dean who has served in faculty and academic administration roles for the past 25 years. As a licensed clinical psychologist she has significant psychotherapy experience with a variety of psychological issues in her private practice. Her areas of expertise include depression, anxiety, relationship/family challenges, work/career challenges, identity concerns, and navigating the impact of privilege and oppression.

Dr. William (Bill) Barkley is dean of the School of Counseling and the School of Human Services and has been in higher education for over 40 years. He is a former elementary school counselor and has extensive experience working with adults who have addiction issues, especially with alcohol abuse. Other areas of expertise include organization development and research methods.

STUDENT REFLECTION 13.3

Drs. Nabors and Barkley discussed their work with older adults and the importance of working with this population through involvement and understanding of their meaningful connections. Think about the older people in your life. How are you connected to them? How do you hold them in a place of reverence, respect, and support? What can you do to actively seek out the wisdom of elders in your life to inform your personal and professional development? Try to spend some time with an older person in your life, and see what new learning can come from that encounter.

SUMMARY

Over the last two chapters, we have discussed the development of people in older adulthood. Our client, Rose, has helped us to get a better understanding of how cultural factors and contextual factors shape the development of people with intersecting identities and different socioenvironmental considerations as they age. In this chapter, we explored several theories of development that can be used as a foundation for examining development among older adults. Many theories of development either do not include consideration of older adults at all, or may do so in only a cursory way, which can further marginalize a group that already experiences ageism, ableism, and other discrimination. We hope what you have gained by our descriptions of theories presented, critiques of those theories, and recent and relevant research and writing on those theories is that our understanding of the developmental process of older adults should be viewed as just another opportunity for individuals to grow, learn, create, and thrive, no matter their age. Rose is facing many challenges and has experienced significant losses. She is dealing with a cognitive decline that does and will continue to impact her well-being and ability to engage in her life and relationships. What we also see, however, is a woman with significant wisdom to share, with stories to tell, and with the capacity for love, humor, and a quest for happiness. Aging is not something to fear, but instead an opportunity to invest in one's best life. The question then becomes, how do we, as helpers, foster those expectations of aging, among our clients, their families, and others in their communities?

This is the consideration we want to leave you with as we close out the final chapter in this book. No matter your clients' ages or stages; no matter their cultural backgrounds, identities, and experiences; no matter their communities, countries, or family histories, you can use your understanding of human development to do your best work. Cicero, the Roman philosopher, published an essay titled "On Old Age" in 44 BC. In this writing, Cicero ponders the life cycle and even talks about stages of life including, "... the fickleness of boyhood, the impetuosity of youth, the sobriety of middle life, and the ripeness of age" (Cicero as cited in Agronin, 2013, p. 31). In focusing on the later years of life (which arguably could have been the 30s and 40s by early Roman standards), Cicero writes, "When the end comes what has passed has flowed away, and all that is left is what you have achieved by virtue and good deeds" (Cicero as cited in Agronin, 2013, p. 32).

REFERENCES

Agronin, M. E. (2013). From Cicero to Cohen: Developmental theories of aging, from antiquity to the present. *The Gerontologist, 54*(1), 30–39. https://doi.org/10.1093/geront/gnt032

Aichele, S., Rabbitt, P., & Ghisletta, P. (2019). Illness and intelligence are comparatively strong predictors of individual differences in depressive symptoms following middle age. *Aging & Mental Health, 23*(1), 122–131. https://doi.org/10.1080/13607863.2017.1394440

Alzheimer's Society. (2019, April). *Dementia and the brain.* https://www.alzheimers.org.uk/sites/default/files/2019-05/456lp-dementia-and-the-brain-190521.pdf

Barnard, D. (2018). Aging as problem and as mystery. *Perspectives in Biology and Medicine, 60*(4), 464–477. https://doi.org/10.1353/pbm.2017.0036

Bronfenbrenner, U. (1995). Development ecology through space and time: A future perspective. In P. Moen, G. H. elder, & K. Lüscher (Eds.), *Examining lives in context: Perspectives on the ecology of human development* (pp. 619–647). https://doi.org/10.1037/10176-000

Cassells, R., & Evans, G. (2020). Concepts from the bioecological model of human development. In L. Tach, R. Dunifon, & D. L. Miller (Eds.), *Confronting inequality: How policies and practices shape children's opportunities* (pp. 221–232). American Psychological Association. https://doi.org/10.1037/0000187-000

Clarke, J. I. (2013). *Four phases of aging: Beyond Erikson's integrity versus despair.* National Council on Family Relations.

Clarke, P., & Latham, K. (2014). Life course health and socioeconomic profiles of Americans aging with disability. *Disability and Health Journal, 7*(1), S15–S23. https://doi.org/10.1016/j.dhjo.2013.08.008

Cohen, G. (2006). Research on creativity and aging: The positive impact of the arts on health and illness. *Generations (San Francisco, Calif.), 30*, 7–15.

Cohen, G. D. (1999). Human potential phases in the second half of life. *The American Journal of Geriatric Psychiatry, 7*(1), 1–7.

Cooper, A. (2021, October 3). *Tony Bennett and Lady Gaga prepare for Bennett's last big concert.* https://www.cbsnews.com/news/tony-bennett-lady-gaga-alzheimers-disease-60-minutes-2021-10-03

Cumming, E. (1963). Further thoughts on the theory of disengagement. *International Social Science Journal, 15*(3), 377–393. https://doi.org/10.1007/978-3-662-38534-0

DeAngelis, T. (2021). Optimizing tech for older adults. *American Psychological Association, 52*(5), 54. https://www.apa.org/monitor/2021/07/tech-older-adults

Dreer, L. E., & Cox, M. K. (2019). Aging and disability. In L. A. Brenner, S. A. Reid-Arndt, T. R. Elliott, R. G. Frank, & B. Caplan (Eds.), *Handbook of rehabilitation psychology* (3rd ed, pp. 203–225). American Psychological Association. https://doi.org/10.1037/0000129-000

Dye, C. J., Williams, J. E., Kemper, K. A., McGuire, F. A., & Aybar-Damali, B. (2012). Impacting mediators of change for physical activity among elderly food stamp recipients. *Educational Gerontology, 38*(11), 788–798. https://doi.org/10.1080/03601277.2011.645444

Erikson, E., & Erikson, J. (1997). *The life cycle completed.* W.W. Norton & Company.

Fazio, S., Pace, D., Flinner, J., & Kallmyer, B. (2017). The fundamentals of person-centered care for individuals with dementia. *The Gerontologist, 58*(suppl_1), S10–S19. https://doi.org/10.1093/geront/gnx122

Fazio, S., Pace, D., Kallmyer, B., & Pike, J. (2018). Alzheimer's Association towards Guidelines for Dementia Care Practice: Recommendations with emphasis on high-quality, person-centered care in long-term and community-based care settings. *Alzheimer's & Dementia: The Journal of the Alzheimer's Association, 14*(4), 520–521. https://doi.org/10.1016/j.jalz.2018.03.001

Fortinsky, R. H., & Downs, M. (2014). Optimizing person-centered transitions in the dementia journey: a comparison of national dementia strategies. *Health Affairs, 33*(4), 566–573. https://doi.org/10.1377/hlthaff.2013.1304

Fried, L. P. (2020). Designing a new social infrastructure to combat loneliness in aging adults. *Generations (San Francisco, Calif.), 44*(3), 1–12.

Geller, H. (2017, December 27). *The importance of skilled human touch in dementia care.* Elder Care Alliance. https://eldercarealliance.org/blog/importance-skilled-human-touch-dementia-care

Gerontological Society of America. (n.d.). *What is gerontology? Geriatrics?.* https://www.geron.org/images/gsa/AGHE/AGHEgerontologyandgeriatrics.pdf

Gleckman, H. (2021, July 6). *Confronting the growing shortage of care workers for older adults.* https://www.forbes.com/sites/howardgleckman/2021

Greenfield, E. A. (2011). Using ecological frameworks to advance a field of research, practice, and policy on aging-in-place initiatives. *The Gerontologist, 52*(1), 1–12. https://doi.org/10.1093/geront/gnr108

Gusky, J. (2012, April 1). *Why aren't they screaming? A counselor's reflection on aging.* Counseling Today. American Counseling Association. https://ct.counseling.org/2012/04/why-arent-they-screaming-a-counselors-reflection-on-aging

Hoare, C. (2008). Models of adult development in Bronfenbrenner's bioecological theory and Erikson's biopsycholosocial life stage theory. In M. C. Smith & N. DeFrates-Densch (Eds.), *Handbook of research on adult learning and development.* Routledge.

Intrieri, R. C., & Kurth, M. L. (2018). Racial differences in attitudes toward aging, aging knowledge, and contact. *Educational Gerontology, 44*(1), 40–53. https://doi.org/10.1080/03601277.2017.1388962

Izal, M., Montorio, I., Márquez, M., & Losada, A. (2005). Caregivers' expectations and care receivers' competence: Lawton's ecological model of adaptation and aging revisited. *Archives of Gerontology and Geriatrics, 41*(2), 129–140. https://doi.org/10.1016/j.archger.2005.01.001

Laranjeira, C. (2021). The "loneliness pandemic": implications for gerontological nursing. *British Journal of Nursing, 30*(11), 652–655. https://doi.org/10.12968/bjon.2021.30.11.652

Lawton, M. P. (1974). Social ecology and the health of older people. *American Journal of Public Health, 64*(3), 257–260. https://doi.org/10.2105/ajph.64.3.257

Lawton, M. P. (2001). The physical environment of the person with Alzheimer's disease. *Aging & Mental Health, 5*(sup1), 56–64. https://doi.org/10.1080/713650004

Lawton, M. P., De Voe, M. R., & Parmelee, P. (1995). Relationship of events and affect in the daily life of an elderly population. *Psychology and Aging, 10*(3), 469–477. https://doi.org/10.1037//0882-7974.10.3.469

Lawton, M. P., & Nahemow, L. (1973). Ecology and the aging process. In C. Eisdorfer & M. P. Lawton (Eds.), *The psychology of adult development and aging* (pp. 619–674).

Levy, B. (1996). Improving memory in old age through implicit self-stereotyping. *Journal of Personality and Social Psychology, 71*(6), 1092–1107. https://doi.org/10.1037/0022-3514.71.6.1092

Levy, B. (2009). Stereotype embodiment: A psychosocial approach to aging. *Current Directions in Psychological Science, 18*(6), 332–336. https://doi.org/10.1111/j.1467-8721.2009.01662.x

Levy, B. R., Slade, M. D., Kunkel, S. R., & Kasl, S. V. (2002). Longevity increased by positive self-perceptions of aging. *Journal of Personality and Social Psychology, 83*(2), 261–270. https://doi.org/10.1037/0022-3514.83.2.261

Macleod, F., Storey, L., Rushe, T., & McLaughlin, K. (2021). Towards an increased understanding of reminiscence therapy for people with dementia: A narrative analysis. *Dementia (Basel, Switzerland), 20*(4), 1375–1407. https://doi.org/10.1177/1471301220941275

Maiden, R. J., Horowitz, B. P., & Howe, J. L. (2010). Workforce training and education gaps in gerontology and geriatrics: what we found in New York State. *Gerontology & Geriatrics Education, 31*(4), 328–348. https://doi.org/10.1080/02701960.2010.532749

McFadden, S. H. (2017). Creative aging and the "existential crack." *The Gerontologist, 57*(3), 593–595. https://doi.org/10.1093/geront/gnx026

Moore, R. C., & Hancock, J. T. (2020). Older adults, social technologies, and the coronavirus pandemic: Challenges, strengths, and strategies for support. *Social Media + Society, 6*, 1–5. https://doi.org/10.1177/2056305120948162

Nilsson, H., Bülow, P. H., & Kazemi, A. (2015). Mindful sustainable aging: Advancing a comprehensive approach to the challenges and opportunities of old age. *Europe's Journal of Psychology, 11*(3), 494–508. https://doi.org/10.5964/ejop.v11i3.949

Pew Research Center. (2014). *Attitudes about aging: A global perspective.* https://www.pewresearch.org/global/2014/01/30/attitudes-about-aging-a-global-perspective

Plunkett, L. B. (2021, July). *It's time to address broadband connectivity issues for older adults.* National Council on Aging. https://www.ncoa.org/article/its-time-to-address-broadband-connectivity-issues-for-older-adults

Pynoos, J., Nishita, C., & Perelma, L. (2003). Advancements in the home modification field: A tribute to M. Powell Lawton. *Journal of Housing For the Elderly, 17*(1–2), 105–116. https://doi.org/10.1300/J081v17n01_08

Rosa, E. M., & Tudge, J. (2013). Urie bronfenbrenner's theory of human development: Its evolution from ecology to bioecology. *Journal of Family Theory & Review, 5*(4), 243–258. https://doi.org/10.1111/jftr.12022

Somes, J. (2021). The loneliness of aging. *Journal of Emergency Nursing, 47*(3), 469–475. https://doi.org/10.1016/j.jen.2020.12.009

Steenbarger, B. N. (1991). All the world is not a stage: Emerging contextualist themes in counseling and development. *Journal of Counseling & Development, 70*(2), 288–296. https://doi.org/10.1002/j.1556-6676.1991.tb01598.x

Stibich, M. (2020). *Functional decline overview and prevention.* https://www.verywellhealth.com/what-is-functional-decline-2223992

Storandt, M. (2003). M. Powell Lawton (1923-2001). *American Psychologist, 58*(9), 761–761. https://doi.org/10.1037/0003-066X.58.9.761

Syme, M. L., & Cohn, T. J. (2021). Aging sexual stereotypes and sexual expression in mid- and later life: examining the stereotype matching effect. *Aging & Mental Health, 25*(8), 1507–1514. https://doi.org/10.1080/13607863.2020.1758909

U.S. Census Bureau. (2021, August 21). *National senior citizens day: August 21, 2021.* https://www.census.gov/newsroom/stories/senior-citizens-day.html

U.S. Department of Health & Human Services. (n.d.). *How do I report elder abuse or abuse of an older person or senior?.* https://www.hhs.gov/answers/programs-for-families-and-children/how-do-i-report-elder-abuse/index.html

Valderas, J. M., Starfield, B., Sibbald, B., Salisbury, C., & Roland, M. (2009). Defining comorbidity: implications for understanding health and health services. *Annals of Family Medicine, 7*(4), 357–363. https://doi.org/10.1370/afm.983

Vauclair, C. M., Hanke, K., Huang, L. L., & Abrams, D. (2017). Are Asian cultures really less ageist than Western ones? It depends on the questions asked. *International Journal of Psychology, 52*(2), 136–144. https://doi.org/10.1002/ijop.12292

Verbrugge, L. M., Latham, K., & Clarke, P. J. (2017). Aging with disability for midlife and older adults. *Research on Aging, 39*(6), 741–777. https://doi.org/10.1177/0164027516681051

Vespa, J., Medina, L., & Armstrong, D. M. (2020). *Demographic turning points for the United States: Population projections for 2020 to 2060.* United States Census Bureau. https://www.census.gov/content/dam/Census/library/publications/2020/demo/p25-1144.pdf

Wagnild, G. (2003). Resilience and successful aging. Comparison among low and high income older adults. *Journal of Gerontological Nursing, 29*(12), 42–49. https://doi.org/10.3928/0098-9134-20031201-09

Wahl, H.-W., Iwarsson, S., & Oswald, F. (2012). Aging well and the environment: Toward an integrative model and research agenda for the future. *The Gerontologist, 52*(3), 306–316. https://doi.org/10.1093/geront/gnr154

Xia, M., Li, X., & Tudge, J. R. H. (2019). Operationalizing urie bronfenbrenner's process-person-context-time mode. *Human Development, 64*(1), 10–20. https://doi.org/10.1159/000507958

Zadworna-Cieślak, M. (2019). Psychometric properties of the developmental tasks questionnaire for seniors. *Current Psychology, 39*(4), 1172–1180. https://doi.org/10.1007/s12144-019-00380-0

Zheng, Z., & Yang, L. (2019). Neighborhood environment, lifestyle, and health of older adults: Comparison of age groups based on ecological model of aging. *Sustainability, 11*(7), 2077. https://doi.org/10.3390/su11072077

Index

AARP. *See* American Association for Retired Persons

ABA. *See* Applied Behavioral Analysis

abductions, 110

accident of birth, 10

accommodation, 35

ACES. *See* Adverse Childhood Experiences Scale

activists, 63

ADD. *See* attention deficit disorder

ADDRESSING framework
  of intersectionality, 63–64
  late adulthood, 334
  middle adulthood, 283–284, 286

ADHD. *See* attention deficit hyperactivity disorder

adolescence, transgender identity development, 183–186. *See also* middle childhood and adolescence

adult development theories
  adulthood, 49
  Arnett and emerging adulthood, 49–50
  Arnett's conceptualization, 270–274
  Carl Jung and personality theory, 258–261
  case study, 253–254
  Daniel Levinson's Theory, 50–53
  Erikson's psychosocial identity development model, 262–266
  psychosocial identity development theory, 261–274
  sequential growth process, 254

adulthood, 49. *See also* emerging adulthood; late adulthood; middle adulthood

Adverse Childhood Experiences Scale (ACES), 156

Adverse Early Experiences and Resiliency Survey, 156

advocacy, 62–63

advocates, 63

African American emerging adults
  African American families, 225–226
  connection and home-leaving, 228
  mothers and sons, 226–227
  otherfathering, 227–228

African American women
  cultural barriers, 347
  distrust of medical providers, 346
  pain management and diagnosis, 346–347

age and sexual orientation
  ageism, 331, 334
  ethnicity intersectionality, 335–336
  LGBT adults, 331, 333

ageism, 331

age-related dementia, 330

aging
  contextual factors, 383–386
  cultural factors, 380–383
  disability, 386–387
  Levy's theory of stereotype embodiment, 381–382
  in rural and urban communities, 348–349
  social support and connection, 349
  technology, 383–385

Ainsworth's social location and personal development
  adjustment, 151
  contingent responsivity, 152
  infant-mother dyads, 151
  quality of care observations, 151

allies, 62

allo-parents, 103

ambivalent–insecure attachment, 47

American Association for Retired Persons (AARP), 294

anal phases, psychosexual development, 22, 24

anally retentive/expulsive character, 24

Anti-Black attitude, 70

Applied Behavioral Analysis (ABA), 111

ASD. *See* Autism Spectrum Disorders

assimilation, 35, 70

attachment network, 48, 150

attachment theories, 46–48, 216
attention deficit disorder (ADD), 112
attention deficit hyperactivity disorder
    (ADHD), 112
Autism Spectrum Disorders (ASD), 111
autonomous level of ego development, 313
avoidant–insecure attachment, 47

baby-wearing, 100
Bandura model of triadic causation, 37
Bandura's Social Cognitive Learning Theory,
    36–39
bi-cultural identity, 72
bidirectional causality, 37
Bioecological Systems model
    contextualist theory, 372
    critiques, 375–376
    process–person–context–time model,
        372–374
BIPOC parents. *See* Black, Indigenous, and
    other People of Color parents
Black, Indigenous, and other People of Color
    (BIPOC) parents, 106–107
Black Lives Matter movement, 232
black male identity development, 232, 234
black male moral development model,
    243–244
Black Nationalism, 71
black otherfathering, 227–228
body-inclusive modality, 144
boomerang effect, 291
Bowlby and Ainsworth's Attachment
    Theory
    ambivalent–insecure attachment, 47
    attachment types, 46–48
    avoidant–insecure attachment, 47
    caregiver–child relationships, 46
    disorganized–insecure attachment, 47–48
    secure attachment, 47
    Strange Situation methodology, 47
Bowlby's social location and personal
    development, 149–151
Bronfenbrenner's bioecological model
    family's role, 79
    federally funded program, 80
    individual's development, 78
    mutually reinforcing themes, 80
    nested systems, 79
    Process–Person–Context–Time model
        (PPCT), 83–84
    social determinants of health, 80
bullying, infancy and early childhood,
    107–108

Carl Jung's personality theory
    criticism, 258–259, 261
    personality, 259–261
Cass's model of sexual identity
    ethnic LGBTQ+ populations, 75–76
    identity acceptance, 75
    identity comparison, 74
    identity confusion, 74
    identity pride, 75
    identity synthesis, 75
    identity tolerance, 74–75
    lesbians, 75–76
character armor, 145, 147
character structure, 145–147
Childhood Trauma Scale, 156
chronosystem, 287
cognitive changes, middle adulthood, 324–325
cognitive development, 6
cognitive development theories
    Bandura's Social Cognitive Learning
        Theory, 36–39
    Piaget's Cognitive Development Theory,
        32–36
cognitive functioning
    dementia and development, 337–338
    late adulthood, 336–338
    neighborhood characteristics, 336–337
cognitive reserve, 337
cognitive structures, 33, 201
commitment, identity process, 216
communal culture, 152–153
conception, 12
concrete operational stage, cognitive
    development, 34, 202
conformist ego stage, 313
conscientious ego stage, 313
contextual factors
    aging, 383–386
    early adulthood, 240–244
    emerging adulthood, 229–236
    late adulthood, 341–352
    middle adulthood, 287–296
    middle childhood and adolescence,
        186–192
conventional morality, 42, 44–45
couple, midlife
    being single, 295
    relationship satisfaction, 295
    renegotiation, 293
    separation and divorce, 294
COVID-19 pandemic
    broadband connectivity and older adults,
        384

healthcare disparities, 346
infancy and early childhood, 113–119
isolation and loneliness, older adults, 385
older adults, urban and rural
   communities, 348
successfully aging, 343
technology and older adults, 383–384
critical race theory, 81
Cross Racial Identity Scale, 72
cultural and contextual development models
   activists, 63
   allies, 62
   dignity, 62
   female identity development, 72–73
   human development and social justice,
      62–63
   identity development models, 63–76
   privileges, 62
   racial and ethnic identity development,
      68–72
   sexual orientation identity development,
      73–76
   systemic and contextual models, 76–81
   theories and models, 61
cultural factors
   aging, 380–383
   early adulthood, 236–237
   emerging adulthood, 224–229
   infancy, 99–102, 99–106
   late adulthood, 331–338
   middle adulthood, 282–287
   middle childhood and adolescence, 173,
      175–186
   toddlerhood, 103–104
cumulative stress, 83
custody, infancy and early childhood, 109

DACA. *See* Deferred Action for Childhood
   Arrivals
death and dying
   mourning myths, 350–351
   rituals of loss, 351–352
   spirituality and loss, 352
Deferred Action for Childhood Arrivals
   (DACA), 109–110
Defining Issues Test (DIT), 322
demand characteristics, person, 373
dementia
   and development, 337–338
   person-centered care, 389
   reminiscence therapy, 388
developmental psychology, 3
developmental theories

adult development, 48–53
attachment theories, 46–48
cognitive development theories, 32–39
ego development theories, 22–32
history, 3–4
human development, 14
infancy and early childhood, 133–154
late adulthood, 359–389
limitations, 4
middle adulthood, 303–326
middle childhood and adolescence, 199–218
moral development theories, 39–45
normative experience, 5
social–emotional development
   perspective, 4
discrimination
   infancy and early childhood, 106–107
   late adulthood, 350
disorganized–insecure attachment, 47–48
DIT. *See* Defining Issues Test

Early Adult Era, 52
early adulthood, 256
   African American women, 241–242
   Arnett's conceptualization, 274
   black male moral development model,
      243–244
   contextual factors, 240–244
   cultural factors, 236–237
   heterosexual partnerships, 241–242
early childhood, cultural factors, 105–106
Ecological Development Theory
   bioecological model, 371–374
   late adulthood, 371–374
Ecological Theory of Aging
   adaptation, 379
   affective responses, 379
   components, 378–379
   environment, 376–377
   environmental press, 378–379
   individual competence, 378
   late adulthood, 376–379
   research, 379
Ecology of Human Development, 287
Ecomap, 297–298
Ego Development Theory
   autonomous level, 313
   conformist, 313
   critical analysis, 315
   cross-racial relationships, 316
   Erikson's Psychosocial Development
      Theory, 26–32
   Freud's Psychosexual Theory, 22–26

Ego Development Theory (*cont.*)
  impulsive and self-protective level, 313
  Loevinger's stages, 312
  middle adulthood, 312–317
  self-awareness, 313
  Washington University Sentence
    Completion Test, 315–316
emerging adulthood, 255
  African American mothers and sons,
    226–227
  Arnett's conceptualization, 270–274
  black male identity development, 232, 234
  black otherfathering, 227–228
  case study, 221–222
  clients, 245–248
  contextual factors, 229–236
  coronavirus disease-19, 222
  cultural factors, 224–229
  demographically distinct, 49
  disabilities, 273–274
  ethnic identity development, 228–229
  identity exploration, 50
  in-between time, 272
  instability, 271
  late adolescence, 263–264
  living at home, 235
  minority status stress, 234
  post-traumatic slave syndrome, 235
  race socialization process, 230–231
  racial identity development, 231–232
  self-determination, 273
  self-focus, 271–272
  subjectively distinct, 49–50
  time of identity exploration, 271
  time period, 223
  uncertainty, 273
  unemployment/underemployment, 235–236
  young adulthood, 264
emotional interdependence, 154
emotion-focused therapy, 156
empty nest, 291–292
epigenetics, 27, 208
equilibration, 35
ERI. *See* ethnic–racial identity
Erikson's Psychosocial Development Theory,
    26–32, 210, 306. *See also* psychosocial
    identity development theory
  attachment theory, 216
  critical analysis, 213–214
  generativity, 310–311
    vs. stagnation, 305, 308
  identity formation, 208
  identity vs. role confusion, 215–216

  industry vs. inferiority, 209, 211
  LGBTQ identity, 215
  middle adulthood, 304–311
  middle childhood and adolescence,
    208–217
  personality development, 26–27
  role confusion, 211
  stages, 27–31, 208–209
  strengths-based framework, 304
  Three-Factor Identity model, 216
established adulthood, 274
ethics of care, 43–45, 72
ethnic identity development, 231
  adulthood and early adulthood, 228–229
  commitment, 69
  exploration, 69
  foreclosed status, 69
  group differences, 69–70
  identity diffuse status, 69
  identity-achieved person, 69
  moratorium, 69
  person's development, 69
  theories, 81–83
ethnic–racial identity (ERI), 175–176
  bi-directional development, 83
  ethnic–racial priming, 81
  healthy adjustment, 82
  model minority myth, 82
  multiracial populations, 82
  perceptual narrowing, 81
  socialization, 82
evolutionary and security theories, 48
exosystem, 287, 374
experience-dependent learning, 142

family income, middle childhood and
    adolescence, 192
FASD. *See* fetal alcohol spectrum disorder
fear system, 48
female identity development, 72–73
feminine goodness, 44
fetal alcohol spectrum disorder (FASD), 111
FirstPlay Infant Storytelling Massage, 156
Flynn effect, 330
force characteristics, person, 373
forethought, Bandura's theory, 345
formal operational stage, cognitive
    development, 34, 202
Fost-Adopt program, 111
foster care and adoption, 110–111
free energy principle, 143
Freud's psychosexual stages
  anal phase, 139–140

core beliefs and somatic self-states, 135
disruptive pattern of needs, 135
free association, 135
neuroscience, 141–144
oral phase, 137–139
phallic stage, 140–141
relational–cultural considerations, 135–137
Freud's Psychosexual Theory
inborn lifeforce, 22
psychoanalysis, 26
psychosexual development stages, 22–26

gender identity
development, 37–39
and gestation, 13
generative caring expressions, 311
generativity, middle-aged adults
and grandparenting, 310
prevalence, 309
and race, 310–311
vs. stagnation, 305, 308
genital libido phases of development, 22, 26
Genogram, 298
GenoPro, 298
gestation, 12–14
gestational period
conception, 12
gestation, 12–14
historical context, 10–11
pre- and perinatal development, 11
Gibson's Model of Disability Identity
Development
acceptance, 338
intact support network, 341
passive awareness, 338
realization, 338
Gilligan's Theory of Moral Development
conventional morality, 44–45
different voice, 43
ethics of care, 43–45
female development, 45
justice and individual rights orientation,
43
postconventional morality, 45
preconventional morality, 44
women, 319–321
gun violence, 108

health and healthcare, late adulthood
African American women, 346–347
patient–provider relationship, 347
healthy adjustment, 82
heterosexism, late adulthood, 350

hierarchy of attachment, 48
hominids, 10
Homo sapiens, 10
human development and social justice
allies, 62
dignity, 62
mental health professionals, 62–63
human potential theory
creativity and aging study, 368–370
critique, 368
encore phase, 367–368
liberation phase, 366–367
midlife re-evaluation phase, 366
summing up phase, 367

identity development models
ethnic identity, 68–70
intersectionality, 63–64
privilege and oppression, 64–68
racial identity development, 70–72
immersion-emersion stage, racial identity, 70
implicit socialization, 82
in-depth exploration, identity process, 216
infancy
co-sleeping, 102
crawling, 101
cruising, 101
cultural preferences for independence, 101
development, 99–100
newborn babies, 100
physical and behavioral traits, 100
pre-term, 100–101
recognizable sounds of discomfort, 100
toddling, 101
tummy time, 101
infancy and early childhood
abductions, 110
Ainsworth's social location and personal
development, 151–154
Bowlby's social location and personal
development, 149–151
bullying and peer abuse, 107–108
case study, 95–96
contextual factors, 106–107
COVID-19 pandemic, 113–119
cultural factors, 99–106
custody, 109
Deferred Action for Childhood Arrivals,
109–110
developmental theories, 133–154
discrimination, 106–107
foster care and adoption, 110–111
Freud's psychosexual stages, 134–142

infancy and early childhood (*cont.*)
  gun violence, 108
  neurodevelopmental differences and
    difficulties, 111–113
  pre-conception, 96
  Reich's life work, 144–149
  relational–cultural considerations, 152–154
  runaways, 110
  secure attachment benefits, 154–155
  secure base provision (SBP), 155–156
  trafficking, 110
  treatment modalities, 156–157
  unaccompanied minors, 109
  Western child development theories, 96
inner speech, 78
instrumental–relativist orientation,
  preconventional morality, 42
intentionality, Bandura's theory, 345
interactive agency, 36–37
internal working model of relationships, 48
internalization stage, racial identity, 71–72
interpersonal concordance orientation, 42
intersectionality, 63–64
intra-personal variability, 207
isolated status, intimacy, 265
isolation, late adulthood, 385–386

justice, 54

Kohlberg's Theory of Moral Development,
  54
  assumptions, 40
  conventional morality, 42
  moral judgment interview, 40
  moral reasoning, 317
  postconventional morality, 42–43
  preconventional morality, 41–42
  stages, 40–43

language, 78
late adulthood
  age and sexual orientation, 331–336
  case study, 329–330
  clinical considerations, 388–389
  cognitive functioning, 336–338
  contextual factors, 341–352
  cultural factors, 331–338
  death and dying, 350–352
  degeneration, 330
  developmental theories, 359–389
  discrimination and heterosexism, 350
  Ecological Development Theory, 371–374
  Ecological Theory of Aging, 376–379

  Erikson's Psychosocial Identity
    Development, 361–366
  Gibson's Model of Disability Identity
    Development, 338–341
  health and healthcare, 345–347
  human potential theory, 366–370
  lifespan development, 361
  living environment, 348–349
  loneliness and social isolation, 385–386
  psychological functioning, 331
  reminiscence therapy, 388
  social support and connection, 349
  successful aging, 343–345
  technology, 349–350
  well-trained helpers, 389
latent phases, psychosexual development,
  22, 25–26
law and order orientation, 42
legalist orientation, 42
lesbian, gay, bisexual, transgender (LGBT)
  adults
  discrimination, 350
  older, 331, 333
Levinson's Theory of Adult Development, 55
  eras and structure, 51–53
  life course, 270
  life course and cycle, 51, 267
  men's adult development, 267–269
  metaphor of seasons, 51
  periodic change, 267
  periods of change, 53
  women's development, 269–270
Levy's theory of stereotype embodiment
  multiple pathways, 382
  self-relevance, 382
  stereotypes internalized, 381–382
  unconscious stereotype operationalization,
    382
libidinal phases, psychosexual development,
  22
life course, 51
life cycle, 51
Life Structures developmental model, 52
lifespan development
  cognitive development, 6
  economic influence, 7
  gestational period, 10–14
  manifestion, 6
  physiological development, 5
  political considerations, 7–8
  social–emotional development, 6
  sociological trends, 8
  theories, 8–9

life-story interview, 311
living environment, late adulthood, 348–349
logico-mathematical experiences, 33
loneliness, late adulthood, 386

macrosystem, 287, 374
macrotime, 374
mad-dogging, 108
Marriage Equality Act, 330
Maslow's hierarchy of needs, 13, 14
maternal deprivation, 150
maternal dew, 154
maternal morality, 44
McGoldrick's family life cycle, 80–81
men's adult development, Levinson's theory
   dream, 269
   early adulthood, 268, 269
   pre-adulthood, 267–268
mental health profession, 3–4
mental health professionals
   activists, 63
   advocacy responsibilities, 62–63
mesosystem, 287
mesotime, 374
microsystem, 287, 373
microtime, 374
middle adulthood
   age and gender, 286–287
   case study, 281–282
   clients, 296–298
   cognitive changes, 324–325
   contextual factors, 287–296
   counseling, 297–298
   cultural factors, 282–287
   developmental theories, 303–326
   Ego Development Theory, 312–316
   moral development, 316–324
   Multicontextual Lifecycle Framework,
     290–295
   personality development, 304
   physical changes, 324
   psychosocial development, 305–311
   self-concept, 287
   sexual changes, 324
   Social Ecology Model, 287–289
Middle Adulthood Era, 52
middle childhood and adolescence
   case study, 171–172
   cognitive developments, 173
   contextual factors, 186–192
   cultural factors, 173, 175–186
   developmental theories, 199–218
   developmental trajectory, 172

   Erikson's psychosocial development,
     208–217
   ethnic and racial identity (ERI), 175–176
   peer relationships, 173
   Piaget's cognitive development theory,
     201–208
   poverty and household structure, 191–192
   religion, 176–177
   social influence, 193
   social media, 190–191
   sociocultural theory, 187–190
   stages, 203, 205
minority status stress, emerging adulthood,
   234
monotropy, 48
moral development theories
   conventional morality, 317
   critical analysis, 321–322
   evolutionary and security theories, 48
   Gilligan's Theory, 43–45, 319–321
   Kohlberg's Theory, 40–43, 317
   middle adulthood, 317–324
   morality, 39
   morality and prejudice, 323–324
   stages, 318
moral judgment interview (MJI), 40
Multicontextual Lifecycle Framework,
    midlife, 300
   couple, 293–295
   developmental view, 290
   empty nest, 291–292
   sandwich generation, 292–293
multicultural identity, 72
Multiculturalist subscale, 72
muscular/character armor, 145
Myers-Briggs Type Indicator, 261

National Child Traumatic Stress Network,
   149
neuroanthropology studies, 153
neurological changes, 6
neuropsychoanalysis, 141
neuroscience, 141–144
neuroses, 23
Nigrescence model, 72, 73
non-violent communication (NVC), 67–68,
   152

obedience, preconventional morality, 42
object permanence, 34
obsessive–compulsive disorder (OCD), 112
Office of Child Labor, Forced Labor, and
   Human Trafficking (OCFT), 110

oogenesis, 12
oral phases, psychosexual development, 22, 23
orgone, 145
otherfathering, 227–228
oxytocin, 155

PANDAS. *See* pediatric autoimmune neuropsychiatric disorders associated with Streptococcal infections
PAST model. *See* privileged and subjugated task model
PCM. *See* Pluralistic and Coalitional model
pediatric autoimmune neuropsychiatric disorders associated with Streptococcal infections (PANDAS), 112
peer abuse, infancy through early childhood, 107–108
person characteristics, 372–373
personality
    attitude and functions, 259–260
    development, 26–27
    extraversion and introversion attitudes, 259–260
    middle adulthood, 304
    perception and judgment, 260
    psyche, 259
    sensing and intuitive functions, 260
    thinking and feeling functions, 260
    typology, 260–261
phallic stage, psychosexual development, 22, 24–25
physical changes, middle adulthood, 324
physical interaction, 33
physiological development, 5
Piaget's Cognitive Development Theory
    accommodation, 35
    age, 205
    age and stage research, 208
    assimilation, 35
    cognitive growth experiences, 33
    concrete operational stage, 34
    critical analysis, 205–206
    cultural background, 36
    equilibration, 35
    formal operational stage, 34
    middle childhood and adolescence, 201–208
    Pluralistic and Coalitional model (PCM), 206–207
    preoperational stage, 34
    schemes, 34–35
    stages, 33–34, 202, 203

Piaget's cognitive model, 54
Pluralistic and Coalitional model (PCM), 206–207
poly-mechanisms, cognitive development, 207
polyvagal-informed therapies, 157
postconventional morality, 42–43, 45
post-traumatic growth, 116
post-traumatic slave syndrome, 235
poverty, middle childhood and adolescence, 191–192
PPCT. *See* Process–Person–Context–Time model
PPN/PPP. *See* pre- and perinatal psychology
pre- and perinatal psychology (PPN/PPP), 11
preconventional morality, 41–42, 44
pre-intimate people, intimacy, 265
prenatal adversity, gestation, 13
preoperational stage, cognitive development, 34
private speech, 78
privilege and oppression
    non-violent communication (NVC), 67–68
    privileged and subjugated task model, 65, 66
    racialized trauma and somatic experiencing, 66–67
privileged and subjugated task (PAST) model, 65, 66
Process–Person–Context–Time model (PPCT), 83–84
    biological and social transitions, 375
    context, 373–374
    interdependent relationship, 375
    objects, 373
    others/other people, 373
    person, 372–373
    proximal processes, 372, 375
    time, 374
productive generativity, 311
proximal processes framework, 80
pseudo-intimate status, intimacy, 265
psyche, 259
psychological subject, 207
psychosexual development stages
    anal phase, 24
    Freud's social location, 22
    latency period, 25–26
    oral phase, 23
    phallic stage, 24–25
psychosocial development
    autonomy vs. shame and doubt, 27, 30
    basic trust vs. basic mistrust, 27

ego integrity vs. despair, 31
epigenetics, 27
generativity vs. stagnation, 31
identity vs. role confusion, 30
industry vs. inferiority, 30
initiative vs. guilt, 30
intimacy vs. isolation, 30–31
middle adulthood, 304–311
psychosocial identity development theory
cognitive decline, 365–366
critiques, 363
ego integrity vs. despair, 362
emerging and early adulthood, 262–266
exploration and commitment status,
264–265
guilt vs. initiative, 364
intimacy statuses, 265
isolation vs. intimacy, 364
late adolescence, 263–264
late adulthood, 361–366
lifespan identity development, 263
mistrust vs. trust, 364
and old-old, 363–366
race socialization, 262–263
role confusion vs. identity, 364
stagnation vs. generativity, 364
young adulthood, 264
psychotic process, 112
punishment orientation, preconventional
morality, 42

race socialization, emerging adulthood,
230–231
racial identity, 231
Cross's model, 70
emerging adulthood, 231–232
immersion–emersion stage, 70
internalization stage, 71–72
pre-encounter stage, 70
theories, 81–83
racialized trauma, 66–67
Reich's Character Analysis, 146
Reich's life work
biographical research, 144–145
body-inclusive modality, 144
body-inclusive psychotherapies, 148
character armor, 145
character structure and analysis, 145–147
formal codes of ethics, 145
mind–body connection, 144
orgone and vegetotherapy, 145
relational–cultural considerations, 147–148
somatic approaches, 149

relational–cultural considerations
communal culture, 152–153
cross-sectional studies, 153
cultural variations, 154
Freud's psychosexual stages, 135–137
group-sustaining preferences, 154
multiple stress sample, 153
neuroanthropology studies, 153
non-violent communication, 152
Reich's life work, 147–148
transgender identity development, 177–186
Relational–Cultural Theory, 116
relational/developmental trauma, 136
religious beliefs, middle childhood and
adolescence, 176–177
repetition compulsion, 144
resource characteristics, person, 373
reunification, 111
runaways, 110

same-sex gendered models, 39
sandwich generation, 292–293
SBP. *See* secure base provision
schemes, 34–35
SCLT. *See* Social Cognitive Learning Theory
secure attachment, 47, 151, 154–155
secure base, 48, 151
secure base provision (SBP), 155–156
self-reactiveness, Bandura's theory, 345
self-reflectiveness, Bandura's theory, 345
Sensitivity–Insensitivity to Infant Signals
and Communications Observational
Scale, 152
sensorimotor stage, cognitive development,
34
sex and gestation, 13
sexual changes, middle adulthood, 324
sexual orientation identity development
gay men and women, 73–74
identity acceptance, 75
identity comparison, 74
identity confusion, 74
identity pride, 75
identity synthesis, 75
identity tolerance, 74–75
SLT. *See* Social Learning Theory
social cognitive learning, successful aging,
344–345
Social Cognitive Learning Theory (SCLT)
Bandura model of triadic causation, 37
gender identity development, 37–39
interactive agency, 36–37
internal developmental process, 36

social competence, 190
social contract, 42
social determinants of health, 80
Social Ecology Model, 287–289
social interaction, 33
Social Learning Theory (SLT), 36
social media, middle childhood and
    adolescence, 190–191
social speech, 78
social-emotional development, 6
sociocultural theory, 187–190
socioeconomic status (SES) communities,
    older adults, 336
socio-political impact, development, 7–8
spirituality and loss, 352
stereotype matching effect (SME), 383
stereotyped status, intimacy, 265
Strange Situation methodology, 47
successful aging
    definition, 343
    protective factors, 344
    social cognitive learning, 344–345
sweetheart placement, 111
systemic and contextual models
    Bronfenbrenner's bioecological model,
        78–80
    McGoldrick's family life cycle, 80–81
    socio-political inequities, 76
    Vygotsky's sociocultural theory, 77–78
systems-inclusive approach, 156

technology
    aging, 383–385
    broadband access, 384
    comfort, 384
    fraud, 384
    late adulthood, 349–350
    overcoming barriers, 384–385
teratogen, 13, 96

Theory of Mind, 107
Three-Factor Identity model, 216
toddlerhood
    caregiving and disciplinary practices, 103
    fine motor skills, 104
    gender-based play, 104
    gross motor skills, 103–104
    neurological development, 103–104
    psychic leash, 103
    receptive language acquisition, 103
transgender identity development
    adolescence, 183–186
    Devor's stages, 178–179
    formation model, 177–180
    gender identity, 177
    middle childhood, 177, 180–183
Transsexual/Transgender Identity Formation
    model, 178–179, 186
traumatology, 141–142
triadic causation, 37, 38

unidirectional causality, 37
universal–ethical principles orientation, 42–43
U.S. Border Patrol (USBP), 109

vegetotherapy, 145
Vygotsky's sociocultural theory
    developmental perspective, 77
    language, 78
    more knowledgeable other, 77
    zone of proximal development, 77–78

Washington University Sentence Completion
    Test (WUSCT), 315–316
Wilhelm Reich Infant Trust, 147
WUSCT. *See* Washington University Sentence
    Completion Test

zone of proximal development, 77–78